14455 North Hayden Road • Suite 220 • Scottsdale, Arizona 85260

Dear Reader:

Coriolis Technology Press was founded to create a very elite group of books: the ones you keep closest to your machine. Sure, everyone would like to have the Library of Congress at arm's reach, but in the real world, you have to choose the books you rely on every day *very* carefully.

To win a place for our books on that coveted shelf beside your PC, we guarantee several important qualities in every book we publish. These qualities are:

- *Technical accuracy*—It's no good if it doesn't work. Every Coriolis Technology Press book is reviewed by technical experts in the topic field, and is sent through several editing and proofreading passes in order to create the piece of work you now hold in your hands.

- *Innovative editorial design*—We've put years of research and refinement into the ways we present information in our books. Our books' editorial approach is uniquely designed to reflect the way people learn new technologies and search for solutions to technology problems.

- *Practical focus*—We put only pertinent information into our books and avoid any fluff. Every fact included between these two covers must serve the mission of the book as a whole.

- *Accessibility*—The information in a book is worthless unless you can find it quickly when you need it. We put a lot of effort into our indexes, and heavily cross-reference our chapters, to make it easy for you to move right to the information you need.

Here at The Coriolis Group we have been publishing and packaging books, technical journals, and training materials since 1989. We're programmers and authors ourselves, and we take an ongoing active role in defining what we publish and how we publish it. We have put a lot of thought into our books; please write to us at **ctp@coriolis.com** and let us know what you think. We hope that you're happy with the book in your hands, and that in the future, when you reach for software development and networking information, you'll turn to one of our books first.

Keith Weiskamp
President and CEO

Jeff Duntemann
VP and Editorial Director

Look For These Other Books From The Coriolis Group

Java Studio Blue Book
by Jennifer Atkinson and Lee Taylor

XML Black Book
by Natanya Pitts-Moultis and Cheryl Kirk

Visual Basic 6 Programming Blue Book
by Peter G. Aitken

Visual Basic 6 Black Book
by Steven Holzner

Visual Basic 6 Core Language Little Black Book
by Steven Holzner

Visual C++ 6 Programming Blue Book
by Bill McCarty and Stephen D. Gilbert

Visual C++ Core Language Little Black Book
by Bill McCarty

For Nancy—now and always!

❧

About The Author

Steven Holzner has written many books on Java, his favorite topic, but this is the big one. He's written a total of 53 books on computing, and his books have been translated into 15 different languages. A former *PC Magazine* contributing editor, he is a graduate of MIT and got his Ph.D. at Cornell University. He and Nancy travel extensively and divide their time between their places near Tanglewood, in the Austrian Alps, and a small, picturesque New England seacoast town.

Acknowledgments

The book you are holding is a result of the dedication of many people. I would especially thank Stephanie Wall, acquisitions editor, for her hard work; Stephanie Palenque, associate project editor, who did such a great job of bringing this project together and shepherding it along; Meg Turecek, the production coordinator who kept things on track; Bart Reed, the copyeditor who waded through everything and got it into such good shape; April Nielsen, who designed the interior, and Jody Winkler who designed the cover. Special thanks to Andrew Indovina for the technical edit. Thanks to all: Great job!

Contents At A Glance

Table Of Contents

Chapter 3
Operators, Conditionals, And Loops 109

Chapter 6
AWT: Applets, Applications, And Event Handling 253

Chapter 12
Swing: Text Fields, Buttons, Toggle Buttons, Check Boxes, And Radio Buttons 541

Chapter 21

In Depth

Immediate Solutions

Chapter 24
Exception Handling, Debugging, And Networking 1057

Introduction

Welcome to the big book of Java. This book is designed to be as comprehensive and easily accessible as it's possible for one book on Java to be. You're going to find as much Java crammed into this book as will fit between the covers.

Java is no ordinary programming language: it inspires devotion, passion, exaltation, and eccentricity—not to mention exasperation and frustration. Hopefully what Java has to offer will prove as irresistible to you as it has to so many other programmers (in fact, Java programming is one of the most lucrative skills that you can have today).

Java has been called "C++ for the Internet," and while there's some truth to that, the Internet is not the only place you'll find Java these days. More and more companies are using Java to build applications that have nothing to do with the Internet, but more to do with cross-platform reliability. I've seen many major corporations making the gradual shift from C++ to Java for in-house programming. Java's influence is spreading, and there's no sign of stopping it—and with each new version, there's more power and more depth to work with.

If you're like me, you'll develop a taste for Java programming, because what you can do with this language is amazing. You'll see what I mean in page after page of this book.

What's In This Book

This book is designed to give you as much of the whole Java story as one book can hold. We'll see not only the full Java syntax—from declaring variables to advanced object-oriented issues—but also see Java in the real world. Setting security permissions for applets, using the Java browser plugin, creating client/server connections over the Internet, creating Java Beans, connecting to databases, and multithreading will all be covered.

There are hundreds of topics covered in this book, and each of them will come with an example showing just how it works. This book is divided into separate, easily accessible topics each addressing a separate programming issue. A few of these topics are listed on the next page.

- The full Java 2 syntax
- Object-oriented programming
- Inheritance and inner classes
- The Abstract Windowing Toolkit (AWT)
- Buttons, check boxes, and radio buttons
- Choosers, lists, and combo boxes
- Graphics, images, text, and fonts
- Menus, dialog boxes, and windows
- Progress bars, sliders, separators, and scrolling
- Image processing and tracking
- Java Swing
- Swing's pluggable look and feel
- All the Swing components
- Swing text components
- Java collections
- Multithreading
- I/O streams
- File handling
- Networking and sockets
- Split panes, editor panes, text panes and more
- Trees and tables
- Java Beans
- Packages, interfaces, and JAR files
- Reading applets from JAR files
- Security issues
- Exception handling
- Java collections
- Keyboard and mouse handling

That's just a partial list—there's really a great deal more coming up. One aspect we'll pay particular attention to—an aspect not covered fully in most books—is Java Swing, the revolutionary new interface classes for Java programming.

There's also one convention that I'll use in this book that you should be aware of. When a particular line of new code needs to be pointed out, I'll shade it this way:

```
public class app
{
    public static void main(String[] args)
    {
        (new printer()).print();
    }
}
```

What You'll Need

In this book, I'll use Java 2, version 1.2.2. If you're not running at least this version, you might get some errors that seem mysterious as you run the code in this book, so pick up the Java Development Kit (JDK) 1.2.2 at **http://java.sun.com/ products/jdk/1.2** (or the most current version).

You'll also need some way of creating Java programs. Such programs are just plain text files filled with Java statements and declarations. To create a Java program, you should have an editor program that can save files in plain text format. See the topic "Writing Code: Creating Code Files" in Chapter 1 for more details.

Just about everything you need to use this book—besides an editor program-you can get from the Sun Java site, **http://java.sun.com**. The JDK has all you need to create standard Java applets and applications, and even has an applet viewer for displaying applets at work.

Besides the JDK, I'll also use the Beans Development Kit (BDK), and the Java Servlet Development Kit (JSDK) in this book, and you can get those from the Java site too. If you want to follow along with the database programming in this book, you'll need to create an ODBC data source on your machine. You'll find the database file that acts as this data source on the CD, along with all the code, images, and other files used in the book—not to mention a great number of other tools.

Finally, Java comes with an immense amount of documentation—hundreds of books' worth, in fact. That documentation is stored in linked HTML pages, and you should have a Web browser to work with and view that documentation.

Other Resources

There are other Java resources that can be of assistance with Java. As mentioned, there are tens of thousands of pages of documentation that comes with Java itself. There are also many, many Web pages out there on Java (a random Web search turns up a mere 10,268,200 pages mentioning Java. In fact, searching for "Java tutorial" alone turns up 11,614 pages). Here are some other useful resources:

- The Java home page is **http://java.sun.com**
- The Sun Java tutorial is at **http://java.sun.com/docs/books/tutorial**
- Sun's online technical support is at **http://developer.java.sun.com/developer/support**
- The Java 2 documentation itself is online at **http://java.sun.com/products/jdk/1.2/docs/index.html**
- To get Java itself, go to **http://java.sun.com/products/jdk/1.2**

Among other topics, you can find tutorials on these topics at the Sun tutorial page **http://java.sun.com/docs/books/tutorial**:

- Collections
- Internationalization
- Servlets
- 2D Graphics
- Security in JDK 1.2
- Sound
- Java Archive (JAR) Files
- Java Beans
- Java Database Connectivity (JDBC)
- Java Native Interface
- Remote Method Invocation (RMI)
- Reflection

There are also a number of Usenet groups for Java programmers, including:

- comp.lang.java.advocacy
- comp.lang.java.announce
- comp.lang.java.beans
- comp.lang.java.corba
- comp.lang.java.databases
- comp.lang.java.gui
- comp.lang.java.help
- comp.lang.java.machine

- comp.lang.java.programmer
- comp.lang.java.security
- comp.lang.java.softwwaretools

There's a lot of help available on Java, but I'm hoping you won't have to turn to any of it. This book is designed to give you what you need (and I hope it does— please write to **ctp@coriolis.com** if you want to see something added in future editions!). Now it's time to get working with Java itself, starting with Chapter 1.

Chapter 1

Essential Java

(continued)

In Depth

Welcome to our big book of Java programming. In this book, we'll cover as much Java programming as can be crammed into one book—in depth and in detail. We won't turn away from the more difficult issues, because the aim of this book is to lay out all of Java for you, making it ready for use. If you're like me, you have a few programming packages you enjoy working with more than others, and my hope is that you'll choose Java as your programming platform of choice.

This first chapter covers the fundamental Java skills you'll rely on in the coming chapters. In the next few chapters, you're going to see a great amount of Java syntax at work, but none of that's any use unless you can get Java running and create programs with it. That fundamental set of skills—creating and running Java programs—is the topic of this chapter, and you can put that information to work in the following chapters to test out the Java syntax we'll develop.

In this chapter, we're going to work through the mechanics of creating Java programs—from installation issues to writing Java code, from making sure your Java program can find what it needs to displaying simple output. These skills are ones you can use in the coming chapters. The material in those chapters is all about the internals of writing Java code; this chapter is all about the rest of the process that makes the code run.

You might know much of the material in this chapter already, in which case it will provide a good review (some of the material is bound to be new—after all, very few people know what *all* the Java compiler command-line switches do). If you've already got a working installation of Java and can write and run basic Java programs, you're already familiar with most of what you'll see in this chapter. Therefore, you can just skim the following pages and continue with Chapter 2, where we start digging into Java syntax—the internals that really make Java work. Otherwise, work through the material in this chapter, because it provides the foundation for the next several chapters to come.

All About Java

Where did Java come from, and why is it so popular? Like other programming languages, Java filled a specific need of its time. Before Java appeared, for example, C was an extremely popular language with programmers, and it seemed that C was the perfect programming language, combining the best elements of low-level assembly language and higher-level languages into a programming language that fit computer architecture well and that programmers liked.

However, C ran into limitations, as previous programming languages had before it. As programs grew longer, C programs became more unwieldy, because there was no easy way to cut a long C program up into self-contained compartments. This meant that code in the first line of a long program could interfere with code in the last line, and the programmer had to keep the whole code in mind while programming.

To cut long programs up into semi-autonomous units, object-oriented programming became popular. With object-oriented programming, the motto is "divide and conquer." In other words, you can divide a program into easily conceptualized parts. For example, suppose you have a complex system that you use to keep food cold. You might watch the temperature of the food using a thermometer, and when the temperature gets high enough, you throw a switch to start the compressor and work the valves so the coolant circulates; then you start a fan to blow air over the cooling vanes, and so on. That's one way to do it. However, another is to connect all those operations together to make them automatic, wrapping the whole into an easily conceptualized unit—a refrigerator. Now all the internals are hidden from view, and all you have to do is to put food into or take it out of the refrigerator.

That's the way objects work: They hide the programming details from the rest of the program, reducing all the interdependencies that spring up in a long C program by setting up a well-defined and controllable interface that handles the connection between the object and the rest of the code. Now you can think of the object in an easy way—for example, you might have an object that handles all the interaction with the screen, an object you call Screen. You can use that object in ways you'll see throughout this book to manipulate what it's intended to work on (in this case, the screen display). After creating that object, you know that the screen is handled by that object, and can put it out of mind—no longer does every part of the code have to set up its own screen handling; you can use the Screen object instead.

When object-oriented programming was added to C, it became C++, and programmers had a new darling. C++ let programmers deal with longer programs, and object-oriented code helped solve many other problems as well. For example, supporting objects made it easier for the manufacturers that supply software to provide you with lots of prewritten code, ready to use. To create an object, you use a *class*, which acts like a template or cookie cutter for that object; that is, a class is to an object what a cookie cutter is to a cookie. In other words, you can think of a class as an object's type, much like a variable's type might be the integer type.

Because C++ supported classes, the software manufacturers could provide you with huge libraries of classes, ready for you to start creating objects from. For example, one of the most popular libraries of C++ classes is the Microsoft Foundation Class (MFC) library that comes with Microsoft's Visual C++, and programmers found the MFC library a tremendous improvement over the old days. When you wrote a Windows program in C, you needed about five pages of solid code just to display a blank window. However, using a class in the MFC library, you could simply create an object of the kind of window you wanted to use—with a border, without a border, as a dialog box, and so on. The object already had all the functionality of the kind of window you wanted to create built in, so all it took to create that window was one line of code—just the line where you create the new window object from the class you've selected.

Even more impressive was the fact that you could use an MFC class as a *base class* for your own classes, adding the functionality you want to that class through a process called *inheritance* in object-oriented programming. For example, suppose you want your window to display a menu bar; you can *derive* your own class from a plain MFC window, adding a menu bar to that class to create a new class. In this way, you can build your own class just by adding a few lines of code to what the Microsoft programmers have already done. (Note that you'll see how object-oriented programming works in depth in this book.)

All this seemed great to programmers, and C++'s star rose high. It appeared to many that the perfect programming language had arrived. What could be better? However, the programming environment itself was about to undergo a great change with the popularization of what amounts to an immense new programming environment—the Internet. And that's what's made Java so popular.

Java Appears

Java was not originally created for the Internet. The first version of Java began in 1991 and was written in 18 months at Sun Microsystems. In fact, it wasn't even called *Java* in those days; it was called Oak, and it was used internally at Sun.

The original idea for Oak was to create a platform-independent, object-oriented language. Many programmers were confining themselves to programming for the IBM PC at that time, but the corporate environment can include all kinds of programming platforms—from the PC to huge mainframes. The driving inspiration behind Oak was to create something that could be used on all those computers (and now that Java has been popularized by the Internet, a huge and increasing number of corporations are adopting it internally instead of C++ for just that reason). The original impetus for Oak was not what you'd call especially glamorous—Sun wanted to create a language it could use in consumer electronics.

Oak was renamed Java in 1995, when it was released for public consumption, and it was a nearly immediate hit. By that time, Java had adopted a model that made it perfect for the Internet—the bytecode model.

All About Bytecodes

A Microsoft Visual C++ program is large, typically starting off at a minimum of 5MB for a full MFC program, and that doesn't even count the dynamic link libraries (DLLs) that the Windows platform needs to run Visual C++ programs. In other words, C++ programs are fully executable on your computer as they stand, which means they have to be large in size. Imagine trying to download all that as part of a Web page to let that page do something interactive on your computer.

Java programs, on the other hand, are constructed differently. Java itself is implemented as the Java Virtual Machine (JVM), which is the application that actually runs your Java program. When JVM is installed on a computer, it can run Java programs. Java programs, therefore, don't need to be self-sufficient, and they don't have to include all the machine-level code that actually runs on the computer. Instead, Java programs are *compiled* into compact bytecodes, and it's these bytecodes that the JVM reads and interprets to run your program. When you download a Java applet on the Internet, you're actually downloading a bytecode file.

In this way, your Java program can be very small, because all the machine-level code to run your program is already on the target computer and doesn't have to be downloaded. To host Java on a great variety of computers, Sun only had to rewrite the JVM to work on those computers. Because your program is stored in a bytecode file, it will run on any computer in which the JVM is installed.

Although Java programs were originally supposed to be *interpreted* by the JVM— that is, executed bytecode by bytecode—interpretation can be a slow process. For that reason, Java 2 introduces a Just In Time (JIT) compiler built into the JVM. The JIT compiler actually reads your bytecodes in sections and compiles them interactively into machine language so the program can run faster (the whole Java program is not compiled at once because Java performs runtime checks on various sections of the code). From your perspective, this means your Java programs will run faster with the new JIT compiler.

Using bytecodes means that Java programs are very compact, which makes them ideal for downloading over the Internet. And there's another advantage of running such programs with the JVM rather than downloading full programs—security.

Java Security

When it executes a program, the JVM can strictly monitor what goes on, which makes it great for Internet applications. As you're no doubt aware, security has become an extremely important issue on the Internet, and Java rises to the task. The JVM can watch all that a program does, and if it does something questionable, such as trying to write a file, it can prevent that operation. That alone makes Java more attractive than C++, which has no such restrictions, for the Internet.

You can also tailor Java security the way you like it, offering a very flexible solution. For example, as you'll see in this book, you can now specify, on a program-by-program basis, just what privileges you want to give to downloaded code. You can now also "sign" your Java code in a way that shows it comes from you without any malicious modifications. We'll take a look at all this and more in this book.

As you can see, Java has a winning combination for the Internet—Java programs are small, secure, platform-independent, object-oriented, and powerful. They also implement other features that programmers like. Java programs are robust (which means they're reliable and can handle errors well), they're often simple to write compared to C++, they're multithreaded (they can perform a number of tasks at the same time, which is useful when you want to continue doing other things while waiting for an entire data file to be downloaded, for example), and they offer high performance. The end result is that you can write your Java program once and it can be easily downloaded and run on all kinds of machines—the perfect recipe for the Internet. That's the reason Java has soared so high.

Java is not only targeted at the Internet, of course; in fact, there are two types of Java programs—one for Internet use and one for local machine use.

Java Programs

Java programs come in two main types: applications and applets. (I'll use the term *program* in this book to refer to both applets and applications.) Applets are Java programs you can download and run in your Web browser, and they're what has made Java so popular. For example, you can see an applet at work in Figure 1.1, where the applet is running in Microsoft Internet Explorer and displaying a greeting.

The major Web browsers have sometimes been slow to implement the most recent versions of Java, so in this book, I'll use the Sun appletviewer utility that comes with Java to look at applets. You'll find this utility, which is called *appletviewer* (with an extension as required by your system, such as appletviewer.exe in Windows), in the Java bin directory along with the other Java

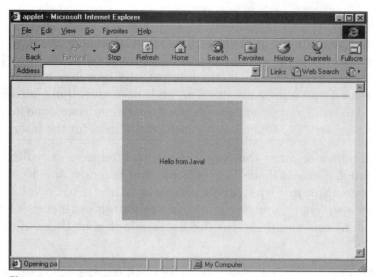

Figure 1.1   An applet at work.

Figure 1.2   An applet at work in the Java appletviewer.

tools we'll be using in this and the next few chapters. You can see the appletviewer at work in Figure 1.2, displaying the same applet shown in Figure 1.1.

TIP: *Does the fact that Web browser manufacturers are slow to upgrade to the latest Java version mean that you can't take advantage of what's new in Java 2 in applets you use in those browsers? No. Sun has taken charge here and created a Java plug-in for Netscape Navigator and Microsoft Internet Explorer that implements the Java 2 JVM as a Netscape plug-in and Internet Explorer ActiveX control, respectively. This means you can now run the latest Java applets in those browsers as long as you make some changes to the Web page the applet is in. You'll see all this in the chapter that formally introduces applets, Chapter 6, after we cover enough Java syntax to start creating applets.*

Besides downloadable applets, Java also supports applications designed to be run on the local machine. Java applications work like other computer applications—you can install and run them on your computer. Because they're installed

Immediate Solutions

Getting And Installing Java

The Big Boss gives you a call—as usual, at the last minute. You have 20 minutes to write a new Web page that will let users get an overview of your company's products. What are you going to do? Knowing how well Java works in cases like this, you select Java as your language of choice to get the task done. Of course, you've got to make sure you have it before you can use it.

It's time to download and install Java, which means downloading the Java Development Kit (JDK), and you can find it currently at **http://java.sun.com/products/jdk/1.2/** (*1.2* refers to the version of the JDK, which is now called the Java 2 Development Kit, version 1.2.2 as of this writing).

After downloading the JDK, usually as one executable package that installs itself, follow the installation instructions on the java.sun.com site; for example, the Windows installation instructions are at **http://java.sun.com/products/jdk/1.2/install-windows.html**, and those for Solaris are at **http://java.sun.com/products/jdk/1.2/install-solaris.html**.

I'd love to be able to provide the actual installation instructions here, but that's one of the biggest pitfalls a Java book can fall into, even one that's designed to be as complete as possible. I've been writing about Java ever since it first came out, and it turns out that the actual installation instructions are often very volatile. Because those instructions changed, the instructions I provided in previous books became instantly obsolete, triggering a landslide of calls and letters. For that reason, the absolute best thing you can do is to see how Sun wants you to install the JDK; therefore, you should refer to the installation instructions as posted on the Java site. The installation process has been getting easier with every version and beta of Java, and now it typically just involves running the file you've downloaded.

One thing you should be sure to do, as indicated in the Sun installation instructions, is to ensure your machine can find the Java tools, including the Java compiler itself. To do that, verify that the Java bin directory is in your computer's path. For example, in Windows 95/98, the bin directory is c:\jdk1.2.2\bin for the

JDK 2, version 1.2.2, and you simply add a line something like this (be sure to include any other directories you want to be in your path) to autoexec.bat:

```
SET PATH=C:\WINDOWS;C:\JDK1.2.2\BIN
```

Also, you must reboot your computer to make these changes take effect. When the bin directory is in the path, you'll be able to use the Java tools directly from the command line, instead of having to preface them with a pathname each time you want to use them on the command line.

What About **CLASSPATH**?

Java veterans will wonder about an environment variable named **CLASSPATH** when they install Java 2. The **CLASSPATH** variable, as you'll see soon in this chapter, tells Java where to find compiled bytecode files—both the ones you create and the system ones that come with the JDK itself. **CLASSPATH** has been the focus of a great deal of confusion when working with Java, and I'm glad to say that Sun has made things easier.

When you install the JDK, you don't have to worry about setting **CLASSPATH** now, because the JDK will know where to find its own installed libraries. However, if you want to search other, custom bytecode files when compiling a file, you'll have to set **CLASSPATH** yourself. You'll see how to do this when we discuss compiling programs in this chapter (there are two ways to indicate to the Java compiler where to find bytecode files you particularly want to search—by setting the **CLASSPATH** environment variable and by using the **-classpath** compiler switch).

There's a lot that's new in Java 2. However, Java 2 has also made some things obsolete—called *deprecated* in Java—and it's as important to know what's obsolete as what's new. In fact, we'll take a look at what was new in Java 1.1 as well to be as complete as possible for programmers coming from Java 1.0. See that topic, coming up next.

What Was New In Java 1.1?

The Novice Programmer comes over, looking, as usual, for some help. "I've been using Java 1.0," the NP says, "and was thinking of upgrading to Java 1.1." "That's fine," you say, "seeing as the current version is 2." The NP ignores that and asks, "So just what's new in Java 1.1?" "Well," you say, "a lot of things—pull up a chair and we'll go over them."

Probably the biggest change between Java 1.0 and 1.1 was the way Java programs handled events. An *event* occurs when the user performs some significant action in the user interface, such as clicking a button, moving the mouse, or typing a key, and you'll see all about the old and the new techniques of handling events in Chapter 6. The new technique in Java 1.1 and 2 uses the *delegated event model*, and it's quite different from the way things were done in Java 1.0. So different, in fact, that if you try to run a Java program that uses the delegated event model in a Web browser that only supports the Java 1.0 event model, things will grind to a halt. (On the other hand, you *can* still use the old event-handling techniques in Java 1.1 and 2, but program performance will be degraded.)

There were a lot of other changes in Java 1.1; here are the bigger changes in overview (note that some of these items might not make a lot of sense right now, but they'll become clearer as the book progresses):

* *Abstract Windowing Toolkit enhancements*—Java 1.1 supported printing, faster scrolling, pop-up menus, the clipboard, a delegation-based event model, imaging and graphics enhancements, and more. In addition, it was faster than ever before (something Java programmers could definitely appreciate).

* *JAR files*—JAR (Java Archive) files let you package a number of files together, zipping them up to shrink their size and letting you download many files at once. You could put many applets and the data they need together into one JAR file, making downloading much faster.

* *Internationalization*—You could now develop *localizable applets*, including using UNICODE characters, a locale mechanism, localized message support, locale-sensitive date, time, time zone and number handling, and more.

* *Signed applets and digital signatures*—You could create digitally signed Java applications. A *digital signature* gives your users a "path" back to you in case something goes wrong. This was part of the new security precautions popular on the World Wide Web.

* *Remote Method Invocation*—RMI lets Java objects have their methods invoked from Java code running in other Java sessions.

* *Object serialization*—Serialization lets you store objects and handle them with binary input/output streams. It's used to allow you to store copies of the objects you serialize, and serialization is also the basis of communication between objects engaged in RMI.

* *Reflection*—Reflection lets Java code examine information about the methods and constructors of loaded classes as well as to make use of those reflected methods and constructors.

* *Inner classes*—These are classes enclosed in other classes, and using inner classes makes it easier to create adapter classes. An *adapter class* is a class

that implements an interface required by an API (application programming interface). Using adapter classes makes it easier to handle events, as you'll see later.

- *A new Java native method interface*—Native code is code written specifically for a particular machine. Writing and calling native code can significantly improve execution speeds. Java 1.1 included a powerful new Java native method interface.

- *Byte and short classes*—Byte and short values could now be handled as "wrapped" numbers when you use the new classes **Byte** and **Short**.

- *JavaBeans*—These are Java components you can plug into other Java programs; this was a powerful new feature.

Quite a number of Java 1.0 methods were made obsolete in Java 1.1, and they're marked as deprecated in the Java 1.1 documentation. In addition, the Java compiler now displays a warning when it compiles code that uses a deprecated feature. Take a look at the next topic for more information.

What Was Deprecated In Java 1.1?

"Hey," says the Novice Programmer, "I'm upgrading to Java 1.1 now, and my code is going all wacky. For example, now I'm getting errors when I use the Java **Date** class." "That's because a lot of the **Date** class was deprecated in Java 1.1," you say.

Quite a number of Java 1.0 features were deprecated in Java 1.1—too many to list here. You can find a list of the items deprecated in Java 1.1 at **http://java.sun.com/ products/jdk/1.1/docs/relnotes/deprecatedlist.html**. However, note that this list won't be of much use to you if you're using Java 2, as I will in this book; instead, take a look at the "What Was Deprecated In Java 2?" topic—it's coming right up.

What's New In Java 2?

"OK," the Novice Programmer says, "you win. Clearly, I should be upgrading to Java 2, not 1.1. So what's new in Java 2?" "Lots of things," you say. "Better get some coffee." "Just when I was getting used to Java 1.1," the NP groans.

Here's an overview of what's new in Java 2 (note that as with the "What's New In Java 1.1?" list, you might not be familiar with the concepts now, but you'll see them at work later in this book):

- *Security enhancements*—Now when code is loaded, it's assigned "permissions" based on the security policy currently in effect. Each permission specifies a permitted access to a particular resource (such as "read" and "write" access to a specified file or directory, "connect" access to a given host and port, and so on). The policy, specifying which permissions are available for code from various signers/locations, can be initialized from an external configurable policy file. Unless a permission is explicitly granted to code, it cannot access the resource that's guarded by that permission.

- *Swing (JFC)*—Swing is the part of the Java Foundation Classes (JFC). It implements a new set of GUI components with a "pluggable" look and feel. Swing is implemented in pure Java and is based on the JDK 1.1 Lightweight UI Framework. The pluggable look and feel lets you design a single set of GUI components that can automatically have the look and feel of any platform (for example, Windows, Solaris, and Macintosh).

- *Java 2D (JFC)*—The Java 2D API is a set of classes for advanced 2D graphics and imaging. It encompasses line art, text, and images in a single comprehensive model.

- *Accessibility (JFC)*—Through the Java Accessibility API, developers are able to create Java applications that can interact with assistive technologies, such as screen readers, speech recognition systems, and Braille terminals.

- *Drag and Drop (JFC)*—Drag and Drop enables data transfer across Java and native applications, between Java applications, and within a single Java application.

- *Collections*—The Java Collections API is a unified framework for representing and manipulating Java collections (you'll see more about them later), allowing them to be manipulated independent of the details of their representation.

- *Java extensions framework*—Extensions are packages of Java classes (and any associated native code) that application developers can use to extend the core Java platform. The extension mechanism allows the Java Virtual Machine (JVM) to use the extension classes in much the same way as the JVM uses the system classes.

- *JavaBeans enhancements*—Java 2 provides developers with a standard means to create more sophisticated JavaBeans components and applications that offer their customers more seamless integration with the rest of the runtime environment, such as the desktop of the underlying operating system or the browser.

- *Input method framework*—The input method framework enables all text-editing components to receive Japanese, Chinese, or Korean text input through standard input methods.

- *Package version identification*—Versioning introduces package-level version control, where applications and applets can identify (at runtime) the version of a specific Java Runtime Environment, JVM, and class package.

- *RMI enhancements*—Remote Method Invocation (RMI) has several new enhancements, including Remote Object Activation, which introduces support for remote objects and automatic object activation, as well as custom socket types, which allow a remote object to specify the custom socket type that RMI will use for remote calls to that object. RMI over a secure transport (such as SSL) can be supported using custom socket types.

- *Serialization enhancements*—Serialization now includes an API that allows the serialized data of an object to be specified independently of the fields of the class. This allows serialized data fields to be written to and read from the stream using the existing techniques (this ensures compatibility with the default writing and reading mechanisms).

- *Reference objects*—A reference object encapsulates a reference to some other object so that the reference, itself, may be examined and manipulated like any other object. Reference objects allow a program to maintain a reference to an object that doesn't prevent the object from being reclaimed by the Java "garbage collector," which manages memory.

- *Audio enhancements*—Audio enhancements include a new sound engine and support for audio in applications as well as applets.

- *Java IDL*—Java IDL adds CORBA (Common Object Request Broker Architecture) capability to Java, providing standards-based interoperability and connectivity. Java IDL enables distributed Web-enabled Java applications to transparently invoke operations on remote network services using the industry standard OMG IDL (Object Management Group Interface Definition Language) and IIOP (Internet Inter-ORB Protocol) defined by the Object Management Group.

- *JAR enhancements*—These enhancements include added functionality for the command-line JAR tool for creating and updating signed JAR files. There are also new standard APIs for reading and writing JAR files.

- *JNI enhancements*—The Java Native Interface is a standard programming interface for writing Java native methods and embedding the Java Virtual Machine into native applications. The primary goal is binary compatibility of native method libraries across all Java Virtual Machine implementations on a given platform. Java 2 extends the JNI to incorporate new features in the Java platform.

- *JVMDI*—A new debugger interface for the Java Virtual Machine now provides low-level services for debugging. The interface for these services is the Java Virtual Machine Debugger Interface (JVMDI).

- *JDBC enhancements*—Java Database Connectivity (JDBC) is a standard SQL database access interface that provides uniform access to a wide range of relational databases. JDBC also provides a common base on which higher-level tools and interfaces can be built. The Java 2 software bundle includes JDBC and the JDBC-ODBC bridge.

Also new in Java 2 is the Java Plug-In. The Java Plug-In software is a product that allows users to direct Java applets or JavaBeans components to run using Sun's Java Runtime Environment (JRE), instead of a Web browser's default Java runtime environment. I'll cover the Java Plug-In in Chapter 6.

What Was Deprecated In Java 2?

"Hey," says the Novice Programmer, "I've upgraded to Java 2 and now my code is going all wacky again—I can't get the multithreaded part of my code to work at all." "That's because you can no longer use the Java **Thread** class's **resume**, **suspend**, and **stop** methods," you say. "They've been deprecated." "Rats," the NP replies.

One of the most important changes in Java 2 is that the Java 1.1 ways of working with threads have been deprecated; you'll see the new ways in the chapter on multithreading later in the book. For a complete list of what's been deprecated in Java 2, take a look at C:\jdk1.2.2\docs\api\deprecated-list.html. I'll mention some important items deprecated in Java 2 throughout the book.

Writing Code: Creating Code Files

The Design Team Coordinator calls to congratulate you on getting Java installed. You accept the accolades gracefully. "So what programs have you been writing?" the DTC asks. "Hmm," you think. "Programs?"

Java programs are just plain text files made up of Java statements and declarations, and we'll start investigating those in the next topic. To create a Java program, you should have a text editor or word processor that can save files in plain text format.

Saving text in plain text format is a simple achievement that's beyond many fancy word processors. You might have trouble w ith word processors such as Microsoft Word, for example, although you can save plain text files with Word using the File|Save As dialog box. The general rule is that if you can type the file out at the command line (note that that's DOS on DOS and Windows-based computers) and don't see any odd, nonalphanumeric characters, it's a plain text file. The real test, of course, is whether the Java compiler, which translates your program into a bytecode file, can read and interpret your program.

In addition, your programs should be stored in files that have the extension ".java". For example, if you're writing an application named *app*, you should store the actual Java program in a file named *app.java*. You pass this file to the Java compiler to create the actual bytecode file, as you'll see in a few pages.

So far so good—we've got the selection of the editor or word processor down. Now, how about writing some code?

Writing Code: Knowing Java's Reserved Words

The Novice Programmer appears and says, "Java is acting all funny—I want to name a variable '**public**', but it's giving me all kinds of problems." "That's because **public** is one of the keywords that Java reserves for itself as part of the Java language," you say. "Rats," says the NP.

When you're writing Java code, you should know that Java reserves certain words for itself as part of the Java language. There aren't too many of them, though. Here they are (I'll cover these keywords throughout the book):

- *abstract*—Specifies that a class or method will be implemented later, in a subclass
- *boolean*—A data type that can hold True and False values only
- *break*—A control statement for breaking out of loops
- *byte*—A data type that can hold 8-bit data values
- *byvalue*—Reserved for future use
- *case*—Used in **switch** statements to mark blocks of text
- *cast*—Reserved for future use
- *catch*—Catches exceptions generated by **try** statements
- *char*—A data type that can hold unsigned 16-bit Unicode characters
- *class*—Declares a new class
- *const*—Reserved for future use
- *continue*—Sends control back outside a loop
- *default*—Specifies the default block of code in a **switch** statement

- *do*—Starts a **do-while** loop
- *double*—A data type that can hold 64-bit floating-point numbers
- *else*—Indicates alternative branches in an **if** statement
- *extends*—Indicates that a class is derived from another class or interface
- *final*—Indicates that a variable holds a constant value or that a method will not be overridden
- *finally*—Indicates a block of code in a **try-catch** structure that will always be executed
- *float*—A data type that holds a 32-bit floating-point number
- *for*—Used to start a **for** loop
- *future*—Reserved for future use
- *generic*—Reserved for future use
- *goto*—Reserved for future use
- *if*—Tests a true/false expression and branches accordingly
- *implements*—Specifies that a class implements an interface
- *import*—References other classes
- *inner*—Reserved for future use
- *instanceof*—Indicates if an object is an instance of a specific class or implements a specific interface
- *int*—A data type that can hold a 32-bit signed integer
- *interface*—Declares an interface
- *long*—A data type that holds a 64-bit integer
- *native*—Specifies that a method is implemented with native (platform-specific) code
- *new*—Creates new objects
- *null*—Indicates that a reference does not refer to anything
- *operator*—Reserved for future use
- *outer*—Reserved for future use
- *package*—Declares a Java package
- *private*—An access specifier indicating that a method or variable may be accessed only in the class it's declared in
- *protected*—An access specifier indicating that a method or variable may only be accessed in the class it's declared in (or a subclasses of the class it's declared in or other classes in the same package)

- *public*—An access specifier used for classes, interfaces, methods, and variables indicating that an item is accessible throughout the application (or where the class that defines it is accessible)

- ~~*rest*—Reserved for future use~~

- *return*—Sends control and possibly a return value back from a called method

- *short*—A data type that can hold a 16-bit integer

- *static*—Indicates that a variable or method is a class method (rather than being limited to one particular object)

- *super*—Refers to a class's base class (used in a method or class constructor)

- *switch*—A statement that executes code based on a test value

- *synchronized*—Specifies critical sections or methods in multithreaded code

- *this*—Refers to the current object in a method or constructor

- *throw*—Creates an exception

- *throws*—Indicates what exceptions may be thrown by a method

- *transient*—Specifies that a variable is not part of an object's persistent state

- *try*—Starts a block of code that will be tested for exceptions

- ~~*var*—Reserved for future use~~

- *void*—Specifies that a method does not have a return value

- *volatile*—Indicates that a variable may change asynchronously

- *while*—Starts a **while** loop

Writing Code: Creating An Application

The Big Boss arrives and says, "So now you can write Java? Give me a demonstration!" You turn to your terminal and immediately your mind goes blank. What will you write?

Here's a sample Java application that I'll develop over the next few sections, all the way through the compiling and running stages. Place this code in a file named app.java:

```
public class app
{
    public static void main(String[] args)
    {
```

```
        System.out.println("Hello from Java!");
    }
}
```

If you're new to Java, this might look strange to you. The idea here is that this application will print out the text "Hello from Java!" when you compile and run it. For example, here's how it looks in a DOS window under Windows:

```
c:\>java app
Hello from Java!
```

Not the most significant of programs, but a good one to get us started. Let's take this program apart line by line.

public class app

Here's the first line in app.java:

```
public class app
{

    .

    .

    .

}
```

This line indicates that we're creating a new Java class named **app**. After we translate this class into bytecodes, the Java Virtual Machine will be able to create objects of this class and run them. You'll learn all about classes in depth in Chapter 4; this code is just to get us started with Java programming.

Note the keyword **public** in the preceding code. This keyword is an *access specifier*, which you'll learn more about in Chapters 4 and 5. The **public** access specifier indicates that this class is available anywhere in a program that makes use of it.

Note also that if you make a class public, Java insists that you name the file after it. That is, you can only have one public class in a .java file. The reason for this is that the Java compiler will translate the .java file into a bytecode file with the extension ".class", which means that app.java will be translated into app.class, and if the JVM needs the **app** class, it'll know to look in the app.class file. Because the JVM uses the name of the file to determine what public classes are in the file, you can only have one public class in a file. For that reason, the code for the **app** class must be in a file named app.java (note that Java is pretty particular about this, and capitalization counts here).

The actual implementation of the class we're defining here will go between the curly braces:

```
public class app
{
        .
        .
        .
}
```

Java always encloses blocks of code within curly braces—that is, "{" and "}". As you'll see in Chapter 4, the code inside the block has its own scope (its visibility to the rest of the program). Right now, however, let's continue building our application by continuing on to the next line of code.

public static void main(String[] args)

Here's the next line of code in our application:

```
public class app
{
    public static void main(String[] args)
    {
            .
            .
            .
    }
}
```

What's happening here is that we're creating a *method* in the **app** class. A method in object-oriented programming is like a function or subroutine in standard programming—a block of code that you can pass control to and that can return a value. Methods provide handy ways of wrapping code into a single functional unit; when you call a method, the code in the method is executed by the Java Virtual Machine.

You'll be introduced to methods formally in Chapter 4, but here the idea is that we're creating a method named **main**, which is the method that the Java Virtual Machine will look for when it starts an application (applets do not have a **main** method). When it finds the **main** method, the JVM passes control to it, and we'll place the code we want to execute in this method's code block.

There are a few things to note before continuing. The **main** method must be declared with the **public** access specifier, which means it may be called outside its class. It must be declared **static** as well, which means, as you'll see in Chapter 4, that **main** is a class method, not an object method. It must not return a value when it's finished executing, which is why we use the keyword **void** in this code (in other words, a return value of type **void** means that there actually is no return value). Finally, note the argument in the parentheses following the word main: **String[] args**. You place an argument list in the parentheses of a method declaration like this to indicate what values are passed to the method and can be used by the code in the method. In this case, we're indicating that **main** is passed an array of string values, called **args**. These string values hold the values passed from the command line when you start the application; for example, if you type **"java app Hello there"**, then "Hello" and "there" would be the two strings in the **args** array. The full details appear in Chapter 4. Because we won't use any command-line arguments in this application, we won't use **args** in the code for the **main** method.

This line of code, then, starts the **main** method. The whole job of this method is to print out the text "Hello from Java!", which is done in the next line of code.

System.out.println("Hello from Java!");

The main method has one line of code in it:

```java
public class app
{
    public static void main(String[] args)
    {
        System.out.println("Hello from Java!");
    }
}
```

This is the actual line of code that does all the work. In this case, we're using some of the code that the programmers at Sun have already created to display the text "Hello from Java!". In particular, the java.lang package's **System** class is used here. Libraries of classes are called *packages* in Java, and the java.lang package is built into every Java program, which means you don't have to take special steps to make use of it, as you do with other Java packages. The java.lang package's **System** class includes a *field* (that is, a data member of the class) called **out**, and this field, in turn, has a method named **println**, which does the actual displaying of text.

To refer to the **System** class's out field, we use the terminology **System.out**. To use the **out** field's **println** method (which stands for "print line"), we use the terminology **System.out.println**. To print the text "Hello from Java!", we pass that text to **System.out.println** by enclosing it in quotes.

Note also that this line of code ends with a semicolon. This end-of-statement convention is something that Java has inherited from C and C++ (in fact, Java has

1. Essential Java

inherited a lot from C and C++), and you end nearly all statements in Java with a semicolon. If this isn't something you're used to, you'll pick it up pretty quickly, because the Java compiler refuses to translate your code into bytecodes until the semicolons are in place.

That's that, then—you've created your new application and stored it in a file named app.java. What's the next step? To get it to actually *run*. Take a look at the next topic.

Compiling Code

The Big Boss is chomping a cigar while standing right behind you as you enter your new Java application into a file. "Hmm," says the Big Boss, clearly not impressed. "What's next?" "Now," you say, "we have to compile the program and then we can run it." "OK," the Big Boss says. "Amaze me."

To translate a Java program into a bytecode file that the Java Virtual Machine can use, you use the Java compiler, which is called *javac* (for example, on Windows machines, this program will be called *javac.exe*, which is in the Java bin directory). Here's how you use javac in general:

```
javac [options] [sourcefiles] [@files]
```

Here are the arguments to javac:

- *options*—Command-line options
- *sourcefiles*—One or more source files to be compiled (such as app.java)
- *@files*—One or more files that list source files

To compile app.java, use this command:

```
C:\>javac app.java
```

The Java compiler, javac, takes the file app.java and (assuming there are no errors) compiles it, translating it and creating a new file called *app.class*. If errors occur, the Java compiler will tell you what they are, including what line of code is wrong—in this case, we've forgotten the **println** method and tried to use one called **printline**:

```
C:\>javac app.java
app.java:5: Method printline(java.lang.String) not found in class
java.io.Print
```

```
Stream.
        System.out.printline("Hello from Java!");
                                    ^
1 error
```

When app.java is successfully compiled to bytecodes, the new file, app.class, contains all the Java Virtual Machine will need to create objects from the **app** class. So now we've created app.class. Now, how do you actually run it in the JVM? See the next topic.

Compiling Code: Using Command-Line Options

"Hmm," says the Novice Programmer, "I've got a problem. I like to keep all my .class files in the same directory, but sometimes I forget to copy the new versions of those files to that directory." You say, "There's a compiler option that's perfect for you: the **-d** option. Using that option, you can have the compiler place bytecode files into any target directory you want." "Swell," says the NP. "Now if I can only remember to use that option...."

There are quite a number of options—that is, command-line directives—you can use with javac. For example, here's how you can use the **-d** option to have javac place the file app.class in the already-existing directory temp, which, in this case, is a subdirectory of the current directory:

```
javac -d temp app.java
```

Here's the list of javac options; note that the options that start with **-X** (called *nonstandard options*) are marked that way by Sun because they may change in the future:

- **-classpath** *classpath*—Sets the user class path, overriding the user class path in the CLASSPATH environment variable. If neither CLASSPATH nor **-classpath** is specified, the user class path will be the current directory. Note that if the **-sourcepath** option is not used, the user class path is searched for source files as well as class files.

- **-d** *directory*—Sets the destination directory for class files. For readers who know what Java packages are, if a class is part of a package, javac puts the class file in a subdirectory that reflects the package name, creating directories as needed. For example, if you specify **-d c:\classes** and the class is called **com.package1.Class1**, the class file is called c:\classes\com\package1\Class1.class. If **-d** is not specified, javac puts the class file in the same directory as the source file. Note that the directory specified by **-d** is not automatically added to your user class path.

- **-deprecation**—Shows a description of each use or override of a deprecated member or class. (Without **-deprecation**, javac only shows the names of source files that use or override deprecated members or classes.)

- **-encoding**—Sets the source file encoding name. If **-encoding** is not specified, the platform default converter is used.

- **-g**—Generates all debugging information, including local variables. By default, only line number and source file information is generated.

- **-g:none**—Makes the compiler not generate any debugging information.

- **-g:***{keyword list}*—Generates only some kinds of debugging information, specified by a comma-separated list of keywords. The valid keywords are **source** (source file debugging information), **lines** (line number debugging information), and **vars** (local variable debugging information).

- **-nowarn**—Disables all warning messages.

- **-O**—Optimizes code for performance in terms of the quickest execution time. Note that using the **-O** option may slow down compilation, produce larger class files, and make the program difficult to debug. Note that before JDK 1.2, the **-g** and **-O** options of javac could not be used together. As of JDK 1.2, you can combine **-g** and **-O**, but you might get odd results, such as missing variables and relocated or missing code. **-O** no longer automatically turns on **-depend** or turns off **–g**.

- **-sourcepath** *sourcepath*—Specifies the source code path to search for class or interface definitions. As with the user class path, source path entries are separated by semicolons (;) and can be directories, .jar (Java Archive) files, or zip files. If you use packages, the local pathname within the directory or archive must reflect the package name, as you'll see later. Note that classes found through the class path are subject to automatic recompilation if their source code files are found.

- **-verbose**—Creates "verbose" output. This includes information about each class loaded and each source file compiled.

- **-X**—Displays information about nonstandard options and quits.

- **-Xdepend**—Searches all reachable classes for more recent source files to recompile. This option will more reliably discover classes that need to be recompiled, but it can slow down the compilation process dramatically.

- **-Xstdout**—Sends compiler messages to **System.out**. By default, compiler messages go to **System.err**, which you'll learn more about later.

- **-Xverbosepath**—Describes how paths and standard extensions were searched to find source and class files.

- **-J*option***—You use this option to pass an option to the java launcher called by javac. For example, **-J-Xms64m** sets the startup memory to 64MB. Although this option does not begin with **-X**, it's not a standard option of javac. It's a common convention for **-J** to pass options to the underlying JVM executing applications written in Java.

Cross-Compilation Options

Cross-compilation options are considered an advanced topic; javac supports *cross-compiling*, where classes are compiled with the bootstrap (default) and extension classes of a different Java platform implementation. You must use **-bootclasspath** and **-extdirs** when cross-compiling. Here are the cross-compilation options:

- **-target *version***—Generates class files that will work on JVMs with the specified version. The default is to generate class files that are compatible with both 1.1 and 1.2 JVMs. The versions supported by javac in JDK 1.2 are 1.1 (ensures that generated class files will be compatible with 1.1 and 1.2 JVMs; this is the default) and 1.2 (generates class files that will run on 1.2 JVMs but will not run on 1.1 JVMs).

- **-bootclasspath *bootclasspath***—Cross-compiles against the specified set of boot classes. As with the user class path, boot class path entries are separated by semicolons (;) and can be directories, .jar files, or zip files.

- **-extdirs *directories***—Cross-compiles against the specified extension directories; *directories* is a semicolon-separated list of directories. Each .jar file in the specified directories is automatically searched for class files.

Compiling Code: Checking For Deprecated Methods

"Jeez," says the Novice Programmer, "how can I keep all the deprecated methods in Java straight? Now that I'm upgrading to Java 2, I don't know what's obsolete and what's not!" "That's an easy one," you say. "The Java compiler, javac, will now tell you if you're using a method that's been deprecated, which it didn't used to do unless you specifically asked it to. Even better, you can use the **-deprecation** option to make sure you get all the details."

The **-deprecation** option is a good one, and it's the standard option I use to make sure I avoid deprecated methods. Suppose you have a 200-line program, and when you try to compile it, javac gives you this result:

```
C:\>javac app.java
Note: app.java uses or overrides a deprecated API.  Recompile with
```

```
"-deprecation" for details.
1 warning
```

That's not much help. However, using the **-deprecation** option, you can pinpoint the exact problem:

```
C:\>javac app.java -deprecation
app.java:109: Note: The method java.awt.Dimension size() in class
java.awt.Component has been deprecated.
        x = (size().width - fontmetrics.stringWidth(text)) / 2;
            ^
Note: app.java uses or overrides a deprecated API.  Please consult
the documentation for a better alternative.
1 warning
```

As you can see, the problem is that app.java uses the **size** method in line 109, and that method has been deprecated; replacing it with the new version, **getSize**, solves the problem.

Running Code

The Big Boss is getting impatient. You've written a new application and compiled it without errors the first time (which you can feel proud of), but nothing has really happened that the BB can see. It's time to run the new application.

You run Java applications with the program named *java* (in Windows, for example, this is the java.exe file in the Java bin file). The java program, called the *java tool*, is what actually runs the JVM. Here's how you can use the java tool:

```
java [options] class [argument ...]
java [options] -jar file.jar [argument ...]
```

Here are the parameters in the preceding lines:

- *options*—Command-line options, which I'll cover in a topic coming right up.

- *class*—The name of the class to be invoked.

- *file.jar*—The name of the Java Archive (JAR) file to be invoked. This is used only with **-jar**. JAR files are covered in Chapter 23 .

- *argument*—A command-line argument passed to the **main** method.

For example, to run the application named app, which is in the file app.class, you could execute the following command at the command line (note that you omit the ".class" part of app.class here):

```
java app
```

The result appears immediately:

```
java app
Hello from Java!
```

You can see how this works in a DOS window under Windows in Figure 1.4.

That's all it takes—now you've written, compiled, and run your first application. Congratulations!

Note that if your application isn't responding or if you want to stop it for some reason, you can type Ctrl+C. If that doesn't work, try the Esc key.

You'll also see how to create windowed applications in this book, and when you run one of these applications with the java tool, you get the results shown in Figure 1.5.

There's one thing to note about Figure 1.5—the console window (a DOS window here) hangs around in the background and waits for the application to finish before continuing (that is, before the DOS prompt reappears in this case). If you don't want a console window associated with your windowed application, you can use the javaw tool, like this:

```
javaw app
```

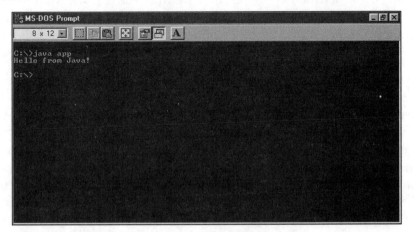

Figure 1.4 Running an application in a DOS window.

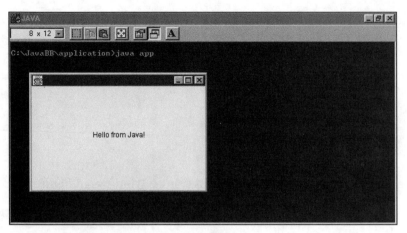

Figure 1.5   Running a windowed application.

Here's how you use javaw in general—just like the java tool:

```
javaw [options] class [argument ...]
javaw [options] -jar file.jar [argument ...]
```

Here are the parameters used by javaw:

- *options*—Command-line options, which I'll cover later in the chapter.

- *class*—The name of the class to be invoked.

- *file.jar*—The name of the Java Archive (JAR) file to be invoked. This is used only with **-jar**. JAR files are covered in Chapter 23.

- *argument*—A command-line argument passed to the **main** method.

When you launch a Java windowed application like this, the console window does not wait for the application to finish; if you're running in DOS, the windowed application appears and the DOS prompt reappears in the DOS window. This gives a more professional feel to those applications that you release for general use.

In fact, there's another launcher in Java 2—the oldjava launcher, which Sun included for backward compatibility. The oldjava launcher does not support the Java Extensions Framework (see the topic "What's New In Java 2?"). It gives you backward compatibility when you have an application that uses a Java 1.1-style security manager, which is incompatible with the 1.2 class-loading techniques (or perhaps the classes you're loading have been generated or changed in some way that's incompatible with the 1.2 class structure). I'm sticking to Java 2 in this book, so there won't be much use for oldjava, but if you're migrating to Java 2 and need to use the old class-loading mechanism, it's good to know it's there. There's also an oldjavaw tool.

That's how you run an application—you use a Java tool such as java, javaw, or oldjava. When you launch a Java 2 application, the Just In Time (JIT) compiler in the launcher compiles the bytecodes in sections and runs the application.

TIP: *If you don't want to use the JIT compiler for some reason, there are two ways to disable it. You can set the environment variable **JAVA_COMPILER** to **NONE**, using, for example, the **SET** command in Windows 95/98 or the System Control Panel in Windows NT. You can also use the **-D** command-line option to set the keyword **java.compiler** to **NONE**, like this: **java -Djava.compiler=NONE app**.*

While we're on the topic of compiling and running code, there's another detail that we should cover—the command-line options you can use with the javac and java commands. We'll take a look at them in the next two topics.

Running Code: Using Command-Line Options

"Well," says the Novice Programmer, "I have another problem. I've stored all my .class files in one directory, but I don't want to keep switching to that directory to run them." "Another easy problem to solve," you say. "You can use the java tool's **-classpath** option or set the CLASSPATH environment variable so that the Java compiler will search for your classes correctly."

TIP: *For more on **CLASSPATH**, an important topic in Java programming, see the upcoming topic "Basic Skills: Finding Java Classes With **CLASSPATH**."*

We'll take a look at using the command-line options in this topic; you use these options with the java, javaw, and oldjava tools, like this (for a discussion of these tools, see the topic "Running Code," earlier in this chapter):

```
java [options] class [argument ...]
java [options] -jar file.jar [argument ...]
javaw [options] class [argument ...]
javaw [options] -jar file.jar [argument ...]
oldjava [options] class [argument ...]
oldjavaw [options] class [argument ...]
```

Here are the command-line options you can use with these tools (note that non-standard options, which means they might not be supported in the future, begin with an **X**):

- **-classpath** *classpath or* **-cp classpath**—Specifies a list of directories, .jar files, or .zip files to search for class files. You separate class path entries with semicolons (;). Note that specifying **-classpath** or **-cp** overrides any setting of the CLASSPATH environment variable. Used with java or javaw, **-classpath** or **-cp** only specifies the class path for user classes. Used with oldjava or oldjavaw, **-classpath** or **-cp** specifies the class path for both user classes and bootstrap classes. If **-classpath** and **-cp** are not used and CLASSPATH is not set, the user class path is limited to the current directory, which is referred to with a dot (.). See the topic "Basic Skills: Finding Java Classes With CLASSPATH," later in this chapter, for more information.

- **-Dproperty=value**—Sets a system property value.

- **-jar**—Executes a program encapsulated in a JAR file. The first argument is the name of a JAR file instead of a startup class name. When you use this option, the JAR file is the source of all user classes, and other user class path settings are ignored. The oldjava and oldjavaw tools do not support the **-jar** option.

- **-verbose** *or* **-verbose:class**—Displays information about each class loaded.

- **-verbose:gc**—Reports on each garbage-collection event. Garbage collection involves automatic memory management in Java.

- **-verbose:jni**—Reports information about the use of native (that is, platform-specific) methods and other Java Native Interface activity.

- **-version**—Displays version information and exits.

- **-?** *or* **-help**—Displays usage information and exits.

- **-X**—Displays information about nonstandard options and exits.

- **-Xbootclasspath:bootclasspath**—Specifies a semicolon-separated list of directories, .jar files, or .zip files to search for boot class files. Note that these will be used in place of the boot class files included with Java itself.

- **-Xdebug**—Starts with the debugger enabled.

- **-Xnoclassgc**—Disables class garbage collection.

- **-Xmsn**—Indicates the initial size of the memory pool you want to use (this value must greater than 1000). To multiply the value by 1000, append the letter k. To multiply the value by 1 million, append the letter m. The default value is **1m**.

- **-Xmxn**—Specifies the maximum size of the memory pool (this value must greater than 1000). To multiply the value by 1000, append the letter k. To multiply the value by 1 million, append the letter m. The default value is **64m**.

- **-Xrunhprof[:help][:<suboption>=<value>,...]**—Enables CPU, heap, or monitor profiling. This option is usually followed by a list of comma-separated pairs of the form **<suboption>=<value>**.

- **-Xrs**—Reduces the use of operating system signals.

- **-Xcheck:jni**—Performs additional checks for Java Native Interface functions.
- **-Xfuture**—Performs strict class-file format checks.

Basic Skills: Commenting Your Code

The Programming Correctness Czar comes in and looks at you reprovingly. "What's wrong, PCC?" you ask. "It's your code," the PCC says. "I can't make heads or tails of what's going on in it." "I guess I forgot to comment it," you say. "I guess you did," the PCC says. "Fix it."

Sometimes, code can be very cryptic and hard to decipher. For that reason, Java lets you place descriptive comments in your code to let you explain to anyone who reads that code how the program works and what it does. As an example, let's add comments to the application we've already developed in the previous topics:

```java
public class app
{
    public static void main(String[] args)
    {
        System.out.println("Hello from Java!");
    }
}
```

Java supports three types of comments, two of which are taken from C++. You can surround a comment of any length with the characters /* and */ like this:

```java
/* This application prints out "Hello from Java!" */

public class app
{
    public static void main(String[] args)
    {
        System.out.println("Hello from Java!");
    }
}
```

The Java compiler will ignore all the text between the **/*** and ***/** markers. You can split comments between these markers across multiple lines, like this:

```java
/* This application prints out "Hello from Java!"
   Created by: G. Whiz, 1/1/00                  */
```

```
public class app
{
    public static void main(String[] args)
    {
        System.out.println("Hello from Java!");
    }
}
```

In fact, in many corporate environments, you're expected to use a standard comment header, created with the /* and */ form of comment, for all new code. It might look something like this:

```
/*******************************************************
*  This application prints out "Hello from Java!"       *
*                                                       *
*  Author: G.Whiz                                       *
*  Imports: None                                        *
*  Parameters: Command-line arguments                   *
*  Returns: None                                        *
*  Assumptions: None                                    *
*  Creation date: 1/1/00                                *
*  Last Update: 1/1/01                                  *
*******************************************************/

public class app
{
    public static void main(String[] args)
    {
        System.out.println("Hello from Java!");
    }
}
```

Java also supports a one-line comment, using a double slash, **//**. The Java compiler will ignore everything on a line after the // marker, so you can create whole lines that are comments or just add a comment to an individual line, like this:

```
/* This application prints out "Hello from Java!" */

public class app     //Create the app class
{
    //Create main(), the entry point for the application.
    public static void main(String[] args)
    {
        //Print out the message with
```

```
        System.out.println("Hello from Java!");
    }
}
```

Finally, Java also supports a documentation comment, which starts with /** and ends with */. This comment is designed to be used with the javadoc tool, which can create documentation for you nearly automatically. We'll take a look at this in Chapter 21. Here's an example using /** and */:

```
/** This application prints out "Hello from Java!" */

public class app
{
    public static void main(String[] args)
    {
        System.out.println("Hello from Java!");
    }
}
```

Commenting your code can be invaluable in team environments where you share your code source files with others. It's also handy if someone else is going to take over a project that you have been working on.

Basic Skills: Importing Java Packages And Classes

"Hmm," says the Novice Programmer, "I've got a problem. The Design Team Co-ordinator told me to use the **Date** class to print out the current date in my application, but Java doesn't seem to have ever heard of the **Date** class—I get an error every time I try to use it." "That's because the **Date** class is part of the Java util package, and you have to import that package before you can use it." "*Import* it?" the NP asks.

The classes that Sun has created for you to use are stored in class libraries called *packages*. To make a class in a package available to your code, you have to import the package, which means the compiler will search that package for classes. You can also import individual classes that are not part of a package. By default, only the basic Java statements are available to you in an application—that is, the ones in the core java.lang Java package. The compiler automatically imports the java.lang package for you, but to use the rest of the classes that come with Java, you'll have to do your own importing with the **import** statement. Here's how you use that statement:

```
import [package1[.package2...].](classname|*);
```

Note that you put a dot (.) between package and class names to keep them separate. The standard java packages, themselves, are stored in a large package called *java*, so the util package is really called the *java.util* package (there are other large packages like the java package available; for example, the extensive swing package is stored in the javax package). You can refer to the **Date** class in java.util as **java.util.Date**. Here's how to import that class into a program:

```
import java.util.Date;

public class app
{
    .
    .
    .
```

Note that if you're going to use **import** statements to import classes into a program, the **import** statements should be at the top of the code. Now we're free to use the **Date** class, like this (note that we're creating an object from the **Date** class using the Java **new** operator, which you'll learn more about in Chapter 4):

```
import java.util.Date;

public class app
{
    public static void main(String[] args)
    {
        System.out.println("Today = " + new Date());
    }
}
```

When you run this application, you'll see the current date displayed, like this:

```
C:\>java app
Today = Mon Aug 02 12:15:13 EDT 2000
```

As you can see by studying the general form of the preceding **import** statement, there's also a shorthand technique that loads in all the classes in a package—you can use an asterisk (*) as a wildcard to stand for all the classes in a particular package. Here's how that would look if you wanted to import all the classes in the java.util package at once:

```
import java.util.*;

public class app
{
```

```
    public static void main(String[] args)
    {
        System.out.println("Today = " + new Date());
    }
}
```

> **TIP:**   *Importing packages and classes only indicates to the compiler where to look for the code it needs—it does not increase the size of your code. For that reason, the bytecode file app.class will be the same size if you use either the* **import java.util.Date;** *statement or the* **import java.util.*;** *statement.*

This is fine if you stick with importing the Sun-provided classes, because Java knows where to look for the classes it was installed with. But what if you want to import your own classes or ones provided by a third party?

Here's an example. Suppose you have a class named **printer** in a file named printer.java, and that class has one method, named **print**:

```
public class printer
{
    public void print()
    {
        System.out.println("Hello from Java!");
    }
}
```

You might want to make use of the **print** method in other classes, as in this case, where we're creating a new object of the **printer** class using the **new** operator and using that object's **print** method in an application named *app*:

```
public class app
{
    public static void main(String[] args)
    {
        (new printer()).print();
    }
}
```

To do this, you can import the **printer** class this way (note that you can also place the code for the **printer** class in the same file as the **app** class, in which case you wouldn't have to import the **printer** class):

```
import printer;

public class app
{
```

```
    public static void main(String[] args)
    {
        (new printer()).print();
    }
}
```

This works just as it should. Congratulations, you've just imported a class into a program.

This technique is fine if **printer.class** is in the same directory in which you're compiling this application, because the Java compiler will search the current directory by default. However, suppose you want to store all your classes in a directory named, say, c:\classes. How will the Java compiler find **printer.class** there? To answer that question, take a look at the next topic on **CLASSPATH**.

Basic Skills: Finding Java Classes With **CLASSPATH**

"That darn Johnson," the Novice Programmer says. "He gave me a new Java class file, johnson.class, to work with, and it's supposed to solve my problems with that spreadsheet. But Java claims it can't find johnson.class!" "Where are you keeping that file?" you ask. "In a special directory I made for it," the NP says, "called darnjohnson." "That's your problem," you say. "You have to include the darnjohnson directory in your class path."

By default, Java will be able to find its bootstrap classes (the ones it comes with), extension classes (those that use the Java Extension Framework; see the topic "What's New In Java 2?" in this chapter), and classes in the current directory (that is, where you're compiling your program). Classes can be stored in .class files, in .jar, and .zip files. Java can search all these types of files.

But what if you want to have Java search for classes in another directory or in a .jar file supplied by a third party? You can do that with the **CLASSPATH** environment variable, because Java uses this variable to determine where you want to search for classes.

Here's an example that I first introduced in the previous topic. Say that you have a class named **printer** in a file named printer.java, and that class has one method, named **print**:

```
public class printer
{
    public void print()
    {
```

```
        System.out.println("Hello from Java!");
    }
}
```

Now say, as in the previous topic, that you want to use the **print** method in another classes—as in this case, where we're creating a new object of the **printer** class using the **new** operator and using that object's **print** method in an application named *app*:

```
import printer;

public class app
{
    public static void main(String[] args)
    {
        (new printer()).print();
    }
}
```

This works if **printer.class** is in the same directory in which you're compiling this application, because the Java compiler will search the current directory by default. But suppose you want to store all your classes in a directory named c:\classes. How will the Java compiler find **printer.class** there?

To make the Java compiler search c:\classes, you can set the **CLASSPATH** environment variable to include that directory. By default, there are no paths or directories in **CLASSPATH**, but you can add a semicolon-separated list to **CLASSPATH**, like this one for Windows (note that it's important here not to have any spaces around the equals sign):

```
SET CLASSPATH=c:\classes;c:\newclasses
```

In Windows NT, you can follow these steps to set the **CLASSPATH** environment variable:

1. Open the Start menu and select Settings|Control Panel. Double-click on the Control Panel to open it.

2. In the Systems Properties dialog box, click on the Environment tab.

3. Click on the **CLASSPATH** variable, making **CLASSPATH's** current setting visible at the bottom of the dialog box.

4. Add the path you want to the **CLASSPATH** setting and click on OK to close the System Properties dialog box.

You can also determine the current setting of **CLASSPATH** using the **SET** command by itself:

```
C:\>SET
TMP=C:\WINDOWS\TEMP
PROMPT=$p$g
winbootdir=C:\WINDOWS
COMSPEC=C:\WINDOWS\COMMAND.COM
PATH=C:\WINDOWS;C:\JDK1.2.2\BIN
windir=C:\WINDOWS
CLASSPATH=C:\CLASSES;C:\NEWCLASSES
```

Now the Java compiler (and other Java tools such as the java tool) will know enough to search c:\classes and c:\newclasses automatically. That means that this code will now work if **printer.class** is in c:\classes, because that directory is in **CLASSPATH**:

```
import printer;

public class app
{
    public static void main(String[] args)
    {
        (new printer()).print();
    }
}
```

You can append the current settings in **CLASSPATH** to a new setting, like this:

```
SET CLASSPATH=c:\classes;c:\newclasses;%CLASSPATH%
```

Note that you can also search .jar and .zip files for classes, as shown here:

```
SET CLASSPATH=server.jar;classes.zip;%CLASSPATH%
```

Originally, **CLASSPATH** was a big headache for beginning Java programmers, because no classes were considered bootstrap classes, which meant that you had to set up and understand **CLASSPATH** before you could use Java at all. That's been fixed with the concept of bootstrap classes, which are the classes that come with Java (and are searched automatically). However, if you want to use nonstandard packages or store your own classes in other directories, it's important to know how to set **CLASSPATH**.

Creating Applets

The Big Boss is getting impatient. "What's all this about applications that print out 'Hello from Java!' in the console window? What we want to use Java for is to create applets that you can look at in Web browsers." "OK," you say, "just give me a minute."

In the chapters that follow, we'll be taking a look at Java syntax, which might make it a hard path for you to follow if you're primarily interested in writing applets. What's more, it seems intolerable that we shouldn't start out a book on a language as visual as Java without at least one applet. Therefore, in this topic, I'll cover the process of creating a Java applet in overview. Knowing how to create a basic applet will help if you want to test the syntax of the next few chapters visually. Applets will be formally introduced in Chapter 6, so consider this a sneak preview.

Standard applets are built on the **Applet** class, which is in the java.applet package. Therefore, we'll start by importing that class in a new Java source code file, which we'll call applet.java:

```
import java.applet.Applet;
    .
    .
    .
```

The **java.applet.Applet** class is the class that forms the base for standard applets, and you can derive your own applet classes from this class using the **extends** keyword:

```
import java.applet.Applet;

public class applet extends Applet
{
    .
    .
    .
}
```

So far so good; now it's time to add code to this new applet. Applets don't have a **main** method like applications do—in fact, that's the primary code difference between applets and applications. So how can you display text directly in an applet?

The actual drawing of an applet is accomplished in its **paint** method, which the Java Virtual Machine calls when it's time to display the applet. The **java.applet.Applet** class has its own **paint** method, but we can *override* that method by defining our own **paint** method, like this (see Chapters 4 and 5 for details on overriding):

```
import java.applet.Applet;
import java.awt.*;

public class applet extends Applet
{
    public void paint(Graphics g)
    {
        .
        .
        .
    }
}
```

This method, **paint**, is actually a part of the Java Abstract Windowing Toolkit (AWT), which you'll see a great deal of in this book, so we've imported the AWT classes with the statement **import java.awt.*** here. You'll see how the following details work later in this book, but for now, here's basically how they work: The **paint** method is passed a Java object of the **Graphics** class (this object is named **g** in the code). You can use this object's **drawString** method to actually draw the text. In this case, we'll draw the text "Hello from Java!" at location (60, 100) in the applet; coordinates are measured in pixels from the upper-left corner of the applet, so this position is 60 pixels from the left border of the applet and 100 pixels from the top. Here's what the code looks like:

```
import java.applet.Applet;
import java.awt.*;

public class applet extends Applet
{
    public void paint(Graphics g)
    {
        g.drawString("Hello from Java!", 60, 100);
    }
}
```

That's all it takes; now you can compile applet.java to applet.class. There's one more step to take—creating a Web page to display the applet in. We'll take a look at that next.

Running Applets

"OK," the Big Boss says, "you've created an applet. Why don't I see it in a Web page?" "Coming right up," you say. "I think...."

To display an applet, you can use a Web page with an HTML (Hypertext Markup Language) **<APPLET>** tag in it. In fact, there's a shortcut in which you can actually store the needed HTML in an applet's source code file itself, as you'll see in Chapter 6; you'll also learn all about the **<APPLET>** tag in that chapter. For now, here's a Web page, applet.html, that will display the applet developed in the previous topic:

```
<HTML>
<HEAD>
<TITLE>APPLET</TITLE>
</HEAD>
<BODY>
<HR>
<CENTER>
<APPLET
    CODE=applet.class
    WIDTH=200
    HEIGHT=200 >
</APPLET>
</CENTER>
<HR>
</BODY>
</HTML>
```

You can open this applet Web page in a Web browser, as shown in Figure 1.6, where the applet is opened in Microsoft Internet Explorer.

You can also use the Sun appletviewer, which comes with Java, to open applet.html, like this:

```
C:\>appletviewer applet.html
```

Figure 1.7 shows the applet in the Sun appletviewer.

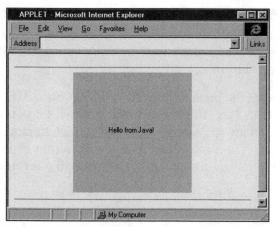

Figure 1.6   An applet at work in Internet Explorer.

Figure 1.7   An applet at work in the Sun appletviewer.

Creating Windowed Applications

The Big Boss is impressed with your new applet and asks, "Can you also make an application display windows?" "Sure," you say. "Coming right up."

You'll learn all about creating windowed applications in depth in Chapter 6, but it's worth taking a sneak preview here. Creating a windowed application is much like creating an applet, except that you have to have a **main** method, and you're responsible for creating the window yourself. To create the window for the application, we'll derive a new class from the AWT **Frame** class and add the same code to the **paint** method that was used in the applet in the previous topic:

```
import java.awt.*;

class AppFrame extends Frame
```

```
{
    public void paint(Graphics g)
    {
        g.drawString("Hello from Java!", 60, 100);
    }
}
```

Now we'll create the application class itself, which we'll name *app*. This is the class that will have a **main** method, and in that method, we'll use the **new** operator to create a new object of the **AppFrame** class, give it a size in pixels, and show it on the screen, all of which looks like this:

```
import java.awt.*;
import java.awt.event.*;

class AppFrame extends Frame
{
    public void paint(Graphics g)
    {
        g.drawString("Hello from Java!", 60, 100);
    }
}

public class app
{
    public static void main(String [] args)
    {
        AppFrame f = new AppFrame();

        f.setSize(200, 200);

        f.addWindowListener(new WindowAdapter() { public void
            windowClosing(WindowEvent e) {System.exit(0);}});

        f.show();
    }
}
```

TIP: *Including the line of code here having to do with the **addWindowListener** method means that when the application window is closed, the application itself will end. You'll learn more about how this very compact and powerful line, which uses inner classes and adapter classes, does its work later in this book.*

Now that the new windowed application is ready to go, how do you actually run it? Take a look at the next topic.

Running Windowed Applications

As with console applications, to run a windowed application, you can use the java or javaw tools, like this:

```
java app
javaw app
```

The java tool launches the application and makes the console window wait until the application is dismissed, whereas the javaw tool launches the application and doesn't wait until the application is dismissed. The running application appears in Figure 1.8.

That's all there is to it—now you're running windowed Java applications.

Figure 1.8   A windowed application.

Designing Java Programs

You've been made the head of program design—and your new office is a stunner. But as you sit there, gazing out of your corner window and stroking your new teak desk, you wonder if you can you handle the new position.

Program design in Java is not necessarily an easy task. Good programming design involves a number of overall aspects, and it's worth taking a look at some of them in this chapter, before we start digging into Java syntax in depth.

In fact, one of the most important aspects of creating a new application is designing that application. Poor choices can end up hampering your application through many revisions of the product. Many books are available on program design. Microsoft, which should know something about it, breaks the process into four areas:

- *Performance*—The responsiveness and overall optimization of speed and resource use.
- *Maintainability*—The ability of the application to be easily maintained.
- *Extensibility*—The ability of the application to be extended in well defined ways.
- *Availability*—How robust the implementation of the application is and how available it is for use.

Let's take a quick look at these four areas now.

Performance

Performance is a design issue that's hard to argue with. If the users aren't getting what they want out of your application, that's clearly a problem. In general, performance depends on the users' needs. For some people, speed is essential; for others, robustness or efficient use of resources is what they're looking for. Overall, the performance of an application is an indication of how well it responds to the users' needs. Here are some general aspects of performance that you should consider when writing Java programs:

- Algorithm efficiency
- CPU speed
- Efficient database design and normalization
- Limiting external accesses
- Network speed
- Security issues
- Speed issues
- Use of resources
- Web access speed

We'll get to more specifics of performance throughout the book.

Maintainability

Maintainability is the measure of how easily you can adapt your application to future needs. This issue comes down to using good programming practices, which I'll talk about throughout the book. Much of this is common sense—simply keeping future coding needs in mind as you write your code. Some major issues in the "best programming" arsenal include the following:

- Avoid deep nesting of loops and conditionals
- Avoid passing global variables to procedures

- Be modular when you write code
- Break code into packages
- Document program changes
- Give each procedure only one purpose
- Make sure your application can scale well for larger tasks and numbers of users
- Plan for code reuse
- Program defensively
- Use access procedures for sensitive data
- Use comments
- Use consistent variable names
- Use constants instead of "magic" numbers

Extensibility

Extensibility is the ability of your application to be extended in a well-defined and relatively easy way. Extensibility is usually a concern only with larger applications, and it often involves an entire interface especially designed for extension modules. In fact, Java, itself, is designed to be extended, using the Java Extension Framework.

Availability

Availability is the measure of how much of the time your application can be used—in comparison to the time users want to use it. This includes everything from not freezing up when performing a long task (at the least, giving the user some feedback of the operation's status), to working with techniques and methods not likely to hang, to making backups of crucial data, to planning for alternate resource use—if possible—when access to a desired resource is blocked.

Overall, the design process is one that involves quite a bit of time. In fact, the whole development cycle is the subject of quite a few studies—you may be surprised to learn that when field testing, in-house testing, planning, design, and user interface testing are added up, some studies allocate as little as 15 percent of total project time to the actual coding.

So much has been written about the development cycle of software that I won't go into much more detail here. But it's worth noting that programmers shouldn't short-change the crucial design steps, because—in serious projects—that can lead to more problems in the long run than time saved in the short run.

Distributing Your Java Program

"Well," the Novice Programmer says, "I've finished my Java program, and I'm ready to sell it." "Oh yes?" you ask. "Better check the licensing agreement first."

In order for users to run your programs, they'll need to have a Java runtime environment on their systems. The Java 2 JDK contains a runtime environment, so users could use that if they happen to have it installed. However, note that most users won't have the whole Java 2 JDK installed, so a better choice for your users will be the Java 2 Runtime Environment (JRE). Here's why distributing the JRE instead of the JDK is a good idea:

- The Java 2 Runtime Environment is redistributable, and the Java 2 JDK is not, which is to say that the JRE license lets you to package it with your software. By distributing the JRE with your application, you can make sure your users will have the correct version of the runtime environment for your software.

- The JRE is smaller than the JDK. The JRE contains all that users need to run your software, but it doesn't include the development tools and applications that are part of the JDK. Because the JRE is small, it's easier for you to package with your software as well as for users to download for themselves from the Java Software Web site.

- In Windows, the JRE installer automatically installs java and javaw in the operating system's path, which means you don't have to worry about finding the launchers to start your application (which means, in turn, that you don't have to give instructions to users for setting up paths on their systems).

You can find more information about the Java 2 Runtime Environment at **http://java.sun.com/products/jdk/1.2/runtime.html**.

Chapter 2

Variables, Arrays, And Strings

(continued)

In Depth

This chapter begins our discussion of Java syntax, and you'll see a great deal in this chapter. Here I'm going to cover how Java stores and retrieves data in variables, arrays, and strings. Working with data is a fundamental part of any significant program, and the information in this chapter is essential for any Java programmer. Even if you already program in Java, take a look at the material in this chapter, because there's a lot coming up here.

Variables

Variables come in different types and serve as placeholders in memory for data. The different types have to do with the format the data is stored in, and how much memory is set aside to hold that data. For example, the integer variable type, the int type, is made up of four bytes (or 32 bits), and you use it to store integer values. This gives the data in the int type a range of possible values from -2,147,483,648 to 2,147,483,647. There are quite a few different variable types built into Java, such as integers, floating-point numbers, and individual characters, and you'll see them all in this chapter.

Before you use a variable in Java, you must *declare* it, specifying its data type. Here's how you declare variables in Java:

```
type name [= value][, name [= value]...];
```

Here's an example showing how to declare a variable of the int type, which means an integer will be stored in it (the variable is named **days**):

```
public class app
{
    public static void main(String[] args)
    {
        int days;



    }
}
```

This code allocates 32 bits of storage in memory and labels the location of that storage, as far as the Java compiler is concerned, as **days**, which means you can now refer to that name in code. Here's how to store a numeric value of 365 in **days**, using the Java assignment operator (=):

```
public class app
{
    public static void main(String[] args)
    {
        int days;

        days = 365;

        .
        .
        .

    }
}
```

Here, the value 365 is an integer *literal*, which means a literal value that you place directly in your code. We'll take a look at what kinds of literals Java allows throughout this chapter. To verify that **days** now holds 365, you can print it out on the console:

```
public class app
{
    public static void main(String[] args)
    {
        int days;

        days = 365;

        System.out.println("Number of days = " + days);
    }
}
```

Here's the result of this code:

```
C:\>java app
Number of days = 365
```

As you can see, we've created a variable, stored data in it, and fetched that data back to print it on the screen. That's how it works.

There's also a convenient shortcut that lets you initialize a variable when you declare it. Here, **days** is declared and initialized to 365 in one step:

```
public class app
{
    public static void main(String[] args)
    {
        int days = 365;

        System.out.println("Number of days = " + days);
    }
}
```

The int type is only one kind of simple variable you can use. Here are all the possibilities:

- *Integers*—These types are byte, short, int, and long, which hold signed, whole-value numbers.

- *Floating-point numbers*—These types are float and double, which hold signed floating-point numbers.

- *Characters*—This is the char type, which holds representations of characters such as letters and numbers.

- *Boolean*—This type is designed to hold only two types of values: true and false.

We'll take a closer look at all these in the "Immediate Solutions" section, including what range of values each can hold. Together, these types make up what are called *simple data types* in Java. Each of these types represents a single data value, not a compound one (as opposed to an array, which is also discussed in this chapter). You can store one data item in a variable made up of any simple data type, and that data item must fit into the range allowed for that data type.

Data Typing

Java puts considerable emphasis on its data types. It's a *strongly typed* language, which means it insists that the simple variables you declare and use must fit into the listed types.

Every simple variable must have a type (and in fact, every expression—every combination of terms that Java can evaluate to a get a value—has a type as well). Also, Java is very particular about maintaining the integrity of those types, especially if you try to assign a value of one type to a variable of another type. In fact, Java is more strongly typed than a language like C++; in C++, for example, you can assign a floating-point number to an integer, and C++ will handle the type conversion for you, but you can't do that in Java. You can, however, convert between certain data types in Java, such as between the integer types, and we'll take a look at that in this chapter.

TIP: *When working with variables, you might find the Java compiler issuing a lot of errors and warnings about data types, which can take some getting used to; bear in mind that the inspiration for making Java very particular about adhering to data types and not mixing them easily is to prevent errors in your code.*

That's an overview of what's going on in Java with simple data types and variables; it's now time to take a look at compound data storage in depth, which as far as this chapter is concerned, means *arrays*.

Arrays

Simple types are fine for storing single data items, but data is often more complex than that. Say, for example, that you want to start a new bank, the Java Programming Bank, and need to keep track of the amount of money in every account, as indexed by account number. A method of working with compound data is best here, and that's what arrays provide.

Using an array, you can group simple data types into a more compound data structure and refer to that new data structure by name. More importantly, you can refer to the individual data items stored in the array by numeric index. That's important, because computers excel at performing millions of operations very quickly, so if your data may be referenced with a numeric index, you can work through a whole set of data very quickly, simply by incrementing the array index and thus accessing all the items in the array.

Here's an example; in this case, I'll start Java Programming Bank out with 100 new accounts, and each one will have its own entry in an array named **accounts[]**. The square braces at the end of **accounts[]** indicate that it's an array, and you place the index number of the item in the array you want to access in the braces. Here's how I create the **accounts[]** array, making each entry in it of the floating-point type double for extra precision. First, I declare the array; then I create it with the **new** operator, which is what Java uses to actually allocate memory:

```
public class app
{
    public static void main(String[] args)
    {
        double accounts[];

        accounts = new double[100];
        .
        .
        .
```

Now that I've created an array with 100 items, I can refer to those items numerically, like this (note that I'm storing $43.95 in account 3 and printing that amount out):

```
public class app
{
    public static void main(String[] args)
    {
        double accounts[];

        accounts = new double[100];

        accounts[3] = 43.95;

        System.out.println("Account 3 has $" + accounts[3]);
    }
}
```

Here's the result of this program:

```
C:\>java app
Account 3 has $43.95
```

As you can see, you can now refer to the items in the array using a numeric index, which organizes them in an easy way. In Java, the lower bound of an array you declare this way is 0, so the statement **accounts = new double[100]** creates an array whose first item is **accounts[0]** and whose last item is **accounts[99]**.

You can combine the declaration and creation steps into one step, like this:

```
public class app
{
    public static void main(String[] args)
    {
        double accounts[] = new double[100];

        accounts[3] = 43.95;

        System.out.println("Account 3 has $" + accounts[3]);
    }
}
```

You can also initialize an array with values when you declare it if you enclose the list of values you want to use in curly braces, as you'll see in this chapter. For example, this code creates four accounts and stores 43.95 in **accounts[3]**:

```
public class app
{
    public static void main(String[] args)
    {
        double accounts[] = {0, 0, 0, 43.95};

        accounts[3] = 43.95;

        System.out.println("Account 3 has $" + accounts[3]);
    }
}
```

It turns out that some of the customers in the Java Programming Bank are unhappy, though; they want a checking account in addition to a savings account.
How will you handle this and still keep things indexed by account number?

The **accounts**[] array is a one-dimensional array, also called a *vector*, which means
you can think of it as a single list of numbers that you can index with one number.
However, arrays can have multiple dimensions in Java, which means you can
have multiple array indexes. In this next example, I'll extend **accounts**[] into a
two-dimensional array—**accounts**[][]—to handle both a savings account and a
checking account. The first index of **accounts**[][] will be 0 for savings accounts
and 1 for checking accounts, and the second index will be the account number, as
before. Here's how this works in code:

```
public class app
{
    public static void main(String[] args)
    {
        double accounts[][] = new double[2][100];

        accounts[0][3] = 43.95;
        accounts[1][3] = 2385489382.06;

        System.out.println("Savings account 3 has $" + accounts[0][3]);
        System.out.println("Checking account 3 has $" + accounts[1][3]);
    }
}
```

Now that **accounts**[][] is a two-dimensional array, each item in it is referred to
using two index values; for example, the savings balance for account 3 is now
accounts[0][3], and the checking balance is **accounts[1][3]**. Here are the results when you run this application:

```
C:\>java app
Savings account 3 has $43.95
Checking account 3 has $2.38548938206E9
```

Note that I've given account 3 a checking balance of $2,385,489,382.06 (wishful thinking) and that Java has printed that out as 2.38548938206E9. This is Java's shorthand for $2.38548938206 \times 10^9$, not an inconsiderable bank balance.

> **TIP:** You'll see a lot of arrays in this chapter, but you should know that Java 2 now supports much more complex data structures than arrays. These data structures are built into the language. Java 2 now supports hashes and maps as well as other types of data structures, as you'll see when we take a look at the new collection classes in Chapter 21.

Strings

You may have noticed that I've been using the **+** operator to create the text to print in the previous examples, like this:

```
public class app
{
    public static void main(String[] args)
    {
        double accounts[][] = new double[2][100];

        accounts[0][3] = 43.95;
        accounts[1][3] = 2385489382.06;

        System.out.println("Savings account 3 has $" + accounts[0][3]);
        System.out.println("Checking account 3 has $" + accounts[1][3]);
    }
}
```

That's because text strings are supported by their own class in Java—the **String** class—and you can think of the **String** class as defining a new data type. For example, here's how I create a string named **greeting** that holds the text "Hello from Java!":

```
public class app
{
    public static void main(String[] args)
    {
        String greeting = "Hello from Java!";
        .
        .
        .
```

Now I can treat this string as I would other types of variables, including printing it out:

```
public class app
{
    public static void main(String[] args)
    {
        String greeting = "Hello from Java!";

        System.out.println(greeting);
    }
}
```

Here's the result of this application:

```
C:\>java app
Hello from Java!
```

Although strings are not one of the simple data types in Java, they deserve a place in this chapter, because most programmers treat them as they would any other data type. In fact, many programmers would argue that strings should be a simple data type in Java, as they are in other languages. The reason they are not has to do with Java's lineage, which stretches back to C. C has no string simple data type; in C, you handle strings as one-dimensional arrays of characters, which is pretty awkward. One of the things that made programmers happy about C++ was that most implementations included a String class, which you could use much as you would any other data type. Java follows this usage, implementing strings as a class, not as an intrinsic data type, but string handling is so fundamental to programming that it makes sense to start looking at string variables in this chapter.

There are two string classes in Java: **String** and **StringBuffer**. You use the **String** class to create text strings that cannot change, and you can use **StringBuffer** to create strings you can modify. As you can see in the preceding code, you can use strings much as you would any simple data type in Java. We'll take a look at using strings in this chapter as well as in the next chapter (which is on using operators such as + and -). We'll also take a look at using operators on strings.

That's enough overview for now—it's time to start creating and using variables, arrays, and strings.

Immediate Solutions

What Data Types Are Available?

"Say," the Big Boss says, "how about writing a Java program to manage the company's debt?" "We're in debt?" you ask. "Just a little," the BB replies. "How little?" you ask. "About $2,848,238,493,902.77," says the BB. "Hmm," you say. "Sounds like a job for floating-point numbers."

What simple data types can you use to create variables in Java? You'll find them in Table 2.1.

The simple data types can be broken up by category, as I did at the beginning of this chapter, like this:

- *Integers*—These types are byte, short, int, and long. They hold signed, whole-value numbers.

Table 2.1   Variable types.

Variable Type	Bytes of Storage	Range
boolean	2	True, False
byte	1	-128 to 127
char	2	N/A
double	8 4	-1.79769313486232E308 to -94065645841247E-324 for negative values and 4.94065645841247E-324 to 1.79769313486232E308 for positive values
float	4	-3.402823E38 to -1.401298E-45 for negative values and 1.401298E-45 to 3.402823E38 for positive values
int	4	-2,147,483,648 to 2,147,483,647
long	8	-9,223,372,036,854,775,808 to 9,223,372,036,854,775,807
short	2	-32,768 to 32,767

- *Floating-point numbers*—These types are float and double. They hold signed, floating-point numbers.

- *Characters*—This is the char type, which holds representations of characters such as letters and numbers.

- *Boolean*—This type is designed to hold only two types of values: true and false.

That's an overview of what simple data types are available; to put each of them to work, see the following topics.

Creating Integer Literals

The Novice Programmer appears and says, "So how do I assign a *hexadecimal* value—that is, base 16—to a variable in Java?"

You say, "You have to use a hexadecimal literal, which starts with the characters *0x* or *0X*."

A literal is a constant value that you can use directly in your Java code, and there are a number of rules that govern them. I've already used integer literals, which are the most common types programmers use, in this chapter. Here's the earlier example:

```
public class app
{
    public static void main(String[] args)
    {
        int days = 365;

        System.out.println("Number of days = " + days);
    }
}
```

Here, I'm assigning an integer literal with a value of 365 to the variable **days**. By default, integer literals are of the int type. However, if you assign them to other integer types, such as short, Java converts the literal's type automatically. On the other hand, longs can have more digits than int values, so Java provides an explicit way of creating long literals: You append an *L* to the end of the literal. Here's an example:

```
public class app
{
```

```
    public static void main(String[] args)
    {
        long value;

        value = 1234567890123456789L;

        System.out.println("The value = " + value);
    }
}
```

Here's the result of this code:

```
C:\>java app
The value = 1234567890123456789
```

You can also create literals in octal format by starting them with a leading zero and in hexadecimal format by starting them with 0x or 0X. Here are some examples:

```
public class app
{
    public static void main(String[] args)
    {
        int value;

        value = 16;

        System.out.println("16 decimal = " + value);

        value = 020;

        System.out.println("20 octal = " + value + " in decimal.");

        value = 0x10;

        System.out.println("10 hexadecimal = " + value + " in decimal.");
    }
}
```

Here's what this program displays:

```
C:\>java app
16 decimal = 16
20 octal = 16 in decimal.
10 hexadecimal = 16 in decimal.
```

Creating Floating-Point Literals

The Novice Programmer appears and says, "I have a problem. I want to put a floating-point number, 1.5, into a floating-point variable, but Java keeps saying 'Incompatible type for =. Explicit cast needed to convert double.' What's going on?" "By default," you say, "floating-point numbers you use as literals are of type double, not of type float. You can change that by adding an f or F to the end of the literal to make it a float or a d or D to make it a double." "Oh," the NP replies.

Floating-point literals are of type double by default in Java code; examples include 3.1415926535, 1.5, and 0.1111111. The standard notation for floating-point literals is to have a whole number followed by a fractional part. You can also indicate a power of 10 with e or E, like this:

```
1.345E10
```

This is the same as 1.345×10^{10} or -9.999E-23, which is the same as -9.999×10^{-23}.

Here's an example in which I'm trying to assign a floating-point literal to a variable of type float:

```
public class app
{
    public static void main(String[] args)
    {
        float value;

        value = 1.5f;

        System.out.println("The value = " + value);
    }
}
```

Unfortunately, the default type for floating-point literals is double, so Java gives me the following error:

```
C:\>javac app.java -deprecation
app.java:7: Incompatible type for =. Explicit cast needed to convert double
to float.
        value = 1.5;
               ^
1 error
```

I can fix this by explicitly making my literal into a float, like this:

```
public class app
{
    public static void main(String[] args)
    {
        float value;

        value = 1.5f;

        System.out.println("The value = " + value);
    }
}
```

Now the code runs as you'd expect:

```
C:\>java app
The value = 1.5
```

Creating Boolean Literals

Boolean values can only be true or false in Java (not 0 or 1 or other numeric values, as in other languages—this is part of Java's strong data typing). This means the only two boolean literals you can use are true and false.

Here's an example using true as a boolean literal:

```
public class app
{
    public static void main(String[] args)
    {
        boolean value;

        value = true;

        System.out.println("The value = " + value);
    }
}
```

Here's the result of this program:

```
C:\>java app
The value = true
```

You can print booleans: true or false

Creating Character Literals

"Hey," says the Novice Programmer, "how do I assign a letter to a variable in Java? I'm evaluating all the company's products and want to assign them letter grades." "You can use character literals, each of which represents a character," you reply. "By the way, does the Big Boss know about this?" "Not yet," says the NP.

The basic form of a Java character literal is just a value that corresponds to a character in the Unicode character set (for more on Unicode, see **www.unicode.org**). Character literals are actually numbers that act as indexes into the Unicode character set, not actual characters. For example, the Unicode code for the letter *C* is 67. Therefore, the following application prints out a *C*:

```
public class app
{
    public static void main(String[] args)
    {
        char char3;

        char3 = 67;

        System.out.println("The third alphabet character = " + char3);
    }
}
```

However, you can also refer to the Unicode code for the letter *C* with a character literal, which you would enclose in single quotes, like this:

```
public class app
{
    public static void main(String[] args)
    {
        char char3;

        char3 = 'C';

        System.out.println("The third alphabet character = " + char3);
    }
}
```

Besides enclosing characters in single quotes to make character literals, you can also enclose special *character escape sequences* in single quotes to make character literals that you couldn't make by typing a single character. Here are the escape sequences:

- \' (single quote)
- \" (double quote)
- \\ (backslash)
- \ b (backspace)
- \ ddd (octal character)
- \ f (form feed)
- \ n (newline; called a *line feed* in DOS and Windows)
- \ r (carriage return)
- \ t (tab)
- \ uxxxx (hexadecimal Unicode character)

For example, if you want to show a double quotation mark in displayed text, you can use the \" escape sequence, like this:

```java
public class app
{
    public static void main(String[] args)
    {
        System.out.println("He said, \"Hello!\"");
    }
}
```

Here's the result of this code:

```
C:\>java app
He said, "Hello!"
```

Creating String Literals

The Novice Programmer is back—this time with some coffee. "OK," the NP says, "here's the problem: I want to use just one **println** statement to print out multiple lines—can I do that?" "Sure," you say, "as long as you use the \ n character literal to stand for a newline." "How's that?" the NP asks.

Here's an example of what the NP wants to do. In this case, I'll print out some multiline text using the \ n character literal to start a new line:

```
public class app
{
    public static void main(String[] args)
    {
        System.out.println("Here is\nsome multiline\ntext.");
    }
}
```

Here's the output of this application:

```
C:\>java app
Here is
some multiline
text.
```

As with most other programming languages, you can enclose text string literals in double quotes (unlike single character literals, which you enclose in single quotes). You can also use the character escape sequences introduced in the previous topic. Note that string literals in Java code are actually converted by the compiler into **String** objects, not inherent simple data types (which means that odd code such as **"Hello".length( )** is perfectly legal and will return the length of the string "Hello").

Declaring Integer Variables

"Now I'm into some real programming," the Novice Programmer says, "and I need to store some integer data. How can I do that?" "With an integer variable," you say. "Pull up a chair and we'll go through it."

Java uses four types of integers, each with its own number of bytes put aside for it in memory: byte (one byte), short (two bytes), int (four bytes), and long (eight bytes). For the range of possible values each type can handle, see the topic "What Data Types Are Available?" in this chapter. Which one you use depends on the range of data you want to use as well as other considerations, such as how much memory is available (in case you want to set up a lot of integers).

Here's an example that puts all the integer types to use, declares an integer of each type, assigns each type some data, and then displays that data:

```
public class app
{
    public static void main(String[] args)
```

```
    {
        byte byte1;
        short short1;
        int int1;
        long long1;


        byte1 = 1;              conversions
        short1 = 100;           (from int)
        int1 = 10000;           automatic
        long1 = 100000000;


        System.out.println("byte1 = " + byte1);
        System.out.println("short1 = " + short1);
        System.out.println("int1 = " + int1);
        System.out.println("long1 = " + long1);
    }
}
```

Here's the result of this application:

```
byte1 = 1
short1 = 100
int1 = 10000
long1 = 100000000
```

Declaring Floating-Point Variables

"Sorry," says the Novice Programmer, "but integers just don't cut it. I'm trying to design a currency converter, and I thought I could ignore the cents part of each value, but the Big Boss told me that every cent counts. Is there any other data type I can use?" "Sure," you say. "You can use floats and doubles."

Java has two built-in types of floating-point variables, each with its own number of bytes set aside for it in memory: float (four bytes) and double (eight bytes). For the range of possible values each type can handle, see the topic "What Data Types Are Available?" in this chapter. Which one you use depends on the range of data you want to use as well as other considerations, such as how much memory is available (in case you want to set up a lot of floating-point values).

Here's an example that declares and uses both a float and a double (note that I explicitly make the literal values either a float or a double literal so there'll be no problem with type conversions):

```
public class app
{
    public static void main(String[] args)
    {
        float float1;
        double double1;

        float1 = 1.11111111111F;
        double1 = 1.1111111111111E+9D;

        System.out.println("float1 = " + float1);
        System.out.println("double1 = " + double1);
    }
}
```

Here's the output of the code (note that I've exceeded the precision allowed for a float, so its value is rounded):

```
C:\>java app
float1 = 1.1111112
double1 = 1.1111111111111E9
```

Declaring Character Variables

You can declare character variables with the keyword **char**. For the possible values you can store in a char variable, see the topic "Character Literals" in this chapter.

Here's an example that declares two char variables: **char1** and **char2**. This example demonstrates that you can assign either a Unicode code or a character literal to a **char** (in fact, the compiler translates character literals into Unicode codes):

```
public class app
{
    public static void main(String[] args)
    {
        char char1, char2;
```

```
        char1 = 65;
        char2 = 'B';

        System.out.println("char1 = " + char1);
        System.out.println("char2 = " + char2);
    }
}
```

Here's the result of this code:

```
C:\>java app
char1 = A
char2 = B
```

Here's a sneak peak at a future topic, in which I add some text to the end of **char1**, converting it to a string, and increment the value in **char2**, changing it from 'B' to 'C':

```
public class app
{
    public static void main(String[] args)
    {
        char char1, char2;

        char1 = 65;
        char2 = 'B';

        System.out.println("char1 = " + char1);
        System.out.println("char2 = " + char2);
        System.out.println("char1 + 1 = " + char1 + 1);
        System.out.println("++char2 = " + ++char2);
    }
}
```

Here's the output of the new version of this program:

```
C:\>java app
char1 = A
char2 = B
char1 + 1 = A1
++char2 = C
```

Declaring Boolean Variables

You declare boolean variables with the **boolean** keyword. Boolean variables can take only two values in Java: true and false (not numerical values such as 0 and 1, as in other programming languages).

Here's an example in which I declare and use two boolean variables:

```
public class app
{
    public static void main(String[] args)
    {
        boolean boolean1, boolean2;

        boolean1 = true;
        boolean2 = false;

        System.out.println("boolean1 = " + boolean1);

        System.out.println("boolean2 = " + boolean2);
    }
}
```

Here's the result of this code:

```
C:\>java app
boolean1 = true
boolean2 = false
```

You usually use boolean values in tests to determine program flow. I'm going to jump the gun here and give you a sneak peak into the next chapter. Here, I'm using these two boolean variables with the Java **if** statement. I test the value in boolean1 with the **if** statement, making the code display the message "boolean1 is true." if it's true and "boolean1 is false." otherwise:

```
public class app
{
    public static void main(String[] args)
    {
        boolean boolean1, boolean2;

        boolean1 = true;
        boolean2 = false;
```

```
        System.out.println("boolean1 = " + boolean1);

        System.out.println("boolean2 = " + boolean2);

        if(boolean1) {
            System.out.println("boolean1 is true.");
        } else {
            System.out.println("boolean1 is false.");
        }
    }
}
```

Here's the new result from this code:

```
C:\>java app
boolean1 = true
boolean2 = false
boolean1 is true.
```

Initializing Variables

"OK," the Novice Programmer says, "I've got it straight now. First, I declare a variable and then I assign a value to it." "Actually," you say, "you can do both in one step." The NP replies, "Tell me how!"

So far, I've been declaring variables and then assigning values to them, like this:

```
public class app
{
    public static void main(String[] args)
    {
        int int1;

        int1 = 1;

        System.out.println("int1 = " + int1);
    }
}
```

However, I can combine these two steps into one by initializing a variable when I declare it, like this:

```
public class app
{
```

```
        public static void main(String[] args)
        {
            int int1 = 1;

            System.out.println("int1 = " + int1);
        }
    }
```

Here's how to declare and initialize multiple variables:

```
public class app
{
    public static void main(String[] args)
    {
        int int1 = 1, int2 = 2, int3 = 3;

        System.out.println("int1 = " + int1 + ", int2 = " + int2 +
        ", int3 = " + int3);
    }
}
```

Here's the result of this program:

```
C:\>java app
int1 = 1, int2 = 2, int3 = 3
```

Dynamic Initialization

Up to this point, I've just assigned constant values to variables, but you can assign any expression (an *expression* is any combination of Java terms that yields a value) to a variable when that variable is declared, as long as the expression is valid at that time. For example, here I'm assigning the value of 2 to **int1** and 3 to **int2** and the value of **int1** times **int2** to **int3** using the Java multiplication operator (*):

```
public class app
{
    public static void main(String[] args)
    {
        int int1 = 2, int2 = 3;
        int int3 = int1 * int2;

        System.out.println("int1 = " + int1 + ", int2 = " + int2 +
        ", int3 = " + int3);
```

```
        }
    }
```

Here's what this code gives you when you run it:

```
C:\>java app
int1 = 2, int2 = 3, int3 = 6
```

Note that the Java compiler has no idea what **int1** times **int2** will be when it creates the bytecodes for this application. This means the actual value with which **int3** is initialized will be determined at runtime, which is why this process is called *dynamic initialization*.

As with C++, in Java you can also intersperse your variable declarations throughout your code, as I'm doing here:

```
public class app
{
    public static void main(String[] args)
    {
        int int1 = 2, int2 = 3;

        System.out.println("int1 = " + int1 + ", int2 = " + int2);

        int int3 = int1 * int2;

        System.out.println("int3 = " + int3);
    }
}
```

Here's the result of this code:

```
C:\>java app
int1 = 2, int2 = 3
int3 = 6
```

Converting Between Data Types

"Uhoh," says the Novice Programmer. "I'm stuck. I have an int variable that I want to assign to a byte variable, but Java keeps giving me an 'Incompatible type for =.' error. What's wrong?" "That's a type conversion problem," you explain, "and you have to use an explicit type cast." "Hmm," says the NP, "how does that work?"

Java is a strongly typed language, and as a result, you're often faced with the situation of assigning a variable of one type to a variable of another. You have two ways you can do this—relying on automatic type conversion and making an explicit type cast. We'll take a look at both here.

Automatic Conversions

When you're assigning one type of data to a variable of another type, Java will convert the data to the new variable type automatically if both the following conditions are true:

- The data type and the variable types are compatible.

- The target type has a larger range than the source type.

For example, you can assign a byte value to an int variable, because byte and int are compatible types, and int variables have a larger range than byte values. Therefore, no data will be lost in the type conversion. Here's an example:

```
public class app
{
    public static void main(String[] args)
    {
        byte byte1 = 1;
        int int1;

        int1 = byte1;

        System.out.println("int1 = " + int1);
    }
}
```

The Java compiler has no problem with this code, and it makes the type conversion automatically. Here's the result of this program:

```
C:\>java app
int1 = 1
```

These types of conversions, where you convert to a data type with a larger range, are called *widening conversions*. In widening conversions, the numeric types, such as the integer and floating-point types, are compatible with each other. On the other hand, char and boolean types are not compatible with each other, or with the numeric types.

Casting To New Data Types

If you're assigning a data value that's of a type that has a larger range than the variable you're assigning it to, you're performing what's called a *narrowing conversion*. The Java compiler will not perform narrowing conversions automatically, because there's the possibility that precision will be lost.

If you want to perform a narrowing conversion, you must use an explicit cast, which looks like this:

```
(target-data-type) value
```

For example, in this code, I'm converting an integer type to a byte type:

```
public class app
{
    public static void main(String[] args)
    {
        byte byte1;
        int int1 = 1;

        byte1 = (byte) int1;

        System.out.println("byte1 = " + byte1);
    }
}
```

Without the explicit type cast, the compiler would object, but with the type cast, there's no problem, because Java decides that you know about the possibility of losing some data when you cram a possibly larger value into a smaller type. In other words, you're taking responsibility for the results. For example, when you put a floating-point number into a long, the fractional part of the number will be truncated, and you may lose more data if the floating-point value is outside the range that a long can hold. Here's the output of this code:

```
C:\>java app
byte1 = 1
```

One thing to note is that the Java compiler also automatically promotes types as needed when it evaluates expressions. For example, consider the following code, in which everything looks like it only involves bytes:

```
public class app
{
    public static void main(String[] args)
```

```
    {
        byte byte1 = 100;
        byte byte2 = 100;
        byte byte3;

        byte3 = byte1 * byte2 / 100;

        System.out.println("byte3 = " + byte3);
    }
}
```

However, because Java knows that multiplying bytes can result in integer-sized values, it automatically promotes the result of the **byte1 * byte2** operation into an integer, which means you actually have to use an explicit cast here to get back to the byte type:

```
public class app
{
    public static void main(String[] args)
    {
        byte byte1 = 100;
        byte byte2 = 100;
        byte byte3;

        byte3 = (byte) (byte1 * byte2 / 100);

        System.out.println("byte3 = " + byte3);
    }
}
```

This code compiles and runs as you'd expect—but it wouldn't without the **(byte)** cast:

```
C:\>java app
byte3 = 100
```

TIP: *In general, the Java compiler promotes bytes and shorts to ints in expressions. If one operand is a long, the entire expression is made a long. Similarly, if one operand is a float, the whole expression is made a float; if one operand is a double, the whole expression is made a double.*

Declaring One-Dimensional Arrays

The Big Boss appears and says, "It's time to start cracking down on customers who are overdue paying their bills to us." "OK," you say, "can I see the accounts?" "We never actually kept any accounts," the BB says. "Oh," you reply. "I guess I'll have to set up an array to store the accounts in."

As explained earlier in this chapter, arrays provide an easy way of handling a set of data by index, which is great for computers, because you can manipulate the index in your code. Java supports one-dimensional and multidimensional arrays, and we'll take a look at both of them here.

Getting an array ready for use is a two-step process. First, you must declare the array. Here's how you declare a one-dimensional array in general:

```
type name[];
```

For example, here's how to declare an array of double values, which I'll name **accounts[]**:

```
public class app
{
    public static void main(String[] args)
    {
        double accounts[];
            .
            .
            .
    }
}
```

TIP: *In fact, there's another way of doing this that follows the pointer-declaration syntax in C++. You can also declare arrays with the brackets ([ ]) after the type, not the name of the variable, like this: **double[ ] accounts**.*

Unlike declaring simple variables, declaring an array does not set aside memory for the array, because Java isn't sure how big you want it to be yet. This means there's another step to the process—actually creating the array. See the next topic for the details.

Creating One-dimensional Arrays

After you've declared a one-dimensional array, the next step is to actually create that array by allocating memory for it. As you'll see in Chapter 4, the Java memory-allocation operator is the **new** operator. Therefore, I can create and use the new array like this:

```
public class app
{
    public static void main(String[] args)
    {
        double accounts[];

        accounts = new double[100];

        accounts[3] = 1335.67;

        System.out.println("Account 3 is overdue by $" + accounts[3]);
    }
}
```

Here, I've created an array of exactly 100 double values, all of which Java initializes to 0. The lower bound of all Java arrays is 0, so the first element in the array is **accounts[0]** and the last element is **accounts[99]**. If the array index is outside the range 0 to 99, Java will create a fatal error, and the program will halt.

Here's the result of this program:

```
C:\>java app
Account 3 is overdue by $1335.67
```

In fact, you can combine the declaration and creation process into one step for arrays, like this:

```
public class app
{
    public static void main(String[] args)
    {
        double accounts[] = new double[100];

        accounts[3] = 1335.67;

        System.out.println("Account 3 is overdue by $" + accounts[3]);
    }
}
```

Initializing One-dimensional Arrays

The Novice Programmer is back with a question. "I know I can initialize simple variables when I declare them," the Novice Programmer says, "but what about initializing arrays when I declare them?" "No problem," you say.

To initialize the data in one-dimensional arrays, you just place the values between curly braces, one value after the other, separated by commas, beginning with the first value in the array. Here's an example that initializes the first four elements of the **accounts[]** array with data:

```
public class app
{
    public static void main(String[] args)
    {
        double accounts[] = {238.45, 999.33, 0, 1335.67};

        accounts[3] = 1335.67;

        System.out.println("Account 3 is overdue by $" + accounts[3]);
    }
}
```

Declaring Multidimensional Arrays

"Hmm," says the Novice Programmer thoughtfully, "I think I need more than a one-dimensional array. I'm supposed to be keeping track of products as indexed by product number, and the array is supposed to store the number of items in inventory, the cost of each item, the number sold, the number...." "Hold it," you say. "Use a multidimensional array."

You can declare multidimensional arrays in much the same way you declare one-dimensional arrays; just include a pair of square brackets for every dimension in the array:

```
type name[][][]...;
```

We looked at declaring multidimensional arrays previously in this chapter; for example, here's how to declare a two-dimensional array with two rows and 100 columns:

```
public class app
{
```

```
public static void main(String[] args)
{
    double accounts[][] = new double[2][100];
        .
        .
        .
}
}
```

TIP: *In fact, there's another way of doing this that follows the pointer-declaration syntax in C++. You can also declare arrays with the brackets ([ ]) after the type, not the name of the variable, like this:* **double[ ][ ] accounts**.

That's how it works with two-dimensional arrays—the left index specifies the row in the array, and the right index specifies the column.

Of course, you don't have to limit yourself to two dimensions; here's how to declare a four-dimensional array:

```
public class app
{
    public static void main(String[] args)
    {
        double accounts[][][][] = new double[2][3][4][5];
            .
            .
            .
    }
}
```

As you can see, it's as easy to declare multidimensional arrays as it is to declare one-dimensional arrays. Now what about actually creating the declared array? See the next topic for the details.

Creating Multidimensional Arrays

The Novice Programmer asks, "Now that I've declared a new multidimensional array, how do I *create* it?" "Coming right up," you say.

You create a new multidimensional array by allocating memory for it with the **new** operator, giving the array the dimensions you want. Here's how this looks in an example:

```
public class app
{
    public static void main(String[] args)
    {
        double accounts[][];

        accounts = new double[2][100];

        accounts[0][3] = 43.95;
        accounts[1][3] = 2385489382.06;

        System.out.println("Savings account 3 has $" + accounts[0][3]);
        System.out.println("Checking account 3 has $" + accounts[1][3]);
    }
}
```

Here's the result of this code:

```
C:\>java app
Savings account 3 has $43.95
Checking account 3 has $2.38548938206E9
```

You can also condense the declaration and memory allocation into one step, like this:

```
public class app
{
    public static void main(String[] args)
    {
        double accounts[][] = new double[2][100];

        accounts[0][3] = 43.95;
        accounts[1][3] = 2385489382.06;

        System.out.println("Savings account 3 has $" + accounts[0][3]);
        System.out.println("Checking account 3 has $" + accounts[1][3]);
    }
}
```

Here's an example that creates and uses a four-dimensional array:

```
public class app
{
    public static void main(String[] args)
    {
        double accounts[][][][] = new double[2][3][4][5];
```

```
        accounts[0][1][2][3] = 43.95;

        System.out.println("Account [0][1][2][3] has $" +
        accounts[0][1][2][3]);
    }
}
```

Here's the result of this program:

```
C:\>java app
Account [0][1][2][3] has $43.95
```

Multidimensional arrays are actually arrays of arrays, which means that if you
have a two-dimensional array (**array[][]**), you can actually treat it as an array of
one dimensional arrays, which you can access as **array[0]**, **array[1]**, **array[2]**,
and so on. Here's a slightly advance example of doing just that using a **for** loop
(which you'll see more of in the next chapter) and the **length** method (which
you'll see in a few topics) to find the length of an array:

```
public class app
{
    public static void main(String[] args)
    {
        double array[][] = {{1, 2, 3},
                            {3, 2, 1},
                            {1, 2, 3}};
        int sum = 0, total = 0;

        for(int outer_index = 0; outer_index < array.length;
            outer_index++) {
            for(int inner_index = 0; inner_index <
                array[outer_index].length; inner_index++) {

                sum += array[outer_index][inner_index];
                total++;

            }
        }

        System.out.println("Average array value = " + (sum / total));
    }
}
```

Here's the result of this code:

```
C:\>java app
Average array value = 2
```

So far, all the arrays we've used have had the same number of elements for each dimension, but you don't need to set things up that way. To learn more, you can take a look at the topic after the next one. But first, let's look at initializing multi-dimensional arrays.

Initializing Multidimensional Arrays

You can initialize multidimensional arrays with data when declaring them in much the same way you initialize one-dimensional arrays; just include a set of curly braces for each dimension and place the values with which you want to initialize the array in those curly braces. For example, here's how to initialize a two-dimensional array:

```
public class app
{
    public static void main(String[] args)
    {
        double accounts[][] = {{10.11, 19.56, 4343.91, 43.95},
                               {11.23, 54.23, 543.62, 2385489382.06}};

        System.out.println("Savings account 3 has $" +
            accounts[0][3]);

        System.out.println("Checking account 3 has $" +
            accounts[1][3]);
    }
}
```

Here's what running this code yields:

```
C:\>java app
Savings account 3 has $43.95
Checking account 3 has $2.38548938206E9
```

Creating Irregular Multidimensional Arrays

"OK," says the Novice Programmer proudly, "now I'm an array expert." "Uh-huh," you say. "Can you give each row in an array a different number of elements?" The NP says, "Excuse me?"

As with many other programming languages, multidimensional arrays are actually arrays of arrays in Java. This means that you can construct arrays as you like, as in this example, in which each row of a two-dimensional array has a different number of elements:

```
public class app
{
    public static void main(String[] args)
    {
        double array[][] = new double[5][];

        array[0] = new double[500];
        array[1] = new double[400];
        array[2] = new double[300];
        array[3] = new double[200];
        array[4] = new double[100];

        array[3][3] = 1335.67;

        System.out.println("Account [3][3] has $" + array[3][3]);
    }
}
```

What's happening here is that I'm treating each row of a two dimensional array as a one-dimensional array by itself and creating each of those one-dimensional arrays separately. Here's the result of this code:

```
C:\>java app
Account [3][3] has $1335.67
```

Getting An Array's Length

It's often useful to know the length of an array, especially if you're iterating over all elements in the array in your code. To find the number of elements in an array named array1, you can use the term **array1.length**. Here's an example from the next chapter that uses a **for** loop to find the average student grade of a set of six grades (here, the term **grades.length** returns a value of 6):

```
public class app
{
    public static void main(String[] args)
    {
        double grades[] = {88, 99, 73, 56, 87, 64};
        double sum, average;

        sum = 0;

        for (int loop_index = 0; loop_index < grades.length;
            loop_index++) {
            sum += grades[loop_index];
        }

        average = sum / grades.length;

        System.out.println("Average grade = " + average);
    }
}
```

Here's the result of this code:

```
C:\>java app
Average grade = 77.83333333333333
```

The **String** Class

"I've been looking through the list of simple data types in Java," the Novice Programmer says, "and I can't find text strings there. Shouldn't there be?" "Some people say so," you reply, "but, in fact, strings are handled as objects in Java. One advantage of this is that a string object has a great variety of methods you can use with it."

In many languages, text strings are fundamental data types inherent to the language, but in Java, strings are handled with the **String** and **StringBuffer** classes. Let's take a look at the **String** class first.

String objects hold text strings that you can't change; if you want to change the actual text in the string, you should use the **StringBuffer** class instead. Here's an example in which I create a string and print it out (notice how much this code makes the **String** class look like any other simple data type):

```
public class app
{
    public static void main(String[] args)
    {
        String s1 = "Hello from Java!";

        System.out.println(s1);
    }
}
```

Here's the result of this code:

```
C:\>java app
Hello from Java!
```

The **String** class is enormously powerful, with methods that enable you to convert the string to a character array, convert numbers into strings, search strings, create substrings, change the case of the string, get a string's length, compare strings, and much more.

The **String** class is a class, not an intrinsic data type, which means you create objects of that class with constructors, which you'll learn all about in Chapter 4. A *constructor* is just like a normal method of a class, except you use it to create an object of that class. You'll get a sneak preview of the **String** class's constructors here. The **String** class also has a data member you use when comparing strings (which we'll take a look at in the next chapter). This data member is shown in Table 2.2. The **String** class's constructors, which you can use to create String objects (see the topic "Creating Strings," coming up in this chapter), appear in Table 2.3, and the methods of the **String** class appear in Table 2.4.

I'll put the material you see in these tables to use in the next few topics, in which we'll create and use String objects.

Table 2.2   String class field summary.

Field	Means
static Comparator CASE_INSENSITIVE_ORDER	Yields a comparator (which we'll see more about later) that orders String objects, as in compareToIgnoreCase.

Table 2.3   String class constructor summary.

Constructor	Means
String( )	Initializes a new String object so that it holds an empty character sequence.
String(byte[ ] bytes)	Constructs a new String object by converting the array of bytes using the platform's default character encoding.
String(byte[ ] ascii, int hibyte)	Deprecated. This method does not properly convert bytes into characters.
String(byte[ ] bytes, int offset, int length)	Constructs a new String object by converting the subarray of bytes using the default character encoding.
String(byte[ ] ascii, int hibyte, int offset, int count)	Deprecated. This method does not properly convert bytes into characters.
String(byte[ ] bytes, int offset, enc)	Constructs a new String object by converting the int length, String subarray of bytes using the specified character encoding.
String(byte[ ] bytes, String enc)	Constructs a new String object by converting the array of bytes using the specified character encoding.
String(char[ ] value)	Allocates a new String object so that it represents the sequence of characters contained in the character array argument.
String(char[ ] value, int offset, int count)	Allocates a new String object that contains characters from a subarray of the character array argument.
String(String value)	Initializes a new String object so that it represents the same sequence of characters as the argument string.
String(StringBuffer buffer)	Allocates a new String object that contains the sequence of characters contained in the string buffer argument.

Table 2.4   String class methods.

Method	Means
char charAt(int index)	Yields the character at the given index.
int compareTo(Object o)	Compares this String object to another object.
int compareTo(String anotherString)	Compares two strings lexicographically.
int compareToIgnoreCase(String str)	Compares two strings lexicographically, ignoring case.
String concat(String str)	Concatenates the given string to the end of this string.
static String copyValueOf(char[ ] data)	Yields a String object that's equivalent to the given character array.
static String copyValueOf(char[ ] int offset, int count)	Yields a String object that's equivalent data to the given character array, using offsets.
boolean endsWith(String suffix)	True if this string ends with the given suffix.
boolean equals(Object anObject)	Compares this string to an object.
boolean equalsIgnoreCase (String anotherString)	Compares this String object to another String object, ignoring case.
byte[ ] getBytes)	Converts this String object into bytes according to the default character encoding, storing the result in a new byte array.
void getBytes(int srcBegin, int srcEnd, byte[ ] dst, int dstBegin)	Deprecated. This method does not properly convert characters into bytes.
byte[ ] getBytes(String enc)	Converts this String object into bytes according to the given character encoding, storing the result in a new byte array.
void getChars(int srcBegin, .int srcEnd, char[ ] dst, int dstBegin)	Copies characters from this string into the destination array.
int hashCode( )	Yields a hashcode for this string.
int indexOf(int ch)	Yields the index within this string of the first occurrence of the given character.
int indexOf(int ch, int fromIndex)	Yields the index within this string of the first occurrence of the given character, starting at the given index.
int indexOf(String str)	Yields the index within this string of the first occurrence of the given substring.
int indexOf(String str, int fromIndex)	Yields the index within this string of the first occurrence of the given substring, starting at the given index.
String intern( )	Yields a representation for the String object.
int lastIndexOf(int ch)	Yields the index within this string of the last occurrence of the given character.

(continued)

Table 2.4   *String class methods* (continued).

Method	Means
int lastIndexOf(int ch, int fromIndex)	Yields the index within this string of the last occurrence of the given character, searching backward from the given index.
int lastIndexOf(String str)	Yields the index within this string of the rightmost occurrence of the given substring.
int lastIndexOf(String str, int fromIndex)	Yields the index within this string of the last occurrence of the given substring.
int length( )	Yields the length of this string.
boolean regionMatches String other, (boolean ignoreCase, int toffset, int ooffset, int len)	Tests whether two string regions are equal, allowing you to ignore case.
boolean regionMatches(int toffset, String other, int ooffset, int len)	Tests whether two string regions are equal.
String replace (char oldChar, char newChar)	Yields a new string by replacing all occurrences of oldChar in this string with newChar.
boolean startsWith(String prefix)	Tests whether this string starts with the given prefix.
boolean startsWith (String prefix, int toffset)	Tests whether this string starts with the given prefix beginning at the given index.
String substring(int beginIndex)	Yields a new string that's a substring of this string.
String substring(int beginIndex, endIndex)	Yields a new string that's a substring of this string, allowing you to int specify the end index.
char[ ] toCharArray( )	Converts this string to a new character array.
String toLowerCase( )	Converts all the characters in this String object to lowercase using the rules of the default locale, which is returned by Locale.getDefault.
String toLowerCase(Locale locale)	Converts all the characters in this String object to lowercase using the rules of the given locale.
String toString( )	This object (which is already a string) is returned.
String toUpperCase( )	Converts all the characters in this String object to uppercase using the rules of the default locale, which is returned by Locale.getDefault.
String toUpperCase(Locale locale)	Converts all the characters in this String object to uppercase using the rules of the given locale.
String trim( )	Removes white space from both ends of this string.
static String valueOf(boolean b)	Yields the string representation of the boolean argument.
static String valueOf(char c)	Yields the string representation of the char argument.

(continued)

Table 2.4   String class methods (continued).

Method	Means
static String valueOf(char[ ] data)	Yields the string representation of the char array argument.
static String valueOf(char[ ] data, offset, int count)	Yields the string representation of a specific subarray of the char int array argument.
static String valueOf(double d)	Yields the string representation of a double.
static String valueOf(float f)	Yields the string representation of a float.
static String valueOf(int i)	Yields the string representation of an int.
static String valueOf(long l)	Yields the string representation of a long.
static String valueOf(Object obj)	Yields the string representation of an object.

Creating Strings

"So Java includes a **String** class to handle text strings," the Novice Programmer says. "That's great, because I'm writing this novel, see, and ...." "Hold it," you say. "I don't want to hear about it."

Let's take a look at some of the many ways of creating String objects. Here's a way you've already seen:

```
public class app
{
    public static void main(String[] args)
    {
        String s1 = "Hello from Java!";
        .
        .
        .
```

In fact, when you use a string literal such as "Hello from Java!" in your code, Java treats it as a String object, so what's really happening here is that I'm assigning one String object to another.

Of course, you can also declare a string first and then assign a value to it:

```
public class app
{
    public static void main(String[] args)
    {
        String s1 = "Hello from Java!";
```

```
        String s2;
        s2 = "Hello from Java!";
            .
            .
            .
```

Here's a case in which I use one of the **String** class's constructors. In this case, I'm just creating an empty string and then assigning data to it:

```
public class app
{
    public static void main(String[] args)
    {
        String s1 = "Hello from Java!";

        String s2;
        s2 = "Hello from Java!";

        String s3 = new String();
        s3 = "Hello from Java!";
            .
            .
            .
```

You can also pass a text string to the **String** class constructor directly to create a new string, like this:

```
public class app
{
    public static void main(String[] args)
    {
        String s1 = "Hello from Java!";

        String s2;
        s2 = "Hello from Java!";

        String s3 = new String();
        s3 = "Hello from Java!";

        String s4 = new String("Hello from Java!");
            .
            .
            .
```

Other **String** class constructors are available that can take character arrays or subsets of character arrays (the **String** class knows which constructor you're using by the number and type of arguments you pass to it). You can even use the **String** class's **valueOf** method to get a string representation of numeric values:

```
public class app
{
    public static void main(String[] args)
    {
        String s1 = "Hello from Java!";

        String s2;
        s2 = "Hello from Java!";

        String s3 = new String();
        s3 = "Hello from Java!";

        String s4 = new String("Hello from Java!");

        char c1[] = {'H', 'i', ' ', 't', 'h', 'e', 'r', 'e'};
        String s5 = new String(c1);

        String s6 = new String(c1, 0, 2);

        double double1 = 1.23456789;
        String s7 = String.valueOf(double1);

        System.out.println(s1);
        System.out.println(s2);
        System.out.println(s3);
        System.out.println(s4);
        System.out.println(s5);
        System.out.println(s6);
        System.out.println(s7);
    }
}
```

Tip: *To convert a string to a number, you can use the numeric wrapper classes, such as **Integer**, **Long**, **Float**, and so on, using methods like **Integer.parseInt** and **Long.parseLong**.*

At the end of this code, I print out all the strings I've created. Here's what appears when the program is run:

```
C:\>java app
Hello from Java!
```

```
Hello from Java!
Hello from Java!
Hello from Java!
Hi there
Hi
1.23456789
```

Getting String Length

The Novice Programmer is breathless. "I've written half my novel," the NP says, "and I need to find out how long it is so far. How can I do that?"

"Use the **String** class's **length** method," you say.

Here's an example that shows how to use the **String** class's **length** method (note that it also shows how Java treats string literals as String objects by using **length** on a string literal):

```
public class app
{
    public static void main(String[] args)
    {
        String s1 = "Hello from Java!";

        System.out.println("\"" + s1 + "\"" + " is " + s1.length()
            + " characters long.");
        System.out.println("\"" + "Hello" + "\"" + " is " +
            "Hello".length() + " characters long.");
    }
}
```

Here's the output of this program:

```
C:\>java app
"Hello from Java!" is 16 characters long.
"Hello" is 5 characters long.
```

Concatenating Strings

Concatenating strings means joining them together, and I've already used the **+** operator in this book to do just that. However, there's another way to concatenate strings—you can use the **String** class's **concat** method to join two strings and create a new one.

How does that look in code? Here's an example where I use both the + operator and the **concat** method to create the same string:

```java
public class app
{
    public static void main(String[] args)
    {
        String s1 = "Hello";

        String s2 = s1 + " from";
        String s3 = s2 + " Java!";

        String s4 = s1.concat(" from");
        String s5 = s4.concat(" Java!");

        System.out.println(s3);
        System.out.println(s5);
    }
}
```

Here's the result of the preceding code:

```
C:\>java app
Hello from Java!
Hello from Java!
```

As you've already seen when printing out numbers, when you concatenate a numeric value with a string, the numeric value is concatenated as a string.

TIP: Note that concatenating numbers does indeed treat them as strings, so be careful—for example, System.out.println("3 + 3 = " + 3 + 3) displays 3 + 3 = 33, not 3 + 3 = 6.

Getting Characters And Substrings

The **String** class provides a number of methods that let you dissect strings into their component characters and substrings. For example, you can use the **charAt** method to get the character at a specific position:

```java
public class app
{
    public static void main(String[] args)
    {
        String s1 = "Hello from Java!";
```

```
        char c1 = s1.charAt(0);
        System.out.println("The first character of \"" + s1 +
            "\" is " + c1);
            .
            .
            .
```

You can use the **toCharArray** method to convert a String object into a char array, and you can use the **getChars** method to get a number of characters:

```
public class app
{
    public static void main(String[] args)
    {
        String s1 = "Hello from Java!";

        char c1 = s1.charAt(0);
        System.out.println("The first character of \"" + s1 +
            "\" is " + c1);

        char chars1[] = s1.toCharArray();
        System.out.println("The second character of \"" +
            s1 + "\" is " + chars1[1]);

        char chars2[] = new char[5];
        s1.getChars(0, 5, chars2, 0);
        System.out.println("The first five characters of \"" + s1
            + "\" are " + new String(chars2));
            .
            .
            .
```

You can also use the **substring** method to create a new string that's a substring of the old one, like this:

```
public class app
{
    public static void main(String[] args)
    {
        String s1 = "Hello from Java!";

        char c1 = s1.charAt(0);
        System.out.println("The first character of \"" + s1 +
            "\" is " + c1);
```

```
        char chars1[] = s1.toCharArray();
        System.out.println("The second character of \"" +
            s1 + "\" is " + chars1[1]);

        char chars2[] = new char[5];
        s1.getChars(0, 5, chars2, 0);
        System.out.println("The first five characters of \"" + s1
            + "\" are " + new String(chars2));

        String s2 = s1.substring(0, 5);
        System.out.println("The first five characters of \"" + s1
            + "\" are " + s2);
    }
}
```

Here's the result of running this program:

```
C:\>java app
The first character of "Hello from Java!" is H
The second character of "Hello from Java!" is e
The first five characters of "Hello from Java!" are Hello
The first five characters of "Hello from Java!" are Hello
```

Searching For And Replacing Strings

You can search strings for characters and substrings using the **indexOf** and **lastIndexOf** methods. The **indexOf** method returns the zero-based location of the first occurrence in a string of a character or substring, and **lastIndexOf** returns the location of the last occurrence of a character or substring.

Here's an example that shows how to use **indexOf** and **lastIndexOf**:

```
public class app
{
    public static void main(String[] args)
    {
        String s1 = "I have drawn a nice drawing.";

        System.out.println("The first occurrence of \"draw\" is " +
            "at location " + s1.indexOf("draw"));

        System.out.println("The last occurrence of \"draw\" is " +
            "at location " + s1.lastIndexOf("draw"));
```

The **String** class also has a **replace** method, which lets you replace all occurrences of a single character with another single character. You might think this violates the idea that you can't change the text in a String object; however, this method creates an entirely new String object. Here's an example showing how this works (note that I turn all occurrences of the letter *h* into the letter *f* in a text string):

```
public class app
{
    public static void main(String[] args)
    {
        String s1 = "I have drawn a nice drawing.";

        System.out.println("The first occurrence of \"draw\" is " +
            "at location " + s1.indexOf("draw"));

        System.out.println("The last occurrence of \"draw\" is " +
            "at location " + s1.lastIndexOf("draw"));

        String s2 = "Edna, you\'re hired!";
        System.out.println(s2.replace('h', 'f'));
    }
}
```

Here's the result of this code:

```
C:\>java app
The first occurrence of "draw" is at location 7
The last occurrence of "draw" is at location 20
Edna, you're fired!
```

Changing Case In Strings

The Novice Programmer says, "The Big Boss told me my program's output wasn't emphatic enough. Do you have any ideas?" "Try the **toUpperCase** method," you say.

You can use the **toLowerCase** method to convert a string to lowercase, and you can use the **toUpperCase** method to convert it to uppercase. Here's how this looks in code:

```
public class app
{
```

```
public static void main(String[] args)
{
    System.out.println("Hello from Java!".toLowerCase());
    System.out.println("Hello from Java!".toUpperCase());
}
}
```

Here's the result of this program:

```
C:\>java app
hello from java!
HELLO FROM JAVA!
```

Formatting Numbers In Strings

You can format numbers in strings using the **Number-Format** class of the java.text package. This class supports the **format**, **set-Minimum-Integer-Digits**, **set-Minimum-Fraction-Digits**, **set-Maximum-Integer-Digits**, and **set-Maximum-Fraction-Digits** methods. Here's an example, using the **set-Maximum-Fraction-Digits** method, in which I round off a double value as I format it:

```
import java.text.*;

public class app
{
    public static void main(String[] args)
    {
        double value = 1.23456789;
        NumberFormat nf = NumberFormat.getNumberInstance();

        nf.setMaximumFractionDigits(6);

        String s = nf.format(value);

        System.out.println(s);
    }
}
```

Here's the result:

```
C:\>java app
1.234568
```

The **StringBuffer** Class

"Hmm," says the Novice Programmer. "I've stored my whole novel in a String object, but now I can't change it. What's wrong?" "You can't change the text in a String object," you say. "You have to use a **StringBuffer** object instead." "Now you tell me," replies the NP.

The **StringBuffer** class gives you much of what the **String** class offers—and something more: the ability to modify the actual string. Here's an example in which I'm using the **StringBuffer** class's **replace** method to change the contents of a **StringBuffer** object from "Hello from Java!" to "Hello to Java!":

```
public class app
{
    public static void main(String[] args)
    {
        StringBuffer s1 = new StringBuffer("Hello from Java!");

        s1.replace(6, 10, "to");

        System.out.println(s1);
    }
}
```

Here's the result of running this code:

```
C:\>java app
Hello to Java!
```

You'll find the **StringBuffer** class's constructors in Table 2.5 and its methods in Table 2.6.

I'll put the **StringBuffer** class to work in the next few topics.

Creating StringBuffers

You can create StringBuffer objects using the **StringBuffer** class's constructors. For example, here's how to create an empty StringBuffer object (which is set up with space for 16 characters, by default) and then insert some text into it:

```
public class app
{
    public static void main(String[] args)
    {
```

```
StringBuffer s1 = new StringBuffer();
s1.insert(0, "Hello from Java!");
System.out.println(s1);
    .
    .
    .
```

Table 2.5   StringBuffer class constructors.

Constructors	Means
StringBuffer( )	Constructs a string buffer with no characters in it and a capacity of 16 characters.
StringBuffer(int length)	Constructs a string buffer with no characters in it and a capacity as given by the length argument.
StringBuffer(String str)	Constructs a string buffer so that it represents the same sequence of characters as the argument string.

Table 2.6   StringBuffer class methods.

Method	Means
StringBuffer append(boolean b)	Appends the string representation of the boolean argument to the string buffer.
StringBuffer append(char c)	Appends the string representation of the char argument to the string buffer.
StringBuffer append(char[ ] str)	Appends the string representation of the char array argument to the string buffer.
StringBuffer append (char[ ] str, int offset, int len)	Appends the string representation of a subarray of the char array argument to the string buffer.
StringBuffer append(double d)	Appends the string representation of the double argument to the string buffer.
StringBuffer append(float f)	Appends the string representation of the float argument to the string buffer.
StringBuffer append(int i)	Appends the string representation of the int argument to the string buffer.
StringBuffer append(long l)	Appends the string representation of the long argument to the string buffer.
StringBuffer append(Object obj)	Appends the string representation of the Object argument to the string buffer.
StringBuffer append(String str)	Appends the string to the string buffer.
int capacity( )	Yields the capacity of the string buffer.

(continued)

Table 2.6   *StringBuffer class methods* (continued).

Method	Means
char charAt(int index)	Yields the given character of the sequence represented by the string buffer, as indicated by the index argument.
StringBuffer delete(int start, int end)	Removes the characters in a substring of this string buffer.
StringBuffer deleteCharAt(int index)	Removes the character at the given position in this string buffer, shortening the string buffer by one character.
void ensureCapacity (int minimumCapacity)	Ensures that the capacity of the buffer is at least equal to the given minimum.
void getChars(int srcBegin, int srcEnd, char[ ] dst, int dstBegin)	Characters are copied from this string buffer into the destination character array.
StringBuffer insert(int offset, boolean b)	Inserts the string representation of the boolean argument into the string buffer.
StringBuffer insert(int offset, char c)	Inserts the string representation of the char argument into the string buffer.
StringBuffer insert(int offset, char[ ] str)	Inserts the string representation of the char array argument into the string buffer.
StringBuffer insert index, char[ ] str, int offset, int len)	Inserts the string representation of a subarray of the str array (int argument into the string buffer.
StringBuffer insert(int offset, double d)	Inserts the string representation of the double argument into the string buffer.
StringBuffer insert(int offset, float f)	Inserts the string representation of the float argument into the string buffer.
StringBuffer insert(int offset, int i)	Inserts the string representation of the second int argument into the string buffer.
StringBuffer insert(int offset, long l)	Inserts the string representation of the long argument into the string buffer.
StringBuffer insert(int offset, Object obj)	Inserts the string representation of the Object argument into the string buffer.
StringBuffer insert(int offset, String str)	Inserts the string into the string buffer.
int length( )	Yields the length (in characters) of this string buffer.
StringBuffer replace start, int end, String str)	Replaces the characters in a substring of the string buffer with the (int characters in the given string.
StringBuffer reverse( )	The character sequence contained in this string buffer is replaced by the reverse of the sequence.

(continued)

2. Variables, Arrays, And Strings

Table 2.6   StringBuffer class methods (continued).

Method	Means
void setCharAt(int index, char ch)	The character at the given index of the string buffer is set to *ch*.
void setLength(int newLength)	Sets the length of the string buffer.
String substring(int start)	Yields a new string that contains a subsequence of characters currently contained in this string buffer. The substring begins at the given index.
String substring(int start, int end)	Yields a new string that contains a subsequence of characters currently contained in this string buffer.
String toString( )	Converts to a string representing the data in this string buffer.

Here's how to initialize a new StringBuffer object with a string:

```
public class app
{
    public static void main(String[] args)
    {
        StringBuffer s1 = new StringBuffer();
        s1.insert(0, "Hello from Java!");
        System.out.println(s1);

        StringBuffer s2 = new StringBuffer("Hello from Java!");
        System.out.println(s2);
        .
        .
        .
```

You can also create a StringBuffer object with a specific length, like this:

```
public class app
{
    public static void main(String[] args)
    {
        StringBuffer s1 = new StringBuffer();
        s1.insert(0, "Hello from Java!");
        System.out.println(s1);

        StringBuffer s2 = new StringBuffer("Hello from Java!");
        System.out.println(s2);

        StringBuffer s3 = new StringBuffer(10);
        s3.insert(0, "Hello from Java!");
```

```
        System.out.println(s3);
    }
}
```

Here's the result of this code:

```
C:\>java app
Hello from Java!
Hello from Java!
Hello from Java!
```

Getting And Setting StringBuffer Lengths And Capacities

You can use the **StringBuffer** class's **length** method to find the lengths of the text in StringBuffer objects, and you can use the **capacity** method to find the amount of memory space allocated for that text. You can also set the length of the text in a StringBuffer object with the **setLength** method, which lets you truncate strings or extend them with null characters (that is, characters whose Unicode codes are 0).

Here's an example that shows how to determine a string's length, how to determine a string's capacity (Java typically makes the capacity 16 characters longer than the length, to save time for future memory allocations), and how to change the length of the string:

```java
public class app
{
    public static void main(String[] args)
    {
        StringBuffer s1 = new StringBuffer("Hello from Java!");

        System.out.println("The length is " + s1.length());

        System.out.println("The allocated length is " +
            s1.capacity());

        s1.setLength(2000);

        System.out.println("The new length is " + s1.length());
    }
}
```

Here's what this program looks like when it's run:

```
C:\>java app
The length is 16
The allocated length is 32
The new length is 2000
```

Setting Characters In StringBuffers

"Help!" the Novice Programmer cries, "I need to change some text in my novel!" "You can try the **setCharAt** method," you say helpfully.

To read characters in a StringBuffer object, you can use the **charAt** and **getChars** methods, just as you can with String objects. However, in StringBuffer objects, you can also set individual characters using the **setCharAt** method.

Here's an example in which I change the text "She had a wild look in her eyes." to "She had a mild look in her eyes." using **setCharAt**:

```
public class app
{
    public static void main(String[] args)
    {
        StringBuffer s1 = new
            StringBuffer("She had a wild look in her eyes.");

        s1.setCharAt(10, 'm');

        System.out.println(s1);
    }
}
```

Here's the result:

```
C:\>java app
She had a mild look in her eyes.
```

Appending And Inserting Using StringBuffers

"The **setCharAt** method doesn't do it for me," the Novice Programmer says. "I really need some way of editing the text in StringBuffer objects as a string, not as individual characters." "OK," you say "use the **append** and **insert** methods."

You can use the **append** method to append strings to the text in a StringBuffer object, and you can use the **insert** method to insert text at a particular location. Here's an example that starts with the text "Hello", appends " Java!", and then inserts "from" into the middle of the text, using **append** and **insert**:

```
public class app
{
    public static void main(String[] args)
    {
        StringBuffer s1 = new StringBuffer("Hello");

        s1.append(" Java!");

        System.out.println(s1);

        s1.insert(6, "from ");

        System.out.println(s1);
    }
}
```

Here's what this code produces:

```
C:\>java app
Hello Java!
Hello from Java!
```

Deleting Text In StringBuffers

You can delete text in a StringBuffer object using the **delete** and **deleteCharAt** methods. For example, here's how to change the text "I'm not having a good time." to "I'm having a good time." with **delete** (to use this method, you just specify the range of the characters you want to delete):

```
public class app
{
    public static void main(String[] args)
    {
        StringBuffer s1 = new
            StringBuffer("I'm not having a good time.");

        s1.delete(4, 8);
```

```
            System.out.println(s1);
    }
}
```

Here's the result:

```
C:\>java app
I'm having a good time.
```

Replacing Text In StringBuffers

"I'm writing a text editor using the **StringBuffer** class," the Novice Programmer says, "but there's one thing I can't figure out—how can I replace text with other text? Do I have to delete it and then insert the new text?" "No," you answer. "It's simple—just use the **replace** method."

In fact, you've already seen how to use **replace**; you just specify a character range and the new text that should replace that range, like this:

```
public class app
{
    public static void main(String[] args)
    {
        StringBuffer s1 = new StringBuffer("Hello from Java!");

        s1.replace(6, 10, "to");

        System.out.println(s1);
    }
}
```

Here's the result of the preceding code:

```
C:\>java app
Hello to Java!
```

Chapter 3

Operators, Conditionals, And Loops

In Depth

In the previous chapter, we took a look at how Java handles data in basic ways. In this chapter, we'll start doing something with that data as we examine the Java operators, conditionals, and loops.

Storing a lot of data in your program is fine, but unless you do something with it, it's not of much use. Using operators, you can manipulate your data—adding, subtracting, dividing, multiplying, and more. With conditionals, you can alter a program's flow by testing the values of your data items. Using loops, you can iterate over all data items in a set, such as an array, working with each data item in succession in an easy way. These three represent the next step up in programming power, and are discussed in this chapter.

Operators

The most basic way to work with the data in a program is with the built-in Java operators. For example, say you've stored a value of 46 in one variable and a value of 4 in another. You can multiply those two values with the Java multiplication operator (*), as shown in this code:

```java
public class app
{
    public static void main(String[] args)
    {
        int operand1 = 46, operand2 = 4, product;

        product = operand1 * operand2;

        System.out.println(operand1 + " * " + operand2 +
            " = " + product);
    }
}
```

Here's the result of this code:

```
C:\>java app
46 * 4 = 184
```

So what operators are available in Java? Here's a list of all of them:

- -- (decrement)
- - (subtraction)
- ! (logical unary **Not**)
- != (not equal to)
- % (modulus)
- %= (modulus assignment)
- & (logical **And**)
- && (short-circuit **And**)
- &= (bitwise **And** assignment)
- * (multiplication)
- *= (multiplication assignment)
- / (division)
- /= (division assignment)
- ?: (ternary **if-then-else**)
- ^ (logical **Xor**)
- ^= (bitwise **Xor** assignment)
- | (logical **Or**)
- || (short-circuit **Or**)
- |= (bitwise **Or** assignment)
- ~ (bitwise unary **Not**)
- + (addition)
- ++ (increment)
- += (addition assignment)
- < (less than)
- << (shift left)
- <<= (shift left assignment)
- <= (less than or equal to)
- = (assignment)
- -= (subtraction assignment)
- == (equal to)
- > (greater than)

- **>=** (greater than or equal to)
- **>>** (shift right)
- **>>=** (shift right assignment)
- **>>>** (shift right with zero fill)
- **>>>=** (shift right zero fill assignment)

You'll see these operators at work in this chapter. Operators that take one oper-and are called *unary* operators. Those that take two operands—for example, addition (a + b)—are called *binary* operators. There's even an operator, ?:, that takes three operands—the *ternary* operator.

NOTE: *Besides the built-in operators, I'll also cover the Java **Math** class in this chapter, which allows you to add a lot more math power to your programs, including exponentiation (unlike other languages, Java has no built-in exponentia-tion operator), logarithms, trigonometric functions, and more.*

Conditionals

The next step up from using simple operators is to use conditional statements, also called *branching statements*, in your code. You use conditional statements to make decisions based on the value of your data and make the flow of the pro-gram go in different directions accordingly.

For example, say you wanted to report on the weather, and if it's under 80 de-grees Fahrenheit, you want to print out a message that reads "It's not too hot." You can do this by checking the current temperature with a Java **if** statement that compares the value in the variable **temperature** to 80, and if that value is under 80, it prints out your message:

```java
public class app
{
    public static void main(String[] args)
    {
        int temperature = 73;

        if (temperature < 80) {
            System.out.println("It\'s not too hot.");
        }
    }
}
```

The **if** statement tests whether its condition (the part that appears in the parentheses) is true, which in this case is **temperature < 80**. The Java < (less than) relational operator is used to test whether the value in **temperature** is less than 80. Because I've set that value to 73, the **if** statement's condition is true, which means the code in the body of the **if** statement will be executed. Here's the result of this code:

```
C:\>java app
It's not too hot.
```

You can make **if** statements more complex by adding **else** clauses. These clauses must follow the **if** statement and are executed when the **if** statement's condition turns out to be false. Here's an example:

```
public class app
{
    public static void main(String[] args)
    {
        int temperature = 73;

        if (temperature < 80) {
            System.out.println("It\'s not too hot.");
        }
        else {
            System.out.println("It\'s too hot!");
        }
    }
}
```

As you'll see, there are other conditional statements as well, and I'll put them to work in this chapter, giving the Java syntax a thorough workout.

Loops

Loops are fundamental programming constructs that let you handle tasks by executing specific code repeatedly. For example, you might want to handle the items in a set of data by working with each item in succession, or you might want to keep performing a task until a particular condition becomes true. The basic loop statement involves the **for** statement, which lets you execute a block of code using a loop index. Each time through the loop, the loop index will have a different value, and you can use the loop index to specify a different data item in your data set, such as when you use the loop index as an index into an array.

Here's how you use a **for** loop in general (note that the statement that makes up the body of the **for** loop can be a compound statement, which means it can be made up of several single statements enclosed in curly braces):

```
for (initialization_expression; end_conditon; iteration_expression) {
    statement
}
```

You can initialize a loop index in the initialization expression (in fact, you can use multiple loop indexes in a **for** loop), provide a test condition for ending the loop when that test condition becomes false in the end condition, and add some way of changing (usually incrementing) the loop index in the iteration expression.

Here's an example to make this clear. In this case, I'll use a **for** loop to sum up the grades of six students in an array and compute the average grade. Here's how this looks in code (note that I'm actually declaring and initializing the loop index to 0 in the initialization expression of the **for** loop, which Java allows, following the same custom in C++):

```
public class app
{
    public static void main(String[] args)
    {
        double grades[] = {88, 99, 73, 56, 87, 64};
        double sum, average;

        sum = 0;

        for (int loop_index = 0; loop_index < grades.length; loop_index++)
        {
            sum += grades[loop_index];
        }

        average = sum / grades.length;

        System.out.println("Average grade = " + average);
    }
}
```

This code loops over all items in the **grades** array and adds them, leaving the result in the variable **sum**, which I then divide by the total number of entries in the array to find the average value. I loop over all elements using a loop index, which starts at 0 and is steadily incremented each time through the loop, up to the last item in the array. Here's the result of this code:

```
C:\>java app
Average grade = 77.83333333333333
```

As you can see, the **for** loop is a powerful one; in fact, it's just one of the many topics coming up in the "Immediate Solutions" section. It's now time to start using operators, conditional statements, and loops.

3. Operators, Conditionals, And Loops

Immediate Solutions

Operator Precedence

"Hey," says the Novice Programmer, "Java's gone all wacky again. I tried adding 12 and 24 and then dividing the result by 6. The answer should have been 6, but Java said it's 16." "Probably an operator precedence problem," you say. "Let me check your code."

Java supports quite a number of operators, which might be a problem if you use a lot of them at once in a single statement. Which operator does Java execute first? For example, take a look at the Novice Programmer's code, in which he tries to add 12 and 24 and then divide the sum by 6:

```java
public class app
{
    public static void main(String[] args)
    {
        double value;

        value = 12 + 24 / 6;

        System.out.println("The value = " + value);
    }
}
```

Here's the actual result of this code:

```
C:\>java app
The value = 16.0
```

Clearly, there's something different going on from what the Novice Programmer expected. In fact, Java sets up a very clear precedence of operators, which means that if it finds two operators at the same level in a statement (that is, not enclosed in parentheses), it'll execute the operator with the higher precedence first. As it happens, the / operator has higher precedence than the + operator, so in the preceding expression, 24 is first divided by 6 and then the result is added to 12, which produces 16.

To specify to Java exactly the order in which you want operators to be evaluated, you can use parentheses to group the operations you want performed first. Here's how this would look for the previous example, where the parentheses around "12 + 24" make sure that this operation is performed first:

```
public class app
{
    public static void main(String[] args)
    {
        double value;

        value = (12 + 24) / 6;

        System.out.println("The value = " + value);
    }
}
```

Here's the result of this code:

```
C:\>java app
The value = 6.0
```

Table 3.1 spells out the Java operator precedence, from highest to lowest (operators on the same line have the same precedence). Note that at the very highest level of precedence, you'll find ( ), [ ] (the array "operator", which you use to get data items at a specific index in an array), and . (the dot operator, which you use to specify methods and data members of objects). This means, for example, that you can always use parentheses to set the execution order of operations in Java statements.

I'll go over all these Java operators, in order of precedence, in this chapter, starting with the incrementing and decrementing operators: ++ and —.

Incrementing And Decrementing: ++ And --

The Programming Correctness Czar appears and says, "C++ has an incrementing operator and a decrementing operator. Does Java support these?" "Sure thing," you say.

The ++ operator increments its operand by one, and the — operator decrements its operand by one. For example, if **value** holds 0, after you execute **value++**, **value** will hold 1. These operators were introduced in C to make incrementing

Table 3.1   Operator Precedence.

Operators			
( )	[ ]	.	
++	--	~	!
*	/	%	
+	-		
>>	>>>	<<	
>	>=	<	<=
==	!=		
&			
^			
|			
&&			
||			
?:			
=	[operator]=		

and decrementing values, which are very common operations, easier. In fact, they were so popular that the incrementing operator was used in C++'s name, indicating that C++ is an incremented version of C.

Here's an important point: ++ and — can be either *postfix* operators (for example, **value++**) or *prefix* operators (for example, **++value**). When used as a postfix operator, they're executed *after* the rest of the statement, and when used as a prefix operator, they're executed *before* the rest of the statement. This is something you have to watch out for. For example, take a look at the following code:

```
value2 = value1++;
```

In this case, when the statement is completed, **value2** will actually be left with the *original* value in **value1**, and the value in **value1** will be incremented. Here's an example showing how this works:

```
public class app
{
    public static void main(String[] args)
    {
        int value1 = 0, value2 = 0;
```

```
        System.out.println("value1 = " + value1);
        System.out.println("value2 = " + value2);


        value2 = value1++;

        System.out.println("After value2 = ++value1...");
        System.out.println("value1 = " + value1);
        System.out.println("value2 = " + value2);

        int value3 = 0, value4 = 0;

        System.out.println();
        System.out.println("value3 = " + value3);
        System.out.println("value4 = " + value4);

        value4 = ++value3;

        System.out.println("After value4 = ++value3...");
        System.out.println("value3 = " + value3);
        System.out.println("value4 = " + value4);
    }
}
```

And here are the results of this code:

```
C:\>java app
value1 = 0
value2 = 0
After value2 = ++value1...
value1 = 1
value2 = 0

value3 = 0
value4 = 0
After value4 = ++value3...
value3 = 1
value4 = 1
```

Unary **Not**: ~ And !

The ~ operator is the bitwise unary **Not** operator, and ! is the logical unary **Not** operator. The ~ operator flips all the bits of numeric arguments, and the ! operator flips true values to false and false values to true.

Here's an example in which I flip all the bits of the most positive short value, 32767, to find the most negative short value, and I also flip a boolean value from true to false:

```
public class app
{
    public static void main(String[] args)
    {
        short short1 = 32767;
        boolean boolean1 = true;

        System.out.println("Most negative short = " + ~short1);
        System.out.println("!true = " + !boolean1);

    }
}
```

Here's the result of this code:

```
C:\>java app
Most negative short = -32768
!true = false
```

If I had set **int1** to 0 and then flipped its bits with the ~ operator to 1111111111111111 in binary, Java would have displayed the resulting value as -1, because it uses two's-complement notation for negative numbers. This means the leading bit is 1 for negative numbers and 0 for zero and positive numbers.

TIP: So why is 1111111111111111 binary equal to -1 in a short variable? If you add it to 1, you end up with 10000000000000000 binary, a number too large for a 16-bit short, so the leading 1 is lost and you end up with 0 —in other words, -1 + 1 = 0.

Multiplication And Division: * And /

The Programming Correctness Czar says, "I expect that Java has multiplication and division operators, just like C++?" "Sure," you say.

You use * to multiply values and / to divide values in Java. Here's an example in which I use * and / on double values, and then I do the same thing on integer values. I perform multiplication and division on integer values to show that the fractional part of math results are truncated when you use integers. Therefore, if you want to perform a division operation and still retain precision, you probably shouldn't be using integers. Here's the code:

```
public class app
{
    public static void main(String[] args)
    {
        double double1 = 4, double2 = 6, double3 = 5, doubleResult;

        doubleResult = double1 * double2 / double3;

        System.out.println("4 * 6 / 5 = " + doubleResult);


        int int1 = 4, int2 = 6, int3 = 5, intResult;

        intResult = int1 * int2 / int3;

        System.out.println("With integer math, 4 * 6 / 5 = " + intResult);
    }
}
```

Here's the result of this code:

```
C:\>java app
4 * 6 / 5 = 4.8
With integer math, 4 * 6 / 5 = 4
```

Modulus: %

You use the modulus operator (%) to return the remainder of a division operation. For example, 10 / 3 equals 3 with a remainder of 1, so 10 % 3 equals 1. Note that the modulus operator is especially useful when converting between bases, because you can use it to successively strip digits off a number by using the modulus operator with the base you're converting to. To see how this works, take a look at the topic "The **while** Loop," later in this chapter. It contains a full example.

Addition And Subtraction: + And -

"The multiplication operator is an asterisk and the division operator is a backslash," the Novice Programmer says, "but those aren't the symbols I learned for these operations in school. What does Java use for plus and minus?" "The usual symbols for plus and minus," you reply.

The old standby numeric operators are + and -, which you use for addition and subtraction, respectively. Here's an example:

```
public class app
{
    public static void main(String[] args)
    {
        int operand1 = 5, operand2 = 4, sum, diff;

        sum = operand1 + operand2;
        diff = operand1 - operand2;

        System.out.println(operand1 + " + " + operand2 + " = " + sum);
        System.out.println(operand1 + " - " + operand2 + " = " + diff);
    }
}
```

Here are the results of this code:

```
C:\>java app
5 + 4 = 9
5 - 4 = 1
```

Shift Operators: >>, >>>, And <<

You use the shift operators to shift all the bits of a number left or right a specified number of binary places. There are three shift operators: right shift (>>), unsigned right shift (>>>), and left shift (<<). Here's how you use these operators:

```
new_value = value << number_places;
new_value = value >> number_places;
new_value = value >>> number_places;
```

For example, 16 >> 2 shifts the number 16 right by two binary places, which is the same as dividing it by 4; therefore, 16 >> 2 equals 4. You commonly use the shift operators when packing binary values into an int or long as fields, because you can add a number to the int or long and then shift it left to make room for the next field of data.

Here's something you should know: The >> operator respects the sign of its operand, and because a negative value means that the leftmost bit is 1, shifting a negative number right introduces a new 1 at the left. Therefore, shifting 1111111111111100, which is -4 as a short, turns it into 1111111111111110, which is -2. Also, shifting -1, which is 1111111111111111, gives you 1111111111111111, which is still -1. If you really want to work with the actual bits in a number when you shift them right and not have a one added to the left when shifting negative numbers, use the unsigned right shift operator (>>>). This introduces a zero at the left, whether the number you're shifting is positive or negative.

Here's an example that puts the shift operators to work:

```java
public class app
{
    public static void main(String[] args)
    {
        int value = 16, negValue = -1;

        System.out.println(value + " << 2 = " + (value << 2));
        System.out.println(value + " >> 2 = " + (value >> 2));
        System.out.println(negValue + " >> 2 = " + (negValue >> 2));
        System.out.println(negValue + " >>> 22 = " + (negValue >>>
        22));
    }
}
```

Here's the result of this code:

```
C:\>java app
16 << 2 = 64
```

```
16 >> 2 = 4
-1 >> 2 = -1
-1 >>> 22 = 1023
```

Relational Operators: >, >=, <, <=, ==, And !=

The Big Boss appears and says, "The budget is just about spent, and we need to make sure it doesn't go negative." "Hmm," you say, "sounds like a job for the less than relational operator. Now, about my raise..." "Forget it," says the BB.

You use relational operators to create logical conditions that you can test with conditional statements such as the **if** statement. For example, here's how you could check to make sure the budget is greater than zero using a Java **if** statement:

```
public class app
{
    public static void main(String[] args)
    {
        int budget = 1;
        if (budget < 0) {
            System.out.println("Uh oh.");
        }
        else {
            System.out.println("Still solvent.");
        }
    }
}
```

Here's the result of this code:

```
C:\>java app
Still solvent.
```

Here's a list of all the relational operators; these operators will return true if their operands match the given descriptions:

- > (greater than; for example, **operand1 > operand2** returns true if **operand1** is greater than **operand2**)

- >= (greater than or equal to)

- < (less than)

- <= (less than or equal to)

- == (equal to)

- != (not equal to)

You can combine the logical conditions you create with a relational operator with the logical operators (see the next topic for the details).

TIP: *Here's a Java pitfall to avoid: When you're creating a logical condition, bear in mind that you probably want to use == instead of =. For example, the expression budget == 0 is true if the value in budget is 0, but the expression budget = 0 assigns a value of 0 to budget. Be careful, because using = instead of == in logical conditions is a very common mistake.*

Bitwise And Bitwise Logical **And, Xor,** And **Or:** &, ^, And |

"Help!" the Novice Programmer says, "I need to find out whether bit number 3 of an integer is set to 1. Is there an easy way to do this?" "Sure," you say, "you can use a bitwise operator."

The bitwise operators let you examine the individual bits of values. For example, when you use the & bitwise operator with two operands, each bit in one operand is logically **And**ed with the corresponding bit in the other operand. If both bits are 1, a one appears in that place in the result; otherwise, a zero will appear in that place. For example, you can have the Novice Programmer test whether the third bit of a value is set to 1 by **And**ing the value with a number for which he knows only one bit—the third bit—is set to 1. If the result of the **And** operation is not zero, the third bit of the original value was set. Here's how this would look in code:

```
public class app
{
    public static void main(String[] args)
    {
        int value = 12;
        int bit3setting = value & 1 << 3;

        if (bit3setting != 0) {
            System.out.println("Bit 3 is set.");
        }
        else {
```

```
                    System.out.println("Bit 3 is not set.");
            }
        }
    }
```

Here's the result:

```
C:\>java app
Bit 3 is set.
```

You can find the bitwise operators in Table 3.2. In overview, here's how they work: The **Or** operator (|) returns 0 when both bits are 0 and returns 1 otherwise. The **And** operator (&) returns 1 when both bits are 1 and returns 0 otherwise. Finally, the **Xor** operator (^, called the *exclusive Or*) returns 1 when one bit is 0 and the other is 1 and returns 0 otherwise.

When the &, ^, and | operators operate on boolean true/false values, they're considered bitwise *logical* operators. The bitwise logical operators work the same as the bitwise operators (substitute false for 0 and true for 1), as you can see in Table 3.3.

In overview, here's how the bitwise logical operators work: The **Or** operator (|) returns false when both operands are false, and it returns true otherwise. The **And** operator (&) returns true when both operands are true, and it returns false otherwise. The **Xor** operator (^) returns true when one operand is false and one is true, and it returns false otherwise.

Table 3.2   The Bitwise Operators.

x	y	x	y (Or)	x & y (And)	x ^ y (Xor)
0	0	0	0	0
1	0	1	0	1
0	1	1	0	1
1	1	1	1	0

Table 3.3   The Bitwise Logical Operators.

x	y	x	y (Or)	x & y (And)	x ^ y (Xor)
false	false	false	false	false
true	false	true	false	true
false	true	true	false	true
true	true	true	true	false

Here's an example in which I tie two logical conditions together, displaying a message if either is true, using the | operator:

```java
public class app
{
    public static void main(String[] args)
    {
        int budget = 1;
        boolean fired = false;

        if (budget < 0 | fired == true) {
            System.out.println("Uh oh.");
        }
        else {
            System.out.println("Still solvent.");
        }
    }
}
```

Here's the result:

```
C:\>java app
Still solvent.
```

In this next example, I insist that the temperature be between 60 and 90 degrees, using the & bitwise logical operator, before printing out a message:

```java
public class app
{
    public static void main(String[] args)
    {
        int temperature = 70;

        if (temperature < 90 & temperature > 60) {
            System.out.println("Time for a picnic.");
        }
    }
}
```

Here's the result:

```
C:\>java app
Time for a picnic.
```

As you can see, the bitwise logical operators can be very useful. Java also includes two logical operators: && and ||. We'll take a look at them next.

Logical && And ||

The two logical operators you usually use in logical expressions are the logical **And** (&&) and logical **Or** (||) operators. Table 3.4 shows how these operators work.

The **Or** operator (||) returns false when both operands are false, and it returns true otherwise. The **And** operator (&&) returns true when both operands are true, and it returns false otherwise. You use these operators to tie logical clauses together in a way that matches their names—use **And** when you want both logical clauses to be true and use **Or** when you only require one of two clauses to be true.

Here's an example taken from the previous topic in which I use &&:

```
public class app
{
    public static void main(String[] args)
    {
        int temperature = 70;

        if (temperature < 90 && temperature > 60) {
            System.out.println("Time for a picnic.");
        }
    }
}
```

Here's the result:

```
C:\>java app
Time for a picnic.
```

The && and || operators also have another interesting property—they're *short-circuit operators*, which means that if they can determine all they need to know by evaluating the left operand, they won't evaluate the right operand. This is very useful in cases such as the following, in which I'm testing both whether a value

Table 3.4 *The Logical Operators.*

x	y	x || y (Or)	x && y (And)
false	false	false	false
true	false	true	false
false	true	true	false
true	true	true	true

holds 0 and its reciprocal is less than 1000. If the value is indeed 0, the second part of the expression, where its reciprocal is calculated, is not executed. This way, a divide-by-zero overflow error doesn't occur. Here's the code:

```
public class app
{
    public static void main(String[] args)
    {
        double value = 0;

        if (value != 0 && 1 / value < 1000) {
            System.out.println("The value is not too small.");
        }
        else {
            System.out.println("The value is too small.");
        }
    }
}
```

Here's the result:

```
C:\>java app
The value is too small.
```

The logical operators differ from the bitwise logical operators, because the logical operators are short-circuit operators. To see this at work, take a look at the following code, where the assignment in the **if** statement is performed when I use the & operator but not when I use the && short-circuit operator:

```
public class app
{
    public static void main(String[] args)
    {
        double int1 = 0, int2 = 1, int3 = 1;

        if (int1 != 0 & (int2 = 2) == 1) {}
        System.out.println("int2 = " + int2);

        if (int1 != 0 && (int3 = 2) == 1) {}
        System.out.println("int3 = " + int3);
    }
}
```

Here's the result:

3. Operators, Conditionals, And Loops

```
C:\>java app
int2 = 2.0
int3 = 1.0
```

The If-Then-Else Operator: ?:

"OK," says the Novice Programmer, "I've mastered the operators. I'm ready for the Java conditional statements." "Not so fast," you say. "What about the ternary conditional operator?" "The *what*?" the NP asks.

There's a Java operator that acts much like an **if-else** statement—the ternary operator (?:). This operator is called a ternary operator because it takes three operands—a condition and two values:

```
value = condition ? value1 : value2;
```

If *condition* is true, the ?: operator returns *value1*, and it returns *value2* otherwise. In this way, the preceding statement works like the following **if** statement:

```
if (condition) {
    value = value1;
}
else {
    value = value2;
}
```

Here's an example in which I convert an integer between 0 and 15 into a hexadecimal digit using the ?: operator. This operator is perfect here, because I can use it to return a string made from the value, itself, if the value is less than 10 or a letter digit if the value is 10 or greater, like this:

```
public class app
{
    public static void main(String[] args)
    {
        int value = 15;
        String digit, chars[] = {"a", "b", "c", "d", "e", "f"};

        digit = value < 10 ? String.valueOf(value) : chars[value - 10];

        System.out.println(value + " = 0x" + digit);
    }
}
```

Here's the result:

```
C:\>java app
15 = 0xf
```

Assignment Operators: = And [operator]=

The most basic operators are the assignment operators, and I've been using these operators throughout the book already. You use the = operator to assign a variable a literal value or the value in another variable, like this:

```
public class app
{
    public static void main(String[] args)
    {
        int value = 12;

        System.out.println("The value = " + value);
    }
}
```

Here's the result:

```
C:\>java app
The value = 12
```

As in C++, you can perform multiple assignments in the same statement (this works because the assignment operator, itself, returns the assigned value):

```
public class app
{
    public static void main(String[] args)
    {
        int value1, value2, value3;

        value1 = value2 = value3 = 12;

        System.out.println("value1 = " + value1);
        System.out.println("value2 = " + value2);
        System.out.println("value3 = " + value3);
    }
}
```

Here's the result:

```
C:\>java app
value1 = 12
value2 = 12
value3 = 12
```

Also, as in C++, you can combine many operators with the assignment operator (=). For example, += is the addition assignment operator, which means *value +=* 2 is a shortcut for *value = value + 2*. Here's an example that puts the multiplication assignment operator to work:

```
public class app
{
    public static void main(String[] args)
    {
        int value = 10;

        value *= 2;

        System.out.println("value * 2 = " + value);
    }
}
```

Here's the result:

```
C:\>java app
value * 2 = 20
```

There are quite a few combination assignment operators. Here's a list of them:

- %= (modulus assignment)
- &= (bitwise **And** assignment)
- *= (multiplication assignment)
- /= (division assignment)
- ^= (bitwise **Xor** assignment)
- |= (bitwise **Or** assignment)
- += (addition assignment)
- <<= (shift left assignment)
- <= (less than or equal to)
- -= (subtraction assignment)

- **>>=** (shift right assignment)

- **>>>=** (shift right zero fill assignment)

That completes the list of Java operators, but there's one more popular way of handling math in Java—the **Math** class. This class is part of the java.lang package (which the Java compiler imports by default). We'll take a look at this class in the next topic.

Using The **Math** Class

"Hey," the Novice Programmer says, "I want to raise 3 to the power 4, but there's no Java operator for exponentiation." "You can use the **Math** class's **pow** method," you say. "And by the way, 3 to the power 4 is 81." "I'll believe it when Java tells me so," says the NP.

You can use the **java.lang.Math** class to perform a great many math operations. For example, here's how to solve the Novice Programmer's problem using the **Math.pow** method:

```
public class app
{
    public static void main(String[] args)
    {
        System.out.println("3 x 3 x 3 x 3 = " + Math.pow(3, 4));
    }
}
```

Here's the result:

```
C:\>java app
3 x 3 x 3 x 3 = 81.0
```

Here are the constants and methods of the **Math** class:

- ***double E***—The constant e (2.7182818284590452354)

- ***double PI***—The constant pi (3.14159265358979323846)

- ***double sin(double a)***—Trigonometric sine

- ***double cos(double a)***—Trigonometric cosine

- ***double tan(double a)***—Trigonometric tangent

- ***double asin(double a)***—Trigonometric arcsine

- *double acos(double a)*—Trigonometric arccosine
- *double atan(double a)*—Trigonometric arctangent
- *double atan2(double a, double b)*—Trigonometric arctangent, two operand version
- *double exp(double a)*—Raise *e* to a power
- *double log(double a)*—Log of a value
- *double sqrt(double a)*—Square root of a value
- *double pow(double a, double b)*—Raise to a power
- *double IEEEremainder(double f1, double f2)*—IEEEremainder method
- *double ceil(double a)*—Ceiling method
- *double floor(double a)*—Floor method
- *double rint(double a)*—Random integer
- *int round(float a)*—Rounds a float
- *long round(double a)*—Rounds a double
- *double random()*—Random number
- *int abs(int a)*—Absolute value of an int
- *long abs(long a)*—Absolute value of a long
- *float abs(float a)*—Absolute value of a float
- *double abs(double a)*—Absolute value of a double
- *int min(int a, int b)*—Minimum of two ints
- *long min(long a, long b)*—Minimum of two longs
- *float min(float a, float b)*—Minimum of two floats
- *double min(double a, double b)*—Minimum of two doubles
- *int max(int a, int b)*—Maximum of two integers
- *long max(long a, long b)*—Maximum of two longs
- *float max(float a, float b)*—Maximum of two floats
- *double max(double a, double b)*—Maximum of two doubles

Comparing Strings

When you're working with the **String** class, there are some methods you can use much like operators. For example, you can use the **equals**, **equalsIgnoreCase**, and **compareTo** methods, like this:

- *s1.equals(s2)*—True if **s1** equals **s2**

- *s1.equalsIgnoreCase(s2)*—True if **s1** equals **s2** (ignoring case)

- *s1.compareTo(s2)*—Returns a value less than zero if **s1** < **s2** lexically, zero if **s1** equals **s2**, or a value greater than zero if **s1** > **s2**

Here's an example putting these methods to work:

```java
public class app
{
    public static void main(String[] args)
    {
        String s1 = "abc";
        String s2 = "abc";
        String s3 = "ABC";
        String s4 = "bcd";
        if (s1.equals(s2)) {
            System.out.println("s1 == s2");
        }
        else {
            System.out.println("s1 != s2");
        }

        if (s1.equalsIgnoreCase(s3)) {
            System.out.println("s1 == s3 when ignoring case");
        }
        else {
            System.out.println("s1 != s3 when ignoring case");
        }

        if (s1.compareTo(s4) < 0){
            System.out.println("s1 < s2");
        }
        else if (s1.compareTo(s4) == 0 ){
            System.out.println("s1 == s2");
        }
        else if (s1.compareTo(s4) > 0 ){
            System.out.println("s1 > s2");
        }
    }
}
```

Here's the result of this code:

```
C:\>java app
s1 == s2
s1 == s3 when ignoring case
s1 < s2
```

The if Statement

"Hmm," says the Novice Programmer, "I'm stuck. I want to write an absolute value routine in Java, and I don't know how to proceed." "I don't suppose you've ever heard of the **Math** class's **Abs** method?" you reply. "The *what*?" asks the NP.

When you want to test conditions and execute code accordingly, it's time to use the Java conditional statements, such as the **if** statement. Here's how you use this statement in general:

```
if (condition) statement1;
else statement2;
```

Note that *statement1* and *statement2* can both be compound statements, which means they can be made up of a number of statements enclosed in curly braces.

One way to get an absolute value, as the Novice Programmer was trying to do, is to start by checking whether the value is greater than zero and, if so, just print out the value itself. Here's how to make that test with an **if** statement:

```
public class app
{
    public static void main(String[] args)
    {
        int value = 10;

        if(value > 0)
            System.out.println("Abs(" + value + ") = " + value);
    }
}
```

Here's the result of this code:

```
C:\>java app
Abs(10) = 10
```

Note that in this case, the statement that's executed if the condition of the **if** statement is true is a single statement, but you can also execute multiple statements if you make them part of a compound statement in a code block, like this:

```
public class app
{
    public static void main(String[] args)
    {
        int value = 10;

        if(value > 0) {
            System.out.println("The number was positive.");
            System.out.println("Abs(" + value + ") = " + value);
        }
    }
}
```

Here's the result of this code:

```
C:\>java app
The number was positive.
Abs(10) = 10
```

The **else** Statement

So far, the **if** statement in the absolute value example only displays an absolute value if the value, itself, is greater than zero. However, I can expand that **if** statement by adding an **else** clause, which is executed if the **if** statement's condition is false. Here's how this looks in code (note that I'm able to handle negative numbers as well as positive ones):

```
public class app
{
    public static void main(String[] args)
    {
        int value = -10;

        if(value > 0) {
            System.out.println("Abs(" + value + ") = " + value);
        }
        else {
            System.out.println("Abs(" + value + ") = " + -value);
        }
    }
}
```

Here's the result of this code:

```
C:\>java app
Abs(-10) = 10
```

Nested **if** Statements

You can also nest **if** statements inside each other (that is, define them inside other **if** statements). Here's an example showing how this technique works:

```
public class app
{
    public static void main(String[] args)
    {
        double value = 2;

        if (value != 0) {
            if (value > 0)
                System.out.println("The result = " + (1 / value));
            else
                System.out.println("The result = " + (-1 / value));
        }
    }
}
```

Here's the result of this code:

```
C:\>java app
The result = 0.5
```

The **if-else** Ladders

It's possible to create an entire sequence of **if-else** statements, which is known as an *if-else ladder*. Here's an example showing how one works (in this case, I test the value in a string variable successively until I find a match to the current day of the week):

```
public class app
{
    public static void main(String[] args)
    {
        String day = "Wednesday";

        if(day == "Monday")
            System.out.println("It\'s Monday.");
        else if (day == "Tuesday")
```

```
        System.out.println("It\'s Tuesday.");
    else if (day == "Wednesday")
        System.out.println("It\'s Wednesday.");
    else if (day == "Thursday")
        System.out.println("It\'s Thursday.");
    else if (day == "Friday")
        System.out.println("It\'s Friday.");
    else if (day == "Saturday")
        System.out.println("It\'s Saturday.");
    else if (day == "Sunday")
        System.out.println("It\'s Sunday.");
    }
}
```

Here's the result of this code:

```
C:\>java app
It's Wednesday.
```

Note that although it's possible to create **if-else** ladders in this way, Java actually includes a statement expressly for situations like this—the **switch** statement. We'll take a look at this statement in the next topic.

The **switch** Statement

"Jeez," says the Novice Programmer, "I'm getting tired of writing **if-else** ladders—the one in my program must be five pages long now." "How about trying a **switch** statement?" you ask. "What's that?" the NP asks.

The **switch** statement is Java's multipath branch statement; it provides the same kind of functionality as an **if-else** ladder (see the previous topic) but in a form that's much easier to work with. Here's what the **switch** statement looks like in general:

```
switch (expression) {
    case value1:
        statement1;
        [break;]
    case value2:
        statement2;
        [break;]
    case value3:
        statement3;
```

```
            [break;]
                .

                .

                .

    default:
        default_statement;
}
```

Here, the value of the *expression*, which must be of type byte, char, short, or int, is compared against the various test values in the **case** statements: ***value1, value2,*** and so on. If the expression matches one of the **case** statements, the code associated with that **case** statement—***statement1, statement2,*** and so on—is executed. If execution reaches a **break** statement, the **switch** statement ends.

Here's an example in which I display the day of the week based on a numeric value using a **switch** statement:

```
public class app
{
    public static void main(String[] args)
    {
        int day = 3;

        switch(day) {
            case 0:
                System.out.println("It\'s Sunday.");
                break;
            case 1:
                System.out.println("It\'s Monday.");
                break;
            case 2:
                System.out.println("It\'s Tuesday.");
                break;
            case 3:
                System.out.println("It\'s Wednesday.");
                break;
            case 4:
                System.out.println("It\'s Thursday.");
                break;
            case 5:
                System.out.println("It\'s Friday.");
                break;
            default:
                System.out.println("It must be Saturday.");
        }
    }
}
```

Here's the result of this code:

```
C:\>java app
It's Wednesday.
```

You can even nest **switch** statements. Note that if you don't specify a **break** statement at the end of a **case** statement, execution will continue with the code in the next **case** statement. Sometimes, that's useful, such as when you want to execute the same code for multiple **case** test values, like this:

```
public class app
{
    public static void main(String[] args)
    {
        int temperature = 68;

        switch(temperature) {
            case 60:
            case 61:
            case 62:
            case 63:
            case 64:
                System.out.println("Too cold.");
                break;
            case 65:
            case 66:
            case 67:
            case 68:
            case 69:
                System.out.println("Cool.");
                break;
            case 70:
            case 71:
            case 72:
            case 73:
            case 74:
            case 75:
                System.out.println("Warm.");
                break;
            default:
                System.out.println("Probably too hot.");
        }
    }
}
```

Here's the result of this code:

```
C:\>java app
Cool.
```

The **while** Loop

"Well," says the Novice Programmer, "I'm in trouble again. The Big Boss wants me to create a commercial program that will calculate factorials, and I don't even know what a factorial is!" "Well," you say, "six factorial, written as '6!', is equal to $6 \times 5 \times 4 \times 3 \times 2 \times 1$. And you can write your program with a **while** loop."

A **while** loops keeps executing the statement in its body (which may be a compound statement, with a number of single statements inside curly braces) while a particular logical condition evaluates to true. Here's what a **while** loop looks like in general:

```
while(condition)
    statement
```

Note that if the *condition* is not true, the body of the loop is not even executed once. Here's an example that puts the **while** loop to work; in this case, I display a value, successively subtract 1 from that value, and then displaying the result, as long as the result is positive. When the value becomes 0, the **while** loop stops, because the condition I've used (value > 0) has become false:

```
public class app
{
    public static void main(String[] args)
    {
        int value = 10;

        while (value > 0) {
            System.out.println("Current value = " + value--);
        }

    }
}
```

Here's what this **while** loop returns:

```
C:\JavaBB\Test>java app
Current value = 10
Current value = 9
```

```
Current value = 8
Current value = 7
Current value = 6
Current value = 5
Current value = 4
Current value = 3
Current value = 2
Current value = 1
```

Here's another **while** loop example in which I'm solving the Novice Programmer's problem and creating a program that will calculate factorials:

```
public class app
{
    public static void main(String[] args)
    {
        int value = 6, factorial = 1, temp;

        temp = value;   //make a destructive copy.

        while (temp > 0) {
            factorial *= temp--;
        }

        System.out.println(value + "! = " + factorial);
    }
}
```

Here's how the program calculates the factorial of 6:

```
C:\>java app
6! = 720
```

Here's a more advanced example. In this case, I'm converting a number to hexadecimal by successively stripping off hex digits with the modulus operator. Because the digits come off in reverse order, I'm using a **while** loop to push them onto a Java *stack*, which you'll see when we discuss the collection classes. After pushing the digits onto the stack, I pop them in another **while** loop to reverse the order of the digits and cause the StringBuffer object to display:

```
import java.util.*;

public class app
{
    public static void main(String[] args)
    {
```

```
        int value = 32, temp = value;
        StringBuffer sb = new StringBuffer();
        Stack st = new Stack();

        while (temp > 0) {
            st.push(String.valueOf(temp % 16));
            temp >>>= 4;
        }

        while(!st.empty()) {
            sb.append(new String((String) st.pop()));
        }

        System.out.println("Converting " + value + " yields 0x" + sb);
    }
}
```

Here's what this program's output looks like:

```
C:\>java app
Converting 32 yields 0x20
```

Here's a fact that can come in handy: Because null statements are valid in Java, a **while** loop doesn't have to have a body at all. Here's an example showing a crude way of calculating an integer square root (note that all the work here takes place in the condition part of the loop):

```
public class app
{
    public static void main(String[] args)
    {
        int target = 144, sqrt = 1;

        while (++sqrt * sqrt != target) ;

        System.out.println("sqrt(" + target + ") = " + sqrt);
    }
}
```

Here's the result:

```
C:\>java app
sqrt(144) = 12
```

Another type of **while** loop—the **do-while** loop—is discussed in the next topic.

The **do-while** Loop

The Programming Correctness Czar says, "So you have a **while** loop in Java. In C++, we have both a **while** loop and a **do-while** loop." "That's funny," you say. "We have both of those in Java too."

The **do-while** loop is just like a **while** loop, except that the test condition is evaluated at the end of the loop, not at the beginning. Here's what the **do-while** loop looks like (bear in mind that the statement can be a compound statement with a number of single statements inside curly braces):

```
do
    statement
while(condition);
```

The biggest reason to use a **do-while** loop instead of a **while** loop is when you need the body of the loop to be run at least once. For example, here's a case where the value I'm testing for isn't even available for testing until the end of the loop:

```
public class app
{
    public static void main(String[] args)
    {
        int values[] = {1, 2, 3, 0, 5}, test, index = 0;

        do {
            test = 5 * values[index++];
        } while (test < 15);
    }
}
```

On the other hand, there are times when you should use a **while** loop instead of a **do-while** loop—times when the body of the loop shouldn't even run once if the condition is not true. For example, take a look at the following code in which a **do-while** loop evaluates the reciprocal of a value but can only test whether the value is a nonzero value at the end of the loop:

```
public class app
{
    public static void main(String[] args)
    {
        double value = 0;
```

```
        do {
            System.out.println("The reciprocal = " + 1 / value);
        } while (value > 0);
    }
}
```

It's far better in this case to use a **while** loop to test for 0 first:

```
public class app
{
    public static void main(String[] args)
    {
        double value = 0;

        while (value > 0) {
            System.out.println("The reciprocal = " + 1 / value);
        }
    }
}
```

The **for** Loop

The Novice Programmer is back and says, "I like **while** loops, but they're not the easiest to work with when handling arrays—I really need an numeric index there. Is there anything else?" "Certainly," you say, "try a **for** loop."

The Java **for** loop is a good choice when you want to use a numeric index that you automatically increment or decrement each time through the loop, such as when you're working with an array. Here's what the **for** loop looks like in general (note that *statement* can be a compound statement, including several single statements inside curly braces):

```
for (initialization_expression; end_conditon; iteration_expression) {
    statement
}
```

You can initialize a loop index in the initialization expression (in fact, you can use multiple loop indexes in a **for** loop), provide a test condition for ending the loop when that test condition becomes false in the end condition, and provide some way of changing—usually incrementing—the loop index in the iteration expression.

Here's an example showing how to put the **for** loop to work (note that I start the loop index at 1 and end it when the loop index exceeds 10, which means that the loop body will execute exactly 10 times):

```
public class app
{
    public static void main(String[] args)
    {
        int loop_index;

        for (loop_index = 1; loop_index <= 10; loop_index++) {
            System.out.println("This is iteration number "
                + loop_index);
        }

    }
}
```

Here's the result:

```
C:\>java app
This is iteration number 1
This is iteration number 2
This is iteration number 3
This is iteration number 4
This is iteration number 5
This is iteration number 6
This is iteration number 7
This is iteration number 8
This is iteration number 9
This is iteration number 10
```

Here's an example that you saw at the beginning of the chapter; this example finds the average student score by looping over the all scores and summing them (note that I'm actually declaring and initializing the loop index to 0 in the initialization expression):

```
public class app
{
    public static void main(String[] args)
    {
        double grades[] = {88, 99, 73, 56, 87, 64};
        double sum, average;

        sum = 0;

        for (int loop_index = 0; loop_index < grades.length;
            loop_index++) {
            sum += grades[loop_index];
        }
```

3. Operators, Conditionals, And Loops

```
        average = sum / grades.length;

        System.out.println("Average grade = " + average);
    }
}
```

Here's the result of this code:

```
C:\>java app
Average grade = 77.83333333333333
```

When you declare a loop variable (such as **loop_index** in this example), the *scope* of that variable is limited to the **for** loop's body (the scope of a variable is the part of the program that you can access it in, as you'll see in the next chapter).

Note that you can use very general expressions in a **for** loop. Java lets you separate expressions in a **for** loop with a comma, as shown in the following example in which I'm using two loop indexes:

```
public class app
{
    public static void main(String[] args)
    {
        for (int loop_index = 0, doubled = 0; loop_index <= 10;
            loop_index++, doubled = 2 * loop_index) {
            System.out.println("Loop index " + loop_index +
                " doubled equals " + doubled);
        }
    }
}
```

Here's the result of this code:

```
C:\>java app
Loop index 0 doubled equals 0
Loop index 1 doubled equals 2
Loop index 2 doubled equals 4
Loop index 3 doubled equals 6
Loop index 4 doubled equals 8
Loop index 5 doubled equals 10
Loop index 6 doubled equals 12
Loop index 7 doubled equals 14
Loop index 8 doubled equals 16
Loop index 9 doubled equals 18
Loop index 10 doubled equals 20
```

You don't have to give a **for** loop any body at all—in fact, you can use a null statement. Here's an example in which I'm summing all the elements of an array in a **for** loop without any code in its body:

```java
public class app
{
    public static void main(String[] args)
    {
        int array[] = {1, 2, 3, 4, 5}, sum = 0;

        for (int loop_index = 0;
            loop_index < array.length;
            sum += array[loop_index++]) ;

        System.out.println("The sum = " + sum);
    }
}
```

Here's the result of this code:

```
C:\>java app
The sum = 15
```

You can even turn a **for** loop into a **while** loop. Here's an example that's adapted from the previous factorial example in the topic "The **while** Loop":

```java
public class app
{
    public static void main(String[] args)
    {
        int value = 6, factorial = 1, temp;

        temp = value;    //make a destructive copy.

        for( ;temp > 0; ) {
            factorial *= temp--;
        }

        System.out.println(value + "! = " + factorial);
    }
}
```

3. Operators, Condition-als, And Loops

Nested Loops

"I'm working with a two-dimensional array," the Novice Programmer says, "and I almost wish I could have a loop *within* a loop so I could loop over both dimensions." "Of course you can use loops within loops," you reply.

Java lets you nest loops, one within another. Here's an example showing how this works (in this case, I'm finding the average value of the elements in a two-dimensional array by looping over all the elements with two **for** loops):

```java
public class app
{
    public static void main(String[] args)
    {
        double array[][] = {{1, 2, 3},
                            {3, 2, 1},
                            {1, 2, 3}};
        int sum = 0, total = 0;

        for(int outer_index = 0; outer_index < array.length;
            outer_index++) {
            for(int inner_index = 0; inner_index <
                array[outer_index].length; inner_index++) {

                sum += array[outer_index][inner_index];
                total++;

            }
        }

        System.out.println("Average array value = " + (sum / total));
    }
}
```

Here's the result of this code:

```
C:\>java app
Average array value = 2
```

Using The **break** Statement

The Novice Programmer has another problem: "I've got a multidimensional array that I'm looping over, and sometimes deep inside five nested loops, the results exceed the maximum allowable value, so I want to end all the loops. How the heck do I do that without letting them all finish naturally?" "By using the **break** statement," you reply.

Some languages include a **goto** statement that you can use to jump to any statement you want to in your code, but most languages consider **goto** too unstructured—as does Java, which does not include a **goto** statement. However, a **goto** statement lets you jump out of a loop that's no longer useful, which is a valid thing to do. Because Java doesn't have a **goto** statement you can use to do that, it supports the **break** statement for this purpose.

You can use the **break** statement to end a loop, as in this case, where I'm ending a loop if a sum becomes greater than 12:

```
public class app
{
    public static void main(String[] args)
    {
        double array[] = {1, 2, 3, 4, 5, 6, 7, 8, 9, 10};
        int sum = 0;

        for(int loop_index = 0; loop_index <
            array.length; loop_index++) {

            sum += array[loop_index];
            if (sum > 12) break;
            System.out.println("Looping...");
        }
        System.out.println("The sum exceeded the maximum value.");
    }
}
```

Here's the result of this code:

```
C:\>java app
Looping...
Looping...
Looping...
Looping...
The sum exceeded the maximum value.
```

3. Operators, Conditionals, And Loops

What if you have multiple loops that you want to break? In this case, you can label the loops and indicate the one you want to break out of. Here's an example in which I break out of a double-nested loop:

```java
public class app
{
    public static void main(String[] args)
    {
        double array[][] = {{1, 2, 3},
                            {3, 2, 1},
                            {1, 2, 3}};
        int sum = 0;

        outer: for(int outer_index = 0; outer_index < array.length;
            outer_index++) {
            inner: for(int inner_index = 0; inner_index <
                array[outer_index].length; inner_index++) {

                sum += array[outer_index][inner_index];
                if (sum > 3) break outer;
            }
            System.out.println("I'm not going to print.");
        }

        System.out.println("The loop has finished.");
    }
}
```

Here's the result of this code:

```
C:\>java app
The loop has finished.
```

Note that if you don't use a label with the **break** statement, you'll only break out of the current loop.

Using The **continue** Statement

"I like loops," the Novice Programmer says, "I really do. There's just one problem, though. Sometimes when I'm looping, I come across a value that I don't want to use and I just want to skip to the next iteration of the loop without executing any more code. Can I do that?" "Yes, indeed," you say. "You can use the **continue** statement."

To skip to the next iteration of a loop, you can use the **continue** statement. Here's an example in which I'm printing out reciprocals, and I want to avoid trying to print out the reciprocal of 0. If the current loop index equals 0, I skip the current iteration and move on to the next one. Here's the code:

```
public class app
{
    public static void main(String[] args)
    {
        for(double loop_index = 5; loop_index > -5; loop_index--) {
            if (loop_index == 0) continue;
            System.out.println("The reciprocal of " + loop_index +
                " = " + (1 / loop_index));
        }

    }
}
```

Here's the result of this code (note that this output skips over the line where the code would try to calculate the reciprocal of 0):

```
C:\>java app
The reciprocal of 5.0 = 0.2
The reciprocal of 4.0 = 0.25
The reciprocal of 3.0 = 0.3333333333333333
The reciprocal of 2.0 = 0.5
The reciprocal of 1.0 = 1.0
The reciprocal of -1.0 = -1.0
The reciprocal of -2.0 = -0.5
The reciprocal of -3.0 = -0.3333333333333333
The reciprocal of -4.0 = -0.25
```

3. Operators, Condition-als, And Loops

Chapter 4

Object-Oriented Programming

(continued)

In Depth

This chapter is all about a topic central to any Java program—object-oriented programming (OOP). I first discussed object-oriented programming in Chapter 1, because you can't write Java code without it. Now that we've come up through the basics of Java syntax, we're ready to work with object-oriented programming in a formal way.

Object-oriented programming is really just another technique to let you implement that famous programming dictum: divide and conquer. The idea is that you *encapsulate* data and methods into objects, making each object semiautonomous, enclosing private (that is, purely internal) data and methods in a way that stops them from cluttering the general namespace. The object can then interact with the rest of the program through a well-defined interface defined by its public (that is, externally callable) methods.

Object-oriented programming was first created to handle larger programs, breaking them up into functional units. It takes the idea of breaking a program into subroutines one step further, because objects can have both multiple subroutines and data inside them. The result of encapsulating parts of your program into an object is that it's easily conceptualized as a single item instead of having to deal with all that makes up that object internally.

As I first discussed in Chapter 1, imagine how your kitchen would look filled with pipes, pumps, a compressor, and all kinds of switches used to keep food cold. Every time the temperature of the food got too high, you'd have to turn on the compressor and open valves and start cranking the pumps manually. Now wrap all that functionality into an object—a refrigerator—in which all those operations are handled internally, with the appropriate feedback between the parts of the object handled automatically inside the object.

That's the idea behind *encapsulation*—taking a complex system that demands a lot of attention and turning it into an object that handles all its own work internally and can be easily conceptualized, much like a refrigerator. If the first dictum of object-oriented programming is "divide and conquer," the second is surely "out of sight, out of mind."

4. Object-Oriented Programming

In Java, object-oriented programming revolves around a few key concepts: classes, objects, data members, methods, and inheritance. Here's what those terms mean in overview:

- A *class* is a template from which you can create objects. The definition of the class includes the formal specifications for the class and any data and methods in it.

- An *object* is an instance of a class, much as a variable is an instance of a data type. You can think of a class as the type of an object, and you can think of the object as an instance of a class. Objects encapsulate methods and instance variables.

- *Data members* are those variables that are part of a class, and they're how you store the data the object uses. Objects support both *instance variables*, whose values are specific to the object, and *class variables*, whose values are shared among the objects of that class.

- A *method* is a function built into a class or object. You can have *instance methods* and *class methods*. You use instance methods with objects, but you can use a class method just by referring to the class by name—no object is required.

- *Inheritance* is the process of deriving one class, called the *derived class*, from another, called the *base class*, and being able to make use of the base class's methods in the derived class.

All these constructs are important to object-oriented programming, and we'll get into more details on each of them now.

TIP: If you're used to working with object-oriented programming in C++, it may surprise you to learn that although Java programs are object oriented, the object-oriented support in Java is less than what's available in languages such as C++. For example, the designers of Java decided to let programmers overload methods but not operators (although Java itself overloads operators such as **+** for the **String** class). Also, Java does not support destructors and does not support multiple inheritance directly—instead Java interfaces are used.

Classes

In object-oriented programming, *classes* provide a sort of template for objects. That is, if you think of a class as a cookie cutter, the objects you create from it are the cookies. You can consider a class an object's *type*—you use a class to create an object and then you can call the object's methods from your code.

To create an object, you call a class's *constructor*, which is a method with the same name as the class itself. This constructor creates a new object of the class. We've been creating classes throughout this book already; each time you create a Java program, you need a class. For example, here's how to create a class named **app**, which is stored in a file named app.java (this class creates a Java application):

```
public class app
{
    public static void main(String[] args)
    {
        System.out.println("Hello from Java!");
    }
}
```

When you use the Java compiler, this file, app.java, is translated into the bytecode file app.class, which holds the complete specification for the **app** class.

So how do you create objects from classes? Take a look at the next section.

Objects

In Java, you call an instance of a class an *object*. To create an object, you call a class's *constructor*, which has the same name as the class itself. Here's an example in which I create an object from the Java **String** class, passing the string I want to enclose in that object to the **String** class's constructor:

```
String s = new String("Hello from Java!");
```

You'll see more about creating objects with constructors throughout this chapter. So what do you do with an object when you have one? You can interact with it using its data members and methods; take a look at the next two sections.

Data Members

Data members of an object are called *instance data members* or *instance variables*. Data items shared by all objects of a class are called *class data members* or *class variables*. You'll see how to create both instance variables and class variables in this chapter. Data members can be accessible outside an object, or you can make them internal to the object for the private use of the methods inside the object.

Here's an example showing how you might use an object's data member; say you have a class named **Data_class**, and you create an object of this class named **data1**:

```
Data_class data1 = new Data_class("Hello from Java!");
    .
    .
    .
```

If **Data_class** defines a publicly accessible data member named **data**, you can refer to the data member of **data1** using the dot operator (**.**), like this:

```
data1.data
```

That means you can print out the data in **data1**, like this:

```
Data_class data1 = new Data_class("Hello from Java!");
```

```
System.out.println(data1.data);
```

In this way, you can refer to the data members of an object that the object makes publicly accessible.

On the other hand, recall that data hiding is one of the motivations behind object-oriented programming, and giving code outside an object access to the internal data of an object might not be a good idea. Instead, you often give code outside an object access to the object's data only through the object's methods (which means you can control the object's interface to the rest of the program, checking data values before those values are stored in the object's data members).

Methods

Methods are the functions built into a class, and therefore built into the objects you create from that class. You usually divide methods into those intended for use inside the class, called *private methods*, those intended for use outside the class, called *public methods*, and those intended for use by the class and those classes you derive from it, called *protected methods*.

Private methods are usually only called inside the object, itself, by other parts of the object. In the refrigerator example introduced at the beginning of this chapter, for instance, the thermostat may call an entirely internal method named **start_compressor** when it's time to get cold.

Once you have an object that supports methods, you can use that object's methods. In the following example, I use the **calculate** method to work with the two values in **operand1** and **operand2** and store the result of the calculation in **result**:

```
Calculator calc1 = new Calculator();
```

```
result = calc1.calculate(operand1, operand2);
```

Java supports two types of methods: class methods and instance methods. Instance methods, like the **calculate** example here, are invoked on objects (that is, objects are instances of a class). Class methods, on the other hand, are invoked on a class. For example, the **java.lang.Math** class has a class method named **sqrt** that calculates a square root, and you can use it like this (no object is needed):

```
public class app
{
    public static void main(String[] args)
    {
        double value = 4, sqrt;

        sqrt = Math.sqrt(value);

        System.out.println("The square root of " + value + " = "
            + sqrt);
    }
}
```

Here's what you see when you run this code:

```
C:\>java app
The square root of 4.0 = 2.0
```

You'll learn how to create both instance and class methods in this chapter.

There's one more object-oriented concept to master before we get to the code—inheritance.

Inheritance

Inheritance is one of the formally defining aspects of object-oriented programming. Using inheritance, you can *derive* a new class from an old class, and the new class will *inherit* all the methods and member data of the old class. The new class is called the *derived class*, and the original class is called the *base class*. The idea here is that you add what you want to the new class to give it more customized functionality than the base class.

For example, if you have class named **vehicle**, you might derive a new class named **car** from **vehicle** and add a new method called **horn** that prints "beep" when called. In that way, you've created a new class from a base class and have augmented that class with an additional method.

Inheritance is an important topic in Java, because you can use the huge class libraries available in Java by deriving your own classes from them. You'll see how to use object-oriented inheritance in the next chapter.

Now that we've gotten OOP concepts down, it's time to turn to the "Immediate Solutions" section and master OOP in detail. All this material is essential for Java programming, so dig into it until you've made it your own.

Immediate Solutions

Declaring And Creating Objects

The Novice Programmer appears, ready to discuss object-oriented programming. "I've know all about objects now," the NP says, "only...." "Only what?" you ask. "Only, I don't know how to actually *create* an object in a program."

You need to declare an object before you can use it. You can declare objects the same way you declare variables of the simple data types, but you use the class as the object's type. Also, you can use the **new** operator to create objects in Java. Let's look at an example using the Java **String** class.

TIP: *Actually, you don't need to declare an object in all cases before using it. In some cases, Java creates an object for you automatically, as is the case with string literals, which Java treats like String objects. This means that expressions such as **"Hello from Java!".length()** are valid.*

To start, I'll declare a new object, **s1**, of the **String** class:

```
public class app
{
    public static void main(String[] args)
    {
        String s1;
        .
        .
        .

}
```

Although declaring a simple variable creates that variable, declaring an object doesn't create it. To actually create the object, I can use the **new** operator using this general form in which I'm passing parameters to the class's constructor:

```
object = new class([parameter1 [, parameter2...]]);
```

The **String** class has several constructors, as you saw in Chapter 2. You can pass quoted strings to one of the **String** class's constructors; therefore, you could create the new object, **s1**, like this:

```java
public class app
{
    public static void main(String[] args)
    {
        String s1;
        s1 = new String("Hello from Java!");
            .
            .
            .
}
```

Now the new object, **s1**, exists and is ready for use. For example, to convert all the characters in **s1** to lowercase, you can use the String class's **toLowerCase** method, like this:

```java
s1.toLowerCase()
```

You can also combine the declaration and creation steps into one step. Here's an example in which I'm declaring a new String object, **s2**, and creating it with the **new** operator, all in one line:

```java
public class app
{
    public static void main(String[] args)
    {
        String s1;
        s1 = new String("Hello from Java!");


        String s2 = new String("Hello from Java!");
            .
            .
            .
}
```

Classes often have several different constructors, each of which can take a different data specification (that is, different parameter types and number of parameters; the Java compiler knows which constructor you want to use by noting how the types of the parameters are used and how many parameters there are). In object-oriented terms, these constructors are *overloaded*, and I'll cover overloading in this chapter. For example, the **String** class's constructor is overloaded to take character arrays as well as text strings, so I can create a new object, **s3**, using a character array, like this:

```java
public class app
{
```

```
    public static void main(String[] args)
    {
        String s1;
        s1 = new String("Hello from Java!");

        String s2 = new String("Hello from Java!");

        char c1[] = {'H', 'i', ' ', 't', 'h', 'e', 'r', 'e'};
        String s3 = new String(c1);
        .
        .
        .
}
```

Sometimes, classes will have methods that return objects, which means they'll use the **new** operator internally (and you don't have to). Here's an example, using the **valueOf** method of the **String** class, -- which I convert a double into a String object:

```
public class app
{
    public static void main(String[] args)
    {
        String s1;
        s1 = new String("Hello from Java!");

        String s2 = new String("Hello from Java!");

        char c1[] = {'H', 'i', ' ', 't', 'h', 'e', 'r', 'e'};
        String s3 = new String(c1);

        double double1 = 1.23456789;
        String s4 = String.valueOf(double1);
        .
        .
        .
}
```

In addition, you can assign one object to another, as I've done here:

```
public class app
{
    public static void main(String[] args)
    {
        String s1;
```

```
        s1 = new String("Hello from Java!");

        String s2 = new String("Hello from Java!");

        char c1[] = {'H', 'i', ' ', 't', 'h', 'e', 'r', 'e'};
        String s3 = new String(c1);

        double double1 = 1.23456789;
        String s4 = String.valueOf(double1);

        String s5;
        s5 = s1;

        System.out.println(s1);
        System.out.println(s2);
        System.out.println(s3);
        System.out.println(s4);
        System.out.println(s5);
    }
}
```

Internally, what's really happening is that the object reference in **s1** is copied to **s5**. What this means in practice is that **s1** and **s5** refer to the *same* object.

That's important to know, because if you change the instance data in **s1**, you're also changing the instance data in **s5**, and vice versa. If two variables refer to the same object, be careful—multiple references to the same object can create some extremely hard-to-find bugs. This usually happens when you think you're really dealing with different objects.

At the end of the preceding code, I print out all the strings I've created. Here's what appears when the program is run:

```
C:\>java app
Hello from Java!
Hello from Java!
Hi there
1.23456789
Hello from Java!
```

That's how to declare and create objects—much the same way you declare and create simple variables, with the added power of configuring objects by passing data to a class's constructor. It's time to start creating our own classes, and we'll start that process in the next topic.

4. Object-Oriented Programming

Declaring And Defining Classes

The Novice Programmer is excited and says, "I've done it! I've created an object—it worked!" "Fine," you say, approvingly, "now how about creating a class?" "Uh-oh," says the NP, "how does that work?"

There are two parts to setting up a class in Java—the class declaration and the class definition. The declaration tells Java what it needs to know about the new class. Here's the general form of a class declaration:

```
[access] class classname [extends ...] [implements ...]
{
    //class definition goes here.
}
```

The actual implementation of the class is called the *class definition*, and it makes up the body of the class declaration you see in the preceding sample code. Here's the general form of a class declaration and definition:

```
access class classname [extends ...] [implements ...]
{
    [access] [static] type instance_variable1;
                        ⤳ class variables
        .
        .
        .
    [access] [static] type instance_variableN;

    [access] [static] type method1 (parameter_list)
    {
                        ⤳ class methods
        .
        .
        .
    }
        .
        .
        .
    [access] [static] type methodN (parameter_list)
    {
        .
        .
        .
    }
}
```

The **static** keyword here turns variables into class variables and methods into class methods (as opposed to instance variables and methods), as you'll see later. The *access* term specifies the accessibility of the class or class member to the rest of the program, and it can be **public**, **private**, or **protected**. There's also a default access if you don't specify an access type; you'll learn about this in a few pages. You use the **extends** and **implements** keywords with inheritance, as you'll see in the next chapter.

An example will make this all clear. To start, I'll just create a very simple class named **printer** that defines one method, **print** (you first saw this example back in Chapter 1). When I call the **print** method, it displays the message "Hello from Java!" on the console. Here's what this class looks like:

```
class printer
{
    public void print()
    {
        System.out.println("Hello from Java!");
    }
}
```

Now I can make use of the **print** method in other classes, as in this example, where I'm creating a new object of the **printer** class using the **new** operator and using that object's **print** method in an application named *app*:

```
class printer
{
    public void print()
    {
        System.out.println("Hello from Java!");
    }
}

public class app
{
    public static void main(String[] args)
    {
        printer printer1 = new printer();

        printer1.print();
    }
}
```

That's all it takes—now I put this code in a file, app.java, compile it, and then run it as follows:

```
C:\>java app
Hello from Java!
```

Take a moment to study this example; note that I'm declaring and defining two classes, **printer** and **app**, in the same file here. Only one class can be declared public in one file, and that's **app** in this case. The file, itself, must be named after that class, which here means the containing file must be app.java. However, you can have as many private or protected classes as you like in the file (and Java will create separate .class files for them when you compile the file).

You can also divide this example into two files, one for each class. Here's printer.java:

```
class printer
{
    public void print()
    {
        System.out.println("Hello from Java!");
    }
}
```

4. Object-Oriented Programming

And here's the new app.java (note that I had to import the **printer** class to be able to use it; see Chapter 1 for more on importing classes):

```
import printer;

public class app
{
    public static void main(String[] args)
    {
        printer printer1 = new printer();

        printer1.print();
    }
}
```

Creating Instance Variables

"Hmm," says the Novice Programmer, "I want to create a class to store data, and I'm all set except for one small thing." "Yes?" you ask. "How do I store data in classes?" the NP asks.

You can store data in classes in two ways—as instance variables or as class variables. Instance variables are specific to objects; if you have two objects (that is, two instances of a class), the instance variables in each object are independent of the instance variables in the other object. On the other hand, the class variables of both objects will refer to the same data and therefore hold the same value. Let's take a look at instance variables first.

Here's how you store instance data in a class:

```
access class classname [extends ...] [implements ...]
{
    [access] type instance_variable1;
        .
        .
        .
    [access] type instance_variableN;
}
```

Here's an example in which I'll create a class named **Data** that holds a String instance variable named **data_string**, which in turn holds the text "Hello from Java!":

```
class Data
{
    public String data_string = "Hello from Java!";
}
```

Now I can create an object, named **data**, of the **Data** class in **main** and refer to the instance variable **data_string** in **data** as **data.data_string**. Here's what this looks like in code:

initialised instance variables

```
class Data
{
    public String data_string = "Hello from Java!";
}

public class app
{
```

```
public static void main(String[] args)
{
    Data data = new Data();

    String string = data.data_string;

    System.out.println(string);
}
```

As you can see, you can access the public instance variables of an object with the dot operator. However, remember that one of the motivations behind object-oriented programming is to keep data private. We'll take a look at this in more detail in the next topic.

Setting Variable Access

"Hey," says the Novice Programmer, "I thought objects were supposed to encapsulate data in a private way—how come that darn Johnson has been able to access the data inside my objects?" "Because you used the wrong access specifier for your data," you say.

You can use an access specifier—called *access* in the following code—to set the visibility of a class's data members as far as the rest of the program is concerned:

```
access class classname [extends ...] [implements ...]
{
    [access] [static] type instance_variable1;
        .
        .
        .
    [access] [static] type instance_variableN;
}
```

The possible values for *access* are **public**, **private**, and **protected**. When you declare a class member **public**, it's accessible from anywhere in your program. If you declare it **private**, it's accessible only in the class it's a member of. If you declare it **protected**, it's available to the current class, other classes in the same package (you can group libraries of classes into Java packages; you've already seen some of the Java packages such as java.lang, and you'll see how to create custom packages later in the book), and classes that are derived from that class. If you don't use an access specifier, the default access is that the class member is visible to the class it's a member of, to classes derived from that class in the same package, and to other classes in the same package. You can find the details in Table 4.1.

For example, if I wanted to make the instance variable **data_string** private to the **Data** class created in the previous topic, I can declare it **private**, like this:

```
class Data
{
    private String data_string = "Hello from Java!";
}

public class app
{
    public static void main(String[] args)
    {
        Data data = new Data();

        String string = data.data_string;

        System.out.println(string);
    }
}
```

Now if I try to access the **data_string** instance variable in another class, as I do previously in the **app** class, the Java compiler will object:

```
C:\>javac app.java -deprecation
app.java:12: Variable data_string in class Data not accessible
from class app.
        String string = data.data_string;
                             ^
1 error
```

Table 4.1   Scope by access specifier (x = in scope).

Location	Private	No Modifier	Protected	Public
Same class	X	X	X	X
Subclass in the same package		X	X	X
Nonsubclass in the same package		X	X	X
Subclass in another package			X	X
Non-subclass in another package				X

Creating Class Variables

"Uh-oh," says the Novice Programmer, "I have a new class named **counter**, and I need to keep track of the total count in a variable named **counter** for *all* objects of that class. Now what? I'm sunk." "You're not sunk," you say. "You just need to use a class variable."

The value in a class variable is shared by all objects of that class, which means it will be the same for all objects. You declare a variable as static with the **static** keyword (which really specifies the way the value is stored, as static data, as opposed to other variables, which are stored dynamically on stacks):

```
access class classname [extends ...] [implements ...]
{
    [access] static type instance_variable1;
        .
        .
        .
    [access] static type instance_variableN;
}
```

Here's an example in which I create a class named **data** with a class data variable named **intdata**:

```
class data
{
    public static int intdata = 0;
}
```

Now I can create two objects of the data class: **a** and **b**. When I set the **intdata** variable for **a** to 1, I find that the **intdata** variable for **b** is also set to 1, as you can see here:

```
class data
{
    public static int intdata = 0;
}

public class app
{
    public static void main(String[] args)
    {
        data a, b;
```

4. Object-Oriented Programming

```
        a = new data();
        b = new data();

        a.intdata = 1;

        System.out.println("The value of b.intdata = " + b.intdata);
    }
}
```

Here's the result of this code:

```
C:\>java app
The value of b.intdata = 1
```

If you need to perform some calculation to initialize static variables, you can do so in a static code block, which you label with the **static** keyword; that code is executed just once, when the class is first loaded:

```
class data
{
    public static int intdata = 1;
    public static int doubledintdata;

    static
    {
        doubledintdata = 2 * intdata;
    }
}


public class app
{
    public static void main(String[] args)
    {
        data a;

        a = new data();

        System.out.println("The value of a.doubledintdata = " +
            a.doubledintdata);
    }
}
```

Here's the result of this code:

```
C:\>java app
The value of a.doubledintdata = 2
```

Creating Methods

"OK," says the Novice Programmer, "I've got instance variables down now. Is there anything more to learning about classes?" "Plenty," you say. "Pull up a chair and we'll talk about creating methods."

We've been using methods ever since printing out our first message with **System.out.println**, so you're certainly familiar with the concept. A *method* is a code block that you can transfer control to and so execute that code. Here's how you create methods in a class:

```
access class classname [extends ...] [implements ...]
{
    [access] [static] type method1 (parameter_list)
    {
        .
        .
        .
    }
    .
    .
    .
    [access] [static] type methodN (parameter_list)
    {
        .
        .
        .
    }
}
```

To declare and define a method, you use an access specifier (see the next topic), specify the return type of the method if you want it to return a value. Examples of these include int, float, an object type, or **void**, if the method doesn't return any value. Give the method's name, and place the list of the parameters you intend to pass to the method after that name. The actual body of the method—the code that will be executed when you call the method—is enclosed in a code block following the method's declaration.

Let's get to an example. In fact, you've already seen one earlier in this chapter—the **printer** class. In that example, I added a public method named **print** to the **printer** class, created an object of the **printer** class, and called the **print** method, like this:

```
class printer
{
    public void print()
    {
        System.out.println("Hello from Java!");
    }
}

public class app
{
    public static void main(String[] args)
    {
        printer printer1 = new printer();

        printer1.print();
    }
}
```

In this case, the **print** method takes no parameters and returns no value, but I still use parentheses after the method's name—this is mandatory when you're calling a method in Java (it's mandatory because that's how the Java compiler knows **print** is a method and not a data member). Here's the output of this code:

```
C:\>java app
Hello from Java!
```

There's a lot to know about creating methods in Java, so I'm going to elaborate on the process over the next few topics. One of the most important aspects of methods is that you can make them purely internal to an object, in keeping with the object-oriented concept of encapsulation—and that's where we'll start.

Setting Method Access

"That darn Johnson," the Novice Programmer says, "has been using the internal method in my objects, even though I clearly named the method **internal_use_only**. Isn't there anything stronger I can use to keep that darn Johnson out?" "Yes," you say, "you can use a stronger access specifier." "Great!" says the NP.

You can add an access specifier to the methods in a class, like this (where *access* is the access specifier):

```
access class classname [extends ...] [implements ...]
{
    [access] [static] type method1 (parameter_list)
    {

         .

         .

         .

    }
    .

    .

    .

    [access] [static] type methodN (parameter_list)
    {

         .

         .

         .

    }
}
```

The possible values for *access* are **public**, **private**, and **protected**. When you declare a class member **public**, it's accessible from anywhere in your program. If you declare it **private**, it's accessible only in the class it's a member of. If you declare it **protected**, it's available to the current class, to other classes in the same package, and to classes that are derived from that class. If you don't use an access specifier, the default access is that the class member is visible to the class it's a member of, to classes derived from that class in the same package, and to other classes in the same package. You can find the details back in Table 4.1.

Here's an example in which I add a **private** method to the **printer** class developed over the last few topics. This method may only be called from other methods in the **printer** class, like this:

```
class printer
{
    public void print()
    {
        internal_use_only();
    }

    private void internal_use_only ()
    {
```

```
        System.out.println("Hello from Java!");
    }
}

public class app
{
    public static void main(String[] args)
    {
        printer printer1 = new printer();

        printer1.print();
    }
}
```

When you call the **printer** class's **print** method, it makes use of the **internal_use_only** method, which is inaccessible outside the object, to do the actual printing. Here's the result of this code:

```
C:\>java app
Hello from Java!
```

Making methods private or protected is often a good idea, because it reduces or controls the method's accessibility from the rest of the code.

Passing Parameters To Methods

The company's Customer Support Specialist gives you a call and says, "We have an issue." "What issue would that be, CSS?" you ask. "Your **printer** class prints out a message, but customers are complaining because they want to be able to set the message that's printed out." "No problem," you say. "I'll set the **print** method up to accept parameters."

When you declare a method, you can specify a comma-separated list of parameters that you want to pass to that method in the parentheses following the method's name:

```
[access] [static] type method1 ([type parameter_name1 [, type
parameter_name1...]])
{
    .
    .
    .

}
```

The values passed to the method will then be accessible in the body of the method, using the names you've given them in the parameter list.

Here's an example in which I pass the string to print to the **print** method. I declare the method like this so that Java knows it will accept one parameter—a String object named **s**:

```
class printer
{
    public void print(String s)
    {
        .
        .
        .
    }
}
```

Now I can refer to the String object passed to the **print** method as **s** in the body of the method:

```
class printer
{
    public void print(String s)
    {
        System.out.println(s);
    }
}

public class app
{
    public static void main(String[] args)
    {
        (new printer()).print("Hello again from Java!");
    }
}
```

Here's the result of this code:

```
C:\>java app
Hello again from Java!
```

If you have more than one parameter to pass, you can specify multiple parameters in the parameter list, separated by commas:

```
class calculator
{
```

```
int addem(int op1, int op2)
{
    int result = op1 + op2;
        .
        .
        .
}
}
```

You can call methods using literals, variables, arrays, or objects, like this:

```
calc.addem(1, int1, array1, obj1)
```

You should note that when you pass a simple variable or literal to a method, the value of the variable or literal is passed to the method—this process is called *passing by value*.

On the other hand, when you pass an object or array, you're really passing a *reference* to that object or array (in fact, when you store an array or object in a variable, what you're really storing is a reference to the array or object). For that reason, the code in the called method has direct access to the original array or object, not a copy of it, so if that code changes some aspect of the array or object, such as an element in the array or a data member of the object, the original array or original object is changed. I'll take another look at this in detail in the topics "Passing Objects To Methods" and "Passing Arrays To Methods" later in this chapter.

Command-line Arguments Passed To **main**

A special array is passed as a parameter to the **main** method in applications—an array of String objects that holds the command-line arguments the user specified when starting Java. For example, suppose you started an application this way:

```
C:\>java app Now is the time
```

In this case, the first element of the array passed to **main** will hold "Now", the second "is", the third "the", and the fourth "time".

Here's an example showing how this works; this application will print out all the command-line arguments passed to it by looping over the **String** array passed as a parameter to the **main** method:

```
public class app
{
    public static void main(String[] args)
    {
        System.out.println("Command line arguments...");

        for(int loop_index = 0; loop_index < args.length;
            loop_index++) {

            System.out.println("Argument " + loop_index +
                " = " + args[loop_index]);
        }
    }
}
```

Here's how I might put this application to work:

```
C:\>java app Now is the time
Command line arguments...
Argument 0 = Now
Argument 1 = is
Argument 2 = the
Argument 3 = time
```

Returning Values From Methods

The Novice Programmer is back and says, "Well, there's another problem. The Big Boss wants me to create a **calculator** class that can perform mathematical operations. I can accept passed parameters in the methods of that class, but...." "Yes?" you ask. "I can't send any results back from the methods of the class after I've done the math." "Ah," you say, "use the **return** statement."

You use the **return** statement in a method to return a value from the method, and you indicate what the return type of the method is when you declare the method:

```
[access] [static] type method1 ([type parameter_name1 [, type
parameter_name1...]])
{
    .
    .
    .
}
```

The return type can be any type that Java recognizes—for example, int, float, double, the name of a class you've defined, **int[]** to return an integer array, or **float[]** to return a float array.

Here's an example in which the class **calculator** has a method named **addem** that takes two integer parameters, adds them, and returns the result. Here's how I declare **addem**:

```
class calculator
{
    int addem(int op1, int op2)
    {
        .
        .
        .
    }
}
```

Here's how I return the sum of the values passed to **addem**, using the **return** statement:

```
class calculator
{
    int addem(int op1, int op2)
    {
        return op1 + op2;
    }
}
```

Here's how I put the **calculator** class to work in a program:

```
class calculator
{
    int addem(int op1, int op2)
    {
        return op1 + op2;
    }
}

public class app
{
    public static void main(String[] args)
    {
```

```
        calculator calc = new calculator();
        System.out.println("addem(2, 2) = " + calc.addem(2, 2));
    }

}
```

Here's the result of this application:

```
C:\>java app
addem(2, 2) = 4
```

Creating Class Methods

"Jeez," says the Novice Programmer, "I've created my new **calculator** class with a terrific method in it named **addem**, but why do I have to go to the trouble of creating an object of that class before I can use the **addem** method? Can't I just call that method directly?" "You can," you say, "if you make **addem** a *class* method instead of an *instance* method."

To make a method into a class method, use the **static** keyword:

```
class calculator
{
    static int addem(int op1, int op2)
    {
        return op1 + op2;
    }
}
```

Now in code, you can call the **addem** method directly using the class name, without creating an object at all. Here's an example:

```
public class app
{
    public static void main(String[] args)
    {
        System.out.println("addem(2, 2) = " + calculator.addem(2, 2));
    }

}
```

Here's the result of this code:

```
C:\>java app
addem(2, 2) = 4
```

You can also use a class method the usual way—as a method of an object:

```
class calculator
{
    static int addem(int op1, int op2)
    {
        return op1 + op2;
    }
}

public class app
{
    public static void main(String[] args)
    {
        calculator calc = new calculator();
        System.out.println("addem(2, 2) = " + calc.addem(2, 2));
    }

}
```

It's worth noting that the **main** method in an application is declared static, because Java must call it before an object actually exists.

If you declare a method static (this includes the **main** method in any application), it can only call other static methods and can only access static data. Also, it cannot use the **this** and **super** keywords, which refer to the current object and the parent object of the current object, respectively, as you'll see in this and the next chapter. Note, in particular, that you can't refer to instance data in a static method.

TIP: So how do you call nonstatic methods from **main**? You do this as we've been doing throughout the book—you create an object of some other class in **main** and call the methods of that object.

Creating Data Access Methods

"That darn Johnson," the Novice Programmer says, "is fiddling around inside my code's objects again. But this time I can't declare everything **private**, because the rest of the code needs access to the data member in question. What can I do?"

"You can set up a data access method," you say, "and restrict access to your data members in a well-defined way." "That'll show that darn Johnson!" the NP says.

You can restrict access to the data in your objects using data access methods, which must be called to fetch the data. Here's an example in which I've got a private String data member called **data_string**:

```
class data
{
    private String data_string = "Hello from Java!";
    .
    .
    .
}
```

I can provide access to this private data member with two methods: **getData** and **setData**. The **getData** method just returns the value in the private variable **data_string**, like this:

```
class data
{
    private String data_string = "Hello from Java!";

    public String getData()
    {
        return data_string;
    }
}
```

However, the **setData** method restricts access to the internal data; in particular, I'll write this method so that the calling code can only set the internal data to a new string if the length of that string is less than 100 characters. Here's how this looks:

```
class data
{
    private String data_string = "Hello from Java!";

    public String getData()
    {
        return data_string;
    }

    public void setData(String s)
    {
```

```
        if (s.length() < 100) {
            data_string = s;
        }
    }
}
```

Now I can use the **getData** method to get the internal string and the **setData** method to set it to a new string. Here's an example that shows how to use **getData**:

```
public class app
{
    public static void main(String[] args)
    {
        System.out.println((new data()).getData());
    }
}
```

Here's the result of this code:

```
C:\>java app
Hello from Java!
```

Using data access methods to grant access to the internal data in your objects is a good idea. By using these methods, you can control the interface to the data, thus blocking operations you consider illegal.

Creating Constructors

"Hmm," says the Novice Programmer, "I know I can use constructors to initialize the data in an object, such as the **String** class's constructors that I use to set the text in a string, but...." "Yes?" you ask. "But how can *I* create constructors for my own classes?" the NP asks.

Creating a constructor for a class is easy; you just add a method to a class with the same name as the class, without any access specifier or return type. Here's an example in which I add a constructor that takes no parameters to the **printer** class we've developed in this chapter. This constructor is called when an object is created of the **printer** class, and in this case, it initializes the internal data **data_string** to "Hello from Java!" (note that I still need the parentheses after the constructor name when declaring it, even though it doesn't take any parameters):

```
class data
{
    private String data_string;

    data()
    {
        data_string = "Hello from Java!";
    }

    public String getData()
    {
        return data_string;
    }
}

public class app
{
    public static void main(String[] args)
    {
        System.out.println((new data()).getData());
    }
}
```

Here's what you see when you run this program:

```
C:\>java app
Hello from Java!
```

This constructor is a particularly simple one because it doesn't take any parameters. I'll enable the constructor take parameters in the next topic.

Passing Parameters To Constructors

"OK," says the Novice Programmer, "Java's gone wacky again. I set up a constructor for my new class, but the object isn't actually initialized with the data I want." "Hmm," you say; "did you pass any data to the constructor?" "Uh-oh," says the NP.

You can pass data to constructors just as you can to other methods. Here's an example, using the **printer** class from the previous topic, in which I pass the string to print out to the **printer** class's constructor:

```
class data
{
    private String data_string;
```

```
    data(String s)
    {
        data_string = s;
    }

    public String getData()
    {
        return data_string;
    }
}

public class app
{
    public static void main(String[] args)
    {
        System.out.println((new data("Hello from Java!")).getData());
    }
}
```

Here's the result of this code:

```
C:\>java app
Hello from Java!
```

And that's all it takes—passing parameters to a constructor works the same as passing parameters to any method.

A Full Class Example

In this topic, I'll present an example using the concepts we've been discussing in the chapter so far. This example involves the simulation of a programming stack. You'll see stacks in more detail when we discuss Java collections, but the theory is a simple one—a programming stack works much like a stack of plates. When you put a plate on top of the stack, you're *pushing* an item onto the stack. When you take a plate off from the stack, you're *popping* an item off the stack. Note that the plates come off in reverse order—if you push plates 1, 2, and then 3, then when you pop the stack, plate 3 comes off first, followed by plates 2 and 1.

To use this **stack** class, you create an object of the class, passing an argument to the constructor indicating how big you want the stack (that is, how many integers you want to be able to store on it). The constructor allocates the memory for the stack in an array named **stack_data**, and it sets up a stack pointer, **stack_ptr**, which points to the current top item on the stack (and this is actually the index I'll use with the **stack_data** array).

You can then use the stack's **push** method to push an item onto the stack, which stores a data item and increments the stack pointer to the next position in the stack array, or you can use the **pop** method to pop an item off the stack—the **pop** method returns the popped item and decrements the stack pointer.

This application is called stacker.java; the test code at the end pushes 10 items onto the stack and then pops them off:

```java
class stack {
    private int stack_data[];
    private int stack_ptr;                  // stack_ptr = -1 --> stack is empty

    stack(int size)
    {
        stack_data = new int[size];
        stack_ptr = -1;
    }

    public int pop()
    {
        if(stack_ptr == -1)      // Stack is empty -- return error
            return 0;
        else                     // Else return data
            return stack_data[stack_ptr--];
    }

    public int push(int push_this)
    {
        if(stack_ptr >= 99)      // Stack is full -- return error
            return 0;
        else {                   // Else store data
            stack_data[++stack_ptr] = push_this;
            return 1;
        }
    }
}

public class stacker {
    public static void main(String args[])
    {
        int popped_value;
        stack stack1 = new stack(100);
```

```
            System.out.println("Pushing values now...");
            for(int loop_index = 0; loop_index < 10; loop_index++){
                stack1.push(loop_index);
                System.out.println("Pushed value--> " + loop_index);
            }

            System.out.println("Popping values now...");
            for(int loop_index = 0; loop_index < 10; loop_index++){
                popped_value = stack1.pop();
                System.out.println("Popped value--> " + popped_value);
            }
        }
    }
```

Here's what this program looks like at work:

```
C:\>java stacker
Pushing values now...
Pushed value--> 0
Pushed value--> 1
Pushed value--> 2
Pushed value--> 3
Pushed value--> 4
Pushed value--> 5
Pushed value--> 6
Pushed value--> 7
Pushed value--> 8
Pushed value--> 9
Popping values now...
Popped value--> 9
Popped value--> 8
Popped value--> 7
Popped value--> 6
Popped value--> 5
Popped value--> 4
Popped value--> 3
Popped value--> 2
Popped value--> 1
Popped value--> 0
```

Understanding Variable Scope

"Hmm" says the Novice Programmer; "I've defined a swell new variable named **the_answer** in a method named **get_the_answer**, and I was trying to use that variable in a method named **get_a_clue**, but Java claims the variable is undefined!" "Hmm," you say, "sounds like a question of variable scope—you can't use variables declared in one method in another method." "You can't?" the NP asks.

The *scope* of a variable is made up of the parts of the program in which that variable can be used in your code, and as you can see from the Novice Programmer's plight, scope is an important concept to understand.

Java defines three main scopes: class-level scope, method-level scope, and code block-level scope.

If you define a data member in a class, that data member is available throughout the class, and possibly beyond, as you've seen with the **private**, **public**, and **protected** access specifiers.

The scope of a method starts when the flow of execution enters the method and ends when the flow of execution leaves the method. Variables declared in the method are only visible in the method itself. The data members of the class are also visible in the class's methods, as are the parameters passed to those methods.

 You can also define a local scope for variables using code blocks, because you can declare variables inside code blocks. The variables you declare inside a code block will be visible only in that code block and in any code blocks contained within the code block.

The easiest way to bear all this in mind is to know that nonstatic variables declared in a code block bounded by curly braces are created and stored on the local stack when you enter that code block, and they're destroyed when you leave the code block (which is why they're called *dynamic variables*). Static variables, on the other hand, are stored in the program's own data allocation, not on any stack, which is why they don't go out of scope. They're as close to global variables (that is, program-wide variables) as Java permits.

Here's an example showing the various levels of scope (class, method, and code block):

```
class Class
{
    int int1 = 1; //visible to all code in the class.
```

```
public void method(int int2) //visible to all code in this method.
{
    int int3 = 3;  //visible to all code in this method.

    if(int1 != int2) {

        int int4 = 4;  //visible only in this code block.

        System.out.println("int1 = " + int1
            + " int2 = " + int2
            + " int3 = " + int3
            + " int4 = " + int4);
    }
}
}

public class app
{
    public static void main(String[] args)
    {
        Class c = new Class();

        c.method(2);
    }
}
```

Here's what you see when this code runs:

```
C:\>java app
int1 = 1 int2 = 2 int3 = 3 int4 = 4
```

Using Recursion

The Novice Programmer comes in still shaking with laughter and says, "You'll never believe what the Programming Correctness Czar just told me—in C++, methods can call themselves!" "It's the same in Java," you reply. "Huh?" the NP says.

Each time you call a method in Java, Java allocates new space on its internal stack for all the variables in the method, which means there's no reason you can't call the same method again—a new set of variables will be allocated on the stack automatically. What's more, a method can call itself in Java—this is a technique called *recursion*.

The classic recursion example is to calculate a factorial, so I'll implement it here. To calculate the factorial of positive integer n, called "n!", you calculate the following:

```
n! = n * (n - 1) * (n - 2) ... * 2 * 1
```

This process lends itself to recursion easily, because each stage of the recursion can calculate one multiplication in which it multiples the number it has been passed by the factorial of the number minus 1. When the number has finally been reduced to 1 through successive calls, the method simply returns, and control comes back through the successive stages, performing one multiplication at each stage until all nested calls have returned and you have the factorial.

Here's what that looks like in code:

```
class calculator
{
    public int factorial(int n)
    {
        if (n == 1) {
            return n;
        }
        else {
            return n * factorial(n - 1);
        }
    }
}

public class app
{
    public static void main(String[] args)
    {
        calculator calc = new calculator();
        System.out.println("6! = " + calc.factorial(6));
    }
}
```

Here's what this program looks like at work:

```
C:\>java app
6! = 720
```

In practice, you probably won't use recursion too often, but it's good to know it's available.

Garbage Collection And Memory Management

"Say," the Novice Programmer says, "I just thought of something—you allocate new memory with the **new** operator, but how do you get rid of it when it's no longer needed? Is there an **old** operator?" "Nope," you say, "Java does all that for you."

In some languages, such as C++, you use the **new** operator to allocate new memory and then you use the **delete** operator to get rid of it when you don't need it anymore. However, Java does not have a **delete** operator. So how do you get rid of allocated memory when it's no longer needed?

In Java, you have to rely on a built-in process called *garbage collection*. This process occurs automatically, although you can't predict when it will happen. Java, itself, will dispose of allocated memory that no longer has any references to it. To make garbage collection happen, you can set any references to an item to **null** (although doing so still does not let you predict when, if ever, garbage collection will happen when your program is executing).

Here's an example in which I'm just creating a new object and then setting its variable to **null**. Because there are no remaining references to the object, the garbage collection process will deallocate it sooner or later. Here's the code:

```
class Data
{
    public int intdata = 0;

    Data()
    {
        intdata = 1;
    }
}

public class app
{
    public static void main(String[] args)
    {
        Data d = new Data();

        //some code...

        d = null;

        //some additional code...
    }
}
```

Here's the thing to remember form this example: When you're done with a data item—including objects and arrays—that you've allocated with the **new** operator, you can set its references to **null**, and if Java needs more memory, it'll start the garbage collection process. However, you have to be careful to avoid circular references.

TIP: *If you're familiar with C++, you may be wondering where pointers are in Java, and the answer is that it doesn't have them. The designers of Java omitted pointers for security reasons, to make sure programmers couldn't access memory beyond legal limits. Instead of pointers, Java uses references, which act very much like pointers behind the scenes. When you create a new object, you get a reference to that object, and when you use that reference, Java dereferences it for you automatically. That's how it works in Java—Java handles references (pointers) for you automatically.*

Avoiding Circular References

Garbage collection—the disposing of memory items that no longer have any references in your program—happens automatically. However, you should watch out for circular references in which one object has a reference to another, and the second object has a reference to the first. When you get rid of any references to these objects in your program, each object still has an internal reference to the other, which means garbage collection can't happen on either object. Worse yet, because there are no external references to either object, you can't reach either object to try to change the situation. Both objects will sit in memory, taking up valuable resources, until your program ends.

Here's a sample program showing what I mean—in this case, class **a** has an internal reference to an object of class **b**, and class **b** has an internal reference to an object of class **a**. When the code in **main** sets the reference it has to one of these objects to **null**, these objects will continue to sit in memory until the program ends. Here's the code:

```
class a
{
    b b1;

    a()
    {
        b1 = new b();
    }
}

class b
{
    a a1;
```

```
    b()
    {
        a1 = new a();
    }
}

public class app
{
    public static void main(String[] args)
    {
        a obj = new a();

        obj = null;    //inaccessible circular references now exist!
    }
}
```

There's only one way to avoid this, and that's to get rid of circular references before cutting them adrift. In practice, this usually means setting an object's references to other objects to **null** before setting the reference to the object, itself, to **null**. Sometimes its possible to do this in the **finalize** method (see the next topic for the details).

While we're discussing memory management, it's also worth noting that you do have some control over memory allocation as a whole—see the **-J** command-line option in Chapter 1, which lets you set the total amount of memory allocated when a program runs. In general, though, Java handles the memory management in your programs.

Garbage Collection And The **finalize** Method

"Hmm," says the Novice Programmer, "so Java has a garbage collector that removes items from memory that are no longer referenced. Is there anything more I should know about this process?" "One thing," you say. "The garbage collector calls a special method named **finalize** in your object if that method exists, and you can use this method for last minute cleanup."

When an object is being "garbage collected" (see the previous topic), the garbage collector will call a method named **finalize** in the object, if it exists. In this method, you can execute cleanup code, and it's often a good idea to get rid of any references to other objects that the current object has in order to eliminate the possibility of circular references (also covered in the previous topic).

Here's an example showing how this looks in code:

```
class Data
{
    public int intdata = 0;
    SuperGiantSizeClass sgsc;

    Data()
    {
        intdata = 1;
        sgsc = new SuperGiantSizeClass(100000000);
    }

    protected void finalize()
    {
        sgsc = null;
    }
}

public class app
{
    public static void main(String[] args)
    {
        Data d = new Data();

        d = null;
    }
}
```

Overloading Methods

"I'm still working on my new program, *SuperDuperMathPro*," says the Novice Programmer, "and I have a great class named **calculator** with a method named **addem** that adds two numbers. I'd also like to add three numbers together, though—I guess I'll have to write a new method." "Not at all," you say. "You can overload the **addem** method to handle either two *or* three operands." "How's that?" the NP asks.

Method overloading is an object-oriented technique that lets you define several different versions of a method, all with the same name, but each with a different parameter list. When you use an overloaded method, the Java compiler will know which one you mean by the number and/or types of the parameters you pass to the method, and will find the version of the method with the right parameter list.

Let's take a look at an example. To overload a method, you just define it more than once, specifying a new parameter list each time. Each parameter list must be different from every other one in some way, such as the number of parameters or the type of one or more of the parameters. I'll create the example the Novice Programmer was worried about here. First, I add a version of the **addem** method to the **calculator** class that will handle two operands:

```
class calculator
{
    int addem(int op1, int op2)
    {
        return op1 + op2;
    }
        .
        .
        .
}
```

Then I add another version of the same method that will take three operands:

```
class calculator
{
    int addem(int op1, int op2)
    {
        return op1 + op2;
    }

    int addem(int op1, int op2, int op3)
    {
        return op1 + op2 + op3;
    }
}
```

Now I can use both methods in code, like this:

```
public class app
{
    public static void main(String[] args)
    {
        calculator calc = new calculator();

        System.out.println("addem(2, 2) = " + calc.addem(2, 2));
        System.out.println("addem(2, 2, 2) = " + calc.addem(2, 2, 2));
    }
}
```

Here's the result of this program:

```
C:\>java app
addem(2, 2) = 4
addem(2, 2, 2) = 6
```

As you can see, overloading provides a powerful technique, especially in code you release to other developers, because being able to pass all different types of parameter lists to a method makes that method easy to use in many ways in code.

You can also overload constructors—see the next topic for the details.

Overloading Constructors

"Wow," says the Novice Programmer, "so I can overload methods in Java to let them handle different parameter lists! Can I also overload constructors?" "Of course," you say. "Consider the Java **String** class, which has a constructor to which you can pass strings, character arrays, and all other kinds of data." "Oh yeah," says the NP.

Overloading constructors works like overloading other methods (see the previous topic for the details): You just define the constructor a number of times, each time with a parameter list with parameters that differ from the other lists in some way.

Here's an example that mimics the Java **String** class's constructors in that this new class, the **data** class, will have a constructor to which you can pass either a character array or a string. This class will simply store the text data you pass to it and make that data available with a **getData** method.

Here's how I declare and define the constructor that takes a character array:

```
class data
{
    private String data_string;

    data(char[] c)
    {
        data_string = new String(c);
    }
}
```

Here's how I declare the constructor that takes a text string:

```
class data
{
    private String data_string;

    data(char[] c)
    {
        data_string = new String(c);
    }

    data(String s)
    {
        data_string = s;
    }
}
```

All that's left is to add the **getData** method:

```
class data
{
    private String data_string;

    data(char[] c)
    {
        data_string = new String(c);
    }

    data(String s)
    {
        data_string = s;
    }

    public String getData()
    {
        return data_string;
    }
}
```

Now I can use both constructors in code, creating objects and printing out the stored text, like this:

```
public class app
{
    public static void main(String[] args)
    {
```

```
        char chararray[] = {'H', 'e', 'l', 'l', 'o'};
        System.out.println((new data(chararray)).getData());

        System.out.println((new data("Hello from Java!")).getData());
    }
}
```

Here's the result of this code:

```
C:\>java app
Hello
Hello from Java!
```

Passing Objects To Methods

The Novice Programmer appears and says, "Java's gone all wacky again. I passed an object to a method because I wanted to do a lot of destructive testing on it in that method, but when control returned from the method, the *original* object was destroyed. What happened?" "Java passes objects by reference," you say. "That's what happened."

When you pass an item of a simple data type to a method, Java passes a copy of the data in the item, which is called *passing by value*. Because the method only gets a copy of the data item, the code in the method cannot affect the original data item at all.

However, when you pass an object to a method, Java actually passes a reference to the object, which is called *passing by reference*. Passing by reference means that the code in the method can reach the original object. In fact, any changes made to the passed object affect the original object.

Here's an example in which I pass an object of class **Data** to the **print** method of the **printer** class in order to print out the data in the object:

```
class Data
{
    public String data_string;

    Data(String data)
    {
        data_string = data;
    }
}

class printer
```

```
{
    public void print (Data d)
    {
        System.out.println(d.data_string);
    }
}

public class app
{
    public static void main(String[] args)
    {
        Data data = new Data("Hello from Java!");
        printer p = new printer();

        p.print(data);
    }
}
```

Here's the result of this code:

```
C:\>java app
Hello from Java!
```

As mentioned previously, because objects are passed by reference, changing a passed object changes the original object. Here's an example in which I pass an object of the **Data** class to a method named **rewrite** that changes the **data_string** instance variable in the object. This variable starts out with the string "Hello from Java!" in it, but the **rewrite** method is able to change the string to "Hello to Java!" in this code:

```
class Data
{
    public String data_string;

    Data(String s)
    {
        data_string = new String(s);
    }
}

class Class
{
    public void rewrite(Data d)
    {
        d.data_string = "Hello to Java!";
    }
}
```

```
public class app
{
    public static void main(String[] args)
    {
        Data d = new Data("Hello from Java!");
        Class c = new Class();

        c.rewrite(d);

        System.out.println(d.data_string);
    }
}
```

Here's the result of this code:

```
C:\>java app
Hello to Java!
```

Passing Arrays To Methods

"So simple variables are passed by value in Java, and objects are passed by reference. I have it all straight now," says the Novice Programmer. "Not quite," you say. "There's one more type of item that's passed by reference—arrays."

You can pass an array to a method as easily as passing a simple variable, but you should keep in mind that arrays are passed by reference, not value, which means that if you make a change to an array passed to a method, the original array is also affected.

Here's an example. In this case, I'll pass an array to a method named **doubler** that doubles each element in the array. Because arrays are passed by reference, the data in the original array is doubled as well. Here's how this looks in code (note that I print out an array before and after the call to the **doubler** method):

```
class Calculate
{
    public void doubler(int a[])
    {
        for (int loop_index = 0; loop_index < a.length;
            loop_index++) {
            a[loop_index] *= 2;
        }
    }
}
```

```
public class app
{
    public static void main(String[] args)
    {
        int array[] = {1, 2, 3, 4, 5};
        Calculate c = new Calculate();

        System.out.println("Before the call to doubler...");
        for (int loop_index = 0; loop_index < array.length;
            loop_index++) {

            System.out.println("array[" + loop_index + "] = " +
                array[loop_index]);
        }

        c.doubler(array);

        System.out.println("After the call to doubler...");
        for (int loop_index = 0; loop_index < array.length;
            loop_index++) {

            System.out.println("array[" + loop_index + "] = " +
                array[loop_index]);
        }
    }
}
```

Here's the result of this code:

```
C:\>java app
Before the call to doubler...
array[0] = 1
array[1] = 2
array[2] = 3
array[3] = 4
array[4] = 5
After the call to doubler...
array[0] = 2
array[1] = 4
array[2] = 6
array[3] = 8
array[4] = 10
```

Using The **this** Keyword

Java objects include a data member named **this** that's actually a reference to the current object. The **this** keyword is useful if you need to refer to the current object—for example, when you want to pass the current object to a method.

Here's an example. In this case, the **Data** class has a method, **printData**, that prints the data in the current object by passing the current object to the **print** method of another object. The **this** keyword is used to refer to the current object. Here's how this looks in code:

```java
class Data
{
    private String data_string;

    Data(String s)
    {
        data_string = s;
    }

    public String getData()
    {
        return data_string;
    }

    public void printData()
    {
        printer p = new printer();
        p.print(this);
    }
}

class printer
{
    void print(Data d)
    {
        System.out.println(d.getData());
    }
}

public class app
{
    public static void main(String[] args)
    {
        (new Data("Hello from Java!")).printData();
```

```
        }
    }
```

Note that when the call to **p.print** is made, a reference to the current object is passed to **p.print**, giving the code in **p.print** access to the **getData** method in the current object, which returns the internal data to print out. Here's the result of this program:

```
C:\>java app
Hello from Java!
```

Returning Objects From Methods

You can return objects from methods, just like other data types. However, this raises a concern: When the method that returned the object goes out of scope, won't the object that it returned also go out of scope?

The answer is no. When you create a new object using the **new** operator, that object is not destroyed when the method that created it goes out of scope, and the object, itself, is not disposed of by the garbage collector until there are no more references to it.

Here's an example. In this case, the class named **ObjectFactory** has a method named **getNewObject** that returns an object of the class **CreatedClass**:

```
class ObjectFactory
{
    public CreatedClass getNewObject()
    {
        return new CreatedClass();
    }
}

class CreatedClass
{
    public String tag = "This is the tag data.";
}

public class app
{
    public static void main(String[] args)
    {
```

```
        ObjectFactory o = new ObjectFactory();
        CreatedClass c = o.getNewObject();

        System.out.println(c.tag);
    }
}
```

When I call the **getNewObject** method, it returns a new object of the **CreatedClass** class, and I can print out the data in that object. Here's what is shown when the program runs:

```
C:\>java app
This is the tag data.
```

Returning Arrays From Methods

You can return arrays from methods just as you can return objects and simple data types. Here's an example in which I create a class called **ArrayFactory** with a method named **getNewArray**. When I call **getNewArray**, it will return an array of integers. Note the return type I specify for **getNewArray** in the declaration—**int[]**. This indicates an integer array. Here's the code:

```
class ArrayFactory
{
    public int[] getNewArray()
    {
        int array[] = {1, 2, 3, 4, 5};

        return array;
    }
}
```

Here's how I put the **ArrayFactory** class to work, creating a new array and printing it out:

```
public class app
{
    public static void main(String[] args)
    {
        ArrayFactory af = new ArrayFactory();

        int array[] = af.getNewArray();
```

```
        for (int loop_index = 0; loop_index < array.length;
            loop_index++) {

            System.out.println("array[" + loop_index + "] = " +
                array[loop_index]);
        }
    }
}
```

Here's the result of this code:

```
C:\>java app
array[0] = 1
array[1] = 2
array[2] = 3
array[3] = 4
array[4] = 5
```

Chapter 5

Inheritance, Inner Classes, And Interfaces

In Depth

This chapter is all about inheritance, a very important topic in Java programming. Using inheritance, you can derive one class, called the *derived class* or *subclass*, from another, called the *base class* or *superclass*. The idea here is that you add what you want to the new class to give it a more customized functionality than the original class.

The previous chapter began our discussion of object-oriented programming, and as I mentioned there, if you have a class named, say, **vehicle**, that contains the basic functionality of some means of transport, you can use that class as the base class of classes you derive from that class, such as **car** and **truck**. The **car** class might, for instance, have a data member named **wheels**, set to 4, whereas the same data member in the **truck** class might be set to 18. You can also use the same **vehicle** class as the base class for other classes, such as a **helicopter** class. All the subclasses will have access to the nonprivate members of the superclass, and they can add their own. In fact, they can *override* the nonprivate members of the superclass, replacing them with their own code. For example, the **vehicle** class may have a method named **go** that prints out "Driving...", and the **helicopter** class may override that method, redefining it so it prints out "Flying...".

Using inheritance, then, you can base your classes on other classes, reusing code and adding to it. You can use or redefine the members of the superclass as you like, customizing that class for your own use. In fact, you can create classes that must be treated as superclasses. These classes are called *abstract classes*. You can't instantiate an abstract class directly into an object; you must instead derive a new class from it first, overriding those members that are specifically declared abstract. You use abstract classes to force developers to customize some or all the members of a class; for example, you may have an abstract method named **printError**, because you want developers to supply their own code for this method as appropriate for the subclasses they create.

That's an overview of what inheritance does. The next question is, why is inheritance so important in Java?

Why Inheritance?

Java is truly an object-oriented language, and it relies on inheritance a great deal. The developers at Sun Microsystems have created huge packages—class libraries—full of classes that you can use as superclasses. This is important if, for example, you want to create an applet in Java, because in that case, you can derive your applet from the java.applet package's **Applet** class. Here's an applet you first saw in Chapter 1 that creates a superclass based on the **Applet** class using the **extends** keyword (more on applets in the next chapter):

```
import java.applet.Applet;
import java.awt.*;

public class applet extends Applet
{
    public void paint(Graphics g)
    {
        g.drawString("Hello from Java!", 60, 100);
    }
}
```

Here's another example you saw in Chapter 1; in this case, I'm creating a windowed application and basing the window, itself, on the Java **java.awt.Frame** class:

```
import java.awt.*;
import java.awt.event.*;

class AppFrame extends Frame
{
    public void paint(Graphics g)
    {
        g.drawString("Hello from Java!", 60, 100);
    }
}

public class app
{
    public static void main(String [] args)
    {
        AppFrame f = new AppFrame();

        f.setSize(200, 200);
```

```
        f.addWindowListener(new WindowAdapter() { public void
            windowClosing(WindowEvent e) {System.exit(0);}});

        f.show();
    }
}
```

As you can see, when it comes to visual elements in your programs, you'll rely on the Java packages a great deal. Buttons, for example, have their own classes, and to customize them, you derive your own classes from them. In fact, if you want to handle mouse actions or button clicks, you have to use inheritance—this time, not using superclasses, but rather *interfaces*.

Why Interfaces?

Suppose you want to create an applet that handles button clicks. To create a standard applet, you can derive a class from the **java.applet.Applet** class, and to handle button clicks, you use another class, **ActionListener**. Therefore, it looks as though you'll have to base your applet on both the **Applet** and **ActionListener** classes.

However, basing a subclass on two or more superclasses is called *multiple inheritance*, and it turns out that Java doesn't support multiple inheritance (although languages such as C++ do). In practice, this means you can only use the **extends** keyword with one class. To solve this problem, Java implements classes such as **ActionListener** as *interfaces*.

In this case, that means you can extend your applet from the **Applet** class and use the **implements** keyword to add the button-click handling. Here's what this looks like in an applet:

```
import java.applet.Applet;
import java.awt.*;
import java.awt.event.*;

public class clicker extends Applet implements ActionListener {

    TextField text1;
    Button button1;

    public void init(){
            text1 = new TextField(20);
            add(text1);
            button1 = new Button("Click Here!");
```

```
        add(button1);
    button1.addActionListener(this);
}

public void actionPerformed(ActionEvent event){
    String msg = new String ("Welcome to Java");
    if(event.getSource() == button1){
        text1.setText(msg);
    }
}
}
```

You can implement as many interfaces as you like; for example, here's part of a program that implements three listeners to enable the program to handle button clicks and mouse actions:

```
import java.awt.Graphics;
import java.awt.*;
import java.awt.event.*;
import java.lang.Math;
import java.applet.Applet;

public class dauber extends Applet implements ActionListener,
MouseListener, MouseMotionListener {
    .
    .
    .
```

You'll see how to create interfaces later in the book. However, you'll get an introduction to them in this chapter so we can use them in the chapters to come.

There's one more topic I'll cover in this chapter—inner classes.

Why Inner Classes?

Java now lets you create classes within classes, and the enclosed class is called an *inner class*. I'll start working with inner classes in this chapter. You might not see much need for defining classes within classes now, but it will become more apparent when we start handling user interface events, such as when the user closes a window.

Events are handled with interfaces, and when you implement an interface, you must also provide implementations of several abstract methods inside the interface. To make this process easier, Java provides *adapter classes*, which already have empty implementations of the required methods. To handle a user interface event of some kind, it's become common to subclass adapter classes as inner classes, overriding just the methods you want in a very compact way. Here's an example in which the code ends an application when the user closes that application's window:

```
public class app
{
    public static void main(String [] args)
    {
        AppFrame f = new AppFrame();

        f.setSize(200, 200);

        f.addWindowListener(new WindowAdapter() {public void
            windowClosing(WindowEvent e) {System.exit(0);}});

        f.show();
    }
}
```

We'll unravel this code in detail when working with events, and I'll get started on that process by introducing inner classes so that this code will make much more sense to you later.

Now that we've gotten the concepts behind inheritance, interfaces, and inner classes down, it's time to turn to the "Immediate Solutions" section.

Immediate Solutions

Creating A Subclass

"OK," the Novice Programmer says, "I want to learn what inheritance is all about. Can you explain it in two words or less?" Counting on your fingers, you say, "No way."

Here's an example showing how to create a subclass using inheritance. Suppose you have a class named **vehicle** that has one method, **start**, that you can use to start the vehicle and that prints out "Starting...":

```
class vehicle
{
    public void start()
    {
        System.out.println("Starting...");
    }
}
```

There are all kinds of vehicles, so if you want to specialize the **vehicle** class into a **car** class, you can use inheritance with the **extends** keyword. Here's how you declare **car** as a subclass of **vehicle**:

```
class car extends vehicle
{
    .
    .
    .
}
```

This syntax indicates that **car** is derived from the **vehicle** class, which means that in this case, **car** will inherit the **start** method from **vehicle**. You can also add your own data members and methods in subclasses. Here's an example in which I add a method named **drive** to the **car** class:

```
class car extends vehicle
{
    public void drive()
```

```
    {
        System.out.println("Driving...");
    }
}
```

Now I can access both the **start** method and the **drive** method in objects of the **car** class, as shown in this example:

```
public class app
{
    public static void main(String[] args)
    {
        System.out.println("Creating a car...");

        car c = new car();
        c.start();
        c.drive();
    }
}
```

Here's the output of the preceding code:

```
C:\>java app
Creating a car...
Starting...
Driving...
```

That's a basic subclassing example. There's a lot more to the process, however. For example, what if you define a method in a subclass with the same name as a method in the superclass? How do you pass data to a superclass's constructor? All that's coming up in this chapter.

Access Specifiers And Inheritance

"Java's gone all wacky again," says the Novice Programmer. "I want to use some methods from the superclass in a subclass, but Java says they don't even exist!" "What's the access specifier for the methods?" you ask. "Private," the NP says. "That's your problem," you say.

You use access specifiers with classes, data members, and methods to specify the visibility of those items in the rest of the program. Here's the general form of a class declaration and definition, showing how to use access specifiers:

```
access class classname [extends ...] [implements ...]
{
    [access] [static] type instance_variable1;
        .
        .
        .

    [access] [static] type instance_variableN;

    [access] [static] type method1 (parameter_list)
    {
        .
        .
        .

    }
    .
    .

    .
    [access] [static] type methodN (parameter_list)
    {
        .
        .
        .

    }
}
```

The possible values for *access* are **public**, **private**, and **protected**. When you declare a class member **public**, it's accessible from anywhere in your program. If you declare it **private**, it's accessible only in the class it's a member of. If you declare it **protected**, it's available to the current class, to other classes in the same package, and to classes that are derived from that class. If you don't use an access specifier, the default access is that the class member is visible to the class it's a member of, to classes derived from that class in the same package, and to other classes in the same package. You can find the details in Table 5.1.

For example, take a look at the Novice Programmer's code, where the **start** method is declared **private** but also accessed in **main**:

```
class vehicle
{
    private void start()
    {
        System.out.println("Starting...");
    }
}
```

Table 5.1   Scope by access specifier (x = in scope).

Location	Private	No Modifier	Protected	Public
Same class	X	X	X	X
Subclass in the same package		X	X	X
Nonsubclass in the same package		X	X	X
Subclass in another package			X	X
Nonsubclass in another package				X

```
class car extends vehicle
{
    public void drive()
    {
        System.out.println("Driving...");
    }
}

public class app
{
    public static void main(String[] args)
    {
        System.out.println("Creating a car...");
        car c = new car();
        c.start();
        c.drive();
    }
}
```

Because declaring a member using **private** restricts that member to its class, Java says it can't find the **start** method as used in **main**:

```
C:\>c:\jdk1.2.2\bin\javac app.java -deprecation
app.java:47: No method matching start() found in class car.
        c.start();
              ^
1 error
```

On the other hand, declaring a member **protected** restricts its scope to code in the same package and subclasses of the class it's declared in. Therefore, the following code works:

```
class vehicle
{
```

```
    protected void start()
    {
        System.out.println("Starting...");
    }
}

class car extends vehicle
{
    public void drive()
    {
        System.out.println("Driving...");
    }
}

public class app
{
    public static void main(String[] args)
    {
        System.out.println("Creating a car...");
        car c = new car();
        c.start();
        c.drive();
    }
}
```

Here's the output of this application:

```
C:\>java app
Creating a car...
Starting...
Driving...
```

Calling Superclass Constructors

"OK," says the Novice Programmer, "I've come up with a problem. I know I can create a subclass from a superclass, but what if the superclass has a constructor? Does it ever get called?" "That," you say, "takes a little thought." "Hmm," says the NP, thinking.

Suppose you have a class named **a** that has a constructor with no parameters:

```
class a
{
```

```
    a()
    {
        System.out.println("In a\'s constructor...");
    }
}
```

Then you derive a subclass, **b**, from **a**:

```
class b extends a
{
}
```

Now when you create an object of class **b**, the constructor in class **a** is called automatically:

```
public class app
{
    public static void main(String[] args)
    {
        b obj = new b();
    }
}
```

Here's the result of the preceding code:

```
C:\>java app
In a's constructor...
```

Now suppose you add a constructor to class **b** that takes no parameters:

```
class a
{
    a()
    {
        System.out.println("In a\'s constructor...");
    }
}

class b extends a
{
    b()
    {
        System.out.println("In b\'s constructor...");
    }
}
```

```
public class app
{
    public static void main(String[] args)
    {
        b obj = new b();
    }
}
```

In this case, when you create an object of class **b**, the constructors from both **a** and **b** are called:

```
C:\>java app
In a's constructor...
In b's constructor...
```

Now suppose you change **b**'s constructor so that it takes one parameter:

```
class a
{
    a()
    {
        System.out.println("In a\'s constructor...");
    }
}

class b extends a
{
    b(String s)
    {
        System.out.println("In b\'s String constructor...");
        System.out.println(s);
    }
}

public class app
{
    public static void main(String[] args)
    {
        b obj = new b("Hello from Java!");
    }
}
```

In this case, the constructors of both classes **a** and **b** are called:

```
C:\>java app
In a's constructor...
```

```
In b's String constructor...
Hello from Java!
```

A constructor with no parameters is called a *default constructor* for a class, be-cause Java will call it automatically when you instantiate subclasses of that class, unless you make other arrangements. What does this mean? Suppose you add another constructor to **a** to handle strings (this is called *overloading*, and you'll see it later in this chapter):

```
class a
{
    a()
    {
        System.out.println("In a\'s constructor...");
    }

    a(String s)
    {
        System.out.println("In a\'s String constructor...");
        System.out.println(s);
    }
}
```

Now say that you want to call the constructor in class **a** with the **String** param-eter instead of the default constructor. How do you do this? You do it by calling the **super** method in class **b**'s constructor, like this:

```
class a
{
    a()
    {
        System.out.println("In a\'s constructor...");
    }

    a(String s)
    {
        System.out.println("In a\'s String constructor...");
        System.out.println(s);
    }
}

class b extends a
{
```

```
    b(String s)
    {
        super(s);
        System.out.println("In b\'s String constructor...");
        System.out.println(s);
    }
}

public class app
{
    public static void main(String[] args)
    {
        b obj = new b("Hello from Java!");
    }
}
```

Now when you instantiate an object of class **b**, the constructor that takes a **String** parameter in class **a** is called, *not* the default constructor:

```
C:\>java app
In a's String constructor...
Hello from Java!
In b's String constructor...
Hello from Java!
```

Why is the constructor that takes a **String** parameter in class **a** called and not the default constructor in class **a**? The reason is simple—Java sees you're using the **super** method to call the superclass's method:

```
class b extends a
{
    b(String s)
    {
        super(s);
        System.out.println("In b\'s String constructor...");
        System.out.println(s);
    }
}
```

If you use **super** to call a superclass's constructor, the line in which you do so must be the very first one in a constructor, which is where Java will look for it (if it's in any line but the first, Java will object).

Creating Multilevel Inheritance

"So," says the Novice Programmer, "can I subclass subclasses?" "Yes," you say. "And can I subclass subclasses of subclasses?" "Yes," you say. The NP is prepared to go farther and asks, "And can I...." You say, "How about some coffee?"

In the first topic of this chapter, I created a class named **vehicle** and a subclass of **vehicle** named **car**:

```
class vehicle
{
    public void start()
    {
        System.out.println("Starting...");
    }
}

class car extends vehicle
{
    public void drive()
    {
        System.out.println("Driving...");
    }
}
```

That class hierarchy only included two levels—the superclass and the subclass— but things can go deeper. Say, for example, that I have a new class, **aircraft**, which subclasses **vehicle** and adds a method named **fly**:

```
class aircraft extends vehicle
{
    public void fly()
    {
        System.out.println("Flying...");
    }
}
```

There are all kinds of aircraft, and I'll derive two further classes from **aircraft**— **whirlybird**, which defines a new method named **whirl**, and **jet**, which defines a method named **zoom**:

```
class whirlybird extends aircraft
{
    public void whirl()
    {
```

```
        System.out.println("Whirling...");
    }
}

class jet extends aircraft
{
    public void zoom()
    {
        System.out.println("Zooming...");
    }
}
```

Here's what the class hierarchy looks like now:

```
vehicle
    |_____ car
    |_____ aircraft
                |_____ whirlybird
                |_____ jet
```

Now I can instantiate objects of these classes, as in this example in which I'm creating objects of class **car** and **jet**:

```
public class app
{
    public static void main(String[] args)
    {
        System.out.println("Creating a car...");
        car c = new car();
        c.start();
        c.drive();

        System.out.println();
        System.out.println("Creating a jet...");
        jet j = new jet();
        j.start();
        j.fly();
        j.zoom();
    }
}
```

Here's what the output of this code looks like:

```
C:\>java app
Creating a car...
Starting...
Driving...
```

```
Creating a jet...
Starting...
Flying...
Zooming...
```

Handling Multilevel Constructors

"Hey!" the Novice Programmer says. "Has Java gone all wacky again?" you ask. "Yes," the NP says, "I've created four levels of subclasses, classes **a** through **d**, where **a** is the superclass everything is derived from. It makes sense that **d**'s constructor should be called first, then **c**'s, then **b**'s, and then **a**'s, right?" "No," you say, "which is why Java calls them in exactly the opposite order." "I knew you'd be on my side," the NP says.

Let's look at an example of multilevel constructor use. Here, I'll implement the Novice Programmer's program with four levels of subclassing, starting with class **a**:

```
class a
{
    a()
    {
        System.out.println("Constructing a...");
    }
}

class b extends a
{
    b()
    {
        System.out.println("Constructing b...");
    }
}

class c extends b
{
    c()
    {
        System.out.println("Constructing c...");
    }
}
```

```
class d extends c
{
    d()
    {
        System.out.println("Constructing d...");
    }
}
```

Next, I'll create an object of class **d**, the last class in the subclassing chain:

```
public class app
{
    public static void main(String[] args)
    {
        d obj = new d();
    }
}
```

Here's what you see when you run this code:

```
C:\>java app
Constructing a...
Constructing b...
Constructing c...
Constructing d...
```

In other words, Java called **a**'s constructor first, then **b**'s, then **c**'s, then **d**'s, not in the reverse order as you might expect. Why does Java do it this way? Because when you create subclasses, you proceed from the general to the specific, which means that class **a** knows nothing about class **b**, class **b** knows nothing about class **c**, and so on. For that reason, Java calls the original subclass's constructor first, then the next, and so on. Because class **b** knows about class **a**, it might rely on certain parts of **a** being initialized before completing its own initialization, and the same for class **c** with respect to class **b**, and so on.

It's also worth noting that you can pass parameters back multiple levels in the ways I outlined in the topic "Calling Superclass Constructors," earlier in this chapter. However, all constructors in the subclassing chain must still be called in ascending order.

Overriding Methods

"Oh well," the Novice Programmer says, "I thought I could use the Java **Button** class in my new program, but I wanted to create a method named **getLabel**, and the **Button** class already has a method named that." "That's no problem," you say, "you can just override the **Button** class's **getLabel** method with a new implementation of that method." "I can do that?" the NP asks.

In the last chapter, you saw that you can overload methods with different implementations that have different parameter lists. You can also *override* methods that you inherit from a superclass, which means that you replace them with a new version.

Here's an example. In this case, I'll start with a general base class named **animal** that has one method: **breathe**. When **breathe** is called, it prints out "Breathing...". Here's the code:

```
class animal
{
    public void breathe()
    {
        System.out.println("Breathing...");
    }
}
```

Now suppose you want to derive a new class from **animal** named **fish**. When you test the **breathe** method in the **fish** class, however, you see that it prints out "Breathing...". You decide it would be better if it prints out "Bubbling..." instead. To do this, you can override the **breathe** method in the **fish** class by simply defining a new version with the same parameter list:

```
class animal
{
    public void breathe()
    {
        System.out.println("Breathing...");
    }
}

class fish extends animal
{
    public void breathe()
    {
        System.out.println("Bubbling...");
    }
}
```

Now you can instantiate new objects of the **animal** and **fish** classes and call their **breathe** methods, like this:

```
public class app
{
    public static void main(String[] args)
    {
        System.out.println("Creating an animal...");
        animal a = new animal();
        a.breathe();

        System.out.println();
        System.out.println("Creating a lungfish...");
        fish f = new fish();
        f.breathe();
    }
}
```

Here's the output of this code, showing that the **breathe** method is indeed overloaded:

```
C:\>java app
Creating an animal...
Breathing...

Creating a lungfish...
Bubbling...
```

Accessing Overridden Members

"Well," the Novice Programmer says, "I think I've run into a problem that no one else has ever encountered in Java." "Oh yes?" you ask. "Yes," the NP says, "I've overridden a superclass's method, and that's fine most of the time, but sometimes I need access to the original overridden method." "That's a common problem" you say, "and you can solve it with the **super** keyword."

 You can use **super** much like you use the **this** keyword, except that **super** doesn't refer to the current object, but rather to its superclass. For example, take a look at this code from the previous topic in which the **fish** class subclasses the **animal** class and overrides the **breathe** method so that it prints out "Bubbling..." instead of "Breathing...":

```
class animal
{
```

```
    public void breathe()
    {
        System.out.println("Breathing...");
    }
}

class fish extends animal
{
    public void breathe()
    {
        System.out.println("Bubbling...");
    }
}
```

Now, however, suppose you realize that a certain type of fish—a lungfish, for example—can indeed breathe as land animals do, so you add a new method to the **fish** class, **newbreathe**. In this method, you'd like to reach the superclass's **breathe** method, and you can do that with the **super** keyword, like this:

```
class animal
{
    public void breathe()
    {
        System.out.println("Breathing...");
    }
}

class fish extends animal
{
    public void breathe()
    {
        System.out.println("Bubbling...");
    }

    public void newbreathe()
    {
        super.breathe();
    }
}
```

Now you can instantiate objects of the **animal** and **fish** classes and use the **newbreathe** method, like this:

```
public class app
{
```

```
    public static void main(String[] args)
    {
        System.out.println("Creating an animal...");
        animal a = new animal();
        a.breathe();

        System.out.println();
        System.out.println("Creating a lungfish...");
        fish lf = new fish();
        lf.newbreathe();
    }
}
```

Here's the result of this code:

```
C:\>java app
Creating an animal...
Breathing...

Creating a lungfish...
Breathing...
```

Using Superclass Variables With Subclassed Objects

The Programming Correctness Czar appears and says, "In C++, you can assign a subclass object reference to a variable of a superclass type. Can you do that in Java?" The Novice Programmer says, "Run that by me again?" "Yes," you say in response to the PCC.

One interesting aspect of object-oriented programming (OOP) in Java—which I'll put to work in the next topic—is that you can assign a subclass object reference to a variable of a superclass type. Say, for example, that class **a** is the superclass of **b** and that you have a variable of class **a**. It turns out that you can assign object references of class **b** to that variable as well as object references of class **a**.

Let's take a look at an example. Here, I'll use the multilevel class hierarchy you saw earlier in this chapter:

```
class vehicle
{
    public void start()
    {
        System.out.println("Starting...");
```

```
        }
    }

    class car extends vehicle
    {
        public void drive()
        {
            System.out.println("Driving...");
        }
    }

    class aircraft extends vehicle
    {
        public void fly()
        {
            System.out.println("Flying...");
        }
    }

    class whirlybird extends aircraft
    {
        public void whirl()
        {
            System.out.println("Whirling...");
        }
    }

    class jet extends aircraft
    {
        public void zoom()
        {
            System.out.println("Zooming...");
        }
    }
```

For example, to create new objects of the **car** and **jet** classes, I can use this code:

```
public class app
{
    public static void main(String[] args)
    {
        System.out.println("Creating a car...");
        car c = new car();
        c.start();
        c.drive();
```

```
            System.out.println();
            System.out.println("Creating a jet...");
            jet j = new jet();
            j.start();
        }
}
```

However, I can also assign the new **jet** object to a variable of class **vehicle**, like this:

```
public class app
{
    public static void main(String[] args)
    {
        System.out.println("Creating a car...");
        car c = new car();
        c.start();
        c.drive();

        System.out.println();
        System.out.println("Creating a jet...");
        vehicle j = new jet();
        j.start();
        //j.fly();
        //j.zoom();
    }
}
```

Here's the output of this code:

```
C:\>java app
Creating a car...
Starting...
Driving...

Creating a jet...
Starting...
```

Note that I commented out the lines **j.fly()** and **j.zoom()** here because those methods are defined in the **aircraft** and **jet** classes, which are subclasses of **vehicle**, which means that those methods can't be used with a variable of class **vehicle**. In general, an object variable **a** will only permit access to those items that are members of its own class, not necessarily all the members of the object variable it happens to hold—in particular, you won't be able to access any members that are not members of **a**'s class.

There's a use for this seemingly arcane piece of information—see the next topic for the details.

Dynamic Method Dispatch (Runtime Polymorphism)

"Hmm," says the Novice Programmer, "I have another problem. My drawing program can create objects of the classes **triangle**, **square**, and **circle**, each of which has a **draw** method, but I'm not sure what type of object the user will want to create until the program runs. Will I have to write the program's main code three times, one for each type of object?" "Not at all," you say. "You can use runtime polymorphism." "Huh?" the NP replies.

Runtime polymorphism, called *dynamic method dispatch* in Java, lets you wait until your program is actually running before specifying the type of object that will be in a particular object variable. This means, in the Novice Programmer's case, that he can write his code calling the **draw** method on various variables and decide what type of object—**triangle**, **square**, or **circle**—is stored in those variables at runtime.

As discussed in the previous topic, you can assign a subclass object reference to a variable of a superclass type. You may be wondering why Java, which is very strict about typing, lets you do this. The answer is to support runtime polymorphism.

Here's an example to make this clearer. In this case, I'll create a superclass named **a**, a subclass of **a** named **b**, a subclass of **b** named **c**, and a subclass of **c** named **d**, each of which has a **print** method:

```
class a
{
    public void print()
    {
        System.out.println("Here's a...");
    }
}

class b extends a
{
    public void print()
    {
        System.out.println("Here's b...");
    }
}
```

```
class c extends a
{
    public void print()
    {
        System.out.println("Here's c...");
    }
}

class d extends a
{
    public void print()
    {
        System.out.println("Here's d...");
    }
}
```

Now I can create an object reference of each class type:

```
public class app
{
    public static void main(String[] args)
    {
        a a1 = new a();
        b b1 = new b();
        c c1 = new c();
        d d1 = new d();
           .
           .
           .
```

To show how runtime polymorphism works, I'll also create a variable named **aref** that holds an object reference to an object of class **a**:

```
public class app
{
    public static void main(String[] args)
    {
        a a1 = new a();
        b b1 = new b();
        c c1 = new c();
        d d1 = new d();
        a aref;
           .
           .
           .
```

Now I can place the object references to objects of all different classes in **aref**, and when I call the **print** method, the **print** method of the corresponding class will be called:

```
public class app
{
    public static void main(String[] args)
    {
        a a1 = new a();
        b b1 = new b();
        c c1 = new c();
        d d1 = new d();
        a aref;

        aref = a1;
        aref.print();

        aref = b1;
        aref.print();

        aref = c1;
        aref.print();

        aref = d1;
        aref.print();
    }
}
```

Here's the result of this code:

```
C:\>java app
Here's a...
Here's b...
Here's c...
Here's d...
```

Using runtime polymorphism, you can write code that will work with many different types of objects and decide on the actual object type at runtime. Note that the restrictions mentioned in the previous topic still apply: An object variable **a** will only permit access to those items that are members of its own class, not necessarily all the members of the object variable it happens to hold—in particular, you won't be able to access any members that are not members of **a**'s class.

Creating Abstract Classes

The Novice Programmer stomps in. "That darn Johnson!" the NP says. "What's wrong?" you ask. "That darn Johnson was using one of my classes that needs to be customized before you can use it, but that darn Johnson didn't. So, it didn't work—right there in front of the Big Boss!" "Well," you say, "next time, make your class abstract, and that darn Johnson will *have* to customize it."

When writing classes, you may run across cases where you can only provide general code, and it's up to the developer who subclasses your class to customize it. To make sure the developer customizes your code, you can make the method *abstract*, which means the developer will have to override your method; otherwise, Java will complain. To make a method abstract, you use the **abstract** keyword. If you make any methods in a class abstract, you also have to make the class, itself, abstract as well.

Here's an example. In this case, I'll create a class named **a** that has a method named **print**, which prints out a string, and it gets the string to print by calling a method named **getData**:

```
class a
{
    String getData();

    public void print()
    {
        System.out.println(getData());
    }
}
```

Note that there's no implementation of the **getData** method because I want developers to specify what data they want to print out. To make sure they know that they must provide an implementation of the **getData** method, I can make the method abstract, which means I must make the class, itself, abstract as well:

```
abstract class a
{
    abstract String getData();

    public void print()
    {
        System.out.println(getData());
    }
}
```

Now when I subclass **a**, I have to provide an implementation of **getData**, like this:

```
class b extends a
{
    String getData()
    {
        return "Hello from Java!";
    }
}
```

Here's how I can put the subclass to work (note that an abstract cannot be instantiated class directly):

```
public class app
{
    public static void main(String[] args)
    {
        b b1 = new b();

        b1.print();
    }
}
```

Here's the result of this code:

```
C:\>java app
Hello from Java!
```

TIP: *This is an important technique to understand because a great many methods in the Java packages, themselves, are abstract and therefore must be overridden.*

Stopping Overriding With **final**

The Novice Programmer says, "That darn Johnson!" "What's wrong?" you ask. "That darn Johnson overrode the **draw** method in my **painter** class and messed it all up," the NP complains. "Don't worry, NP," you say, "you can mark that method as *final*, and no one can override it then." "Swell!" says the NP.

Earlier in this chapter, you saw an example in which the **fish** class overrode the method called **breathe** in the **animal** class:

```
class animal
{
    void breathe()
    {
        System.out.println("Breathing...");
    }
}

class fish extends animal
{
    public void breathe()
    {
        System.out.println("Bubbling...");
    }
}
```

If for some reason you don't want to let anyone override the **breathe** method, you can declare it **final**, like this:

```
class animal
{
    final void breathe()
    {
        System.out.println("Breathing...");
    }
}

class fish extends animal
{
    public void breathe()
    {
        System.out.println("Bubbling...");
    }
}
```

Now let's say you try to use these classes in some code:

```
public class app
{
    public static void main(String[] args)
    {
        System.out.println("Creating an animal...");
        animal a = new animal();
        a.breathe();
```

```
            System.out.println();
            System.out.println("Creating a lungfish...");
            fish f = new fish();
            f.breathe();
    }
}
```

Java will object that you can't override **breathe**, like this:

```
C:\>javac app.java -deprecation
app.java:11: The method void breathe() declared in class fish cannot
override the final method of the same signature declared in class animal.
Final methods cannot be overridden.
    public void breathe()
                ^
1 error
```

Stopping Inheritance With **final**

You can prevent a class from being subclassed by declaring the entire class **final**, as you see here:

```
final class animal
{
    public void breathe()
    {
        System.out.println("Breathing...");
    }
}

class fish extends animal
{
    public void breathe()
    {
        System.out.println("Bubbling...");
    }
}

public class app
{
    public static void main(String[] args)
    {
```

```
        System.out.println("Creating an animal...");
        animal a = new animal();
        a.breathe();

        System.out.println();
        System.out.println("Creating a lungfish...");
        fish f = new fish();
        f.breathe();
    }
}
```

Here's what happens when you try to execute this code:

```
C:\>javac app.java -deprecation
app.java:9: Can't subclass final classes: class animal
class fish extends animal
                   ^

1 error
```

Creating Constants With **final**

In the previous two topics, I showed two uses for **final**: to prevent method over-riding and to prevent subclassing. There's another use for **final** in Java—you can use it to declare constants.

Here's an example in which I make a variable into a constant with **final** and then try to assign a value to it:

```
public class app
{
    public static void main(String[] args)
    {
        final int a = 5;

        a = 6;
    }
}
```

Here's how the Java compiler objects to this code:

```
C:\> javac app.java -deprecation
app.java:7: Can't assign a value to a final variable: a
        a = 6;
```

```
          ^
1 error
```

Is-a Vs. Has-a Relationships

The Programming Correctness Czar arrives and says, "In C++, you can have is-a and has-a relationships in inheritance." "Same in Java," you say.

You may come across the terms *is-a* and *has-a* when working with inheritance, because they specify two of the ways classes can relate to each other. Standard inheritance is what you usually think of in terms of an is-a relationship, as in the following example. In this case, class **a** extends class **b**, so you can say class **a** *is-a* **b**:

```
class a extends b
{
    a()
    {
        print();
    }
}

class b
{
    void print()
    {
        System.out.println("This comes from class b...");
    }
}

public class app
{
    public static void main(String[] args)
    {
        a obj = new a();
    }
}
```

When you call **a**'s **print** method, you're actually calling the **print** method **a** inherited from **b**, and it's this method that does the printing:

```
C:\>java app
This comes from class b...
```

In a has-a relationship, on the other hand, one object includes an object reference to another, as in this case, where objects of class **a** will include an internal object of class **b**:

```
class a
{
    b b1;

    a()
    {
        b1 = new b();
        b1.print();
    }
}

class b
{
    void print()
    {
        System.out.println("This comes from class b...");
    }
}

public class app
{
    public static void main(String[] args)
    {
        a obj = new a();
    }
}
```

Now class **b**'s **print** method is accessible from the object named **b1** in the object of class **a**:

```
C:\>java app
This comes from class b...
```

The Java Object Class

"All I want," the Novice Programmer says, "is to write a simple class, no inheritance whatsoever and...." "Too late," you say. "All classes in Java are subclasses of one master class, **java.lang.Object,** so anything you do already involves inheritance."

Every class in Java is derived automatically from the **java.lang.Object** class, and there's certain advantages to knowing this, including knowing that all objects have already inherited quite a few methods, ready for you to use. The methods of class **Object** appear in Table 5.2.

Here's an example in which I use the **getClass** method to determine the class of an object reference in a superclass variable. This is useful because a superclass variable can hold references to objects of any of its subclasses. I start with a superclass named **a** and three subclasses: **b**, **c**, and **d**. The **print** method in each of these classes prints out the name of the class. Here's the code:

```java
class a
{
    public void print()
    {
        System.out.println("Here's a...");
    }
}
```

Table 5.2   The Java Object class methods.

Constructors methods	Means
protected Object clone( )	Yields a copy of this object
boolean equals(Object obj)	Indicates whether another object is equal to this one
protected void finalize( )	Called by the garbage collector on an object when garbage collection is about to dispose of the object
Class getClass( )	Yields the runtime class of an object
int hashCode( )	Yields a hashcode value for the object
void notify( )	Wakes up a single thread that's waiting on this object
void notifyAll( )	Wakes up all threads that are waiting on this object
String toString( )	Yields a string representation of the object
void wait( )	Makes the current thread wait until another thread invokes the notify method or the notifyAll method
void wait(long timeout)	Makes the current thread wait until either another thread invokes the notify method or the notifyAll method or a specified amount of time has passed
void wait(long timeout, int nanos)	Causes the current thread to wait until another thread invokes the notify method or the notifyAll method for this object, some other thread interrupts this thread, or a certain amount of real time has passed

```
class b extends a
{
    public void print()
    {
        System.out.println("Here's b...");
    }
}

class c extends a
{
    public void print()
    {
        System.out.println("Here's c...");
    }
}

class d extends a
{
    public void print()
    {
        System.out.println("Here's d...");
    }
}
```

Next, I create an instance of each class and a variable of class **a** named **aref**:

```
public class app
{
    public static void main(String[] args)
    {
        a a1 = new a();
        b b1 = new b();
        c c1 = new c();
        d d1 = new d();
        a aref;
        .
        .
        .
```

Now I can determine the class of the object in **aref**, no matter which of the subclasses it is:

```
public class app
{
    public static void main(String[] args)
```

```
        {
            a a1 = new a();
            b b1 = new b();
            c c1 = new c();
            d d1 = new d();
            a aref;

            aref = a1;
            System.out.println("aref\'s class is now " + aref.getClass());
            aref.print();

            aref = b1;
            System.out.println("aref\'s class is now " + aref.getClass());
            aref.print();

            aref = c1;
            System.out.println("aref\'s class is now " + aref.getClass());
            aref.print();

            aref = d1;
            System.out.println("aref\'s class is now " + aref.getClass());
            aref.print();
        }
}
```

Here's the result:

```
C:\>java app
aref's class is now class a
Here's a...
aref's class is now class b
Here's b...
aref's class is now class c
Here's c...
aref's class is now class d
Here's d...
```

As you can see, each object's built-in methods—such as **getClass**—can be very useful.

Using Interfaces For Multiple Inheritance

"Hmm," says the Novice Programmer, "I have a class named **animal** and an entirely separate class named **mineral**, and I want to inherit from both of those classes at the same time to create something entirely new." "Sorry," you say, "Java doesn't support multiple inheritance directly—you'll have to make one of those classes an *interface*."

In other languages such as C++, one class can inherit from multiple classes at once, but this technique doesn't work directly in Java—that is, you can only use the **extends** keyword with one class at a time. Therefore, you can't do this:

```
class a extends b, c      //Won't work!
{
      .
      .
      .
}
```

However, there are two ways to implement what amounts to multiple inheritance in Java. The first is to use single inheritance in stages (if that will work for the classes you want to inherit from), like this:

```
class c
{
      .
      .
      .
}

class b extends c
{
      .
      .
      .
}

class a extends b
{
      .
      .
      .
}
```

The other way is to use interfaces. Interfaces will start becoming important in the next chapter, so I'll introduce them now.

An *interface* specifies the form of its methods but does not give any implementation details; therefore, you can think of it much like the declaration of a class. As you'll see later in the book, you can create interfaces with the **interface** keyword:

```
interface c
{
        .
        .
        .

}
```

```
interface b
{
        .
        .
        .

}
```

Now you can use these two interfaces with the **implements** keyword:

```
class a implements b, c
{
        .
        .
        .

}
```

Because the interfaces declare but do not define methods, it's up to you to implement the interfaces' methods. For example, in the applet shown at the beginning of this chapter, I implemented the Java **ActionListener** interface to handle button clicks (you'll see all the details of applets like this in the next chapter). That interface declares one method, **actionPerformed**, which I defined like this:

```
import java.applet.Applet;
import java.awt.*;
import java.awt.event.*;

public class clicker extends Applet implements ActionListener {

    TextField text1;
    Button button1;
```

```
public void init(){
        text1 = new TextField(20);
        add(text1);
        button1 = new Button("Click Here!");
        add(button1);
    button1.addActionListener(this);
}

public void actionPerformed(ActionEvent event){
        String msg = new String ("Welcome to Java");
        if(event.getSource() == button1){
            text1.setText(msg);
        }
    }
}
```

If you don't define the **actionPerformed** method, the Java compiler will give you a message like this one:

```
C:\>javac clicker.java -deprecation
clicker.java:5: class clicker must be declared abstract. It does not define
void actionPerformed(java.awt.event.ActionEvent) from interface
java.awt.event.ActionListener.
public class clicker extends Applet implements ActionListener {
        ^
1 error
```

You can implement as many interfaces as you want, as in this example, which implements the **ActionListener** interface for button clicks and the **MouseListener** and **MouseMotionListener** interfaces to work with the mouse:

```
import java.awt.Graphics;
import java.awt.*;
import java.awt.event.*;
import java.applet.Applet;

public class dauber extends Applet implements ActionListener,
    MouseListener, MouseMotionListener {

        Button buttonDraw, buttonLine, buttonOval, buttonRect,
            button3DRect;
        Button buttonRounded;

        Point pts[] = new Point[1000];
        Point ptAnchor, ptDrawTo, ptOldAnchor, ptOldDrawTo;
```

```
        int ptindex = 0;
               .
               .
               .
```

Creating Inner Classes

"OK," says the Novice Programmer, "I'm an expert now. Is there anything about classes that I don't know?" You smile and say, "Plenty. For example, what do you know about inner classes?" "What classes?" the NP asks.

Beginning in Java 1.1, you could nest class definitions inside each other. Nested classes can be static or nonstatic; however, static classes cannot refer to the members of its enclosing class directly but must instantiate and use an object instead, so they're not often used. *Inner classes*, on the other hand, are nonstatic nested classes, and they're quite popular for reasons having to do with event handling, which we'll get into in the next chapter.

Here's an example of an inner class; in this case, class **b** is defined inside class **a**, and I instantiate an object of class **b** in class **a**'s constructor:

```
class a
{
    b obj;

    a()
    {
        obj = new b();
        obj.print();
    }

    class b
    {
        public void print()
        {
            System.out.println("Inside b...");
        }
    }
}

public class app
{
    public static void main(String[] args)
```

```
    {
        a obj = new a();
    }
}
```

When this code runs, it instantiates an object of class **a**, which instantiates an internal object of class **b** and calls that object's **print** method. Here's the result:

```
C:\>java app
Inside b...
```

Besides inner classes as demonstrated in this example, you can also have *anonymous* (unnamed) inner classes—see the next topic for the details.

Creating Anonymous Inner Classes

One type of shorthand that's handy for working with event handling is to use *anonymous inner classes*. I'll introduce them here, and we'll use them in the next chapter. An anonymous inner class is one that doesn't have a name, and you create it using this syntax:

```
new SuperType(constructor parameters)
{
    //methods and data
}
```

Here, *SuperType* is the name of a class or interface you're subclassing (you must specify a superclass type when creating anonymous inner classes), and you can define the anonymous inner class's methods and data in a code block.

Let's look at an example. In this case, I'll create an anonymous inner class inside a new class—class **a**. This anonymous inner class will subclass another class, class **b**, and define a method named **print**, which I call immediately, like this:

```
class a
{
    a()
    {
        (new b() {public void print()
            {System.out.println("Hello from Java!");}}).print();
    }
}

class b{}
```

All that's left is to create an object of class **a** and to call that class's constructor, which I do like this:

```
public class app
{
    public static void main(String[] args)
    {
        a obj = new a();
    }
}
```

Here's the result of this code:

```
C:\>java app
Hello from Java!
```

You'll learn more about anonymous inner classes in the next chapter.

Chapter 6

AWT: Applets, Applications, And Event Handling

In Depth

We've worked through a lot of Java syntax to get to this point, and this is one of the payoff chapters. Here, we'll start working with graphical programs, both applets and applications. This chapter introduces the Java Abstract Windowing Toolkit (AWT), Java's original way of working with graphics. AWT is now supplemented with the Swing package, which you'll see in a few chapters. AWT provides the foundation of graphics work in Java, and even the Swing package is based on AWT.

In this chapter, I'll put AWT to work, creating applets and windowed applications. Before we begin, it's worth putting AWT in some historical perspective. AWT was developed very quickly for the first release of Java—in fact, in only six weeks. The original AWT developers used one window for each component of AWT, so each button, text field, check box, and so on had its own window as far as the underlying operating system was concerned. That turned out to be a considerable use of system resources as programs became larger. Recently Sun introduced the Swing package, in which components are displayed using graphical methods of their containing applet or application windows—they don't have their own operating system windows. AWT components are now called *heavyweight components* because of their significant use of system resources, and the Swing components are called *lightweight components*, because they're just drawn and don't need their own windows.

What does this mean for you? It's clear that, to Sun, Swing is the future. There are far more Swing components than AWT ones, and in fact, there's a Swing replacement component for each of AWT components. Sun probably won't be expanding AWT component set much in the future, whereas Swing is expected to grow. On the other hand, Swing, itself, is *based* on AWT—the windows that Swing uses to display Swing components in—that is, windows, frame windows, applets, and dialogs—are all based on AWT containers. AWT isn't going away, and in order to work with Swing, you need a thorough background in AWT. For that reason, and because so much development is still done with AWT—and more will be done in the future—I'll spend this and the next few chapters on AWT. I'll start with an overview of AWT itself.

The Abstract Windowing Toolkit

It's no exaggeration to say that the Abstract Windowing Toolkit was the driving force behind Java's popularity. You can create and display buttons, labels, menus, combo boxes, text fields, and the other user-interface controls you'd expect in windowed programs using AWT. Here's an overview of the most popular AWT classes:

- *Applet*—Creates an applet
- *Button*—Creates a button
- *Canvas*—Creates a canvas you can draw on
- *Checkbox*—Creates a check box
- *Choice*—Creates a choice control
- *Label*—Creates a label
- *Menu*—Creates a menu
- *ComboBox*—Creates a combo box
- *List*—Creates a list control
- *Frame*—Creates a frame for windowed applications
- *Dialog*—Creates a dialog box
- *Panel*—Creates a panel that can contain other controls
- *PopupMenu*—Creates a pop-up menu
- *RadioButton*—Creates a radio button
- *ScrollBar*—Creates a scrollbar
- *ScrollPane*—Creates a scrollable surface
- *TextArea*—Creates a two-dimensional text control
- *TextField*—Creates a one-dimensional text field (called a *text box* in other languages)
- *TextPane*—Creates a text surface
- *Window*—Creates a freestanding window

The AWT **Applet** class is what you base AWT applets on, and we'll take a look at that class first.

Applets

So just what is an AWT applet? An applet is just a class file that's specially written to display graphics in a Web browser; you embed applets in Web pages using the HTML **<APPLET>** tag. When run in a Web page, Java applets are downloaded automatically and run by the Web browser, displaying themselves in the space you've allocated for them in the page. They can do anything from working with graphics, to displaying animation, to handling controls (like the ones we'll work on in this chapter), text fields, and buttons. Using applets makes your Web pages *active*, not passive—that's their main attraction.

The process goes like this when working with AWT: You create a new applet, basing it on the **java.applet.Applet** class, which, in turn, is based on AWT **Component** class. Here's an example you've seen before, and I'll go through it again in this chapter. This example just displays the text "Hello from Java!" in a Web page:

```
import java.applet.Applet;
import java.awt.*;

public class applet extends Applet
{
    public void paint(Graphics g)
    {
        g.drawString("Hello from Java!", 60, 100);
    }
}
```

You compile the applet into a bytecode .class file. When you have your .class file, you upload it to an Internet Service Provider (ISP). You can give the applet the same protection you would give a Web page, making sure anyone can read the applet .class file (for example, in Unix, you might give the applet the permission setting 644, which lets anyone read the file).

TIP: *Unix file permissions make up three octal digits corresponding to, in order, the file owner's permission, the permission of others in the same user group, and the permission of all others. In each octal digit, a value of 4 indicates read permission, a value of 2 indicates write permission, and a value of 1 indicates execute permission. You add these values together to set the individual digits in a permission setting—for example, a permission of 0600 means that the file's owner, and only the file's owner, can both read and write to the file.*

You can embed the new applet in a Web page with the **<APPLET>** tag, indicating the name of the .class file for the applet as well as telling the Web browser how much space (in pixels) to leave for the applet. Here's an example:

```
<HTML>

<BODY>

<CENTER>
<APPLET
    CODE = "newApplet.class"
    WIDTH = 300
    HEIGHT = 200
>
</APPLET>
</CENTER>

</BODY>
</HTML>
```

In this case, I've set up a centered 300 x 200 pixel space in a Web page in which to display the applet, and I told the Web browser to download the newApplet.class file and run it. I'll cover the details, including the details on the **<APPLET>** tag, in this chapter. When the browser loads this page, it'll display the applet.

TIP: One useful item to know about is the Java Web browser plug-in. Web browser manufacturers have been notoriously slow to implement the latest Java versions, so Sun took matter into its own hands by creating the Java plug-in, which is a plug-in for Netscape Navigator and an ActiveX control for the Microsoft Internet Explorer. The plug-in is a complete implementation of the Java Runtime Environment, and it lets you run applets using the latest Java version. Note, however, that you must specially configure your Web pages to use the plug-in. I'll cover using the plug-in in this chapter.

Applications

AWT windowed applications are based on AWT **Frame** class, which creates a window with a frame that displays buttons and a title. Here's an example that you'll see more of in this chapter. Like the previous applet, this application displays "Hello from Java!" in a frame window:

```java
import java.awt.*;
import java.awt.event.*;

class AppFrame extends Frame
{
    public void paint(Graphics g)
    {
        g.drawString("Hello from Java!", 60, 100);
    }
}
```

```
public class app
{
    public static void main(String [] args)
    {
        AppFrame f = new AppFrame();

        f.setSize(200, 200);

        f.addWindowListener(new WindowAdapter() { public void
            windowClosing(WindowEvent e) {System.exit(0);}});

        f.show();
    }
}
```

I'll go through the process of creating windowed applications in detail in this chapter.

Handling Events

One of the biggest aspects of creating applets and applications is letting the user interact with the program, and you do that with *events*. When the user performs some action—clicking a button, closing a window, selecting an item in a list, or using the mouse, for example—Java considers that an event. We'll handle events throughout the rest of this book, and we'll take a look at how event handling works in this chapter.

To start working with events, I'll also introduce two basic controls in this chapter: buttons and text fields. The user can use the mouse to click buttons that initiate some action in your program, such as placing some text in a text field. In fact, button clicks are perhaps the most basic event Java supports. To see how event handling works in Java, I'll create programs in this chapter that support buttons and text fields. The full details on these controls appear in the next chapter.

Now that you have an overview of applets, applications, and event handling, it's time to get to the details in the "Immediate Solutions" section.

Immediate Solutions

Using The Abstract Windowing Toolkit

"OK," says the Novice Programmer, "I'm ready to start working with the Abstract Windowing Toolkit. Where does it start?" "With the **Component** class," you say. "Get some coffee and we'll take a look at it."

The most basic AWT class is the **java.awt.Component** class, on which all AWT visual components are based . For example, AWT **Button** class, **java.awt.Button**, is derived directly from **java.awt.Component**. The **java.awt.Component** class, itself, is derived directly from the **java.lang.Object** class, which you saw in the previous chapter.

The **Component** class includes a huge number of methods, many of which you'll see in this and the upcoming chapter. I've listed them all in Table 6.1 for reference. This is a long table, but it's worth glancing through and coming back to later for reference.

Table 6.1 Methods of AWT *Component* class.

Method	Does This
boolean action(Event evt, Object what)	Deprecated. You should register the component with an ActionListener.
void add(PopupMenu popup)	Adds the pop-up menu to the component.
void addComponentListener (ComponentListener l)	Adds the component listener to receive component events.
void addFocusListener(FocusListener l)	Adds the focus listener to receive focus events.
void addInputMethodListener (InputMethodListener l)	Adds the input method listener to receive input method events.
void addKeyListener(KeyListener l)	Adds the key listener to receive key events.
void addMouseListener (MouseListener l)	Adds the mouse listener to receive mouse events.
void addMouseMotionListener (MouseMotionListener l)	Adds the mouse motion listener to receive mouse motion events.

(continued)

Table 6.1   Methods of AWT _Component_ class (continued).

Method	Does This
void addNotify( )	Makes a component "displayable" by connecting it to a native screen resource.
void addPropertyChangeListener (PropertyChangeListener listener)	Adds a PropertyChangeListener.
void addPropertyChangeListener (String propertyName, PropertyChange Listener listener)	Adds a PropertyChangeListener for a property.
Rectangle bounds( )	Deprecated. Replaced by **getBounds**( ).
int checkImage(Image image, ImageObserver observer)	Gets the status of the screen representation of the image.
int checkImage(Image image, int width, int height, ImageObserver observer)	Gets the status of the screen representation of the image.
protected AWTEvent coalesceEvents (AWTEvent existingEvent, AWTEvent newEvent)	Coalesces an event being posted with another event.
boolean contains(int x, int y)	Checks whether this component contains the indicated point.
boolean contains(Point p)	Checks whether this component contains the indicated point.
Image createImage (ImageProducer producer)	Creates an image from the indicated image producer.
Image createImage (int width, int height)	Creates an offscreen image to be used for double buffering.
void deliverEvent(Event e)	Deprecated. Replaced by **dispatchEvent(AWTEvent e)**.
void disable( )	Deprecated. Replaced by **setEnabled(boolean)**.
protected void disableEvents (long eventsToDisable)	Disables the events defined by the indicated event mask parameter from being sent to this component.
void dispatchEvent(AWTEvent e)	Dispatches an event to this component or one of its subcomponents.
void doLayout( )	Makes the layout manager lay out this component.
void enable( )	Deprecated. Replaced by setEnabled(boolean).
void enable(boolean b)	Deprecated. Replaced by setEnabled(boolean).
protected void enableEvents (long eventsToEnable)	Enables the events defined by the indicated event mask parameter to be sent to this component.
void enableInputMethods (boolean enable)	Enables or disables input method support.

Table 6.1   Methods of AWT *Component* class (continued).

Method	Does This
protected void firePropertyChange (String propertyName, Object oldValue, Object newValue)	Sets up support for reporting bound property changes.
float getAlignmentX( )	Gets the alignment along the x axis.
float getAlignmentY( )	Gets the alignment along the y axis.
Color getBackground( )	Gets the background color of this component.
Rectangle getBounds( )	Ties the bounds of this component in a Rectangle object.
Rectangle getBounds(Rectangle rv)	Stores the bounds of this component into **rv** and **return rv**.
ColorModel getColorModel( )	Gets the instance of ColorModel used to display the component.
Component getComponentAt (int x, int y)	Determines whether this component or one of its immediate subcomponents contains the (x, y) location and gets the containing component.
Component getComponentAt(Point p)	Gets the component or subcomponent that contains the indicated point.
ComponentOrientation get ComponentOrientation( )	Retrieves the language-sensitive orientation to be used to order the elements or text within this component.
Cursor getCursor	Gets the cursor set in the component.
DropTarget getDropTarget( )	Get the DropTarget connected to this component.
Font getFont( )	Gets the font of this component.
FontMetrics getFontMetrics(Font font)	Gets the font metrics for the indicated font.
Color getForeground( )	Gets the foreground color of this component.
Graphics getGraphics( )	Creates a graphics context for this component.
int getHeight( )	Returns the current height of this component.
InputContext getInputContext( )	Gets the input context used by this component.
InputMethodRequests getInputMethodRequests( )	Gets the input method request handler.
Locale getLocale( )	Gets the locale of this component.
Point getLocation( )	Gets the location of this component in the form of a point specifying the component's top-left corner.
Point getLocation(Point rv)	Stores the x,y origin of this component into **rv** and **return rv**.
Point getLocationOnScreen( )	Gets the location of this component in the form of a point specifying the component's top-left corner.
Dimension getMaximumSize( )	Gets the maximum size of this component.

(continued)

Table 6.1   Methods of AWT Component class (continued).

Method	Does This
Dimension getMinimumSize( )	Gets the minimum size of this component.
String getName( )	Gets the name of the component.
Container getParent( )	Gets the parent of this component.
java.awt.peer.Component) Peer getPeer(	Deprecated. Replaced by **boolean isDisplayable( )**.
Dimension getPreferredSize( )	Gets the preferred size of this component.
Dimension getSize( )	Gets the size of this component in a Dimension object.
Dimension getSize(Dimension rv)	Stores the width/height of this component into **rv** and **return rv**.
Toolkit getToolkit( )	Gets the toolkit of this component.
Object getTreeLock( )	Gets the locking object for AWT component tree.
int getWidth( )	Gets the current width of this component.
int getX( )	Gets the current x coordinate of the component's origin.
int getY( )	Gets the current y coordinate of the component's origin.
boolean gotFocus (Event evt, Object what)	Deprecated. Replaced by **processFocusEvent(FocusEvent)**.
boolean handleEvent(Event evt)	Deprecated. Replaced by **processEvent(AWTEvent)**.
boolean hasFocus( )	True if this component has the keyboard focus.
void hide( )	Deprecated. Replaced by **setVisible(boolean)**.
boolean imageUpdate (Image img, int flags, int x, int y, int w, int h)	Repaints the component when the image has changed.
boolean inside(int x, int y)	Deprecated. Replaced by **contains(int, int)**.
void invalidate( )	Invalidates the component.
boolean isDisplayable( )	Determines whether the component can be displayed.
boolean isDoubleBuffered( )	True if this component is painted to an offscreen image that's copied to the screen later.
boolean isEnabled( )	Indicates whether this component is enabled.
boolean isFocusTraversable( )	Indicates whether this component can be traversed using Tab or Shift+Tab.
boolean isLightweight( )	Indicates whether the component is lightweight.
boolean isOpaque( )	True if this component is completely opaque; false by default.
boolean isShowing( )	Determines whether this component is visible onscreen.

(continued)

Table 6.1 **Methods of AWT *Component* class (continued).**

Method	Does This
boolean isValid( )	Determines whether this component is valid.
boolean isVisible( )	Determines whether this component should be visible when its parent is visible.
boolean keyDown(Event evt, int key)	Deprecated. Replaced by **processKeyEvent(KeyEvent)**.
boolean keyUp(Event evt, int key)	Deprecated. Replaced by **processKeyEvent(KeyEvent)**.
void layout( )	Deprecated. Replaced by **doLayout( )**.
void list( )	Prints a listing of this component to **System.out.**
void list(PrintStream out)	Prints a listing of this component to the indicated output stream.
void list(PrintStream out, int indent)	Prints out a list, starting at the indicated indention, to the indicated print stream.
void list(PrintWriter out)	Prints a listing to the indicated print writer.
void list(PrintWriter out, int indent)	Prints out a list, starting at the indicated indention, to the indicated print writer.
Component locate(int x, int y)	Deprecated. Replaced by **getComponentAt(int, int)**.
Point location( )	Deprecated. Replaced by **getLocation( )**.
boolean lostFocus(Event evt, Object what)	Deprecated. Replaced by **processFocusEvent(FocusEvent)**.
Dimension minimumSize( )	Deprecated. Replaced by **getMinimumSize( )**.
boolean mouseDown (Event evt, int x, int y)	Deprecated. Replaced by **processMouseEvent(MouseEvent)**.
boolean mouseDrag (Event evt, int x, int y)	Deprecated. Replaced by **processMouseMotionEvent(MouseEvent)**.
boolean mouseEnter (Event evt, int x, int y)	Deprecated. Replaced by **processMouseEvent(MouseEvent)**.
boolean mouseExit (Event evt, int x, int y)	Deprecated. Replaced by **processMouseEvent(MouseEvent)**.
boolean mouseMove (Event evt, int x, int y)	Deprecated. Replaced by **processMouseMotionEvent(MouseEvent)**.
boolean mouseUp (Event evt, int x, int y)	Deprecated. Replaced by **processMouseEvent(MouseEvent)**.
void move(int x, int y)	Deprecated. Replaced by **setLocation(int, int)**.
void nextFocus( )	Deprecated. Replaced by **transferFocus( )**.
void paint(Graphics g)	Paints this component.

(continued)

Table 6.1   Methods of AWT *Component* class (continued).

Method	Does This
void paintAll(Graphics g)	Paints this component and all subcomponents.
protected String paramString( )	Gets a string representing the state of this component.
boolean postEvent(Event e)	Deprecated. Replaced by **dispatchEvent(AWTEvent)**.
Dimension preferredSize( )	Deprecated. Replaced by **getPreferredSize( )**.
boolean prepareImage (Image image, ImageObserver observer)	Prepares an image for rendering on this component.
boolean prepareImage(Image image, int width, int height, ImageObserver observer)	Prepares an image for rendering on this component at the indicated width and height.
void print(Graphics g)	Prints the component.
void printAll(Graphics g)	Prints the component and all its subcomponents.
protected void processComponent Event(ComponentEvent e)	Processes component events occurring in this component by sending them to any registered ComponentListeners.
protected void processEvent (AWTEvent e)	Processes events occurring in this component.
protected void processFocusEvent (FocusEvent e)	Processes focus events occurring in this component by dispatching them to any registered FocusListener objects.
protected void processInputMethod Event(InputMethodEvent e)	Processes input method events occurring in this component by sending them to any registered InputMethodListener objects.
protected void processKeyEvent (KeyEvent e)	Processes key events occurring in this component by sending them to any registered KeyListener objects.
protected void processMouseEvent (MouseEvent e)	Processes mouse events occurring in this component by sending them to any registered MouseListener objects.
protected void processMouseMotion Event(MouseEvent e)	Processes mouse motion events occurring in this component by sending them to any registered MouseMotionListener objects.
void remove(MenuComponent popup)	Removes the indicated pop-up menu from the component.
void removeComponentListener (ComponentListener l)	Removes the indicated component listener so that it no longer receives component events.
void removeFocusListener (FocusListener l)	Removes the indicated focus listener so that it no longer receives focus events.
void removeInputMethodListener (InputMethodListener l)	Removes the indicated input method listener so that it no longer receives input method events.

(continued)

Table 6.1   Methods of AWT Component class (continued).

Method	Does This
void removeKeyListener(KeyListener l)	Removes the indicated key listener so that it no longer receives key events.
void removeMouseListener (MouseListener l)	Removes the indicated mouse listener so that it no longer receives mouse events.
void removeMouseMotionListener (MouseMotionListener l)	Removes the indicated mouse motion listener so that it no longer receives mouse motion events.
void removeNotify( )	Disallows displaying the component by destroying its native screen resource.
void removePropertyChangeListener (PropertyChangeListener listener)	Removes a PropertyChangeListener.
void removePropertyChangeListener (String propertyName, Property ChangeListener listener)	Removes a PropertyChangeListener for a given property.
void repaint( )	Repaints the component.
void repaint(int x, int y, int width, int height)	Repaints the indicated rectangle of this component.
void repaint(long tm)	Repaints the component.
void repaint(long tm, int x, int y, int width, int height)	Repaints the indicated rectangle of this component within **tm** int milliseconds.
void requestFocus( )	Requests the input focus.
void reshape(int x, int y, int width, int height)	Deprecated. Replaced by **setBounds(int, int, int, int)**.
void resize(Dimension d)	Deprecated. Replaced by **setSize(Dimension)**.
void resize(int width, int height)	Deprecated. Replaced by **setSize(int, int)**.
void setBackground(Color c)	Sets the background color.
void setBounds(int x, int y, int width, int height)	Moves and resizes the component.
void setBounds(Rectangle r)	Moves and resizes the component to conform to the new bounding rectangle **r**.
void setComponentOrientation (ComponentOrientation o)	Set the language-sensitive orientation to be used to order the elements or text.
void setCursor(Cursor cursor)	Sets the cursor image to the indicated cursor.
void setDropTarget(DropTarget dt)	Associate a DropTarget with this component.

(continued)

Table 6.1   Methods of AWT Component class (continued).

Method	Does This
void setEnabled(boolean b)	Enables or disables this component, depending on the value of the parameter **b**.
void setFont(Font f)	Sets the font of the component.
void setForeground(Color c)	Sets the foreground color of the component.
void setLocale(Locale l)	Sets the locale of the component.
void setLocation(int x, int y)	Moves this component to a new location.
void setLocation(Point p)	Moves this component to a new location.
void setName(String name)	Sets the name of the component to the indicated string.
void setSize(Dimension d)	Resizes this component so that it has width **d.width** and height **d.height**.
void setSize(int width, int height)	Resizes this component so that it has width and height.
void setVisible(boolean b)	Shows or hides this component as specified by the value of parameter **b**.
void show( )	Deprecated. Replaced by **setVisible(boolean)**.
void show(boolean b)	Deprecated. Replaced by **setVisible(boolean)**.
Dimension size( )	Deprecated. Replaced by **getSize( )**.
String toString( )	Gets a string representation of the component.
void transferFocus( )	Transfers the focus to the next component.
void update(Graphics g)	Updates the component.
void validate( )	Ensures that the component has a valid layout in effect.

Another important AWT class is the **Container** class. This class is derived from AWT **Component** class, and it's the basis of AWT containers, which can hold other components. Applets and windowed applications, which can display AWT components, are based on the **Container** class. Because you run across the **Container** class often in AWT programming—as in the next topic coming up—I've listed its methods in Table 6.2.

Table 6.2   Methods of the Container class.

Method	Does This
Component add(Component comp)	Adds the indicated component to this container.
Component add (Component comp, int index)	Adds the indicated component to this container at a specific position.

(continued)

Table 6.2   Methods of the *Container* class (continued).

Method	Does This
void add(Component comp, Object constraints)	Adds the indicated component to this container.
void add(Component comp, Object constraints, int index)	Adds the indicated component to this container with the indicated constraints at the indicated index.
Component add(String name, Component comp)	Adds a component to this container.
void addContainerListener (ContainerListener l)	Adds a container listener to get container events from the container.
protected void addImpl(Component comp, Object constraints, int index)	Adds the indicated component to the container at the given index.
void addNotify( )	Allows displaying the container by connecting it to a native screen resource.
int countComponents( ) (int x, int y)	Deprecated. Replaced by **getComponentCount( )**.
void deliverEvent(Event e)	Deprecated. Replaced by **dispatchEvent(AWTEvent e)**.
void doLayout( )	Makes the container lay out its components.
Component findComponentAt	Locates the visible child component containing the indicated position.
Component findComponentAt(Point p)	Locates the visible child component containing the indicated point.
float getAlignmentX( )	Gets the alignment along the x axis.
float getAlignmentY( )	Gets the alignment along the y axis.
Component getComponent(int n)	Gets the *n*th component in this container.
Component getComponentAt (int x, int y)	Locates the component that contains the x,y position.
Component getComponentAt(Point p)	Gets the component that contains the indicated point.
int getComponentCount( )	Gets the number of components in this panel.
Component[ ] getComponents( )	Gets all the components in the container.
Insets getInsets( )	Determines the insets of the container, which indicate the size of the container's border.
LayoutManager getLayout( )	Gets the layout manager for the container.
Dimension getMaximumSize( )	Gets the maximum size of the container.
Dimension getMinimumSize( )	Gets the minimum size of the container.
Dimension getPreferredSize( )	Gets the preferred size of the container.

(continued)

Table 6.2   Methods of the *Container* class (continued).

Method	Does This
Insets insets( )	Deprecated. Replaced by **getInsets( )**.
void invalidate( )	Invalidates the container.
boolean isAncestorOf(Component c)	Checks whether the component is contained in the hierarchy of this container.
void layout( )	Deprecated. Replaced by **doLayout( )**.
void list(PrintStream out, int indent)	Prints a listing of this container to the indicated output stream.
void list(PrintWriter out, int indent)	Prints out a list, starting at the indicated indention, to the indicated print writer.
Component locate(int x, int y)	Deprecated. Replaced by **getComponentAt(int, int)**.
Dimension minimumSize( )	Deprecated. Replaced by **getMinimumSize( )**.
void paint(Graphics g)	Paints the container.
void paintComponents(Graphics g)	Paints each component in the container.
protected String paramString( )	Gets the parameter string representing the state of the container.
Dimension preferredSize( )	Deprecated. Replaced by **getPreferredSize( )**.
void print(Graphics g)	Prints the container.
void printComponents(Graphics g)	Prints each of the components in this container.
protected void processContainerEvent (ContainerEvent e)	Processes container events occurring in this container by sending them to ContainerListener.
protected void processEvent (AWTEvent e)	Processes events in this container.
void remove(Component comp)	Removes the indicated component from the container.
void remove(int index)	Removes the component at the index from the container.
void removeAll( )	Removes all the components from this container.
void removeContainerListener (ContainerListener l)	Removes the indicated container listener so that it no longer receives container events from this container.
void removeNotify( )	Makes this container undisplayable by removing its connection to its native screen resource.
void setCursor(Cursor cursor)	Sets the cursor image to the indicated cursor.
void setFont(Font f)	Sets the font of this container.
void setLayout(LayoutManager mgr)	Sets the layout manager for this container.
void update(Graphics g)	Updates the container.
void validate( )	Validates this container and all its subcomponents.
protected void validateTree( )	Recursively descends the container tree and recomputes the layout for any subtrees marked as needing it (those marked as invalid).

Creating Applets

"Finally!" says the Novice Programmer. "At last I'm ready to create an applet." "That's right," you say. "Now which one would you like to create?" "Hmm," says the NP.

You base applets on the **java.applet.Applet** class, which is itself subclassed from the **java.awt.Container** class:

```
java.lang.Object
|____java.awt.Component
     |____java.awt.Container
          |____java.awt.Panel
               |____java.applet.Applet
```

For the sake of reference, you'll find the methods of the **Applet** class in Table 6.3.

Table 6.3   Methods of the Applet class.

Method	Does This
void destroy( )	Called when the applet is about to be disposed of.
AppletContext getAppletContext( )	Determines this applet's context. The context allows the applet to query the environment in which it runs.
String getAppletInfo( )	Gets information about this applet.
AudioClip getAudioClip(URL url)	Gets the AudioClip object specified by the **URL** argument.
AudioClip getAudioClip(URL url, String name)	Gets the AudioClip object specified by the **URL** and **name** arguments.
URL getCodeBase( )	Gets the base URL.
URL getDocumentBase( )	Gets the document URL.
Image getImage(URL url)	Gets an image that can then be painted on the screen.
Image getImage(URL url, String name)	Gets an image that can then be painted on the screen.
Locale getLocale( )	Gets the locale for the applet.
String getParameter(String name)	Gets the value of the named parameter in the HTML tag.
String[ ][ ] getParameterInfo( )	Gets information about the applet parameters.
void init( )	Called by the browser or applet viewer to allow you to initialize the applet.
boolean isActive( )	Determines whether this applet is active.
static AudioClip newAudioClip(URL url)	Gets an audio clip from the given URL.

(continued)

Table 6.3   Methods of the Applet class (continued).

Method	Does This
void play(URL url)	Plays the audio clip at the specified absolute URL.
void play(URL url, String name)	Plays the audio clip given the URL and a specifier that's relative to it.
void resize(Dimension d)	Requests that this applet be resized.
void resize(int width, int height)	Requests that this applet be resized.
void setStub(AppletStub stub)	Sets this applet's stub.
void showStatus(String msg)	Requests that the string be displayed in the status window of the applet.
void start( )	Called by the browser or applet viewer to tell the applet it should start execution.
void stop( )	Called by the browser or applet viewer to tell the applet it should stop execution.

Let's look at an example. Here, I'll create the applet you saw at the beginning of the chapter that displays the text "Hello from Java!" in the file applet.java. I start by deriving a new class, **applet**, from the **java.applet.Applet** class, like this:

```
import java.applet.Applet;

public class applet extends Applet
{
        .
        .
        .
}
```

To display the message in the applet, I'll use the **paint** method, which the applet inherits from the **Component** class. When an applet is displayed, its **paint** method is called, and you can place the code for drawing the applet in that method. The **paint** method is passed an object of the **Graphics** class, which you'll meet in a few chapters. It's the basis of graphical work in applets. This object supports a method named **drawString**, which I'll use to draw a string of text in the applet. The **Graphics** class is an AWT class, so I'll import AWT classes when I override the default **Applet paint** method:

```
import java.applet.Applet;
import java.awt.*;

public class applet extends Applet
{
```

```
    public void paint(Graphics g)
    {
        .
        .
        .
    }
}
```

Now I customize the overridden **paint** method to draw the text "Hello from Java!" at location (60, 100) in the applet. Applet coordinates are in pixels; therefore, (60, 100) is at 60 pixels from the left edge of the applet and 100 pixels below the bottom of the title bar. Here's the code:

```
import java.applet.Applet;
import java.awt.*;

public class applet extends Applet
{
    public void paint(Graphics g)
    {
        g.drawString("Hello from Java!", 60, 100);
    }
}
```

This new **paint** method draws directly on the surface of the applet. Note that you can also place controls such as buttons and text fields directly on the surface of the applet. You'll see how that works in this chapter as well.

I can compile applet.java into applet.class using javac—and now we've just created an applet. Now it's time to see the applet at work.

6. AWT: Applets, Applications, And Event Handling

Using The **<APPLET>** HTML Tag

"OK," says the Novice Programmer, "I've created an applet and compiled it into a .class file. How do I actually *look* at it?" "You have to use the HTML **<APPLET>** tag," you reply.

When you've created an applet's .class file, you can upload the applet to an ISP (or view it on your own machine) and set its protection (see the introduction to this chapter) so that it may be read. Next, you can create a Web page using the **<APPLET>** tag to display the applet. Here's what the **<APPLET>** tag looks like:

```
<APPLET
    [CODEBASE = URL]
```

```
        CODE = filename
        [ALT = alternateText]
        [NAME = instancename]
        WIDTH = pixels
        HEIGHT = pixels
        [ALIGN = alignment]
        [VSPACE = pixels]
        [HSPACE = pixels]
>
[<PARAM NAME = name VALUE = value>]
        .
        .
        .
[<PARAM = NAME name VALUE = value>]
</APPLET>
```

Here are the attributes of the **<APPLET>** tag:

- **CODEBASE**—The URL that specifies the directory in which the applet code is to be found.
- **CODE**—The name of the applet file, including the extension .class.
- **ALT**—The text to be displayed if a browser supports applets but cannot run this one for some reason.
- **NAME**—The name of the applet in the Web browser. Applets must be given names if you want other applets to be able to find and interact with them.
- **WIDTH**—The width of the space reserved for the applet.
- **HEIGHT**—The height of the space reserved for the applet.
- **ALIGN**—Specifies the alignment of the applet: **LEFT**, **RIGHT**, **TOP**, **BOTTOM**, **MIDDLE**, **BASELINE**, **TEXTTOP**, **ABSMIDDLE**, or **ABSBOTTOM**.
- **VSPACE**—The space allocated above and below the applet.
- **HSPACE**—The space allocated to the right and left around the applet.
- **PARAM NAME**—The name of a parameter to pass to the applet.
- **PARAM VALUE**—The value of a parameter.

Here's a Web page, applet.html, that displays the applet created in the previous topic (note that the only required attributes are the **CODE**, **WIDTH**, and **HEIGHT** attributes):

```
<HEAD>
<TITLE>APPLET</TITLE>
</HEAD>
```

```
<BODY>
<HR>
<CENTER>
<APPLET
    CODE=applet.class
    WIDTH=200
    HEIGHT=200
>
</APPLET>
</CENTER>
<HR>
</BODY>
</HTML>
```

In this case, I'm not specifying a code base, so I place applet.class in the same directory as applet.html. This Web page, as opened in Netscape Navigator, appears in Figure 6.1.

You can also use the Sun appletviewer, which comes with Java, to view the applet. You open the Web page like this:

```
C:\>appletviewer applet.html
```

The result appears in Figure 6.2. The appletviewer always supports the latest version of Java, so if your Web browser doesn't, and you don't want to install the Java plug-in, you can always use the appletviewer to test your applets.

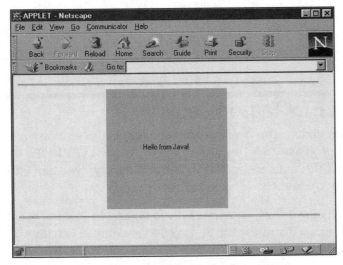

Figure 6.1   An applet at work in Netscape Navigator.

Figure 6.2   An applet at work in the appletviewer.

Handling Non-Java Browsers

"Uh-oh," says the Novice Programmer, "there's a problem. Some users are using a slightly nonstandard Web browser named *SuperWildcat14b*...." "That does sound slightly nonstandard," you say. "And," the NP continues, "it doesn't support Java. Is there any way of informing the users that they're missing something?" "There sure is," you say. "Pull up a chair and we'll go through it."

If you enclose text inside an **<APPLET>** tag, that text will be displayed if the Web browser does not support Java. For example, here's how you might alert users that they're missing your applet:

```
<APPLET code = "applet.class" width = 100 height = 100>
Sorry, you don't have Java, so you can't see my beautiful applet.
</APPLET>
```

Embedding <APPLET> Tags In Code

The Novice Programmer sighs. "I've been writing applets, and it's always a little bit of a pain." "What is?" you ask. "Writing a Web page with an **<APPLET>** tag to test the applet out—isn't there an easier way?" "Sure," you say, "you can embed the **<APPLET>** tag directly in the source code file."

The developers at Sun realized that sometimes it's annoying to have to create a Web page to test an applet, so if you use the Sun appletviewer, you can now place an **<APPLET>** tag directly into the applet's .java file in a comment, like this:

```
import java.applet.Applet;
import java.awt.*;
import java.awt.event.*;

/*
<APPLET
    CODE=applet.class
    WIDTH=200
    HEIGHT=200 >
</APPLET>
*/

import java.applet.Applet;
import java.awt.*;

public class applet extends Applet
{
    public void paint(Graphics g)
    {
        g.drawString("Hello from Java!", 60, 100);
    }
}
```

After creating the .class file, you can now start the appletviewer with the .java file directly:

```
C:\>appletviewer applet.html
```

Using The **init, start, stop, destroy, paint,** And **update** Methods

The Novice Programmer is back and says, "My browser has gone all wacky—it draws my applets in gray!" "That's the default for many Web browsers," you say. "However, you can change that by adding some initialization code to your applet in the **init** method."

Here are a number of important applet methods you should know about:

- *init*—The first method to be called; it's called only once. You initialize the applet here.

- *start*—Called after **init**. This method is called each time an applet appears again on the screen. That is, if the user moves to another page and then comes back, the **start** method is called again.

- **stop**—Called when the browser moves to another page. You can use this method to stop additional execution threads your applet may have started.

- **destroy**—Called when the applet is about to be removed from memory. You can perform cleanup here.

- **paint**—Called when the applet is to be redrawn. This method is passed an object of the **Graphics** class, and you can use that object's methods to draw in the applet.

- **update**—Called when a portion of the applet is to be redrawn. The default version fills the applet with the background color before redrawing the applet, which can lead to flickering when you're performing animation, in which case you would override this method.

You can override these methods to customize them as you like. I've already overridden the **paint** method to draw a string of text; here I override the **init** method to change the background of the applet to white, using the applet **setBackground** method and passing it the **white** field of the Java **Color** class. This applet also provides a skeletal implementation of the other methods listed previously. Here's the code:

```java
import java.applet.Applet;
import java.awt.*;

/*
<APPLET
    CODE=applet.class
    WIDTH=200
    HEIGHT=200 >
</APPLET>
*/

public class applet extends Applet
{
    public void init()
    {
        setBackground(Color.white);
    }

    public void start()
    {
    }

    public void paint(Graphics g)
    {
```

```
        g.drawString("Hello from Java!", 60, 100);
    }

    public void stop()
    {
    }

    public void destroy()
    {
    }
}
```

The **init** method is a very useful one, and it's commonly overridden because it lets you initialize your applet. In this case, I've changed the background color from gray (the default in many browsers) to white. Applets excel at graphics; the next topic provides an overview of handling graphics in applets.

Drawing Graphics In Applets

You'll learn much more about drawing in applets in a few chapters, but it's worth covering some of the graphics methods you'll use here:

- *paint*—Called when the applet is to be redrawn.
- *repaint*—Call this method to force the applet to be painted.
- *drawString*—Draws a string of text.
- *setBackground*—Sets the background color.
- *setForeground*—Sets the foreground (drawing) color.
- *draw3DRect*—Draws a 3D rectangle.
- *drawBytes*—Draws text, given a byte array.
- *drawImage*—Draws an image.
- *drawOval*—Draws an oval (including circles).
- *drawPolyLine*—Draws a line with multiple segments.
- *drawRoundRect*—Draws a rounded rectangle.
- *drawArc*—Draws an arc.
- *drawChars*—Draws text, given a character array.
- *drawLine*—Draws a line.

- **drawPolygon**—Draws a polygon.
- **drawRect**—Draws a rectangle.

Two methods that are particularly worth noticing are the **paint** method, in which you paint the applet, and the **repaint** method, which forces the **paint** method to be called.

Using The Java Browser Plug-In

"Hey," says the Novice Programmer, "I have a problem. I'm using the big two Web browsers, but they don't support the latest Java features. What can I do?" "There's an easy solution," you say. "Use the Java plug-in."

The Java plug-in lets you run the latest Java version applets in Netscape Navigator and Microsoft Internet Explorer by implementing the Java Runtime Environment as a plug-in for Netscape and an ActiveX control for Internet Explorer. You can get the plug-in from **http://java.sun.com/ products/plugin**. It's also installed automatically when you install the JDK.

To use Web pages with the plug-in, you need to convert their HTML first, using the Sun HTML Converter, which you can also get at **http://java.sun.com/ products/ plugin**. The HTML Converter is a Java .class file that you run on HTML pages to convert the **<APPLET>** tag to use the plug-in. You can see the HTML Converter in Figure 6.3.

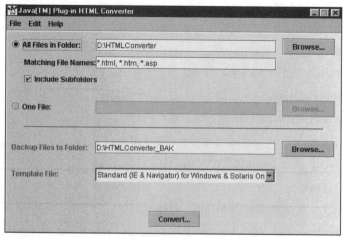

Figure 6.3   The Sun HTML Converter.

To convert a Web page to use the plug-in, you select an HTML file or files in the HTML Converter and click the Convert... button. The Converter will change an **<APPLET>** tag such as

```
<APPLET code=adder.class width=200 height=200></APPLET>
```

into something like this:

```
<!--"CONVERTED_APPLET"-->
<!-- CONVERTER VERSION 1.0 -->
<OBJECT classid="clsid:8AD9C840-044E-11D1-B3E9-00805F499D93"
WIDTH = 200 HEIGHT = 200  codebase="http://java.sun.com/products/plugin/1.2/
jinstall-12-
win32.cab#Version=1,2,0,0">
<PARAM NAME = CODE VALUE = adder.class >

<PARAM NAME="type" VALUE="application/x-java-applet;version=1.2">
<COMMENT>
<EMBED type="application/x-java-applet;version=1.2" java_CODE =
adder.class WIDTH = 200 HEIGHT = 200
pluginspage="http://java.sun.com/products/plugin/1.2/plugin-
install.html"><NOEMBED></COMMENT>

</NOEMBED></EMBED>
</OBJECT>

<!--
<APPLET  CODE = adder.class WIDTH = 200 HEIGHT = 200 >


</APPLET>
-->
<!--"END_CONVERTED_APPLET"-->
```

The new HTML file will use the Java plug-in instead of the browser's default Java Virtual Machine. For example, Figure 6.4 shows the Swing TicTacToe demo applet at **http://192.9.48.9/products/plugin /1.2.2/demos/applets/TicTacToe/ example1.html** in Internet Explorer.

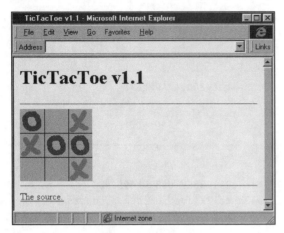

Figure 6.4   Using the Java plug-in.

Reading Parameters In Applets

The Big Boss appears, chomping on a cigar, and says, "We need to personalize the greeting in our applet by customer." "But there are thousands of customers," you say. "We can't recompile the applet for each one and store each new version on the Web site." "What do you suggest?" the BB asks.

What will you say?

You can pass parameters to applets in the **<APPLET>** tag, and the applet code can read the values of those parameters, which means that to customize the applet, you only need to supply different parameters in the **<APPLET>** tag. To actually get the value of a parameter, you use the **Applet** class's **getParameter** method, passing it the name of the parameter as specified in the **<PARAM>** tag. The **getParameter** method will return the value of the parameter that was set in the **<PARAM>** tag.

Here's an example in which I pass a parameter named **string** to an applet; the value of this parameter is the text that the applet should display. Here's how this looks in code:

```
import java.applet.Applet;
import java.awt.*;

/*
<APPLET
    CODE=applet.class
```

```
    WIDTH=200
    HEIGHT=200 >
    <PARAM NAME = string VALUE = "Hello from Java!">
</APPLET>
*/


public class applet extends Applet
{
    public void paint(Graphics g)
    {
        g.drawString(getParameter("string"), 60, 100);
    }
}
```

Using Java Consoles In Browsers

"All this **drawString** stuff is OK," the Novice Programmer says, "but what about the Java console? What if I use **System.out.println** in an applet?" "That depends," you say, "on your browser."

Here's an applet that displays a message and uses **System.out.println** to print to the console:

```
import java.applet.Applet;
import java.awt.*;

public class applet extends Applet
{
    public void paint(Graphics g)
    {
        g.drawString("Hello from Java!", 60, 100);
        System.out.println("Hello from Java!");
    }
}
```

If you run this applet with the Sun appletviewer, the applet will open in a separate window, and you'll see "Hello from Java!" in the console window.

Web browsers often have a Java console as well, although you often have to enable them before using them. The way to enable the Java console differs, unfortunately, from browser to browser as well as from version to version. Currently, you enable the Java console in Internet Explorer by selecting View|Internet

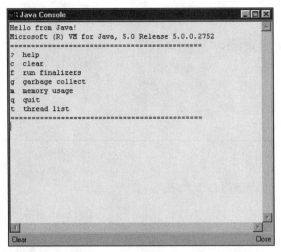

Figure 6.5   Using Internet Explorer's Java console.

Options, clicking the Advanced tab, and selecting the Java Console Enabled check box. Figure 6.5 shows the result of the preceding applet as it appears in the Internet Explorer Java console, which pops up when you print to it.

In Netscape Navigator, you can open the Java console with the Communicator|Java Console menu item.

Adding Controls To Applets: Text Fields

"OK," says the Novice Programmer, "I can draw text in an applet now. But what if I want to let the user *enter* some text?" "For that," you say, "you can use all kinds of text controls, such as text fields."

Text fields are about the most basic controls you can use in AWT, so they provide a good starting point. A text field displays text on a single line and lets the user edit that text. We'll discuss text fields formally in the next chapter, but I'll put them to use here, too, when talking about event handling. Here's a text field example in which I'm creating a text field 20 characters wide in an applet's **init** method (note that I'm importing AWT classes to be able to use text fields):

```
import java.applet.Applet;
import java.awt.*;

/*
<APPLET
```

```
    CODE=applet.class
    WIDTH=200
    HEIGHT=200 >
</APPLET>
*/

public class applet extends Applet
{
    public TextField text1;

    public void init()
    {
        text1 = new TextField(20);
        .
        .
        .
    }
}
```

After creating a new control, you must add it to the applet so that it's displayed.
Here's an example:

```
    public void init()
    {
        text1 = new TextField(20);
        add(text1);
        .
        .
        .
    }
```

The **add** method adds the control to the current layout manager, which decides where the control should be placed (you'll see the details on layout
managers in the next chapter). Now that the text field has been added to the
applet, I can place the text "Hello from Java!" in the text field with the **setText**
method, like this:

```
    public void init()
    {
        text1 = new TextField(20);
        add(text1);
        text1.setText("Hello from Java!");
    }
```

Figure 6.6   Adding a text field to an applet.

The result of this code appears in Figure 6.6, where you can see the text field with the message I've put into it. The user can also edit this text. We'll take a closer look at text fields in the next chapter.

Another basic control is AWT Button control; we'll use buttons and text fields to discuss event handling, so I introduce the Button control in the next topic. You'll learn about buttons and text fields in more detail in the next chapter.

Adding Controls To Applets: Buttons

"I'm ready for the next step," the Novice Programmer reports. "I've added text fields to my applets. What's next?" "Buttons," you say. "Pull up a chair and let's talk about them."

Users can click buttons in your applet to signal that they want to perform some action; for example, you may have a button labeled "Change Color" that, when clicked, changes the background color of the applet using the **setBackground** method. Buttons are supported in the **java.awt.Button** class, which we'll discuss in detail in the next chapter. It's easy enough to add a button to an applet— you do it in much the same way as adding a text field to an applet, as demonstrated in the previous example. Here, I'm creating and adding a button with the caption "Click Here!":

```
public class applet extends Applet
{
    TextField text1;
    Button button1;

    public void init()
    {
```

```
        text1 = new TextField(20);
        add(text1);
        button1 = new Button("Click Here!");
        add(button1);
             .
             .
             .
    }
```

The real trick is to get something to happen when the user clicks on the button, and for that, we'll have to take a look at event handling (see the next topic).

Handling Events

"Hey," says the Novice Programmer, "I've put a button in my applet, but when I click on it, nothing happens. What gives?" "What gives," you say, "is that you have to implement event handling."

Event handling—the process of responding to button clicks, mouse movements, and so on—has become a complex topic in Java. Starting with Java 1.1, event handling changed significantly in Java; the current model is called *delegated event handling*. In this event-handling model, you must specifically *register* with Java if you want to handle a specific event such as a button click. The idea is that performance is improved if only code that needs to handle specific events is informed of those events, and not the rest of your code.

You register for events by implementing an event listener interface. Here are the available event listeners and the kinds of events they handle:

- *ActionListener*—Handles action events such as button clicks.

- *AdjustmentListener*—Handles adjustment events such as scrollbar movements.

- *ComponentListener*—Handles cases in which a component is hidden, moved, resized, or shown.

- *ContainerListener*—Handles the cases in which a component is added or removed from a container.

- *FocusListener*—Handles the case in which a component gains or loses the focus.

- *ItemListener*—Handles the case in which the state of an item changes.

- *KeyListener*—Listens for keyboard events.

- *MouseListener*—Listens for cases in which the mouse is clicked, enters a component, exits a component, or is pressed.

- *MouseMotionListener*—Listens for the case in which the mouse is dragged or moved.

- *TextListener*—Listens for text value changes.

- *WindowListener*—Handles cases in which a window is activated, deactivated, iconified, deiconified, opened, closed, or quit.

Each listener is an interface, and it's up to you to implement the methods of the interface (for more on interfaces, see the previous chapter). Each of these methods is passed a type of event object that corresponds to the kind of event:

- *ActionEvent*—Handles buttons, list double-clicks, menu item clicks.

- *AdjustmentEvent*—Handles scrollbar movements.

- *ComponentEvent*—Handles the case in which a component is hidden, moved, resized, or becomes visible.

- *FocusEvent*—Handles the case in which a component gains or loses the focus.

- *InputEvent*—Handles check box and list item clicks, choice control selections, and checkable menu item selections.

- *KeyEvent*—Handles input from the keyboard.

- *MouseEvent*—Handles the case in which the mouse is dragged, moved, clicked, pressed, released, or enters or exits a component.

- *TextEvent*—Handles the value of a text field or text area being changed.

- *WindowEvent*—Handles the case in which a window is activated, deactivated, iconified, deiconified, opened, closed, or quit.

Standard Event Handling

It's time to put some of what we've covered to work. I'll start by adding a new button with the text "Click Me!" to an applet as well as adding an action listener that will be notified when the button is clicked. To add an action listener to the button, you use the button's **addActionListener** method, passing it an object that implements the methods of the **ActionListener** interface. This object can be an object of the applet's main class or another class. I'll go over both variations here, starting with sending event notifications to the **main** applet class.

TIP: You can also unregister an event listener using the **removeListener** method.

Here's how I add an action listener to a button, sending event notifications to the current applet object (note that I indicate that the **applet** class now implements the **ActionListener** interface):

```
import java.applet.Applet;
import java.awt.*;
import java.awt.event.*;

/*
<APPLET
    CODE=applet.class
    WIDTH=200
    HEIGHT=200 >
</APPLET>
*/

public class applet extends Applet implements ActionListener
{
    TextField text1;
    Button button1;

    public void init()
    {
        text1 = new TextField(20);
        add(text1);
        button1 = new Button("Click Here!");
        add(button1);
        button1.addActionListener(this);
    }
}
```

register the applet class as an actionListener

Now I have to implement the methods of the **ActionListener** interface. It turns out that this interface has only one method, **actionPerformed**, which is passed an object of the **ActionEvent** class when the button is clicked:

```
void actionPerformed(ActionEvent e)
```

ActionEvent objects (which we'll discuss in the next chapter) inherit a method named **getSource** from the **EventObject** class, and this method returns the object that caused the event. That means I can check whether this event was caused by the button, **button1**, and if so, place the text "Hello from Java!" into the text field **text1** this way:

```
import java.applet.Applet;
import java.awt.*;
import java.awt.event.*;

/*
<APPLET
    CODE=applet.class
    WIDTH=200
    HEIGHT=200 >
</APPLET>
*/

public class applet extends Applet implements ActionListener
{
    TextField text1;
    Button button1;

    public void init()
    {
        text1 = new TextField(20);
        add(text1);
        button1 = new Button("Click Here!");
        add(button1);
        button1.addActionListener(this);
    }

    public void actionPerformed(ActionEvent event)
    {
        String msg = new String ("Hello from Java!");
        if(event.getSource() == button1){
            text1.setText(msg);
        }
    }
}
```

This applet appears in Figure 6.7. When you click the button, the text "Hello from Java!" appears in the text field.

The class you register to listen for events doesn't need to be the main applet class (and in fact, the Sun developers originally intended that it not be, although it's now become common practice). We'll take a look at using other classes to listen for events next.

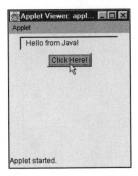

Figure 6.7   Supporting button clicks.

Using Delegated Classes

Here's an example in which I'm creating a new class to implement the **ActionListener** interface. Note that this is a little clumsy, because I want to work with the text field and button controls in the main applet object, so I have to pass and store references to that object in the new class's constructor:

```
import java.applet.Applet;
import java.awt.*;
import java.awt.event.*;

/*
<APPLET
    CODE=applet.class
    WIDTH=200
    HEIGHT=200 >
</APPLET>
*/

public class applet extends Applet
{
    public TextField text1;
    public Button button1;

    public void init()
    {
        text1 = new TextField(20);
        add(text1);
        button1 = new Button("Click Here!");
        add(button1);
        a obj = new a(this);
        button1.addActionListener(obj);
```

```
        }
    }

class a implements ActionListener {
    applet c;

    a(applet appletobject)
    {
        c = appletobject;
    }

    public void actionPerformed(ActionEvent event)
    {
        String msg = new String ("Hello from Java!");
        if(event.getSource() == c.button1){
            c.text1.setText(msg);
        }
    }
}
```

This code works the same as the previous version of this applet, except that internally it uses a new class to handle events, not the main applet class. There are
times when this is useful, such as when you have many events to handle and don't
want to make your main applet class huge.

In addition, there are other ways of determining which object caused the event;
for example, you can use *commands*.

Using Action Commands

Java lets you associate commands with events caused by AWT buttons and menu
items. When working with buttons, the command is just the caption of the button
by default (you'll see how to create custom commands in the next chapter), so
you can determine which button was clicked by looking at its caption (not a good
idea if your program changes captions). You can get the command for a button
with the **getActionCommand** method. Here's how I implement the preceding
applet using commands:

```
import java.applet.Applet;
import java.awt.*;
import java.awt.event.*;

/*
<APPLET
    CODE=applet.class
```

```
    WIDTH=200
    HEIGHT=200 >
</APPLET>
*/

public class applet extends Applet implements ActionListener {

    TextField text1;
    Button button1;

    public void init()
    {
        text1 = new TextField(20);
        add(text1);
        button1 = new Button("Click Here!");
        add(button1);
        button1.addActionListener(this);
    }

    public void actionPerformed(ActionEvent event)
    {
        String msg = new String ("Hello from Java!");
        String caption = event.getActionCommand();

        if(caption.equals("Click Here!")){
            text1.setText(msg);
        }
    }
}
```

This introduces you to the process of handling events the modern way. However, the old, Java 1.0 way still runs in Java, although it's considered deprecated. For the sake of completeness, we'll take a look at it in the next topic.

Handling Events The Old Way

Java 1.0 uses a nondelegated approach to events. In the Java 1.0 event model, you don't need to register to get events, they are just passed to you anyway, and you can handle them in a method named **action**. For example, here's how the previous applet looks using the old event model:

```
import java.applet.Applet;
import java.awt.*;

public class First extends Applet
```

```
{
    TextField text1;
    Button button1;

    public void init()
    {
        text1 = new TextField(20);
        add(text1);
        button1 = new Button("Click Me");
        add(button1);
    }

    public boolean action (Event e, Object o)
    {
        String caption = (String)o;
        String msg = "Hello from Java!";
        if(e.target instanceof Button){
            if(caption == "Click Me"){
                text1.setText(msg);
            }
        }
        return true;
    }
}
```

The problem was that the **action** method often became huge, so the Java designers introduced the delegated event model in which you can send events where you want and are not restricted to an **action** method.

In fact, there's one more way of handling events—by extending components.

Extending Components

If you like being sneaky, you can handle events by deriving new classes from components and overriding the methods in the components that handle events. In fact, this way of doing things ends up much like the Java 1.0 technique of event handling, because all event handling takes place in one method; therefore, it's discouraged. However, I'll cover it here to be complete.

Here's how I implement the applet by extending the **Button** class in a derived class named **newButton**. In this new class, I override the **Button** class's **processActionEvent** method, displaying the text "Hello from Java!" in the applet's text field after calling the **Button** class's **processActionEvent** method:

```
import java.applet.Applet;
import java.awt.*;
import java.awt.event.*;
```

```
/*
<APPLET
    CODE=applet.class
    WIDTH=200
    HEIGHT=200 >
</APPLET>
*/

class newButton extends Button
{
    applet a;

    newButton(applet aref, String s)
    {
        super(s);
        a = aref;
        enableEvents(AWTEvent.ACTION_EVENT_MASK);
    }

    protected void processActionEvent (ActionEvent e)
    {
        super.processActionEvent(e);
        a.text1.setText("Hello from Java!");
    }
}
```

Now all I have to do is to create a new button of this class and add it to the applet:

```
public class applet extends Applet {

    TextField text1;
    Button button1;

    public void init()
    {
        text1 = new TextField(20);
        add(text1);
        button1 = new newButton(this, "Click Here!");
        add(button1);
    }
}
```

That's all it takes; now this applet works like the others.

Using Adapter Classes

"Ugh," says the Novice Programmer, "I understand about the delegated event model that uses listener interfaces, but sometimes it's a pain to have to implement all the methods of an interface when you just want to use one method." "That's true," you say, "which is why Sun introduced adapter classes to make the whole process much easier."

Adapter classes are classes that have already implemented the various event interfaces available. Each method of an interface is implemented as an empty method without any code in an adapter class, and all you need to do is to override the method or methods you want to provide code for.

Let's look at an example. In this case, I'll start with an applet that stores a string to print, which is "Hello from Java!" by default, and displays that string in the **paint** method. Then I'm going to add a mouse listener (which you'll learn more about in the next chapter) to the applet so that when the user clicks on the applet, the message "Hello to Java!" appears. Unlike the **ActionListener** interface, the **MouseListener** interface has five methods that must be implemented. However, I just want to use the **mouseClicked** method to handle mouse clicks, so I'll use the **MouseAdapter** class instead.

I start by adding a class that implements a mouse listener to the program. This class will subclass the **MouseAdapter** class, and I'll call it **ma**:

```
import java.applet.Applet;
import java.awt.*;
import java.awt.event.*;

/*
<APPLET
    CODE=applet.class
    WIDTH=200
    HEIGHT=200 >
</APPLET>
*/

public class applet extends Applet
{
    public String s = "Hello from Java!";

    public void init() {
        addMouseListener(new ma(this));
    }
```

```
    public void paint(Graphics g)
    {
        g.drawString(s, 60, 100);
    }
}
```

I pass an object of the main applet class to the **ma** class's constructor so it can reach the fields in the applet. When the mouse is clicked, the text string in the applet is replaced with the text "Hello to Java!" and then the applet is repainted, causing the new string to appear on the screen:

```
class ma extends MouseAdapter {
    applet a;

    ma(applet appletobject)
    {
        a = appletobject;
    }

    public void mouseClicked(MouseEvent me)
    {
        a.s = "Hello to Java!";
        a.repaint();
    }
}
```

The result of this code appears in Figure 6.8.

Note that this was a little awkward because I had to pass the **applet** object to the **ma** class's constructor so that the class could reach the fields in the **applet** class. On the other hand, inner classes have access to the fields of their enclosing classes, so adapters are often implemented as inner classes. We'll take a look at that next.

Figure 6.8   Supporting button clicks with adapter classes.

Using Anonymous Inner Adapter Classes

You first saw anonymous inner classes in the previous chapter. These classes have the following special format:

```
new SuperType(constructor parameters)
{
    //methods and data
}
```

Here, *SuperType* is the class or interface the anonymous inner class is derived from. In this case, I'm going to derive an anonymous inner class from the **MouseAdapter** class to implement the applet you first saw in the previous topic. Here's how that looks (note that I'm overriding the **mouseClicked** method as I did in the previous topic, but this time I'm using an anonymous inner class, which makes the code much more compact):

```
import java.applet.Applet;
import java.awt.*;
import java.awt.event.*;

/*
<APPLET
    CODE=applet.class
    WIDTH=200
    HEIGHT=200 >
</APPLET>
*/

public class applet extends Applet
{
    public String s = "Hello from Java!";

    public void init() {
        addMouseListener(new MouseAdapter(){
        public void mousePressed(MouseEvent me) {
            s = "Hello to Java!";
            repaint();
        }});
    }

    public void paint(Graphics g)
    {
```

```
        g.drawString(s, 60, 100);
    }
}
```

Creating Windowed Applications

The Novice Programmer appears and says, "OK, I can create applets now, but what about applications that use windows?" "Coming right up," you say.

Unlike writing applets, when you write a windowed application, you're responsible for creating your own window in which to display that application. The most common type of window to use for this purpose is the Java frame window, as supported in the **java.awt.Frame** class. Here's the inheritance diagram for that class (this class is derived from the **java.awt.Window** class, which we'll cover in a few chapters):

```
java.lang.Object
|____java.awt.Component
     |____java.awt.Container
          |____java.awt.Window
               |____java.awt.Frame
```

You'll find the constructors for the **Frame** class in Table 6.4 and its methods in Table 6.5.

Tip: One important thing to note: although the **Applet** class's default layout manager is the flow layout manager, the default layout manager in the **Frame** class is the border layout manager. If you want to use another layout when adding components to a **Frame** window, you'll have to change the layout manager yourself.

Here's an example in which I'll derive a new class, **AppFrame**, from the **Frame** class and customize this new class to display the string "Hello from Java!" to make it look like the applet developed earlier.

Table 6.4   Constructors of the Frame class.

Constructor	Does this
Frame( )	Constructs a new instance of **Frame** that's initially invisible
Frame(String title)	Constructs a new Frame object that's invisible, with the given title

Table 6.5   Methods of the *Frame* class.

Methods	Does this
void addNotify( )	Makes this frame displayable by connecting it to a native screen resource.
protected void finalize( )	Called when the frame is about to be garbage collected.
int getCursorType( )	Deprecated. Replaced by **Component.getCursor( )**.
static Frame[ ] getFrames( )	Gets an array containing all frames created by the application.
Image getIconImage( )	Gets the image to be displayed in the minimized icon.
MenuBar getMenuBar( )	Gets the menu bar.
int getState( )	Gets the state of the frame.
String getTitle( )	Gets the title of the frame.
boolean isResizable( )	Indicates whether this frame is resizable by the user.
protected String paramString( )	Returns the parameter **String** of this frame.
void remove(MenuComponent m)	Removes the specified menu bar from this frame.
void removeNotify( )	Makes this frame undisplayable by removing its connection to its native screen resource.
void setCursor(int cursorType)	Deprecated. Replaced by **Component.setCursor(Cursor)**.
void setIconImage(Image image)	Sets the image to be displayed in the minimized icon for this frame.
void setMenuBar(MenuBar mb)	Sets the menu bar for this frame to the specified menu bar.
void setResizable(boolean resizable)	Sets whether this frame is resizable by the user.
void setState(int state)	Sets the state of this frame.
void setTitle(String title)	Sets the title for this frame to the specified string.

As with the **java.applet.Applet** class, the **java.awt.Frame** class is derived from the **java.awt.Component** class, so I can use the **paint** method to display graphics in the **Frame** class. In fact, the **paint** method will look just as it did in the applet created earlier in the application's code file, app.java. Here's the code:

```
import java.awt.*;
import java.awt.event.*;

class AppFrame extends Frame
{
    public void paint(Graphics g)
    {
        g.drawString("Hello from Java!", 60, 100);
    }
}
```

A **main** method is needed to start the application itself, so I create that method in a new class named **app**:

```
public class app
{
    public static void main(String [] args)
    {
        .
        .
    }
}
```

To display the application's frame window, I create an object of the **AppFrame** class, like this:

```
public class app
{
    public static void main(String [] args)
    {
        AppFrame f = new AppFrame();
        .
        .
        .
    }
}
```

Now I give the frame window object a size of 200×200 pixels and display it on the screen with the **show** method:

```
public class app
{
    public static void main(String [] args)
    {
        AppFrame f = new AppFrame();

        f.setSize(200, 200);

        f.show();
    }
}
```

TIP: *If you don't give a frame window a size before displaying it, all you'll see is a title bar; in graphical user interface (GUI) terms, there will be no client area, which is the area under the title bar in which the application displays itself.*

Figure 6.9   Creating a windowed application.

The results of this code appear in Figure 6.9. As you can see, the message "Hello from Java!" appears in the application, as intended. You can also add controls to this application, just as I did with the button applet earlier in this chapter.

There are a few things to mention here: First, if you launch the application with the java tool (that is, as **java app**), that tool will wait until the application endsbefore returning control to the console. From the user's point of view, the console appears to hang until the application is exited. If you want control to return immediately to the console after the application is launched and displays its own window, use the javaw tool instead. See Chapter 1 for more information.

Another important point is that if you want to distribute your applications to users who don't have the JDK installed, you can use the Java Runtime Environment (JRE). Again, see Chapter 1 for the details.

Finally, it's important to point out that there's no easy way to exit the application in Figure 6.9—clicking the close button has no effect at all. You can press Ctrl+C to end execution of the java tool in the console window, but that's pretty awkward. Instead, you have to handle window-closing events to end the application when its window is closed. We'll take a look at that in the next topic.

Exiting An Application When Its Window Is Closed

"Hey," says the Novice Programmer, "I found it a little difficult to end my first windowed application—clicking the close button didn't do anything." "So how did you end the application?" you ask. "Turned off my computer," the NP says sheepishly.

Java expects you to handle the case in which the user clicks the close button in an application's window yourself (although this has been made easier with Swing windows). To end an application when the user clicks the close button, you must catch window events, which you can do with the **WindowListener** interface. I'll show a compact way of doing that here by modifying the application developed in the previous chapter using the **WindowAdapter** class, which implements the **WindowListener** interface with an empty implementation of each method in **WindowListener**. In this case, I'll use an anonymous inner adapter class (see the topic "Using Anonymous Inner Adapter Classes" in this chapter for more details) and override the **windowClosing** event. In that event's method, I'll add code to exit the application—**System.exit(0)**. This ends the application with an exit code of 0 (which means a normal termination). Here's the code:

```
import java.awt.*;
import java.awt.event.*;

class AppFrame extends Frame
{
    public void paint(Graphics g)
    {
        g.drawString("Hello from Java!", 60, 100);
    }
}

public class app
{
    public static void main(String [] args)
    {
        AppFrame f = new AppFrame();

        f.setSize(200, 200);

        f.addWindowListener(new WindowAdapter() {public void
            windowClosing(WindowEvent e) {System.exit(0);}});

        f.show();
    }
}
```

That's all it takes. Now when you click the application window's close button, the window closes and the application exits.

Applications You Can Run As Applets

The Big Boss arrives and says, "We've got to cut development costs. From now on, all applets must also double as applications." "Hmm," you say, "when do you need that in place?" "Aren't you done yet?" the BB asks.

> If you add a **main** method to an applet, that applet can run as both an applet and an application; Java will ignore the **main** method when it runs as an applet, and it will run the **main** method when it runs as an application.

Here's an example in which I've combined the applet and application developed in this chapter into one program:

```
import java.applet.Applet;
import java.awt.*;
import java.awt.event.*;

/*
<APPLET
    CODE=applet.class
    WIDTH=200
    HEIGHT=200 >
</APPLET>
*/

import java.applet.Applet;
import java.awt.*;

public class applet extends Applet
{
    public static void main(String [] args)
    {
        AppFrame f = new AppFrame();

        f.setSize(200, 200);

        f.addWindowListener(new WindowAdapter() {public void
            windowClosing(WindowEvent e) {System.exit(0);}});

        f.show();
    }

    public void paint(Graphics g)
    {
```

```
            g.drawString("Hello from Java!", 60, 100);
    }
}

class AppFrame extends Frame
{
    public void paint(Graphics g)
    {
        g.drawString("Hello from Java!", 60, 100);
    }
}
```

You can run this code as either an applet or application (the big boss would be proud.)

Chapter 7

AWT: Text Fields, Buttons, Check Boxes, Radio Buttons, And Layouts

In Depth

This chapter is all about a number of important AWT components: text fields, buttons, check boxes, and radio buttons. Now that we're dealing with visible components, we'll also take a look at Java layout managers, which let you arrange the components in an applet or in an application as you like. We'll also take a look at Java panels, which let you assemble components together on one surface and submit the resulting surface to a layout manager. We'll start by taking a look at text fields.

Text Fields

Text fields are the basic text-handling components of the AWT. These components handle a one-dimensional string of text; they let you display text, let the user enter text, allow you to take passwords by masking typed text, allow you to read the text the user has entered, and more. In addition to buttons, these components are the most fundamental AWT components.

Buttons

Buttons provide users with a quick way to start some action—all they have to do is to click them. Every user is familiar with buttons, and we've already taken a look at how buttons work in code when we discussed event handling in the previous chapter. You can give buttons a caption, such as "Click Me!" When the user does click the button, your code is notified, if you've registered to handle events from the button.

Check Boxes

Check boxes are much like buttons, except that they're *dual state*, which means they can appear as selected or unselected. When selected, they display a visual indication of some kind, such as a check mark or an X (the type of visual indication varies by operating system in AWT programming, which is one of the reasons Sun introduced Swing, which can display components with the same look across many operating systems). The user can check a check box to select an option of some kind, such as the items on a sandwich, to enable automatic spell checking, or to enable printing while he or she is doing something else. You use check boxes to let the user select nonexclusive options; for example, both automatic spell checking and background printing may be enabled at the same time. Radio buttons, however, are a different story.

Radio Buttons

You let the user select one of a set of mutually exclusive options by using radio buttons. Only one out of a set of option buttons can be selected at one time; for example, using radio buttons, you can let the user select a printing color or the day of the week. In the AWT, radio buttons are actually a type of check box, and when selected, they display a round dot or a clicked square or some other indication (again, the visual indication depends on the operating system). You use radio buttons in groups, and we'll see how that works in this chapter.

Layouts

So far, we've just added components to applets and applications using the **add** method. This method is actually a method of the default layout manager—the *flow layout manager*. This layout manager is responsible for arranging components in AWT applets, by default. The flow layout manager arranges components much like a word processor might arrange words—across the page and then wrapped to the next line as needed, creating what Sun calls a *flow of components*. You'll see that you can customize flow layouts to some extent. However, the limitations of the flow layout are clear, especially if you're counting on components to maintain some position with respect to the others, because if the user resizes your applet or application, the components will all move around. On the other hand, there are other AWT layout managers (and quite a few new ones in Swing), and we'll cover the AWT grid, border, card, and grid bag layout managers in this chapter.

Why can't you just set where a component goes and then forget it? Novice Java programmers are often frustrated by having to deal with AWT layout managers and want to know why they can't just give the coordinates for the components they want to use and be done with it. In fact, you can, although you're responsible for handling the case in which windows are resized and components should be moved. To position components where you want them, you can indicate that you want no layout manager at all, and then size and locate components as you want them, using **add** to display them like this:

```
setLayout(null);
text1 = new TextField(20);
text1.setSize(200, 50);
text1.setLocation(20, 20);
add(text1);
```

This adds a text field of size (200, 50) at location (20, 20) in a container such as an applet window. So as you can see, you can add components to containers without any layout manager at all, something that's useful to bear in mind if the AWT layouts frustrate you too much.

One very useful AWT container to use with layouts is the Panel component. You can arrange components in a panel and then add the panel, itself, to the layout of an applet or application. You'll see how to do that in this chapter.

That's it. Now that we've reviewed what's in this chapter, it's time to turn to the "Immediate Solutions" section.

Immediate Solutions

Using Text Fields

"Hey," says the Novice Programmer, "I want to let users type in a password, but that darn Johnson keeps standing over peoples' shoulders and watching as they type their passwords." "That's easily fixed," you say. "Just set the echo character of the text field to an asterisk or some similar character. Problem solved!"

You first saw and used text fields in the previous chapter; these components can display a single line of text, and the user can edit that text. Here's the inheritance diagram for the text field class, **TextField**:

```
java.lang.Object
|____java.awt.Component
      |____java.awt.TextComponent
            |____java.awt.TextField
```

You can find the constructors of the **TextField** class in Table 7.1 and its methods in Table 7.2.

Let's look at an example. In this case, I'll create a password text field that will display an asterisk (*) each time the user types a character. You may be wondering how you can read the typed password in the text field. The answer is by using the text field's **getText** method, which the text field inherits from the **Component** class. In fact, I'll add a second text field to this program and display the

Table 7.1 Constructors of the TextField class.

Constructor	Does This
TextField( )	Constructs a new text field
TextField(int columns)	Constructs a new, empty text field with the indicated number of columns
TextField(String text)	Constructs a new text field with the indicated text
TextField(String text, int columns)	Constructs a new text field initialized with the indicated text and with the indicated number of columns

Table 7.2   Methods of the TextField class.

Method	Does This
void addActionListener (ActionListener l)	Adds the indicated action listener to receive events.
void addNotify( )	Creates the TextField object's peer.
boolean echoCharIsSet( )	Indicates whether the text field has a character set to use for echoing.
int getColumns( )	Gets the number of columns in the text field.
char getEchoChar( )	Gets the character to be used for echoing.
Dimension getMinimumSize( )	Gets the minimum dimensions for the text field.
Dimension getMinimumSize (int columns)	Gets the minimum dimensions for a text field with the indicated number of columns.
Dimension getPreferredSize( )	Gets the preferred size of the text field.
Dimension getPreferredSize (int columns)	Gets the preferred size of the text field with the indicated number of columns.
Dimension minimumSize( )	Deprecated. Replaced by **getMinimumSize( )**.
Dimension minimumSize(int columns)	Deprecated. Replaced by **getMinimumSize(int)**.
protected String paramString( )	Gets the parameter string representing the state of the text field.
Dimension preferredSize( )	Deprecated. Replaced by **getPreferredSize( )**.
Dimension preferredSize(int columns)	Deprecated. Replaced by **getPreferredSize(int)**.
protected void processActionEvent (ActionEvent e)	Processes events occurring in the text field by sending them to ActionListener objects.
protected void processEvent (AWTEvent e)	Processes events in the text field.
void removeActionListener (ActionListener l)	Removes the indicated action listener so that it no longer receives events.
void setColumns(int columns)	Sets the number of columns in the text field.
void setEchoChar(char c)	Sets the echo character for the text field.
void setEchoCharacter(char c)	Deprecated. Replaced by **setEchoChar(char)**.
void setText(String t)	Sets the text in this text field to the indicated text.

password in that text field when the user presses the Enter key. I start by adding two text fields, each 30 characters wide:

```
import java.applet.Applet;
import java.awt.*;
import java.awt.event.*;
```

```
/*
<APPLET
    CODE=password.class
    WIDTH=200
    HEIGHT=200 >
</APPLET>
*/

public class password extends Applet implements ActionListener
{
    public TextField text1;
    public TextField text2;

    public void init()
    {
        text1 = new TextField(30);
        add(text1);
        text2 = new TextField(30);
        add(text2);
            .
            .
            .
```

Next, I set the echo character in **text1** (the password text field) to * and add an action listener to that text field:

```
    public void init()
    {
        text1 = new TextField(30);
        add(text1);
        text2 = new TextField(30);
        add(text2);

        text1.setEchoChar('*');
        text1.addActionListener(this);
    }
```

When the user presses Enter, the **actionPerformed** method is called, so I override that method to set the text in the second text field to the text in the password component:

```
    public void actionPerformed(ActionEvent e)
    {
        if(e.getSource() == text1){
            text2.setText(text1.getText());
        }
    }
```

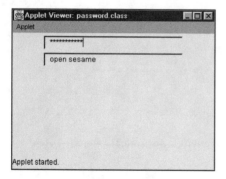

Figure 7.1   Reading passwords in text fields.

The result of this code appears in Figure 7.1. When the user types a password in the top text field and presses Enter, that password appears in the lower text field (not exactly what you'd call high security).

You can find this example on this book's CD in the file password.java.

TIP: Another useful text field method is **getSelectedText,** which lets you get the selected text in a text field.

Using Labels

AWT labels are much like AWT text fields, except that the user can't edit the text in them. You can use labels to present noneditable text, or, as their name implies, to *label* other components. Here's the inheritance diagram for the **Label** class:

```
java.lang.Object
|____java.awt.Component
     |____java.awt.Label
```

You can find the **Label** class's constructors in Table 7.3 and its methods in Table 7.4.

Table 7.3   Constructors of the Label class.

Constructor	Does This
Label( )	Constructs an empty label
Label(String text)	Constructs a new label with the specified string of text, left justified
Label(String text, int alignment)	Constructs a new label that presents the specified string of text with the specified alignment

Table 7.4   Methods of the *Label* class.

Method	Does This
void addNotify( )	Creates the peer for this label
int getAlignment( )	Gets the current alignment of this label
String getText( )	Gets the text of this label
protected String paramString( )	Returns the parameter string representing the state of this label
void setAlignment(int alignment)	Sets the alignment for this label to the specified alignment
void setText(String text)	Sets the text for this label to the specified text

You can justify the text in a label by passing the fields **Label.LEFT**, **Label.CENTER**, and **Label.RIGHT** to the label's constructor. Here's an example that creates three labels with the various possible text justifications:

```
import java.applet.Applet;
import java.awt.*;
import java.awt.event.*;

/*
<APPLET
    CODE=label.class
    WIDTH=200
    HEIGHT=200 >
</APPLET>
*/

public class label extends Applet
{
    Label label1;
    Label label2;
    Label label3;

    public void init()
    {
        label1 = new Label("Hello from Java!", Label.LEFT);
        add(label1);
        label2 = new Label("Hello from Java!", Label.CENTER);
        add(label2);
        label3 = new Label("Hello from Java!", Label.RIGHT);
        add(label3);
    }
}
```

Figure 7.2   Justifying text in a label.

The result of this applet appears in Figure 7.2. This example is in the file label.java on the CD.

Using Buttons

"I want to let users interact with my program," says the Novice Programmer. "I want to let them indicate what they want to do with just a click of the mouse, I want them to be able to select an action quickly and easily, I want...." "Buttons," you say. "What you want are buttons." "Right," replies the NP.

Every GUI user is familiar with buttons, those elementary controls you click to signal to a program to start some action; for example, you might let the user click on a button to change the background color of an application. Buttons are supported in the **java.awt.Button** class. Here's the lineage of that class:

```
java.lang.Object
|____java.awt.Component
      |____java.awt.Button
```

You'll find the constructors for the **Button** class in Table 7.5 and the methods of this class in Table 7.6.

To handle button events, you use the **ActionListener** interface, as you saw in the previous chapter. This interface has only one method, **actionPerformed**, which is passed an object of the **ActionEvent** class when the button is clicked:

```
void  actionPerformed(ActionEvent e)
{
      .
      .
      .
}
```

Table 7.5   Constructors of the *Button* class.

Constructor	Does This
Button( )	Constructs a button without any label
Button(String label)	Constructs a button with the indicated label

Table 7.6   Methods of the *Button* class.

Method	Does This
void addActionListener (ActionListener l)	Adds the indicated action listener to receive events from the button
void addNotify( )	Creates the peer of the button
String getActionCommand( )	Gets the command of the event caused by the button
String getLabel( )	Gets the label of the button
protected String paramString( )	Gets the parameter string representing the state of the button
protected void processActionEvent (ActionEvent e)	Processes action events occurring on the button by sending them to any registered ActionListener objects
protected void processEvent (AWTEvent e)	Processes events in the button
void removeActionListener (ActionListener l)	Removes the action listener so that it no longer receives events from the button
void setActionCommand (String command)	Sets the command name for the action event caused by the button
void setLabel(String label)	Sets the button's label to the indicated string

Here's the inheritance diagram of the **ActionEvent** class:

```
java.lang.Object
|____java.util.EventObject
      |____java.awt.AWTEvent
            |____java.awt.event.ActionEvent
```

You'll find the methods of the **ActionEvent** class in Table 7.7.

Table 7.7   Methods of the *ActionEvent* class.

Method	Does This
String getActionCommand( )	Gets the command string
int getModifiers( )	Gets the modifier keys held down during the event
String paramString( )	Gets a parameter string identifying the event

7. AWT: Text Fields, Buttons, Check Boxes, Radio Buttons, And Layouts

As you saw in the previous chapter, there are two main ways to determine which button was selected—using the **getSource** method and using commands. We'll take a look at the **getSource** way of doing things first. Here's an example with a button that, when clicked, displays the message "Hello from Java!" in a text field (note that I register an action listener with the button and find out which button was clicked by using the **getSource** method before setting the appropriate text in the text field):

```
import java.applet.Applet;
import java.awt.*;
import java.awt.event.*;

public class button extends Applet implements ActionListener {

/*
<APPLET
    CODE=button.class
    WIDTH=200
    HEIGHT=200 >
</APPLET>
*/

    TextField text1;
    Button button1;

    public void init()
    {
        text1 = new TextField(20);
        add(text1);
        button1 = new Button("Click Here!");
        add(button1);
        button1.addActionListener(this);
    }

    public void actionPerformed(ActionEvent event)
    {
        String msg = new String ("Hello from Java!");
        if(event.getSource() == button1){
            text1.setText(msg);
        }
    }
}
```

The result of this code appears in Figure 7.3. You can find this applet in button.java on the CD.

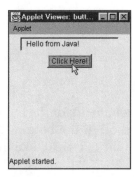

Figure 7.3 Handling button clicks.

You can also use commands with buttons; in the previous chapter, you saw that the default command associated with a button is its caption. However, because captions can change during program execution (for example, by using the **setLabel** method), you should associate a command with the button yourself. You can give a button a command string with the **setActionCommand** method, like this:

```
import java.applet.Applet;
import java.awt.*;
import java.awt.event.*;

/*
<APPLET
    CODE=button2.class
    WIDTH=200
    HEIGHT=200 >
</APPLET>
*/

public class button2 extends Applet implements ActionListener {

    TextField text1;
    Button button1;

    public void init()
    {
        text1 = new TextField(20);
        add(text1);
        button1 = new Button("Click Here!");
        add(button1);
        button1.setActionCommand("buttonClicked");
        button1.addActionListener(this);
```

```
    }
    .
    .
    .
}
```

Now, in the **actionPerformed** method, you can get the command for the button that was clicked by using the **getActionCommand** method. If the button that was clicked is the right one, you can place the message in the text field, like this:

```
public void actionPerformed(ActionEvent event)
{
    String msg = new String ("Hello from Java!");
    String command = event.getActionCommand();

    if(command.equals("buttonClicked")){
        text1.setText(msg);
    }
}
}
```

You can find this applet in button2.java on the CD.

Using Check Boxes

"Now I have another problem," the Novice Programmer says. "I want to let users select what they want on a pizza, so I'd like a button that, when clicked, stays clicked so that the users know what they've already selected." "No problem at all," you say. "Don't use buttons." "No?" the NP asks. "No," you say. "Use check boxes instead."

A check box allows the user to select options; when the user clicks on a check box, a visual indication of some kind, such as a check mark (the indicator varies by operating system when using the AWT), is used to indicate that the option is selected. Clicking the check box again deselects the check box. In AWT, check boxes are supported with the **java.awt.Checkbox** class, which has the following inheritance diagram:

```
java.lang.Object
|____java.awt.Component
      |____java.awt.Checkbox
```

Table 7.8   Constructors of the *Checkbox* class.

Constructor	Does This
Checkbox( )	Creates a check box without a label
Checkbox(String label)	Creates a check box with the indicated label
Checkbox(String label, boolean state)	Creates a check box with the indicated label and sets the state
Checkbox(String label, boolean state, CheckboxGroup group)	Creates a check box in the indicated check box group and sets its state
Checkbox(String label, Checkbox Group group, boolean state)	Constructs a check box with the indicated label in the indicated check box group

Table 7.9   Methods of the *Checkbox* class.

Method	Does This
void addItemListener(ItemListener l)	Adds the indicated item listener to the check box
void addNotify( )	Creates the peer of the check box
CheckboxGroup getCheckboxGroup( )	Gets the check box's group
String getLabel( )	Gets the label of the check box
Object[ ] getSelectedObjects( )	Gets an array (of length1) that contains the check box label (or null if the check box is not selected)
boolean getState( )	Determines whether the check box is in the selected or deselected state
protected String paramString( )	Gets a parameter string representing the state of the check box
protected void processEvent (AWTEvent e)	Processes events in the check box
protected void processItemEvent (ItemEvent e)	Processes item events occurring in the check box by sending them to any registered ItemListener objects
void removeItemListener (ItemListener l)	Removes the indicated item listener so that the item listener no longer gets item events from the check box
void setCheckboxGroup (CheckboxGroup g)	Sets the check box's group to the given check box group
void setLabel(String label)	Sets the check box's label to the string
void setState(boolean state)	Sets the state of the check box to the given state

You can find the constructors for the **Checkbox** class in Table 7.8 and the methods of this class in Table 7.9. Note, in particular, that you can set the state of a check box with **setState** and get the state with **getState**.

Here's an example in which I add four check boxes to an applet, and when the user clicks on a check box, I indicate which check box was clicked by using a text field. Note that check boxes do not use the **ActionListener** interface as buttons do; instead, they use the **ItemListener** interface, which is set up to handle components that can be selected or deselected. The **ItemListener** interface has only one method, **itemStateChanged**, which is passed a parameter of class **ItemEvent**:

```
void itemStateChanged(ItemEvent e)
```

You can find the methods of the **ItemEvent** class in Table 7.10.

Here's how I add the check boxes to an applet and add an **ItemListener** to each one:

```
import java.applet.Applet;
import java.awt.*;
import java.awt.event.*;

/*
<APPLET
    CODE=checks.class
    WIDTH=200
    HEIGHT=200 >
</APPLET>
*/

public class checks extends Applet implements ItemListener {

    Checkbox checkbox1, checkbox2, checkbox3, checkbox4;
    TextField text1;

    public void init()
    {
        checkbox1 = new Checkbox("1");
        add(checkbox1);
        checkbox1.addItemListener(this);
        checkbox2 = new Checkbox("2");
```

Table 7.10   Methods of the *ItemEvent* class.

Method	Does This
Object getItem( )	Gets the item affected by the event
ItemSelectable getItemSelectable( )	Gets the originator of the event
int getStateChange( )	Gets the type of state change (that is, selected or deselected)
String paramString( )	Gets a parameter string matching this item event

```
        add(checkbox2);
        checkbox2.addItemListener(this);
        checkbox3 = new Checkbox("3");
        add(checkbox3);
        checkbox3.addItemListener(this);
        checkbox4 = new Checkbox("4");
        add(checkbox4);
        checkbox4.addItemListener(this);
        text1 = new TextField(20);
        add(text1);
    }
```

Now I override the **itemStateChanged** method, determining which check box was clicked by using the **ItemEvent** object's **getItemSelectable** method:

```
public void itemStateChanged(ItemEvent e)
{
    if(e.getItemSelectable() == checkbox1){
        text1.setText("Check box 1 clicked!");
    } else if(e.getItemSelectable() == checkbox2){
        text1.setText("Check box 2 clicked!");
    } else if(e.getItemSelectable() == checkbox3){
        text1.setText("Check box 3 clicked!");
    } else if(e.getItemSelectable() == checkbox4){
        text1.setText("Check box 4 clicked!");
    }
}
```

Note that you can also use the **ItemEvent** object's **getStateChanged** method to determine whether a check box is selected or deselected. This method returns **Checkbox.SELECTED** or **Checkbox.DESELECTED**. And, of course, you can use the check box's **getState** method to make the same determination. You can also set the state of the check box with the **setState** method.

The result of this applet appears in Figure 7.4. You can find this applet in checks.java on the CD.

Because it's tedious to have so many **if** statements in the **if-else** ladder in the preceding code, I can just display the check box that was clicked by getting its label directly, like this:

```
import java.applet.Applet;
import java.awt.*;
import java.awt.event.*;
```

Figure 7.4   Handling check box clicks.

```
/*
<APPLET
    CODE=checks.class
    WIDTH=200
    HEIGHT=200 >
</APPLET>
*/

public class checks2 extends Applet implements ItemListener {

    Checkbox checkbox1, checkbox2, checkbox3, checkbox4;
    TextField text1;

    public void init()
    {
        checkbox1 = new Checkbox("1");
        add(checkbox1);
        checkbox1.addItemListener(this);
        checkbox2 = new Checkbox("2");
        add(checkbox2);
        checkbox2.addItemListener(this);
        checkbox3 = new Checkbox("3");
        add(checkbox3);
        checkbox3.addItemListener(this);
        checkbox4 = new Checkbox("4");
        add(checkbox4);
        checkbox4.addItemListener(this);
        text1 = new TextField(20);
        add(text1);
    }
```

```
    public void itemStateChanged(ItemEvent e)
    {
        text1.setText("Check box " +
            ((Checkbox) e.getItemSelectable()).getLabel() + " clicked!");
    }
}
```

This new version of the applet appears in checks2.java on the CD. There's another kind of check box you can use—radio buttons—and we'll take a look at them in the next topic.

Using Radio Buttons

"Uh-oh," says the Novice Programmer, "I have another problem. I put some check boxes in my program so the users could select the day of the week, but one user selected Wednesday *and* Friday." "Well," you say, "you should use radio buttons, not check boxes to display exclusive options such as the day of the week."

In AWT programming, radio buttons are a special kind of check box, and you use radio buttons in groups. Only one radio button in a group may be selected at one time; when the user selects one radio button in a group, the others in the group are automatically deselected.

When you add check boxes to a check box *group*, they become radio buttons automatically. The AWT supports check box groups with the **CheckboxGroup** class. This class has only one constructor, **CheckboxGroup**, which takes no parameters, and you'll find the methods of this class in Table 7.11. Note that because radio buttons are really check boxes, you can use **Checkbox** methods with them, such as **getState** and **setState**.

Table 7.11   Methods of the CheckboxGroup class.

Method	Does This
Checkbox getCurrent( )	Deprecated. Replaced by **getSelectedCheckbox( )**.
Checkbox getSelectedCheckbox( )	Gets the current selected check box in this check box group.
void setCurrent(Checkbox box)	Deprecated. Replaced by **setSelectedCheckbox(Checkbox)**.
void setSelectedCheckbox (Checkbox box)	Sets the currently selected check box in this group.
String toString( )	Returns a string representing the check box group, including the value of its current selection.

Note, for example, that you can determine which radio button is selected in a group with the **CheckboxGroup** class's **getSelectedCheckbox** method, and you can set which one is selected with the **setSelectedCheckbox** method.

Here's an example in which I create a check box group named **radios**, and I add four radio buttons to that group. You add a radio button to a check box group by adding the group as a parameter in a check box's constructor, which turns the check box into a radio button. Here's what this looks like:

```
import java.applet.Applet;
import java.awt.*;
import java.awt.event.*;

/*
<APPLET
    CODE=radios.class
    WIDTH=200
    HEIGHT=200 >
</APPLET>
*/

public class radios extends Applet implements ItemListener {

    CheckboxGroup radios;
    Checkbox radio1, radio2, radio3, radio4;
    TextField text1;

    public void init()
    {
        radios = new CheckboxGroup();

        radio1 = new Checkbox("1", false, radios);
        add(radio1);
        radio1.addItemListener(this);

        radio2 = new Checkbox("2", false, radios);
        add(radio2);
        radio2.addItemListener(this);

        radio3 = new Checkbox("3", false, radios);
        add(radio3);
        radio3.addItemListener(this);

        radio4 = new Checkbox("4", false, radios);
        add(radio4);
        radio4.addItemListener(this);
```

```
        text1 = new TextField(20);
        add(text1);
    }
```

Note that I've added an **ItemListener** to each radio button, so I can implement the **ItemListener** interface and the **itemStateChanged** method to indicate which radio button was clicked, like this:

```
    public void itemStateChanged(ItemEvent e)
    {
        text1.setText("Radio button " +
            ((Checkbox) e.getItemSelectable()).getLabel() + " clicked!");
    }
}
```

The result of this code appears in Figure 7.5, and you'll find this applet on the CD as radios.java.

Now that we're working with components in visual programs, it's time to give some consideration as to how those components are arranged, and I'll do that in the next few topics.

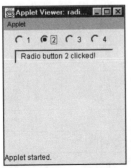

Figure 7.5   Handling radio button clicks.

Flow Layouts

"Uh-oh," says the Novice Programmer, "Java's gone all wacky again." "What's it done this time?" you ask. The NP says, "Well, I'm creating a multiplying calculator, and I want all the text fields to be stacked vertically, but they keep rearranging themselves into rows." "That's because you're using a flow layout," you say.

Java has a number of AWT layout managers that handle how components are displayed in containers, and you can install those layout managers into those containers. By default, applets use the flow layout manager, which arranges components like

Table 7.12   Constructors of the FlowLayout class.

Constructor	Does This
FlowLayout( )	Constructs a new flow layout with centered alignment. The horizontal and vertical gap will be 5 pixels.
FlowLayout(int align)	Constructs a new flow layout with the given alignment. The horizontal and vertical gap will be 5 pixels.
FlowLayout (int align, int hgap, int vgap)	Creates a new flow layout manager with the given alignment and the given horizontal and vertical gaps between components.

Table 7.13   Methods of the FlowLayout class.

Method	Does This
void addLayoutComponent (String name, Component comp)	Adds the specified component to the layout
int getAlignment( )	Gets the alignment for the layout
int getHgap( )	Gets the horizontal gap between components
int getVgap( )	Gets the vertical gap between components
void layoutContainer(Container target)	Lays out the container
Dimension minimumLayoutSize (Container target)	Returns the minimum dimensions needed to lay out the components in the target container
Dimension preferredLayoutSize (Container target)	Returns the preferred dimensions for the layout given the components in the target container
voidremoveLayoutComponent (Component comp)	Removes the component from the layout
void setAlignment(int align)	Sets the alignment
void setHgap(int hgap)	Sets the horizontal gap between components
void setVgap(int vgap)	Sets the vertical gap between components
String toString( )	Returns a string representation of this FlowLayout object

text in a word processor, including wrapping them to the next line. The constructors of the **FlowLayout** class appear in Table 7.12, and its methods appear in Table 7.13.

You do have some control over how the components in a flow layout are arranged; you can specify their alignment using these **FlowLayout** fields:

- *CENTER*—Indicates that each row of components should be centered
- *LEADING*—Indicates that each row of components should be justified to the leading edge of the container
- *LEFT*—Indicates that each row of components should be left-justified

- *RIGHT*—Indicates that each row of components should be right-justified
- *TRAILING*—Indicates that each row of components should be justified to the trailing edge of the container

The default flow layout is to center each component in a row, but here's how I create a new flow layout manager that right-justifies components using the **setLayout** method:

```
import java.applet.Applet;
import java.awt.*;

/*
  <APPLET
    CODE=flow.class
    WIDTH=200
    HEIGHT=200 >
  </APPLET>
*/

public class flow extends Applet {

    TextField text1, text2, text3;

    public void init(){
        setLayout(new FlowLayout(FlowLayout.RIGHT));
        text1 = new TextField(10);
        add(text1);
        text2 = new TextField(10);
        add(text2);
        text3 = new TextField(10);
        add(text3);
    }
}
```

After a few text fields are added to this new flow manager, you can see that they're indeed right-justified, as shown in Figure 7.6.

However, sometimes a flow layout just isn't right. For example, take a look at this applet, which presents the multiplying calculator the Novice Programmer was trying to create:

```
import java.applet.Applet;
import java.awt.*;
import java.awt.event.*;
```

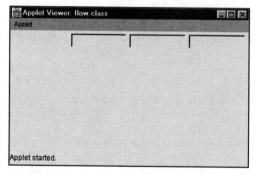

Figure 7.6   Right-justifying components in a flow layout.

```
/*
  <APPLET
     CODE=multiplier.class
     WIDTH=200
     HEIGHT=200 >
  </APPLET>
*/


public class multiplier extends Applet implements ActionListener {

    TextField text1, text2, text3;
    Label multiplylabel;
    Button b1;

    public void init()
    {
        text1 = new TextField(10);
        add(text1);

        multiplylabel = new Label("*");
        add(multiplylabel);

        text2 = new TextField(10);
        add(text2);

        b1 = new Button("=");
        add(b1);
        b1.addActionListener(this);

        text3 = new TextField(10);
        add(text3);
    }
```

```
    public void actionPerformed(ActionEvent e) {
        if(e.getSource() == b1){
            int product = Integer.parseInt(text1.getText()) *
                Integer.parseInt(text2.getText());
            text3.setText(String.valueOf(product));
        }
    }
}
```

The result appears in Figure 7.7, and this applet is in multiplier.java on the CD. As you can see in the figure, the text fields are arranged to suit the flow layout manager, and the result is hardly what the Novice Programmer intended. To fix this situation, we'll take a look at another layout manager, the grid layout manager, next.

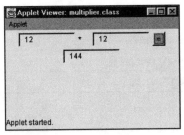

Figure 7.7   A first attempt at a multiplying calculator.

Grid Layouts

"So how do I fix my multiplying calculator? The text fields are all over the place," the Novice Programmer asks. "You have to use a different layout manager," you say, "such as the grid layout manager."

The grid layout manager lets you add components to a container, positioning them in a grid. You tell the grid layout manager what the dimensions of your grid will be—such as five rows and four columns—and when you add components to the layout, they'll be added starting left of the first row. After the first row is filled, components are placed into the first column of the second row, and that row is then filled, and so on. Note that each component is given the same size and dimensions. Here's the inheritance diagram for the grid layout manager:

```
java.lang.Object
|____java.awt.GridLayout
```

*Table 7.14   Constructors of the **GridLayout** class.*

Constructor	Does This
GridLayout( )	Creates a grid layout with one column per component, in one row
GridLayout(int rows, int cols)	Creates a grid layout with the given number of rows and columns
GridLayout(int rows, int cols, int hgap, int vgap)	Creates a grid layout with the given number of rows, columns, and spacing

*Table 7.15   Methods of the **GridLayout** class.*

Method	Does This
void addLayoutComponent (String name, Component comp)	Adds the indicated component to the layout
int getColumns( )	Gets the number of columns in the layout
int getHgap( )	Gets the horizontal gap between components
int getRows( )	Gets the number of rows in the layout
int getVgap( )	Gets the vertical gap between components
void layoutContainer(Container parent)	Lays out the container using the layout
Dimension minimumLayoutSize (Container parent)	Determines the minimum size of the container using this grid layout
Dimension preferredLayoutSize (Container parent)	Determines the preferred size of the container using this grid layout
void removeLayoutComponent (Component comp)	Removes the indicated component from the layout
void setColumns(int cols)	Sets the number of columns in the layout
void setHgap(int hgap)	Sets the horizontal gap between components
void setRows(int rows)	Sets the number of rows in the layout
void setVgap(int vgap)	Sets the vertical gap between components
String toString( )	Gets a string representation of this layout

You'll find the constructors for the **GridLayout** class in Table 7.14 and the methods of this class in Table 7.15.

Here's an example in which I create a grid of five rows and one column by passing those dimensions to the grid layout manager's constructor as **GridLayout(5, 1)**. When I start adding components to this layout, they'll be stacked one on top of the other. Here's how that looks:

```java
import java.applet.Applet;
import java.awt.*;
import java.awt.event.*;

/*
<APPLET
    CODE=multiplier2.class
    WIDTH=200
    HEIGHT=200 >
</APPLET>
*/

public class multiplier2 extends Applet implements ActionListener {

    TextField text1, text2, text3;
    Label multiplylabel;
    Button button1;

    public void init()
    {
        setLayout(new GridLayout(5, 1));

        text1 = new TextField(10);
        add(text1);

        multiplylabel = new Label("*", Label.CENTER);
        add(multiplylabel);

        text2 = new TextField(10);
        add(text2);

        button1 = new Button("=");
        add(button1);
        button1.addActionListener(this);

        text3 = new TextField(10);
        add(text3);
    }

    public void actionPerformed(ActionEvent e)
    {
        if(e.getSource() == button1){
            int product = Integer.parseInt(text1.getText()) *
                Integer.parseInt(text2.getText());
            text3.setText(String.valueOf(product));
        }
    }
}
```

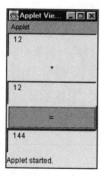

Figure 7.8   A second version of the multiplying calculator.

The result of this code appears in Figure 7.8. As you can see in the figure, the components in this applet are stacked vertically, as intended.

One way of working with layouts is to divide your program's components into panels and to add those panels to the layout. This gives you more control over what controls go where. We'll take a look at panels in the next topic.

Using Panels

The Novice Programmer is still dissatisfied with layout issues and says, "I need finer control in my layout—I've got a lot of components to display." "OK," you say, "you can use Java panels to get that kind of control." "Great! Tell me all about it," replies the NP.

The Java **Panel** class is a container you can use in your layouts. You add components to a panel and then add the panel to a layout. Because panels are containers, you can set their layout managers using the **setLayout** methods. Panels, themselves, are not visual containers—they don't have borders, for example—and exist only to contain components. Here's the inheritance diagram for the **Panel** class:

```
java.lang.Object
|____java.awt.Component
        |____java.awt.Container
                |____java.awt.Panel
```

The constructor for the **Panel** class appears in Table 7.16 and the method of this class appears in Table 7.17.

*Table 7.16   The constructor of the **Panel** class.*

Constructor	Does This
Panel(LayoutManager layout)	Creates a new panel with the specified layout manager

*Table 7.17   The method of the **Panel** class.*

Method	Does This
addNotify( )	Creates the panel's peer

Here's an example in which I derive a new class, **buttonpanel**, from the **Panel** class and add a few buttons to the panel in the **buttonpanel** constructor:

```
import java.applet.Applet;
import java.awt.*;

/*
<APPLET
    CODE=panels.class
    WIDTH=200
    HEIGHT=200 >
</APPLET>
*/

class buttonpanel extends Panel
{
    Button button1, button2, button3, button4;

    buttonpanel()
    {
        button1 = new Button("1");
        add(button1);
        button2 = new Button("2");
        add(button2);
        button3 = new Button("3");
        add(button3);
        button4 = new Button("4");
        add(button4);
    }
}
```

Now I can arrange panels of this new class in a grid layout, like this:

```
public class panels extends Applet {

    buttonpanel panel1, panel2, panel3, panel4, panel5, panel6;

    public void init(){
        setLayout(new GridLayout(2, 3));

        panel1 = new buttonpanel();
        panel2 = new buttonpanel();
        panel3 = new buttonpanel();
        panel4 = new buttonpanel();
        panel5 = new buttonpanel();
        panel6 = new buttonpanel();

        add(panel1);
        add(panel2);
        add(panel3);
        add(panel4);
        add(panel5);
        add(panel6);
    }
}
```

The result of this code appears in Figure 7.9, and you can find the code for this applet in panels.java on the CD. As you can see in this figure, each panel has been added to the grid layout; in this way, using panels gives you finer layout control.

Figure 7.9   Arranging components using panels.

Border Layouts

The Novice Programmer is back and asks, "Are there any more layouts I should know about?" "Of course," you say. "You should know the border layout, for example." The NP asks, "Does that arrange borders?" "Sort of," you say.

The border layout lets you arrange components around the border of a container, which is useful if you want to support, say, scrollbars and scroll a central component. Border layouts are the default in AWT windows, frame windows, and dialog boxes. You indicate where you want a component to go by passing text strings such as "North", "East", and so on to the **BorderLayout** constructor. Here's the inheritance diagram for **BorderLayout**:

```
java.lang.Object
|____java.awt.BorderLayout
```

You can find the constructors of the **BorderLayout** class in Table 7.18 and its methods in Table 7.19.

Table 7.18   Constructors of the *BorderLayout* class.

Constructor	Does This
BorderLayout( )	Constructs a new border layout
BorderLayout(int hgap, int vgap)	Constructs a border layout with the indicated gaps between components

Table 7.19   Methods of the *BorderLayout* class.

Method	Does This
void addLayoutComponent (Component comp, Object constraints)	Adds the component to the layout, using the given constraint object
void addLayoutComponent (String name, Component comp)	Adds the given component with the given name to the layout
int getHgap( )	Gets the horizontal gap between components
float getLayoutAlignmentX (Container parent)	Gets the alignment along the x axis
float getLayoutAlignmentY (Container parent)	Gets the alignment along the y axis
int getVgap( )	Gets the vertical gap between components
void invalidateLayout(Container target)	Invalidates the layout
void layoutContainer(Container target)	Lays out the container

(continued)

Table 7.19   Methods of the *BorderLayout* class (continued).

Method	Does This
Dimension maximumLayoutSize (Container target)	Gets the maximum dimensions for the layout given the components in the given target
Dimension minimumLayoutSize (Container target)	Determines the minimum size of the target using the layout manager
Dimension preferredLayoutSize (Container target)	Determines the preferred size of the target using the layout manager
void removeLayoutComponent (Component comp)	Removes the given component from this layout
void setHgap(int hgap)	Sets the horizontal gap between components
void setVgap(int vgap)	Sets the vertical gap between components
String toString( )	Gets a string representation of this layout

Here's an example in which I create a panel containing a text field and add four buttons around the border of the panel. When the user clicks a button, the applet will indicate which button was clicked on in the text field.

Here's how I create the panel that displays a text field:

```java
import java.applet.Applet;
import java.awt.*;
import java.awt.event.*;

/*
  <APPLET
    CODE=border.class
    WIDTH=200
    HEIGHT=200 >
  </APPLET>
*/

class textPanel extends Panel
{
    TextField Text1;

    textPanel(){
        Text1 = new TextField(30);
        add(Text1);
    }
}
```

Now I create a border layout, placing the text field panel in the center and adding four buttons around the border. You can specify where you want to place a component with strings such as "North", "West", "Center" and so on. Therefore, creating the layout looks like this:

```
public class border extends Applet implements ActionListener
{

    Button button1, button2, button3, button4;
    textPanel Panel1;

    public void init()
    {
        setLayout(new BorderLayout());

        button1 = new Button("1");
        add("North", button1);
        button1.addActionListener(this);

        button2 = new Button("2");
        add("West", button2);
        button2.addActionListener(this);

        button3 = new Button("3");
        add("South", button3);
        button3.addActionListener(this);

        button4 = new Button("4");
        add("East", button4);
        button4.addActionListener(this);

        Panel1 = new textPanel();
        add("Center", Panel1);
        Panel1.Text1.setLocation(0, 0);
    }

    public void actionPerformed(ActionEvent e)
    {
        Panel1.Text1.setText("Button " +
            ((Button) e.getSource()).getLabel() + " clicked.");
    }
}
```

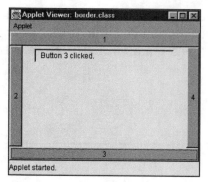

Figure 7.10   Creating a border layout.

The result of this code appears in Figure 7.10. As you can see in this figure, the buttons appear around the perimeter of the central text field panel.

Card Layouts

"So," the Novice Programmer says, "are there any other AWT layouts?" "There sure are," you say, "such as the card layout." "You're making that up," says the NP.

The card layout manager displays the containers you pass to it as *cards*. You give each card a name; then you can move from card to card with the card layout's **show** method. Here's the inheritance diagram for the **CardLayout** class:

```
java.lang.Object
|____java.awt.CardLayout
```

Besides the **show** method, you can also display specific cards using the **first**, **last**, **next**, and **previous** methods of the **CardLayout** class. You'll find the **CardLayout** class's constructors in Table 7.20 and the methods of this class in Table 7.21.

Table 7.20   Constructors of the *CardLayout* class.

Constructor	Does This
CardLayout( )	Creates a new card layout
CardLayout(int hgap, int vgap)	Creates a new card layout with the given horizontal and vertical gaps

Table 7.21   Methods of the *CardLayout* class.

Method	Does This
void addLayoutComponent (Component comp, Object constraints)	Adds the given component to the layout
void addLayoutComponent (String name, Component comp)	Adds the given component with the given name to the layout
void first(Container parent)	Goes to the first card of the container
int getHgap( )	Gets the horizontal gap between components
float getLayoutAlignmentX (Container parent)	Gets the alignment along the x axis
float getLayoutAlignmentY (Container parent)	Gets the alignment along the y axis
int getVgap( )	Gets the vertical gap between components
void invalidateLayout(Container target)	Invalidates the layout
void last(Container parent)	Goes to the last card of the container
void layoutContainer(Container parent)	Lays out the given container using this card layout
Dimension maximumLayoutSize (Container target)	Gets the maximum dimensions for the layout, given the components in the given target container
Dimension minimumLayoutSize (Container parent)	Calculates the minimum size for the given panel
void next(Container parent)	Goes to the next card of the given container
Dimension preferredLayoutSize (Container parent)	Determines the preferred size of the container argument using this card layout
void previous(Container parent)	Goes to the previous card of the given container
void removeLayoutComponent (Component comp)	Removes the given component from the layout
void setHgap(int hgap)	Sets the horizontal gap between components
void setVgap(int vgap)	Sets the vertical gap between components
void show(Container parent, String name)	Goes to the component that was added to the layout with the given name
String toString( )	Gets a string representation of this layout

Here's an example in which I create a panel class, **cardPanel**, that displays a button the user can click to move to the next card and a label to indicate what the present card number is. The constructor for this class takes two parameters: an object of the main applet class, so the applet, itself, can handle button clicks that occur in each panel, and a string representing the current panel's number:

```java
import java.awt.*;
import java.applet.Applet;
import java.awt.event.*;

/*
<APPLET
    CODE=card.class
    WIDTH=200
    HEIGHT=200 >
</APPLET>
*/

class cardPanel extends Panel
{
    Button button;
    Label label;

    cardPanel(card applet, String cardnumber)
    {
        button = new Button("Next card");
        button.addActionListener(applet);
        add(button);
        label = new Label("This is card " + cardnumber);
        add(label);
    }
}
```

In the main applet class, I create three panels of the **cardPanel** class. Then I add them to a card layout, giving them the names "first", "second", and "third":

```java
public class card extends Applet implements ActionListener
{
    int index = 1;
    CardLayout cardlayout;
    cardPanel panel1, panel2, panel3;

    public void init()
    {
```

```
        cardlayout = new CardLayout();
        setLayout(cardlayout);

        panel1 = new cardPanel(this, "one");
        panel2 = new cardPanel(this, "two");
        panel3 = new cardPanel(this, "three");

        add("first", panel1);
        add("second", panel2);
        add("third", panel3);

        cardlayout.show(this, "first");
    }
```

When the user clicks on a button, I can iterate over the available cards using an index value that I increment and check with a **switch** statement:

```
    public void actionPerformed(ActionEvent event)
    {
        switch(++index){
            case 1:
                cardlayout.show(this, "first");
                break;
            case 2:
                cardlayout.show(this, "second");
                break;
            case 3:
                cardlayout.show(this, "third");
                break;
        }
        if(index == 3) index = 0;
        repaint();
    }
}
```

The result appears in Figure 7.11. When the user clicks on the "Next card" button, the applet switches to the next card in the layout, cycling through the cards over and over. That's what a card layout looks like and how it works; you can find this applet in card.java on the CD.

There's one more AWT layout to take a look at—grid bag layouts.

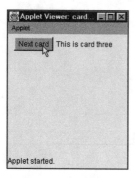

Figure 7.11   Using a card layout.

Grid Bag Layouts

"OK," says the Novice Programmer, "I'm an expert with AWT layouts now." "No you're not," you say. "Not until you master the grid bag layout." The NP asks, "What the heck is a grid bag?"

Grid bag layouts are the most complex and most flexible of AWT layouts, letting you specify more exactly than any of the other AWT layout managers where you want your components to go. Here's the inheritance diagram for the **GridBagLayout** class:

```
java.lang.Object
|_____java.awt.GridBagLayout
```

You can find the constructor of the **GridBagLayoutClass** in Table 7.22 and its methods in Table 7.23.

Table 7.22   Constructor of the GridBagLayout class.

Constructor	Does This
GridBagLayout( )	Creates a grid bag layout manager

Table 7.23   Methods of the GridBagLayout class.

Method	Does This
void addLayoutComponent (Component comp, Object constraints)	Adds the given component to the layout, using the constraint object
void addLayoutComponent (String name, Component comp)	Adds the given component to the layout

(continued)

Table 7.23 Methods of the *GridBagLayout* class (continued).

Method	Does This
protected void AdjustForGravity (GridBagConstraints constraints, Rectangle r)	Adjusts for gravity setting
protected void ArrangeGrid (Container parent)	Arranges the grid in the parent
GridBagConstraints getConstraints (Component comp)	Gets the constraints for the given component
float getLayoutAlignmentX (Container parent)	Gets the alignment along the x axis
float getLayoutAlignmentY (Container parent)	Gets the alignment along the y axis
int[ ][ ] getLayoutDimensions( )	Determines column widths and row heights for the layout grid
protected java.awt.GridBagLayoutIn fo GetLayoutInfo(Container parent, int sizeflag)	Gets the layout constraints
Point getLayoutOrigin( )	Determines the origin of the layout grid
double[ ][ ] getLayoutWeights( )	Determines the weights of the layout grid's columns and rows
protected Dimension GetMinSize (Container parent, java.awt.GridBag LayoutInfo info)	Gets the minimum size of the container
void invalidateLayout(Container target)	Invalidates the layout
void layoutContainer(Container parent)	Lays out the container
Point location(int x, int y)	Determines which cell in the layout grid contains a point
protected GridBagConstraints lookup Constraints(Component comp)	Retrieves the constraints for a given component
Dimension maximumLayoutSize (Container target)	Gets the maximum dimensions for the layout given the components in the container
Dimension minimumLayoutSize (Container parent)	Determines the minimum size of the container using this layout
Dimension preferredLayoutSize (Container parent)	Determines the preferred size of the container using this layout
void removeLayoutComponent (Component comp)	Removes the given component from the layout

(continued)

7. AWT: Text Fields, Buttons, Check Boxes, Radio Buttons, And Layouts

Table 7.23   Methods of the GridBagLayout class (continued).

Method	Does This
void setConstraints(Component comp, GridBagConstraints constraints)	Sets the constraints for the given component in the layout
String toString( )	Gets a string representation of this layout

Adding components to a container using a grid bag layout is something like using a grid layout, except you have more options, such as setting the relative widths and heights of the components. Setting up a grid bag layout is a two-step process: You first configure how you want a component to appear relative to the other components and then you add the component to the layout. You configure components using the **GridBagConstraints** class; the fields of that class appear in Table 7.24, its constructors in Table 7.25, and its method in Table 7.26.

Table 7.24   Fields of the GridBagConstraints class.

Field	Does This
int anchor	Used when the component is smaller than its display area.
static int BOTH	Resizes the component both horizontally and vertically.
static int CENTER	Puts the component in the center of its display area.
static int EAST	Puts the component on the right side of its display area, centered vertically.
int fill	This field is used when the component's display area is larger than the component's requested size.
int gridheight	Indicates the number of cells in a column for the component's display area.
int gridwidth	Indicates the number of cells in a row for the component's display area.
int gridx	Indicates the cell at the left of the component's display area.
int gridy	Indicates the cell at the top of the component's display area.
static int HORIZONTAL	Resizes the component horizontally.
Insets insets	Indicates the external padding of the component.
int ipadx	Indicates the internal x padding of the component.
int ipady	Indicates the internal y padding.

(continued)

*Table 7.24   Fields of the **GridBagConstraints** class* (continued).

Field	Does This
static int NONE	Indicates not to resize the component.
static int NORTH	Puts the component at the top of its display area, centered horizontally.
static int NORTHEAST	Puts the component at the top-right corner of its display area.
static int NORTHWEST	Puts the component at the top-left corner of its display area.
static int RELATIVE	Indicates that this component is the next-to-last component in its column or row or that this component be placed next to the previously added component.
static int REMAINDER	Specifies that this component is the last component in its column or row.
static int SOUTH	Puts the component at the bottom of its display area, centered horizontally.
static int SOUTHEAST	Puts the component at the bottom-right corner of its display area.
static int SOUTHWEST	Puts the component at the bottom-left corner of its display area.
static int VERTICAL	Resizes the component vertically but not horizontally.
double weightx	Specifies how to distribute extra horizontal space.
double weighty	Specifies how to distribute extra vertical space.
static int WEST	Puts the component on the left side of its display area, centered vertically.

*Table 7.25   Constructors of the **GridBagConstraints** class.*

Constructor	Does This
GridBagConstraints( )	Creates a GridBagConstraint object.
GridBagConstraints(int gridx, int gridy, int gridwidth, int gridheight, double weightx, double weighty, int anchor, int fill, Insets insets, int ipadx, int ipady)	Creates a GridBagConstraints object with all fields set to the passed values.

*Table 7.26   Method of the **GridBagConstraints** class.*

Method	Does This
Object clone( )	Creates a copy of this grid bag constraint.

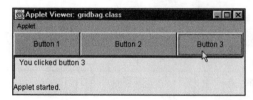

Figure 7.12   Using a grid bag layout.

Let's look at an example of putting a grid bag layout to work. In this example, I'll create the applet you see in Figure 7.12; here, I've put three buttons into the top row of the layout, making the middle button twice as wide as the others, and I added a text field underneath. When the user clicks on a button, the applet reports which button was clicked, as you see in Figure 7.12.

You can specify both x and y constraints for the components you add to a grid bag layout using the **weightx** and **weighty** fields. These values represent the relative weights you want to give to components in the same row or column. In this case, I'll give each component the same y weight but give the second button twice the x weight as the other buttons.

I start by creating a grid bag layout and a constraints object:

```
import java.applet.Applet;
import java.awt.*;
import java.awt.event.*;

/*
<APPLET
    CODE=gridbag.class
    WIDTH=400
    HEIGHT=80 >
</APPLET>
*/

public class gridbag extends Applet implements ActionListener
{
    Button button1, button2, button3;
    TextField text1;

    public void init()
    {
        GridBagLayout gridbag = new GridBagLayout();
        GridBagConstraints constraints = new GridBagConstraints();
        setLayout(gridbag);
```

```
        constraints.weighty = 1;
        constraints.fill = GridBagConstraints.BOTH;
      .
      .
      .
```

Note that I'm setting the constraints object's fill field to **GridBagConstraints.BOTH**, which means the layout manager will expand components in both dimensions to fill them out. Next, I create the first button and add it to the layout, like this:

```
public void init()
{
    GridBagLayout gridbag = new GridBagLayout();
    GridBagConstraints constraints = new GridBagConstraints();
    setLayout(gridbag);
    constraints.weighty = 1;
    constraints.fill = GridBagConstraints.BOTH;

    constraints.weightx = 1;
    button1 = new Button("Button 1");
    gridbag.setConstraints(button1, constraints);
    button1.setActionCommand("button 1");
    add(button1);
    button1.addActionListener(this);
      .
      .
      .
```

This first button has an x weight of 1, but I'll give the next button an x weight of 2, to make it twice as wide as the others in the same row:

```
public void init()
{
    GridBagLayout gridbag = new GridBagLayout();
    GridBagConstraints constraints = new GridBagConstraints();
    setLayout(gridbag);
    constraints.weighty = 1;
    constraints.fill = GridBagConstraints.BOTH;

    constraints.weightx = 1;
    button1 = new Button("Button 1");
    gridbag.setConstraints(button1, constraints);
    button1.setActionCommand("button 1");
    add(button1);
    button1.addActionListener(this);
```

```
        constraints.weightx = 2;
        button2 = new Button("Button 2");
        gridbag.setConstraints(button2, constraints);
        button2.setActionCommand("button 2");
        add(button2);
        button2.addActionListener(this);

        constraints.weightx = 1;
        button3 = new Button("Button 3");
        constraints.gridwidth = GridBagConstraints.REMAINDER;
        gridbag.setConstraints(button3, constraints);
        button3.setActionCommand("button 3");
        add(button3);
        button3.addActionListener(this);

        text1 = new TextField();
        constraints.gridwidth = GridBagConstraints.REMAINDER;
        gridbag.setConstraints(text1, constraints);
        add(text1);
    }
```

All that's left is to handle button clicks, and I do that by displaying the number of the button that was clicked :

```
public void actionPerformed(ActionEvent e)
{
    text1.setText("You clicked " +
        ((Button) e.getSource()).getActionCommand());
}
```

And that's all it takes. Now this code will create the applet you see in Figure 7.12. You can find this example in the file gridbag.java on the CD.

Using Insets And Padding

"Say," says the Novice Programmer, "is there any way of adding a border around the components in a layout?" "There sure is," you say. "You can use insets and padding."

Using insets, you can add space between the container edges and your components. You create insets with the **Insets** class, which has the following constructor:

```
Insets (int top, int left, int bottom, int right)
```

Here's an example in which I add insets of 20 pixels on all edges to the applet developed in the previous topic:

```
public Insets getInsets()
{
    return new Insets(20, 20, 20, 20);
}
```

The result appears in Figure 7.13. As you can see in this figure, there's an inset of 20 pixels all around the components in the container.

You can also pad individual components. You can do this with the **setHgap** and **setVgap** methods in card layouts, flow layouts, border layouts, and grid layouts as well as by using the **ipadx** and **ipady** members in grid bag layouts. For example, I can modify the multiplying calculator I wrote earlier in the chapter to add a vertical space of 10 pixels between components, like this:

```
import java.applet.Applet;
import java.awt.*;
import java.awt.event.*;

/*
<APPLET
    CODE=multiplier2.class
    WIDTH=200
    HEIGHT=200 >
</APPLET>
*/

public class multiplier2 extends Applet implements ActionListener {

    TextField text1, text2, answertext;
    Label multiplylabel;
```

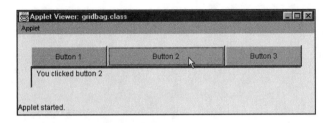

Figure 7.13   Using insets.

```
    Button button1;
    GridLayout g;

    public void init()
    {
        g = new GridLayout(5, 1);
        g.setVgap(10);

        setLayout(g);

        text1 = new TextField(10);
        add(text1);

        multiplylabel = new Label("*", Label.CENTER);
        add(multiplylabel);

        text2 = new TextField(10);
        add(text2);

        button1 = new Button("=");
        add(button1);
        button1.addActionListener(this);

        answertext = new TextField(10);
        add(answertext);
    }

    public void actionPerformed(ActionEvent e)
    {
        if(e.getSource() == button1){
            int product = Integer.parseInt(text1.getText()) *
                Integer.parseInt(text2.getText());
            answertext.setText(String.valueOf(product));
        }
    }
}
```

The result appears in Figure 7.14.

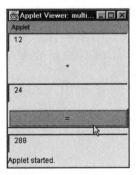

Figure 7.14   Using padding.

Creating Your Own Layout Manager

You can lay out the components in a container yourself if you uninstall any layout manager from the container—see the introduction to this chapter for the details. In fact, you can even create your own layout manager if you implement the **LayoutManager2** interface in a class (the **LayoutManager** interface does not support constraints). Here are the methods you'll have to override from **LayoutManager2**:

- *public void addLayoutComponent(String name, Component component)*—This method adds a component to the layout. It's called by the container class; override this method if you want to know the names of the components to layout.

- *public void removeLayoutComponent(Component component)*—Removes a component from the layout.

- *public float getLayoutAlignmentX(Container target) and public float getLayoutAlignmentX(Container target)*—Specifies how to align components in the x and y directions; returning a value of 0 aligns the component at the origin, returning 1 aligns it as far as possible from the origin, and returning 0.5 centers the component.

- *public void invalidateLayout(Container target)*—Invalidates a layout, which means you should discard any cached information if this method is called.

- *public Dimension preferredLayoutSize(Container parent)*—Returns the ideal size of the parent container.

- *public Dimension maximumLayoutSize(Container target)*—Returns the maximum size of the component.

- *public Dimension minimumLayoutSize(Container target)*—Returns the minimum size of the component.

- *public void layoutContainer(Container parent)*—Uses the **resize**, **move**, and **reshape** methods to arrange the components.

Chapter 8

AWT: Lists, Choices, Text Areas, Scrollbars, And Scroll Panes

In Depth

This chapter is all about a number of important AWT components: lists, choices, text areas, scrollbars, and scroll panes. These components are all fundamental to AWT programming—they're familiar to nearly all GUI users—and we'll take a look at them in overview in this section. Note that one of the major themes of this chapter is *scrolling*; all the controls in this chapter support scrolling in one way or another, letting the user move around large documents with ease.

Lists

As its name suggests, a list control presents the user with a list of items—text strings—from which he or she can select. In windowing environments, space is often at a premium, so it's a good idea to place items in lists, because using scrollbars, you can hide long lists in short list components. The user can select the item in the list he or she wants, double-click on it, and initiate some action.

Lists can also support multiple selections at the same time, using the Shift and Ctrl keys. However, if you support multiple selections, you have to think about how to use the mouse in a list control; because clicking an item selects it, the user can't just make multiple selections and then double-click on one to initiate some action—when one item is double-clicked on, all the others are deselected. To solve this problem, Sun suggests you use some other event, such as a button click, to initiate an action when dealing with multiple selections.

Choices

Choice controls also present the user with a list of items to select from, but there's a difference—choice controls are even more compact than lists. Choice controls look much like text fields—although you can't edit the text in them—with a small button on the right that has a downward-pointing arrow. When the user clicks on the arrow, a list opens displaying all the available choices, and the user can select from one of them. After the selection is made, the choice control closes the list and displays the current selection. If the user opens the list again, the current selection is highlighted.

Note that choice controls are only designed to display one choice at a time, which means you can't select more than one item in the list at a time. Using Shift+click and Ctrl+click is the same as just clicking an item. Like the other components in this chapter, choice controls support scrolling—if the list of items is long, scrollbars will appear on the side of the list automatically.

Text Areas

Text areas are much like text fields, except they support text in two-dimensions, with both rows and columns, so you can display considerably more text in them. You indicate the size, in rows and columns (as measured in characters), that you want the text area to have when you create it. The result is just like a text field that has the specified number of rows and columns. You use text areas when you want to work with entire documents, not just single lines of text.

As with the other components in this chapter, text areas support scrolling. You can specify whether you want a horizontal scrollbar, a vertical scrollbar, both, or none. If you don't have a horizontal scrollbar (and only if you don't have a horizontal scrollbar), the word-wrapping feature is automatically enabled.

Scrollbars

Scrollbars are, of course, the zenith of scrolling controls, and every GUI user knows about them. The user uses the mouse to manipulate the *thumb*—also called the scroll box, elevator, or bubble—in a scrollbar to select a value from a continuous range. You set that range when you create the scrollbar, and after the user selects a new value, you can catch scrollbar events to read that new value.

The user can also click on the arrow buttons at the ends of a scrollbar to increment or decrement the scrollbar's setting by an amount you specify. The user can also click on the scrollbar's track (that is, the part that's not the thumb or the arrow buttons) to increment or decrement the scrollbar's setting by an amount you specify.

Scroll Panes

You might want to use scrollbars to scroll other components, such as a long text field, but Java controls either support scrollbars, themselves, or don't support scrolling at all. To make scrolling of other components easier, Java has the **ScrollPane** class. You use scroll panes by adding components to them and letting the scroll pane handle the scrolling. After you've added a large component to a scroll pane, only part of it is visible at once, and you can use the scroll pane's scrollbars to scroll to other parts of that component.

That's it. Now that we've reviewed what's in this chapter, it's time to turn to the "Immediate Solutions" section.

Immediate Solutions

Using Text Areas

"Uh-oh," says the Novice Programmer, "I've got a problem. I've been writing my novel in a Java text field, and...." You smile and say, "And you've run out of space?" "Well," says the NP, "it's just not very convenient to write an entire novel as one line of text." "Try text areas," you suggest.

A text area is much like a two-dimensional text field; in fact, that's its big advantage—you can display whole documents in text areas, including word wrapping at the end of lines. You can also use scrollbars to move through the text. Note, however, that if you've enabled a horizontal scrollbar, word wrapping will be turned off. Here's the inheritance diagram for the AWT **TextArea** class:

```
java.lang.Object
|____java.awt.Component
     |____java.awt.TextComponent
          |____java.awt.TextArea
```

You'll find the fields of the **TextArea** class, which you use in the **TextArea** class's constructors, in Table 8.1, its constructors in Table 8.2, and its methods in Table 8.3.

Let's look at an example. In this case, I'll create a text area with 10 rows and 20 columns (note that these dimensions are measured in characters). I'll also add a button that the user can click on to display the text "Hello from Java!" in the text area.

Table 8.1   Fields of the *TextArea* class.

Field	Does This
static int SCROLLBARS_BOTH	Adds both vertical and horizontal scrollbars.
static int SCROLLBARS_HORIZONTAL_ONLY	Adds a horizontal scrollbar only.
static int SCROLLBARS_NONE	Indicates not to create any scrollbars for the text area.
static int SCROLLBARS_VERTICAL_ONLY	Displays a vertical scrollbar only.

Table 8.2   Constructors of the *TextArea* class.

Constructor	Does This
TextArea( )	Constructs a new text area.
TextArea(int rows, int columns)	Constructs a new empty text area with the given number of rows and columns.
TextArea(String text)	Constructs a new text area with the given text.
TextArea(String text, int rows, int columns)	Constructs a new text area with the given text and with the given number of rows and columns.
TextArea(String text, int rows, int columns, int scrollbars)	Constructs a new text area with the given text and sets the visibility of the rows, columns, and scrollbar.

Table 8.3   Methods of the *TextArea* class.

Method	Does This
void addNotify( )	Creates the text area's peer.
void append(String str)	Appends text to the text area's current text.
void appendText(String str)	Deprecated. Replaced by append(String).
int getColumns( )	Gets the number of columns in the text area.
Dimension getMinimumSize( )	Sets the minimum size of the text area.
Dimension getMinimumSize(int rows, int columns)	Sets the minimum size of a text area with the given number of rows and columns.
Dimension getPreferredSize( )	Sets the preferred size of the text area.
Dimension getPreferredSize(int rows, int columns)	Sets the preferred size of a text area to the given number of rows and columns.
int getRows( )	Gets the number of rows in the text area.
int getScrollbarVisibility( )	Gets an enumerated value that indicates scrollbar visibility.
void insert(String str, int pos)	Inserts the given text at the given position in the text area.
void insertText(String str, int pos)	Deprecated. Replaced by insert(String, int).
Dimension minimumSize( )	Deprecated. Replaced by getMinimumSize( ).
Dimension minimumSize(int rows, int columns)	Deprecated. Replaced by getMinimumSize(int, int).
protected String paramString( )	Returns a string representing the state of the text area.
Dimension preferredSize( )	Deprecated. Replaced by getPreferredSize( ).
Dimension preferredSize(int rows, int columns)	Deprecated. Replaced by getPreferredSize(int, int).

(continued)

8. AWT: Lists, Choices, Text Areas, Scrollbars, And Scroll Panes

Table 8.3 Methods of the TextArea class (continued).

Method	Does This
void replaceRange(String str, int start, int end)	Replaces text between the start and end positions.
void replaceText(String str, int start, int end)	Deprecated. Replaced by replaceRange(String, int, int).
void setColumns(int columns)	Sets the number of columns.
void setRows(int rows)	Sets the number of rows.

There are several ways to place text in a text area. For example, you can use the **insert** method to insert text at a specific character position (starting at 0) in the string that the text area holds, or you can use the **append** method to append text to the end of the current text. Here's how I use the **insert** method:

```
import java.applet.Applet;
import java.awt.*;
import java.awt.event.*;

/*
<APPLET
    CODE=textarea.class
    WIDTH=200
    HEIGHT=200 >
</APPLET>
*/

public class textarea extends Applet implements ActionListener {

    TextArea textarea1;
    Button button1;

    public void init(){
        textarea1 = new TextArea("", 10, 20, TextArea.SCROLLBARS_BOTH);
        add(textarea1);
        button1 = new Button("Click Me!");
        add(button1);
        button1.addActionListener(this);
    }
```

```
    public void actionPerformed (ActionEvent e)
    {
        String msg = "Hello from Java!";
        if(e.getSource() == button1){
            textarea1.insert(msg, 0);
        }
    }
}
```

Note also that I've added both horizontal and vertical scrollbars to the text area. The result appears in Figure 8.1. This example can be found as textarea.java on the CD accompanying this book.

You can do even more with text areas—for example, you can select and replace text. See the next topic for the details.

Replacing Text In Text Areas

The Product Support Specialist is unhappy, as usual, and says, "Users have a complaint about the new word processor you've written in Java." "Yes?" you ask. "They want to be able to select and replace text," the PSS says. "Some people," you say, "are never satisfied."

You can use the **replaceRange** method to replace a range of text in a text area:

```
void replaceRange(String str, int start, int end);
```

Here, *str* is the string you want to replace the old text with, *start* is the beginning of the range of characters to replace, and *end* is the end of the range.

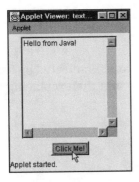

Figure 8.1   Using a text area.

Here's an example in which I display the text "Now is the time." in a text area. The user can select any or all of that text and click on a button to replace the selected text with the message "Hello from Java!". I start by creating the new text area and initializing it with the text "Now is the time.":

```
import java.applet.Applet;
import java.awt.*;
import java.awt.event.*;

/*
<APPLET
    CODE=replace.class
    WIDTH=200
    HEIGHT=200 >
</APPLET>
*/

public class replace extends Applet implements ActionListener
{
    TextArea textarea1;
    Button button1;

    public void init()
    {
        textarea1 = new TextArea("Now is the time.", 5, 20,
            TextArea.SCROLLBARS_BOTH);
        add(textarea1);
        button1 = new Button("Replace selected text");
        add(button1);
        button1.addActionListener(this);
    }
    .
    .
    .

}
```

When the user clicks on the button, I can determine what text is selected by using the **getSelectionStart** and **getSelectionEnd** methods and then replacing the selected text with "Hello from Java!", like this:

```
public void actionPerformed (ActionEvent e){
    if(e.getSource() == button1){
        textarea1.replaceRange("Hello from Java!",
            textarea1.getSelectionStart(),
```

```
                        textarea1.getSelectionEnd()) ;
    }
```

The result appears in Figure 8.2, and you'll find this example on the CD as replace.java.

Besides replacing text, you can also search for it—see the next topic.

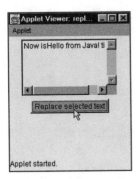

Figure 8.2   Replacing selected text in a text area.

Searching For And Selecting Text In Text Areas

The Product Support Specialist is back and unhappy again. "Now users want to be able to search for text when they use your word processor," the PSS reports. "What next?" you ask, exasperated. "Spell checking?"

The **TextArea** class does not support any direct methods for searching for text, but the **String** class does. Therefore, you can copy the text in a text area into a String object and search that object for the text you want using the **indexOf** method.

Here's an example in which I let the user click on a button to find and select the word *time* in the text "Now is the time." in a text area. I start by creating a new text area, and then initializing it with the text "Now is the time.":

```
import java.applet.Applet;
import java.awt.*;
import java.awt.event.*;
```

8. AWT: Lists, Choices,
Text Areas, Scrollbars,
And Scroll Panes

```
/*
<APPLET
    CODE=find.class
    WIDTH=200
    HEIGHT=200 >
</APPLET>
*/

public class find extends Applet implements ActionListener
{
    TextArea textarea1;
    Button button1;

    public void init()
    {
        textarea1 = new TextArea("Now is the time.", 5, 20,
            TextArea.SCROLLBARS_BOTH);
        add(textarea1);
        button1 = new Button("Find \"time\"");
        add(button1);
        button1.addActionListener(this);
    }
            .
            .
            .
}
```

Now when the user clicks on the button, the text in the text area is loaded into a string called **s**:

```
    public void actionPerformed (ActionEvent e)
    {
        if(e.getSource() == button1){
            String s = textarea1.getText();
                .
                .
                .

        }
    }
```

Now the text "time" can be searched for using the **String** class's **indexOf** method:

```
    public void actionPerformed (ActionEvent e)
    {
        if(e.getSource() == button1){
```

```
        String s = textarea1.getText();
        String s2 = new String("time");

        int location = s.indexOf(s2);
            .
            .
            .
    }
}
```

After the string "time" is found, the **TextArea select** method (inherited from the AWT **TextComponent** class) is used to highlight that text. Here's how you use **select** in general:

```
void select(int selectionStart, int selectionEnd);
```

Here's how I use the **select** method in code:

```
    public void actionPerformed (ActionEvent e)
    {
        if(e.getSource() == button1){
            String s = textarea1.getText();
            String s2 = new String("time");

            int location = s.indexOf(s2);
            textarea1.select(location, location + s2.length()) ;
        }
    }
```

The result of this code appears in Figure 8.3. When the user clicks on the button, the code finds and highlights the text "time" in the text area. This example is in find.java on the CD.

Figure 8.3   Finding and selecting text in a text area.

Using Lists

The Product Support Specialist is back and says, "There's a problem." "Yes?" you ask. "About your catalog of all the classical music CDs in your most recent program—there's more than a hundred-thousand listings." "That's right," you say proudly. "Of course, I guess that makes the list a little tall on the screen." "About two-thousand feet tall," says the PSS.

If you have a long list of items that you want to present, consider using a list control. You can fill a list with many text items (using the **List** class's **add** method) and present only a few at a time—you can choose how many—to the user. The user can highlight an item in the list by clicking on the item and can double-click on that item to initiate some action. In fact, the user can select multiple items in a list and initiate some action, typically by clicking on a button. Here's the inheritance diagram for the **List** class:

```
java.lang.Object
|____java.awt.Component
       |____java.awt.List
```

You'll find the constructors for the **List** class in Table 8.4 and the methods for this class in Table 8.5. Take a close look at the methods table; a lot of useful ones are listed, such as **getItemCount**, which returns the number of items in the list.

Let's look at an example. In this case, I'll add nine items to a list control, making only four of them visible at once. When the user double-clicks on an item, I'll report which one was chosen in a text field. I start by creating the list control and making only four lines visible, like this:

```
import java.applet.Applet;
import java.awt.*;
import java.awt.event.*;

/*
<APPLET
```

Table 8.4   Constructors of the List class.

Constructor	Does This
List( )	Creates a new scrolling list.
List(int rows)	Creates a new list with the specified number of visible lines.
List(int rows, boolean multipleMode)	Creates a new list with the specified number of rows, and multiple selection is enabled if multipleMode is true.

Table 8.5   Methods of the List class.

Method	Does This
void add(String item)	Adds the given item to the end of list.
void add(String item, int index)	Adds the given item to the list at the position given by the index.
void addActionListener (ActionListener l)	Adds the given action listener to get action events from the list.
void addItem(String item)	Deprecated. Replaced by add(String).
void addItem(String item, int index)	Deprecated. Replaced by add(String, int).
void addItemListener(ItemListener l)	Adds the given item listener to get item events from the list.
void addNotify( )	Creates the peer for the list.
boolean allowsMultipleSelections( )	Deprecated. Replaced by isMultipleMode( ).
void clear( )	Deprecated. Replaced by removeAll( ).
int countItems( )	Deprecated. Replaced by getItemCount( ).
void delItem(int position)	Deprecated. Replaced by remove(String) and remove(int).
void delItems(int start, int end)	Deprecated. It's no longer for public use.
void deselect(int index)	Deselects the item at the given index.
String getItem(int index)	Gets the item associated with the given index.
int getItemCount( )	Gets the number of items in the list.
String[ ] getItems( )	Gets the items in the list.
Dimension getMinimumSize( )	Determines the minimum size of this list.
Dimension getMinimumSize(int rows)	Gets the minimum screen dimensions for a list with the given number of rows.
Dimension getPreferredSize( )	Gets the preferred size of this list.
Dimension getPreferredSize(int rows)	Gets the preferred dimensions for a list with the given number of rows.
int getRows( )	Gets the number of visible lines in the list.
int getSelectedIndex( )	Gets the index of the selected item on the list.
int[ ] getSelectedIndexes( )	Gets the selected indexes on the list.
String getSelectedItem( )	Gets the selected item on this list.
String[ ] getSelectedItems( )	Gets the selected items on this list.
Object[ ] getSelectedObjects( )	Gets the selected items on the list in an array of objects.
int getVisibleIndex( )	Gets the index of the item that was last made visible by the method makeVisible.

(continued)

Table 8.5   Methods of the List class (continued).

Method	Does This
boolean isIndexSelected(int index)	Determines if the given item in this list is selected.
boolean isMultipleMode( )	Determines whether the list allows multiple selections.
boolean isSelected(int index)	Deprecated. Replaced by isIndexSelected(int).
void makeVisible(int index)	Makes the item at the given index visible at the top of the list.
Dimension minimumSize( )	Deprecated. Replaced by getMinimumSize( ).
Dimension minimumSize(int rows)	Deprecated. Replaced by getMinimumSize(int).
protected String paramString( )	Gets the parameter string representing the state of this list.
Dimension preferredSize( )	Deprecated. Replaced by getPreferredSize( ).
Dimension preferredSize(int rows)	Deprecated. Replaced by getPreferredSize(int).
protected void processActionEvent (ActionEvent e)	Processes action events occurring on this component by sending them to registered ActionListener objects.
protected void processEvent (AWTEvent e)	Processes events in this list.
protected void processItemEvent (ItemEvent e)	Processes item events occurring in the list by sending them to registered ItemListener objects.
void remove(int position)	Removes the item at the given position from the list.
void remove(String item)	Removes the first occurrence of an item from the list.
void removeActionListener (ActionListener l)	Removes the given action listener so that it no longer gets action events from the list.
void removeAll( )	Removes all items from the list.
void removeItemListener (ItemListener l)	Removes the given item listener so that it no longer gets item events from the list.
void removeNotify( )	Removes the peer for the list.
void replaceItem(String newValue, int index)	Replaces the item at the given index in the list with the new string.
void select(int index)	Selects the item at the given index in the list.
void setMultipleMode(boolean b)	Sets the flag that determines whether the list allows multiple selections.
void setMultipleSelections(boolean b)	Deprecated. Replaced by setMultipleMode(boolean).

8. AWT: Lists, Choices, Text Areas, Scrollbars, And Scroll Panes

```
        CODE=list.class
        WIDTH=200
        HEIGHT=200 >
    </APPLET>
    */
```

```
public class list extends Applet implements ActionListener {

    List list1;
    TextField text1;

    public void init()
    {
        text1 = new TextField(20);
        add(text1);

        list1 = new List(4);
        .
        .
        .
    }
}
```

Now I add nine items using the **add** method:

```
public void init()
{
    text1 = new TextField(20);
    add(text1);

    list1 = new List(4);
    list1.add("Item 1");
    list1.add("Item 2");
    list1.add("Item 3");
    list1.add("Item 4");
    list1.add("Item 5");
    list1.add("Item 6");
    list1.add("Item 7");
    list1.add("Item 8");
    list1.add("Item 9");
    add(list1);
    .
    .
    .
}
```

After adding the list to the layout, I add a listener to it. It turns out that lists use **ActionListener** interfaces, just as buttons do. Here's how I add this to the code:

8. AWT: Lists, Choices,
Text Areas, Scrollbars,
And Scroll Panes

367

```
public void init()
{
    text1 = new TextField(20);
    add(text1);

    list1 = new List(4);
    list1.add("Item 1");
    list1.add("Item 2");
    list1.add("Item 3");
    list1.add("Item 4");
    list1.add("Item 5");
    list1.add("Item 6");
    list1.add("Item 7");
    list1.add("Item 8");
    list1.add("Item 9");
    add(list1);

    list1.addActionListener(this);
}
```

Now I'll need to add an **actionPerformed** method to the main applet class to handle double clicks (this method is not called for single clicks, which just selects items in a list):

```
public void actionPerformed(ActionEvent e)
{
    .
    .
    .
}
```

In this case, I'll get the item the user double-clicked on by using the **List** class's **getSelectedItem** method (the first click of the double-click selects the item) and then displaying that item in the text field, like this:

```
public void actionPerformed(ActionEvent e)
{
    if(e.getSource() == list1){
        text1.setText(((List) e.getSource()).getSelectedItem());
    }
}
```

The result of this code appears in Figure 8.4. When the user double-clicks on an item in the list, that item is displayed in the text field. Note also that only four items of the nine total are visible in the list, because the actual list is larger than the number of visible items. The list control has automatically added a vertical scrollbar. This example is list.java on the CD.

You can do more with lists—for example, you can let the user make multiple selections. We'll take a look at that in the next topic.

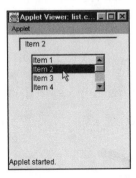

Figure 8.4   Using a list.

Using Multiple Selection Lists

"Uh-oh," says the Novice Programmer, "I've got a problem. My new program lets users order groceries using a list, but so far, they can only order one item at a time." "No problem," you say, "just enable multiple selection in a list."

If you pass a second parameter with the value true to the **List** class's constructor, you'll create a list component that can support multiple selection. The user can select multiple items with Ctrl+click or select a range of items with Shift+click.

Let's look at an example. In this case, I'll let the user select multiple items, and when he or she clicks a button, I'll list the selected items in a text field. I start by creating and populating a multiselect list:

```
import java.applet.Applet;
import java.awt.*;
import java.awt.event.*;


/*
<APPLET
    CODE=multiselect.class
```

```
        WIDTH=300
        HEIGHT=200 >
</APPLET>
*/

public class multiselect extends Applet implements ActionListener {

    List list1;
    TextField text1;
    Button button1;

    public void init(){
        text1 = new TextField(40);
        add(text1);
        list1 = new List(4, true);
        list1.add("Item 1");
        list1.add("Item 2");
        list1.add("Item 3");
        list1.add("Item 4");
        list1.add("Item 5");
        list1.add("Item 6");
        list1.add("Item 7");
        list1.add("Item 8");
        list1.add("Item 9");
        add(list1);
        button1 = new Button("Show selections");
        button1.addActionListener(this);
        add(button1);
    }
```

Next, I add an **ActionListener** to the list and add the button the user can click on to display the selections made in the list:

```
    public void init(){
        text1 = new TextField(40);
        add(text1);
        list1 = new List(4, true);
        list1.add("Item 1");
        list1.add("Item 2");
        list1.add("Item 3");
        list1.add("Item 4");
        list1.add("Item 5");
        list1.add("Item 6");
        list1.add("Item 7");
        list1.add("Item 8");
```

```
        list1.add("Item 9");
        add(list1);
        button1 = new Button("Show selections");
        button1.addActionListener(this);
        add(button1);
    }
```

Here, I need to use a button to show what multiple selections have been made (note that I don't let the user initiate an action involving multiple selections using the mouse in the list because clicking or double-clicking any item will deselect all the other items).

When the user clicks the button, the **List** component's **getSelectedItems** method is used to get a **String** array of the selected items:

```
String selections[];

public void actionPerformed(ActionEvent e)
{
    if(e.getSource() == button1){
        selections = list1.getSelectedItems();
        .
        .
        .

    }
}
```

Next, I loop over that array, adding all the items to a string that starts "You selected:":

```
public void actionPerformed(ActionEvent e)
{
    String outString = new String("You selected:");

    if(e.getSource() == button1){
        selections = list1.getSelectedItems();
        for(int loopIndex = 0; loopIndex < selections.length;
            loopIndex++){
            outString += " " + selections[loopIndex];
        }
        .
        .
        .

    }
}
```

Finally, I place the string with all the selections in the text field:

```
public void actionPerformed(ActionEvent e)
{
    String outString = new String("You selected:");

    if(e.getSource() == button1){
        selections = list1.getSelectedItems();
        for(int loopIndex = 0; loopIndex < selections.length;
            loopIndex++){
            outString += " " + selections[loopIndex];
        }
        text1.setText(outString);
    }
}
```

And that's it. The result appears in Figure 8.5. As you can see in this figure, the user can make multiple selections in this new list, and when he or she clicks on the button, the selections made will appear in the text field. This example is multiselect.java on the CD.

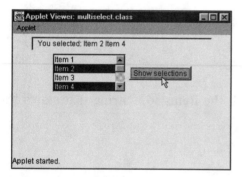

Figure 8.5   Using multiple selection in a list.

Using Choice Controls

"Jeez," says the Novice Programmer, "the Big Boss is cutting costs again, and he says all the controls must be half their original size. But the list control I'm using is already too small!" "No problem," you say, "just use a choice control instead."

Choice controls are much like list controls that just display one item. To display the entire list in a choice control, you click on the button that appears on the right side of the control. This causes a drop-down list to appear, and then you can select an item with the mouse. Then the list closes. The current choice appears in the choice control when the list is closed (note that you can't make multiple selections in a choice control). Here's the inheritance diagram for choice controls:

```
java.lang.Object
|____java.awt.Component
      |____java.awt.Choice
```

You'll find the constructor for the **Choice** class in Table 8.6 and the methods of this class in Table 8.7.

Table 8.6   The constructor of the Choice class.

Constructor	Does This
Choice( )	Creates a new choice menu.

Table 8.7   Methods of the Choice class.

Method	Does This
void add(String item)	Adds an item to this choice control.
void addItem(String item)	Adds an item to this choice control.
void addItemListener(ItemListener l)	Adds the given item listener to get events from this choice control.
void addNotify( )	Creates the choice control's peer.
int countItems( )	Deprecated. Replaced by getItemCount( ).
String getItem(int index)	Gets the string at the given index in this choice control.
int getItemCount( )	Gets the number of items in this choice control.
int getSelectedIndex( )	Gets the index of the currently selected item.
String getSelectedItem( )	Gets a string representation of the current choice.
Object[ ] getSelectedObjects( )	Gets an array (length 1) containing the currently selected item.
void insert(String item, int index)	Inserts the item into this choice at the given position.
protected String paramString( )	Gets the parameter string representing the state of this choice control.
protected void processEvent (AWTEvent e)	Processes events on this choice.
protected void processItemEvent (ItemEvent e)	Processes item events occurring in this choice control by sending them to any registered ItemListener objects.
void remove(int position)	Removes an item from the choice control at the given position.
void remove(String item)	Removes the first occurrence of an item from the choice control.

(continued)

Table 8.7   Methods of the Choice class (continued).

Method	Does This
void removeAll( )	Removes all items from the choice control.
void removeItemListener (ItemListener l)	Removes an item listener so that it no longer gets item events from this choice control.
void select(int pos)	Sets the selected item in this choice control to the given position.
void select(String str)	Sets the selected item in this choice control to the item with the name that's the same as the given string.

Let's look at an example. In this case, I'll add a choice control to a program and use the control's **add** method to add items to its internal list. When the user makes a selection, I'll display that new selection in a text field.

I start by creating a new choice control and populating its internal list with choices (note that you don't have a lot of options when creating choice controls—there's only one constructor, and it doesn't take any parameters):

```
import java.applet.Applet;
import java.awt.*;
import java.awt.event.*;

/*
<APPLET
    CODE=choice.class
    WIDTH=200
    HEIGHT=200 >
</APPLET>
*/

public class choice extends Applet implements ItemListener {

    TextField text1;
    Choice choice1;

    public void init(){
        text1 = new TextField(20);
        add(text1);

        choice1 = new Choice();
        choice1.add("Item 1");
        choice1.add("Item 2");
        choice1.add("Item 3");
```

```
        choice1.add("Item 4");
        choice1.add("Item 5");
        choice1.add("Item 6");
        choice1.add("Item 7");
        choice1.add("Item 8");
        choice1.add("Item 9");
        choice1.add("Item 10");
        choice1.add("Item 11");
        choice1.add("Item 12");
    }
    .
    .
    .
}
```

With a large number of items like this, the choice control will add a vertical scrollbar to the list automatically.

Now I'll handle events in the choice control. You use **ItemListener** interfaces with choice controls, not **ActionListener** interfaces as you do with list controls. The **ItemListener** interface has only one method, **itemStateChanged**:

```
void itemStateChanged(ItemEvent e)
```

This method is passed an object of the **ItemEvent** class. This class's fields appear in Table 8.8, its constructor in Table 8.9, and its methods in Table 8.10.

*Table 8.8   Fields of the **ItemEvent** class.*

Field	Does This
static int DESELECTED	Indicates that a selected item was unselected.
static int ITEM_FIRST	The first number in the range of IDs used for item events.
static int ITEM_LAST	The last number in the range of IDs used for item events.
static int ITEM_STATE_CHANGED	Indicates that an item's state changed.
static int SELECTED	Indicates that an item was selected.

*Table 8.9   The constructor of the **ItemEvent** class.*

Constructor	Does This
ItemEvent(ItemSelectable source, int id, Object item, int stateChange)	Constructs an ItemEvent object.

Table 8.10   Methods of the ItemEvent class.

Method	Does This
Object getItem( )	Gets the item affected by the event.
ItemSelectable getItemSelectable( )	Gets the originator of the event.
int getStateChange( )	Gets the type of state change (that is, selected or deselected).
String paramString( )	Gets a string identifying this event.

I next add an **ItemListener** to the choice control, like this:

```
public void init()
{
    text1 = new TextField(20);
    add(text1);

    choice1 = new Choice();
    choice1.add("Item 1");
    choice1.add("Item 2");
    choice1.add("Item 3");
    choice1.add("Item 4");
    choice1.add("Item 5");
    choice1.add("Item 6");
    choice1.add("Item 7");
    choice1.add("Item 8");
    choice1.add("Item 9");
    choice1.add("Item 10");
    choice1.add("Item 11");
    choice1.add("Item 12");
    add(choice1);

    choice1.addItemListener(this);
}
```

When the user does make a selection from the choice control's internal list, I'll use the choice control's **getSelectedItem** method to determine which item was selected and then display it in a text field:

```
public void itemStateChanged(ItemEvent e)
{
    if(e.getItemSelectable() == choice1){
        text1.setText("You chose " +
            ((Choice)e.getItemSelectable()).getSelectedItem());
    }
}
```

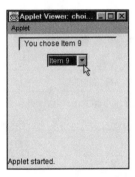

Figure 8.6   Using a choice control.

The result appears in Figure 8.6. As you can see in this figure, users can select an item from the choice control's list, and when they do, the program displays that item in the text field.

Using Scrollbars

The Novice Programmer appears and says, "I have a problem. I want to let users select the drawing color in my new program, but they're getting tired of typing in color values in hexadecimal format." You smile and say, "Why not use scrollbars instead? They're the perfect component when you want to let users select from a continuous numeric range." "Sounds perfect," the NP says.

Every GUI user is familiar with scrollbars. In Java, scrollbars consist of arrows (the buttons at each end of the scrollbar), a thumb or bubble (the scrollable box you slide), and a track (the part of the scrollbar you slide the thumb in). The AWT supports scrollbars with the **Scrollbar** class, which has the following inheritance diagram:

```
java.lang.Object
|____java.awt.Component
     |____java.awt.Scrollbar
```

You'll find the constructors for the **Scrollbar** class in Table 8.11 and its methods in Table 8.12.

Scrollbars do not use **ActionListener** or **ItemListener** interfaces; instead they use **AdjustmentListener** interfaces. The **AdjustmentListener** interface has only one method, **adjustmentValueChanged**:

```
void adjustmentValueChanged(AdjustmentEvent e)
```

Table 8.11   Constructors of the Scrollbar class.

Constructor	Does This
Scrollbar( )	Creates a new vertical scrollbar.
Scrollbar(int orientation)	Creates a new scrollbar with the given orientation.
Scrollbar(int orientation, int value, int visible, int minimum, int maximum)	Creates a new scrollbar with the given orientation, initial value, page size, and minimum and maximum values.

Table 8.12   Methods of the Scrollbar class.

Method	Does This
void addAdjustmentListener (AdjustmentListener l)	Adds the given adjustment listener to get adjustment events.
void addNotify( )	Creates the scrollbar's peer.
int getBlockIncrement( )	Gets the block increment of the scrollbar.
int getLineIncrement( )	Deprecated. Replaced by getUnitIncrement( ).
int getMaximum( )	Gets the maximum value of the scrollbar.
int getMinimum( )	Gets the minimum value of the scrollbar.
int getOrientation( )	Gets the orientation of the scrollbar.
int getPageIncrement( )	Deprecated. Replaced by getBlockIncrement( ).
int getUnitIncrement( )	Gets the unit increment for this scrollbar.
int getValue( )	Gets the current value of the scrollbar.
int getVisible( )	Deprecated. Replaced by getVisibleAmount( ).
int getVisibleAmount( )	Gets the visible amount of the scrollbar.
protected String paramString( )	Gets a string representing the state of the scrollbar.
protected void processAdjustment Event(AdjustmentEvent e)	Processes adjustment events occurring in this scrollbar by sending them to any registered AdjustmentListener objects.
protected void processEvent (AWTEvent e)	Processes events on the scrollbar.
void removeAdjustmentListener (AdjustmentListener l)	Removes the given adjustment listener so that it no longer gets adjustment events from the scrollbar.
void setBlockIncrement(int v)	Sets the block increment for the scrollbar.
void setLineIncrement(int v)	Deprecated. Replaced by setUnitIncrement(int).
void setMaximum(int newMaximum)	Sets the maximum value.
void setMinimum(int newMinimum)	Sets the minimum value.

(continued)

Table 8.12   Methods of the *Scrollbar* class (continued).

Method	Does This
void setOrientation(int orientation)	Sets the orientation.
void setPageIncrement(int v)	Deprecated. Replaced by setBlockIncrement( ).
void setUnitIncrement(int v)	Sets the unit increment.
void setValue(int newValue)	Sets the value of the scrollbar.
void setValues(int value, int visible, int minimum, int maximum)	Sets four values for the scrollbar.
void setVisibleAmount (int newAmount)	Sets the visible amount of the scrollbar.

This method, **adjustmentValueChanged**, is passed an object of class **AdjustmentEvent**. You'll find the fields of the **AdjustmentEvent** class in Table 8.13, its constructor in Table 8.14, and its methods in Table 8.15.

Note, in particular, that you can use the **AdjustmentEvent** class's **getAdjustmentType** method to determine what kind of scrollbar event occurred, as specified by the fields you see in Table 8.13.

Table 8.13   Fields of the *AdjustmentEvent* class.

Field	Does This
ADJUSTMENT_FIRST	The first integer ID for the range of adjustment event IDs.
ADJUSTMENT_LAST	Marks the last integer ID for the range of adjustment event IDs.
ADJUSTMENT_VALUE_CHANGED	The adjustment value changed event occurred.
TRACK	The user dragged the scrollbar's thumb.
UNIT_INCREMENT	The user clicked on the left arrow of a horizontal scrollbar or the top arrow of a vertical scrollbar (or performed the equivalent keyboard action).
UNIT_DECREMENT	The user clicked on the right arrow of a horizontal scrollbar or the bottom arrow of a vertical scrollbar (or performed the equivalent keyboard action).
BLOCK_INCREMENT	The user clicked in the track, to the left of the thumb on a horizontal scrollbar, or above the thumb on a vertical scrollbar. The Page Up key is the keyboard equivalent.
BLOCK_DECREMENT	The user clicked in the track, to the right of the thumb on a horizontal scrollbar, or below the thumb on a vertical scrollbar. The Page Down key is the keyboard equivalent.

8. AWT: Lists, Choices, Text Areas, Scrollbars, And Scroll Panes

Table 8.14   The constructor of the *AdjustmentEvent* class.

Constructor	Does This
AdjustmentEvent(Adjustable source, int type, int value)	Constructs a AdjustmentEvent object with the given adjustable int id, source, event type, adjustment type, and value.

Table 8.15   Methods of the *AdjustmentEvent* class.

Method	Does This
Adjustable getAdjustable( )	Gets the adjustable object where this event originated.
int getAdjustmentType( )	Gets the type of adjustment that caused the value changed event.
int getValue( )	Gets the current value in the adjustment event.
String paramString( )	Gets a string representing the state of this event.

Let's look at an example. Here, I'll just add two scrollbars to a program and display their settings when the user moves them. When you construct a scrollbar, you can specify its orientation (horizontal or vertical), its initial value, a page size, and its numeric range. The *page size* indicates how big you want the thumb to be (it's customary to let the size of the thumb give an indication of the total range—you use a smaller thumb for a longer range and a larger thumb for a smaller range, as you see in word processors when they work with documents of varying sizes). Here's how I add a scrollbar to a program, giving it a horizontal orientation, an initial value of 1, a page size of 20, and a range from 1 to 200:

```
import java.applet.Applet;
import java.awt.event.*;
import java.awt.*;

/*
<APPLET
    CODE=scroll.class
    WIDTH=400
    HEIGHT=100 >
</APPLET>
*/

public class scroll extends Applet implements AdjustmentListener
{
    TextField text1;
    Scrollbar scroll1, scroll2;
```

```
public void init()
{
    scroll1 = new Scrollbar(Scrollbar.HORIZONTAL, 1, 20, 1, 200);
    add(scroll1);
    scroll1.addAdjustmentListener(this);
    .
    .
    .
```

Note that I also add an **AdjustmentListener** to this new scrollbar.

TIP: *You might think that this scrollbar can return any value in the range of 1 to 200, but in fact, the thumb must also be represented in the track, so the scrollbar can only return values from 1 to 200 minus the page size (20, in this case), which equals 180. That's something to think about when you're creating scrollbars.*

You can also configure the scrollbar by using the **setUnitIncrement** and **setBlockIncrement** methods. The **setUnitIncrement** method sets the amount the scrollbar's setting changes when the user clicks on an arrow button (the default is 1), and the **setBlockIncrement** method sets the amount the setting changes when the user clicks on the scrollbar track (the default is 10).

Next, I add a text field to display the new settings of the scrollbars as well as a vertical scrollbar:

```
public void init()
{
    scroll1 = new Scrollbar(Scrollbar.HORIZONTAL, 1, 20, 1, 200);
    add(scroll1);
    scroll1.addAdjustmentListener(this);
    text1 = new TextField(20);
    add(text1);
    scroll2 = new Scrollbar(Scrollbar.VERTICAL, 1, 20, 1, 200);
    add(scroll2);
    scroll2.addAdjustmentListener(this);
}
```

All that's left is to update the display in the text field when the user uses the scrollbars. I do that in the **adjustmentValueChanged** method, checking the **AdjustmentEvent** object's **getAdjustable** method to make sure I'm dealing with one of the scrollbars and using the scrollbar's **getValue** method to display the new settings in the text field. Here's how this looks in code:

```
public void adjustmentValueChanged(AdjustmentEvent e)
{
```

```
        if(e.getAdjustable() == scroll1 ||
            e.getAdjustable() == scroll2) {
            text1.setText("Horizontal: " + scroll1.getValue() +
                " Vertical: " + scroll2.getValue());
        }
    }
```

The result appears in Figure 8.7. As you can see in this figure, the user can move the scrollbars, and the new settings of those scrollbars will appear in the text field. This example is in scroll.java on the CD.

That's fine if you just want to use freestanding scrollbars to let the user easily specify numbers from a continuous range, but what if you want to use scrollbars to scroll something? Next, we'll take a look at another example that scrolls a text string around an applet.

In this case, I'll move the string "Hello from Java!" around the applet to match the setting of a scrollbar. I start by creating the scrollbar and painting the string at the location (**x**, 60), where I'll adjust **x** when the scrollbar is moved:

```
import java.applet.Applet;
import java.awt.event.*;
import java.awt.*;

/*
<APPLET
    CODE=scroll2.class
    WIDTH=200
    HEIGHT=200 >
</APPLET>
*/
```

```
public class scroll2 extends Applet implements AdjustmentListener
{
```

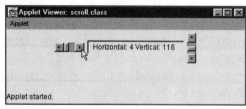

Figure 8.7   Using scrollbars.

```
Scrollbar scroll1;
int x = 0;

public void init()
{
    scroll1 = new Scrollbar(Scrollbar.HORIZONTAL, 1, 10, 1, 100);
    add(scroll1);
    scroll1.addAdjustmentListener(this);
}

public void paint(Graphics g)
{
    g.drawString("Hello from Java!", x, 60);
}
    .
    .
    .
}
```

When scroll events occur, I'll be notified in the **adjustmentValueChanged** method, and I can set the value in the variable **x** to reflect the new horizontal location of the string and redraw the applet (note that I'm using the **Applet** class's **getSize** method here to determine the width of the applet and scale the motions of the text string accordingly):

```
public void adjustmentValueChanged(AdjustmentEvent e)
{
    if(e.getAdjustable() == scroll1) {
        x = (int) (getSize().width * (float) scroll1.getValue() / 100);
        repaint();
    }
}
```

The result appears in Figure 8.8. As you can see in this figure, the user can scroll the text string around the applet just by manipulating the horizontal scrollbar. This example is in scroll2.java on the CD.

We'll take a closer look at scrolling text with scrollbars in the next topic.

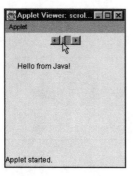

Figure 8.8   Scrolling a text string.

Scrollbars And Border Layouts

"Jeez," says the Novice Programmer, "now the Big Boss wants me to add horizontal and vertical scrollbars to my program, but they just don't want to stay where I put them." "That's because you should use a border layout," you say.

Because border layouts let you add controls around the perimeter of a program, they're a natural to use with scrollbars. Here's an example in which I add four scrollbars around a central panel. This panel displays the text "Hello from Java!" at the location (**x**, **y**), like this:

```
class textPanel extends Panel
{
    TextField Text1;

    public int x = 0, y = 0;

    public void paint (Graphics g)
    {
        g.drawString("Hello from Java!", x, y);
    }
}
```

Next, I can add an object of this new panel class to the center of a border layout, surrounding it with scrollbars, like this:

```
import java.applet.Applet;
import java.awt.*;
import java.awt.event.*;
```

```
/*
<APPLET
    CODE=scrollborder.class
    WIDTH=200
    HEIGHT=200 >
</APPLET>
*/

public class scrollborder extends Applet implements AdjustmentListener
{

    Scrollbar hScroll1, hScroll2, vScroll1, vScroll2;
    textPanel t1;

    public void init()
    {
        setLayout(new BorderLayout());

        hScroll1 = new Scrollbar(Scrollbar.HORIZONTAL, 1, 1, 1, 100);
        add("North", hScroll1);
        hScroll1.addAdjustmentListener(this);

        vScroll1 = new Scrollbar(Scrollbar.VERTICAL, 1, 1, 1, 100);
        add("West", vScroll1);
        vScroll1.addAdjustmentListener(this);

        hScroll2 = new Scrollbar(Scrollbar.HORIZONTAL, 1, 1, 1, 100);
        add("South", hScroll2);
        hScroll2.addAdjustmentListener(this);

        vScroll2 = new Scrollbar(Scrollbar.VERTICAL, 1, 1, 1, 100);
        add("East", vScroll2);
        vScroll2.addAdjustmentListener(this);

        t1 = new textPanel();
        add("Center", t1);
    }
        .
        .
        .
}
```

8. AWT: Lists, Choices, Text Areas, Scrollbars, And Scroll Panes

The only trick here is that when the user moves one scrollbar, I have to move the corresponding one on the other side of the central panel to keep the scrollbars coordinated. Here's how this looks in the **adjustmentValueChanged** method:

```
public void adjustmentValueChanged(AdjustmentEvent e)
{
    if(e.getAdjustable() == hScroll1){
        hScroll2.setValue(hScroll1.getValue());
    }
    if(e.getAdjustable() == vScroll1){
        vScroll2.setValue(vScroll1.getValue());
    }
    if(e.getAdjustable() == hScroll2){
        hScroll1.setValue(hScroll2.getValue());
    }
    if(e.getAdjustable() == vScroll2){
        vScroll1.setValue(vScroll2.getValue());
    }
        .
        .
        .
}
```

All that's left is to get the new scrollbar settings, adjust the **x** and **y** location of the text string in the panel to match, and then redraw the panel. The process looks like this:

```
public void adjustmentValueChanged(AdjustmentEvent e)
{

    if(e.getAdjustable() == hScroll1){
        hScroll2.setValue(hScroll1.getValue());
    }
    if(e.getAdjustable() == vScroll1){
        vScroll2.setValue(vScroll1.getValue());
    }
    if(e.getAdjustable() == hScroll2){
        hScroll1.setValue(hScroll2.getValue());
    }
    if(e.getAdjustable() == vScroll2){
        vScroll1.setValue(vScroll2.getValue());
    }

    t1.x = (int) (getSize().width * (float) hScroll1.getValue() / 100);
    t1.y = (int) (getSize().height * (float) vScroll1.getValue() /
```

```
          100);
      t1.repaint();
  }
```

And that's all it takes. The result appears in Figure 8.9. As you can see in this figure, the scrollbars appear around the perimeter of the applet. This example is in scrollborder.java on the CD.

There's another way to make scrolling text in panels easy—you can use scroll panes, which is coming up next.

Figure 8.9   Scrollbars in a border layout.

Using Scroll Panes

"I want to scroll some text," the Novice Programmer says, "but setting up the scrollbars is too much work. Isn't there an easier way?" "There sure is," you say. "You can use scroll panes." "Great!" says the NP.

You can add a component to a scroll pane, and the scroll pane will let you scroll that component around. If the component is larger than the scroll pane, only part of the component will be visible at any one time. Here's the inheritance diagram for the **ScrollPane** class:

```
java.lang.Object
|____java.awt.Component
     |____java.awt.Container
          |____java.awt.ScrollPane
```

You'll find the fields of the **ScrollPane** class in Table 8.16, its constructors in Table 8.17, and its methods in Table 8.18.

Table 8.16   Fields of the ScrollPane class.

Field	Does This
static int SCROLLBARS_ALWAYS	Indicates that horizontal/vertical scrollbars should always be shown.
static int SCROLLBARS_AS_NEEDED	Indicates that horizontal/vertical scrollbars should be shown only when the size of the child is greater than the size of the scroll pane.
static int SCROLLBARS_NEVER	Indicates that horizontal/vertical scrollbars should never be shown.

Table 8.17   Constructors of the ScrollPane class.

Constructor	Does This
ScrollPane( )	Creates a new scroll pane.
ScrollPane(int scrollbarDisplayPolicy)	Creates a new scroll pane using a display policy.

Table 8.18   Methods of the ScrollPane class.

Method	Does This
protected void addImpl(Component comp, Object constraints, int index)	Adds the given component to this scroll pane.
void addNotify( )	Creates the scroll pane's peer.
void doLayout( )	Lays out this container by resizing the contained component to its preferred size.
Adjustable getHAdjustable( )	Gets the horizontal scrollbar.
int getHScrollbarHeight( )	Gets the height that would be occupied by a horizontal scrollbar.
int getScrollbarDisplayPolicy( )	Gets the display policy for the scrollbars.
Point getScrollPosition( )	Gets the current **x,y** position within the child, which is displayed at the origin of the scrolled panel's view port.
Adjustable getVAdjustable( )	Gets the vertical scrollbar.
Dimension getViewportSize( )	Gets the current size of the scroll pane's view port.
int getVScrollbarWidth( )	Gets the width that would be occupied by a vertical scrollbar.
void layout( )	Deprecated. Replaced by doLayout( ).
String paramString( )	Gets a string representing the state of this container.
void printComponents(Graphics g)	Prints the component in this scroll pane.
void setLayout(LayoutManager mgr)	Sets the layout manager for this container.
void setScrollPosition(int **x**, int **y**)	Scrolls to the given position within the child component.
void setScrollPosition(Point p)	Scrolls to the given position within the child component.

Let's look at an example. It's easy enough to just add a component to a scroll pane; you simply use the **ScrollPane** class's **add** method. Here's how this looks when I add a text field to a scroll pane:

```java
import java.applet.Applet;
import java.awt.*;

/*
<APPLET
    CODE=scrollpane.class
    WIDTH=200
    HEIGHT=200 >
</APPLET>
*/

public class scrollpane extends Applet
{
    ScrollPane scrollpane1;
    TextField text1;

    public void init()
    {
        scrollpane1 = new ScrollPane();
        text1 = new TextField("Hello from Java!");
        scrollpane1.add(text1);
        add(scrollpane1);
    }
}
```

However, it looks odd when only part of a text field is visible in a scroll pane. A more interesting example would involve scrolling text in a panel, and I'll create that example here. In this case, I'll create a new panel class, **TextPanel**, that displays a long string of text:

```java
class TextPanel extends Panel
{
    public void paint (Graphics g)
    {
        g.drawString ("This is a long string of text that just " +
            "seems to go on and on and on and on....", 0, 60);
    }
}
```

There's an important point here that most other books never cover—when you use an object that has no predefined size, such as a panel in a scroll pane, you have to give it a size. In the case of containers such as panels, this means overriding the **getPreferredSize** method so that the method can be called by the scroll pane. Here, I return an object of the Java **Dimension** class, which just has two data members—**width** and **height**. I can set those values like this:

```java
class TextPanel extends Panel
{
    public Dimension getPreferredSize()
    {
        return new Dimension(400, 400);
    }

    public void paint (Graphics g)
    {
        g.drawString ("This is a long string of text that just " +
            "seems to go on and on and on and on....", 0, 60);
    }
}
```

Now I just add an object of the **TextPane** class to a scroll pane, like this:

```java
import java.applet.Applet;
import java.awt.*;

/*
<APPLET
    CODE=scrollpane.class
    WIDTH=200
    HEIGHT=200 >
</APPLET>
*/

public class scrollpane extends Applet
{
    ScrollPane scrollpane1;
    TextPanel t1;

    public void init(){
        scrollpane1 = new ScrollPane(ScrollPane.SCROLLBARS_ALWAYS);
```

```
        t1 = new TextPanel();
        scrollpanel.add(t1);
        add(scrollpanel);
    }
}
```

The result appears in Figure 8.10. As you can see in this figure, the user ends up scrolling text around inside a scroll pane instead of scrolling around some control such as a text field. This example is in scrollpane.java on the CD.

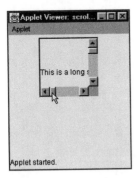

Figure 8.10   Scroll text position in a scroll pane.

Chapter 9

AWT: Graphics, Images, Text, And Fonts

In Depth

This chapter is all about some very powerful topics in Java—graphics, images, text handling, and working with fonts. Java is a very visual language, and all these areas are popular with programmers. I'll start with an overview of these items.

Graphics

The graphics capability in the AWT is pretty solid, and it's based on the huge **Graphics** class. You can use this class to draw all kinds of figures—lines, points, rectangles, ovals, polygons, and more. You can also select colors, drawing modes, and fill figures in with color. You'll see all this in this chapter, including a special component—the **Canvas** component—that exists expressly so you can draw in it.

Images

The AWT excels at handling images, and you'll see what it's capable of in this chapter. We'll take a look at various ways of loading images in formats such as GIF and JPG, resizing images, waiting until images are fully loaded before displaying them, drawing images offscreen before displaying them (a process called *double buffering*), and animating images. In fact, you can even gain access to the individual pixels in images, and we'll do that here, copying images, brightening them, converting them to grayscale, and giving them an engraved appearance.

TIP: *You'll learn all about animating images and double buffering when we discuss multithreading, later in the book.*

Text And Fonts

You might be surprised to see text and fonts in a chapter on graphics, but when you draw text directly, not inserting it into a control such as a text field, you're creating a graphic, and Java treats it as such. In this chapter, you'll see that there's quite a bit to working with text as graphics. For example, you'll see how to set the font and font style of text —such as italics or bold—as well as how to measure the screen length of a string of text so you can center it in a window.

The Keyboard And Mouse

In this chapter, we'll be writing code that can display text directly, without any controls such as text fields or text areas, which means we'll have to read that text directly from the keyboard. Therefore, we'll take a look at handling keyboard input here. In addition, when you're letting the user create graphics, the mouse is a very handy tool to have—in fact, we'll create a mouse-driven drawing program in this chapter—so we'll also take a look at working with the mouse in code. In fact, I'll start this chapter by taking a look at using the mouse and keyboard.

That's it. Now you have an overview of what's in this chapter. There's a lot coming up here, so it's time to turn to the "Immediate Solutions" section.

9. AWT: Graphics, Images, Text, And Fonts

Immediate Solutions

Using The Mouse

"OK," says the Novice Programmer, "in my program, the user can select text with Ctrl+Alt+F8, move the insertion point with Shift+Alt+F3, and...." "Wait a minute," you say. "Have you ever thought about adding mouse support to your program too? It might make things easier for the user." "Hmm," says the NP thoughtfully.

You can work with the mouse using two AWT interfaces—**MouseListener**, which handles mouse clicks, presses, and releases as well as the case in which the mouse enters a component and then leaves it, and **MouseMotionListener**, which handles mouse movements and drag operations. You can find the methods of the **MouseListener** interface in Table 9.1 and the methods of the **MouseMotionListener** interface in Table 9.2.

TIP: Bear in mind that you need to override all the methods in an interface if you want to implement that interface, which can get a little tedious in the case of **MouseListener**, which has five methods. To make things easier, you can use adapter classes such as **MouseAdapter** instead and just override the methods you want to use. For more on adapter classes, see Chapter 6.

Table 9.1   Methods of the MouseListener interface.

Method	Does This
void mouseClicked(MouseEvent e)	Called when the mouse has been clicked on a component.
void mouseEntered(MouseEvent e)	Called when the mouse enters a component.
void mouseExited(MouseEvent e)	Called when the mouse exits a component.
void mousePressed(MouseEvent e)	Called when a mouse button has been pressed on a component.
void mouseReleased(MouseEvent e)	Called when a mouse button has been released on a component.

Table 9.2   Methods of the MouseMotionListener interface.

Method	Does This
void mouseDragged(MouseEvent e)	Called when a mouse button is pressed on a component and then dragged.
void mouseMoved(MouseEvent e)	Called when the mouse button has been moved over a component (with no buttons down.

Each of the mouse interface methods are passed an object of class **MouseEvent**, and the inheritance diagram for that class looks like this:

```
java.lang.Object
|____java.util.EventObject
     |____java.awt.AWTEvent
          |____java.awt.event.ComponentEvent
               |____java.awt.event.InputEvent
                    |____java.awt.event.MouseEvent
```

The **MouseEvent** class adds only fields to its base classes, and you can find the fields of this class in Table 9.3.

*Table 9.3   Fields of the **MouseEvent** class.*

Field	Does This
static int MOUSE_CLICKED	Indicates the "mouse clicked" event.
static int MOUSE_DRAGGED	Indicates the "mouse dragged" event.
static int MOUSE_ENTERED	Indicates the "mouse entered" event.
static int MOUSE_EXITED	Indicates the "mouse exited" event.
static int MOUSE_FIRST	Indicates the first number in the range of IDs used for mouse events.
static int MOUSE_LAST	Indicates the last number in the range of IDs used for mouse events.
static int MOUSE_MOVED	Indicates the "mouse moved" event.
static int MOUSE_PRESSED	Indicates the "mouse pressed" event.
static int MOUSE_RELEASED	Indicates the "mouse released" event.

Let's look at an example. This applet, mouse.java, will display most of what the mouse can do. To catch particular mouse actions, you just override the corresponding mouse listener method. To get the current location of the mouse from a **MouseEvent** object, you can use the **getX** and **getY** methods. To determine which button was pressed, you can use the **MouseEvent** class's **getModifiers** method and then **And** the result with the following fields from the **InputEvent** class: **ALT_GRAPH_MASK, ALT_MASK, BUTTON1_MASK, BUTTON2_MASK, BUTTON3_MASK, CTRL_MASK, META_MASK**, and **SHIFT_MASK**. Here's what this applet, mouse.java, looks like, with all this work put together:

```java
import java.applet.Applet;
import java.awt.*;
import java.awt.event.*;

/*
<APPLET
    CODE=mouse.class
    WIDTH=300
    HEIGHT=200 >
</APPLET>
*/

public class mouse extends Applet implements MouseListener,
    MouseMotionListener
{
    TextField text1;

    public void init(){
        text1 = new TextField(30);
        add(text1);
        addMouseListener(this);
        addMouseMotionListener(this);
    }

    public void mousePressed(MouseEvent e)
    {
        if((e.getModifiers() & InputEvent.BUTTON1_MASK) ==
            InputEvent.BUTTON1_MASK){
            text1.setText("Left mouse button down at " + e.getX() + "," +
                e.getY());
        }
        else{
            text1.setText("Right mouse button down at " + e.getX() + "," +
                e.getY());
        }
    }

    public void mouseClicked(MouseEvent e)
    {
        text1.setText("You clicked the mouse at " + e.getX() + "," +
            e.getY());
    }

    public void mouseReleased(MouseEvent e)
    {
```

```
        text1.setText("The mouse button went up.");
    }

    public void mouseEntered(MouseEvent e)
    {
        text1.setText("The mouse entered.");
    }

    public void mouseExited(MouseEvent e)
    {
        text1.setText("The mouse exited.");
    }

    public void mouseDragged(MouseEvent e)
    {
        text1.setText("The mouse was dragged.");
    }

    public void mouseMoved(MouseEvent e)
    {
        text1.setText("The mouse was moved.");
    }
}
```

You can see this applet at work in Figure 9.1. When you move the mouse or use a mouse button, the applet lets you know what's going on. This example is in mouse.java on the CD that accompanies this book.

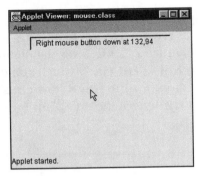

Figure 9.1   Using the mouse.

Using The Keyboard

"Say," says the Novice Programmer, "I'm writing a word processor, *SuperDuperTextPro*, in Java and I want to read text directly from the keyboard. How does that work?" "With the key listener," you say. "I knew it'd be something like that," the NP says.

You use the **KeyListener** interface to work with the keyboard, and you can find the methods of the **KeyListener** interface in Table 9.4.

TIP: *Bear in mind that you need to override all the methods in an interface if you want to implement that interface, which can get a little tedious. To make things easier, you can use adapter classes such as **KeyAdapter** instead and just override the methods you want to use. For more on adapter classes, see Chapter 6.*

Note that there are three different key events—key pressed, released, and typed. You usually use the "key typed" event when working with the keyboard, because you can use the **getKeyChar** method in **keyTyped** to get the Unicode character that was typed. In the **keyPressed** and **KeyReleased** methods, on the other hand, you can use the **getKeyCode** (not **getKeyChar**) method to get a *virtual key code*; this code just tells you what key was pressed or released—you're responsible for determining whether the Shift, Ctrl, or other key was pressed down, which you can do with the **KeyEvent** object passed to the key event methods. To determine which modifier keys (such as Shift) were pressed down, you can use the **KeyEvent** object's **getModifiers** method and then **And** the result with these fields from the **InputEvent** class: **ALT_GRAPH_MASK**, **ALT_MASK**, **CTRL_MASK**, **META_MASK**, and **SHIFT_MASK**.

In general, it's not very easy to work with virtual key codes because there's a separate constant you have to use for each key as returned by **getKeyCode**—for example, **VK_F1** for the F1 key, **VK_A** for the character A, **VK_5** for the number 5, and so on, as enumerated in the fields of the **KeyEvent** class, which you can see in Table 9.5. You can also find the constructors for the **KeyEvent** class in Table 9.6 and its methods in Table 9.7. Here's the inheritance diagram for the **KeyEvent** class:

```
java.lang.Object
|____java.util.EventObject
     |____java.awt.AWTEvent
          |____java.awt.event.ComponentEvent
               |____java.awt.event.InputEvent
                    |____java.awt.event.KeyEvent
```

Table 9.4   Methods of the *KeyListener* interface.

Method	Does This
void keyPressed(KeyEvent e)	Called when a key has been pressed.
void keyReleased(KeyEvent e)	Called when a key has been released.
void keyTyped(KeyEvent e)	Called when a key has been typed.

Table 9.5   Fields of the *KeyEvent* Class

CHAR_UNDEFINED	KEY_FIRST	KEY_LAST
KEY_PRESSED	KEY_RELEASED	KEY_TYPED
VK_0 to VK_9	VK_A to	VK_Z
VK_ACCEPT	VK_ADD	VK_AGAIN
VK_ALL_CANDIDATES	VK_ALPHANUMERIC	VK_ALT
VK_ALT_GRAPH	VK_AMPERSAND	VK_ASTERISK
VK_AT	VK_BACK_QUOTE	VK_BACK_SLASH
VK_BACK_SPACE	VK_BRACELEFT	VK_BRACERIGHT
VK_CANCEL	VK_CAPS_LOCK	VK_CIRCUMFLEX
VK_CLEAR	VK_CLOSE_BRACKET	VK_CODE_INPUT
VK_COLON	VK_COMMA	VK_COMPOSE
VK_CONTROL	VK_CONVERT	VK_COPY
VK_CUT	VK_DEAD_ABOVEDOT	VK_DEAD_ABOVERING
VK_DEAD_ACUTE	VK_DEAD_BREVE	VK_DEAD_CARON
VK_DEAD_CEDILLA	VK_DEAD_CIRCUMFLEX	VK_DEAD_DIAERESIS
VK_DEAD_DOUBLEACUTE	VK_DEAD_GRAVE	VK_DEAD_IOTA
VK_DEAD_MACRON	VK_DEAD_OGONEK	VK_DEAD_SEMIVOICED_SOUND
VK_DEAD_TILDE	VK_DEAD_VOICED_SOUND	VK_DECIMAL
VK_DELETE	VK_DIVIDE	VK_DOLLAR
VK_DOWN	VK_END	VK_ENTER
VK_EQUALS	VK_ESCAPE	VK_EURO_SIGN
VK_EXCLAMATION_MARK	VK_F1 to VK_F24	VK_FINAL
VK_FIND	VK_FULL_WIDTH	VK_GREATER
VK_HALF_WIDTH	VK_HELP	VK_HIRAGANA
VK_HOME	VK_INSERT	VK_INVERTED_EXCLAMATION_MARK

(continued)

Table 9.5   Fields of the *KeyEvent Class* (continued).

VK_JAPANESE_HIRAGANA	VK_JAPANESE_KATAKANA	VK_JAPANESE_ROMAN
VK_KANA	VK_KANJI	VK_KATAKANA
VK_KP_DOWN	VK_KP_LEFT	VK_KP_RIGHT
VK_KP_UP	VK_LEFT	VK_LEFT_PARENTHESIS
VK_LESS	VK_META	VK_MINUS
VK_MODECHANGE	VK_MULTIPLY	VK_NONCONVERT
VK_NUM_LOCK	VK_NUMBER_SIGN	VK_NUMPAD0 to VK_NUMPAD9
VK_OPEN_BRACKET	VK_PAGE_DOWN	VK_PAGE_UP
VK_PASTE	VK_PAUSE	VK_PERIOD
VK_PLUS	VK_PREVIOUS_CANDIDATE	VK_PRINTSCREEN
VK_PROPS	VK_QUOTE	VK_QUOTEDBL
VK_RIGHT	VK_RIGHT_PARENTHESIS	VK_ROMAN_CHARACTERS
VK_SCROLL_LOCK	VK_SEMICOLON	VK_SEPARATER
VK_SHIFT	VK_SLASH	VK_SPACE
VK_STOP	VK_SUBTRACT	VK_TAB
VK_UNDEFINED	VK_UNDERSCORE	VK_UNDO
VK_UP		

Table 9.6   Constructors of the *KeyEvent* class.

Constructor	Does This
KeyEvent(Component source, int id, long when, int modifiers, int keyCode)	Creates a **KeyEvent** object.
KeyEvent(Component source, int id, long when, int modifiers, int keyCode, char keyChar)	Creates a **KeyEvent** object.

Table 9.7   Methods of the *KeyEvent* class.

Method	Does This
char getKeyChar( )	Gets the character associated with the key in this event.
int getKeyCode( )	Gets the integer key-code associated with the key in this event.
static String getKeyModifiersText (int modifiers)	Gets a String describing the modifier key(s), such as "Shift" or "Ctrl+Shift".
static String getKeyText(int keyCode)	Gets a String describing the keycode, such as "HOME", "F1", or "A".

(continued)

Table 9.7 **Methods of the *KeyEvent* class (continued).**

Method	Does This
boolean isActionKey( )	Determines whether the key in this event is an "action" key, as defined in **Event.java**.
String paramString( )	Gets a parameter string identifying this event.
void setKeyChar(char keyChar)	Set the **keyChar** value to indicate a character.
void setKeyCode(int keyCode)	Set the **keyCode** value to indicate a physical key.
void setModifiers(int modifiers)	Set the modifiers to indicate additional keys that were held down (Shift, Ctrl, Alt, Meta, and so on). Defined as part of **InputEvent**.

Let's look at an example. This simple applet reads and display keys from the keyboard using the **keyTyped** event and the **getKeyChar** method to actually read the key. Every time the user types a key, the corresponding character is added to the end of the displayed string. Here's what the applet looks like:

```
import java.awt.*;
import java.awt.event.*;
import java.applet.Applet;

/*
  <APPLET
      CODE=key.class
      WIDTH=300
      HEIGHT=200 >
  </APPLET>
*/

public class key extends Applet implements KeyListener {

    String text = "";

    public void init()
    {
        addKeyListener(this);
        requestFocus();
    }

    public void paint(Graphics g)
    {
        g.drawString(text, 0, 100);
    }
```

```
public void keyTyped(KeyEvent e)
{
    text = text + e.getKeyChar();
    repaint();
}

public void keyPressed(KeyEvent e) {}
public void keyReleased(KeyEvent e) {}
}
```

There's one thing to note here: In order for the applet, itself, to receive keystrokes, you have to give it the focus. (In a GUI, an element that has focus is the one that receives keystrokes.) We do that with the applet's **requestFocus** method; if you don't give the applet the focus explicitly, you won't see any of the typed characters.

The results of this code appear in Figure 9.2. As you can see in the figure, the user can type text directly into this applet—this applet works as intended. This example is in key.java on the CD.

That's just the beginning of working with text. Now let's take a look at the next topic, where we start working with fonts.

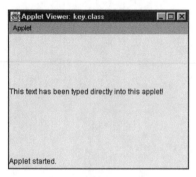

Figure 9.2   Using the keyboard.

Using Fonts

"The banner you created for the Company Pride Picnic was good," the Big Boss says, "but it didn't seem to be bursting with pride." "Why not?" you ask. "Well for one thing," the BB says, "it was only a quarter of an inch tall." "Hmm," you say, "guess I better use a bigger font."

You can select the type and style of text fonts with the **Font** class. Using this class, you can select a font (such as Helvetica, Arial, or Courier), set its size, and specify if it's bold, italic, and so on. You'll find the fields of the **Font** class in Table 9.8, its constructors in Table 9.9, and its methods in Table 9.10.

As if all the methods in Table 9.10 weren't enough, there's another important class here—the **FontMetrics** class, which tells you about the physical dimensions of fonts. The **FontMetrics** class's field appears in Table 9.11, its constructor in Table 9.12, and its methods in Table 9.13. One of the most common uses of the **FontMetrics** class is to determine the height of text when you're displaying multiline text. It's worthwhile going through the tables in this topic to see what's available when working with fonts.

*Table 9.8   Fields of the **Font** class.*

Field	Does This
protected Font font	The font from which the font metrics are to be created.
static int BOLD	The bold style.
static int CENTER_BASELINE	The baseline used in ideographic scripts (such as Japanese).
static int HANGING_BASELINE	The baseline used when laying out scripts such as Devanagari.
static int ITALIC	The italicized style.
protected String name	The logical name of this font.
static int PLAIN	The plain style.
protected float pointSize	The point size of this font in a float.
static int ROMAN_BASELINE	The baseline used in most roman scripts when laying out text.
protected int size	The point size of this font.
protected int style	The style of this font.

*Table 9.9   Constructors of the **Font** class.*

Constructor	Does This
Font(Map attributes)	Creates a new font with the given attributes.
Font(String name, int style, int size)	Creates a new font from the given name, style, and point size.

*Table 9.10   Methods of the **Font** class.*

Method	Does This
boolean canDisplay(char c)	Checks whether the font has a glyph for the given character.
int canDisplayUpTo(char[ ] text, int start, int limit)	Indicates whether this font can display the characters in the given text.

(continued)

9. AWT: Graphics, Images, Text, And Fonts

Table 9.10 Methods of the Font class (continued).

Method	Does This
int canDisplayUpTo(CharacterIterator iter, int start, int limit)	Indicates whether this font can display a string.
int canDisplayUpTo(String str)	Indicates whether this font can display a given string.
GlyphVector createGlyphVector(Font RenderContext frc, char[ ] chars)	Gets a new **GlyphVector** object.
GlyphVector createGlyphVector(Font RenderContext frc, CharacterIterator ci)	Gets a new **GlyphVector** object with the given character iterator.
GlyphVector createGlyphVector(Font RenderContext frc, int[ ] glyphCodes)	Gets a new **GlyphVector** object with the given integer array and the given **FontRenderContext**.
GlyphVector createGlyphVector(Font RenderContext frc, String str)	Gets a new **GlyphVector** object created with the given **FontRenderContext**.
static Font decode(String str)	Gets the font that the string describes.
Font deriveFont(AffineTransform trans)	Creates a new **Font** object by duplicating the current **Font** object and applying a new transform, which maps one set of coordinates to another.
Font deriveFont(float size)	Creates a new **Font** object by duplicating the current **Font** object and applying a new size.
Font deriveFont(int style)	Creates a new **Font** object by duplicating the current **Font** object and applying a new style.
Font deriveFont(int style, Affine and Transform trans)	Creates a new **Font** object by duplicating the current **Font** object applying a new style and transform.
Font deriveFont(int style, float size)	Creates a new **Font** object by duplicating the current **Font** object and applying a new style and size.
Font deriveFont(Map attributes)	Creates a new **Font** object by duplicating the current **Font** object and applying a new set of font attributes to it.
boolean equals(Object obj)	Compares this **Font** object to the given object.
protected void finalize( )	Disposes of the native **Font** object.
Map getAttributes( )	Gets a map of font attributes in this font.
AttributedCharacterIterator.Attribute [ ] getAvailableAttributes( )	Gets the keys of all the font attributes.
byte getBaselineFor(char c)	Gets the baseline for displaying this character.
String getFamily( )	Gets the family name of this font.

(continued)

Table 9.10   Methods of the *Font* class (continued).

Method	Does This
String getFamily(Locale l)	Gets the family name of this font, localized for the given locale.
static Font getFont(Map attributes)	Gets a font appropriate to the attributes.
static Font getFont(String nm)	Gets a **Font** object from the system properties list.
static Font getFont(String nm, Font font)	Gets the given font from the system properties list.
String getFontName( )	Gets the font face name.
String getFontName(Locale l)	Gets the font face name, localized for the given locale.
float getItalicAngle( )	Gets the italic angle of this font.
LineMetrics getLineMetrics(char[ ] chars, int beginIndex, int limit, FontRenderContext frc)	Gets a **LineMetrics** object using the given arguments.
LineMetrics getLineMetrics (CharacterIterator ci, int beginIndex, int limit, FontRenderContext frc)	Gets a **LineMetrics** object using the given arguments.
LineMetrics getLineMetrics (String str, FontRenderContext frc)	Gets a **LineMetrics** object created with the given string and **FontRenderContext**.
LineMetrics getLineMetrics(String str, int beginIndex, int limit, FontRenderContext frc)	Gets a **LineMetrics** object created with the given arguments.
Rectangle2D getMaxCharBounds (FontRenderContext frc)	Gets the bounds for the character with the maximum bounds, as defined in the given **FontRenderContext**.
int getMissingGlyphCode( )	Gets the glyph code used when this font does not have a glyph for a given Unicode character.
String getName( )	Gets the font's logical name.
int getNumGlyphs( )	Gets the number of glyphs in this font.
java.awt.peer.FontPeer getPeer( )	Deprecated. Font rendering is now supposed to be platform independent.
String getPSName( )	Gets the Postscript name of the font.
int getSize( )	Gets the point size of the font.
float getSize2D( )	Gets the point size of this font in a float value.
Rectangle2D getStringBounds (char[ ] chars, int beginIndex, int limit, FontRenderContext frc)	Gets the bounds of the array of characters in the **FontRenderContext**.

(continued)

Table 9.10   Methods of the Font class (continued).

Method	Does This
Rectangle2D getStringBounds (CharacterIterator ci, int beginIndex, int limit, FontRenderContext frc)	Gets the bounds of the characters in the given character iterator in the **FontRenderContext**.
Rectangle2D getStringBounds(String str, FontRenderContext frc)	Gets the bounds of the given string in a **FontRenderContext**.
Rectangle2D getStringBounds(String str, int beginIndex, int limit, FontRenderContext frc)	Gets the bounds of the given string in a **FontRenderContext**.
int getStyle( )	Gets the style of this font.
AffineTransform getTransform( )	Gets a copy of the transform associated with this font.
int hashCode( )	Gets a hashcode for this font.
boolean hasUniformLineMetrics( )	Checks whether this font has uniform line metrics.
boolean isBold( )	Indicates whether this **Font** object's style is bold.
boolean isItalic( )	Indicates whether this **Font** object's style is italic.
boolean isPlain( )	Indicates whether this **Font** object's style is plain.
String toString( )	Converts the **Font** object into a string representation.

Table 9.11   The field of the FontMetrics class.

Field	Does This
protected Font font	Determines the font from which the font metrics are created.

Table 9.12   The constructor of the FontMetrics class.

Constructor	Does This
protected FontMetrics(Font font)	Creates a new **FontMetrics** object.

Table 9.13   Methods of the FontMetrics class.

Method	Does This
int bytesWidth(byte[ ] data, int off, int len)	Gets the total advance width for showing the given array of bytes in this font.
int charsWidth(char[ ] data, int off, intlen)	Gets the total advance width for showing the given array of characters in this font.
int charWidth(char ch)	Gets the advance width of the given character in this font.

(continued)

Table 9.13   *Methods of the FontMetrics class* (continued).

Method	Does This
int charWidth(int ch)	Gets the advance width of the given character in this font.
int getAscent( )	Indicates the font ascent of the font.
int getDescent( )	Indicates the font descent of the font.
Font getFont( )	Gets the font described by this **FontMetrics** object.
int getHeight( )	Gets the standard height of a line of text in this font.
int getLeading( )	Indicates the leading of the font.
LineMetrics getLineMetrics(char[ ] chars, int beginIndex, int limit, Graphics context)	Gets the **LineMetrics** object for the given character array.
LineMetrics getLineMetrics(Characterl terator ci, int beginIndex, int limit, Graphics context)	Gets the **LineMetrics** object for the character iterator.
LineMetrics getLineMetrics(String str, Graphics context)	Gets the **LineMetrics** object for the given string.
LineMetrics getLineMetrics(String str, graphics int beginIndex, int limit, Graphics context)	Gets the **LineMetrics** object for the given string in the given context.
int getMaxAdvance( )	Gets the maximum advance width of any character in this font.
int getMaxAscent( )	Indicates the maximum ascent of the font described by this **FontMetrics** object.
Rectangle2D getMaxCharBounds (Graphics context)	Gets the bounds for the character with the maximum bounds in the given graphics context.
~~int getMaxDecent( )~~	Deprecated. Replaced by **getMaxDescent( )**.
int getMaxDescent( )	Indicates the maximum descent of the font described by this **FontMetrics** object.
Rectangle2D getStringBounds(char chars, int beginIndex, int limit, Graphics context)	Gets the bounds of the given array of characters in the given [ ] graphics context.
Rectangle2D getStringBounds(CharacterIterator ci, int beginIndex, int limit, Graphics context)	Gets the bounds of the characters indexed in the given character iterator in the given graphics context.
Rectangle2D getStringBounds(String str, Graphics context)	Gets the bounds of the given string in the given graphics context.

(continued)

Table 9.13   Methods of the FontMetrics class (continued).

Method	Does This
Rectangle2D getStringBounds(String str, int beginIndex, int limit, Graphics context)	Gets the bounds of the given string in the given graphics context.
int[ ] getWidths( )	Gets the advance widths of the first 256 characters in the font.
boolean hasUniformLineMetrics( )	Checks whether the font has uniform line metrics.
int stringWidth(String str)	Gets the total advance width for showing the given string in this font.
String toString( )	Gets this **FontMetrics** object's values as a string.

Let's look at an example. In this case, I'll let the user type characters and display them in Courier font, centered in an applet, by determining the screen size of the text using the **FontMetrics** class's **stringWidth** and **getHeight** methods and the width and height of the applet with the applet's **getSize** method. I'll also let the user specify the size of the text, as well as whether it should be in italics or bold, and set a **Font** object accordingly. To actually install the font so that when you print text it appears in that font, you use a **Graphics** object's **setFont** method. Here's what the applet looks like:

```
import java.awt.*;
import java.awt.event.*;
import java.applet.Applet;

/*
  <APPLET
      CODE=fonts.class
      WIDTH=600
      HEIGHT=200 >
  </APPLET>
*/

public class fonts extends Applet implements ActionListener, KeyListener {

    String text = "";

    Button boldbutton, italicbutton, largebutton;
    boolean bold = false;
    boolean italic = false;
    boolean large = false;

    public void init()
    {
```

```
        boldbutton = new Button("Bold font");
        italicbutton = new Button("Italic font");
        largebutton = new Button("Large font");

        boldbutton.addActionListener(this);
        italicbutton.addActionListener(this);
        largebutton.addActionListener(this);

        add(boldbutton);
        add(italicbutton);
        add(largebutton);

        addKeyListener(this);
        requestFocus();
    }

    public void actionPerformed(ActionEvent event)
    {
        if(event.getSource() == boldbutton) bold = !bold;
        if(event.getSource() == italicbutton) italic = !italic;
        if(event.getSource() == largebutton) large = !large;
        requestFocus();
        repaint();
    }

    public void paint(Graphics g)
    {
        String fontname = "Courier";
        int type = Font.PLAIN;
        int size = 36;
        Font font;
        FontMetrics fm;

        if(bold) type = type | Font.BOLD;
        if(italic) type = type | Font.ITALIC;
        if(large) size = 72;

        font = new Font(fontname, type, size);
        g.setFont(font);

        fm = getFontMetrics(font);
        int xloc = (getSize().width - fm.stringWidth(text)) / 2;
        int yloc = (getSize().height + fm.getHeight()) / 2;

        g.drawString(text, xloc, yloc);
    }
```

9. AWT: Graphics, Images, Text, And Fonts

```
        public void keyTyped(KeyEvent e)
        {
            text = text + e.getKeyChar();
            repaint();
        }

        public void keyPressed(KeyEvent e) {}
        public void keyReleased(KeyEvent e) {}
}
```

You can see the result in Figure 9.3. When the user types text, that text appears centered in the applet. Also, when the Bold font, Italic font, and Large font buttons are used, the text appears with the corresponding attributes, which is also shown in Figure 9.3.

Now it's time to move on to working with images—take a look at the next topic.

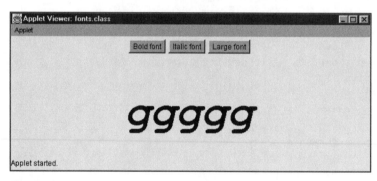

Figure 9.3   Using fonts.

Using Images

The Big Boss says, "About this photo essay you wrote for the company newspaper...." "Yes?" you ask. "Where are the photos?" the BB asks. "Hmm," you say, "this looks like a job for the **Image** class."

You can support images in the AWT with the **Image** class, which is derived directly from **java.lang.Object**:

```
java.lang.Object
|____java.awt.Image
```

You'll find the fields of the **Image** class in Table 9.14, its constructor in Table 9.15, and its methods in Table 9.16.

Table 9.14   Fields of the Image class.

Field	Does This
static int SCALE_AREA_AVERAGING	Indicates that the area-averaging image-scaling algorithm is used.
static int SCALE_DEFAULT	Indicates that the default image-scaling algorithm is used.
static int SCALE_FAST	Indicates that an image-scaling algorithm that gives higher priority to scaling speed has been chosen.
static int SCALE_REPLICATE	Indicates that the image-scaling algorithm in the **ReplicateScaleFilter** class is used.
static int SCALE_SMOOTH	Indicates that an image-scaling algorithm that gives higher priority to image smoothness has been chosen.
static Object UndefinedProperty	The **UndefinedProperty** object should be returned whenever a property that was not defined for a particular image is requested.

Table 9.15   The constructor of the Image class.

Constructor	Does This
Image( )	Creates an **Image** object.

Table 9.16   Methods of the Image class.

Method	Does This
abstract void flush( )	Flushes all resources used by the image.
abstract Graphics getGraphics( )	Creates a graphics context for drawing an offscreen image.
abstract int getHeight(ImageObserver observer)	Indicates the height of the image.
abstract Object getProperty(String name, ImageObserver observer)	Gets a property of this image by name.
Image getScaledInstance(int width, int height, int hints)	Creates a scaled version of this image.
abstract ImageProducer getSource( )	Gets the object that produces the pixels for the image.
abstract int getWidth(ImageObserver observer)	Indicates the width of the image.

9. AWT: Graphics, Images, Text, And Fonts

To load an image into an applet, you can use the **Applet** class's **getImage** method:

```
Image getImage(URL url)
Image getImage(URL url, String name)
```

Here, you can specify the URL of the image file you want to read using the **URL** class. You can create a **URL** object using the **URL** class's constructor like this: **URL("http://java.sun.com/products/jdk/1.2")**, as you'll see later in this book. As far as this chapter is concerned, however, I'll use the **Applet** class's **getCodeBase** and **getDocumentBase** methods to get the URL for the applet, itself, and use that as the same location to find the image file.

Here's a short example that just reads in an image, image.jpg, and then displays it. To read in the image, I use the **getImage** method. To draw the image, I use the **Graphics** class's **drawImage** method. For a lot more on the **Graphics** class, see the topic "Drawing Graphics," later in this chapter. Here's the form of **drawImage** I'll use here, which lets me specify the image object to draw and its position in the applet:

```
boolean drawImage(Image img, int x, int y, ImageObserver observer)
```

Note that you have to pass an object that implements the **ImageObserver** interface to **drawImage**. **ImageObserver** objects let you monitor the progress of image-loading operations, and we'll take a look at them later in this chapter. There's a default implementation of this interface in the **Applet** class, so I just use the **this** keyword as the **ImageObserver** object:

```
import java.awt.*;
import java.applet.*;

/*
  <APPLET
      CODE=image.class
      WIDTH=500
      HEIGHT=150 >
  </APPLET>
*/

public class image extends Applet
{
    Image image;
```

```
public void init()
{
    image = getImage(getDocumentBase(), "image.jpg");
}

public void paint(Graphics g)
{
    g.drawImage(image, 10, 10, this);
}
}
```

ImageObserver's default implementation in the Applet class

The result appears in Figure 9.4, where you can see the loaded image. This example is a success, and you'll find it in image.java on the CD.

Of course, there's a lot more you can do with images. For example, you can resize them (see the next topic).

Figure 9.4   Displaying an image.

Resizing Images

The Novice Programmer is working on a graphics program and needs your help. "I want to let the user resize images," the NP says. "How the heck does that work?" "No problem," you say. "You just specify the new height and width of the image in the **drawImage** method."

To resize an image, you can use this overloaded version of the **Graphics** class's **drawImage** method, which lets you specify an image's width and height:

```
drawImage(Image img, int x, int y, int width, int height,
    ImageObserver observer)
```

Here's an example. In this applet, you just need to press the mouse at one point and release it at another; the applet will draw the image you saw in the previous topic, resized to fit the rectangle you've defined:

```java
import java.awt.*;
import java.lang.Math;
import java.awt.event.*;
import java.applet.Applet;

/*
  <APPLET
    CODE=resizer.class
    WIDTH=600
    HEIGHT=300 >
</APPLET>
*/

public class resizer extends Applet implements MouseListener
{
    Image image;
    boolean mouseUp = false;
    Point start, end;

    public void init()
    {
        image = getImage(getDocumentBase(), "image.jpg");
        addMouseListener(this);
    }

    public void mousePressed(MouseEvent e)
    {
        mouseUp = false;
        start = new Point(e.getX(), e.getY());
    }

    public void mouseReleased(MouseEvent e)
    {
        mouseUp = true;
        end = new Point(Math.max(e.getX(), start.x),
            Math.max(e.getY(), start.y));
        start = new Point(Math.min(e.getX(), start.x),
            Math.min(e.getY(), start.y));
        repaint();
    }
```

```
    public void mouseClicked(MouseEvent e){}
    public void mouseEntered(MouseEvent e){}
    public void mouseExited(MouseEvent e){}

    public void paint (Graphics g)
    {
        if(mouseUp){
            int width = end.x - start.x;
            int height = end.y - start.y;
            g.drawImage(image, start.x, start.y, width, height, this);
        }
    }
}
```

The result of this code appears in Figure 9.5, where you can see that I've resized the image from the previous topic.

We've used a few variations of the handy **drawImage** method, which is part of the **Graphics** class. Now it's time to take a look at the **Graphics** class, itself, and all it contains (which is a truckload of methods). See the next topic for the details.

Figure 9.5   Resizing an image.

Drawing Graphics

The Big Boss appears in a puff of cigar smoke and says, "The design team has come up with a winner program that I want you to write." "What does it do?" you ask. "It lets the user draw lines, rectangles, and ovals as well as freehand with the mouse," the BB says. "Real cutting-edge stuff," you reply.

The real core of AWT graphics is the huge AWT **Graphics** class, which is derived directly from **java.lang.Object**. You'll find the constructor of this class in Table 9.17 and its methods in Table 9.18.

*Table 9.17   The constructor of the **Graphics** class.*

Constructor	Does This
protected Graphics( )	Creates a new **Graphics** object.

*Table 9.18   Methods of the **Graphics** class.*

Method	Does This
abstract void clearRect(int x, int y, int width, int height)	Clears a rectangle by filling it with the background color.
abstract void clipRect(int x, int y, int width, int height)	Intersects the current clip region with the rectangle.
abstract void copyArea(int x, int y, int width, int height, int dx, int dy)	Copies an area of the component by a region given by **dx** and **dy**.
abstract Graphics create( )	Creates a new **Graphics** object that's a copy of this one.
Graphics create(int x, int y, int width, height)	Creates a new **Graphics** object based on this one, with a new int translation and clip area.
abstract void dispose( )	Disposes of this graphics context.
void draw3DRect(int x, int y, int width, int height, boolean raised)	Displays a 3D highlighted outline of a rectangle.
abstract void drawArc(int x, int y, int width, int height, int startAngle, int arcAngle)	Displays the outline of a circular or elliptical arc.
void drawBytes(byte[ ] data, int offset, int length, int x, int y)	Draws the text given by the given byte array.
void drawChars(char[ ] data, int offset, int length, int x, int y)	Shows the text given by the given character array.
abstract boolean drawImage(Image img, int x, int y, Color bgcolor, ImageObserver observer)	Shows as much of the given image as is available.
abstract boolean drawImage(Image img, int x, int y, ImageObserver observer)	Shows as much of the given image as is available.

(continued)

Table 9.18   Methods of the *Graphics* class (continued).

Method	Does This
abstract boolean drawImage(Image img, int x, int y, int width, int height, Color bgcolor, ImageObserver observer)	Shows as much of the given image as has been scaled to fit inside the rectangle.
abstract boolean drawImage(Image img, int x, int y, int width, int height, ImageObserver observer)	Shows as much of the given image as has been scaled to fit inside the rectangle.
abstract boolean drawImage(Image img, int dx1, int dy1, int dx2, int dy2, int sx1, int sy1, int sx2, int sy2, Color bgcolor, ImageObserver observer)	Shows as much of the image as is available, scaling it to fit inside the given area.
abstract boolean drawImage(Image img, int dx1, int dy1, int dx2, int dy2, int sx1, int sy1, int sx2, int sy2, ImageObserver observer)	Shows as much of the area of the image as is available, scaling it to fit inside the given area of the destination surface.
abstract void drawLine(int x1, int y1, int x2, int y2)	Shows a line, using the current color, between the points (x1, y1) and (x2, y2).
abstract void drawOval(int x, int y, int width, int height)	Shows the outline of an oval.
abstract void drawPolygon(int[ ] x Points, int[ ] yPoints, int nPoints)	Shows a closed polygon defined by arrays of x and y coordinates.
void drawPolygon(Polygon p)	Shows the outline of a polygon defined by the given **Polygon** object.
abstract void drawPolyline(int[ ] x Points, int[ ] yPoints, int nPoints)	Shows a sequence of connected lines defined by arrays of x and y coordinates.
void drawRect(int x, int y, int width, int height)	Shows the outline of the given rectangle.
abstract void drawRoundRect(int x, int y, int width, int height, int arcWidth, int arcHeight)	Shows an outlined rounded-corner rectangle.
abstract void drawString(Attributed CharacterIterator iterator, int x, int y)	Shows the text given by the given iterator.
abstract void drawString(String str, int x, int y)	Shows the text given by the given string.

(continued)

Table 9.18   Methods of the *Graphics* class (continued).

Method	Does This
void fill3DRect(int x, int y, int width, int height, boolean raised)	Paints a 3D highlighted rectangle filled with the current color.
abstract void fillArc(int x, int y, int width, int height, int startAngle, int arcAngle)	Fills a circular or elliptical arc covering the given rectangle.
abstract void fillOval(int x, int y, int width, int height)	Fills an oval bounded by the given rectangle with the current color.
abstract void fillPolygon(int[ ] xPoints, int[ ] yPoints, int nPoints)	Fills a closed polygon defined by arrays of x and y coordinates.
void fillPolygon(Polygon p)	Fills the polygon defined by the given **Polygon** object with the graphics context's current color.
abstract void fillRect(int x, int y, int width, int height)	Fills the given rectangle.
abstract void fillRoundRect(int x, int y, int width, int height, int arcWidth, int arcHeight)	Fills the given rounded-corner rectangle.
void finalize( )	Handles garbage collection of this graphics context.
abstract Shape getClip( )	Gets the clipping area.
abstract Rectangle getClipBounds( )	Gets the bounding rectangle of the clipping area.
Rectangle getClipBounds(Rectangle r)	Gets the bounding rectangle of the clipping area.
~~Rectangle getClipRect( )~~	Deprecated. Replaced by **getClipBounds( )**.
abstract Color getColor( )	Gets this graphics context's current color.
abstract Font getFont( )	Gets the font.
FontMetrics getFontMetrics( )	Gets the font metrics of the font.
abstract FontMetrics getFontMetrics(Font f)	Gets the font metrics for the given font.
boolean hitClip(int x, int y, int width, int height)	Returns True if the rectangular area intersects the rectangle of the clipping area.
abstract void setClip(int x, int y, int width, int height)	Sets the current clip to the rectangle given by the given coordinates.
abstract void setClip(Shape clip)	Sets the clipping area to an arbitrary shape.
abstract void setColor(Color c)	Sets this graphics context's color to the given color.

(continued)

Table 9.18   Methods of the *Graphics* class (continued).

Method	Does This
abstract void setFont(Font font)	Sets this graphics context's font to the given font.
abstract void setPaintMode( )	Sets the paint mode to overwrite the destination with this graphics context's current color.
abstract void setXORMode(Color c1)	Sets the paint mode to alternate between this graphics context's current color and the new given color by using **XOR** painting.
String to String( )	Gets a **String** object representing this **Graphics** object.
abstract void translate(int x, int y)	Translates the origin of the graphics context to the point (x, y).

I'm going to put the **Graphics** class to work here by creating the program the Big Boss wanted—a graphics program that lets the user draw lines, ovals, rectangles, rounded rectangles, and freehand with the mouse, as shown in Figure 9.6.

This program is called draw.java on the CD, and here's how it works: The user clicks on a button indicating what kind of figure he or she wants to draw, which sets a boolean flag inside the program. When the user next presses the mouse in the drawing area, that location is stored as **start**, using a Java **Point** object (which has two data members: **x** and **y**). When the user releases the mouse in a new location, that location is stored as **end**. Releasing the mouse also repaints the program, and the user can select what figure to draw—a line, oval, rectangle, or rounded rectangle—between **start** and **end** based on the boolean flags set by clicking the buttons.

Drawing freehand with the mouse is a little different, though. In that case, I store up to 1,000 points that the mouse moves over. When it's time to draw the program, I just connect the dots with lines (note that a mouse event is not generated for each pixel the mouse moves over, so I need to draw lines between the mouse

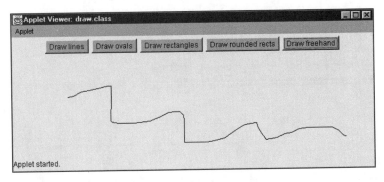

Figure 9.6   Drawing freehand with the mouse.

9. AWT: Graphics, Images, Text, And Fonts

locations that Java does report). Here's what draw.java looks like (we'll take a look at the drawing sections in detail in the following pages):

```java
import java.awt.*;
import java.lang.Math;
import java.awt.event.*;
import java.awt.Graphics;
import java.applet.Applet;

/*
  <APPLET
      CODE=draw.class
      WIDTH=600
      HEIGHT=200 >
  </APPLET>
*/

public class draw extends Applet implements ActionListener, MouseListener,
MouseMotionListener {
    Button bDraw, bLine, bOval, bRect, bRounded;
    Point dot[] = new Point[1000];
    Point start, end;
    int dots = 0;

    boolean mouseUp = false;
    boolean draw = false;
    boolean line = false;
    boolean oval = false;
    boolean rectangle = false;
    boolean rounded = false;

    public void init()
    {
        bLine = new Button("Draw lines");
        bOval = new Button("Draw ovals");
        bRect = new Button("Draw rectangles");
        bRounded = new Button("Draw rounded rects");
        bDraw = new Button("Draw freehand");

        add(bLine);
        add(bOval);
        add(bRect);
        add(bRounded);
        add(bDraw);
```

```
    bLine.addActionListener(this);
    bOval.addActionListener(this);
    bRect.addActionListener(this);
    bRounded.addActionListener(this);
    bDraw.addActionListener(this);

    addMouseListener(this);
    addMouseMotionListener(this);
}

public void mousePressed(MouseEvent e)
{
    mouseUp = false;
    start = new Point(e.getX(), e.getY());
}

public void mouseReleased(MouseEvent e)
{
    if(line){
        end = new Point(e.getX(), e.getY());
    } else {
        end = new Point(Math.max(e.getX(), start.x),
            Math.max(e.getY(), start.y));
        start = new Point(Math.min(e.getX(), start.x),
            Math.min(e.getY(), start.y));
    }
    mouseUp = true;
    repaint();
}

public void mouseDragged(MouseEvent e)
{
    if(draw){
        dot[dots] = new Point(e.getX(), e.getY());
        dots++;
        repaint();
    }
}

public void mouseClicked(MouseEvent e){}
public void mouseEntered(MouseEvent e){}
public void mouseExited(MouseEvent e){}
public void mouseMoved(MouseEvent e){}
```

[handwritten note: o ponto final tem que ser abaixo e à direita do inicial]

[handwritten note: the points reported when the mouse is dragged]

[handwritten note: why not used the adapter class??]

```java
public void paint (Graphics g)
{
    if (mouseUp) {
        int width = end.x - start.x;
        int height = end.y - start.y;

        if(line){
            g.drawLine(start.x, start.y, end.x, end.y);
        }
        else if(oval){
            g.drawOval(start.x, start.y, width, height);
        }
        else if(rectangle){
            g.drawRect(start.x, start.y, width, height);
        }
        else if(rounded){
            g.drawRoundRect(start.x, start.y, width, height, 10, 10);
        }
        else if(draw){
            for(int loop_index = 0; loop_index < dots - 1;
                loop_index++){
                g.drawLine(dot[loop_index].x, dot[loop_index].y,
                    dot[loop_index + 1].x, dot[loop_index + 1].y);
            }
        }
    }
}

public void actionPerformed(ActionEvent e)
{
    setFlagsFalse();
    if(e.getSource() == bDraw)draw = true;
    if(e.getSource() == bLine)line = true;
    if(e.getSource() == bOval)oval = true;
    if(e.getSource() == bRect)rectangle = true;
    if(e.getSource() == bRounded)rounded = true;
}

void setFlagsFalse()
{
    rounded = false;
    line = false;
    oval = false;
    rectangle = false;
    draw = false;
}
```

That's what draw.java looks like. Now let's take a look at some of its drawing functions. All these drawing functions, except for the freehand drawing functions, draw a figure between the locations **start** and **end**, which the user indicates by dragging the mouse.

Drawing Lines

Using a **Graphics** object, you can draw a line between the points (x1, y1) and (x2, y2) with the **drawLine** method:

```
drawLine(int x1, int y1, int x2, int y2);
```

Here's how that looks in draw.java:

```
g.drawLine(start.x, start.y, end.x, end.y);
```

You can see the result in draw.java, as shown in Figure 9.7.

Drawing Ovals

Ellipses, including circles, are called *ovals* in the AWT, and you can draw them with the **Graphics** class's **drawOval** method:

```
drawOval(int x, int y, int width, int height);
```

Here's how ovals are drawn, as specified by the user when running draw.java:

```
int width = end.x - start.x;
int height = end.y - start.y;
g.drawOval(start.x, start.y, width, height);
```

You can see the result in draw.java, as shown in Figure 9.8.

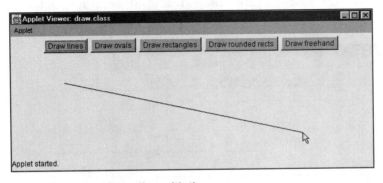

Figure 9.7   Drawing a line with the mouse.

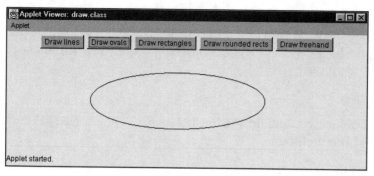

Figure 9.8   Drawing an oval with the mouse.

Drawing Rectangles

You can draw rectangles using the **Graphics** class's **drawRect** method:

```
drawRect(int x, int y, int width, int height);
```

Here's how I do it in draw.java:

```
int width = end.x - start.x;
int height = end.y - start.y;
g.drawRect(start.x, start.y, width, height);
```

You can see the result in draw.java, as shown in Figure 9.9.

Drawing Rounded Rectangles

You can draw rounded rectangles (rectangles with rounded corners, that is) using the **Graphics** class's **drawRoundRect** method:

```
drawRoundRect(int x, int y, int width, int height, int arcWidth, int
    arcHeight);
```

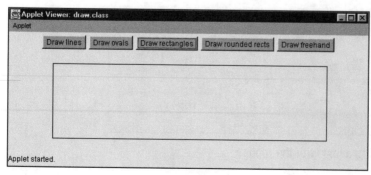

Figure 9.9   Drawing a rectangle with the mouse.

Here, you specify the arc width and height, in pixels, which specifies the rounding of the corners. Here's how I create a rounded rectangle in draw.java:

```
int width = end.x - start.x;
int height = end.y - start.y;
g.drawRoundRect(start.x, start.y, width, height, 10, 10);
```

You can see the result in draw.java, as shown in Figure 9.10.

Drawing Freehand

You can draw freehand with the mouse using the AWT **Graphics** class, but you'll have to implement it yourself in code. Here's how I do it in draw.java using the **mouseDragged** method: After checking to make sure the user is drawing freehand by making sure the **draw** flag is True, I save all the mouse locations in an array named **dot[]** as the mouse is dragged:

```
public void mouseDragged(MouseEvent e)
{
    if(draw){
        dot[dots] = new Point(e.getX(), e.getY());
        dots++;
        repaint();
    }
}
```

Then, when it's time to draw the figure, I just connect the dots using lines, like this:

```
for(int loop_index = 0; loop_index < dots - 1; loop_index++){
    g.drawLine(dot[loop_index].x, dot[loop_index].y,
        dot[loop_index + 1].x, dot[loop_index + 1].y);
}
```

You can see the result in Figure 9.6 (shown previously).

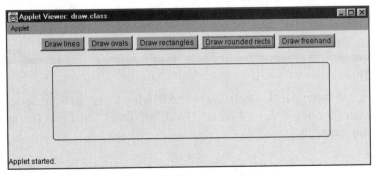

Figure 9.10   Drawing a rounded rectangle with the mouse.

Drawing Arcs

You can use the **Graphics** class's **drawArc** method to draw arcs (you specify angles in degrees):

```
drawArc(int x, int y, int width, int height, int startAngle, int arcAngle);
```

Drawing Polygons

There are a number of ways to draw polygons and multiple-segment lines with the AWT:

```
drawPolygon(int[] xPoints, int[] yPoints, int nPoints);
```

```
drawPolygon(Polygon p);
```

```
drawPolyline(int[] xPoints, int[] yPoints, int nPoints);
```

Setting Drawing Modes

The AWT also allows you to alternate between two drawing modes—straight painting mode and **XOR** mode—with these methods:

```
setXORMode(Color c1);
```

```
setPaintMode();
```

In painting mode, whatever you paint just covers what's underneath, but in **XOR** mode, what you draw will be exclusively **OR**ed with a particular color that's already on the screen. This is very useful, because when you **XOR** A with B twice, B is restored, which means you can draw something on the screen and then draw it using **XOR** drawing. Then, whatever was on the screen originally is restored. For example, you may want to let the user "stretch" the figures he or she is drawing in draw.java interactively. Here's how to do this: You let the user draw a figure; then, when the user moves the mouse, you redraw the figure using **XOR** mode to erase it. Then you redraw it with its new size.

Selecting Colors

"My graphics work has been a little drab," says the Novice Programmer, "because everything's appearing in one color—black." "Well," you say, "you can select the drawing color easily enough."

No discussion of graphics would be complete without discussing colors, and you handle colors in the AWT with the **Color** class. You'll find the fields of this class in Table 9.19, its constructors in Table 9.20, and its methods in Table 9.21.

For example, to create a new color, you can specify red, green, and blue values (in the range 0 to 255) to the **Color** class's constructor, like this:

```
Color c = new Color(red, green, blue);
```

Now you're free to set this new color as the drawing color, using **setForeground**:

```
setForeground(c);
```

Now drawing operations will take place in the color you've specified. You can also use a predefined color, such as **Color.blue**, as in this case, where I'm setting the background color:

```
setBackground(Color.blue);
```

In fact, you can also fill in figures using the color you've specified with **Graphics** methods, such as **fillArc**, **fillOval**, and so on.

Table 9.19   Fields of the Color class.

Field	Does This
static Color black	Stands for the color black.
static Color blue	Stands for the color blue.
static Color cyan	Stands for the color cyan.
static Color darkGray	Stands for the color dark gray.
static Color gray	Stands for the color gray.
static Color green	Stands for the color green.
static Color lightGray	Stands for the color light gray.
static Color magenta	Stands for the color magenta.
static Color orange	Stands for the color orange.
static Color pink	Stands for the color pink.
static Color red	Stands for the color red.
static Color white	Stands for the color white.
static Color yellow	Stands for the color yellow.

9. AWT: Graphics, Images, Text, And Fonts

Table 9.20 Constructors of the Color class.

Constructor	Does This
Color(ColorSpace cspace, float[ ] components, float alpha)	Creates a color in the color space of the supplied **ColorSpace** .
Color(float r, float g, float b)	Creates an opaque color with the given red, green, and blue values in the range 0.0 to 1.0.
Color(float r, float g, float b, float a)	Creates a color with the given red, green, blue, and alpha values in the range 0.0 to 1.0.
Color(int rgb)	Creates an opaque color with the given combined RGB value, consisting of the red value in bits 16-23, the green value in bits 8-15, and the blue value in bits 0-7.
Color(int rgba, boolean hasalpha)	Creates a color with the given combined RGBA value, consisting of the alpha value in bits 24-31, the red value in bits 16-23, the green value in bits 8-15, and the blue value in bits 0-7.
Color(int r, int g, int b)	Creates an opaque color with the given red, green, and blue values in the range 0 to 255.
Color(int r, int g, int b, int a)	Creates a color with the given red, green, blue, and alpha values in the range 0 to 255.

Table 9.21 Methods of the Color class.

Method	Does This
Color brighter( )	Makes a brighter version of the color.
PaintContext createContext(Color Model cm, Rectangle r, Rectangle2D r2d, AffineTransform xform, Rendering Hints hints)	Creates and returns a paint context to generate a pattern in solid color.
Color darker( )	Makes a darker version of the color.
static Color decode(String nm)	Converts a string to an integer and returns that color.
boolean equals(Object obj)	Determines whether another color is equal to this color.
int getAlpha( )	Gets the alpha value.
int getBlue( )	Gets the blue value.
static Color getColor(String nm)	Finds a color in the system properties.
static Color getColor (String nm, Color v)	Finds a color in the system properties.
static Color getColor(String nm, int v)	Finds a color in the system properties.
float[ ] getColorComponents(Color Space cspace, float[ ] compArray)	Gets a float array containing the color components of the Color object in the color space.

(continued)

*Table 9.21   Methods of the **Color** class* (continued).

Method	Does This
float[ ] getColorComponents(float [ ] compArray)	Gets a float array containing the color components (no alpha) of the Color object.
ColorSpace getColorSpace( )	Gets the color space of the Color object.
float[ ] getComponents(ColorSpace cspace, float[ ] compArray)	Gets a float array containing the color and alpha components of the Color object in the color space.
float[ ] getComponents(float[ ] compArray)	Gets a float array containing the color and alpha components of the Color object.
int getGreen( )	Gets the green value.
static Color getHSBColor(float h, float s, float b)	Creates a Color object based on HSB values.
int getRed( )	Gets the red value.
int getRGB( )	Gets the RGB value representing the color in the default color model.
float[ ] getRGBColorComponents (float[ ] compArray)	Gets a float array containing the color components (no alpha) of the Color object in the default color space.
float[ ] getRGBComponents (float[ ] compArray)	Gets a float array containing the color and alpha components of the Color object, as represented in the default color space.
int getTransparency( )	Returns the transparency mode for this color.
int hashCode( )	Computes the hashcode for this color.
static int HSBtoRGB	(float hue, float Converts the composaturation, float brightness). nents of a color given by the HSB model to the default RGB model
static float[ ] RGBtoHSB(int r, int g, int b, float[ ] hsbvals)	Converts the components of a color, as given by the RGB model, to an equivalent set of values for the HSB model.
String toString( )	Gets a string representation of this color.

Using Canvases

The canvas component is specially built to support graphics operations. As the name suggests, canvases provide a blank space for you to draw on, using the **Graphics** object passed to the **paint** method. Here's the inheritance diagram for the AWT **Canvas** class:

```
java.lang.Object
|____java.awt.Component
     |____java.awt.Canvas
```

Table 9.22   Constructors of the Canvas class.

Constructor	Does This
Canvas( )	Creates a new canvas.
Canvas(GraphicsConfiguration config)	Creates a new canvas given a **GraphicsConfiguration** object.

Table 9.23   Methods of the Canvas class.

Method	Does This
void addNotify( )	Creates the peer of the canvas.
void paint(Graphics g)	This method is called to repaint the canvas.

You'll find the constructors for this class in Table 9.22 and its methods in Table 9.23.

One common use for canvases is to support an elementary form of animation, because you can use AWT **Component** class's **setLocation** method to move a canvas (or any other component) around. Here's an applet that does just that when it's clicked :

```
import java.applet.Applet;
import java.awt.*;
import java.awt.event.*;

/*
  <APPLET
      CODE=canvas.class
      WIDTH=400
      HEIGHT=200 >
  </APPLET>
*/

public class canvas extends java.applet.Applet implements MouseListener {

    graphicsCanvas gc;
    Button button1;

    public void init()
    {
        gc = new graphicsCanvas();
        gc.setSize(100, 100);
        add(gc);
```

```
            addMouseListener(this);
    }

    public void mousePressed(MouseEvent e){}

    public void mouseClicked(MouseEvent e)
    {
        for(int loop_index = 0; loop_index < 150; loop_index++){
            gc.setLocation(loop_index, 0);
        }
    }
    public void mouseReleased(MouseEvent e){}
    public void mouseEntered(MouseEvent e){}
    public void mouseExited(MouseEvent e){}
}

class graphicsCanvas extends java.awt.Canvas
{
    public void paint (Graphics g)
    {
        g.drawOval(10, 50, 40, 40);
        g.drawLine(10, 50, 50, 90);
        g.drawLine(50, 50, 10, 90);
    }
}
```

The result appears in Figure 9.11. When you click the applet, the canvas, which displays a small figure, moves to the left and then sweeps to the right. This example is in canvas.java on the CD. Note that because a **Graphics** object is passed in a canvas's **paint** method, you can use any **Graphics** method in a canvas.

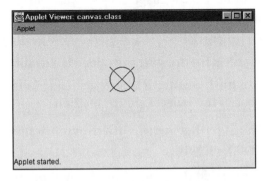

Figure 9.11   Simple animation with a canvas.

Using The **ImageObserver** Interface

The Product Support Specialist appears and sadly says, "There have been complaints about how your program draws images downloaded from the Internet—only part of the image appears at first, and the rest arrives gradually." "That's the way the Internet works," you say, surprised. "Can't you fix it?" the PSS asks.

You can use the methods in the **ImageObserver** interface to watch as images are loaded; as you saw earlier, you need to indicate an **ImageObserver** interface when loading an image into an applet and specify the **Applet** class's own default implementation of that interface. In this topic, I'll create my own implementation of this interface. The **ImageObserver** interface has only one method, **imageUpdate**:

```
boolean imageUpdate(Image img, int infoflags, int x, int y, int width,
    int height)
```

This method is called when information about an image that's being loaded asynchronously becomes available. Here are the flags passed in the *infoflags* parameter in the **imageUpdate** method:

- *ABORT*—Indicates that an image that was being tracked was aborted

- *ALLBITS*—Indicates that a static image that was previously drawn is now complete

- *ERROR*—Indicates that an image that was being tracked has developed an error

- *FRAMEBITS*—Indicates that another complete frame of a multiframe image is now available to be drawn

- *HEIGHT*—Indicates that the height of the base image is now available (and can be read from the **height** argument of the **imageUpdate** method)

- *PROPERTIES*—Indicates that the properties of the image are now available

- *SOMEBITS*—Indicates that more pixels for drawing the image are available

- *WIDTH*—Indicates that the width of the base image is now available (and can be read from the **width** argument of the **imageUpdate** method)

The **imageUpdate** method returns True if further updates are required; it returns False if you've received the information you want.

Here's an example. In this case, I just override the **imageUpdate** method to call **repaint** to display an image, but only when it's completely loaded:

```
import java.awt.*;
import java.applet.*;
```

```
/*
  <APPLET
      CODE=iobserver.class
      WIDTH=600
      HEIGHT=150 >
  </APPLET>
*/

public class iobserver extends Applet
{
    Image image;

    public void init()
    {
        image = getImage(getDocumentBase(), "image.jpg");
    }

    public void paint(Graphics g)
    {
        g.drawImage(image, 10, 10, this);
    }

    public boolean imageUpdate(Image img, int flags, int x, int y,
        int w, int h)
    {
        if ((flags & ALLBITS) != 0) {
            repaint(x, y, w, h);
        }
        return (flags & ALLBITS) == 0;
    }
}
```

The result is shown in Figure 9.12, where the image appears only after it's been fully loaded—no f lickering involved at all. This example is in iobserver.java on the CD.

Programmers have told Sun that they find the **ImageObserver** interface to be too complex, especially when dealing with multiple downloads; therefore, Sun created the **MediaTracker** class (see the next topic).

9. AWT: Graphics, Images, Text, And Fonts

Figure 9.12   Using an **ImageObserver** interface.

Using The **MediaTracker** Class

The **MediaTracker** class provides an easy way (easier than using **ImageObserver** objects) to monitor the downloading of images. To start, you just pass the **addImage** method an image as well as an ID you want to use for that image (you can use the same ID for a number of images if you want to keep track of them as a group):

```
void addImage(Image image, int id)
void addImage(Image image, int id, int w, int h)
```

You can check whether an image or image group has finished loading with the **checkID** method, like this:

```
boolean checkID(int id)
boolean checkID(int id, boolean load)
```

This method return True if the image or image group concerned is finished loading; otherwise, False is returned. You can also use the **waitForAll** method; this method returns only when all tracked images have been loaded.

You'll find the fields of the **MediaTracker** class in Table 9.24, its constructor in Table 9.25, and its methods in Table 9.26.

Table 9.24   Fields of the *MediaTracker* class.

Field	Does This
static int ABORTED	Indicates that the downloading was aborted.
static int COMPLETE	Indicates that the downloading of media was completed.
static int ERRORED	Indicates that the downloading of some media developed an error.
static int LOADING	Indicates some data is currently being loaded.

Table 9.25   The constructor of the *MediaTracker* class.

Constructor	Does This
MediaTracker(Component comp)	Creates a media tracker.

Table 9.26   Methods of the *MediaTracker* class.

Method	Does This
void addImage(Image image, int id)	Adds an image to the images being tracked
void addImage(Image image, int id, int w, int h)	Adds a scaled image to the list of images being tracked
boolean checkAll( )	Checks to see if all images being tracked have finished loading
boolean checkAll(boolean load)	Checks to see if all images being tracked by this media tracker have finished loading
boolean checkID(int id)	Checks to see if all images tracked by this media tracker that have the given identifier are finished loading
boolean checkID(int id, boolean load)	Checks to see if all images tracked by this media tracker that are tagged with the given identifier have finished loading
Object[ ] getErrorsAny( )	Gets a list of all images that have developed an error
Object[ ] getErrorsID(int id)	Gets a list of images with the given ID that have encountered an error
boolean isErrorAny( )	Checks the error status of all the images
boolean isErrorID(int id)	Checks the error status of all the images with the given identifier
void removeImage(Image image)	Removes an image from this media tracker
void removeImage(Image image, int id)	Removes the given image from the given tracking ID
void removeImage(Image image, int id, int width, int height)	Removes the given image with the given width, height, and ID from this media tracker
int statusAll(boolean load)	Gets the bitwise inclusive **OR** of the status of all media tracked by this media tracker
int statusID(int id, boolean load)	Gets the bitwise inclusive **OR** of the status of all media with the given identifier that are tracked by this media tracker
void waitForAll( )	Starts loading all images
boolean waitForAll(long ms)	Starts loading all images
void waitForID(int id)	Starts loading all images with the given identifier
boolean waitForID(int id, long ms)	Starts loading all images with the given identifier

9. AWT: Graphics, Images, Text, And Fonts

Here's an example. In this case, I use the **waitForAll** method to wait until an image is fully loaded (note the **try/catch** statement, which is there to handle exceptions—you'll see this in more detail later in this book):

```java
import java.awt.*;
import java.applet.*;

/*
  <APPLET
      CODE=mediatracker.class
      WIDTH=600
      HEIGHT=150 >
  </APPLET>
*/

public class mediatracker extends Applet
{
    Image image;

    public void init()
    {
        MediaTracker tracker = new MediaTracker(this);
        image = getImage(getDocumentBase(), "image.jpg");
        tracker.addImage(image, 0);
        try {
            tracker.waitForAll();
        }
        catch (InterruptedException ex) { }
    }

    public void paint(Graphics g)
    {
        g.drawImage(image, 10, 10, this);
    }
}
```

The results appear in Figure 9.13. This example is in mediatracker.java on the CD.

Figure 9.13   Using a MediaTracker Object.

Working Pixel By Pixel: The **PixelGrabber** And **MemoryImageSource** Classes

"OK," says the Novice Programmer, "there are some things that I want to do graphically that I can only do by gaining direct access to the pixels in the image themselves. Guess I can't use Java for that." "Of course you can," you say. The NP says, "Tell me more!"

You can use **PixelGrabber** objects to place the pixels from an image into an array and thus gain direct access to those pixels. Here's the inheritance diagram for **PixelGrabber**:

```
java.lang.Object
|____java.awt.image.PixelGrabber
```

You'll find the constructors for the **PixelGrabber** class in Table 9.27 and the methods for this class in Table 9.28.

Table 9.27   Constructors of the **PixelGrabber** *class.*

Constructor	Does This
PixelGrabber(Image img, int x, int y, int w, int h, boolean forceRGB)	Creates a PixelGrabber object to grab the (x, y, w, h) section of pixels.
PixelGrabber(Image img, int x, int y, scansize) pixels int w, int h, int[ ] pix, and places them in an array	Creates a **PixelGrabber** object to grab the (x, y, w, h) section of from the given image int off, int.
PixelGrabber(ImageProducer ip, int x, int y, int w, int h, int[ ] pix, int off, int scansize)	Creates a **PixelGrabber** object to grab the (x, y, w, h) rectangular section of pixels from the image produced by the image producer.

Table 9.28   Methods of the **PixelGrabber** *class.*

Method	Does This
void abortGrabbing( )	Asks the **PixelGrabber** object to abort the image fetch.
ColorModel getColorModel( )	Gets the color model for the pixels in the array.
int getHeight( )	Gets the height of the pixel buffer.
Object getPixels( )	Gets the pixel buffer.
int getStatus( )	Gets the status of the pixels.
int getWidth( )	Gets the width of the pixel buffer.
boolean grabPixels( )	Requests the image or image producer to start delivering pixels.

(continued)

Table 9.28   Methods of the *PixelGrabber* class (continued).

Method	Does This
boolean grabPixels(long ms)	Asks the image or image producer to start delivering pixels and wait for all the pixels until the given timeout has elapsed.
void imageComplete(int status)	This is part of the ImageConsumer API, which this class must implement to retrieve the pixels.
void setColorModel(ColorModel model)	This is part of the ImageConsumer API, which this class must implement to retrieve pixels.
void setDimensions(int width, int height)	This is part of the ImageConsumer API, which this class must implement to retrieve pixels.
void setHints(int hints)	This is part of the ImageConsumer API, which this class must implement to retrieve pixels.
void setPixels(int srcX, int srcY, intsrcW, int srcH, ColorModel model, byte[ ] pixels, int srcOff, int srcScan)	This is part of the ImageConsumer API, which this class must implement to retrieve pixels.
void setPixels(int srcX, int srcY, intsrcW, int srcH, ColorModel model, int[ ] pixels, int srcOff, int srcScan)	This is part of the ImageConsumer API, which this class must implement to retrieve pixels.
void setProperties(Hashtable props)	This is part of the ImageConsumer API, which this class must implement to retrieve the pixels.
void startGrabbing( )	Asks the **PixelGrabber** object to start fetching pixels.
int status( )	Deprecated. Replaced by **getStatus( )**.

To create an image from an array of pixels, you can use the **MemoryImageSource** class. The inheritance diagram for this class looks like this:

```
java.lang.Object
|____java.awt.image.MemoryImageSource
```

You'll find the constructors for the **MemoryImageSource** class in Table 9.29 and the methods for this class in Table 9.30.

Here's an example using the **PixelGrabber** and **MemoryImageSource** classes.

In this case, I just read in an image and copy it to a new image object. I do this by loading in the image I've used in the previous examples in this chapter, which is 485 by 88 pixels. First, I load the image into **image**, place the pixels in that image into an array named **pixels** using a **PixelGrabber** object's **grabPixels** method,

Table 9.29   Constructors of the *MemoryImageSource* class.

Constructor	Does This
MemoryImageSource(int w, int h, ColorModel cm, byte[ ] pix, int off, int scan)	Creates an ImageProducer object that uses an array of bytes.
MemoryImageSource(int w, int h, ColorModel cm, byte[ ] pix, int off, int scan, Hashtable props)	Creates an ImageProducer object that uses an array of bytes and properties.
MemoryImageSource(int w, int h, ColorModel cm, int[ ] pix, int off, int scan)	Creates an ImageProducer object that uses an array of integers.
MemoryImageSource(int w, int h, ColorModel cm, int[ ] pix, int off, int scan, Hashtable props)	Creates an ImageProducer object that uses an array of integers and properties.
MemoryImageSource(int w, int h, int[ ] pix, int off, int scan)	Creates an ImageProducer object that uses an array of integers in the default RGB color model.
MemoryImageSource(int w, int h, int[ ] pix, int off, int scan, Hashtable props)	Creates an ImageProducer object that uses an array of integers in the default RGB color model and properties.

Table 9.30   Methods of the *MemoryImageSource* class.

Method	Does This
void addConsumer (ImageConsumer ic)	Adds an **ImageConsumer** object to the list of consumers.
boolean isConsumer (ImageConsumer ic)	Indicates whether an **ImageConsumer** object is on the list of consumer images..
void newPixels( )	Sends a whole new buffer of pixels to any **ImageConsumer** objects.
void newPixels(byte[ ] newpix, ColorModel newmodel, int offset, int scansize)	Changes to a new byte array.
void newPixels(int[ ] newpix, ColorModel newmodel, int offset, int scansize)	Changes to a new int array.
void newPixels(int x, int y, int w, int h)	Sends a rectangular region of the buffer of pixels to **ImageConsumer** objects.

(continued)

9. AWT: Graphics, Images, Text, And Fonts

Table 9.30   Methods of the *MemoryImageSource* class (continued).

Method	Does This
void newPixels(int x, int y, int w,	Sends a rectangular region of the buffer of pixels to **ImageConsumer** int h, boolean framenotify) objects
void removeConsumer (ImageConsumer ic)	Removes an **ImageConsumer** object from the list of consumers
void requestTopDownLeftRight Resend(ImageConsumer ic)	Requests that the image data be delivered one more time in top-down, left-right order
void setAnimated(boolean animated)	Changes this memory image into a multiframe animation or a single-frame static image
void setFullBufferUpdates (boolean fullbuffers)	Indicates whether this animated memory image should always be updated by sending the complete buffer of pixels
void startProduction (ImageConsumer ic)	Adds an **ImageConsumer** object to the list of consumers and starts delivery of the image data

and then create a new image, **image2**, using a **MemoryImageSource** object and the **Applet** class's **createImage** method:

```
import java.awt.*;
import java.applet.*;
import java.awt.image.*;

/*
  <APPLET
     CODE=copier.class
     WIDTH=600
     HEIGHT=150 >
  </APPLET>
*/

public class copier extends Applet {
    Image image, image2;

    public void init()
    {
        image = getImage(getDocumentBase(), "image.jpg");
        int pixels[] = new int[485 * 88];

        PixelGrabber pg = new PixelGrabber(image, 0, 0, 485, 88,
            pixels, 0, 485);
        try {
            pg.grabPixels();
```

```
        }
      catch (InterruptedException e) {}

      for (int loop_index = 0; loop_index < 485 * 88; loop_index++){
          int p = pixels[loop_index];
          int red = 0xff & (p >> 16);
          int green = 0xff & (p >> 8);
          int blue = 0xff & p;
          pixels[loop_index] = (0xff000000 | red << 16 | green << 8 |
              blue);
      }

      image2 = createImage(new MemoryImageSource(485, 88, pixels, 0 ,
          485));
  }

    public void paint(Graphics g)
    {
        g.drawImage(image2, 10, 10, this);
    }
}
```

That's all there is to it—now the image is copied into **image2** and displayed. This example is in copier.java on the CD. Now that we have access to the pixels in the image, I'll do a few more things with the image, such as brightening it, as discussed in the next topic.

Brightening Images

You can brighten images just by increasing their red, green, and blue color values by the same amount. In the following code, I add 20 to each color value:

```
import java.awt.*;
import java.applet.*;
import java.awt.image.*;

/*
  <APPLET
      CODE=brighten.class
      WIDTH=600
      HEIGHT=150 >
  </APPLET>
*/
```

```
public class brighten extends Applet {
    Image image, image2;

    public void init()
    {
        image = getImage(getDocumentBase(), "image.jpg");
        int pixels[] = new int[485 * 88];

        PixelGrabber pg = new PixelGrabber(image, 0, 0, 485,
            88, pixels, 0, 485);
        try {
            pg.grabPixels();
        }
        catch (InterruptedException e) {}

        for (int loop_index = 0; loop_index < 485 * 88; loop_index++){
            int p = pixels[loop_index];
            int red = (0xff & (p >> 16)) + 20;
            int green = (0xff & (p >> 8)) + 20;
            int blue = (0xff & p) + 20;
            if (red > 255) red = 255;
            if (green > 255) green = 255;
            if (blue > 255) blue = 255;
            pixels[loop_index] = (0xff000000 | red << 16 | green << 8 |
                blue);
        }

        image2 = createImage(new MemoryImageSource(485, 88, pixels, 0 ,
            485));
    }

    public void paint(Graphics g)
    {
        g.drawImage(image2, 10, 10, this);
    }
}
```

The result appears in Figure 9.14. Now we're really manipulating images in code.

Figure 9.14   Using a **MediaTracker** object.

Converting Images To Grayscale

You can convert images to gray by averaging the red, green, and blue color values for each pixel. In this case, I convert a color wheel image—whirl1.gif (a red and white image that you'll see later in this book when we discuss graphics animation)—to gray. Here's how this looks in code:

```java
import java.awt.*;
import java.applet.*;
import java.awt.image.*;

/*
  <APPLET
      CODE=grayscale.class
      WIDTH=300
      HEIGHT=300 >
  </APPLET>
*/

public class grayscale extends Applet {
    Image image, image2;

    public void init()
    {
        image = getImage(getDocumentBase(), "whirl1.gif");
        int pixels[] = new int[248 * 248];

        PixelGrabber pg = new PixelGrabber(image, 0, 0, 248, 248,
            pixels, 0, 248);
        try {
            pg.grabPixels();
        }
        catch (InterruptedException e) {}
```

```
    for (int loop_index = 0; loop_index < 248 * 248; loop_index++){
        int p = pixels[loop_index];
        int red = (0xff & (p >> 16));
        int green = (0xff & (p >> 8));
        int blue = (0xff & p);
        int avg = (int) ((red + green + blue) / 3);
        pixels[loop_index] = (0xff000000 | avg << 16 | avg << 8 | avg);
    }

    image2 = createImage(new MemoryImageSource(248, 248, pixels, 0 ,
        248));
}

public void paint(Graphics g)
{
    g.drawImage(image2, 10, 10, this);
}
}
```

The result appears in Figure 9.15. Of course, seeing a grayscale image in this figure might not be too convincing in a book full of black and white images. Instead, try running the example from the CD—it's graysscale.java.

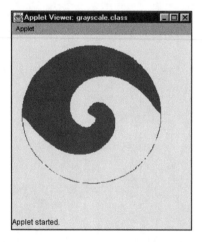

Figure 9.15   Converting an image to gray.

Embossing Images

"Embossing" images is a powerful effect in which images appear to be raised from the viewing surface; we'll take a look at this effect here. Embossing images is most convenient when you work in terms of a two-dimensional array. However, the **PixelGrabber** and **MemoryImageSource** classes only work with one-dimensional arrays, so I'll simulate two-dimensional addressing by multiplying and adding array indexes in this example. Here, I emboss the whirl1.gif image you saw in the previous topic:

```java
import java.awt.*;
import java.awt.image.*;
import java.applet.*;

/*
  <APPLET
      CODE=emboss.class
      WIDTH=300
      HEIGHT=300 >
  </APPLET>
*/

public class emboss extends Applet
{
    Image image, image2;

    public void init()
    {
        image = getImage(getDocumentBase(), "whirl1.gif");
        int pixels[] = new int[248 * 248];

        PixelGrabber pg = new PixelGrabber(image, 0, 0, 248, 248,
            pixels, 0, 248);
        try {
            pg.grabPixels();
        }
        catch (InterruptedException e) {}

        for (int x = 2; x < 247; x++){
            for (int y = 2; y < 247; y++){

                int red = ((pixels[(x + 1) * 248 + y + 1] & 0xFF) -
                    (pixels[x * 248 + y] & 0xFF)) + 128;
```

```
                int green = (((pixels[(x + 1) * 248 + y + 1] & 0xFF00) /
                    0x100) % 0x100 - ((pixels[x * 248 + y] & 0xFF00) /
                    0x100) % 0x100) + 128;

                int blue = (((pixels[(x + 1) * 248 + y + 1] &
                    0xFF0000) / 0x10000) % 0x100 - ((pixels[x * 248 + y] &
                    0xFF0000) / 0x10000) % 0x100) + 128;

                int avg = (red + green + blue) / 3;

                pixels[x * 248 + y] = (0xff000000 | avg << 16 | avg << 8 |
                    avg);
            }
        }

        image2 = createImage(new MemoryImageSource(248, 248, pixels, 0 ,
            248));
    }

    public void paint(Graphics g)
    {
        g.drawImage(image2, 0, 0, this);
    }
}
```

The result appears in Figure 9.16. As you can see, the figure does indeed appear as though it were embossed. This example is embossed.java on the CD.

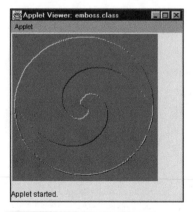

Figure 9.16   Embossing an image.

Chapter 10

AWT: Windows, Menus, And Dialog Boxes

In Depth

This chapter is all about taking the next step beyond creating controls in AWT programs. In this chapter, we'll create and display AWT windows and see all that goes into the process, using the AWT **Window** and **Frame** classes. We'll also look at how to use the **Dialog** class to create dialog boxes and the **FileDialog** class to create file dialog boxes for specifying a file. This is also where we'll take a look at menus, because in AWT programming, you need a window before you can display menus. First, we'll take a brief look at all these items in overview.

Windows

Windows, of course, are the foundation of GUI programming. Just about everything having to do with the user interface in a graphical environment happens in a window, and every GUI user is familiar with windows. You host the components that make up an applet or windowed application in windows, and there are three types of windows available to AWT programmers.

The first type of window is the applet window, where the **Applet** class manages the window itself and automatically creates and handles the window. You can also create frame windows, which are what you normally think of windows, because they support a frame around the window and a title bar, as well as minimize, maximize, and close buttons. I'll create one here using the **Frame** class.

TIP: *When launching a frame window from an applet, Java adds a large warning at the bottom of the window for security purposes announcing "Warning: Applet Window". It's not very pretty, but there you are.*

There's another window class you can use—the **Window** class. This class just presents a blank window—no title bar, no frame, just a blank rectangle. You're responsible for displaying what you want in these windows. As you might expect, the **Frame** class is derived from the **Window** class. Paradoxically, however, you can't create a direct **Window** object in your own programs unless you already have a **Frame** window, because the publicly available **Window** constructor requires you to pass either a **Frame** window object or another **Window** object.

Menus

Every GUI user knows about menus—they're those indispensable controls that hide all the options a program can present by category. Imagine if all the options a word processor could present were available as buttons, visible all at once—there would be no space to enter text. Menus let you store those options away in a compact way. This is a very attractive GUI technique, because space is always at a premium in windowed environments.

In AWT programming, you need a frame window to use menus. You create a **MenuBar** object and add that menu bar to a frame window with the window's **setMenuBar** method. You also create objects of the **Menu** class to create the individual menus (such as File, Edit, and so on) that appear in the menu bar, and you create objects of the **MenuItem** class to create the actual items in each menu (such as New, Open, Help, Exit, and so on).

You can also support some nice options in menus—submenus that open when you select a menu item and check boxes that let you toggle menu items on and off (such as Automatic Spell Checking or View Toolbar). We'll look at all this in the chapter.

Dialog Boxes

Windowed programs frequently use dialog boxes to get user input, such as the name of a file to open, a password, or a color that's selected from many colors. Like the other visual elements in this chapter, dialog boxes are familiar to nearly all GUI users. You use dialog boxes when you want to get user input, but you don't want to display a dedicated control, such as a text field, for that option at all times in your main window. That is, dialog boxes are temporary windows you can fill with controls for user input.

We'll see two types of dialog boxes in this chapter, as supported by the **Dialog** and **FileDialog** classes. You use the **Dialog** class as a base class for the dialog boxes you create and customize. On the other hand, you don't usually need to derive a class from the **FileDialog** class—this class presents a file dialog box, which the user can use to select a file. The methods and data members of this class are sufficient for most file-selection purposes, and all you need to do is to instantiate an object of this class and use it. You'll see all this in the chapter too.

That's it. Now you have an overview of what's in this chapter. There's a lot coming up here, so let's turn to the "Immediate Solutions" section.

Immediate Solutions

Creating Frame Windows

"OK," says the Novice Programmer, "I'm working on my word processor in Java and want to present various views of the document—each view is a window into a different place in the document. What do you think?" You say, "I think you should think about letting the user launch new frame windows."

You've already seen the **Frame** window class in this book, because you use that class as the foundation of applications in AWT programming. Here's the inheritance diagram for frame windows:

```
java.lang.Object
|____java.awt.Component
      |____java.awt.Container
            |____java.awt.Window
                  |____java.awt.Frame
```

You can see the constructors and methods of this class in Chapter 6, in Tables 6.4 and 6.5, respectively. I'll create a frame window over the next few topics, showing and hiding it as needed, giving it a size, adding controls to it, and handling events in it. To start, I'll create a new class, **labelFrame**, based on the **Frame** class, and I'll display a label with the text "Hello from Java! This is a frame window.".

First, I declare this new class by extending the **Frame** class:

```
import java.awt.*;

class labelFrame extends Frame
{
      .
      .
      .
}
```

Next, I create a constructor for the class. I'm going to use the **Frame** class constructor, which takes a title for the window. Therefore, I add a title parameter to the constructor and pass that back to the **Frame** class, like this:

```
import java.awt.*;

class labelFrame extends Frame
{
    labelFrame(String title)
    {
        super(title);
        .
        .
        .
    }
}
```

Here's an important point—the default layout manager in frame windows is the **BorderLayout** manager (unlike applet windows, which use the **FlowLayout** manager). Note that this applies for both frame windows you display from applets and frame windows you use in windowed applications. If you want to use a different layout manager, you have to install it yourself. In this case, I install a flow layout manager using the **setLayout** method, like this:

```
import java.awt.*;

class labelFrame extends Frame
{
    labelFrame(String title)
    {
        super(title);
        setLayout(new FlowLayout());
        .
        .
        .
    }
}
```

Now I'm ready to create a label and add it to the layout:

```
import java.awt.*;

class labelFrame extends Frame
{
    Label label;
```

```
    labelFrame(String title)
    {
        super(title);
        setLayout(new FlowLayout());
        label = new Label("Hello from Java! This is a frame window.");
        add(label);
    }
}
```

That completes the frame window class—the next step is to display it. See the following topic for the details.

Showing And Hiding Windows

"I've created a frame window class," the Novice Programmer says. "Now how do I display a window of that class on the screen?" "That's not so hard," you say, "after giving the window a size, you just use the **setVisible** method."

Here's the frame window class, **labelFrame**, I developed in the previous topic:

```
class labelFrame extends Frame
{
    Label label;

    labelFrame(String title)
    {
        super(title);
        setLayout(new FlowLayout());
        label = new Label("Hello from Java! This is a frame window.");
        add(label);
    }
}
```

I'll launch this window from an applet. To do that, I display two buttons in the applet: Display the window and Hide the window. Here's how I add these buttons in the applet:

```
import java.awt.*;
import java.awt.event.*;
import java.applet.Applet;
```

```
/*
<APPLET
    CODE=frame.class
    WIDTH=300
    HEIGHT=200 >
</APPLET>
*/

public class frame extends Applet implements ActionListener
{
    Button b1, b2;

    public void init()
    {
        b1 = new Button("Display the window");
        add(b1);
        b1.addActionListener(this);

        b2 = new Button("Hide the window");
        add(b2);
        b2.addActionListener(this);
            .
            .
            .
    }
}
```

Now I'll create a new object of the **labelFrame** class, giving it the title "Java window":

```
public class frame extends Applet implements ActionListener
{
    Button b1, b2;
    labelFrame window;

    public void init()
    {
        b1 = new Button("Display the window");
        add(b1);
        b1.addActionListener(this);

        b2 = new Button("Hide the window");
        add(b2);
        b2.addActionListener(this);
```

```
        window = new labelFrame("Java window");
            .
            .
            .
    }
```

Before you can display a window, you must give it a size, using the **setSize** method; otherwise, it won't appear on the screen. Here's how I use **setSize** to give this window the dimensions 300 by 200 pixels:

```
    public void init()
    {
        b1 = new Button("Display the window");
        add(b1);
        b1.addActionListener(this);

        b2 = new Button("Hide the window");
        add(b2);
        b2.addActionListener(this);

        window = new labelFrame("Java window");
        window.setSize(300, 200);
    }
```

The new window object is ready to go. To display the window, I can use the **setVisible** method. I pass it a value of True to display the window and False to hide the window. Here's what this looks like for the two buttons in this applet:

```
    public void actionPerformed(ActionEvent event)
    {
        if(event.getSource() == b1){
            window.setVisible(true);
        }
        if(event.getSource() == b2){
            window.setVisible(false);
        }
    }
```

That's all that's needed. Now the applet is ready to go, as you can see in Figure 10.1. When you click the Display the window button, the frame window appears, with a colorful warning at the bottom of the window (which is not visible when you use a frame window in an application), as you can see in the figure. When you click the Hide the window button, the window is dismissed from the screen. This applet is a success.

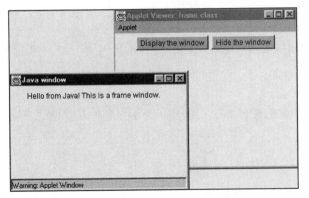

Figure 10.1   Displaying a frame window.

Handling Window Events

"Hmm," says the Novice Programmer, "I've put three hundred buttons in a frame window, but when you click on them, nothing happens." You smile and say, "Do you handle button click events in your frame window?" "Uh-oh," says the NP.

You can handle events in windows just as you can handle them anywhere—by implementing the methods of listener interfaces or by using adapter classes. Here's an example in which I handle mouse events in the frame window developed over the previous two topics by implementing the methods in the **MouseListener** interface and then displaying what the mouse is doing with messages in the label in that window:

```java
class labelFrame extends Frame implements MouseListener
{
    Label label;

    labelFrame(String title)
    {
        super(title);
        setLayout(new FlowLayout());
        label = new Label("Hello from Java! This is a frame window.");
        add(label);
        addMouseListener(this);
    }

    public void mousePressed(MouseEvent e)
    {
```

```
        if((e.getModifiers() & InputEvent.BUTTON1_MASK) ==
            InputEvent.BUTTON1_MASK){
            label.setText("Left mouse button down at " + e.getX() + "," +
                e.getY());
        }
        else{
            label.setText("Right mouse button down at " + e.getX() + "," +
                e.getY());
        }
    }

    public void mouseClicked(MouseEvent e)
    {
        label.setText("You clicked the mouse at " + e.getX() + "," +
            e.getY());
    }

    public void mouseReleased(MouseEvent e)
    {
        label.setText("The mouse button went up.");
    }

    public void mouseEntered(MouseEvent e)
    {
        label.setText("The mouse entered.");
    }

    public void mouseExited(MouseEvent e)
    {
        label.setText("The mouse exited.");
    }
}
```

The result appears in Figure 10.2. As you can see in the figure, the frame window now handles **MouseListener** events by displaying messages. That's it; this program is a success. You'll find it in frame.java on the CD that accompanies this book.

There are also events specific to windows—that is, there's an entire **WindowListener** interface, and you can see the methods of this interface in Table 10.1.

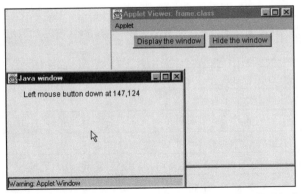

Figure 10.2   Handling mouse events in a frame window.

*Table 10.1   Methods of the **WindowListener** interface.*

Methods	Does This
void windowActivated (WindowEvent e)	Called when the window is set to the user's active window, which means the window will receive keyboard events.
void windowClosed(WindowEvent e)	Called when a window has been closed.
void windowClosing(WindowEvent e)	Called when the user closes the window from the window's system menu.
void windowDeactivated (WindowEvent e)	Called when a window is no longer the user's active window.
void windowDeiconified (WindowEvent e)	Called when a window is changed from a minimized to a normal state.
void windowIconified(WindowEvent e)	Called when a window is changed from a normal to a minimized state.
void windowOpened(WindowEvent e)	Called the first time a window is made visible.

Note that you can also use the **WindowAdapter** class to handle window events; this class already implements all the methods of the **WindowListener** interface, and you just override the methods you want to use. The methods of the **WindowListener** interface and **WindowAdapter** class are passed an object of the **WindowEvent** class. You'll find the fields of this class in Table 10.2, its constructor in Table 10.3, and its methods in Table 10.4.

I put one of the **WindowInterface** methods to work—the **windowClosing** event—in the next topic.

*Table 10.2   Fields of the **WindowEvent** class.*

Field	Does This
static int WINDOW_ACTIVATED	"Window activated" event.
static int WINDOW_CLOSED	"Window closed" event.
static int WINDOW_CLOSING	"Window closing" event.
static int WINDOW_DEACTIVATED	"Window deactivated" event.
static int WINDOW_DEICONIFIED	"Window deiconified" event.
static int WINDOW_FIRST	The first number in the range of IDs used for window events.
static int WINDOW_ICONIFIED	"Window iconified" event.
static int WINDOW_LAST	The last number in the range of IDs used for window events.
static int WINDOW_OPENED	"Window opened" event.

*Table 10.3   The constructor of the **WindowEvent** class.*

Constructor	Does This
WindowEvent(Window source, int id)	Creates a **WindowEvent** object.

*Table 10.4   Methods of the **WindowEvent** class.*

Method	Does This
Window getWindow( )	Gets the originator of the event.
String paramString( )	Gets a parameter string identifying this event.

Automatically Hiding Windows Upon Closing

"Hey," says the Novice Programmer, "Java's gone all wacky again. When I try to close a frame window, nothing happens. I'm emailing Sun Microsystems about it—what a bug!" "It's not a bug," you say. "It's just up to you to close a window yourself, that's all." "Oh," says the NP, "how does that work?"

To close a frame window when the user clicks the close button in the upper-right corner of the title bar, you can handle the **windowClosing** event. Here, I'm using an anonymous adapter inner class to do it (see Chapter 6 for more details). In this case, I'm just hiding the window when the user clicks the close button:

```
class labelFrame extends Frame implements MouseListener
{
    Label label;
```

```
labelFrame(String title)
{
    super(title);
    setLayout(new FlowLayout());
    label = new Label("Hello from Java! This is a frame window.");
    add(label);
    addMouseListener(this);
    addWindowListener(new WindowAdapter() {public void
        windowClosing(WindowEvent e) {setVisible(false);}});
    }
}
```

Here's something useful to note: When you close a window this way, it still exists as an object, which means you can still access its methods and data members. This will be useful when we're working with dialog boxes and want to retrieve the data the user entered.

Using The **Window** Class

"I want to customize the appearance of my windows entirely," the Novice Programmer says. "I'm going to be displaying works of the old painting masters and want to make the frame look like a real gilt painting frame." "Hmm," you say, "sounds like a big seller. You should use the **Window** class and customize it."

You can use the **Window** class to create an entirely blank window that's ready to be customized. You'll find the constructors for the **Window** class in Table 10.5 and its methods in Table 10.6.

*Table 10.5   Constructors of the **Window** class.*

Constructor	Does This
Window(Frame owner)	Creates a new invisible window.
Window(Window owner)	Creates a new invisible window with the given window as its owner.

*Table 10.6   Methods of the **Window** class.*

Method	Does This
void addNotify( )	Makes the window displayable by connecting the window to the underlying operating system.
void addWindowListener (WindowListener l)	Adds the given window listener to get window events from this window.

(continued)

Table 10.6   Methods of the Window class (continued).

Method	Does This
void applyResourceBundle (ResourceBundle rb)	Applies the settings in the given resource bundle to this window.
void applyResourceBundle (String rbName)	Loads the resource bundle with the given name.
void dispose( )	Releases all the native screen resources used by this window.
protected void finalize( )	Disposes of the input methods and context.
Component getFocusOwner( )	Gets the child component of this window, which has focus if and only if the window is active.
InputContext getInputContext( )	Gets the input context for this window.
Locale getLocale( )	Gets the **Locale** object associated with this window if the locale has been set.
Window[ ] getOwnedWindows( )	Returns an array containing all the windows this window currently owns.
Window getOwner( )	Gets the owner of this window.
Toolkit getToolkit( )	Gets the frame's toolkit.
String getWarningString( )	Gets the warning string displayed with this window.
void hide( )	Hides this window.
boolean isShowing( )	Checks whether this window is visible.
void pack( )	Causes this window to be sized to fit the preferred size and layouts of its components.
boolean postEvent(Event e)	Deprecated. Replaced by **dispatchEvent(AWTEvent)**.
protected void processEvent (AWTEvent e)	Processes events in this window.
protected void processWindowEvent (WindowEvent e)	Processes window events occurring on this window by sending them to any registered **WindowListener** objects.
void removeWindowListener (WindowListener l)	Removes the given window listener.
void setCursor(Cursor cursor)	Set the cursor image to a given cursor.
void show( )	Makes the window visible.
void toBack( )	Sends this window to the back.
void toFront( )	Brings this window to the front.

Let's look at an example. In this case, I create a new window class named **labelWindow** that displays a label with the text "Hello from Java!". I start by declaring this new class:

```
class labelWindow extends Window
{
    .
    .
    .
}
```

I have to pass the **Window** class's constructor a **Frame** window object or another **Window** object. To make things simpler, I use this new window in an application, so I'll pass the main frame window object to the **labelWindow** class's constructor and then pass that object back to the **Window** class's constructor, like this:

```
class labelWindow extends Window
{
    Label label;

    labelWindow(AppFrame af)
    {
        super(af);
        .
        .
        .
    }
}
```

As is the case with frame windows, the default layout manager here is a border layout manager, so I'll install a flow layout and display the label with its message in the window:

```
class labelWindow extends Window
{
    Label label;

    labelWindow(AppFrame af)
    {
        super(af);
        setLayout(new FlowLayout());
        label = new Label("Hello from Java!");
        add(label);
    }
    .
    .
    .
}
```

Windows of the **Window** class are simply blank white spaces, so I'll also override the **paint** method of this window to add a very simple frame—just a rectangle—like this. Note that I can determine the dimensions of the window with the **getSize** method, the same as with applet:

```
class labelWindow extends Window
{
    Label label;

    labelWindow(AppFrame af)
    {
        super(af);
        setLayout(new FlowLayout());
        label = new Label("Hello from Java!");
        add(label);
    }

    public void paint (Graphics g)
    {
        int width = getSize().width;
        int height = getSize().height;

        g.drawRect(0, 0, --width, --height);
    }
}
```

That completes the **labelWindow** class. I'll put this class to work in an application now. In this case, I'll just instantiate an object of the class and set its size—this is required before the window can be displayed. I'll also set its screen location using **setLocation**, because there's currently no way for the user to move this window when it appears, and if I just show it with the **setVisible** method, it'll appear at (0, 0) on the screen, which is at the extreme upper-left corner. When the user clicks on the Display the window button in this application, the window will appear. When the user clicks on the Hide the window button, the window will disappear. Here's the code:

```
import java.awt.*;
import java.awt.event.*;
import java.applet.Applet;

public class window
{
    public static void main(String [] args)
    {
        AppFrame f = new AppFrame();
```

```
        f.setSize(200, 200);

        f.addWindowListener(new WindowAdapter() { public void
            windowClosing(WindowEvent e) {System.exit(0);}});

        f.show();
    }
}

class AppFrame extends Frame implements ActionListener
{
    Button b1, b2;
    labelWindow window;

    AppFrame()
    {
        setLayout(new FlowLayout());
        b1 = new Button("Display the window");
        add(b1);
        b1.addActionListener(this);

        b2 = new Button("Hide the window");
        add(b2);
        b2.addActionListener(this);

        window = new labelWindow(this);
        window.setSize(300, 200);
        window.setLocation(300, 300);
    }

    public void actionPerformed(ActionEvent event)
    {
        if(event.getSource() == b1){
            window.setVisible(true);
        }
        if(event.getSource() == b2){
            window.setVisible(false);
        }
    }
}
```

You can see the result in Figure 10.3. As you can see in this figure, the window appears with its minimal border and the label control, which displays a message. This application is a success, and you can find it in window.java on the CD.

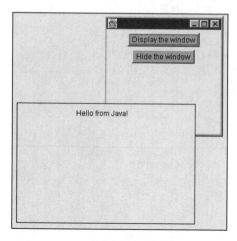

Figure 10.3   Creating a window of the **Window** class.

Creating Menus

"OK," says the Novice Programmer, "I've been waiting to ask you this one." "Oh boy," you say. The NP asks, "How do I create menus?" You sit back and say, "Better get some coffee."

You can add AWT menus to **Frame** class windows using three AWT classes: **MenuBar**, **Menu**, and **MenuItem**. I list the details for these classes here. The first class you use is the **MenuBar** class, which adds a menu bar to a frame window. After you've added a menu bar to a frame window, you can add menus, such as a File menu and an Edit menu, to that menu bar using the **Menu** class. Finally, you add menu items to the menus in your program using the **MenuItem** class.

I'll create and use menus over the next few topics while developing an applet named menu.java, which you'll find on the CD. This applet will display a frame window with a menu in it. Here's the applet:

```
import java.awt.*;
import java.awt.event.*;
import java.applet.Applet;

/*
<APPLET
    CODE=menu.class
    WIDTH=200
    HEIGHT=200 >
</APPLET>
*/
```

```java
public class menu extends Applet implements ActionListener
{
    Button b1;
    frame menuWindow;

    public void init()
    {
        b1 = new Button("Display the menu window");
        add(b1);
        b1.addActionListener(this);

        menuWindow = new frame("Menus");
        menuWindow.setSize(200, 200);
    }

    public void actionPerformed(ActionEvent event)
    {
        if(event.getSource() == b1){
            menuWindow.setVisible(true);
        }
    }
}

class frame extends Frame implements ActionListener
{
    Menu menu;
    MenuBar menubar;
    MenuItem menuitem1, menuitem2, menuitem3;

    Label label;

    frame(String title)
    {
        super(title);
        label = new Label("Hello from Java!");
        setLayout(new GridLayout(1, 1));
        add(label);
        menubar = new MenuBar();

        menu = new Menu("File");

        menuitem1 = new MenuItem("Item 1");
        menu.add(menuitem1);
        menuitem1.addActionListener(this);
```

```
                    menuitem2 = new MenuItem("Item 2");
                    menu.add(menuitem2);
                    menuitem2.addActionListener(this);

                    menuitem3 = new MenuItem("Item 3");
                    menu.add(menuitem3);
                    menuitem3.addActionListener(this);

                    menubar.add(menu);

                    setMenuBar(menubar);

                     addWindowListener(new WindowAdapter() {public void
                         windowClosing(WindowEvent e) {setVisible(false);}});
                }

                public void actionPerformed(ActionEvent event)
                {
                    if(event.getSource() == menuitem1){
                        label.setText("You chose item 1");
                    }
                    if(event.getSource() == menuitem2){
                        label.setText("You chose item 2");
                    }
                    if(event.getSource() == menuitem3){
                        label.setText("You chose item 3");
                    }
                }
            }
        }
```

You can see this applet at work in Figure 10.4.

The menu work in this applet takes place in the **Frame** window class I've
named **frame**. I develop this class throughout the examples shown in the next
few topics.

Figure 10.4   Creating a window of the Window class.

Creating A **MenuBar** Object

"I'm ready to create a menu system in my frame window," says the Novice Programmer. "Where do I start?" You say, "You start by creating a **MenuBar** object. Sit down and I'll show you how."

To create a menu bar in a frame window, you use the **MenuBar** class. Here's the inheritance diagram for the **MenuBar** class:

```
java.lang.Object
|____java.awt.MenuComponent
     |____java.awt.MenuBar
```

You'll find the constructor for the **MenuBar** class in Table 10.7 and its methods in Table 10.8.

Table 10.7   The constructor of the *MenuBar* class.

Constructor	Does This
MenuBar( )	Creates a new menu bar.

Table 10.8   Methods of the *MenuBar* class.

Method	Does This
Menu add(Menu m)	Adds the given menu to the menu bar.
void addNotify( )	Creates the menu bar's peer.
int countMenus( )	Deprecated. Replaced by **getMenuCount( )**.
void deleteShortcut(MenuShortcut s)	Deletes the given menu shortcut.
Menu getHelpMenu( )	Gets the Help menu on the menu bar.
Menu getMenu(int i)	Gets the given menu.
int getMenuCount( )	Gets the number of menus on the menu bar.
MenuItem getShortcutMenuItem (MenuShortcut s)	Gets the instance of **MenuItem** associated with the given **MenuShortcut** object.
void remove(int index)	Removes the menu located at the given index from this menu bar.
void remove(MenuComponent m)	Removes the given menu component from this menu bar.
void removeNotify( )	Removes the menu bar's peer.
void setHelpMenu(Menu m)	Sets the Help menu on this menu bar to be the given menu.
Enumeration shortcuts( )	Gets an enumeration of all menu shortcuts.

Here's how I create a menu bar in the frame window of the menu.java applet introduced in the "Creating Menus" topic (note that I install the menu bar in the frame window with the **Frame** class's **setMenuBar** method):

```
class frame extends Frame implements ActionListener
{
    MenuBar menubar;
    Label label;

    frame(String title)
    {
        super(title);
        label = new Label("Hello from Java!");
        setLayout(new GridLayout(1, 1));
        add(label);
        menubar = new MenuBar();
          .
          .
          .
        setMenuBar(menubar);
    }
}
```

All this does, however, is display a blank menu bar—it's time to add some menus to the menu bar. See the next topic for the details.

Creating Menu Objects

"Well," says the Novice Programmer, "I've found that after creating a new menu bar, nothing appears in it. How do I add menus to my menu bar?" "That's easy," you say, "just use the **Menu** class."

You create the individual menus in a menu bar with the **Menu** class. Here's the inheritance diagram for that class:

```
java.lang.Object
|____java.awt.MenuComponent
     |____java.awt.MenuItem
          |____java.awt.Menu
```

You'll find the **Menu** class's constructors in Table 10.9 and its methods in Table 10.10.

*Table 10.9   Constructors of the **Menu** class.*

Constructor	Does This
Menu( )	Creates a new menu.
Menu(String label)	Creates a new menu with the given label.
Menu(String label, boolean tearOff)	Creates a new menu with the given label, indicating whether the menu can be torn off.

*Table 10.10   Methods of the **Menu** class.*

Method	Does This
MenuItem add(MenuItem mi)	Adds the given menu item to this menu.
void add(String label)	Adds an item with the given label to this menu.
void addNotify( )	Creates the menu's peer.
void addSeparator( )	Adds a separator line or a hyphen to the menu at the current position.
int countItems( )	Deprecated. Replaced by **getItemCount( )**.
MenuItem getItem(int index)	Gets the item located at the given index.
int getItemCount( )	Get the number of items.
void insert(MenuItem menuitem, int index)	Inserts a menu item into this menu at the given position.
void insert(String label, int index)	Inserts a menu item with the given label into this menu.
void insertSeparator(int index)	Inserts a separator at the given position.
boolean isTearOff( )	Indicates whether this menu is a tear-off menu.
String paramString( )	Gets the parameter string representing the state of this menu.
void remove(int index)	Removes the menu item at the given index from this menu.
void remove(MenuComponent item)	Removes the given menu item from this menu.
void removeAll( )	Removes all items from this menu.
void removeNotify( )	Removes the menu's peer.

Here's how I create a File menu in the menu.java applet and add that menu to the menu bar (note that I name the menu simply by passing that name to the **Menu** class's constructor):

```
class frame extends Frame implements ActionListener
{
    Menu menu;
    MenuBar menubar;
    Label label;
```

```
        frame(String title)
        {
            super(title);
            label = new Label("Hello from Java!");
            setLayout(new GridLayout(1, 1));
            add(label);
            menubar = new MenuBar();

            menu = new Menu("File");

                .
                .
                .

            menubar.add(menu);

            setMenuBar(menubar);
        }
    }
```

TIP: *One powerful way of creating menus is as tear-off menus, which you can accomplish by using the third form of the **Menu** constructor in Table 10.9. Users can "tear off" these menus with the mouse and place them where they like.*

Creating **MenuItem** Objects

The Novice Programmer is back and says, "Hey, I've created a new menu. How would I add menu items to that menu?" "It's not so hard," you say, "you just use the **MenuItem** class."

Each menu item you add to an AWT menu is actually an object of the **MenuItem** class. Here's the inheritance diagram for this class:

```
java.lang.Object
|____java.awt.MenuComponent
     |____java.awt.MenuItem
```

You'll find the constructors for the **MenuItem** class in Table 10.11 and its methods in Table 10.12.

To add a menu item to a menu, you just create a new **MenuItem** object, passing the **MenuItem** constructor the name of the new item and then using the **Menu**

*Table 10.11   Constructors of the **MenuItem** class.*

Constructor	Does This
MenuItem( )	Creates a new menu item.
MenuItem(String label)	Creates a new menu item with the given label and no keyboard shortcut.
MenuItem(String label, MenuShortcut s)	Creates a menu item with an associated keyboard shortcut.

*Table 10.12   Methods of the **MenuItem** class.*

Method	Does This
void addActionListener (ActionListener l)	Adds the given action listener to receive action events from this menu item.
void addNotify( )	Creates the menu item's peer.
void deleteShortcut( )	Delete any **MenuShortcut** object associated with this menu item.
void disable( )	Deprecated. Replaced by **setEnabled(boolean)**.
protected void disableEvents (long eventsToDisable)	Disables event delivery to this menu item.
void enable( )	Deprecated. Replaced by **setEnabled(boolean)**.
void enable(boolean b)	Deprecated. Replaced by **setEnabled(boolean)**.
protected void enableEvents (long eventsToEnable)	Enables event delivery to this menu item.
String getActionCommand( )	Gets the command name of the action event that's caused by this menu item.
String getLabel( )	Gets the label for this menu item.
MenuShortcut getShortcut( )	Get the **MenuShortcut** object associated with this menu item.
boolean isEnabled( )	Checks whether this menu item is enabled.
String paramString( )	Gets the parameter string representing the state of this menu item.
protected void processActionEvent (ActionEvent e)	Processes action events occurring on this menu item by sending them to any registered **ActionListener** objects.
protected void processEvent (AWTEvent e)	Processes events on this menu item.
void removeActionListener (ActionListener l)	Removes the given action listener so it no longer gets action events from this menu item.
void setActionCommand (String command)	Sets the command name of the action event that's fired by this menu item.

(continued)

Table 10.12   Methods of the MenuItem class (continued).

Method	Does This
void setEnabled(boolean b)	Sets whether this menu item can be chosen.
void setLabel(String label)	Sets the label for this menu item to the given label.
void setShortcut(MenuShortcut s)	Set the **MenuShortcut** object associated with this menu item.

object's **add** method to add the new item to a menu. Here's an example in which I add items to the File menu in the menu.java applet:

```
class frame extends Frame implements ActionListener
{
    Menu menu;
    MenuBar menubar;
    MenuItem menuitem1, menuitem2, menuitem3;

    Label label;

    frame(String title)
    {
        super(title);
        label = new Label("Hello from Java!");
        setLayout(new GridLayout(1, 1));
        add(label);
        menubar = new MenuBar();

        menu = new Menu("File");

        menuitem1 = new MenuItem("Item 1");
        menu.add(menuitem1);

        menuitem2 = new MenuItem("Item 2");
        menu.add(menuitem2);

        menuitem3 = new MenuItem("Item 3");
        menu.add(menuitem3);

        menubar.add(menu);

        setMenuBar(menubar);
    }
}
```

TIP: *Java menu items support shortcuts, which you can create by using the third form of the **MenuItem** constructor in Table 10.11. Users can access menus items with shortcuts by typing those shortcuts at the keyboard.*

This is all fine as far as it goes, except that nothing happens when these menu items are clicked on. To learn how to support menu events, see the next topic.

Handling **Menu** Events

The Novice Programmer is back and says, "Well, I've set up my entire menu system, but there's a problem. Nothing happens when I click on the items in my menus." "That's because you have to add an action listener to each item," you say, smiling. "Oh," says the NP.

You use action listeners with menu items, just as you do with buttons. Here's an example in which I enable menu event handling in the menu.java applet. In this case, I indicate which menu item the user selected by displaying a message in a label. First, I add an action listener to each menu item:

```
class frame extends Frame implements ActionListener
{
    Menu menu;
    MenuBar menubar;
    MenuItem menuitem1, menuitem2, menuitem3;
    Label label;

    frame(String title)
    {
        super(title);
        label = new Label("Hello from Java!");
        setLayout(new GridLayout(1, 1));
        add(label);
        menubar = new MenuBar();

        menu = new Menu("File");

        menuitem1 = new MenuItem("Item 1");
        menu.add(menuitem1);
        menuitem1.addActionListener(this);

        menuitem2 = new MenuItem("Item 2");
        menu.add(menuitem2);
        menuitem2.addActionListener(this);
```

```
        menuitem3 = new MenuItem("Item 3");
        menu.add(menuitem3);
        menuitem3.addActionListener(this);

        menubar.add(menu);

        setMenuBar(menubar);

         addWindowListener(new WindowAdapter() {public void
             windowClosing(WindowEvent e) {setVisible(false);}});
    }

    public void actionPerformed(ActionEvent event)
    {
        if(event.getSource() == menuitem1){
            label.setText("You chose item 1");
        } else if(event.getSource() == menuitem2){
            label.setText("You chose item 2");
        } else if(event.getSource() == menuitem3){
            label.setText("You chose item 3");
        }
    }
}
```

That's it. Now the user can run the menu.java applet and report on the items he or she selected, as shown in Figure 10.5.

It's worth noting that although I used the **ActionEvent** class's **getSource** method to determine which menu item was clicked in this topic, you can also give each menu item an action command with the **setActionCommand** method, as I did for buttons in Chapter 6, and use the **ActionEvent** class's **getActionCommand** method to read the action command.

Figure 10.5   Creating and using a menu system.

More Menu Options

In the previous few topics, I created an applet, menu.java, that examined the basic construction of a menu system. In the following few topics, I'll elaborate on my menu system explanation, and include menu separators, disabled menu items, check box menu items, and submenus—all in a new applet called menu2.java. Here's what this new applet looks like:

```java
import java.applet.Applet;
import java.awt.*;
import java.awt.event.*;

/*
<APPLET
    CODE=menu2.class
    WIDTH=200
    HEIGHT=200 >
</APPLET>
*/

public class menu2 extends Applet implements ActionListener
{
    Button b1;
    frame menuWindow;

    public void init()
    {
        b1 = new Button("Display the menu window");
        add(b1);
        b1.addActionListener(this);

        menuWindow = new frame("Menus");
        menuWindow.setSize(200, 200);
    }

    public void actionPerformed(ActionEvent event)
    {
        if(event.getSource() == b1){
            menuWindow.setVisible(true);
        }
    }
}

class frame extends Frame implements ActionListener, ItemListener
{
```

```
Menu menu, submenu;
MenuBar menubar;
Label label;
MenuItem menuitem1, menuitem2, menuitem4;
MenuItem subitem1, subitem2, subitem3;
CheckboxMenuItem menuitem3;

frame(String title)
{
    super(title);
    label = new Label("Hello from Java!");
    setLayout(new GridLayout(1, 1));
    add(label);
    menubar = new MenuBar();
    menu = new Menu("File");

    menuitem1 = new MenuItem("Item 1");
    menuitem1.addActionListener(this);
    menu.add(menuitem1);

    menuitem2 = new MenuItem("Item 2");
    menuitem2.addActionListener(this);
    menu.add(menuitem2);

    menu.addSeparator();

    menuitem3 = new CheckboxMenuItem("Check Item");
    menuitem3.addItemListener(this);
    menu.add(menuitem3);

    menu.addSeparator();

    submenu = new Menu("Sub menus");
    subitem1 = new MenuItem("Sub item 1");
    subitem2 = new MenuItem("Sub item 2");
    subitem3 = new MenuItem("Sub item 3");
    subitem1.addActionListener(this);
    subitem2.addActionListener(this);
    subitem3.addActionListener(this);
    menuitem2.addActionListener(this);
    menuitem2.addActionListener(this);
    submenu.add(subitem1);
    submenu.add(subitem2);
    submenu.add(subitem3);
```

```
        menu.add(submenu);

        menu.addSeparator();

        menuitem4 = new MenuItem("Exit");
        menuitem4.addActionListener(this);
        menu.add(menuitem4);

        menubar.add(menu);
        setMenuBar(menubar);

         addWindowListener(new WindowAdapter() {public void
             windowClosing(WindowEvent e) {setVisible(false);}});
    }

    public void actionPerformed(ActionEvent event)
    {
        if(event.getSource() == menuitem1){
          label.setText("You chose item 1");
        } else if(event.getSource() == menuitem2){
          menuitem2.setEnabled(false);
          label.setText("You chose item 2");
        } else if(event.getSource() == subitem1){
          label.setText("You chose sub item 1");
        } else if(event.getSource() == subitem2){
          label.setText("You chose sub item 2");
        } else if(event.getSource() == subitem3){
          label.setText("You chose sub item 3");
        } else if(event.getSource() == menuitem4){
          setVisible(false);
        }
    }

    public void itemStateChanged (ItemEvent event)
    {
        if(event.getSource() == menuitem3){
            if(((CheckboxMenuItem)event.getItemSelectable()).getState())
                label.setText("Item 3 is checked");
            else
                label.setText("Item 3 is not checked");
        }
    }
}
```

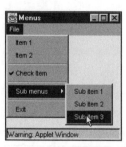

Figure 10.6   Elaborating a menu system.

You can see this applet in Figure 10.6. I'll develop the various new aspects of this applet, menu2.java, over the next few topics, as you see how to handle its various parts in code.

Adding Menu Separators

You can combine menu items into groups using *menu separators*—the thin horizontal lines that appear in menus (see Figure 10.6). Adding a menu separator to a menu is easy; you just use the **addSeparator** method, like this:

```
frame(String title)
{
    super(title);
    label = new Label("Hello from Java!");
    setLayout(new GridLayout(1, 1));
    add(label);
    menubar = new MenuBar();
    menu = new Menu("File");

    menuitem1 = new MenuItem("Item 1");
    menuitem1.addActionListener(this);
    menu.add(menuitem1);

    menuitem2 = new MenuItem("Item 2");
    menuitem2.addActionListener(this);
    menu.add(menuitem2);

    menu.addSeparator();
    .
    .
    .
}
```

Disabling Menu Items

"That darn Johnson," the Novice Programmer says, "has been messing around with my program again by selecting menu items that don't apply, such as spell checking when the program was drawing graphics. It crashed my program right in front of the Big Boss!" "Hmm," you say, "how about disabling menu items when they're not appropriate?" The NP smiles and says, "That'll show that darn Johnson!"

When you disable a menu item, the menu item is displayed in gray and cannot be selected or clicked. To disable a menu item, you use that item's **setEnabled** method, passing the method a value of False. For example, I can disable the second menu item in menu2.java when the user clicks it, like this:

```
class frame extends Frame implements ActionListener, ItemListener
{
    Menu menu, submenu;
    MenuBar menubar;
    Label label;
    MenuItem menuitem1, menuitem2, menuitem4;
    MenuItem subitem1, subitem2, subitem3;
    CheckboxMenuItem menuitem3;

    frame(String title){
        super(title);
        label = new Label("Hello from Java!");
        setLayout(new GridLayout(1, 1));
        add(label);
        menubar = new MenuBar();
        menu = new Menu("File");

        menuitem1 = new MenuItem("Item 1");
        menuitem1.addActionListener(this);
        menu.add(menuitem1);

        menuitem2 = new MenuItem("Item 2");
        menuitem2.addActionListener(this);
        menu.add(menuitem2);

        menubar.add(menu);
        setMenuBar(menubar);
    }

    public void actionPerformed(ActionEvent event)
    {
```

```
        if(event.getSource() == menuitem1){
          label.setText("You chose item 1");
        } else if(event.getSource() == menuitem2){
          menuitem2.setEnabled(false);
          label.setText("You chose item 2");
        }
      }
    }
}
```

The result appears in Figure 10.7, where you can see the disabled menu item.

Now that the item is disabled, the user has no way to click on it again to enable it.

Figure 10.7   Disabling a menu item.

Adding Check Marks To Menus

The Product Support Specialist is back and unhappy. "There's a problem in your new application," the PSS says, "because the user has no way to know if the Auto-translate to German menu option is on or off, and the results can prove to be pretty startling." "Hmm," you say, "I suppose I can add a check mark to that menu option to show when it's in effect."

You can create menu items that display check marks next to them to indicate when specific options are in effect. Also, you can toggle a check mark when the user selects it. To support check marks in menu items, use the **CheckboxMenuItem** class, which has the following inheritance diagram:

```
java.lang.Object
|____java.awt.MenuComponent
     |____java.awt.CheckboxMenuItem
```

You'll find the constructors for **CheckboxMenuItem** in Table 10.13 and its methods in Table 10.14.

Table 10.13   Constructors of the *CheckboxMenuItem* class.

Constructor	Does This
CheckboxMenuItem( )	Creates a check box menu item.
CheckboxMenuItem(String label)	Creates a check box menu item with the given label.
CheckboxMenuItem(String label, boolean state)	Creates a check box menu item with the given label and state.

Table 10.14   Methods of the *CheckboxMenuItem* class.

Method	Does This
void addItemListener(ItemListener l)	Adds the given item listener to receive item events from this check box menu item.
void addNotify( )	Creates the peer of the check box item.
Object[ ] getSelectedObjects( )	Gets an array of length 1 containing the check box menu item label.
boolean getState( )	Determines whether the state of this check box menu item is on or off.
String paramString( )	Gets a string representing the state of this check box menu item.
protected void processEvent (AWTEvent e)	Processes events in this check box menu item.
protected void processItemEvent (ItemEvent e)	Processes item events occurring in this check box menu item by sending them to **ItemListener** objects.
void removeItemListener (ItemListener l)	Removes the given item listener so that it no longer receives item events from this check box menu item.
void setState(boolean b)	Sets this check box menu item to the specified state.

Note that you use item listeners, not action listeners, with check box menu items. Here's how I add a check mark item to the applet menu2.java using an **ItemListener** object:

```
class frame extends Frame implements ActionListener, ItemListener
{
    Menu menu, submenu;
    MenuBar menubar;
    Label label;
    MenuItem menuitem1, menuitem2, menuitem4;
    MenuItem subitem1, subitem2, subitem3;
    CheckboxMenuItem menuitem3;

    frame(String title)
    {
```

```
            super(title);
            label = new Label("Hello from Java!");
            setLayout(new GridLayout(1, 1));
            add(label);
            menubar = new MenuBar();
            menu = new Menu("File");

            menuitem1 = new MenuItem("Item 1");
            menuitem1.addActionListener(this);
            menu.add(menuitem1);

            menuitem2 = new MenuItem("Item 2");
            menuitem2.addActionListener(this);
            menu.add(menuitem2);

            menu.addSeparator();

            menuitem3 = new CheckboxMenuItem("Check Item");
            menuitem3.addItemListener(this);
            menu.add(menuitem3);
                .
                .
                .
            menubar.add(menu);
            setMenuBar(menubar);

            addWindowListener(new WindowAdapter() {public void
                windowClosing(WindowEvent e) {setVisible(false);}});
    }
```

As the user selects this item time after time, Java will toggle the check mark on and off automatically. To handle events from this item, you have to override the **itemStateChanged** method. In this case, I determine the state of the menu item and display that state in a label, like this:

```
    public void itemStateChanged (ItemEvent event)
    {
        if(event.getSource() == menuitem3){
            if(((CheckboxMenuItem)event.getItemSelectable()).getState())
                label.setText("Item 3 is checked");
            else
                label.setText("Item 3 is not checked");
        }
    }
}
```

Figure 10.8   Using a check box menu item.

You can see the check box menu item in menu2.java at work in Figure 10.8.

Creating Submenus

Another powerful aspect of working with menus in AWT programming involves *submenus*. Submenus are attached to a menu item, and when the user selects the menu item, the submenu opens, as you can see in Figure 10.9. The user can select items from the submenu just as he or she can for normal menus.

Using submenus is a very powerful technique when you need another level of detail; for example, you may want to let the user select a drawing color with a menu item, and when that item is selected, a submenu opens indicating possible colors such as red, green, magenta, and blue.

Creating a submenu is easy—you just add menu items to another menu item using the **add** method. Here's an example showing how that works. In this case, I add the submenu items you see in Figure 10.9 to the Sub Menus menu item you see in the figure. Here's how this looks in code:

```
frame(String title)
{
    super(title);
    label = new Label("Hello from Java!");
    setLayout(new GridLayout(1, 1));
    add(label);
    menubar = new MenuBar();
    menu = new Menu("File");

    menuitem1 = new MenuItem("Item 1");
    menuitem1.addActionListener(this);
    menu.add(menuitem1);
```

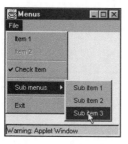

Figure 10.9   Using submenus.

```
menuitem2 = new MenuItem("Item 2");
menuitem2.addActionListener(this);
menu.add(menuitem2);

menu.addSeparator();

menuitem3 = new CheckboxMenuItem("Check Item");
menuitem3.addItemListener(this);
menu.add(menuitem3);

menu.addSeparator();

submenu = new Menu("Sub menus");
subitem1 = new MenuItem("Sub item 1");
subitem2 = new MenuItem("Sub item 2");
subitem3 = new MenuItem("Sub item 3");
subitem1.addActionListener(this);
subitem2.addActionListener(this);
subitem3.addActionListener(this);
menuitem2.addActionListener(this);
menuitem2.addActionListener(this);
submenu.add(subitem1);
submenu.add(subitem2);
submenu.add(subitem3);

menu.add(submenu);

menu.addSeparator();

menuitem4 = new MenuItem("Exit");
menuitem4.addActionListener(this);
menu.add(menuitem4);
```

```
        menubar.add(menu);
        setMenuBar(menubar);
    }
```

Here's how I handle submenu item clicks in the **actionPerformed** method:

```
    public void actionPerformed(ActionEvent event)
    {
        if(event.getSource() == menuitem1){
          label.setText("You chose item 1");
        } else if(event.getSource() == menuitem2){
          menuitem2.setEnabled(false);
          label.setText("You chose item 2");
        } else if(event.getSource() == subitem1){
          label.setText("You chose sub item 1");
        } else if(event.getSource() == subitem2){
          label.setText("You chose sub item 2");
        } else if(event.getSource() == subitem3){
          label.setText("You chose sub item 3");
        } else if(event.getSource() == menuitem4){
          setVisible(false);
        }
    }
```

You can see the submenu in Figure 10.9. When the user selects one of the submenu items, the applet displays the item that was selected in the label in the frame window.

Pop-up Menus

"Hey," says the Novice Programmer, "I saw that you can right-click some applications and a pop-up menu appears. Can I do that in Java?" "Sure thing," you say, "nothing to it. Just use the **PopupMenu** class."

You use the **PopupMenu** class to create pop-up menus that don't need to be attached to a menu bar. Here's the inheritance diagram for this class:

```
java.lang.Object
|____java.awt.MenuComponent
      |____java.awt.MenuItem
            |____java.awt.Menu
                  |____java.awt.PopupMenu
```

Table 10.15   Constructors of the PopupMenu class.

Constructor	Does This
PopupMenu( )	Creates a new pop-up menu.
PopupMenu(String label)	Creates a new pop-up menu with the given name.

Table 10.16   Methods of the PopupMenu class.

Method	Does This
void addNotify( )	Creates the pop-up menu's peer.
void show(Component origin, int x, int y)	Shows the pop-up menu at the x, y position.

You can find the constructors for the **PopupMenu** class in Table 10.15 and the methods of this class in Table 10.16.

Let's look at an example. Here, I create a new pop-up menu and add four items to it (note that I also install a **MouseListener** interface to handle right-clicks):

```
import java.awt.*;
import java.awt.event.*;
import java.applet.Applet;

/*
<APPLET
CODE=popup.class
WIDTH=200
HEIGHT=200 >
</APPLET>
*/

public class popup extends Applet implements ActionListener,
    MouseListener {

    Label label;
    PopupMenu popup;
    MenuItem menuitem1, menuitem2, menuitem3, menuitem4;

    public void init()
    {
        popup = new PopupMenu("Menu");
        menuitem1 = new MenuItem("Item 1");
        menuitem1.addActionListener(this);
        menuitem2 = new MenuItem("Item 2");
```

```
        menuitem2.addActionListener(this);
        menuitem3 = new MenuItem("Item 3");
        menuitem3.addActionListener(this);
        menuitem4 = new MenuItem("Item 4");
        menuitem4.addActionListener(this);
        popup.add(menuitem1);
        popup.addSeparator();
        popup.add(menuitem2);
        popup.addSeparator();
        popup.add(menuitem3);
        popup.addSeparator();
        popup.add(menuitem4);
        add(popup);
        label = new Label("Hello from Java!");
        add(label);
        addMouseListener(this);
    }
```

When the user right-clicks the applet window, I can use the **PopupMenu** class's
show method to display the menu, passing that method a **this** keyword pointing
to the applet and the position at which to display the pop-up menu (here, I display
the pop-up menu at the location where the mouse was clicked):

```
public void mousePressed(MouseEvent e)
{
    if(e.getModifiers() != 0){
        popup.show(this, e.getX(), e.getY());
    }
}
```

When the user clicks on a submenu item, I can display which item was clicked in
the **actionPerformed** method:

```
    public void actionPerformed(ActionEvent event)
    {
        if(event.getSource() == menuitem1)
            label.setText("You chose item 1");
        else if(event.getSource() == menuitem2)
            label.setText("You chose item 2");
        else if(event.getSource() == menuitem3)
            label.setText("You chose item 3");
        else if(event.getSource() == menuitem4)
            label.setText("You chose item 4");
    }
```

Dialog Boxes

"Uh-oh," says the Novice Programmer, "I need some text input from the user, but the Big Boss said that if I put one more text field into my program, I would live to regret it." "How many text fields do you have in your program?" you ask. "About four hundred," the Novice Programmer says. "Hmm," you say, "well, you can always use a dialog box to get input from the user if you don't want to use another text field." The NP says, "Great!"

The result appears in Figure 10.10. As you can see in this figure, the user can open the pop-up menu just by right-clicking on the applet. When the user selects an item in the menu, the applet reports which item was selected. This example is popup.java on the CD.

The AWT supports a special window class—the **Dialog** class—that you can use to create dialog boxes. The windows created with this class look more like standard dialog boxes than the ones you create with frame windows—for example, dialog windows do not have a minimize or maximize button. Here's the inheritance diagram for the **Dialog** class:

```
java.lang.Object
|____java.awt.Component
     |____java.awt.Container
          |____java.awt.Window
               |____java.awt.Dialog
```

You'll find the constructors of the **Dialog** class in Table 10.17 and its methods in Table 10.18.

There are a few things to note in Tables 10.17 and 10.18. One is that you can create either modal dialog boxes (that is, the user must dismiss the dialog box

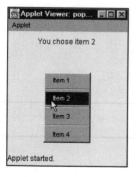

Figure 10.10   Using pop-up menus.

Table 10.17   Constructors of the Dialog class.

Constructor	Does This
Dialog(Dialog owner)	Creates an initially invisible, nonmodal **Dialog** object with an empty title and the given owner dialog box.
Dialog(Dialog owner, String title)	Creates an initially invisible, nonmodal **Dialog** object with the given owner dialog box and title.
Dialog(Dialog owner, String dialog title, boolean modal)	Creates an initially invisible **Dialog** object with the given owner box, title, and modality.
Dialog(Frame owner)	Creates an initially invisible, nonmodal **Dialog** object with an empty title and the given owner frame.
Dialog(Frame owner, boolean modal)	Creates an initially invisible **Dialog** object with an empty title as well asthe given owner frame and modality.
Dialog(Frame owner, String title)	Creates an initially invisible, nonmodal **Dialog** object with the given owner frame and title.
Dialog(Frame owner, String title, frame, boolean modal)	Creates an initially invisible **Dialog** object with the given owner title, and modality.

Table 10.18   Methods of the Dialog class.

Method	Does This
void addNotify( )	Makes this dialog box displayable by connecting it to a native peer.
void dispose( )	Disposes of the dialog box.
String getTitle( )	Gets the title of the dialog box.
void hide( )	Hides the dialog box.
boolean isModal( )	Indicates whether the dialog box is modal.
boolean isResizable( )	Indicates whether this dialog box can be resized by the user.
protected String paramString( )	Gets the parameter string representing the state of this dialog box.
void setModal(boolean b)	Specifies whether this dialog box should be modal.
void setResizable(boolean resizable)	Sets whether this dialog box can be resized by the user.
void setTitle(String title)	Sets the title of the dialog box.
void show( )	Makes the dialog box visible.

from the screen before interacting with the rest of the program) or nonmodal dialog boxes, depending on which **Dialog** constructor you use or if you use the **setModal** method. Another point is that you can use the **setResizeable** method to create a dialog box that the user can resize.

Let's look at an example that puts the **Dialog** class to work. I'll start by creating a new dialog box class named **okcanceldialog** that displays a text field and two buttons: OK and Cancel. If the user types text into the text field and clicks the OK button, that text will appear in the main window of the application; otherwise, if the user clicks the Cancel button, no text will appear. I start by extending **okcanceldialog** from the **Dialog** class, creating a new dialog box, and then installing the controls I'll need in it:

```
class okcanceldialog extends Dialog implements ActionListener
{
    Button ok, cancel;
    TextField text;

    okcanceldialog(Frame hostFrame, String title, boolean dModal)
    {
        super(hostFrame, title, dModal);
        setSize(300, 100);
        setLayout(new FlowLayout());
        ok = new Button("OK");
        add(ok);
        ok.addActionListener((ActionListener)this);
        cancel = new Button("Cancel");
        add(cancel);
        cancel.addActionListener(this);
        text = new TextField(30);
        add(text);
        data = new String("");
    }
        .
        .
        .
}
```

When the user clicks on the OK button, I store the text the user typed in a public data member named **data** so that it'll be accessible to the rest of the program in the **actionPerformed** method. If the user clicks on Cancel, I place an empty string in that data member. When the user clicks on either button, I also hide the dialog box. Here's the code:

```
class okcanceldialog extends Dialog implements ActionListener
{
    Button ok, cancel;
    TextField text;
    public String data;
```

```
    public void actionPerformed(ActionEvent event)
    {
        if(event.getSource() == ok){
            data = text.getText();
        } else {
            data = "";
        }
        setVisible(false);
    }
    .
    .
    .
}
```

That's it. I can make use of the new **okcanceldialog** class in an application, displaying a dialog box of that class when the user selects the item Dialog box in the File menu:

```
import java.awt.*;
import java.awt.event.*;
import java.applet.Applet;

public class dialog
{
    public static void main(String [] args)
    {
        dialogframe f = new dialogframe("Dialogs");

        f.setSize(200, 200);

        f.addWindowListener(new WindowAdapter() { public void
            windowClosing(WindowEvent e) {System.exit(0);}});

        f.show();
    }
}

class dialogframe extends Frame implements ActionListener
{
    Menu Menu1;
    MenuBar Menubar1;
    MenuItem menuitem1;
    Label label;
    okcanceldialog dialog;
```

```
dialogframe(String title)
{
    super(title);
    label = new Label("Hello from Java!");
    setLayout(new GridLayout(1, 1));
    add(label);
    Menubar1 = new MenuBar();

    Menu1 = new Menu("File");

    menuitem1 = new MenuItem("Dialog box...");
    Menu1.add(menuitem1);
    menuitem1.addActionListener(this);

    Menubar1.add(Menu1);

    setMenuBar(Menubar1);
    dialog = new okcanceldialog(this, "Dialog", true);
}

public void actionPerformed(ActionEvent event)
{
    if(event.getSource() == menuitem1){
        dialog.setVisible(true);
        label.setText(dialog.data);
    }
}
}
```

Note that I also recover the text data from the dialog box using the public data
member named **data** and place it in a label in the application. When this application runs and the Dialog box... item in the File menu is clicked, the dialog box
appears, as shown in Figure 10.11.

When the user enters text into the text field in the dialog box and clicks OK, the
dialog box closes and that text appears in the label in the main application window, as shown in Figure 10.12.

This application is a success. There's another kind of dialog box that's worth taking a look at—the file dialog box. We'll take a look at it next.

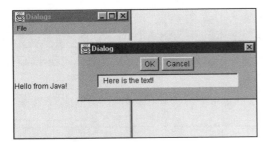

Figure 10.11   Displaying a dialog box.

Figure 10.12   Displaying text from a dialog box.

File Dialog Boxes

You can use the special AWT class **FileDialog** to create and display file dialog boxes that let the user browse directories and select files. Here's the inheritance diagram for the **FileDialog** class:

```
java.lang.Object
|____java.awt.Component
     |____java.awt.Container
          |____java.awt.Window
               |____java.awt.Dialog
                    |____java.awt.FileDialog
```

You'll find the fields of the **FileDialog** class in Table 10.19, its constructors in Table 10.20, and its methods in Table 10.21.

TIP: *Note that you can create file dialog boxes that indicate to the user that they are specifically intended for loading or saving files, depending on which constant from Table 10.19 you use with the **FileDialog** constructor. If you don't specify which purpose the file dialog box is for, you'll just get a generic version.*

Table 10.19   Fields of the FileDialog class.

Field	Does This
static int LOAD	Indicates that the purpose of the file dialog box is to locate a file from which to read.
static int SAVE	Indicates that the purpose of the file dialog box is to locate a file to which to write.

Table 10.20   Constructors of the FileDialog class.

Constructor	Does This
FileDialog(Frame parent)	Creates a file dialog box for loading a file.
FileDialog(Frame parent, String title)	Creates a file dialog box with the given title for loading a file.
FileDialog(Frame parent, String title, int mode)	Creates a file dialog box with the given title for loading or saving a file.

Table 10.21   Methods of the FileDialog class.

Method	Does This
void addNotify( )	Creates the file dialog box's peer.
String getDirectory( )	Gets the directory of this file dialog box.
String getFile( )	Gets the selected file of this file dialog box.
FilenameFilter getFilenameFilter( )	Determines this file dialog box's file name filter.
int getMode( )	Indicates whether this file dialog box is for loading from a file or for saving to a file.
protected String paramString( )	Gets the parameter string representing the state of this file dialog box.
void setDirectory(String dir)	Sets the directory of this file dialog box to be the given directory.
void setFile(String file)	Sets the selected file for this file dialog box to be the given file.
void setFilenameFilter(Filename Filter filter)	Sets the file name filter for this file dialog box to the given filter.
void setMode(int mode)	Sets the mode of the file dialog box.

Here's an example in which I let the user browse through directories with a file dialog box. When the user selects a file, I display the file name in the main application window. Doing this is easy; I just create a **FileDialog** object, show it with the **setVisible** method, and then read the name of the file the user selected by using the **getFile** method:

```
import java.awt.*;
import java.awt.event.*;
```

```java
public class filedialog
{
    public static void main(String [] args)
    {
        dialogframe f = new dialogframe("Dialogs");

        f.setSize(200, 200);

        f.addWindowListener(new WindowAdapter() { public void
            windowClosing(WindowEvent e) {System.exit(0);}});

        f.show();
    }
}

class dialogframe extends Frame implements ActionListener
{
    Menu Menu1;
    MenuBar Menubar1;
    MenuItem menuitem1;
    Label label;
    FileDialog dialog;

    dialogframe(String title)
    {
        super(title);
        label = new Label("Hello from Java!");
        setLayout(new GridLayout(1, 1));
        add(label);
        Menubar1 = new MenuBar();

        Menu1 = new Menu("File");

        menuitem1 = new MenuItem("Open file...");
        Menu1.add(menuitem1);
        menuitem1.addActionListener(this);

        Menubar1.add(Menu1);

        setMenuBar(Menubar1);
        dialog = new FileDialog(this, "File Dialog");
    }

    public void actionPerformed(ActionEvent event){
        if(event.getSource() == menuitem1){
```

```
                        dialog.setVisible(true);
                        label.setText("You chose " + dialog.getFile());
            }
        }
}
```

Figure 10.13 shows the result in Windows (so a Windows file dialog box is used). In this figure, I'm navigating to a file. In Figure 10.14, I've selected a file and closed the dialog box, and the main application is displaying the file I selected.

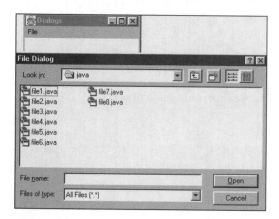

Figure 10.13   Using a file dialog box.

Figure 10.14   Reading a file name from a file dialog box.

Chapter 11

Swing: Applets, Applications, And Pluggable Look And Feel

In Depth

This chapter begins a section of the book that a lot of programmers have been waiting for—a discussion of Swing. Let's get right into the topic with a look at some Java history.

The Java Foundation Classes

The AWT was a powerful toolkit when introduced, and it was the original driving force behind Java's popularity. Now that Swing, which has about four times the number of user interface (UI) components as the AWT, is part of the standard Java distribution, it's become fashionable to deride the AWT. However the AWT was a significant advance for its day. Nonetheless, the AWT is, by today's standards, a limited implementation, not designed to provide a serious, main UI for the needs of millions of programmers. The AWT component set wasn't designed for the popularity that it was received with, and in the context of today's programming needs, it's rather limited in range, has a lot of bugs, and takes up a lot of system resources.

As mentioned earlier in this book, the original AWT took only six weeks to write, was modeled after HTML controls, and allocated one operating system window per component. Because there are a lot more controls out there that programmers have become used to using, third parties began producing their own control sets for use with Java, which Sun Microsystems watched somewhat nervously. When Netscape introduced its Internet Foundation Classes (IFC) library for use with Java, and those classes became very popular, Sun decided to act, and the joint effort between Sun and Netscape produced the original Swing set of components as part of the Java Foundation Classes (JFC).

Many programmers think that JFC and Swing are the same thing, but that's not so; the JFC contains Swing and quite a number of other items. Here's what's in the JFC:

- *Swing*—The large UI package
- *Cut and paste*—Clipboard support
- *Accessibility features*—Aimed at users with disabilities
- *The Desktop Colors features*—First introduced in Java 1.1

- *Java 2D*—Improved color, image, and text support

- *Printing*—Originally enabled in Java 1.1

Swing introduced three significant advances: it uses fewer system resources, adds a lot more sophisticated components, and lets you tailor the look and feel of your programs. We'll take a closer look at Swing next.

Swing

Swing is a set of packages built on top of the AWT that provides you with a great number of prebuilt classes (over 250 classes and 40 UI components). From a programmer's point of view, the UI components are probably the most interesting, and I'll list them here (note that each UI component begins with **J**, which is one of the reasons so many programmers mistakenly use the terms *JFC* and *Swing* interchangeably):

- *JApplet*—An extended version of **java.applet.Applet** that adds support for root panes and other panes

- *JButton*—A push or command button

- *JCheckBox*—A check box that can be selected or deselected, displaying its state visually

- *JCheckBoxMenuItem*—A menu item that can be selected or deselected and that displays its state visually

- *JColorChooser*—A pane of controls to allow a user to select a color

- *JComboBox*—A combo box, which is a combination of a text field and drop-down list

- *JComponent*—The base class for Swing components

- *JDesktopPane*—A container used to create a multiple-document interface or a desktop

- *JDialog*—The base class for creating a dialog window

- *JEditorPane*—A text component that allows the user to edit various kinds of content

- *JFileChooser*—Lets the user choose a file

- *JFrame*—An extended version of **java.awt.Frame** that adds support root panes and other panes

- *JInternalFrame*—A lightweight object that provides many of the features of a heavyweight frame

- *JInternalFrame.JDesktopIcon*—Represents an iconified version of a **JInternalFrame**

- *JLabel*—A display area for a short text string or an image (or both)
- *JLayeredPane*—Adds layers to a Swing container, allowing components to overlap each other
- *JList*—A component that allows the user to select one or more objects from a list
- *JMenu*—A pop-up menu containing **JMenuItems** that's displayed when the user selects it in the **JMenuBar** component
- *JMenuBar*—An implementation of a menu bar
- *JMenuItem*—An implementation of a menu item
- *JOptionPane*—Makes it easy to pop up a standard dialog box
- *JPanel*—A generic lightweight container
- *JPasswordField*—Allows editing of a single line of text where the view does not show the original characters
- *JPopupMenu*—A pop-up menu
- *JPopupMenu.Separator*—A pop-up menu-specific separator
- *JProgressBar*—A component that displays an integer value within an interval
- *JRadioButton*—A radio button that can be selected or deselected, displaying its state visually
- *JRadioButtonMenuItem*—An radio button menu item
- *JRootPane*—The fundamental component in the container hierarchy
- *JScrollBar*—An implementation of a scrollbar
- *JScrollPane*—A container that manages a viewport, optional vertical and horizontal scrollbars, and optional row and column heading viewports
- *JSeparator*—A menu separator
- *JSlider*—A component that lets the user select a value by sliding a knob within an interval
- *JSplitPane*—Divides two components
- *JTabbedPane*—Lets the user switch between a group of components by clicking tabs
- *JTable*—Presents data in a two-dimensional table format
- *JTextArea*—A multiline area that displays plain text
- *JTextField*—Allows the editing of a single line of text
- *JTextPane*—A text component that can be marked up with attributes

- **JToggleButton**—A two-state button
- **JToggleButton.ToggleButtonModel**—The toggle button model
- **JToolBar**—A toolbar, useful for displaying commonly used controls
- **JToolBar.Separator**—A toolbar-specific separator
- **JToolTip**—Displays a tooltip for a component
- **JTree**—Displays a set of hierarchical data as an outline
- **JTree.DynamicUtilTreeNode**—Can wrap vectors/hashtables/arrays/strings and create appropriate children tree nodes
- **JTree.EmptySelectionModel**—A trees election model that does not allow anything to be selected
- **JViewport**—The viewport through which you see the information
- **JWindow**—A window that can be displayed anywhere on the desktop

One thing you might note in this list is that there's a Swing replacement for every AWT control and container except **JCanvas**; the reason is that the **JPanel** class already supports all that the **Canvas** component did, so Sun didn't find it necessary to add a separate **JCanvas** component.

Heavyweight Vs. Lightweight Components

Why couldn't all these enhancements and new components simply be added to AWT? It turns out that there's a fundamental philosophical difference between AWT and Swing UI components. Each AWT component gets its own operating platform window (and therefore ends up looking like a standard control in that operating platform). In extended programs, a large number of such windows slows performance and uses up a great deal of memory. Such components have come to be called *heavyweight*. Swing controls, on the other hand, are simply *drawn* as images in their containers and don't have a operating platform window of their own at all, so they use far fewer system resources. Therefore, they're called *lightweight* components.

All Swing components are derived from the **JComponent** class, and this class is, in turn, derived from the AWT **Container** class, which has no heavyweight window (called a peer), so **JComponent** is a lightweight class. As you'll see in this chapter, **JComponent** adds a tremendous amount of programming support to the AWT component class. Note that because all Swing components are derived from **JComponent**, and **JComponent** is derived from the AWT **Container** class, all Swing components are also AWT components in that way, and you can mix AWT controls with Swing controls in your programs. However, because Swing controls are merely drawn in their container, you can end up with strange results, because AWT controls will appear on top of them.

Not all Swing components are lightweight; to display anything in a windowed environment, you need some operating system windows, if only in which to draw lightweight controls. For that reason, Swing supports these heavyweight classes: **JFrame**, **JDialog**, **JWindow**, and **JApplet**.

Just as you build AWT applets using the **Applet** class and AWT applications using the **Frame** class, you build Swing applets on the **JApplet** class and Swing applications using the **JFrame** class. The fact that Swing is built on top of AWT is by no means seamless to the programmer, and the Swing heavyweight containers in fact have a complex structure that takes some getting used to. In fact, Swing often has the feeling of something added on by a third party, not by Sun itself. For example, to paint components, you don't override the paint method anymore, because Swing needs to do that to draw component borders and so on, and you have direct access to the parts of the program in which menus and dialog boxes are drawn, and so on. All in all, it takes some additional programming effort to move from AWT to Swing, as you'll see in this chapter.

Swing Features

Besides the large array of components in Swing and the fact that they're lightweight, Swing introduces many other innovations. Here are some of the major ones:

- *Borders*—You can draw borders in many different styles around components using the **setBorder** method.

- *Graphics debugging*—You can use the **setDebuggingGraphicsOptions** method to set up graphics debugging, which means, among other things, that you can watch each line as it's drawn and make it flash.

- *Easy mouseless operation*—It's now easy to connect keystrokes to components.

- *Tooltips*—You can use the **JComponent setToopTipText** method to give components a *tooltip*, one of those small windows that appears when the mouse hovers over a component and that gives explanatory text.

- *Easy scrolling*—You can now connect scrolling to various components, something that was impossible in AWT.

- *Pluggable look and feel*—You can set the appearance of applets and applications to one of three standard looks: Windows, Motif (Unix), or Metal (the standard Swing look).

- *New layout managers*—Swing introduces the **BoxLayout** and **OverlayLayout** layout managers.

Of these, the pluggable look and feel is probably the most important, because it allows you to select the appearance style of your program. In the AWT, controls were built on windows from the operating platform and therefore looked like other controls in that platform—something that gave AWT programs a very platform-specific appearance, which was not a good idea for a language that prides itself on being cross-platform. For example, because different fonts and controls are used in different platforms, the layout of programs could appear very different in different platforms. Swing introduces the Metal look, which is the new Java look, and it will appear the same across all platforms. In addition, you can give your programs a Windows or Motif look if you so choose. We'll take a look at this process in this chapter.

TIP: *Sun has created several other looks and feels that don't ship with the JDK, including one for the Apple Macintosh and another platform-independent look and feel called Organic.*

We have two essential programming differences between AWT and Swing programming to take a look at before jumping into the "Immediate Solutions" section. One is that you work with panes when creating Swing applets and applications, and the other is Model View Controller programming architecture. We'll take a look at working with Swing panes first, because you have to understand how panes work before setting them anywhere at all in Swing.

TIP: *Here's another difference between AWT and Swing; When you redraw items on the screen in AWT, the **update** method is called first to redraw the item's background, and programmers often override **update** to just call the **paint** method directly to avoid flickering. In Swing, on the other hand, the **update** method does not redraw the item's background, because components can be transparent; instead, **update** just calls **paint** directly.*

Graphics Programming Using Panes

The classes that are the basis of applets and applications, **JApplet** and **JFrame**, have a child object that does all the graphics work, and this object is of the **JRootPane** class. In AWT programming, you could just add components directly to applets or frame windows, but in Swing, it's a little more complex. Although you actually can add components directly to **JFrame** or **JApplet**, you'll get an error unless you turn off some error checking first, because you're expected to add them to the *content pane* in the **JRootPane** object.

Here's the structure of a **JRootPane**: This pane itself has two other panes—a layered pane and a glass pane. The glass pane is actually an AWT **Component** object that "rides" above everything else and that intercepts mouse events when you make this pane visible (although it's usually transparent) and add a mouse listener to it. The layered pane, which is of class **JLayeredPane**, is where most of the action takes place. There are specific layers you have access to, which display menus and dialog boxes when they're opened. From a programmer's point of view, probably the most interesting elements in the layered pane are usually the menu bar and content pane. The *content pane* is actually an object of the AWT **Container** class (there is no **JContentPane** class), and it's where applets and applications display their components. In practice, this means that when you add components to your program, you add them to the content pane, which means you must first get a reference to that pane. If you have a menu bar in your program, it's supported with a **JMenuBar** object, which is displayed right above the content pane.

TIP: *Swing content panes use a border layout manager by default, whereas AWT applets use a flow layout by default and AWT frame windows use border layouts by default.*

Model View Controller Architecture

There's one last topic to discuss before jumping into Swing programming—Model View Controller (MVC) architecture. MVC architecture is at the heart of Swing UI component programming, and an understanding of the term is essential. Here's what this term means: The *model* of a component is where the component's data is stored, such as the state of a button or the items in a list. The *view* is the screen representation of the component, such as the way a button or list appears. Finally, the *controller* is that part of the component that handles input, such as mouse clicks.

It's become standard to divide larger programs into views and documents, as in Microsoft Visual C++. There, a view provides a window into a document, which is where the data in the program is stored; multiple views can provide multiple windows into the document. Swing, inspired by the Smalltalk language, goes one step further and bases its UI components on the MVC architecture. As you can imagine, separating the view from the model is very useful in Swing, where the look and feel of components can change with a few lines of code. You'll see more about MVC architecture soon.

That's it. Now that we have an overview of Swing, it's time to turn to the "Immediate Solutions" section.

Immediate Solutions

Working With Swing

The Novice Programmer appears and says, "OK, I'm ready to start working with Swing. Where do I start?" "Well," you say, "probably with the **JComponent** class."

The **JComponent** class is the basis of all Swing components. **JComponent** is a lightweight class derived from the AWT **Container** class. Formally speaking, **JComponent** is actually the **javax.swing.JComponent** class, because **javax** is the package that contains Swing. Here's the inheritance diagram for **JComponent**:

```
java.lang.Object
|____java.awt.Component
      |____java.awt.Container
            |____javax.swing.JComponent
```

The **JComponent** class adds a lot to the AWT **Container** class, such as the ability to draw predefined borders around UI components, add **PropertyChangeListener** objects, which are notified when a property's value changes, and much more. For the sake of reference, you should take a look through Tables 11.1, 11.2, and 11.3, which list the fields, the constructor, and the methods, respectively, of this large class.

Table 11.1   Fields of the JComponent class.

Field	Does This
protected AccessibleContext accessibleContext	Accessibility support
protected EventListenerList listenerList	List of the current event listeners.
static String TOOL_TIP_TEXT_KEY	A comment to display when the cursor is over the component.
protected ComponentUI ui	The user interface.
static int UNDEFINED_CONDITION	A constant used to mean that no condition is defined.
static int WHEN_ANCESTOR_OF mand _FOCUSED_COMPONENT	Used for **registerKeyboardAction( )**, indicating that the command should be invoked when the receiving component is an ancestor of the focused component.

(continued)

*Table 11.1   Fields of the **JComponent** class* (continued).

Field	Does This
static int WHEN_FOCUSED	Constant used for **registerKeyboardAction( )**, indicating that the command should be invoked when the component has the focus.
static int WHEN_IN_FOCUSED _WINDOW	Constant used for **registerKeyboardAction( )**, indicating that the command should be invoked when the receiving component gets the focus.

*Table 11.2   The constructor of the **JComponent** class.*

Constructor	Does This
JComponent( )	The default **JComponent** constructor.

*Table 11.3   Methods of the **JComponent** class.*

Method	Does This
void addAncestorListener(Ancestor Listener listener)	Registers listener so that it will receive **AncestorEvents**.
void addNotify( )	Notification that this component now has a parent component.
void addPropertyChangeListener (PropertyChangeListener listener)	Adds a **PropertyChangeListener** to the listener list.
void addPropertyChangeListener (String propertyName, Property ChangeListener listener)	Adds a **PropertyChangeListener** for a specific property.
void addVetoableChangeListener (VetoableChangeListener listener)	Adds a **VetoableChangeListener** to the listener list.
void computeVisibleRect(Rectangle visibleRect)	Gets the component's visible rectangle.
boolean contains(int x, int y)	Determines if the component contains the given point.
JToolTip createToolTip( )	Gets the instance of **JToolTip** that should be used to display the tooltip.
void firePropertyChange(String propertyName, boolean oldValue, boolean newValue)	Reports a bound property change.
void firePropertyChange(String propertyName, byte oldValue, byte newValue)	Reports a bound property change.

(continued)

Table 11.3   Methods of the *JComponent* class (continued).

Method	Does This
void firePropertyChange(String propertyName, char oldValue, char newValue)	Reports a bound property change.
void firePropertyChange(String propertyName, double oldValue, double newValue)	Reports a bound property change.
void firePropertyChange(String propertyName, float oldValue, float newValue)	Reports a bound property change.
void firePropertyChange(String propertyName, int oldValue, int newValue)	Reports a bound property change.
void firePropertyChange(String propertyName, long oldValue, long newValue)	Reports a bound property change.
protected void firePropertyChange (String propertyName, Object oldValue, Object newValue)	Provides support for reporting bound property changes.
void firePropertyChange(String propertyName, short oldValue, short newValue)	Reports a bound property change.
protected void fireVetoableChange (String propertyName, Object old Value, Object newValue)	Provides support for reporting constrained property changes.
AccessibleContext getAccessible Context( )	Gets the **AccessibleContext** associated with this **JComponent**.
ActionListener getActionForKey Stroke(KeyStroke aKeyStroke)	Gets the object that will perform the action registered for a given keystroke.
float getAlignmentX( )	Gets the vertical alignment.
float getAlignmentY( )	Gets the horizontal alignment.
boolean getAutoscrolls( )	Yields True if this component automatically scrolls its contents when dragged.
Border getBorder( )	Gets the border of this component or null if no border is set.

(continued)

11. Swing: Applets, Applications, And Pluggable Look And Feel

Table 11.3   Methods of the *JComponent* class (continued).

Method	Does This
Rectangle getBounds(Rectangle rv)	Stores the bounds of this component into **rv** and returns **rv**.
Object getClientProperty(Object key)	Gets the value of the property with the specified key.
protected Graphics getComponent Graphics(Graphics g)	Gets the graphics object used to paint this component.
int getConditionForKeyStroke(Key Stroke aKeyStroke)	Get the condition that determines if an action occurs for the specified keystroke.
int getDebugGraphicsOptions( )	Gets the state of graphics debugging.
Graphics getGraphics( )	Gets this component's graphics context.
int getHeight( )	Gets the current height of this component.
Insets getInsets( )	If a border has been set on this component, the method gets the border's insets. Otherwise, it calls **super.getInsets**.
Insets getInsets(Insets insets)	Gets an **Insets** object for this component.
Point getLocation(Point rv)	Stores the x,y origin of this component into **rv** and returns **rv**.
Dimension getMaximumSize( )	Gets the component's maximum size.
Dimension getMinimumSize( )	Gets the component's minimum size.
Component getNextFocusable Component( )	Gets the next focusable component or null.
Dimension getPreferredSize( )	If the preferred size has been set to a nonnull value, this method returns it.
KeyStroke[ ] getRegisteredKeyStrokes( )	Gets the keystrokes that initiate actions.
JRootPane getRootPane( )	Gets the ancestor for a component.
Dimension getSize(Dimension rv)	Stores the width/height of this component into **rv** and returns **rv**.
Point getToolTipLocation(Mouse Event event)	Gets the tooltip location in the component coordinate system.
String getToolTipText( )	Gets the tooltip string that has been set with **setToolTipText( )**.
String getToolTipText(Mouse Event event)	Gets the string to be used as the tooltip for the event.
Container getTopLevelAncestor( )	Gets the top-level ancestor of this component.
String getUIClassID( )	Gets the **UIDefaults** key used to find the name of the **swing.plaf.ComponentUI** class.
Rectangle getVisibleRect( )	Gets the component's visible rectangle.

(continued)

Table 11.3   Methods of the JComponent class (continued).

Method	Does This
int getWidth( )	Gets the current width.
int getX( )	Gets the current x coordinate of this component's origin.
int getY( )	Gets the current y coordinate of this component's origin.
void grabFocus( )	Sets the focus on the component.
boolean hasFocus( )	Returns True if this component has the keyboard focus.
boolean isDoubleBuffered( )	Indicates if the receiving component should use a buffer to paint.
boolean isFocusCycleRoot( )	Returns True if the component is the root of a component tree with a focus cycle.
boolean isFocusTraversable( )	Specifies whether if this component can receive the focus.
static boolean isLightweight Component(Component c)	Returns True if this component is a lightweight component.
boolean isManagingFocus( )	Returns True if the component manages focus.
boolean isOpaque( )	Returns True if the component is opaque.
boolean isOptimizedDrawingEnabled( )	Returns True if the component tiles its children.
boolean isPaintingTile( )	Returns True if the component is painting a tile.
boolean isRequestFocusEnabled( )	Returns True if the receiving component can get the focus.

Preparing To Create A Swing Applet

"OK," the Novice Programmer reports, "I'm ready to start creating applets using Swing. How do I proceed?" "With the **JApplet** class," you say. "Pull up a chair and we'll go through it."

The **JApplet** class is a heavyweight container that's the foundation of Swing applets and extension of the AWT **Applet** class. The **JApplet** class has one child, an object of the **JRootPane** class, and that's where the drawing goes on as well as where you add components. Here's the inheritance diagram for **JApplet**:

```
java.lang.Object
|____java.awt.Component
      |____java.awt.Container
            |____java.awt.Panel
                  |____java.applet.Applet
                        |____javax.swing.JApplet
```

You can find the fields of the **JApplet** class in Table 11.4, its constructor in Table 11.5, and its methods in Table 11.6.

To start a Swing applet, I just derive a class from the **JApplet** class like this (note that I import **javax.swing.*** in order to use **JApplet**):

```
import java.awt.*;
import javax.swing.*;

/*
<APPLET
    CODE=applet.class
    WIDTH=300
    HEIGHT=200 >
</APPLET>
*/

public class applet extends JApplet
{
        .
        .
        .
}
```

Unfortunately, things get more complex at this point (when you want to draw in an applet or add controls to it), because you normally work with the content pane in the applet rather than directly with the applet itself.

Table 11.4   Fields of the JApplet class.

Field	Does This
protected AccessibleContext accessibleContext	An accessibility context.
protected JRootPane rootPane	The root pane.
protected boolean rootPane CheckingEnabled	Indicates if attempting to add components to the root pane will cause errors.

Table 11.5   The constructor of the JApplet class.

Constructor	Does This
JApplet( )	Creates a swing applet instance.

Table 11.6   Methods of the *JApplet* class.

Method	Does This
protected void addImpl(Component comp, Object constraints, int index)	Adds children to the content pane instead.
protected JRootPane create RootPane( )	Called by the constructor methods to create the default root pane.
AccessibleContext getAccessible Context( )	Get the accessible context associated with this **JApplet**.
Container getContentPane( )	Gets the **contentPane** object for this applet.
Component getGlassPane( )	Gets the **glassPane** object for this applet.
JMenuBar getJMenuBar( )	Gets the menu bar set on this applet.
JLayeredPane getLayeredPane( )	Gets the **layeredPane** object for this applet.
JRootPane getRootPane( )	Gets the **rootPane** object for this applet.
protected boolean isRootPane CheckingEnabled( )	Returns true if root pane checking is enabled.
protected String paramString( )	Gets a string representation of this **JApplet**.
protected void processKeyEvent (KeyEvent e)	Processes key events occurring in this component by sending them to **KeyListener** objects.
void remove(Component comp)	Removes the specified component from this container.
void setContentPane(Container contentPane)	Sets the **contentPane** property.
void setGlassPane(Component glassPane)	Sets the **glassPane** property.
void setJMenuBar(JMenuBar menuBar)	Sets the menu bar for this applet.
void setLayeredPane(JLayeredPane layeredPane)	Sets the **layeredPane** property.
void setLayout(LayoutManager manager)	Set the layout of its content pane instead.
protected void setRootPane (JRootPane root)	Sets the **rootPane** property.
protected void setRootPaneChecking Enabled(boolean enabled)	If True, calls to **add** and **setLayout** will cause an exception to be thrown.
void update(Graphics g)	Calls **paint(g)**. Does not redraw the background.

Both **JApplet** and **JFrame** have one child object, an object of class **JRootPane**, and the content pane is part of the root pane. We'll take a look at root panes in the next topic.

Understanding Root Panes

The **JRootPane** class is the class that manages the appearance of **JApplet** and **JFrame** objects, and it's worth taking a look at what's in **JRootPane**, because all its functionality is available to you in applets and applications. In particular, the root pane contains the glass pane, content pane, and layered pane, which you'll see a lot about in Swing programming.

Here's the inheritance diagram for **JRootPane**:

```
java.lang.Object
|____java.awt.Component
      |____java.awt.Container
            |____javax.swing.JComponent
                  |____javax.swing.JRootPane
```

You'll find the fields of the **JRootPane** class in Table 11.7, its constructor in Table 11.8, and its methods in Table 11.9.

Table 11.7   Fields of the JRootPane class.

Field	Does This
protected Container contentPane	The content pane.
protected JButton defaultButton	The button that gets activated when the pane has the focus and an action such as pressing the Enter key happens.
protected javax.swing.JRootPane. DefaultAction defaultPressAction	The action to take when the default button is pressed.
protected javax.swing.JRootPane. DefaultAction defaultReleaseAction	The action to take when the default button is released.
protected Component glassPane	Glass panes overlay the menu bar and content pane so they can intercept mouse movements.
protected JLayeredPane layeredPane	The layered pane that manages the menu bar and content pane.
protected JMenuBar menuBar	The menu bar.

Table 11.8   The constructor of the JRootPane class.

Constructor	Does This
JRootPane( )	Creates a **JRootPane** component, setting up its **glassPane**, **LayeredPane**, and **contentPane** components.

Table 11.9 Methods of the JRootPane class.

Method	Does This
protected void addImpl(Component comp, Object constraints, int index)	Overridden by Swing to ensure the glass component as the zero child.
void addNotify( )	Registers as a new root pane.
protected Container create ContentPane( )	Called by the constructor methods to create the default content pane.
protected Component createGlass Pane( )	Called by the constructor methods to create the default glass pane.
protected JLayeredPane create pane.LayeredPane( )	Called by the constructor methods to create the default layered
protected LayoutManager createRoot Layout( )	Called by the constructor methods to create the default layout manager.
Component findComponentAt(int x, int y)	Locates the visible child component that contains the specified position.
AccessibleContext getAccessible Context( )	Gets the accessible context.
Container getContentPane( )	Gets the content pane.
JButton getDefaultButton( )	Gets the default button.
Component getGlassPane( )	Gets the glass pane.
JMenuBar getJMenuBar( )	Gets the menu bar from the layered pane.
JLayeredPane getLayeredPane( )	Get the layered pane used by the root pane.
JMenuBar getMenuBar( )	Deprecated. Replaced by **getJMenubar( )**.
boolean isFocusCycleRoot( )	Makes the root of a focus cycle.
boolean isValidateRoot( )	If a descendant of this **JRootPane** calls **revalidate**, validation will occur from here on down.
protected String paramString( )	Gets a string representation of the root pane.
void removeNotify( )	Unregisters from **SystemEventQueueUtils**.
void setContentPane (Container content)	Sets the content pane.
void setDefaultButton(JButton defaultButton)	Sets the current default button.
void setGlassPane(Component glass)	Sets a specified component to be the glass pane for this root pane.
void setJMenuBar(JMenuBar menu)	Adds or changes the menu bar used in the layered pane.
void setLayeredPane(JLayeredPane layered)	Set the layered pane for the root pane.
void setMenuBar(JMenuBar menu)	Deprecated. Replaced by **setJMenuBar**.

As far as constructing applets and applications goes, you usually work with the content pane of the root pane. The content pane itself, however, is part of another pane—the layered pane. We'll take a look at layered panes in the next topic.

Understanding Layered Panes

The layered pane inside the root pane holds the actual components that appear in applets and applications, including menu bars and the content pane. Here's the inheritance diagram for the layered pane class, **JLayeredPane**:

```
java.lang.Object
|____java.awt.Component
      |____java.awt.Container
            |____javax.swing.JComponent
                  |____javax.swing.JLayeredPane
```

For convenience, **JLayeredPane** divides the depth range into several different layers. Putting a component into one of these layers makes it easy for you to ensure that components overlap properly, without having to worry about specifying numbers for specific depths:

- *DEFAULT_LAYER*—The standard, bottommost layer, where most components go.

- *PALETTE_LAYER*—The palette layer sits over the default layer and is useful for floating toolbars and palettes.

- *MODAL_LAYER*—The layer used for modal dialog boxes.

- *POPUP_LAYER*—The pop-up layer displays above the dialog layer.

- *DRAG_LAYER*—When you drag a component, assigning it to the drag layer makes sure it's positioned over all other component in the container.

You can use the **JLayeredPane** methods **moveToFront**, **moveToBack**, and **setPosition** to reposition a component within its layer. The **setLayer** method can also be used to change the component's current layer. You'll find the fields of the **JLayeredPane** class in Table 11.10, its constructor in Table 11.11, and its methods in Table 11.12.

As far as typical drawing operations go in applets and applications, the most important part of the layered pane is the content pane. We'll take a look at this next.

*Table 11.10   Fields of the **JLayeredPane** class.*

Field	Does This
static Integer DEFAULT_LAYER	The default layer.
static Integer DRAG_LAYER	The drag layer.
static Integer FRAME_CONTENT _LAYER	The frame content layer.
static String LAYER_PROPERTY	A bound property.
static Integer MODAL_LAYER	The modal layer.
static Integer PALETTE_LAYER	The palette layer.
static Integer POPUP_LAYER	The pop-up layer.

*Table 11.11   The constructor of the **JLayeredPane** class.*

Constructor	Does This
JLayeredPane( )	Creates a new **JLayeredPane** object.

*Table 11.12   Methods of the **JLayeredPane** class.*

Method	Does This
protected void addImpl(Component indexcomp, Object constraints, int index)	Adds the indicated component to this container at the indicated.
AccessibleContext getAccessible Context( )	Get the accessible context.
int getComponentCountInLayer (int layer)	Gets the number of children in the indicated layer.
Component[ ] getComponentsInLayer (int layer)	Gets an array of the components in the indicated layer.
protected Hashtable getComponent ToLayer( )	Gets the hashtable, which maps components to layers.
int getIndexOf(Component c)	Gets the index of the indicated component.
int getLayer(Component c)	Gets the layer attribute for the indicated component.
static int getLayer(JComponent c)	Gets the layer property for a **JComponent** and does not cause any side effects like **setLayer( )**.
static JLayeredPane getLayeredPane Above(Component c)	Gets the first **JLayeredPane**, which contains the indicated component protected Integer getObjectForLayer(int layer). Gets the **Integer** object with a indicated layer.

(continued)

Table 11.12   Methods of the JLayeredPane class (continued).

Method	Does This
int getPosition(Component c)	Gets the relative position of the component within its layer.
int highestLayer( )	Gets the highest layer value from all current children.
protected int insertIndexForLayer(int layer, int position)	Determines the proper location in which to insert a new child based on layer and position requests.
boolean isOptimizedDrawingEnabled( )	Returns False if components in the pane can overlap.
int lowestLayer( )	Gets the lowest layer value from all current children.
void moveToBack(Component c)	Moves the component to the bottom of the components in its current layer.
void moveToFront(Component c)	Moves the component to the top of the components in its current layer.
void paint(Graphics g)	Paints the layered pane using a graphics context.
protected String paramString( )	Gets a string representation of this **JLayeredPane**.
static void putLayer(JComponent c, int layer)	Sets the layer property on a **JComponent**.
void remove(int index)	Removes the indexed component from this pane.
void setLayer(Component c, int layer)	Sets the layer attribute on the indicated component, making it the bottommost component in that layer.
void setLayer(Component c, int layer, int position)	Sets the layer attribute for the indicated component and also sets its position within that layer.
void setPosition(Component c, int position)	Moves the component to position within its current layer.

Understanding Content Panes

You usually place controls and graphics in the content pane of an applet or application. You may be expecting the content pane to be supported by its own class, but in fact, a content pane is just an AWT **Container** object (which is itself a lightweight class). You can get access to the content pane in the layered pane of an applet or application using the **getContentPane** method of the **JApplet** and **JFrame** classes.

The importance of the content pane is that it's where you usually add components to applets and applications as well as where you draw graphics; this is a major difference from AWT programming. Another important point to know is that content panes use border layouts by default. To see how this actually works in code, take a look at the next topic.

Creating A Swing Applet

"OK," says the Novice Programmer, "I'm ready to create a Swing applet and add items to the content pane. How does it work?" "Sit down and let's discuss it," you reply.

Painting In Swing Vs. AWT

If you've gone through the AWT material earlier in this chapter, you may be expecting there to be a **paint** method you can use to handle painting operations and graphics in Swing applets and applications. In fact, there is a **paint** method, but you should not override it unless you really know what you're doing, because Swing, itself, uses that method to draw the borders around the component as well as to draw any child components inside the component, among other tasks.

Instead of using the **paint** method for painting operations, you now use the **paintComponent** method. This has some ramifications for you when creating applets and applications compared to AWT programming. Instead of just overriding the applet or frame window class's **paint** method, you now have to create a component to do your painting in. You must do this because the content pane in a program is not a class that you can override methods in—it's an object (one alternative is to create a custom content pane class and use the **setContentPane** method to install it in your program). In addition, note that when you work with **paintComponent**, the first thing you should do is call **super.paintComponent**, the super class's **paintComponent** method, to let the super class do additional painting.

Displaying Controls In Swing Vs. AWT

To add controls to a content pane, you use the content pane's **add** method. The content pane in both applets and applications uses a border layout by default, unlike AWT programming, in which applets use flow layouts by default and frame windows use border layouts by default.

To add controls to a content pane, you first set the layout manager to whatever you like or use the default border layout. To actually add the controls, you use the **add** method, just as you do in AWT programming.

Let's get to an example. In this case, I just display the text "Hello from Swing!" in an applet. How does that text get displayed? I can't just display it in the default content pane of an applet, because that pane is an object, not a class, so I can't override its **paintComponent** method. On the other hand, I can add a panel, as represented by the **JPanel** class, to the applet so that it covers the content pane. I can also draw in that panel by overriding its **paintComponent** method. Note that I could create a new content pane class, override its **paintComponent** method, and install it with the **setContentPane** method, but **JPanel** is generally used to create content panes anyway, so that just represents needless work.

TIP: *If you ever want to find out exactly what values were used to construct a visual component such as a **JApplet**, give it the focus, press Shift+Ctrl+F1, and watch the console window for a complete overview.*

Using The **JPanel** Class

The **JPanel** class is the all-purpose container class of Swing, and it's an important one to know about. Here's the inheritance diagram for **JPanel**:

```
java.lang.Object
|____java.awt.Component
     |____java.awt.Container
          |____javax.swing.JComponent
               |____javax.swing.JPanel
```

Unlike the heavyweight Swing containers, **JPanel** uses a flow layout by default. You'll find the constructors of the **JPanel** class in Table 11.13 and its methods in Table 11.14.

Table 11.13   Constructors of the JPanel class.

Constructor	Does This
JPanel( )	Constructs a new **JPanel** with a double buffer and a flow layout.
JPanel(boolean isDoubleBuffered)	Constructs a new **JPanel** with flow layout and the specified buffering strategy.
JPanel(LayoutManager layout)	Constructs a new buffered **JPanel** with the specified layout manager.
JPanel(LayoutManager layout, boolean isDoubleBuffered)	Constructs a new **JPanel** with the specified layout manager and buffering strategy.

Table 11.14   Methods of the JPanel class.

Methods	Does This
AccessibleContext getAccessible Context( )	Gets the accessible context .
String getUIClassID( )	Gets a string that specifies the name of the "look and feel" class that renders this component.
protected String paramString( )	Gets a string representation of the **JPanel**.
void updateUI( )	Called when the look and feel has changed.

Here's how I create a **JPanel** class that displays the text "Hello from Swing!" (note that I'm giving this panel a white background and am overriding the **paintComponent** method; **paintComponent** is passed an AWT **Graphics** object, with which I can use to draw the text):

```
class jpanel extends JPanel
{
    jpanel()
    {
        setBackground(Color.white);
    }

    public void paintComponent (Graphics g)
    {
        super.paintComponent(g);
        g.drawString("Hello from Swing!", 0, 60);
    }
}
```

Now I can add an object of this new class to the content pane of an applet by using the **JApplet** class's **getContentPane** method and then use the content pane's **add** method to actually add the panel:

```
import java.awt.*;
import javax.swing.*;

/*
<APPLET
    CODE=applet.class
    WIDTH=300
    HEIGHT=200 >
</APPLET>
*/

public class applet extends JApplet
{
    jpanel j;

    public void init()
    {
        Container contentPane = getContentPane();

        j = new jpanel();
        contentPane.add(j);
    }
}
```

```
class jpanel extends JPanel
{
    jpanel()
    {
        setBackground(Color.white);
    }

    public void paintComponent (Graphics g)
    {
        super.paintComponent(g);
        g.drawString("Hello from Swing!", 0, 60);
    }
}
```

That's all it takes—now I can compile and run this applet, as you see in Figure 11.1.

You'll find this example in applet.java on the CD accompanying this book.

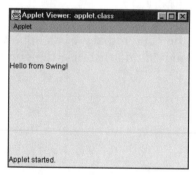

Figure 11.1   A Swing applet.

Creating A Swing Application

"OK," says the Novice Programmer, "I'm ready to create an application using Swing. Where do I start?" "By creating a frame window," you say. "Using the **Frame** class?" the NP asks. "Nope," you say, "the **JFrame** class."

Just as in AWT applications, you usually use a frame window when creating applications in Swing, and in Swing, that means using a **JFrame** object, which has a root pane child. Here's the inheritance diagram for **JFrame** (note that it's derived from the **Frame** class and is therefore a heavyweight container):

```
java.lang.Object
|____java.awt.Component
```

```
|____java.awt.Container
    |____java.awt.Window
        |____java.awt.Frame
            |____javax.swing.JFrame
```

You'll find the fields of the **JFrame** class in Table 11.15, its constructors in Table 11.16, and its methods in Table 11.17. Note that the default layout in a **JFrame** is a border layout.

TIP: *If you ever want to find out exactly what values were used to construct a visual component such as a **JFrame**, give it the focus, press Shift+Ctrl+F1, and watch the console window for a complete overview.*

Table 11.15   Fields of the JFrame class.

Field	Does This
protected AccessibleContext accessibleContext	The accessible context.
protected JRootPane rootPane	The root pane that manages the content pane, menu bar, and glass pane.
protected boolean rootPane CheckingEnabled	If this is True, calls to **add** and **setLayout** cause an exception to be thrown.

Table 11.16   Constructors of the JFrame class.

Constructor	Does This
JFrame( )	Constructs a new frame.
JFrame(String title)	Constructs a new frame with the specified title.

Table 11.17   Methods of the JFrame class.

Method	Does This
protected void addImpl(Component comp, Object constraints, int index)	Adds children to the content pane instead.
protected JRootPane createRootPane( )	Called by the constructor methods to create the default root pane.
protected void frameInit( )	Called by the constructors to initialize the **JFrame** properly.
AccessibleContext getAccessible Context( )	Gets the accessible context associated with this **JFrame**.
Container getContentPane( )	Gets the content pane object for this frame.
int getDefaultCloseOperation( )	Gets the operation that occurs when the user closes the frame.
Component getGlassPane( )	Gets the **glassPane** object.

(continued)

Table 11.17   Methods of the JFrame class (continued).

Method	Does This
JMenuBar getJMenuBar( )	Gets the menu bar.
JLayeredPane getLayeredPane( )	Gets the layered pane.
JRootPane getRootPane( )	Gets the root pane.
protected boolean isRootPane CheckingEnabled( )	Indicates whether calls to **add** and **setLayout** cause an exception to be thrown.
protected String paramString( )	Gets a string representation of this **JFrame**.
protected void processKey Event(KeyEvent e)	Processes key events occurring in this component.
protected void processWindowEvent (WindowEvent e)	Processes window events occurring in this component.
void remove(Component comp)	Removes the component from this container.
void setContentPane(Container contentPane)	Sets the **contentPane** property.
void setDefaultCloseOperation (int operation)	Sets the operation that will happen by default when the user closes this frame.
void setGlassPane(Component glassPane)	Sets the **glassPane** property.
void setJMenuBar(JMenu Bar menubar)	Sets the menu bar for this frame.
void setLayeredPane(JLayeredPane layeredPane)	Sets the **layeredPane** property.
void setLayout(LayoutManager manager)	By default, you should set the layout of the content pane instead.
protected void setRootPane(JRootPane root)	Sets the **rootPane** property.
protected void setRootPaneChecking Enabled(boolean enabled)	Determines whether calls to **add** and **setLayout** cause an exception to be thrown.
void update(Graphics g)	Calls **paint**.

I'll put the **JFrame** class to work in an application now. In this case, I'll create a **JPanel** object (as in the previous topic), install the panel in a **JFrame** object, and display the text "Hello from Swing!" in the panel. The default background color of **JFrame** is gray, but I'll make this panel white by setting its background color. Here's the code:

```
class jpanel extends JPanel
{
```

```
    jpanel()
    {
        setBackground(Color.white);
    }

    public void paintComponent (Graphics g)
    {
        super.paintComponent(g);
        g.drawString("Hello from Swing!", 0, 60);
    }
}
```

Next, I create an object of this new class and add it to the content pane of the
JFrame in an application, like this:

```
import java.awt.*;
import javax.swing.*;
import java.awt.event.*;

public class app extends JFrame
{
    jpanel j;

    public app()
    {
        super("Swing application");

        Container contentPane = getContentPane();
        j = new jpanel();
        contentPane.add(j);
    }

    public static void main(String args[])
    {
        final JFrame f = new app();

        f.setBounds(100, 100, 300, 300);
        f.setVisible(true);
    }
}

class jpanel extends JPanel
{
    jpanel()
    {
        setBackground(Color.white);
    }
```

```
public void paintComponent (Graphics g)
{
    super.paintComponent(g);
    g.drawString("Hello from Swing!", 0, 60);
}
}
```

Note also that I've used the **setBounds** method to set the screen location and size of the **JFrame** window. The result appears in Figure 11.2. You'll find this example in app.java on the CD.

However, there's a problem with the application you see in Figure 11.2. When you close the application window by clicking on the close button, it disappears from the screen (which is more than an AWT application window would do), but the application doesn't end. To remedy this situation, take a look at the next topic.

Figure 11.2   Displaying a Swing application in a frame window.

Closing **JFrame** Windows

"Hey," says the Novice Programmer, "Java's gone all wacky again. When I try to close a Swing **JFrame** window, nothing happens." "Well," you say, "you can take care of that in several ways." "I'll get some coffee," the NP says.

When you close an AWT window, nothing happens by default, but you can handle window events yourself and end the application if you like. Swing **JFrame** windows, on the other hand, let you set a default close operation with the **setDefaultCloseOperation** method. Here are the possible values to pass to this method:

• *DO_NOTHING_ON_CLOSE*—The default. Nothing happens when the window is closed.

- **HIDE_ON_CLOSE**—Hides the window when it's closed.

- **DISPOSE_ON_CLOSE**—Disposes of the window when it's closed. You cannot redisplay the window, although the window object is still available in memory.

Note that these possibilities only deal with the window itself; if you want to end the application when the application window is closed, you'll still have to handle that yourself. Here, I dispose of the window and end the application with a window adapter inner class:

```
import javax.swing.*;
import java.awt.*;
import java.awt.event.*;

public class app extends JFrame
{
    jpanel j;

    public app()
    {
        super("Swing application");

        Container contentPane = getContentPane();
        j = new jpanel();
        contentPane.add(j);
    }

    public static void main(String args[])
    {
        final JFrame f = new app();

        f.setBounds(100, 100, 300, 300);
        f.setVisible(true);
        f.setDefaultCloseOperation(DISPOSE_ON_CLOSE);

        f.addWindowListener(new WindowAdapter() {
            public void windowClosed(WindowEvent e) {
                System.exit(0);
            }
        });
    }
}

class jpanel extends JPanel
{
```

```
jpanel()
{
    setBackground(Color.white);
}

public void paintComponent (Graphics g)
{
    super.paintComponent(g);
    g.drawString("Hello from Swing!", 0, 60);
}
}
```

Selecting Component Borders

"Say," says the Novice Programmer, "the Big Boss wants our programs to look more decorative, more visually interesting. Any ideas?" "Well," you say, "you can use different kinds of borders for components in Swing. That's easy enough." "How does it work?" the NP asks, enthralled.

To create a border for a component, you can use the **BorderFactory** class, which can create borders of these classes: **BevelBorder**, **SoftBevelBorder**, **EtchedBorder**, **LineBorder**, **TitledBorder**, and **MatteBorder**. You can also use the **EmptyBorder**, **CompoundBorder**, and **AbstractBorder** classes to create your own borders.

Here's the inheritance diagram for the **BorderFactory** class:

```
java.lang.Object
|____javax.swing.BorderFactory
```

You'll find the **BorderFactory** class methods in Table 11.18.

The **BorderFactory** class creates objects that implement the **Border** interface; you'll find the methods of this interface in Table 11.19.

Using Insets

One important aspect of working with borders is knowing about *insets*, which indicate the distance you must allow along each edge to account for the border. You can get the insets of a border with the **getBorderInsets** method of the **Border** interface; this method returns an object of class **Insets**. Here's the inheritance diagram for the **Insets** class:

```
java.lang.Object
|____java.awt.Insets
```

Table 11.18   Methods of the *BorderFactory* class.

Methods	Does This
static Border createBevelBorder (int type)	Creates a beveled border of the indicated type.
static Border createBevelBorder (int type, Color highlight, Color shadow)	Creates a beveled border of the indicated type with the indicated highlighting and shadowing.
static Border createBevelBorder (int type, Color highlightOuter, highlightInner, Color shadowOuter, Color shadowInner)	Creates a beveled border of the indicated type, using the indicated Color colors for the inner and outer highlight and shadow areas .
static CompoundBorder create CompoundBorder( )	Creates a compound border.
static CompoundBorder create CompoundBorder(Border Border, Border insideBorder)	Creates a compound border, indicating the border objects for the outside and inside edges.
static Border createEmptyBorder( )	Returns an empty border that takes up no space. Returns an empty border
static Border createEtchedBorder( )	Creates a border with an etched look using the component's current background color for highlighting and shading.
static Border createEtchedBorder(Color highlight, Color shadow)	Creates a border with an etched look using the indicated highlighting and shading colors.
static Border createLineBorder (Color color)	Returns a line border with the indicated color.
static Border createLineBorder (Color color, int thickness)	Returns a line border with the indicated color and width.
static Border createLowered BevelBorder( )	Returns a border with a lowered beveled edge.
static MatteBorder createMatte Border(int top, int left, int bottom, int right, Color color)	Returns a matted border using a solid color.
static MatteBorder createMatte Border(int top, int left, int bottom, int right, Icon tileIcon)	Returns a matted border made up of multiple tiles of an indicated icon.
static Border createRaisedBevel Border( )	Returns a border with a raised beveled edge.
static TitledBorder createTitledBorder (Border border)	Returns a new title border with an empty title.

(continued)

Table 11.18 **Methods of the BorderFactory class (continued).**

Methods	Does This
static TitledBorder createTitledBorder (Border border, String title)	Adds a title to an existing border, indicating the text of the title.
static TitledBorder createTitledBorder (Border border, String title, int title Justification, int titlePosition)	Adds a title to a border, indicating the text of the title along with its positioning.
static TitledBorder createTitledBorder (Border border, String title, int title Justification, int titlePosition, Font titleFont)	Adds a title to a border, indicating the text of the title along with its positioning and font.
static TitledBorder createTitledBorder (Border border, String title, int title Justification, int titlePosition, Font titleFont, Color titleColor)	Adds a title to a border, indicating the text of the title along with its positioning, font, and color.
static TitledBorder createTitledBorder (String title)	Creates a new title border, indicating the text of the title and using default settings.
boolean isBorderOpaque( )	Determines whether the border is opaque.
void paintBorder(Component c, Graphics g, int x, int y, int width, int height)	Paints the border for the specified component.

Table 11.19 **Methods of the Border interface.**

Methods	Does This
Insets getBorderInsets(Component c)	Gets the insets of the border.

You'll find the fields of the **Insets** class in Table 11.20, its constructor in Table 11.21, and its methods in Table 11.22.

Table 11.20 **Fields of the Insets class.**

Field	Does This
int bottom	The inset from the bottom.
int left	The inset from the left.
int right	The inset from the right.
int top	The inset from the top.

*Table 11.21 The constructor of the **Border** class.*

Constructor	Does This
Insets(int top, int left, int bottom, int right)	Creates and initializes a new **Insets** object.

*Table 11.22 Methods of the **Border** class.*

Method	Does This
Object clone( )	Creates a copy of this object.
boolean equals(Object obj)	Checks whether two objects are equal.
String toString( )	Gets a string representing this **Insets** object.

Let's look at an example. In this case, I add a border to the **JPanel** used in the applet example a few topics ago. To do that, I just use the panel's **setBorder** method (which most visual components have in Swing) and create a new raised bevel border with the **BorderFactory** class's **createRaisedBevelBorder** method:

```java
import javax.swing.*;
import java.awt.*;
import java.awt.event.*;
import java.util.*;

/*
<APPLET
    CODE=bordered.class
    WIDTH=300
    HEIGHT=200 >
</APPLET>
*/

public class bordered extends JApplet
{
    jpanel j;

    public void init()
    {
        Container contentPane = getContentPane();

        j = new jpanel();
        j.setBorder(BorderFactory.createRaisedBevelBorder());
        contentPane.add(j);
    }
}
```

Besides adding a new border to the panel, I'll take the insets of this border into account to draw the message "Hello from Swing!" without overlapping the border. To do that, I'll use the **getBorder** method to get the current border, the **getBorderInsets** method of the object that supports the **Border** interface, and the left data member of that object to determine where to start printing the message so as not to overlap the border:

```
class jpanel extends JPanel
{
    public void paintComponent (Graphics g)
    {
        g.drawString("Hello from Swing!",
        getBorder().getBorderInsets(this).left, 60);
    }
}
```

The results appear in Figure 11.3. As you can see in the figure, the text appears inside the thin beveled border that encloses the panel. This example is in bordered.java on the CD.

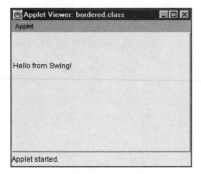

Figure 11.3   Adding a border to a **JPanel** object.

Setting The Pluggable Look And Feel

The Big Boss is back and says, "I understand you can set the appearance of a Swing program to match various programming platforms." "That's right," you say. The BB asks, "Do you have anything in burnished mahogany?" "Sorry," you reply.

By default, the appearance of Swing programs is set to the Java Metal look, a cross-platform look that Sun has designed. However, you can change that by using the **UIManager** class. Here's the inheritance diagram for this class:

```
java.lang.Object
|_____javax.swing.UIManager
```

You'll find the constructor of the **UIManager** class in Table 11.23 and its methods in Table 11.24.

To change the look and feel as a program is tuning, you can use the **UIManager** class's **setLookAndFeel** method, passing it one of these arguments as a string:

- **javax.swing.plaf.metal.MetalLookAndFeel**—The Metal look and feel
- **com.sun.java.swing.plaf.motif.MotifLookAndFeel**—The Motif look and feel
- **com.sun.java.swing.plaf.windows.WindowsLookAndFeel**—The Windows look and feel

Table 11.23   The constructor of the UIManager class.

Constructor	Does This
UIManager( )	Constructs a new **UIManager** object.

Table 11.24   Methods of the UIManager class.

Method	Does This
static void addAuxiliaryLookAndFeel	Adds a **LookAndFeel** (LookAndFeel laf) object to the list of look and feels.
static void addPropertyChangeListener (PropertyChangeListener listener)	Adds a **PropertyChangeListener**.
static Object get(Object key)	Gets an object from the defaults table.
static LookAndFeel[ ] getAuxiliary LookAndFeels( )	Gets the list of look and feels.
static Border getBorder(Object key)	Gets a border from the defaults table.
static Color getColor(Object key)	Gets a drawing color from the defaults table.
static String getCrossPlatformLookAnd FeelClassName( )	Gets the name of the **LookAndFeel** class that supports the default cross-platform look and feel.
static UIDefaults getDefaults( )	Gets the defaults for this look and feel.
static Dimension getDimension (Object key)	Gets a dimension from the defaults.
static Font getFont(Object key)	Gets a font from the defaults.
static Icon getIcon(Object key)	Gets an icon from the defaults.
static Insets getInsets(Object key)	Gets an **Insets** object from the defaults.

(continued)

Table 11.24 *Methods of the UIManager class* (continued).

Method	Does This
static UIManager.LookAndFeelInfo[ ] getInstalledLookAndFeels( )	Gets an array of objects that hold information about the **LookAndFeel** implementations installed.
static int getInt(Object key)	Gets an integer from the defaults.
static LookAndFeel getLookAndFeel( )	Gets the current default look and feel.
static UIDefaults getLookAndFeel Defaults( )	Gets the default values for this look and feel.
static String getString(Object key)	Gets a string from the defaults.
static String getSystemLookAndFeel ClassName( )	Gets the name of the **LookAndFeel** class that implements the native systems look and feel.
static ComponentUI getUI (JComponent target)	Gets the look and feel object that draws the target component.
static void installLookAndFeel (String name, String className)	Creates a new look and feel and adds it to the current array.
static void installLookAndFeel(UIManager.LookAndFeelInfo info)	Installs the specified look and feel.
static Object put(Object key, Object value)	Stores an object in the defaults.
static boolean removeAuxiliaryLook AndFeel(LookAndFeel laf)	Removes a **LookAndFeel** object from the list of look and feels.
static void removePropertyChange Listener(PropertyChangeListener listener)	Removes a **PropertyChangeListener** object.
static void setInstalledLookAndFeels (UIManager.LookAndFeelInfo[ ] infos)	Replaces the current array of installed **LookAndFeelInfo** objects.
static void setLookAndFeel(LookAnd Feel newLookAndFeel)	Sets the current default look and feel with a **LookAndFeel** object .
static void setLookAndFeel(String className)	Sets the current default look and feel with a class name.

After changing the look and feel of the content pane, you make it take effect with the **updateComponentTreeUI** method of the **SwingUtilities** class, like this:

```
SwingUtilities.updateComponentTreeUI(getContentPane());
```

Here's an example in which I add a lot of Swing controls that we haven't worked with yet to an applet so you can see what they look like in various looks and feels. There are three radio buttons in this applet, labeled Metal, Motif, and Windows, and when you click a radio button, the applet changes to the corresponding look and feel. Here's the code (you'll see how to use all these controls in the following chapters):

```java
import java.awt.*;
import javax.swing.*;
import java.awt.event.*;
import javax.swing.plaf.metal.MetalLookAndFeel;
import com.sun.java.swing.plaf.motif.MotifLookAndFeel;
import com.sun.java.swing.plaf.windows.WindowsLookAndFeel;

/*
<APPLET
    CODE=plaf.class
    WIDTH=210
    HEIGHT=200 >
</APPLET>
*/

public class plaf extends JApplet
{
    JRadioButton b1 = new JRadioButton("Metal"),
    b2 = new JRadioButton("Motif"),
    b3 = new JRadioButton("Windows");

    public void init()
    {
        Container contentPane = getContentPane();
        contentPane.add(new jpanel(), BorderLayout.CENTER);
    }

    class jpanel extends JPanel implements ActionListener
    {
        public jpanel()
        {
            add(new JButton("JButton"));
            add(new JTextField("JTextField"));
            add(new JCheckBox("JCheckBox"));
            add(new JRadioButton("JRadioButton"));
            add(new JLabel("JLabel"));
            add(new JList(new String[] {
                "JList Item 1", "JList Item 2", "JList Item 3"}));
            add(new JScrollBar(SwingConstants.HORIZONTAL));
```

```
            ButtonGroup group = new ButtonGroup();
            group.add(b1);
            group.add(b2);
            group.add(b3);

            b1.addActionListener(this);
            b2.addActionListener(this);
            b3.addActionListener(this);

            add(b1);
            add(b2);
            add(b3);
        }

        public void actionPerformed(ActionEvent e)
        {
            JRadioButton src = (JRadioButton)e.getSource();

            try {
                if((JRadioButton)e.getSource() == b1)
                    UIManager.setLookAndFeel(
                      "javax.swing.plaf.metal.MetalLookAndFeel");
                else if((JRadioButton)e.getSource() == b2)
                    UIManager.setLookAndFeel(
                        "com.sun.java.swing.plaf.motif.MotifLookAndFeel");
                else if((JRadioButton)e.getSource() == b3)
                    UIManager.setLookAndFeel(
                      "com.sun.java.swing.plaf.windows.WindowsLookAndFeel"
                      );
            }
            catch(Exception ex) {}

            SwingUtilities.updateComponentTreeUI(getContentPane());
        }
    }
}
```

You can see the applet in the Metal look and feel in Figure 11.4, in the Motif look and feel in Figure 11.5, and the Windows look and feel in Figure 11.6. Switching between these looks is as easy as clicking a radio button. You'll find this example in plaf.java on the CD.

Figure 11.4   The Java Metal look and feel.

Figure 11.5   The Motif look and feel.

Figure 11.6   The Windows look and feel.

Setting The Pluggable Look And Feel For Components

"Jeez," says the Novice Programmer, "wouldn't it be great if all components used the same fonts and borders?" "Well," you say, "I'm not sure about that, but you can actually make that happen in Swing." The NP asks, "You can?"

You can set the look and feel of individual components in Swing using the **LookAndFeel** class. Here's the inheritance diagram for that class:

```
java.lang.Object
|____javax.swing.LookAndFeel
```

You'll find the constructor for the **LookAndFeel** class in Table 11.25 and its methods in Table 11.26.

*Table 11.25   The constructor of the **LookAndFeel** class.*

Constructor	Does This
LookAndFeel( )	Creates a **LookAndFeel** object.

*Table 11.26   Methods of the **LookAndFeel** class.*

Method	Does This
UIDefaults getDefaults( )	Called by **UIManager.setLookAndFeel** to create the look and feel defaults.
abstract String getDescription( )	Gets a one-line description of this look-and-feel implementation.
abstract String getID( )	Gets a string that identifies this look and feel.
abstract String getName( )	Gets a short string that identifies this look and feel.
void initialize( )	**UIManager.setLookAndFeel** calls this method before the first call to **getDefaults( )**.
static void installBorder(JComponent c, String defaultBorderName)	Installs a component's default **Border** object.
static void installColors(JComponent c, String defaultBgName, String defaultFgName)	Installs a component's foreground and background color properties with values from the current defaults.
static void installColorsAndFont (JComponent c, String defaultBg Name, String defaultFgName, String defaultFontName)	Installs a components foreground background and font properties with values from the defaults.
abstract boolean isNative LookAndFeel( )	If True, this is an implementation of the platform's native look and feel.
abstract boolean isSupportedLook AndFeel( )	If True, the underlying platform supports and or permits this look and feel.
static Object makeIcon(Class base Class, String gifFile)	Creates a **UIDefaults.LazyValue** that creates an **ImageIcon** for the specified **gifFile** filename.

(continued)

Table 11.26 Methods of the *LookAndFeel* class (continued).

Method	Does This
static JTextComponent.KeyBinding[ ] makeKeyBindings(Object[ ] key BindingList)	Builds lists of key bindings.
String toString( )	Gets a string that identifies this object's properties.
void uninitialize( )	**UIManager.setLookAndFeel** calls this method just before a new default look and feel is installed, replacing this one.
static void uninstallBorder (JComponent c)	Uninstalls a component's default border if the border is an instance of **UIResource**.

Here's an example in which I give a Swing text field the look and feel of a Swing label using the **LookAndFeel** class's **installBorder** and **installColorsAndFont** methods. Note that you haven't seen these controls at work formally yet; this example is just to indicate what can be done with look and feels. I'll create a Swing label here and a class extended from the text field class to look like a label. Here's the code:

```
import java.awt.*;
import javax.swing.*;

/*
<APPLET
    CODE=plafcomponent.class
    WIDTH=210
    HEIGHT=200 >
</APPLET>
*/

public class plafcomponent extends JApplet
{
    public void init()
    {
        Container contentPane = getContentPane();

        JNewLabel jnewlabel = new JNewLabel(
                "This is a fake label.");

        contentPane.setLayout(new FlowLayout());

        contentPane.add(new JLabel("This is a real label."));
        contentPane.add(jnewlabel);
    }
}
```

```
class JNewLabel extends JTextField
{
    public JNewLabel(String s)
    {
        super(s);
    }
    public void updateUI()
    {
        super.updateUI();

        setHighlighter(null);
        setEditable(false);

        LookAndFeel.installBorder(this, "Label.border");

        LookAndFeel.installColorsAndFont(this, "Label.background",
            "Label.foreground", "Label.font");
    }
}
```

The result appears in Figure 11.7. As you can see in the figure, the text field, which appears under the label, has been given the look and feel of the label. This gives you an indication of how powerful the look-and-feel handling is in Swing. This example is in plafcomponent.java on the CD.

Figure 11.7   Setting the look and feel of a text field to be like a label.

Chapter 12

Swing: Text Fields, Buttons, Toggle Buttons, Check Boxes, And Radio Buttons

In Depth

This chapter begins the discussion of Swing controls; specifically, we'll take a look at Swing labels, buttons, text fields, toggle buttons, check boxes, and radio buttons. All these are essential controls that make up a big part of the foundation of Swing. With the exception of toggle buttons, all these controls should be familiar to you from AWT programming. However, each of these Swing controls has a lot more functionality than the corresponding AWT controls, and I'll emphasize what's new here. (Bear in mind that all Swing controls appear differently in the various look and feels; this is important to remember when you starting to program with them.)

Labels And Text Fields

Labels are basic Swing controls that just display one line of text. There was reason to believe that labels would support multiple lines of text in Swing, but they turned out only supporting one line. On the other hand, they do support something that AWT labels don't—images. We'll see how to use the **ImageIcon** class to add images to labels.

Text handling in Swing text components has become a somewhat involved topic that we'll look into later in this book. Here, we'll get a start on handling text in Swing with text fields, seeing how they work fundamentally in this chapter and in more depth later.

Buttons

In Swing, buttons of all kinds are built into the **AbstractButton** class, and we'll take a look at that class in this chapter. As you might expect, Swing buttons have more capabilities than their AWT counterparts, including the capabilities to display images, use mnemonics (keyboard shortcuts), designate a button as a window's default button, and set a button's margins and text alignment. You can also assign multiple images to a button to handle the case where the mouse moves over the button, and more. You'll see all this in the chapter.

Toggle Buttons

Swing introduces toggle buttons, which are buttons that, when pressed, stay pressed until they're pressed again. Toggle buttons are much like check boxes and radio buttons that look like standard buttons—and, in fact, the **JToggleButton** class is the base class for the Swing check box and radio button classes, but you can also instantiate objects of this class directly. As with check boxes and radio buttons, you can also put toggle buttons into groups and use images with them.

Check Boxes And Radio Buttons

The AWT has check boxes and radio buttons, but handling these controls in Swing is a little different. For one thing, radio buttons have their own class in Swing (radio buttons are just glorified check boxes in AWT), and you can use images with them. In fact, you'll see that there are a few issues to consider when you use images with check boxes and radio buttons.

That's it for the overview of what's in this chapter. It's time to turn to the "Immediate Solutions" section.

Immediate Solutions

Using Labels

The Novice Programmer appears and says, "I'm creating a new Swing applet and I want to label the controls in it, so I'm starting with a **Label** object and...." "Hold it," you say. "You should be using a **JLabel** object." The NP says, "Oh."

The lightweight Swing label class is **JLabel**. Here's the inheritance diagram for this class:

```
java.lang.Object
|____java.awt.Component
     |____java.awt.Container
          |____javax.swing.JComponent
               |____javax.swing.JLabel
```

You'll find the constructors for the **JLabel** class in Table 12.1 and its methods in Table 12.2.

Table 12.1   Constructors of the JLabel class.

Constructor	Does This
JLabel( )	Constructs a **JLabel** object with no image.
JLabel(Icon image)	Constructs a **JLabel** object with the indicated image.
JLabel(Icon image, int horizontal Alignment)	Constructs a **JLabel** object with the indicated image and horizontal alignment.
JLabel(String text)	Constructs a **JLabel** object with the indicated text.
JLabel(String text, Icon icon, int horizontalAlignment)	Constructs a **JLabel** object with the indicated text, image, and horizontal alignment.
JLabel(String text, int horizontal Alignment)	Constructs a **JLabel** object with the indicated text and horizontal alignment.

Table 12.2   Methods of the JLabel class.

Method	Does This
protected int checkHorizontalKey(int key, String message)	Verifies a legal value for the **horizontalAlignment** properties.
protected int checkVerticalKey(int message)	Verifies a legal value for the **verticalAlignment** or key, String **verticalTextPosition** property.
AccessibleContext getAccessible Context( )	Gets the accessible context.
Icon getDisabledIcon( )	Gets the value of the **disabledIcon** property if it has been set.
int getDisplayedMnemonic( )	Gets the keycode that indicates a mnemonic key.
int getHorizontalAlignment( )	Gets the alignment of the label's contents along the x axis.
int getHorizontalTextPosition( )	Gets the horizontal position of the label's text, relative to its image.
Icon getIcon( )	Gets the graphic image (glyph or icon) that the label displays.
int getIconTextGap( )	Gets the amount of space between the text and the icon displayed in this label.
Component getLabelFor( )	Gets the component this object is a label for.
String getText( )	Gets the text string that the label displays.
LabelUI getUI( )	Gets the look and feel object that renders this component.
String getUIClassID( )	Gets a string that indicates the name of the look and feel class that renders this component.
int getVerticalAlignment( )	Gets the alignment of the label's contents along the y axis.
int getVerticalTextPosition( )	Gets the vertical position of the label's text, relative to its image.
protected String paramString( )	Gets a string representation of this **JLabel** object.
void setDisabledIcon(Icon disabledI con)	Sets the icon to be displayed if this **JLabel** object is "disabled."
void setDisplayedMnemonic (char aChar)	Specifies the displayed mnemonic as a char value.
void setDisplayedMnemonic(int key)	Specifies a keycode that indicates a mnemonic key.
void setHorizontalAlignment(int alignment)	Sets the alignment of the label's contents along the x axis.
void setHorizontalTextPosition(int t extPosition)	Sets the horizontal position of the text relative to its image.
void setIcon(Icon icon)	Defines the icon this component will display.

(continued)

Table 12.2   Methods of the JLabel class (continued).

Method	Does This
void setIconTextGap(int iconTextGap)	If both the icon and text properties are set, this property defines the space between them.
void setLabelFor(Component c)	Sets the component this object is labeling.
void setText(String text)	Defines the single line of text this component will display.
void setUI(LabelUI ui)	Sets the look and feel object that renders this component.
void setVerticalAlignment (int alignment)	Sets the alignment of the label's contents along the y axis.
void setVerticalTextPosition(int textPosition)	Sets the vertical position of the text relative to the image.
void updateUI( )	Called by the **UIFactory** class that the look and feel has changed.

Here's a basic example that shows how to create a Swing label with the text "Hello from Swing!":

```
import java.awt.*;
import javax.swing.*;

/*
<APPLET
    CODE=label.class
    WIDTH=300
    HEIGHT=200 >
</APPLET>
*/

public class label extends JApplet
{
    public label()
    {
        Container contentPane = getContentPane();
        JLabel jlabel = new JLabel("Hello from Swing!");
        contentPane.setLayout(new FlowLayout());
        contentPane.add(jlabel);
    }
}
```

The result of this code appears in Figure 12.1; this example is in label.java on the CD accompanying this book.

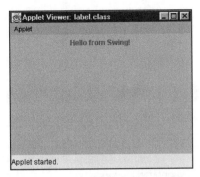

Figure 12.1   A Swing label.

There's a lot more you can do with Swing labels. For example, you can set the alignment of the text in a label as well as use images, and we'll take a look at the possibilities over the next couple of topics. To display an image in a label, you need an object that implements the **Icon** interface, and you'll find the methods of this interface in Table 12.3.

Fortunately, there's an easy way to create icons from images in Swing—you can use the **ImageIcon** class, coming up in the next topic.

*Table 12.3   Methods of the **Icon** interface.*

Method	Does This
int getIconHeight( )	Gets the icon's height.
int getIconWidth( )	Gets the icon's width.
void paintIcon(Component c, Graphics g, int x, int y)	Draws the icon at the indicated location.

Using Image Icons

"Hey," says the Novice Programmer, "I was just taking a look at the **Icon** interface. Do I have to paint images in icons myself in Swing?" "Of course not," you say. "You can use the **ImageIcon** class to make things a lot easier." "Tell me all about it," the NP says.

The **ImageIcon** class lets you create an icon from an image file for use in a Swing control. Here's the inheritance diagram for this class:

```
java.lang.Object
|____javax.swing.ImageIcon
```

You'll find the constructors of the **ImageIcon** class in Table 12.4 and its methods in Table 12.5.

Table 12.4   Constructors of the *ImageIcon* class.

Constructor	Does This
ImageIcon( )	Constructs an image icon.
ImageIcon(byte[ ] imageData)	Constructs an image icon from an array of bytes.
ImageIcon(byte[ ] imageData, String description)	Constructs an image icon from an array of bytes that were read from an image file containing a supported image format.
ImageIcon(Image image)	Constructs an image icon from an image object.
ImageIcon(Image image, String description)	Constructs an image icon from the given image.
ImageIcon(String filename)	Constructs an image icon from the given file.
ImageIcon(String filename, String description)	Constructs an image icon from the given file.
ImageIcon(URL location)	Constructs an image icon from the indicated URL.
ImageIcon(URL location, String description)	Constructs an image icon from the indicated URL.

Table 12.5   Methods of the *ImageIcon* class.

Method	Does This
String getDescription( )	Gets the description of the image.
int getIconHeight( )	Gets the height of the icon.
int getIconWidth( )	Gets the width of the icon.
Image getImage( )	Gets the icon's image.
int getImageLoadStatus( )	Gets the status of the image-loading operation.
ImageObserver getImageObserver( )	Gets the image observer for the image.
protected void loadImage (Image image)	Waits for the image to load.
void paintIcon(Component c, Graphics g, int x, int y)	Paints the icon.
void setDescription(String description)	Sets the description of the image.
void setImage(Image image)	Sets the image displayed by this icon.
void setImageObserver(Image Observer observer)	Sets the image observer for the image.

The **ImageIcon** class is an extremely useful one in Swing, because many Swing components can display icons. I'll put this class to work in the next topic.

Using Images In Labels

The Big Boss appears and says, "We need to jazz things up a bit in our programs, because there's some heavy competition in the GUI field now." "OK," you say, "I can add image icons to each label in the code." "Swell," says the BB, "your new code is due yesterday."

You can use several of the **JLabel** constructors to add images to labels, and you can specify the alignment of images and text in a label with methods like these:

- *setVerticalTextAlignment*—Sets the vertical text alignment relative to the image.

- *setHorizontalTextAlignment*—Sets the horizontal text alignment relative to the image.

- *setVerticalAlignment*—Sets the vertical alignment of the label's contents.

- *setHorizontalAlignment*—Sets the horizontal alignment of the label's contents.

You can use constants like these to specify alignments: **BOTTOM**, **CENTER**, **EAST**, **HORIZONTAL**, **LEADING**, **LEFT**, **NORTH**, **NORTH_EAST**, **NORTH_WEST**, **RIGHT**, **SOUTH**, **SOUTH_EAST**, **SOUTH_WEST**, **TOP**, **TRAILING**, **VERTICAL**, and **WEST**.

Here's an example in which I add a label with an image and text to an applet. The text will be centered under the image. To create the image, I use the **ImageIcon** class, passing that class's constructor the name of the file that holds the image I want to use (which, in this case, is label.jpg):

```
import java.awt.*;
import javax.swing.*;

/*
<APPLET
    CODE=labelimage.class
    WIDTH=500
    HEIGHT=200 >
</APPLET>
*/
```

```
public class labelimage extends JApplet
{

  public void init()
  {
    Container contentPane = getContentPane();

    JLabel jlabel = new JLabel("Label", new ImageIcon("label.jpg"),
        JLabel.CENTER);
    jlabel.setVerticalTextPosition(JLabel.BOTTOM);
    jlabel.setHorizontalTextPosition(JLabel.CENTER);

    contentPane.add(jlabel);
  }
}
```

The result appears in Figure 12.2, and you can find this example in labelimage.java on the CD. Note how easy it is to add images to labels in Swing—because it's so simple, it's a very common thing to do.

Figure 12.2   A Swing label with an image.

Using Text Fields

"Don't tell me," the Novice Programmer says. "I bet I can guess—the name of the Swing text field class is **JTextField**, right?" "Exactly," you smile.

For compatibility, Swing text fields work much like AWT text fields, with some added capabilities. Here's the inheritance diagram for the Swing **JTextField** class:

```
java.lang.Object
|____java.awt.Component
      |____java.awt.Container
            |____javax.swing.JComponent
                  |____javax.swing.text.JTextComponent
                        |____javax.swing.JTextField
```

You'll see more on using Swing text components later in this book, but for now I'll introduce the **JTextField** class so we can get user input before that point. You'll find the constructors of the **JTextField** class in Table 12.6 and its methods in Table 12.7.

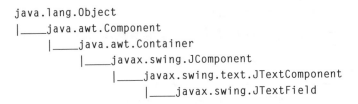

Table 12.6 **Constructors of the *JTextField* class.**

Constructor	Does This
JTextField( )	Constructs a new text field.
JTextField(Document doc, String text, int columns)	Constructs a new **JTextField** object that uses the given storage model and the given columns.
JTextField(int columns)	Constructs a new empty text field with the indicated columns.
JTextField(String text)	Constructs a new text field initialized with the indicated text.
JTextField(String text, int columns)	Constructs a new text field initialized with the indicated text and columns.

Table 12.7 **Methods of the *JTextField* class.**

Method	Does This
void addActionListener(Action Listener l)	Adds the action listener to get action events from this text field.
protected Document createDefault Model( )	Constructs the default implementation of the model.
protected void fireActionPerformed( )	Notifies listeners that have this event type.
AccessibleContext getAccessible Context( )	Gets the accessible context.
Action[ ] getActions( )	Gets the command list for the editor.
int getColumns( )	Gets the number of columns.
protected int getColumnWidth( )	Gets the column width.
int getHorizontalAlignment( )	Gets the horizontal alignment of the text.

(continued)

Table 12.7   Methods of the *JTextField* class (continued).

Method	Does This
BoundedRangeModel getHorizontalVisibility( )	Gets the visibility of the text field.
Dimensio getPreferredSize( )	Gets the preferred size dimensions needed for this text field.
int getScrollOffset( )	Gets the scroll offset.
String getUIClassID( )	Gets the class ID for a UI.
boolean isValidateRoot( )	Revalidate calls that come from the text field will be handled by validating the text field.
protected String paramString( )	Gets a string representation of this text field.
void postActionEvent( )	Processes action events occurring on this text field by sending them to any registered **ActionListener** objects.
void removeActionListener(Action Listener I)	Removes the indicated action listener.
void scrollRectToVisible(Rectangle r)	Scrolls the field left or right.
void setActionCommand(String command)	Sets the command string used for action events.
void setColumns(int columns)	Sets the number of columns.
void setFont(Font f)	Sets the current font.
void setHorizontalAlignment(int alignment)	Sets the horizontal alignment of the text.
void setScrollOffset(int scrollOffset)	Sets the scroll offset.

Here's a quick example that does nothing more than display a text field with the text "Hello from Swing!" in it:

```
import java.awt.*;
import javax.swing.*;

/*
<APPLET
    CODE=textfield.class
    WIDTH=300
    HEIGHT=200 >
</APPLET>
*/

public class textfield extends JApplet {
    JTextField text = new JTextField(20);
```

```
    public void init()
    {
        Container contentPane = getContentPane();

        contentPane.setLayout(new FlowLayout());
        contentPane.add(text);
        text.setText("Hello from Swing!");
    }
}
```

The result of this code—textfield.java on the CD—appears in Figure 12.3.

This is only the very beginning of using text components in Swing, but it gets us started and provides an easy way for our programs to display output. For example, I'll connect a text field to a button over the next couple topics.

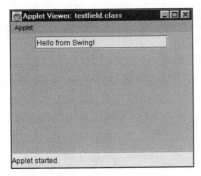

Figure 12.3   A Swing label with an image.

Abstract Button: The Foundation Of Swing Buttons

"But I don't want to use the **AbstractButton** class," the Novice Programmer says. "I want to use the **JButton** class. Why do I have to learn about **AbstractButton**?" "All buttons in Swing are derived from **AbstractButton**," you say, "and there's a tremendous number of methods in that class you should know about, even if only for reference. Really, it'll do you good." "Oh," says the NP.

The **AbstractButton** class provides the foundation of the button classes in Java, and like **JComponent**, it provides so many methods that we can't ignore it here. Here's the inheritance diagram for **AbstractButton**:

```
java.lang.Object
|____java.awt.Component
     |____java.awt.Container
          |____javax.swing.JComponent
               |____javax.swing.AbstractButton
```

You'll find the fields of the **AbstractButton** class in Table 12.8, its constructor in Table 12.9, and its methods in Table 12.10.

Table 12.8   Fields of the *AbstractButton* class.

Field	Does This
protected ActionListener actionListener	The action listener.
static String BORDER_PAINTED_ CHANGED_ PROPERTY	Indicates a change to the border painting.
protected ChangeEvent changeEvent	The button's **changeEvent**.
protected ChangeListener changeListener	The button's model listeners.
static String CONTENT_AREA_FILLED _CHANGED_ PROPERTY	Indicates a change from rollover enabled to disabled or back to enabled.
static String DISABLED_ICON_ CHANGED_ PROPERTY	Indicates a change to the icon used when the button has been disabled.
static String DISABLED_SELECTED _ICON_CHANGED_ PROPERTY	Indicates a change to the icon shown when the button has been disabled and selected.
static String FOCUS_PAINTED _CHANGED_ PROPERTY	Indicates a change to having the border highlighted when it has the focus (or not).
static String HORIZONTAL _ALIGNMENT_CHANGED _ PROPERTY	Indicates a change in the button's horizontal alignment.
static String HORIZONTAL_TEXT _POSITION_CHANGED_ PROPERTY	Indicates a change in the button's horizontal text position.
static String ICON_CHANGED _ PROPERTY	Indicates a change to the icon that represents the button.
protected ItemListener itemListener	The ItemListener for this button.
static String MARGIN_CHANGED _ PROPERTY	Indicates a change in the button's margins.
static String MNEMONIC_CHANGED _ PROPERTY	Indicates a change to the button's mnemonic.

(continued)

Table 12.8   Fields of the *AbstractButton* class (continued).

Field	Does This
protected ButtonModel model	The data model that determines the button's state.
static String MODEL_CHANGED _ PROPERTY	Indicates a change in the button model.
static String PRESSED_ICON _CHANGED_ PROPERTY	Indicates a change to the icon used when the button has been pressed.
static String ROLLOVER_ENABLED _CHANGED_ PROPERTY	Indicates a change in the button's "rollover enabled" property.
static String ROLLOVER_ICON _CHANGED_ PROPERTY	Indicates a change to the icon used when the cursor is over the button.
static String ROLLOVER_SELECTED _ICON_CHANGED_ PROPERTY	Indicates a change to the icon used when the cursor is over the button and the button is selected.
static String SELECTED_ICON _CHANGED_ PROPERTY	Indicates a change to the icon used when the button has been selected.
static String TEXT_CHANGED _ PROPERTY	Indicates a change in the button's text.
static String VERTICAL_ALIGNMENT _CHANGED_ PROPERTY	Indicates a change in the button's vertical alignment.
static String VERTICAL_TEXT _POSITION_CHANGED_ PROPERTY	Indicates a change in the button's vertical text position.

Table 12.9   The constructor of the *AbstractButton* class.

Constructor	Does This
AbstractButton( )	Constructs a new **AbstractButton** object.

Table 12.10   Methods of the *AbstractButton* class.

Method	Does This
void addActionListener (ActionListener I)	Adds an action listener.
void addChangeListener (ChangeListener I)	Adds a change listener.
void addItemListener(ItemListener I)	Adds an item listener to a check box.
protected int checkHorizontalKey(int properkey, String exception)	Verifies that key is a legal value for the **horizontalAlignment** ties.

(continued)

Table 12.10   Methods of the *AbstractButton* class (continued).

Method	Does This
protected int checkVerticalKey(int key, exception)	Verifies that key is a legal value for the **verticalAlignment** String properties.
protected ActionListener create ActionListener( )	Creates an action listener.
protected ChangeListener create implementationChangeListener( )	Override this method to return another **ChangeListener**
protected ItemListener createItem Listener( )	Creates an item listener.
void doClick( )	Programmatically clicks the button.
void doClick(int pressTime)	Programmatically clicks the button at a certain time.
protected void fireActionPerformed (ActionEvent event)	Fires an action event.
protected void fireItemStateChanged (ItemEvent event)	Fires an "item changed" event.
protected void fireStateChanged( )	Fires a "state changed" event.
String getActionCommand( )	Gets the action command for this button.
Icon getDisabledIcon( )	Gets the disabled icon.
Icon getDisabledSelectedIcon( )	Gets the disabled selected icon.
int getHorizontalAlignment( )	Gets the horizontal alignment of the icon and text.
int getHorizontalTextPosition( )	Sets the horizontal position of the text relative to the icon.
Icon getIcon( )	Gets the default icon.
String getLabel( )	Deprecated. Replaced by **getText( )**.
Insets getMargin( )	Gets the margin between the button's border and the label.
int getMnemonic( )	Gets the keyboard mnemonic from the current model.
ButtonModel getModel( )	Gets the model that this button represents.
Icon getPressedIcon( )	Gets the pressed icon for the button.
Icon getRolloverIcon( )	Gets the rollover icon for the button.
Icon getRolloverSelectedIcon( )	Gets the rollover selected icon for the button.
Icon getSelectedIcon( )	Gets the selected icon for the button.
Object[ ] getSelectedObjects( )	Gets an array of length 1 containing the label or null if the button is not selected.
String getText( )	Gets the button's text.
ButtonUI getUI( )	Gets the button's current UI.

(continued)

Table 12.10   Methods of the *AbstractButton* class (continued).

Method	Does This
int getVerticalAlignment( )	Gets the vertical alignment of the text and icon.
int getVerticalTextPosition( )	Gets the vertical position of the text relative to the icon.
protected void init(String text, Icon icon)	For internal use.
boolean isBorderPainted( )	Determines whether the border should be painted.
boolean isContentAreaFilled( )	Checks whether the "content area" of the button should be filled.
boolean isFocusPainted( )	Determines whether focus should be painted.
boolean isRolloverEnabled( )	Checks whether rollover effects are enabled.
boolean isSelected( )	Gets the state of the button.
protected void paintBorder(Graphics g)	Paints the button's border.
protected String paramString( )	Gets a string representation of this **AbstractButton** object.
void removeActionListener (ActionListener l)	Removes an action listener.
void removeChangeListener (ChangeListener l)	Removes a change listener.
void removeItemListener(I temListener l)	Removes an item listener.
void setActionCommand(String actionCommand)	Sets the action command.
void setBorderPainted(boolean b)	Sets whether the border should be painted.
void setContentAreaFilled(boolean b)	Specifies whether the button should paint the content area.
void setDisabledIcon(Icon disabledIcon)	Sets the disabled icon for the button.
void setDisabledSelectedIcon(Icon disabledSelectedIcon)	Sets the disabled selected icon for the button.
void setEnabled(boolean b)	Enables (or disables) the button.
void setFocusPainted(boolean b)	Sets whether focus should be painted.
void setHorizontalAlignment (int alignment)	Sets the horizontal alignment of the icon and text.
void setHorizontalTextPosition (int textPosition)	Sets the horizontal position of the text relative to the icon.
void setIcon(Icon defaultIcon)	Sets the button's default icon.
void setLabel(String label)	Deprecated. Replaced by **setText(text)**.

(continued)

Table 12.10   Methods of the AbstractButton class (continued).

Method	Does This
void setMargin(Insets m)	Sets space for margins.
void setMnemonic(char mnemonic)	Specifies the mnemonic value.
void setMnemonic(int mnemonic)	Sets the keyboard mnemonic.
void setModel(ButtonModel newModel)	Sets the model that this button represents.
void setPressedIcon(Icon pressedIcon)	Sets the pressed icon.
void setRolloverEnabled(boolean b)	Sets whether rollover effects should be enabled.
void setRolloverIcon(Icon rolloverIcon)	Sets the rollover icon for the button.
void setRolloverSelectedIcon (Icon rolloverSelectedIcon)	Sets the rollover selected icon for the button.
void setSelected(boolean b)	Sets the state of the button.
void setSelectedIcon(Icon selectedIcon)	Sets the selected icon for the button.
void setText(String text)	Sets the button's text.
void setUI(ButtonUI ui)	Sets the button's UI.
void setVerticalAlignment(int alignment)	Sets the vertical alignment of the icon and text.
void setVerticalTextPosition (int textPosition)	Sets the vertical position of the text relative to the icon.
void updateUI( )	Gets a new UI object from the default UIFactory class.

Using Buttons

The Novice Programmer arrives and says, "I'm ready to start working with Swing buttons. What can they do?" "Hmm," you say, "quite a lot! Better pull up a chair."

Swing buttons are supported in the **JButton** class. Here's the inheritance diagram for this class:

```
java.lang.Object
|____java.awt.Component
      |____java.awt.Container
            |____javax.swing.JComponent
                  |____javax.swing.AbstractButton
                        |____javax.swing.JButton
```

Swing buttons let you do a lot more than AWT buttons. Some of the things you can do with the **JButton** class include using **setToolTipText** to add a tooltip to the button, using **setMargin** to set the insets in the button itself, using **doClick** to click the button from code, adding images to the button, and adding mnemonics (keyboard shortcuts) to the button. Of course, you can do standard AWT things with **JButton** too, such as using **setEnabled** to enable or disable the button, using **addActionListener** to register an action listener with the button, and adding action commands to **JButton** objects with **setActionCommand**.

You'll find the constructors of the **JButton** class in Table 12.11 and its methods in Table 12.12. Note that this class is based on the **AbstractButton** class, which means it inherits all of that class's functionality (see the previous topic for the details).

Let's look at an example that puts the **JButton** class to work. Here, I just display the message "Hello from Swing!" when the user clicks a button. This example, button.java on the CD, is very simple, as you can see in the following code:

Table 12.11   Constructors of the JButton class.

Constructor	Does This
JButton( )	Constructs a button.
JButton(Icon icon)	Constructs a button with an icon.
JButton(String text)	Constructs a button with the given text.
JButton(String text, Icon icon)	Constructs a button with text and an icon.

Table 12.12   Methods of the JButton class.

Method	Does This
AccessibleContext getAccessible Context( )	Gets the accessible context.
String getUIClassID( )	Gets a string that indicates the name of the look and feel.
boolean isDefaultButton( )	Indicates whether this button is the default button on the root pane.
boolean isDefaultCapable( )	Indicates whether this button is capable of being the default button on the root pane.
protected String paramString( )	Gets a string representation of this **JButton** object.
void setDefaultCapable(boolean defaultCapable)	Specifies whether this button is capable of being the default button on the root pane.
void updateUI( )	Called by the **UIFactory** class when the look and feel has changed.

```
import java.awt.*;
import javax.swing.*;
import java.awt.event.*;

/*
<APPLET
    CODE=button.class
    WIDTH=300
    HEIGHT=200 >
</APPLET>
*/

public class button extends JApplet {
    JButton button = new JButton("Click Me");
    JTextField text = new JTextField(20);

    public void init()
    {
        Container contentPane = getContentPane();

        contentPane.setLayout(new FlowLayout());
        contentPane.add(button);
        contentPane.add(text);

        button.addActionListener(new ActionListener()
        {
            public void actionPerformed(ActionEvent event) {
                text.setText("Hello from Swing!");
            }
        });
    }
}
```

The result of this code appears in Figure 12.4. As you can see in the figure, when the user clicks the button, the applet displays its message in the text field.

There's a lot more you can do with **JButton** objects, however, and we'll take a look at the possibilities over the following few topics.

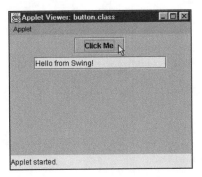

Figure 12.4   Using a Swing button.

Displaying Images In Buttons

"I know that you can display images in Swing labels," the Novice Programmer says, "but what about displaying them in buttons?" "No problem at all," you say, "as long as you have an **Icon** object."

It's easy to display images in buttons using the **ImageIcon** class, because several **JButton** constructors let you add icons to buttons. You can also set the alignment of the text and image using these **AbstractButton** methods:

- *setVerticalTextAlignment*—Sets the vertical text alignment relative to the image.

- *setHorizontalTextAlignment*—Sets the horizontal text alignment relative to the image.

- *setVerticalAlignment*—Sets the vertical alignment of the button's contents.

- *setHorizontalAlignment*—Sets the horizontal alignment of the button's contents.

Let's look at an example in which I add an image from button.jpg to the button example from the previous topic:

```
import java.awt.*;
import javax.swing.*;
import java.awt.event.*;

/*
<APPLET
    CODE=imagebutton.class
    WIDTH=600
    HEIGHT=200 >
```

```
</APPLET>
*/

public class imagebutton extends JApplet {
    JButton button = new JButton("Button", new ImageIcon("button.jpg"));
    JTextField text = new JTextField(20);

    public void init()
    {
        Container contentPane = getContentPane();

        contentPane.setLayout(new FlowLayout());
        contentPane.add(button);
        contentPane.add(text);

        button.addActionListener(new ActionListener()
        {
            public void actionPerformed(ActionEvent event) {
                text.setText("Hello from Swing!");
            }
        });
    }
}
```

The result appears in Figure 12.5. As you can see in the figure, the button now displays a large image, making the whole program more visually interesting. This example is in imagebutton.java on the CD.

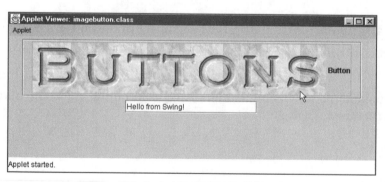

Figure 12.5   Using a Swing button with an image.

Using Rollover And Disabled Images

The Big Boss is distraught and says, "We've got to jazz our programs up!" "OK," you say, "I can add rollover images with the buttons so they'll display an image when the mouse is over them. By the way, why do we have to jazz things up?" "Because," the Big Boss says, "our competitors have invested years of work and money to make their programs twice as useful as ours." "Shouldn't we do the same?" you ask. The BB says, "Don't be ridiculous."

You can set a number of icons for buttons. Here are the possibilities (rollover icons appear when the mouse moves over the button):

- Normal icon
- Rollover icon
- Rollover selected icon
- Selected icon
- Pressed icon
- Disabled icon
- Disabled selected icon

I'll put these possibilities to work in an example (it's named buttonicons.java on the CD). To install these icons, I just use a method with the matching name: **setIcon**, **setRolloverIcon**, **setRolloverSelectedIcon**, **setSelectedIcon**, **setPressedIcon**, **setDisabledIcon**, and **setDisabledSelectedIcon**. Here's how this looks in code (note that to enable rollover events, I call **setRolloverEnabled** with a value of **true**):

```
import java.awt.*;
import javax.swing.*;

/*
<APPLET
    CODE=buttonicons.class
    WIDTH=300
    HEIGHT=200 >
</APPLET>
*/

public class buttonicons extends JApplet
{
    public void init()
    {
```

```
        Container contentPane = getContentPane();

        Icon normal = new ImageIcon("normal.jpg");
        Icon rollover = new ImageIcon("rollover.jpg");
        Icon pressed = new ImageIcon("pressed.jpg");
        Icon disabled = new ImageIcon("disabled.jpg");
        Icon selected = new ImageIcon("selected.jpg");
        Icon rolloverSelected = new
            ImageIcon("rselected.jpg");
        Icon disabledSelected = new
            ImageIcon("dselected.jpg");

        JButton jbutton = new JButton();

        jbutton.setRolloverEnabled(true);

        jbutton.setIcon(normal);
        jbutton.setRolloverIcon(rollover);
        jbutton.setRolloverSelectedIcon(rolloverSelected);
        jbutton.setSelectedIcon(selected);
        jbutton.setPressedIcon(pressed);
        jbutton.setDisabledIcon(disabled);
        jbutton.setDisabledSelectedIcon(disabledSelected);

        contentPane.setLayout(new FlowLayout());
        contentPane.add(jbutton);
    }
}
```

You can see the result in Figure 12.6. In the figure, the mouse is moving over the button, so the rollover image is visible.

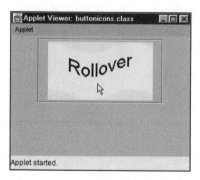

Figure 12.6   Using rollover and other images in a button.

Default Buttons And Mnemonics

If you've taken a look at dialog boxes for your operating system, you'll see that one button is usually marked as the *default* button, and that button is automatically clicked if the user performs some keyboard action such as pressing the Enter key. You can make a button the default button in Swing using the **setDefaultButton** method.

Besides making buttons into default buttons, you can also give each button a *mnemonic*, which is a keyboard shortcut, much like those you see in menus. You underline one (case-insensitive) letter in a button's caption, and when the button has the focus, typing that character activates the button. If the button does not have a caption, typing the meta key (for example, that's the Alt key in Windows) and the button's mnemonic activates the button.

Let's see this in code. In this case, I add two buttons to an applet and make the second button the default button. The second button will have the caption Click Me, and I'll make the letter *C* the button's mnemonic. Here's what this looks like in code (note that I give the root pane the focus at the end of the code so it can intercept key events and therefore activate the default button when the user presses Enter):

```
import java.awt.*;
import javax.swing.*;
import java.awt.event.*;

/*
<APPLET
    CODE=defaultbutton.class
    WIDTH=300
    HEIGHT=200 >
</APPLET>
*/

public class defaultbutton extends JApplet {
    JButton button1 = new JButton("Click Me");
    JButton button2 = new JButton("Click Me");
    JTextField text = new JTextField(20);

    public void init()
    {
        Container contentPane = getContentPane();

        contentPane.setLayout(new FlowLayout());
```

```
        button2.setMnemonic('C');
        getRootPane().setDefaultButton(button2);

        contentPane.add(button1);
        contentPane.add(button2);
        contentPane.add(text);
        getRootPane().requestFocus();

        button1.addActionListener(new ActionListener()
        {
            public void actionPerformed(ActionEvent event)
            {
                text.setText("Hello from Swing!");
            }
        });

        button2.addActionListener(new ActionListener()
        {
            public void actionPerformed(ActionEvent event)
            {
                text.setText("Hello from Swing!");
            }
        });
    }
}
```

The result appears in Figure 12.7. As you can see in the figure, the second button appears with a heavy border, indicating it's the default button, and the *C* in its caption is underlined, indicating that it's the button's mnemonic. When the user presses Enter, the default button is clicked automatically, displaying the message shown in Figure 12.7.

Figure 12.7   Using a default button with a mnemonic.

Using Toggle Buttons

The Novice Programmer is back with a question. "Does Swing add any fundamentally new types of buttons to Java?" "Well," you say, "yes and no." "I knew you'd say that," the NP says. "Toggle buttons are new," you say, "but they're really just the base class of check boxes and radio buttons." "Tell me more!" the NP says.

Toggle buttons are new in Swing, and they present a two-state button (actually three states if you count the disabled state) that can appear as selected or deselected. Here's the inheritance diagram for **JToggleButton**, the toggle button class:

```
java.lang.Object
|_____java.awt.Component
      |_____java.awt.Container
            |_____javax.swing.JComponent
                  |_____javax.swing.AbstractButton
                        |_____javax.swing.JToggleButton
```

You'll find the constructors of the **JToggleButton** class in Table 12.13 and its methods in Table 12.14.

I'll put **JToggleButton** to use in an example. In this example, I draw a few toggle buttons, most with icons and some with text. Here's what the code looks like:

Table 12.13   Constructors of the JToggleButton class.

Constructor	Does This
JToggleButton( )	Constructs a toggle button.
JToggleButton(Icon icon)	Constructs an unselected toggle button with the indicated image.
JToggleButton(Icon icon, boolean selected)	Constructs a toggle button with the indicated image and selection state.
JToggleButton(String text)	Constructs an unselected toggle button with the indicated text.
JToggleButton(String text, boolean state.selected)	Constructs a toggle button with the indicated text and selection.
JToggleButton(String text, Icon icon)	Constructs a toggle button that has the indicated text and image and that's initially unselected.
JToggleButton(String text, Icon icon, boolean selected)	Constructs a toggle button with the indicated text, image, and selection state.

Table 12.14   Methods of the JToggleButton class.

Method	Does This
AccessibleContext getAccessible Context( )	Gets the accessible context.
String getUIClassID( )	Gets a string holding the name of the look and feel.
protected String paramString( )	Gets a string representation of this toggle button.
void updateUI( )	Called by the **UIFactory** class to indicate that the look and feel has changed.

```java
import java.awt.*;
import javax.swing.*;
import java.awt.event.*;

/*
<APPLET
    CODE=toggle.class
    WIDTH=400
    HEIGHT=400 >
</APPLET>
*/

public class toggle extends JApplet
{
    public toggle()
    {
        Container contentPane = getContentPane();

        Icon icon = new ImageIcon("toggle.jpg");

        JToggleButton toggle1 = new JToggleButton(icon);
        JToggleButton toggle2 = new JToggleButton(icon, true);
        JToggleButton toggle3 = new JToggleButton("Toggle Me!");
        JToggleButton toggle4 = new JToggleButton("Toggle Me!", icon);
        JToggleButton toggle5 = new JToggleButton("Toggle Me!", icon,
        true);

        contentPane.setLayout(new FlowLayout());

        contentPane.add(toggle1);
        contentPane.add(toggle2);
        contentPane.add(toggle3);
        contentPane.add(toggle4);
```

```
        contentPane.add(toggle5);
    }
}
```

You can see the result of this code in Figure 12.8. As you can see in the figure, you can set the state of a toggle button by passing a value of True to its constructor if you want it to appear selected initially. This example is in toggle.java on the CD.

Figure 12.8   Using toggle buttons.

Creating Toggle Button Groups

The Novice Programmer says, "Toggle buttons are new in Swing—do they do anything new besides present the user with a selected or deselected state?" "Sure," you say; "you can also put them into groups."

You can group toggle buttons as you do other kinds of buttons—with the **ButtonGroup** class. This means that only one of the buttons in a group can be selected at once, just as with radio buttons.

Here's an example where I add an array of five toggle buttons to a group:

```
import java.awt.*;
import javax.swing.*;
import java.awt.event.*;

/*
<APPLET
    CODE=togglegroup.class
```

```
        WIDTH=300
        HEIGHT=200 >
</APPLET>
*/


public class togglegroup extends JApplet
{
    public togglegroup()
    {
        Container contentPane = getContentPane();
        ButtonGroup group = new ButtonGroup();

        JToggleButton[] buttons = new JToggleButton[] {
            new JToggleButton(new ImageIcon("toggle.jpg")),
            new JToggleButton(new ImageIcon("toggle.jpg")),
            new JToggleButton(new ImageIcon("toggle.jpg")),
            new JToggleButton(new ImageIcon("toggle.jpg")),
            new JToggleButton(new ImageIcon("toggle.jpg"))
        };

        contentPane.setLayout(new FlowLayout());
        for(int i=0; i < buttons.length; ++i) {
            group.add(buttons[i]);
            contentPane.add(buttons[i]);
        }
    }
}
```

The result appears in Figure 12.9. The toggle buttons in that figure are indeed acting as a group; therefore, when you click one, any other toggle button that was selected is deselected automatically. This example is in togglegroup.java on the CD.

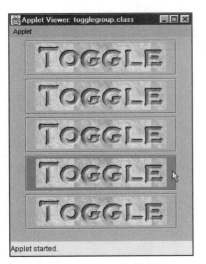

Figure 12.9   Using toggle buttons in a group.

Using Check Boxes

The Novice Programmer says, "I need some way for the user to select an option. I need some way for the user to select from many options, in fact. I need some way for the user to select multiple options from many options. I need...." "Check boxes," you say. "What you need are check boxes." "Right," says the NP.

The **JCheckBox** class has some advantages over the AWT **CheckBox** class, such as being able to display images. Here's the inheritance diagram for the **JCheckBox** class:

```
java.lang.Object
|____java.awt.Component
     |____java.awt.Container
          |____javax.swing.JComponent
               |____javax.swing.AbstractButton
                    |____javax.swing.JToggleButton
                         |____javax.swing.JCheckBox
```

You'll find the constructors for the **JCheckBox** class in Table 12.15 and the methods of this class in Table 12.16.

TIP: *In future Java releases, check boxes will support HTML text.*

Table 12.15   Constructors of the JCheckBox class.

Constructor	Does This
JCheckBox( )	Constructs a check box.
JCheckBox(Icon icon)	Constructs a check box with an icon.
JCheckBox(Icon icon, boolean selected)	Constructs a check box with an icon and indicates whether it's initially selected.
JCheckBox(String text)	Constructs a check box with text.
JCheckBox(String text, boolean selected)	Constructs a check box with text and indicates whether it's initially selected.
JCheckBox(String text, Icon icon)	Constructs a check box with the indicated text and icon.
JCheckBox(String text, Icon icon, boolean selected)	Constructs a check box with text and an icon and indicates whether it's initially selected.

Table 12.16   Methods of the JCheckBox class.

Method	Does This
AccessibleContext getAccessible Context( )	Gets the accessible context.
String getUIClassID( )	Gets a string that indicates the name of the look and feel class.
protected String paramString( )	Gets a string representation of this check box.
void updateUI( )	Called by the **UIFactory** class to indicate that the look and feel has changed.

Let's take a look at an example. Here, I just display four check boxes and indicate which one the user clicked (note that, as with AWT check boxes, **ItemListener** is used with **JCheckBox** objects, not **ActionListener**):

```
import java.awt.*;
import javax.swing.*;
import java.awt.event.*;

/*
<APPLET
    CODE=checkbox.class
    WIDTH=340
    HEIGHT=200 >
</APPLET>
*/
```

```java
public class checkbox extends JApplet implements ItemListener
{
    JCheckBox check1, check2, check3, check4;
    JTextField text;

    public void init()
    {
        Container contentPane = getContentPane();
        contentPane.setLayout(new FlowLayout());

        check1 = new JCheckBox("Check 1");
        check2 = new JCheckBox("Check 2");
        check3 = new JCheckBox("Check 3");
        check4 = new JCheckBox("Check 4");

        check1.addItemListener(this);
        check2.addItemListener(this);
        check3.addItemListener(this);
        check4.addItemListener(this);

        contentPane.add(check1);
        contentPane.add(check2);
        contentPane.add(check3);
        contentPane.add(check4);

        text = new JTextField(20);

        contentPane.add(text);
    }

    public void itemStateChanged(ItemEvent e)
    {
        if (e.getItemSelectable() == check1) {
            text.setText("You clicked check box 1.");
        } else if (e.getItemSelectable() == check2) {
            text.setText("You clicked check box 2.");
        } else if (e.getItemSelectable() == check3) {
            text.setText("You clicked check box 3.");
        } else if (e.getItemSelectable() == check4) {
            text.setText("You clicked check box 4.");
        }
    }
}
```

12. Text Fields, Buttons,
Toggle Buttons, Check
Boxes, And Radio Buttons

You can see the result in Figure 12.10. As you can see in the figure, the applet reports which check box you clicked when you do click one. This example is checkbox.java on the CD. There's more to using check boxes in Swing, which you'll learn in the topics following the next one on radio buttons.

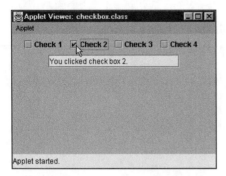

Figure 12.10   Using check boxes.

Using Radio Buttons

"OK," says the Novice Programmer, "I need some radio buttons in my Swing code. Do I make them using the **JCheckBox** class?" "Nope," you say. "Although you use the **CheckBox** class to make radio buttons in AWT programming, radio buttons have their own class in Swing—**JRadioButton**." "Cool!" says the NP.

Here's the inheritance diagram for the **JRadioButton** class:

```
java.lang.Object
|____java.awt.Component
      |____java.awt.Container
            |____javax.swing.JComponent
                  |____javax.swing.AbstractButton
                        |____javax.swing.JToggleButton
                              |____javax.swing.JRadioButton
```

Unlike in AWT programming, radio buttons have their own class in Swing—the **JRadioButton** class. You can find the constructors of the **JRadioButton** class in Table 12.17 and its methods in Table 12.18.

TIP: *In future Java releases, radio buttons will support HTML text.*

Table 12.17   Constructors of the JRadioButton class.

Constructor	Does This
JRadioButton( )	Constructs a radio button with no set text.
JRadioButton(Icon icon)	Constructs a radio button with the indicated image but no text.
JRadioButton(Icon icon, boolean selected)	Constructs a radio button with the indicated image and selection state.
JRadioButton(String text)	Constructs a radio button with the indicated text.
JRadioButton(String text, boolean selected)	Constructs a radio button with the indicated text and selection state.
JRadioButton(String text, Icon icon)	Constructs a radio button that has the indicated text and image.
JRadioButton(String text, Icon icon, boolean selected)	Constructs a radio button that has the indicated text, image, and selection state.

Table 12.18   Methods of the JRadioButton class.

Method	Does This
AccessibleContext getAccessibleContext( )	Get the accessible context.
String getUIClassID( )	Gets the name of the look and feel class.
protected String paramString( )	Gets a string representation of this radio button.
void updateUI( )	Called by the **UIFactory** class to indicate that the look and feel has changed.

Let's take a look at an example. Here, I just display four radio buttons and put them into the same button group so that only one of the four can be selected at one time. Here's what the code looks like:

```
import java.awt.*;
import javax.swing.*;
import java.awt.event.*;

/*
<APPLET
    CODE=radiogroup.class
    WIDTH=340
    HEIGHT=200 >
</APPLET>
*/
```

```
public class radiogroup extends JApplet implements ItemListener
{
    JRadioButton radio1, radio2, radio3, radio4;
    ButtonGroup group;
    JTextField text;

    public void init()
    {
        Container contentPane = getContentPane();
        contentPane.setLayout(new FlowLayout());

        group = new ButtonGroup();

        radio1 = new JRadioButton("Radio 1");
        radio2 = new JRadioButton("Radio 2");
        radio3 = new JRadioButton("Radio 3");
        radio4 = new JRadioButton("Radio 4");

        group.add(radio1);
        group.add(radio2);
        group.add(radio3);
        group.add(radio4);

        radio1.addItemListener(this);
        radio2.addItemListener(this);
        radio3.addItemListener(this);
        radio4.addItemListener(this);

        contentPane.add(radio1);
        contentPane.add(radio2);
        contentPane.add(radio3);
        contentPane.add(radio4);

        text = new JTextField(20);

        contentPane.add(text);
    }

    public void itemStateChanged(ItemEvent e)
    {
        if (e.getItemSelectable() == radio1) {
            text.setText("You clicked radio button 1.");
        } else if (e.getItemSelectable() == radio2) {
            text.setText("You clicked radio button 2.");
        } else if (e.getItemSelectable() == radio3) {
```

```
        text.setText("You clicked radio button 3.");
    } else if (e.getItemSelectable() == radio4) {
        text.setText("You clicked radio button 4.");
    }
}
}
```

You can see the result of this code in Figure 12.11. All the radio buttons in the figure act together, as part of one group. When you click one, any other radio buttons that were selected in the group become deselected. This example is in radiogroup.java on the CD.

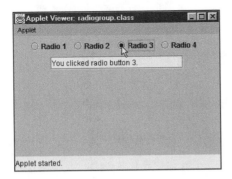

Figure 12.11   Using radio buttons.

Using Check Box And Radio Button Images

"Uh-oh," the Novice Programmer says, "Java's gone all wacky again. I added an image to a check box, and now it doesn't work anymore." You smile and say, "That's because you also have to add a selected image to the check box. Otherwise, the check box's appearance won't change when you click it."

Now that you can add images to check boxes and radio buttons, there's one important point to know—if you use images in check boxes or radio buttons, there's no visual indication in the control (such as a check mark) to show whether it's selected, so you must add a selected image to the control.

Here's an example showing how that works. Here, I add a selected image to a check box:

```
import java.awt.*;
import javax.swing.*;
import java.awt.event.*;
```

```
/*
<APPLET
    CODE=checkimages.class
    WIDTH=340
    HEIGHT=200 >
</APPLET>
*/

public class checkimages extends JApplet implements ItemListener
{
    JCheckBox check1;
    JTextField text;

    public void init()
    {
        Container contentPane = getContentPane();
        contentPane.setLayout(new FlowLayout());

        check1 = new JCheckBox("Check 1", new ImageIcon("normal.jpg"));

        check1.setSelectedIcon(new ImageIcon("selected.jpg"));

        check1.addItemListener(this);

        contentPane.add(check1);

        text = new JTextField(20);

        contentPane.add(text);
    }

    public void itemStateChanged(ItemEvent e)
    {
        if (e.getItemSelectable() == check1) {
            text.setText("You clicked check box 1.");
        }
    }
}
```

You can see the result in Figure 12.12. When the user clicks the check box, the selected image appears, as shown in the figure. This example is in checkimages.java on the CD.

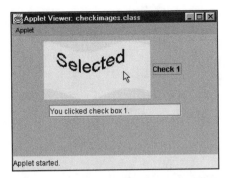

Figure 12.12   Using images in check boxes.

Getting And Setting The State Of Check Boxes And Radio Buttons

It's easy enough to respond to check box and radio button events, but there are times when you want to work with these controls outside event-handling methods. For example, the user may select a number of options using check boxes in a dialog box that don't go into effect until he or she dismisses the dialog box. At that time, you need to determine which check boxes are selected.

You can use the **isSelected** method to determine whether a check box or radio button is selected and the **setState** method to set the state of a check box or radio button. Here's an example in which I display four check boxes and list which ones are checked when the user clicks any of them. I start by creating an array of four check boxes and displaying them:

```
import java.awt.*;
import javax.swing.*;
import java.awt.event.*;

/*
<APPLET
    CODE=checkselected.class
    WIDTH=500
    HEIGHT=200 >
</APPLET>
*/

public class checkselected extends JApplet implements ItemListener
{
```

```
JCheckBox checks[];
JTextField text;

public void init()
{
    Container contentPane = getContentPane();
    contentPane.setLayout(new FlowLayout());

    checks = new JCheckBox[4];

    for(int loop_index = 0; loop_index <= checks.length - 1;
        loop_index++){
        checks[loop_index] = new JCheckBox("Check " + loop_index);
        checks[loop_index].addItemListener(this);
        contentPane.add(checks[loop_index]);
    }

    text = new JTextField(40);

    contentPane.add(text);
}
    .
    .
    .

}
```

Now when the user clicks a check box, I loop over all the check boxes, using the **isSelected** method to see whether they're selected, and list the check boxes that are selected:

```
public void itemStateChanged(ItemEvent e)
{
    String outString = new String("Currently selected: ");

    for(int loop_index = 0; loop_index <= checks.length - 1;
loop_index++){
        if(checks[loop_index].isSelected()) {
            outString += " check box " + loop_index;
        }
    }
    text.setText(outString);
}
```

The result appears in Figure 12.13. As you can see in the figure, when the user selects check boxes, the applet indicates which ones were checked. This example is in checkselected.java on the CD.

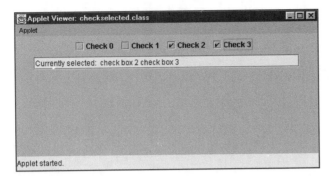

Figure 12.13   Determining which check boxes are selected.

Chapter 13

Swing: Viewports, Scrolling, Sliders, And Lists

In Depth

In this chapter, I'm going to cover some important Swing topics: viewports, scroll panes, sliders, scroll bars, and list controls. The controls in this chapter all have one thing in common—scrolling. The list control, in particular, is a very important control in Swing, but it doesn't handle scrolling by itself, so you need to understand how to work with scrolling before working with lists and many other Swing controls. We'll take an overview of the topics in this chapter before digging into the code.

Viewports

The **JViewport** class is at the heart of scrolling in Swing. A *viewport* is a window into a view, displaying a section of your data. You can scroll viewports yourself. Using viewports, you can move around in your displayed data, much like handling the scrolling by yourself. We'll take a look at using the **JViewport** class to scroll images.

Scroll Panes

A common way to implement scrolling in Swing is to use scroll panes, because you can scroll components using scroll panes. A number of Swing controls, such as the **JList** control, implement the **Scrollable** interface in order to work with scroll panes. In fact, scroll panes are commonly used with **JList** controls to create scrolling lists.

Sliders

Another scrollable control is the Swing slider control, supported by the **JSlider** class. Sliders are much like the controls you see in audio devices that let you slide a knob along a track. In fact, sliders are much like scroll bars, except you explicitly use sliders to let the user select a value from a continuous range. You can do the same with scroll bars, of course, but sliders were introduced because users have come to expect that scroll bars will be used to scroll other controls, such as text areas.

Scroll Bars

Every GUI user knows about scroll bars, of course, and Swing supports them just as the AWT does. We'll put the **JScrollBar** class to use in this chapter, scrolling text around in an applet. When the scroll box (also called the *thumb* or *bubble*) is moved, the value of the scroll bar changes. You can click the arrow buttons at the end of the scroll bar to change the value of the scroll bar by its *block increment*, and you can also click the track of the scroll bar to change its value by its *unit increment*.

Lists

Lists, supported by the **JList** class in Swing, are very popular controls, because they let you present a list of items in an easily handled way, hiding a long list of items by making the list control scrollable. I'll show you how to scroll long lists here as well as cover a number of other Swing topics. For example, you can make multiple selections in various ways in Swing list boxes. You can also display images, handle double- and even triple-clicks, and more. You'll see how all this works in the chapter. We'll also take a look at how to implement a new model for lists as well as for cell renderers, in order to handle the actual display of each item in the list in a custom manner.

That's it for the overview of this chapter. As you can see, there's a lot coming up. It's time to turn to the "Immediate Solutions" section.

13. Swing: Viewports, Scrolling, Sliders, And Lists

Immediate Solutions

Handling Viewports

"Hmm," says the Novice Programmer, "I want to move an image around under programmatic control, without displaying any scroll bars to the user. Is there any easy way to do that?" "As it happens," you say, "there is—you can use a viewport."

Viewports represent windows or portals into a view. Imagine, for example, that you have a huge document, not all of which will fit on the screen at one time. To present the user with only part of that document at once, you can set up a viewport into that document, moving the viewport around the document as you see fit. In fact, you can have multiple viewports to let the user move around inside the data in your program's model at will. Viewports are supported by the **JViewport** class, which is the foundation of scrolling in Swing. Here's the inheritance diagram for this class:

```
java.lang.Object
|____java.awt.Component
       |____java.awt.Container
              |____javax.swing.JComponent
                     |____javax.swing.JViewport
```

You'll find the fields for the **JViewport** class in Table 13.1, its constructor in Table 13.2, and its methods in Table 13.3.

Table 13.1   Fields of the *JViewport* class.

Field	Does This
protected boolean backingStore	Returns True when the viewport is maintaining an offscreen image of its contents.
protected Image backingStoreImage	The image used for a backing store.
protected boolean isViewSizeSet	Returns True when the viewport dimensions have been set.
protected Point lastPaintPosition	The last viewPosition painted.
protected boolean scrollUnderway	The **scrollUnderway** flag indicates whether a scrolling operation is underway.

Table 13.2   The Constructor of the *JViewport* class.

Constructor	Does This
JViewport( )	Constructs a **JViewport** object.

Table 13.3   Methods of the *JViewport* class.

Method	Does This
void addChangeListener (ChangeListener l)	Adds a ChangeListener.
protected void addImpl(Component child, Object constraints, int index)	Sets the viewport's lightweight child, which can be null.
protected boolean computeBlit(int dx, int dy, Point blitFrom, Point blitTo, Dimension blitSize, Rectangle blitPaint)	Computes the parameters for a **blit** operation.
protected LayoutManager create LayoutManager( )	Override this to install a different layout manager (or null) in the constructor.
protected JViewport.ViewListener createViewListener( )	Constructs a listener for the view.
protected void firePropertyChange (String propertyName, Object oldValue, Object newValue)	Notifies listeners of a property change.
protected void fireStateChanged( )	Notifies listeners of a state change.
AccessibleContext getAccessible Context( )	Gets the accessible context.
Dimension getExtentSize( )	Gets the size of the visible part of the view.
Insets getInsets( )	Gets the inset (border) dimensions as (0,0,0,0). Borders are not supported on a **JViewport** object.
Insets getInsets(Insets insets)	Gets an **Insets** object containing this **JViewport** object's inset values.
Component getView( )	Gets the viewport's one child or null.
Point getViewPosition( )	Gets the view coordinates that appear in the upper-left corner of the viewport (0,0 if there's no view).
Rectangle getViewRect( )	Returns a rectangle whose origin is **getViewPosition** and size is **getExtentSize( )**.
Dimension getViewSize( )	Gets the preferred size if the size has been set; otherwise, returns the view's current size.

(continued)

Table 13.3   Methods of the JViewport class (continued).

Method	Does This
boolean isBackingStoreEnabled( )	Returns True if this viewport is maintaining an offscreen image.
boolean isOptimizedDrawingEnabled( )	**JViewport** overrides this method to return False.
void paint(Graphics g)	Paints the image.
protected String paramString( )	Gets a string representation of this **JViewport** object.
void remove(Component child)	Removes the viewport's lightweight child.
void removeChangeListener (ChangeListener l)	Removes a change listener from the list.
void repaint(long tm, int x, int y, int w, int h)	Repaints the list.
void reshape(int x, int y, int w, int h)	Sets the bounds of this viewport.
void scrollRectToVisible(Rectangle contentRect)	Overridden to scroll the view so that the rectangle within the view becomes visible.
void setBackingStoreEnabled (boolean x)	If **x** is True, the viewport will maintain an offscreen image.
void setBorder(Border border)	Sets a border.
void setExtentSize(Dimension new Extent)	Sets the size of the visible part of the view using view coordinates.
void setView(Component view)	Sets the viewport's lightweight child (its view).
void setViewPosition(Point p)	Sets the view coordinates that appear in the upper-left corner of the viewport.
void setViewSize(Dimension newSize)	Sets the view coordinates that appear in the upper-left corner of the viewport as well as the size of the view.
Dimension toViewCoordinates (Dimension size)	Converts a size in pixel coordinates to view coordinates.
Point toViewCoordinates(Point p)	Converts a point in pixel coordinates to view coordinates.

Let's take a look at a viewport example that enables the user to scroll the viewport, not with scroll bars, but with buttons. Here, I add a viewport with an image in it to a program as well as add a panel containing buttons with the captions Scroll left, Scroll up, Scroll down, and Scroll right. The user can scroll the image in the viewport by clicking the buttons.

I start by creating a new viewport and then a new panel. I add a label with an image in it to the panel and then add the panel to the viewport. When the user scrolls the viewport, he or she is actually scrolling the panel. Here's how I create the viewport and add it to the program (note that to actually add the panel to the viewport, I use the **JViewport** class's **setView** method, which sets the viewport's view object):

```java
import java.awt.*;
import javax.swing.*;
import java.awt.event.*;

/*
<APPLET
    CODE=viewport.class
    WIDTH=700
    HEIGHT=200 >
</APPLET>
*/

public class viewport extends JApplet
{
    public viewport()
    {
        Container contentPane = getContentPane();

        JViewport jviewport = new JViewport();
        JPanel jpanel = new JPanel();

        jpanel.add(new JLabel(new ImageIcon("viewport.jpg")));

        jviewport.setView(jpanel);

        contentPane.add(jviewport, BorderLayout.CENTER);
            .
            .
            .

    }
}
```

I also need another panel that's not part of the viewport in which to display the buttons the user can use for scrolling. I'll call this panel **buttonpanel**. Note that I must pass the viewport to this class's constructor so it can scroll the viewport. Here's how I store the viewport passed to the constructor and add the buttons needed for scrolling:

```java
class buttonpanel extends JPanel implements ActionListener
{
    JViewport jviewport;
```

```
JButton button1 = new JButton("Scroll left");
JButton button2 = new JButton("Scroll up");
JButton button3 = new JButton("Scroll down");
JButton button4 = new JButton("Scroll right");

public buttonpanel(JViewport vport)
{
    jviewport = vport;

    add(button1);
    add(button2);
    add(button3);
    add(button4);

    button1.addActionListener(this);
    button2.addActionListener(this);
    button3.addActionListener(this);
    button4.addActionListener(this);
}
    .
    .
    .
}
```

All that's left is to implement scrolling when the user clicks a button. To do that, I use the **JViewport** class's **getViewPosition** method to get the current view position. Then I change that position—according to which button was clicked—by 10 pixels, and I use the **setViewPosition** method to set the new viewport position:

```
public void actionPerformed(ActionEvent e)
{
    Point position = jviewport.getViewPosition();

    if(e.getSource() == button1) position.x += 10;
    else if(e.getSource() == button2) position.y += 10;
    else if(e.getSource() == button3) position.y -= 10;
    else if(e.getSource() == button4) position.x -= 10;

    jviewport.setViewPosition(position);
}
```

Now I install a **buttonpanel** object in the applet at the bottom, like this:

```
public class viewport extends JApplet
{
    public viewport()
    {
        Container contentPane = getContentPane();

        JViewport jviewport = new JViewport();
        JPanel jpanel = new JPanel();

        jpanel.add(new JLabel(new ImageIcon("viewport.jpg")));

        jviewport.setView(jpanel);

        contentPane.add(jviewport, BorderLayout.CENTER);
        contentPane.add(new buttonpanel(jviewport), BorderLayout.SOUTH);
    }
}
```

The result appears in Figure 13.1. As you can see in the figure, the scroll buttons appear at the bottom of the applet. When the user clicks a button, the image moves accordingly. This applet is a success, and you'll find it in viewport.java on the CD accompanying this book.

Normally, you won't go all the way to the **JViewport** class to handle your scrolling; instead, you'll use components such as scroll panes, which is coming up next.

Figure 13.1   Scrolling a viewport.

Creating Scroll Panes

The Novice Programmer appears and says, "Hey, Java's gone all wacky again! I created a new Swing list control, put 40,000 items in it, made only two visible at once, and there are no scroll bars! This is definitely a bug, I'm going to file a report and...." "Hold it," you say. "The **JList** control does not implement scrolling by itself, but you can put it into a scroll pane." The NP asks, "Really? Is that the way it's *supposed* to work?"

The **JScrollPane** class is the Swing lightweight implementation of a scroll pane, and you use it to scroll other controls. In fact, whenever you display a list, it's standard to display it in a scroll pane to allow the user to scroll the list.

Thanks to the new Swing **Scrollable** interface, scroll operations are much more closely coordinated with the control being scrolled (the **JViewport**, **JScrollPane**, and **JScrollbar** classes all implement this interface). Here's the inheritance diagram for **JScrollPane**:

```
java.lang.Object
|_____java.awt.Component
      |_____java.awt.Container
            |_____javax.swing.JComponent
                  |_____javax.swing.JScrollPane
```

You'll find the fields for the **JScrollPane** class in Table 13.4, its constructors in Table 13.5, and its methods in Table 13.6.

Table 13.4   Fields of the *JScrollPane* class.

Field	Does This
protected JViewport columnHeader	The column header child.
protected JScrollBar horizontal ScrollBar	The scroll pane's horizontal scroll bar child.
protected int horizontalScrollBarPolicy	The display policy for the horizontal scroll bar.
protected Component lowerLeft	The component to display in the lower-left corner.
protected Component lowerRight	The component to display in the lower-right corner.
protected JViewport rowHeader	The row header child.
protected Component upperLeft	The component to display in the upper-left corner.
protected Component upperRight	The component to display in the upper-right corner.
protected JScrollBar verticalScrollBar	The scroll pane's vertical scroll bar child.
protected int verticalScrollBarPolicy	The display policy for the vertical scroll bar.
protected JViewport viewport	The scroll pane's viewport child.

Table 13.5   Constructors of the *JScrollPane* class.

Constructor	Does This
JScrollPane( )	Constructs an empty **JScrollPane** object.
JScrollPane(Component view)	Constructs a **JScrollPane** object that displays the contents of the indicated component.
JScrollPane(Component view, int vsb Policy, int hsbPolicy)	Constructs a **JScrollPane** object that displays the view component in a viewport whose view position can be controlled with a pair of scrollbars.
JScrollPane(int vsbPolicy, int hsbPolicy)	Constructs an empty **JScrollPane** object with indicated scrollbar policies.

Table 13.6   Methods of the *JScrollPane* class.

Method	Does This
JScrollBar createHorizontalScrollBar( )	Creates the horizontal scroll bar.
JScrollBar createVerticalScrollBar( )	Creates the vertical scroll bar.
protected JViewport createViewport( )	Gets a new **JViewport** object by default.
AccessibleContext getAccessible Context( )	Gets the accessible context associated with this **JComponent** object.
JViewport getColumnHeader( )	Gets the column header.
Component getCorner(String key)	Gets the component at the indicated corner.
JScrollBar getHorizontalScrollBar( )	Gets the horizontal scroll bar.
int getHorizontalScrollBarPolicy( )	Gets the horizontal scroll bar policy value.
JViewport getRowHeader( )	Gets the row header.
ScrollPaneUI getUI( )	Gets the look and feel object that renders this component.
String getUIClassID( )	Gets the key used to look up the **ScrollPaneUI** class that provides the look and feel for **JScrollPane**.
JScrollBar getVerticalScrollBar( )	Gets the vertical scroll bar.
int getVerticalScrollBarPolicy( )	Gets the vertical scroll bar policy value.
JViewport getViewport( )	Gets the current **JViewport** object.
Border getViewportBorder( )	Gets the value of the **viewportBorder** property.
Rectangle getViewportBorderBounds( )	Gets the bounds of the viewport border.
boolean isOpaque( )	Returns True if this component paints every pixel in its range.
boolean isValidateRoot( )	Checks the root.

(continued)

13. Swing: Viewports, Scrolling, Sliders, And Lists

Table 13.6   Methods of the *JScrollPane* class (continued).

Method	Does This
protected String paramString( )	Gets a string representation of this **JScrollPane** object.
void setColumnHeader (JViewport columnHeader)	If an old column header exists, this method removes it.
void setColumnHeaderView (Component view)	Constructs a column-header viewport, if necessary, sets its view, and then adds the column-header viewport to the scroll pane.
void setCorner(String key, Component corner)	Adds a child that will appear in one of the scroll panes corners (if there's room).
void setHorizontalScrollBar(JScroll horizontalScrollBar)	Adds the scroll bar that controls the viewport's horizontal view bar position to the scroll pane.
void setHorizontalScrollBarPolicy(int policy)	Determines when the horizontal scroll bar appears in the scroll pane.
void setLayout(LayoutManager layout)	Sets the layout manager for this **JScrollPane** object.
void setRowHeader(JViewport rowHeader)	Sets the new row header.
void setRowHeaderView (Component view)	Constructs a row-header viewport if, necessary, and then adds the row-header viewport to the scroll pane.
void setUI(ScrollPaneUI ui)	Sets the object that provides the look and feel.
void setVerticalScrollBar(JScrollBar verticalScrollBar)	Adds the scroll bar that controls the viewport's vertical view position.
void setVerticalScrollBarPolicy (int policy)	Determines when the vertical scroll bar appears in the scroll pane.
void setViewport(JViewport viewport)	Forces the view position of the new viewport to be in the +x,+y quadrant.
void setViewportBorder(Border viewportBorder)	Adds a border around the viewport.
void setViewportView(Component view)	Constructs a viewport, if necessary, and then sets its view.
void updateUI( )	Called when the default look and feel changes.

Let's look at an example in which I add a grid layout of text fields to a panel and scroll that panel in a scroll pane. I'll start by creating a **JPanel** object full of text fields:

```
import java.awt.*;
import javax.swing.*;
```

```
/*
<APPLET
    CODE=scrollpane.class
    WIDTH=300
    HEIGHT=200 >
</APPLET>
*/

public class scrollpane extends JApplet
{
    public void init()
    {
        Container contentPane = getContentPane();

        JPanel jpanel = new JPanel();
        jpanel.setLayout(new GridLayout(11, 16));

        for(int outer = 0; outer <= 10; outer++) {
            for(int inner = 0; inner <= 15; inner++) {
                jpanel.add(new JTextField("Text Field " + outer +
                    ", " + inner));
            }
        }
            .
            .
            .
    }
}
```

Now I'll add this new panel to a scroll pane. When you create a scroll pane object, you pass the object to be scrolled and you can specify when and where you want scroll bars with these constants: **HORIZONTAL_SCROLLBAR _ALWAYS, HORIZONTAL_SCROLLBAR_AS_NEEDED, HORIZONTAL_ SCROLLBAR_ NEVER, VERTICAL_SCROLLBAR, VERTICAL_SCROLLBAR_ ALWAYS, VERTICAL_ SCROLLBAR_AS_NEEDED, VERTICAL_SCROLLBAR_ NEVER.** In this case, I'll always let the scroll pane display scroll bars:

```
import java.awt.*;
import javax.swing.*;

/*
<APPLET
    CODE=scrollpane.class
    WIDTH=300
```

```
        HEIGHT=200 >
</APPLET>
*/

public class scrollpane extends JApplet
{
    public void init()
    {
        Container contentPane = getContentPane();

        JPanel jpanel = new JPanel();
        jpanel.setLayout(new GridLayout(11, 16));

        for(int outer = 0; outer <= 10; outer++) {
            for(int inner = 0; inner <= 15; inner++) {
              jpanel.add(new JTextField("Text Field " + outer +
                  ", " + inner));
            }
        }

        JScrollPane jscrollpane = new JScrollPane(jpanel,
            ScrollPaneConstants.VERTICAL_SCROLLBAR_ALWAYS,
            ScrollPaneConstants.HORIZONTAL_SCROLLBAR_ALWAYS);

        contentPane.add(jscrollpane);
    }
}
```

The result of adding the scroll pane to the applet's content pane is shown in Figure 13.2. As you see in the figure, the whole grid of text fields appears in the scroll pane, and the user can scroll that grid with the scroll bars. This example is in scrollpane.java on the CD.

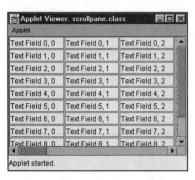

Figure 13.2   Using a scroll pane.

Creating Scroll Pane Headers And Borders

The Programming Correctness Czar appears and says, "So Java has scroll panes? Well, they don't seem to be very professional—with professional controls, you could specify labels or even images to use as row and column headers." "No problem," you say. "You can do that in Java, and you can even select the border type as well." "Oh," says the PCC.

You can customize a scroll pane by adding header images or text with the **setColumnHeaderView** and **setRowHeaderView** methods. You can also customize the border used in a scroll pane with the **setViewportBorder** method.

TIP: *In fact, you can even customize the corners of a scroll pane with the **setCorner** method.*

As an example, I'll put this customization to work in the scroll pane example I developed in the previous topic. In this case, I'll use labels as the row and column headers and add an etched border:

```java
import java.awt.*;
import javax.swing.*;

/*
<APPLET
    CODE=scrollpane.class
    WIDTH=300
    HEIGHT=200 >
</APPLET>
*/

public class scrollpane extends JApplet
{
    public void init()
    {
        Container contentPane = getContentPane();
        contentPane.setLayout(new BorderLayout());

        JPanel jpanel = new JPanel();
        jpanel.setLayout(new GridLayout(11, 16));

        for(int outer = 0; outer <= 10; outer++) {
            for(int inner = 0; inner <= 15; inner++) {
                jpanel.add(new JTextField("Text Field " + outer +
```

```
                              ", " + inner));
                    }
          }

          JScrollPane jscrollpane = new JScrollPane(jpanel,
              ScrollPaneConstants.VERTICAL_SCROLLBAR_ALWAYS,
              ScrollPaneConstants.HORIZONTAL_SCROLLBAR_ALWAYS);

          JLabel jlabel1 = new JLabel("Horizontal label");
          JLabel jlabel2 = new JLabel("Vertical label");

          jscrollpane.setColumnHeaderView(jlabel1);
          jscrollpane.setRowHeaderView(jlabel2);
          jscrollpane.setViewportBorder(BorderFactory.createEtchedBorder());

          contentPane.add(jscrollpane);
      }
}
```

You can see the result of this code in Figure 13.3.

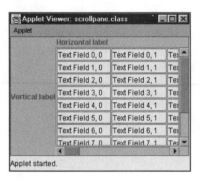

Figure 13.3   Adding headers to a scroll pane.

Scrolling Images

Scroll panes provide an ideal way to scroll images—all you have to do is display
the image in a label (or a similar component) and add that label to a scroll pane.
Here's an example showing how this works:

```
import java.awt.*;
import javax.swing.*;
```

```
/*
<APPLET
    CODE=scrollpaneimage.class
    WIDTH=300
    HEIGHT=200 >
</APPLET>
*/

public class scrollpaneimage extends JApplet
{
    public scrollpaneimage()
    {
        Container contentPane = getContentPane();

        JLabel jlabel = new JLabel(new ImageIcon("scrollpane.jpg"));
        JScrollPane jscrollpane = new JScrollPane(jlabel);

        contentPane.add(jscrollpane);
    }
}
```

The result appears in Figure 13.4. Now the user can scroll a large image, as needed, to handle images that can't be displayed all at once. This example is in scrollpaneimage.java on the CD.

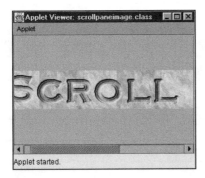

Figure 13.4   Scrolling an image.

13. Swing: Viewports, Scrolling, Sliders, And Lists

Creating Sliders

The Novice Programmer is back and says, "I've seen a new control in various programs—sliders. When do you think we'll get those in Java?" You smile and say, "Quite a while ago."

You can use scroll bars to let the user select a value from a continuous range, but users have become more familiar with using scroll bars to scroll other controls, such as lists. For that reason, Swing adds the **JSlider** class to support slider controls.

Sliders present the user with controls that look like those you see in audio equipment; they're clearly intended to let the user select a value from a range. To use the slider, the user moves a knob around with the mouse. Here's the inheritance diagram for the **JSlider** class:

```
java.lang.Object
|____java.awt.Component
     |____java.awt.Container
          |____javax.swing.JComponent
               |____javax.swing.JSlider
```

You can find the fields for the **JSlider** class in Table 13.7, its constructors in Table 13.8, and its methods in Table 13.9.

Table 13.7   Fields of the JSlider class.

Field	Does This
protected ChangeEvent changeEvent	The change event.
protected ChangeListener change Listener	The change listener.
protected int majorTickSpacing	The number of values between the major tick marks.
protected int minorTickSpacing	The number of values between the minor tick marks.
protected int orientation	The orientation of the slider.
protected BoundedRangeModel sliderModel	The data model, which handles the numeric maximum value, minimum value, and current-position value for the slider.
protected boolean snapToTicks	If True, the thumb resolves to the closest tick mark next to where the user positioned the thumb.

Table 13.8   Constructors of the JSlider class.

Constructor	Does This
JSlider( )	Constructs a horizontal slider with the range 0 to 100 and an initial value of 50.
JSlider(BoundedRangeModel brm)	Constructs a horizontal slider using the indicated bounded range model.
JSlider(int orientation)	Constructs a slider using the indicated orientation with the range 0 to 100 and an initial value of 50.
JSlider(int min, int max)	Constructs a horizontal slider using the indicated minimum and maximum values with an initial value of 50.
JSlider(int min, int max, int value)	Constructs a horizontal slider using the indicated min, max, and initial values.
JSlider(int orientation, int min, max, int value)	Constructs a slider with the indicated orientation and the indicated int minimum, maximum, and initial values.

Table 13.9   Methods of the JSlider class.

Method	Does This
void addChangeListener (ChangeListener I)	Adds a change listener to the slider.
protected ChangeListener create ChangeListener( )	Override this method to return your own change listener implementation.
Hashtable createStandardLabels (int increment)	Constructs a hashtable that will draw text labels starting at the slider minimum.
Hashtable createStandardLabels (int increment, int start)	Constructs a hashtable that will draw text labels starting at the start point indicated.
protected void fireStateChanged( )	Sends a change event, whose source is this slider, to each listener.
AccessibleContext getAccessible Context( )	Gets the accessible context.
int getExtent( )	Gets the extent, which is the range of values covered by the thumb.
boolean getInverted( )	Returns True if the value range shown for the slider is reversed.
Dictionary getLabelTable( )	Gets the dictionary of what labels to draw.
int getMajorTickSpacing( )	Returns the major tick spacing.
int getMaximum( )	Gets the maximum value supported by the slider.
int getMinimum( )	Gets the minimum value supported by the slider.
int getMinorTickSpacing( )	Returns the minor tick spacing.

(continued)

13. Swing: Viewports, Scrolling, Sliders, And Lists

Table 13.9   Methods of the JSlider class (continued).

Method	Does This
BoundedRangeModel getModel( )	Gets the data model that handles the sliders three fundamental properties: minimum, maximum, and value.
int getOrientation( )	Returns this slider's vertical or horizontal orientation.
boolean getPaintLabels( )	Indicates whether labels are to be painted.
boolean getPaintTicks( )	Indicates whether tick marks are to be painted.
boolean getPaintTrack( )	Indicates whether the track is to be painted.
boolean getSnapToTicks( )	Returns True if the thumb resolves to the closest tick mark next to where the user positioned the thumb.
SliderUI getUI( )	Gets the UI object, which implements the look and feel for this component.
String getUIClassID( )	Gets the name of the look and feel class that renders this component.
int getValue( )	Gets the slider's value.
boolean getValueIsAdjusting( )	Returns True if the slider thumb is being dragged.
protected String paramString( )	Gets a string representation of this **JSlider** object.
void removeChangeListener(ChangeListener l)	Removes a change listener from the slider.
void setExtent(int extent)	Sets the size of the range covered by the thumb.
void setInverted(boolean b)	Passes a value of True to reverse the value range.
void setLabelTable(Dictionary labels)	Used to specify what label will be drawn at any given value.
void setMajorTickSpacing(int n)	Sets the major tick spacing.
void setMaximum(int maximum)	Sets the model's maximum property.
void setMinimum(int minimum)	Sets the model's minimum property.
void setMinorTickSpacing(int n)	Sets the minor tick spacing.
void setModel(BoundedRangeModel newModel)	Sets the model that handles the sliders three fundamental properties: minimum, maximum, and value.
void setOrientation(int orientation)	Set the scroll bar's orientation to either **VERTICAL** or **HORIZONTAL**.
void setPaintLabels(boolean b)	Determines whether labels are painted on the slider.
void setPaintTicks(boolean b)	Determines whether tick marks are painted on the slider.
void setPaintTrack(boolean b)	Determines whether the track is painted on the slider.
void setSnapToTicks(boolean b)	Specifying True makes the thumb resolve to the closest tick mark next to where the user positioned the thumb.

(continued)

Table 13.9   Methods of the *JSlider* class (continued).

Method	Does This
void setUI(SliderUI ui)	Sets the UI object, which implements the look and feel for this component.
void setValue(int n)	Sets the slider's current value.
void setValueIsAdjusting(boolean b)	Sets the model's **valueIsAdjusting** property.
protected void updateLabelUIs( )	Called internally to replace the label UIs with the latest versions from the **UIFactory** class.
void updateUI( )	Notification from the **UIFactory** class that the look and feel has changed.

Let's put the **JSlider** class to work in an example. In this case, I'll just create a slider that can return values from 0 to 100 and report the current value in an applet's status bar. Here's how I create a horizontal slider with the constant **SwingConstants.HORIZONTAL** (as you might guess, the other possibility is **SwingConstants.VERTICAL**) with a minimum value of 0, a maximum value of 100, and an initial value of 0:

```
import java.awt.*;
import javax.swing.*;
import java.awt.event.*;
import javax.swing.event.*;

/*
<APPLET
    CODE=slider.class
    WIDTH=300
    HEIGHT=200 >
</APPLET>
*/

public class slider extends JApplet implements ChangeListener
{
    JSlider jslider = new JSlider(SwingConstants.HORIZONTAL, 0, 100, 0);

    public void init()
    {
        .
        .
        .
    }
    .
```

```
        .
        .
        .
}
```

Now, in the **init** method, I'll add this slider to the applet's content pane. You use *change listeners* with sliders, not adjustment listeners, as you do with scroll bars. The **ChangeListener** interface has only one method, **stateChanged**, which you can see in Table 13.10.

I add a change listener to the slider in this applet and then add the slider to the applet's layout like this:

```
public void init()
{
    Container contentPane = getContentPane();
    contentPane.setLayout(new FlowLayout());

    jslider.addChangeListener(this);

    contentPane.add(jslider);
}
```

In the **stateChanged** method, I use the **JSlider** methods **getMimimum**, **getMaximum**, and **getValue** to display the settings for the slider in the status bar:

```
public void stateChanged(ChangeEvent e)
{
    JSlider jslider1 = (JSlider) e.getSource();
    showStatus("Slider minimum: " + jslider1.getMinimum() +
        ", maximum: " + jslider1.getMaximum() +
        ", value: " + jslider1.getValue());
}
```

The result appears in Figure 13.5. As you can see in the figure, the user can move the knob on the slider, and the new value appears. This example is in slider.java on the CD.

Table 13.10   The method of the *ChangeListener* interface.

Method	Does This
void stateChanged(ChangeEvent e)	Invoked when the target of the listener has changed its state.

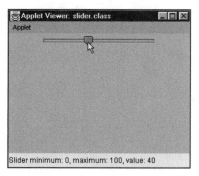

Figure 13.5   Using a slider.

Filling A Slider

If you're using the default Metal look in Swing, you can *fill in* your sliders, which means that their tracks will appear filled from the origin to the slider's knob. To do that, you must set the **JSlider's isFilled** *client property* to True, which you can do like this (note that I'm adding this code to the slider example from the previous topic):

```
public void init()
{
    Container contentPane = getContentPane();
    contentPane.setLayout(new FlowLayout());

    jslider.addChangeListener(this);
    jslider.putClientProperty("JSlider.isFilled", Boolean.TRUE);

    contentPane.add(jslider);
}
```

The result appears in Figure 13.6. As you can see, the slider in the figure is filled.

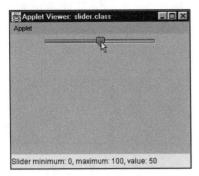

Figure 13.6   Filling a slider.

Painting Slider Tick Marks

"Hmm," says the Novice Programmer, "users are complaining about the sliders in my program—they say they can't get their bearings using a single long slider." "Well," you say, "you can fix that by adding tick marks."

To paint tick marks in a slider control, you pass a value of True to the **setPaintTicks** method and then indicate the spacing you want for the major (that is, *longer*) and minor (*shorter*) ticks using the **setMajorTickSpacing** and **MinorTickSpacing** methods, like this (note that I'm adding this code to the existing slider example):

```
public void init()
{
    Container contentPane = getContentPane();
    contentPane.setLayout(new FlowLayout());

    jslider.addChangeListener(this);
    jslider.setPaintTicks(true);
    jslider.setMajorTickSpacing(20);
    jslider.setMinorTickSpacing(10);

    contentPane.add(jslider);
}
```

The result appears in Figure 13.7. As you can see in the figure, the slider now displays tick marks.

You can also paint the numeric values for the major tick marks—see the next topic for the details.

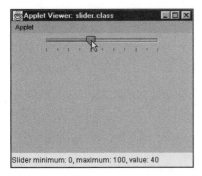

Figure 13.7   Painting tick marks in a slider.

Painting Slider Labels

You can use the **JSlider** class' **setPaintLabels** method to display the numeric value for the major tick marks in the slider. Here's how I do that by adding one line of code to the existing slider example:

```
public void init()
{
    Container contentPane = getContentPane();
    contentPane.setLayout(new FlowLayout());

    jslider.addChangeListener(this);
    jslider.putClientProperty("JSlider.isFilled", Boolean.TRUE);
    jslider.setPaintTicks(true);
    jslider.setPaintLabels(true);
    jslider.setMajorTickSpacing(20);
    jslider.setMinorTickSpacing(10);

    contentPane.add(jslider);
}
```

The result appears in Figure 13.8. As you can see in the figure, the major tick marks are labeled.

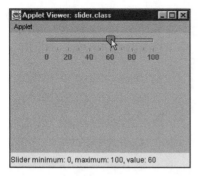

Figure 13.8   Painting slider labels.

Setting The Slider Extent

You can set a slider's *extent*, which bounds the maximum value in the slider. If you do set the extent of a slider, and its maximum value is *maximum*, the slider's value can never exceed the value of *maximum - extent*.

As an example, I'll add a button to the slider example I've been developing over the last few topics that lets the user set the slider's extent to 60:

```
public class slider extends JApplet implements ActionListener,
    ChangeListener
{
    JSlider jslider = new JSlider(SwingConstants.HORIZONTAL, 0, 100, 0);
    JButton jbutton = new JButton("Set extent to 60");

    public void init()
    {
        Container contentPane = getContentPane();
        contentPane.setLayout(new FlowLayout());

        jslider.addChangeListener(this);
        jslider.putClientProperty("JSlider.isFilled", Boolean.TRUE);
        jslider.setPaintTicks(true);
        jslider.setPaintLabels(true);
        jslider.setMajorTickSpacing(20);
        jslider.setMinorTickSpacing(10);

        contentPane.add(jslider);

        jbutton.addActionListener(this);
        contentPane.add(jbutton);
    }
```

```
public void stateChanged(ChangeEvent e)
{
    JSlider jslider1 = (JSlider) e.getSource();
    showStatus("Slider minimum: " + jslider1.getMinimum() +
        ", maximum: " + jslider1.getMaximum() +
        ", value: " + jslider1.getValue() +
        ", extent: " + jslider1.getExtent());
}

public void actionPerformed(ActionEvent e)
{
    jslider.setExtent(60);
    jslider.revalidate();
}
}
```

When the user clicks the button, the slider's extent is set to 60, and because its maximum value is 100, that means its value can't exceed 40. You can see the result in Figure 13.9. Note that even though the slider is at its maximum setting, its value is only 40.

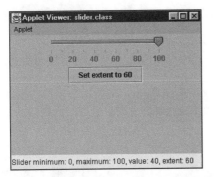

Figure 13.9   Setting a slider's extent.

Creating Scroll Bars

"OK," says the Novice Programmer, "I want to let the users move through the data in my program. I want to let them adjust values. I want to let them navigate through the items in a long list. I want...." "Scroll bars," you say. "What you want are scroll bars." "Right," says the NP.

The Swing lightweight scroll bar class is **JScrollBar**, and its inheritance diagram looks like this:

13. Swing: Viewports, Scrolling, Sliders, And Lists

```
java.lang.Object
|____java.awt.Component
     |____java.awt.Container
          |____javax.swing.JComponent
               |____javax.swing.JScrollBar
```

You can find the fields of the **JScrollBar** class in Table 13.11, its constructors in
Table 13.12, and its methods in Table 13.13.

Table 13.11   Fields of the *JScrollBar* class.

Field	Does This
protected int blockIncrement	The block increment.
protected BoundedRangeModel model	The model that represents the scroll bar's minimum, maximum, extent, and current values.
protected int orientation	The scroll bar's orientation.
protected int unitIncrement	The unit increment.

Table 13.12   Constructors of the *JScrollBar* class.

Constructor	Does This
JScrollBar( )	Constructs a vertical scroll bar.
JScrollBar(int orientation)	Constructs a scroll bar with the indicated orientation and the following initial values.
JScrollBar(int orientation, int value, extent, int min, int max)	Constructs a scroll bar with the indicated orientation, value, extent, int minimum, and maximum values.

Table 13.13   Methods of the *JScrollBar* class.

Method	Does This
void addAdjustmentListener (AdjustmentListener l)	Adds an adjustment listener.
protected void fireAdjustmentValue Changed(int id, int type, int value)	Fires an adjustment event.
AccessibleContext getAccessible Context( )	Gets the AccessibleContext.
int getBlockIncrement( )	Used for backwards compatibility with **java.awt.Scrollbar** only.
int getBlockIncrement(int direction)	Gets the amount to change the scroll bar's value by, given a block change request.
int getMaximum( )	The maximum value of the scroll bar equals the maximum value minus the extent.

(continued)

Table 13.13 **Methods of the *JScrollBar* class** (continued).

Method	Does This
Dimension getMaximumSize( )	Gets the scroll bar's maximum size.
int getMinimum( )	Gets the minimum value supported by the scroll bar.
Dimension getMinimumSize( )	Gets the scroll bar's minimum size.
BoundedRangeModel getModel( )	Gets the data model that handles the scroll bar's four fundamental properties: minimum, maximum, value, and extent.
int getOrientation( )	Gets the component's orientation (horizontal or vertical).
ScrollBarUI getUI( )	Gets the delegate that implements the look and feel for this component.
String getUIClassID( )	Gets the name of the **LookAndFeel** class for this component.
int getUnitIncrement( )	Used for backwards compatibility with **java.awt.Scrollbar** only.
int getUnitIncrement(int direction)	Gets the amount to change the scroll bar's value by, given a unit change request.
int getValue( )	Gets the scroll bar's value.
boolean getValueIsAdjusting( )	Returns True if the scroll bar knob is being dragged.
int getVisibleAmount( )	Gets the scroll bar's extent.
protected String paramString( )	Gets a string representation of the scroll bar.
void removeAdjustmentListener (AdjustmentListener l)	Removes an **AdjustmentEvent** listener.
void setBlockIncrement (int blockIncrement)	Sets the **blockIncrement** property.
void setEnabled(boolean x)	Enables the component so that the knob position can be changed.
void setMaximum(int maximum)	Sets the model's maximum property.
void setMinimum(int minimum)	Sets the model's minimum property.
void setModel(BoundedRangeModel newModel)	Sets the model that handles the scroll bar's four fundamental properties: minimum, maximum, value, and extent.
void setOrientation(int orientation)	Sets the scroll bar's orientation to either **VERTICAL** or **HORIZONTAL**.
void setUnitIncrement(int unitIncrement)	Sets the **unitIncrement** property.
void setValue(int value)	Sets the scroll bar's value.
void setValueIsAdjusting(boolean b)	Sets the model's **valueIsAdjusting** property.
void setValues(int newValue, int new Extent, int newMin, int newMax)	Sets the four **BoundedRangeModel** properties.
void setVisibleAmount(int extent)	Sets the model's extent property.
void updateUI( )	Overrides **JComponent.updateUI**.

13. Swing: Viewports, Scrolling, Sliders, And Lists

Here's an example in which I use a scroll bar to scroll some text in an applet. To do that, I'll create a new panel that displays a label with the text "Hello from Swing!" at the vertical position given by the public data member named **y**. Here's what the panel class looks like:

```
class jpanel extends JPanel
{
    JLabel jlabel = new JLabel("Hello from Swing!");
    int y = 0;

    jpanel()
    {
        jlabel = new JLabel("Hello from Swing!");
        add(jlabel);
    }

    public void paintComponent(Graphics g)
    {
        super.paintComponent(g);

        jlabel.setLocation(0, y);
    }

    public void setScrolledPosition(int newposition)
    {
        y = newposition;
    }
}
```

Now I can add an object of this new panel class to an applet as well as a vertical scroll bar in a border layout, like this:

```
import java.awt.*;
import javax.swing.*;
import java.awt.event.*;

/*
<APPLET
    CODE=scrollbar.class
    WIDTH=300
    HEIGHT=200 >
</APPLET>
*/
```

```
public class scrollbar extends JApplet
{
    private JScrollBar vsb = new JScrollBar(JScrollBar.VERTICAL, 0,
        0, 0, 180);
    private jpanel j = new jpanel();

    public void init()
    {
        Container contentPane = getContentPane();

        contentPane.add(j, BorderLayout.CENTER);
        contentPane.add(vsb, BorderLayout.EAST);

        vsb.addAdjustmentListener(new AdjustmentListener()
        {
            public void adjustmentValueChanged(
                                        AdjustmentEvent e) {
                JScrollBar sb = (JScrollBar)e.getSource();
                j.setScrolledPosition(e.getValue());
                j.repaint();
            }
        });
    }
}
```

The result appears in Figure 13.10. As you can see in the figure, the user can use the scroll bar to move the text up and down in the panel. This example is in scrollbar.java on the CD.

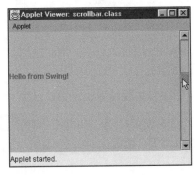

Figure 13.10   Creating and using a scroll bar.

Creating Lists

The Big Boss appears in a cloud of cigar smoke and says, "We've got 14,389 products now for the user to select from. How are we going to display all those in a program?" "No problem," you say, "I'll just use a list control." The Big Boss smiles and says, "Here are the product names to type in."

The **JList** class is the Swing lightweight list control. Here's the inheritance diagram for the **JList** class:

```
java.lang.Object
|____java.awt.Component
     |____java.awt.Container
          |____javax.swing.JComponent
               |____javax.swing.JList
```

You can do more with **JList** controls than you can with AWT **List** controls; for example, you can display images in Swing lists. In fact, we'll take a look at what you can do with Swing lists from this point to the end of the chapter. You can find the constructors of the **JList** class in Table 13.14 and its methods in Table 13.15.

Table 13.14   Constructors of the JList class.

Constructor	Does This
JList( )	Constructs a **JList** object.
JList(ListModel dataModel)	Constructs a **JList** object that displays the elements in the indicated data model.
JList(Object[ ] listData)	Constructs a **JList** object that displays the elements in the indicated array.
JList(Vector listData)	Constructs a **JList** object that displays the elements in the indicated vector.

Table 13.15   Methods of the JList class.

Method	Does This
void addListSelectionListener(List SelectionListener listener)	Adds a list selection listener.
void addSelectionInterval(int anchor, lead)	Makes the selection to be the union of the indicated interval with current selection.
void clearSelection( )	Clears the selection.

(continued)

Table 13.15   Methods of the JList class (continued).

Method	Does This
protected ListSelectionModel create SelectionModel( )	Gets an instance of **DefaultListSelectionModel**.
void ensureIndexIsVisible(int index)	Scrolls the viewport to make sure an item is visible.
protected void fireSelectionValue Changed (int firstIndex, int lastIndex, boolean isAdjusting)	Notifies **JList** list selection listeners that the selection model has changed.
AccessibleContext getAccessible Context( )	Gets the accessible context.
int getAnchorSelectionIndex( )	Gets the first index argument from the most recent **addSelectionInterval** or **setSelectionInterval** call.
Rectangle getCellBounds(int index1, int index2)	Gets the bounds of the indicated range of items.
ListCellRenderer getCellRenderer( )	Gets the object that renders the list items.
int getFirstVisibleIndex( )	Returns the index of the cell in the upper-left corner of the **JList** object.
int getFixedCellHeight( )	Gets the fixed cell height value.
int getFixedCellWidth( )	Gets the fixed cell width value.
int getLastVisibleIndex( )	Returns the index of the cell in the lower-right corner of the **JList** object.
int getLeadSelectionIndex( )	Gets the second index argument from the most recent **addSelectionInterval** or **setSelectionInterval** call.
int getMaxSelectionIndex( )	Gets the maximum selected cell index.
int getMinSelectionIndex( )	Gets the minimum selected cell index.
ListModel getModel( )	Gets the data model that holds the list of data items.
Dimension getPreferredScrollable ViewportSize( )	Computes the size of the viewport needed to display **visibleRowCount** rows.
Object getPrototypeCellValue( )	Gets the cell width of the prototypical cell (a cell used for the calculation of cell widths).
int getScrollableBlockIncrement (Rectangle visibleRect, int orientation, int direction)	Gets the block increment amount.
boolean getScrollableTracksViewport Height( )	Gets the height of the track's viewport.

(continued)

Table 13.15   Methods of the JList class (continued).

Method	Does This
boolean getScrollableTracksViewport Width( )	Gets the width of the track's viewport.
int getScrollableUnitIncrement(Rectangle visibleRect, int orientation, int direction)	Returns the list's font size.
int getSelectedIndex( )	Returns the first selected index.
int[ ] getSelectedIndices( )	Returns an array of all the selected indexes in increasing order.
Object getSelectedValue( )	Returns the first selected value or null, if the selection is empty.
Object[ ] getSelectedValues( )	Returns an array of the values for the selected cells.
Color getSelectionBackground( )	Gets the background color for selected cells.
Color getSelectionForeground( )	Gets the foreground color.
int getSelectionMode( )	Gets whether single-item or multiple-item selections are allowed.
ListSelectionModel getSelection Model( )	Gets the value of the current selection model.
ListUI getUI( )	Gets the look and feel object that renders this component.
String getUIClassID( )	Gets the name of the **UIFactory** class that generates the look and feel for this component.
boolean getValueIsAdjusting( )	Gets the value of the data model's **isAdjusting** property.
int getVisibleRowCount( )	Returns the preferred number of visible rows.
Point indexToLocation(int index)	Gets the origin of the indicated item in **JList** coordinates. Gets null if the index isn't valid.
boolean isSelectedIndex(int index)	Returns True if the indicated index is selected.
boolean isSelectionEmpty( )	Returns True if nothing is selected. This is a convenience method that just delegates to the selection model.
int locationToIndex(Point location)	Converts a point in **JList** coordinates to the index of the cell at that location.
protected String paramString( )	Gets a string representation of this **JList** object.
void removeListSelectionListener (ListSelectionListener listener)	Removes a listener from the list that's notified each time a change to the selection occurs.
void removeSelectionInterval(int index0, int index1)	Sets the selection to be the set difference of the indicated interval and the current selection.
void setCellRenderer(ListCell Renderer cellRenderer)	Sets the delegate that's used to paint each cell in the list.

(continued)

Table 13.15   Methods of the JList class (continued).

Method	Does This
void setFixedCellHeight(int height)	Defines the height of every cell in the list.
void setFixedCellWidth(int width)	Defines the width of every cell in the list.
void setListData(Object[ ] listData)	Constructs a list model from an array of objects and then applies **setModel** to it.
void setListData(Vector listData)	Constructs a list model from a vector and then applies **setModel** to it.
void setModel(ListModel model)	Sets the model that represents the contents of the list and clears the list selection.
void setPrototypeCellValue(Object prototypeCellValue)	Used to compute **fixedCellWidth** and **fixedCellHeight**.
void setSelectedIndex(int index)	Selects a single cell.
void setSelectedIndices(int[ ] indices)	Selects a set of cells.
void setSelectedValue(Object an Object, boolean shouldScroll)	Selects the indicated object from the list.
void setSelectionBackground (Color selectionBackground)	Sets the background color for selected cells.
void setSelectionForeground (Color selectionForeground)	Sets the foreground color for selected cells.
void setSelectionInterval(int anchor, int lead)	Selects the indicated interval.
void setSelectionMode int selectionMode)	Determines whether single-item or multiple-item selections are allowed.
void setSelectionModel(List selectionModel)	Sets the selection model for the list to a non-null SelectionModel **ListSelectionModel** implementation.
void setUI(ListUI ui)	Sets the look and feel object that renders this component.
void setValueIsAdjusting(boolean b)	Sets the data model's **isAdjusting** property to True.
void setVisibleRowCount(int visible RowCount)	Sets the preferred number of rows in the list that can be displayed without a scroll bar.
void updateUI( )	Sets the UI property with the **ListUI** object from the default **UIFactory** class.

Note that you can get the currently selected item's index with the **JList** class **getSelectedIndex** method, multiple selections with **getSelectedIndices**, the actual selected item with **getSelectedValue**, and the actual selected items with **getSelectedValues**.

TIP: One thing to bear in mind is that the data in a list is actually maintained by its model, so if you want access to an item that's not selected, you can use the **JList** class's **getModel** method to get the model and then the model's **getElementAt** method to get the actual item.

I'll put the **JList** class to work in this and the following few topics. To start, I create a simple **JList** example that just displays 12 items and reports which one the user clicks. I start by creating a list control with those items in it:

```java
import java.awt.*;
import javax.swing.*;
import javax.swing.event.*;

/*
<APPLET
    CODE=list.class
    WIDTH=300
    HEIGHT=200 >
</APPLET>
*/

public class list extends JApplet implements ListSelectionListener
{
    JList jlist;

    public void init()
    {
        Container contentPane = getContentPane();
        String[] items = new String[12];

        for(int loop_index = 0; loop_index <= 11; loop_index++) {
            items[loop_index] = "Item " + loop_index;
        }

        jlist = new JList(items);
            .
            .
            .
    }
        .
        .
        .
}
```

Next, I add this list control to a scroll pane to enable scrolling, set it so it will display five rows, and add a selection listener to it:

```
    public void init()
    {
        Container contentPane = getContentPane();
        String[] items = new String[12];

        for(int loop_index = 0; loop_index <= 11; loop_index++) {
            items[loop_index] = "Item " + loop_index;
        }

        jlist = new JList(items);
        JScrollPane jscrollpane = new JScrollPane(jlist);
        jlist.setVisibleRowCount(5);
        jlist.addListSelectionListener(this);


        contentPane.setLayout(new FlowLayout());
        contentPane.add(jscrollpane);
    }
```

Now, in the **valueChanged** method, I can use the **getSelectedIndex** method to get the item the user clicks and display the number of that item in the status bar:

```
    public void valueChanged(ListSelectionEvent e)
    {
        String outString = "You chose item: ";
        outString += " jlist.getSelectedIndex();
        showStatus(outString);
    }
```

That's all there is to it. Now when the user clicks an item in the list, the applet displays which item was clicked, as you see in Figure 13.11. This example is in list.java on the CD.

Note, however, that there's more than one way to select items in a list—you can make multiple selections in lists as well. See the next topic for the details.

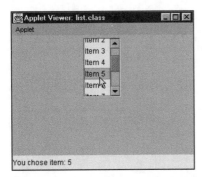

Figure 13.11   Handling selections in a list control.

Handling Multiple List Selections

The Product Support Specialist appears and says, "Users are unhappy about your new program. They want to order a dozen products at once, but the list control in the program only lets them order one." "So?" you ask. "So the Big Boss is going to be very unhappy," the PSS says. "OK," you say, "I'll set up a multiple-selection list control."

List Selection Modes

By default, there are three selection modes for **JList** objects, and you can set the one you want to use with the **setSelectionMode** method. Here are the constants you can pass to this method and what they mean:

- *SINGLE_SELECTION*—Single selection.

- *SINGLE_INTERVAL_SELECTION*—One interval selection. The user can select one, but only one, interval of items.

- *MULTIPLE_INTERVAL_SELECTION*—Multiple selection intervals.

I'll create a multiple-interval selection list control here and show how to determine what items are selected when the user makes a selection. To start, I just create a list control as in the previous topic, making it a multiple-interval selection list control. Here's the code:

```
import java.awt.*;
import javax.swing.*;
import javax.swing.event.*;

/*
<APPLET
    CODE=listmultiple.class
    WIDTH=300
    HEIGHT=200 >
</APPLET>
*/

public class listmultiple extends JApplet implements ListSelectionListener
{
    JList jlist;

    public void init()
    {
        Container contentPane = getContentPane();
        String[] items = new String[12];
```

13. Swing: Viewports, Scrolling, Sliders, And Lists

```
        for(int loop_index = 0; loop_index <= 11; loop_index++) {
            items[loop_index] = "Item " + loop_index;
        }

        jlist = new JList(items);
        JScrollPane jscrollpane = new JScrollPane(jlist);
        jlist.setVisibleRowCount(5);
        jlist.setSelectionMode(
    ListSelectionModel.MULTIPLE_INTERVAL_SELECTION
);

        jlist.addListSelectionListener(this);

        contentPane.setLayout(new FlowLayout());
        contentPane.add(jscrollpane);
    }
        .
        .
        .
}
```

Now when the user makes a selection, I can determine what items were selected in the **valueChanged** method, using the **getSelectedIndices** method, which returns an array of the selected indexes. The end result is that I can report these indexes in the applet's status bar, like this:

```
public void valueChanged(ListSelectionEvent e)
{
    int[] indexes = jlist.getSelectedIndices();
    String outString = "You chose:";

    for(int loop_index = 0; loop_index < indexes.length; loop_index++){
        outString += " item " + indexes[loop_index];
    }

    showStatus(outString);
}
```

You can see the result in Figure 13.12. The user can click an item to select it and then use the Ctrl key to select other items or the Shift key to select an interval of items. Whenever a selection is made, the applet reports the selection in its status bar, as you see in Figure 13.12. This example is a success, and it appears in listmultiple.java on the CD.

13. Swing: Viewports, Scrolling, Sliders, And Lists

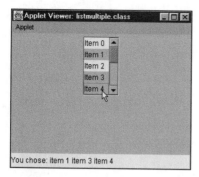

Figure 13.12   Handling multiple selections in a list control.

Displaying Images In Lists

"We've just got to jazz things up," the Big Boss says, "the competition is getting too tough." "Well," you ask, "how about adding more features?" "That costs money," the BB growls. "Hmm," you say, "I suppose I could display images in the list controls." "Swell," says the BB, "get to it."

Getting a Swing list control to display images is not as easy as adding images to a Swing label. In particular, you have to create your own model and renderer class for the list control, and I'll do that here. The result we're aiming for appears in Figure 13.13. This example is in listimages.java on the CD.

To handle images in a list control, I create a new list control model, **newModel**, and a new list control cell renderer, **newRenderer**. To install the new model,

Figure 13.13   Adding images to a list control.

which will hold the string for each list item and an image icon for each item, I can pass an object of the **newModel** class to the **JList** constructor. To install the new renderer, I can use the **setCellRenderer** method. Here's the code:

```
import java.awt.*;
import javax.swing.*;
import java.awt.event.*;

/*
<APPLET
    CODE=listimages.class
    WIDTH=300
    HEIGHT=300 >
</APPLET>
*/

public class listimages extends JApplet
{
    public void init()
    {
        Container contentPane = getContentPane();

        newModel newmodel = new newModel();
        newRenderer newrenderer = new newRenderer();

        JList jlist = new JList(newmodel);
        jlist.setCellRenderer(newrenderer);
        jlist.setVisibleRowCount(6);

        contentPane.add(new JScrollPane(jlist));
    }
}
```

This installs the new model and renderers—all that's left is to actually create the corresponding classes, and I'll do that in the next two topics.

Creating A Custom List Model

Creating a new model for a list is not difficult; all you have to do is store your data using the **addElement** method. In this case, I'll create the new model for the list example in the previous topic, which will display images and text in a list control.

In this case, I just make each data element in the model a two-element array; the first array element will hold the text for the list item, and the second array element will hold the image icon for the list item. Here's the code:

```
class newModel extends DefaultListModel
{
    public newModel()
    {
        for(int loop_index = 0; loop_index <= 12; loop_index++) {
            addElement(new Object[] {"Item " + loop_index,
                new ImageIcon("item.jpg")});
        }
    }
}
```

That's all it takes. Now a new model for a list control has been created. To actually draw the icon image, however, you have to handle the cell rendering yourself. I'll do just that in the next topic.

Creating A Custom List Cell Renderer

Each list item is actually of class **JLabel**, so you can use the methods of **JLabel**, such as **setText** and **setIcon**, to display images in a list's cells. Here, I'll do that by creating a new cell renderer that will draw the items in the list I've developed over the previous two topics. To create a cell renderer, you have to implement the **ListCellRenderer** interface, which has only one method: **getListCellRendererComponent**. This object is passed the object to render (which in this case is the two-element array holding the item's text and icon) and returns a cell renderer. Here's what the code looks like (note that I also indicate whether an item is selected by adjusting its background):

```
class newRenderer extends JLabel implements ListCellRenderer
{
    public newRenderer()
    {
        setOpaque(true);
    }

    public Component getListCellRendererComponent(
        JList jlist, Object obj, int index, boolean isSelected,
        boolean focus)
    {
        newModel model = (newModel)jlist.getModel();
```

```
        setText((String)((Object[])obj)[0]);
        setIcon((Icon)((Object[])obj)[1]);

        if(!isSelected) {
            setBackground(jlist.getBackground());
            setForeground(jlist.getForeground());
        }
        else {
            setBackground(jlist.getSelectionBackground());
            setForeground(jlist.getSelectionForeground());
        }

        return this;
    }
```

That's all it takes. Now the list control will display images, as you see in Figure 13.13. This example is in listimages.java on the CD.

Handling Double-Clicks In Lists

"Hey," says the Novice Programmer, "I want to let the user launch an item from a list control by double-clicking it, but the **ListSelectionListener** interface's **valueChanged** method is called for single clicks, and I can't tell whether the list has been double-clicked." "Well," you say, "you can handle mouse clicks yourself to intercept double-clicks." The NP says, "Really? Tell me more!"

If you intercept mouse events, you can determine the number of mouse clicks, and by accessing the list's model, you can determine what list item was clicked.

Let's see this in code. Here, I just add a list with a number of items in it to an applet and then add a mouse listener to the list:

```
import java.awt.*;
import javax.swing.*;
import java.awt.event.*;

/*
<APPLET
    CODE=listdouble.class
    WIDTH=300
    HEIGHT=200 >
</APPLET>
*/
```

```
public class listdouble extends JApplet implements MouseListener
{
    public void init()
    {
        Container contentPane = getContentPane();

        String[] items = {"Item 1", "Item 2", "Item 3", "Item 4",
                          "Item 5", "Item 6", "Item 7", "Item 8",
                          "Item 9", "Item 10", "Item 11", "Item 12"};

        JList list = new JList(items);

        contentPane.setLayout(new FlowLayout());

        contentPane.add(new JScrollPane(list));

        list.addMouseListener(this);
    }
        .
        .
        .
}
```

Now, in the **mouseClicked** method, I determine where the mouse was double-clicked; then I use the **locationToIndex** method of the list to determine what list item was clicked. Finally, I can determine how many times the item was clicked with the **MouseEvent getClickCount** method and therefore report the number of times each item is clicked, like this:

```
public void mouseClicked(MouseEvent e)
{
    JList jlist = (JList)e.getSource();
    int index = jlist.locationToIndex(e.getPoint());

    String outString = new String("Number of clicks for item " +
    ++index + ": " + e.getClickCount());

    showStatus(outString);
}

public void mouseEntered(MouseEvent e) {}
public void mouseExited(MouseEvent e) {}
public void mousePressed(MouseEvent e) {}
public void mouseReleased(MouseEvent e) {}
}
```

The result appears in Figure 13.14. As you can see in the figure, the applet reports the number of clicks each time a list item is clicked. This way, you can handle double- and even triple-clicks. This example is in listdouble.java on the CD.

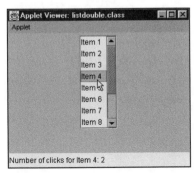

Figure 13.14   Handling double-clicks in a list control.

Chapter 14

Swing: Combo Boxes, Progress Bars, Tooltips, Separators, And Choosers

In Depth

In this chapter, we're going to cover some important Swing controls: combo boxes, progress bars, separators, and choosers. We'll also take a look at adding tooltips, those small windows that display explanatory text when you let the mouse rest over a control. All these topics—especially combo boxes—are important topics in Java, and we'll take an overview of them before digging into the code.

Combo Boxes

Combo boxes are one of the most common controls in GUI programming, but the AWT doesn't have a combo box. Swing rectifies that. Combo boxes are combinations of text fields and drop-down lists. They're very useful in that they let the user either select an item from the list or enter his or her own value into the text field. Combo boxes are also very compact controls, because they only display one item and a button that the user can use to display the drop-down list of other items. Combo boxes can function as drop-down lists, presenting the user with an even more compact way of displaying a list of items than a list control could manage, and they've become very popular for that reason. In fact, Swing makes the default combo box into a drop-down list only, because the default setting for combo boxes is to make them noneditable, which turns them into drop-down lists.

Progress Bars

Progress bars are relatively new controls, made popular as a way to give the user some indication of the progress of a long operation. Originally introduced as a way to show how an installation program is progressing, progress bars are now used for all kinds of time-consuming operations, such as downloading files from the Internet. Progress bars display a colored bar inside them that grows (or shrinks), much like the mercury in a thermometer, to display visually how an operation is proceeding. You can orient progress bars either horizontally or vertically, select the colors and labels used in them, and handle their events. Even so, progress bars remain simple controls, because they really only have one function—displaying the progress of some task. We'll see all the possibilities in this chapter.

Choosers

Like the AWT, Swing supports dialog boxes. Unlike the AWT, Swing also supports two dialog boxes that you don't have to create or customize yourself—file choosers and color choosers. File choosers let the user select a file for opening or saving to, much like any standard file dialog box. Color choosers let the user select a color from among many. Both of these choosers represent standard dialog boxes, and Sun has simply saved you time by creating them for you. We'll work with both of these choosers in this chapter. The color chooser we can use in programs immediately, but actually using the filenames returned by file choosers will have to wait until we start working with files in a few chapters.

Tooltips

Tooltips are those small windows that appear and display explanatory text (such as Download Now or Open New Folder) when the mouse rests over a control. Tooltips can be very useful because GUI users have a great resistance to reading manuals. All the user has to do is let the mouse ride over your program to see what the various controls do. On the other hand, bear in mind that too many tooltips—connected with many different text items in a text control, for example—can be a burden and make your program feel difficult to use.

Separators

Separators are horizontal or vertical bars that let you organize your controls into groups. Although mostly used in menus to divide menu items into logical groupings, you can also use separators in **JApplet** and **JFrame** components like any other control, as we'll see in this chapter.

That's it for the overview of what's in this chapter. As you can see, there's a lot coming up. It's time to turn to the "Immediate Solutions" section now, starting with combo boxes.

Immediate Solutions

Creating Combo Boxes

"Hmm," says the Novice Programmer, "I want to let the user select a word to spell check from a list of words, but now users say they want to enter their own words, too." "Sounds reasonable," you say, "what about using a combo box?" "OK," says the NP, "can you add one to my code?"

Combo boxes can be used in two ways in Swing: as normal combo boxes and as drop-down lists. Drop-down lists let the users make a selection from a list that appears when they click a downwards pointing arrow. Normal combo boxes, on the other hand, are combinations of text fields and drop-down lists; the users can select an item from the drop-down list or enter their own text into the text field. Note that unlike list controls, only one item may be selected at a time in a combo box.

Combo boxes are supported by the **JComboBox** class in Swing, and here's the inheritance diagram for that class:

```
java.lang.Object
|____java.awt.Component
      |____java.awt.Container
            |____javax.swing.JComponent
                  |____javax.swing.JComboBox
```

You'll find the fields for the **JComboBox** class in Table 14.1, its constructors in Table 14.2, and its methods in Table 14.3.

The actual data in the combo box is stored in its model, which by default is an object of the **DefaultComboBoxModel** class. You can find the methods of this class in Table 14.4. Note that to add and delete items, you can use the model's methods, as shown in the table. To get the model object, you can use the **getModel** method of **JComboBox**.

*Table 14.1   Fields of the **JComboBox** class.*

Field	Does This
protected String actionCommand	The action command.
protected ComboBoxModel dataModel	The data model.
protected ComboBoxEditor editor	The editor, which is responsible for the text field.
protected boolean isEditable	Indicates whether the combo box is editable.
protected JComboBox.KeySelection Manager keySelectionManager	The key selection manager.
protected boolean lightWeightPopup Enabled	Indicates whether the drop-down list is enabled as a lightweight component.
protected int maximumRowCount	Holds the row count.
protected ListCellRenderer renderer	The cell renderer.
protected Object selectedItem Reminder	A reminder for the selected item.

*Table 14.2   Constructors of the **JComboBox** class.*

Constructor	Does This
JComboBox( )	Constructs a **JComboBox** object.
JComboBox(ComboBoxModel aModel)	Constructs a **JComboBox** object that takes items from an existing combo box model.
JComboBox(Object[ ] items)	Constructs a **JComboBox** object that contains the elements in the indicated array.
JComboBox(Vector items)	Constructs a **JComboBox** object that contains the elements in the indicated vector.

*Table 14.3   Methods of the **JComboBox** class.*

Method	Does This
void actionPerformed(ActionEvent e)	Public as an implementation side effect.
void addActionListener (ActionListener l)	Adds an action listener.
void addItem(Object anObject)	Adds an item to the item list.
void addItemListener(ItemListener aListener)	Adds an item listener.
void configureEditor(ComboBox Editor anEditor, Object anItem)	Initializes the editor.

(continued)

Table 14.3   Methods of the *JComboBox* class (continued).

Method	Does This
void contentsChanged (ListDataEvent e)	Public as an implementation side effect.
protected JComboBox.KeySelection Manager createDefaultKey SelectionManager( )	Gets an instance of the default key-selection manager.
protected void fireActionEvent( )	Notifies all listeners that have registered interest for notification on this event type.
protected void fireItemStateChanged (ItemEvent e)	Notifies all listeners that have registered interest for notification on this event type.
AccessibleContext getAccessible Context( )	Gets the accessible context.
String getActionCommand( )	Gets the action command.
ComboBoxEditor getEditor( )	Gets the editor used to edit the selected item in the **JComboBox** text field.
Object getItemAt(int index)	Gets the list item at the indicated index.
int getItemCount( )	Gets the number of items in the list.
JComboBox.KeySelectionManager getKeySelectionManager( )	Gets the list's key-selection manager.
int getMaximumRowCount( )	Gets the maximum number of items the combo box can display at once.
ComboBoxModel getModel( )	Gets the data model.
ListCellRenderer getRenderer( )	Gets the renderer.
int getSelectedIndex( )	Gets the index of the currently selected item in the list.
Object getSelectedItem( )	Gets the currently selected item.
Object[ ] getSelectedObjects( )	Gets an array containing the selected item.
ComboBoxUI getUI( )	Gets the look and feel object that renders this component.
String getUIClassID( )	Gets the name of the look and feel class that renders this component.
void hidePopup( )	Causes the combo box to close its pop-up window.
void insertItemAt(Object anObject, int index)	Inserts an item into the item list at a given index.
protected void installAncestorListener( )	Installs an ancestor listener.
void intervalAdded(ListDataEvent e)	Invoked when items have been added to the internal data model.
void intervalRemoved(ListDataEvent e)	Invoked when values have been removed from the data model.
boolean isEditable( )	Returns True if the **JComboBox** object is editable.

(continued)

Table 14.3   Methods of the *JComboBox* class (continued).

Method	Does This
boolean isFocusTraversable( )	Returns True if the component can receive the focus.
boolean isLightWeightPopupEnabled( )	Returns True if lightweight pop-ups are in use. Returns false if heavyweight pop-ups are used.
boolean isPopupVisible( )	Determines the visibility of the pop-up.
protected String paramString( )	Gets a string representation of this **JComboBox** object.
void processKeyEvent(KeyEvent e)	Handles key events, looking for the Tab key.
void removeActionListener (ActionListener l)	Removes an action listener.
void removeAllItems( )	Removes all items from the item list.
void removeItem(Object anObject)	Removes an item from the item list.
void removeItemAt(int anIndex)	Removes the item at **anIndex**. This method works only if the **JComboBox** object uses the default data model.
void removeItemListener(Item Listener aListener)	Removes an item listener.
protected void selectedItemChanged( )	Called when the selected item changes.
boolean selectWithKeyChar (char keyChar)	Selects the list item that corresponds to the indicated keyboard character.
void setActionCommand (String aCommand)	Sets the action command that should be included in the event sent to action listeners.
void setEditable(boolean aFlag)	Sets the editable flag.

Table 14.4   Methods of the *DefaultComboBoxModel* class.

Method	Does This
void addElement(Object anObject)	Adds an item to the end of the model.
Object getElementAt(int index)	Gets the value at the indicated index.
int getIndexOf(Object anObject)	Gets the index-position of the indicated object in the list.
Object getSelectedItem( )	Returns the selected item.
int getSize( )	Gets the length of the list.
void insertElementAt(Object anObject, int index)	Adds an item at a specific index.
void removeAllElements( )	Empties the list.
void removeElement(Object anObject)	Adds an item to the end of the model.
void removeElementAt(int index)	Removes an item at a specific index.
void setSelectedItem(Object anObject)	Sets the selected item.

To add items to a combo box, you can use the **addItem** convenience method, passing it an object that it will pass on to its internal model. I put together an example here showing how this works. In this case, I just create a combo box and add five items—that is, five **String** objects—to it. Here's the code:

```
import java.awt.*;
import javax.swing.*;

/*
<APPLET
    CODE = combobox.class
    WIDTH = 200
    HEIGHT = 200 >
</APPLET>
*/

public class combobox extends JApplet
{
    JComboBox jcombobox = new JComboBox();

    public void init()
    {
        Container contentPane = getContentPane();

        jcombobox.addItem("Item 1");
        jcombobox.addItem("Item 2");
        jcombobox.addItem("Item 3");
        jcombobox.addItem("Item 4");
        jcombobox.addItem("Item 5");

        contentPane.setLayout(new FlowLayout());
        contentPane.add(jcombobox);
    }
}
```

The result appears in Figure 14.1, where you can see the combo box with its drop-down list open, displaying all five items. When the user selects an item from that list and releases the mouse button, that item becomes the newly selected item in the combo box, and it also appears in the text field. This example is in combobox.java on the CD that accompanies this book. Note that by default, the text field in the combo box is not editable—I'll show how to change that in a few pages.

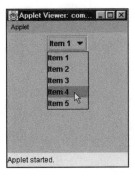

Figure 14.1   Creating a combo box.

So how do you retrieve elements from a combo box? Because only one item in a combo box can be selected at one time, you can get that item with the **getSelectedItem** method, which returns the item itself (note that the item is an object). You can also use **getSelectedIndex** to determine the index of the currently selected item in the combo box's list, like this:

```
String string = (String) jcombobox.getSelectedItem();
int index = (String) jcombobox.getSelectedIindex();
```

To get an item at a specific index, use the model's **getElementAt** method. You can also use the model's **insertElementAt** and **removeElementAt** methods to edit the list.

Note that you can also respond to combo box events. We'll take a look at that in the next topic.

Handling Combo Box Selection Events

The Novice Programmer is back and says, "I want to change the drawing color in my program as soon as the user selects a new color from a combo box—how can I do that?" "It's easy," you say, "just make your code respond to selection events." "Aha," says the NP. "Here's my code, can you fix it?"

You can use two types of listeners with combo boxes—action listeners and item listeners. You use action listeners to handle editing events in the text field, and you use item listeners to handle list selections. We'll take a look at list selections in this topic and editing events in the next topic.

To handle selection events, I'll just add an item listener to the combo box example developed in the previous topic:

```java
import java.awt.*;
import javax.swing.*;
import java.awt.event.*;

/*
<APPLET
    CODE = comboboxevents.class
    WIDTH = 300
    HEIGHT = 200 >
</APPLET>
*/

public class comboboxevents extends JApplet implements ItemListener
{
    JComboBox jcombobox = new JComboBox();
    String outString = "";

    public void init()
    {
        Container contentPane = getContentPane();

        jcombobox.addItem("Item 1");
        jcombobox.addItem("Item 2");
        jcombobox.addItem("Item 3");
        jcombobox.addItem("Item 4");
        jcombobox.addItem("Item 5");

        contentPane.setLayout(new FlowLayout());

        contentPane.add(jcombobox);

        jcombobox.addItemListener(this);
    }
        .
        .
        .
}
```

Now I add the **itemStateChanged** method to this applet that the **ItemListener** interface needs:

```
public void itemStateChanged(ItemEvent e)
{
    .
    .
    .
}
```

This method is passed an object of the **ItemEvent** class, and I can determine whether the corresponding item in the combo box list was selected by using the **getStateChange** method like this:

```
public void itemStateChanged(ItemEvent e)
{
    if(e.getStateChange() == ItemEvent.SELECTED)
        .
        .
        .
}
```

I'll indicate whether an item was selected or deselected in the status bar of the applet like this:

```
public void itemStateChanged(ItemEvent e)
{
    if(e.getStateChange() == ItemEvent.SELECTED)
        outString += "Selected: " + (String)e.getItem();
    else
        outString += "Deselected: " + (String)e.getItem();

    showStatus(outString);
}
```

The result of this code appears in Figure 14.2. As you can see at the bottom of the applet in the figure, the code reports every time the user deselects one item and selects another. This program is a success, and you'll find it in comboboxevents.java on the CD.

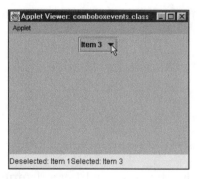

Figure 14.2   Working with combo box selection events.

Creating Editable Combo Boxes

"Darn," says the Novice Programmer, "I can't get the text field in my combo box to work—I can't seem to enter any text in it." You smile and say, "That's because you have to make it *editable*." "Oh," says the NP. "How do you do that?"

To make the text field in a combo box editable, you use the **setEditable** method. To handle editing events, you use an action listener. Here's an example where I make a combo box editable and add an action listener to it:

```
import java.awt.*;
import javax.swing.*;
import java.awt.event.*;

/*
<APPLET
    CODE = comboboxedit.class
    WIDTH = 200
    HEIGHT = 200 >
</APPLET>
*/

public class comboboxedit extends JApplet implements ActionListener
{
    private JComboBox jcombobox = new JComboBox();

    public void init()
    {
        Container contentPane = getContentPane();
```

```
jcombobox.addItem("Item 1");
jcombobox.addItem("Item 2");
jcombobox.addItem("Item 3");
jcombobox.addItem("Item 4");
jcombobox.addItem("Item 5");

jcombobox.setEditable(true);

contentPane.setLayout(new FlowLayout());

contentPane.add(jcombobox);

jcombobox.getEditor().addActionListener(this);

}
.
.
.

}
```

Note that I'm not adding an action listener to the combo box directly but rather to the *editor* in the combo box, which is an object that implements the **ComboBoxEditor** interface. You get this object with the **getEditor** method. The editor is responsible for the editing actions in the text field in the combo box, and you'll find the methods of **ComboBoxEditor** in Table 14.5.

In this example, I display the item's text before it's edited and the text after it has been edited and the user pressed Enter. To get the item's text before it's edited, I use the **getSelectedItem** method, and to get the item after it has been edited, I use the editor's **getItem** method, like this:

```
public void actionPerformed(ActionEvent e)
{
    String outString = (String)jcombobox.getSelectedItem()
        + " was changed to " + (String)jcombobox.getEditor().getItem();

    showStatus(outString);
}
```

The result appears in Figure 14.3. When the user edits an item in the text field and presses Enter, the old and new text in the combo box appears in the applet's status bar, as you can see in the figure. This example is in comboboxedit.java on the CD.

Table 14.5   Methods of the ComboBoxEditor interface.

Method	Does This
void addActionListener(ActionListener l)	Adds an action listener.
Component getEditorComponent( )	Returns the editor component.
Object getItem( )	Returns the edited item.
void removeActionListener(ActionListener l)	Removes an action listener.
void selectAll( )	Asks the editor to start editing and to select everything.
void setItem(Object anObject)	Sets the item that should be edited.

Figure 14.3   Editing the text field in a combo box.

Adding Images To Combo Boxes

"Say," says the Novice Programmer, "isn't there any way to display images in a combo box?" "There sure is," you say, "just sit down and we'll take a look at it."

You can add images to combo boxes just as you can to list controls. In fact, when you add images to combo boxes, you actually add images to the list part of the combo box, so the process is much the same as adding images to lists.

Here's an example in which I create a new model, **newModel**, and cell renderer, **newRenderer**, for a combo box. Here's how I install them in the combo box:

```
import java.awt.*;
import javax.swing.*;
import java.awt.event.*;
```

```
/*
<APPLET
    CODE = comboimages.class
    WIDTH = 400
    HEIGHT = 200 >
</APPLET>
*/

public class comboimages extends JApplet
{
    public void init()
    {
        Container contentPane = getContentPane();
        contentPane.setLayout(new FlowLayout());

        newModel newmodel = new newModel();
        newRenderer newrenderer = new newRenderer();

        JComboBox jcombobox = new JComboBox(newmodel);
        jcombobox.setRenderer(newrenderer);

        contentPane.add(new JScrollPane(jcombobox));
    }
}
```

This new model and renderer will store and display the images in the combo box, and the result appears in Figure 14.4. Now all that remains is to create the new model and renderer, and I'll do that in the next two topics. This example is in comboimages.java on the CD.

Figure 14.4   Adding images to combo boxes.

Creating A Combo Box Model

I'll create a new combo box model in this topic for use with the combo box in the previous topic (the one that displays images). This new model, which extends the **DefaultComboBoxModel** class, will use the **addElement** method to store data elements in the model. Each element is made up of a text string and an image icon, like this:

```
class newModel extends DefaultComboBoxModel
{
    public newModel()
    {
        for(int loop_index = 0; loop_index <= 12; loop_index++) {
            addElement(new Object[] {"Item " + loop_index,
                new ImageIcon("combo.jpg")});
        }
    }
}
```

Creating A Combo Box Custom Renderer

In this topic, I'll create a renderer that displays images in a combo box (this renderer is for use in the code in the previous two topics). To create the cell renderer for a combo box, you can just extend the **JLabel** class, which is the class of each item in a combo box, and implement the **ListCellRenderer** interface. To implement that interface, I override the **getListCellRenderer** method using the **JLabel** class's **setText** and **setIcon** methods to install the text and images in the combo box:

```
class newRenderer extends JLabel implements ListCellRenderer
{
    public newRenderer()
    {
        setOpaque(true);
    }

    public Component getListCellRendererComponent(
        JList jlist, Object obj, int index, boolean isSelected,
        boolean focus)
    {
        newModel model = (newModel)jlist.getModel();

        setText((String)((Object[])obj)[0]);
        setIcon((Icon)((Object[])obj)[1]);

        if(!isSelected) {
            setBackground(jlist.getBackground());
            setForeground(jlist.getForeground());
        }
        else {
            setBackground(jlist.getSelectionBackground());
            setForeground(jlist.getSelectionForeground());
        }

        return this;
    }
}
```

The result appears in Figure 14.4, where you can see the images displayed in the combo box.

Creating Progress Bars

"Well," the Novice Programmer says, "it's true that it takes three hours for my program to sort its internal data, but is that any reason for users to complain?" "It sure is," you say, "unless you give them some kind of visual indication of what's going on. How about adding a progress bar to your program." "Sure!" says the NP. "What's a progress bar?"

A progress bar control draws an updated, colored bar inside itself that displays the progress of some operation. You can set the minimum and maximum values for a progress bar when you call the **JProgressBar** constructor, or you can use the **setMinimum** and **setMaximum** methods. You can then repeatedly update the progress bar by calling its **setValue** method to indicate the progressive status of an operation. Here's the inheritance diagram for the **JProgressBar** class:

```
java.lang.Object
|____java.awt.Component
      |____java.awt.Container
            |____javax.swing.JComponent
                  |____javax.swing.JProgressBar
```

You can find the fields of the **JProgressBar** class in Table 14.6 (note that it also inherits two constants from **SwingConstants** that you use for orientation: **HORIZONTAL** and **VERTICAL**), its constructors in Table 14.7, and its methods in Table 14.8.

Table 14.6   Fields of the JProgressBar class.

Field	Does This
protected ChangeEvent changeEvent	The change event.
protected ChangeListener change Listener	The change listener.
protected BoundedRangeModel model	The data model that holds data values for the progress bar.
protected int orientation	The orientation in which to display the progress bar.
protected boolean paintBorder	Returns True if there should be a border around the progress bar.
protected boolean paintString	Returns True if there should be a string label in the progress bar.
protected String progressString	A optional string that can be displayed on the progress bar.

Table 14.7   Constructors of the *JProgressBar* class.

Constructor	Does This
JProgressBar( )	Constructs a horizontal progress bar.
JProgressBar(BoundedRangeModel newModel)	Constructs a horizontal progress bar (the default orientation).
JProgressBar(int orient)	Constructs a progress bar with the indicated orientation, which can be either **JProgressBar.VERTICAL** or **JProgressBar.HORIZONTAL**.
JProgressBar(int min, int max)	Constructs a horizontal progress bar, which is the default.
JProgressBar(int orient, int min, int max)	Constructs a progress bar using the indicated orientation, minimum, and maximum values.

Table 14.8   Methods of the *JProgressBar* class.

Method	Does This
void addChangeListener(Change Listener l)	Adds a change listener.
protected ChangeListener create ChangeListener( )	Creates a change listener.
protected void fireStateChanged( )	Notifies all listeners that have registered interest for notification on this event type.
AccessibleContext getAccessible Context( )	Gets the accessible context associated with this **JProgressBar** object.
int getMaximum( )	Gets the model's maximum value.
int getMinimum( )	Gets the model's minimum value.
BoundedRangeModel getModel( )	Gets the data model.
int getOrientation( )	Returns **JProgressBar.VERTICAL** or **JProgressBar.HORIZONTAL**.
double getPercentComplete( )	Gets the percentage/percent complete for the progress bar.
String getString( )	Gets the current value of the progress string.
ProgressBarUI getUI( )	Gets the look and feel object that renders this component.
String getUIClassID( )	Gets the name of the look and feel class that renders this component.

(continued)

Table 14.8   Methods of the *JProgressBar* class (continued).

Method	Does This
int getValue( )	Gets the model's current value.
boolean isBorderPainted( )	Returns True if the progress bar has a border and false if it does not.
boolean isStringPainted( )	Returns True if a string will be drawn in the progress bar.
protected void paintBorder(Graphics g)	Paints the progress bar's border (as long as the **BorderPainted** property is True).
protected String paramString( )	Gets a string representation of the **JProgressBar** object.
void removeChangeListener (ChangeListener l)	Removes a change listener from the button.
void setBorderPainted(boolean b)	Sets whether the progress bar should paint its border.
void setMaximum(int n)	Sets the model's maximum value to **x**.
void setMinimum(int n)	Sets the model's minimum value to **x**.
void setModel(BoundedRangeModel newModel)	Sets the data model used by the **JProgressBar** object.
void setOrientation(int newOrientation)	Sets the progress bar's orientation to **newOrientation**.
void setString(String s)	Sets the value of the progress string.
void setStringPainted(boolean b)	Specifies whether the progress bar will render a string.
void setUI(ProgressBarUI ui)	Sets the look and feel object that renders this component.
void setValue(int n)	Sets the model's current value to **x**.
void updateUI( )	Called by the **UIFactory** class to indicate that the look and feel has changed.

There are quite a few ways to display progress bars. For example, you can make them horizontal or vertical when you call the class's constructor or use the **setOrientation** method. You can also select the drawing color for the actual bar, display a label inside the progress bar that indicates the current value, and more. The basic use of all progress bars, however, is the same no matter what they look like—you set a minimum and maximum value for the progress bar (the default values are 0 and 100) and then update its display with the **setValue** method, as appropriate. Here are a few examples showing some of the ways you can display progress bars:

```
import java.awt.*;
import javax.swing.*;

/*
<APPLET
```

```
    CODE = progressbar.class
    WIDTH = 500
    HEIGHT = 200 >
</APPLET>
*/

public class progressbar extends JApplet
{
    JProgressBar jprogressbar1, jprogressbar2, jprogressbar3,
        jprogressbar4, jprogressbar5, jprogressbar6;

    public void init()
    {
        Container contentPane = getContentPane();

        contentPane.setLayout(new FlowLayout());

        jprogressbar1 = new JProgressBar();
        jprogressbar1.setValue(50);
        contentPane.add(jprogressbar1);


        jprogressbar2 = new JProgressBar();
        jprogressbar2.setMinimum(100);
        jprogressbar2.setMaximum(200);
        jprogressbar2.setValue(180);
        jprogressbar2.setForeground(Color.red);
        contentPane.add(jprogressbar2);


        jprogressbar3 = new JProgressBar();
        jprogressbar3.setOrientation(JProgressBar.VERTICAL);
        jprogressbar3.setForeground(Color.blue);
        jprogressbar3.setValue(50);
        jprogressbar3.setStringPainted(true);
        jprogressbar3.setBorder(BorderFactory.createRaisedBevelBorder());
        contentPane.add(jprogressbar3);


        jprogressbar4 = new JProgressBar();
        jprogressbar4.setOrientation(JProgressBar.VERTICAL);
        jprogressbar4.setForeground(Color.red);
        jprogressbar4.setValue(80);
        jprogressbar4.setStringPainted(true);
        jprogressbar4.setBorderPainted(false);
        contentPane.add(jprogressbar4);


        jprogressbar5 = new JProgressBar();
```

```
        jprogressbar5.setOrientation(JProgressBar.VERTICAL);
        jprogressbar5.setStringPainted(true);
        jprogressbar5.setString("Hello from Swing!");
        jprogressbar5.setValue(90);
        contentPane.add(jprogressbar5);
    }
}
```

The result of this code appears in Figure 14.5, where you can see various progress bars displayed in a number of ways. There's a lot of possibilities here (note, in particular, that you can add a label to the progress bar to indicate its current setting, and you can customize the progress bar's border). This example is in progressbar.java on the CD.

On the other hand, static progress bars, like the ones shown in Figure 14.5, aren't much use, because they don't do anything. To see how to update a progress bar, take a look at the next topic.

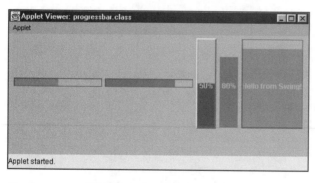

Figure 14.5   Displaying progress bars.

Updating Progress Bars

The Novice Programmer says, "Jeez, I put progress bars into my program, but they're not doing anything—what's wrong?" "Well," you say, "that's because you have to call the **setValue** method yourself to update them." "Oh," says the NP.

After creating and displaying a progress bar, it's up to you to update it with the **setValue** method. You'll usually do that by dividing your time-consuming task into parts, and you'll update the progress bar as each part completes.

Here's an example—progressbarupdate.java on the CD—that increments a progress bar each time a button is clicked:

```java
import java.awt.*;
import javax.swing.*;
import java.awt.event.*;

/*
<APPLET
    CODE = progressbarupdate.class
    WIDTH = 400
    HEIGHT = 200 >
</APPLET>
*/

public class progressbarupdate extends JApplet
{
    JProgressBar jprogressbar = new JProgressBar();
    JButton jbutton = new JButton("Increment the progress bar");

    public void init()
    {
        Container contentPane = getContentPane();

        contentPane.setLayout(new FlowLayout());

        contentPane.add(jprogressbar);
        contentPane.add(jbutton);

        jprogressbar.setStringPainted(true);

        jbutton.addActionListener(new ActionListener() {
            public void actionPerformed(ActionEvent e)
            {
                jprogressbar.setValue(jprogressbar.getValue() + 10);
            }
        });
    }
}
```

The result appears in Figure 14.6. Note that you can update the progress bar just by clicking the button. Usually, of course, your code will update the progress bar itself, because progress bars are used to indicate to the user the progress of time-consuming operations.

14. Swing: Combo Boxes, Progress Bars, Tooltips, Separators, And Choosers

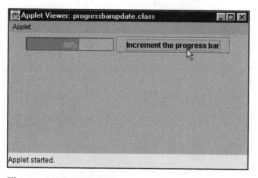

Figure 14.6   Updating a progress bar.

Handling Progress Bar Events

Progress bars events occur every time the progress bar's value changes, and you can work with change listeners to catch those events. Here's an example—progressbarevents.java on the CD—that lets the user update a progress bar with a button. It catches the events that occur as they do. In this case, I report the new value of the progress bar each time it's changed as well as its minimum and maximum values, like this:

```
import java.awt.*;
import javax.swing.*;
import java.awt.event.*;
import javax.swing.event.*;

/*
<APPLET
    CODE = progressbarevents.class
    WIDTH = 400
    HEIGHT = 200 >
</APPLET>
*/

public class progressbarevents extends JApplet
{
    JProgressBar jprogressbar = new JProgressBar();
    JButton jbutton = new JButton("Increment the progress bar");

    public void init()
    {
        Container contentPane = getContentPane();
```

```
        contentPane.setLayout(new FlowLayout());

        contentPane.add(jbutton);

        jprogressbar.setForeground(Color.blue);
        contentPane.add(jprogressbar);

        jbutton.addActionListener(new ActionListener() {
            public void actionPerformed(ActionEvent e)
            {
                jprogressbar.setValue(jprogressbar.getValue() + 10);
            }
        });

        jprogressbar.addChangeListener(new ChangeListener() {
            public void stateChanged(ChangeEvent e)
            {
                showStatus("Progress bar minimum: " +
                    jprogressbar.getMinimum()
                    + " maximum: " + jprogressbar.getMaximum() +
                    " value: " + jprogressbar.getValue());
            }
        });
    }
}
```

The result of this code appears in Figure 14.7. As you can see in the figure, each time the user updates the progress bar, its new value appears in the applet's status bar. This example is a success, and you can find it in progressbarevents.java on the CD.

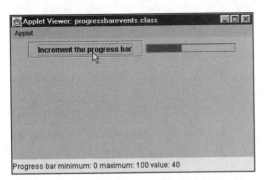

Figure 14.7   Handling progress bar events.

Creating Tooltips

"Say," says the Product Support Specialist, "no one seems to read the manuals, ever. Isn't there some way to make our programs self-explanatory?" "Well," you say, "we could reduce everything to a series of cartoons." "Hmm," says the PSS thoughtfully. "Just kidding," you say quickly. "I'll add tooltips to the controls in the program."

Tooltips are small windows that appear when the user lets the mouse rest on a component. They display some text that explains the purpose of the control. For example, a Cut button's tooltip might read "Cut selected text." Tooltips are supported with the Swing **JToolTip** class, and here's that class's inheritance diagram:

```
java.lang.Object
|_____java.awt.Component
      |_____java.awt.Container
            |_____javax.swing.JComponent
                  |_____javax.swing.JToolTip
```

You'll find the constructor of the **JToolTip** class in Table 14.9 and its methods in Table 14.10.

Table 14.9   The constructor of the JToolTip class.

Constructor	Does This
JToolTip( )	Constructs a tooltip.

Table 14.10   Methods of the JToolTip class.

Method	Does This
AccessibleContext getAccessible Context( )	Get the accessible context.
JComponent getComponent( )	Gets the component the tooltip applies to.
String getTipText( )	Gets the text that's shown in the tooltip.
ToolTipUI getUI( )	Gets the look and feel object that renders this component.
String getUIClassID( )	Gets the name of the look and feel class that renders this component.
protected String paramString( )	Gets a string representation of this **JToolTip** object.
void setComponent(JComponent c)	Sets the component that the tooltip describes.
void setTipText(String tipText)	Sets the text shown when the tooltip appears.
void updateUI( )	Called by the **UIFactory** class when the look and feel has changed.

Many components already have a method, **setToolTipText**, that you can use to add a tooltip. Here's an example in which I add a tooltip to a button:

```java
import java.awt.*;
import javax.swing.*;
import java.awt.event.*;

/*
<APPLET
    CODE=tooltip.class
    WIDTH=300
    HEIGHT=200 >
</APPLET>
*/

public class tooltip extends JApplet
{
    JButton button = new JButton("Click Me");
    JTextField text = new JTextField(20);

    public void init()
    {
        Container contentPane = getContentPane();

        contentPane.setLayout(new FlowLayout());

        button.setToolTipText("This is a button.");

        contentPane.add(button);
        contentPane.add(text);

        button.addActionListener(new ActionListener()
        {
            public void actionPerformed(ActionEvent event) {
                text.setText("Hello from Swing!");
            }
        });
    }
}
```

It's as easy as that to add a tooltip to most components. The result appears in Figure 14.8, where you can see the tooltip with its explanatory text. This example is in tooltip.java on the CD.

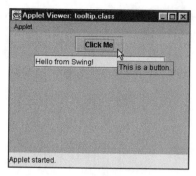

Figure 14.8   Using tooltips.

Creating Separators

The Novice Programmer says, "The Big Boss told me that there are too many text fields in my program and I should divide them into groups." "You can do that in several easy ways," you say, "such as adding text fields to panels and giving the panels various background colors. You can even use separators. By the way, how many text fields are there in your program?" "About 2,413," the NP says. "Uh-oh," you say.

Separators are horizontal or vertical lines, and they usually appear in menus to separate menu items into logical groups, but you can also use them to separate components in a layout. They're supported by the **JSeparator** class in Swing, and here's that class's inheritance diagram:

```
java.lang.Object
|____java.awt.Component
      |____java.awt.Container
            |____javax.swing.JComponent
                  |____javax.swing.JSeparator
```

You can find the constructors of the **JSeparator** class in Table 14.11 and its methods in Table 14.12.

Table 14.11   Constructors of the JSeparator class.

Constructor	Does This
JSeparator( )	Creates a new horizontal separator.
JSeparator(int orientation)	Creates a new separator with the indicated horizontal or vertical orientation.

Table 14.12   Methods of the *JSeparator* class.

Method	Does This
AccessibleContext getAccessible Context( )	Gets the accessible context.
int getOrientation( )	Gets the orientation of this separator.
SeparatorUI getUI( )	Gets the look and feel object that renders this component.
String getUIClassID( )	Gets the name of the look and feel class that renders this component.
boolean isFocusTraversable( )	Indicates whether this component can receive the focus.
protected String paramString( )	Gets a string representation of this **JSeparator** object.
void setOrientation(int orientation)	Sets the orientation of the separator.
void setUI(SeparatorUI ui)	Sets the look and feel object that renders this component.
void updateUI( )	Called by the **UIFactory** class when the look and feel has changed.

Let's look at an example. Here, I put a separator between two text fields in a flow layout. To make a separator visible, you have to do more than just add it to a layout—you also have to give it a preferred size using its **setPreferredSize** method. The usual way to do that is to use the separator's **getPreferredSize** method to get the current width of the separator and then pass that and the new length you want to **setPreferredSize**. The **setPreferredSize** and **setPreferredSize** methods work with objects of the AWT **Dimension** class, which has two fields: **width** and **height**. Here's how I create the new separator and get its dimensions:

```
import java.awt.*;
import javax.swing.*;

/*
<APPLET
    CODE = separator.class
    WIDTH = 400
    HEIGHT = 200 >
</APPLET>
*/

public class separator extends JApplet
{
    JSeparator jseparator = new JSeparator(JSeparator.VERTICAL);
```

```
Dimension dimension = jseparator.getPreferredSize();
        .
        .
        .
```

Now I can put the separator between two text fields, like this, making it 100 pixels high:

```
public class separator extends JApplet
{
    JSeparator jseparator = new JSeparator(JSeparator.VERTICAL);
    Dimension dimension = jseparator.getPreferredSize();

    public void init()
    {
        Container contentPane = getContentPane();

        contentPane.setLayout(new FlowLayout());

        contentPane.add(new JTextField("Hello from Swing!"));
        contentPane.add(jseparator);
        contentPane.add(new JTextField("Hello from Swing!"));

        jseparator.setPreferredSize(new Dimension(dimension.width, 100));
    }
}
```

The result of this code—separator.java on the CD—appears in Figure 14.9. As you can see in the figure, the separator appears between the two text fields.

There's one problem here, though—what if the user resizes the applet? In that case, you might want to resize the separator to match. You can do that by handling resizing events—see the next topic for the details.

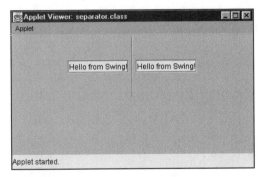

Figure 14.9   Creating a separator.

Resizing Separators Automatically

To resize a separator, you can catch component resizing events by using the
ComponentListener interface, which handles the resizing events for compo-
nents, including applets and windows. The methods of this interface appear in
Table 14.13.

For example, when you resize an applet, you can resize a separator to the new
size you want. Here's an example in which I create a separator between two text
fields that goes from the top of an applet window's client area to the bottom and
maintains that extent even when the applet is resized. Here's what the code looks

Table 14.13   Methods of the *ComponentListener* interface.

Constructor	Does This
void componentHidden (ComponentEvent e)	Called when the component is made invisible.
void componentMoved (ComponentEvent e)	Called when the component's position changes.
void componentResized (ComponentEvent e)	Called when the component's size changes.
void componentShown (ComponentEvent e)	Called when the component is made visible.

like—note the resizing code in the **ComponentShown** (to display the separator the first time) and **ComponentResized** methods:

```
import java.awt.*;
import javax.swing.*;
import java.awt.event.*;

/*
<APPLET
    CODE = separatorevents.class
    WIDTH = 400
    HEIGHT = 200 >
</APPLET>
*/

public class separatorevents extends JApplet implements ComponentListener
{
    JSeparator jseparator = new JSeparator(JSeparator.VERTICAL);
    Dimension dimension = jseparator.getPreferredSize();

    public void init()
    {
        Container contentPane = getContentPane();

        contentPane.setLayout(new FlowLayout());

        contentPane.add(new JTextField("Hello from Swing!"));
        contentPane.add(jseparator);
        contentPane.add(new JTextField("Hello from Swing!"));

        addComponentListener(this);
    }

    public void componentShown(ComponentEvent e)
    {
        jseparator.setPreferredSize(new Dimension(dimension.width,
            getSize().height));
        jseparator.revalidate();
    }

    public void componentResized(ComponentEvent e)
    {
```

```
        jseparator.setPreferredSize(new Dimension(dimension.width,
            getSize().height));
        jseparator.revalidate();
    }

    public void componentMoved(ComponentEvent e) {}
    public void componentHidden(ComponentEvent e) {}
}
```

The result of this code appears in Figure 14.10. As you can see in the figure, the separator extends from the top of the client area in the applet to the bottom—and it'll resize itself as the applet does. This example is in separatorevents.java on the CD.

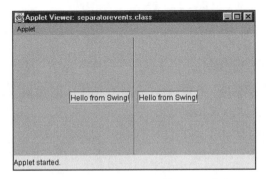

Figure 14.10   Creating a separator that resizes itself.

Creating Color Choosers

"Now I've got a real problem," the Novice Programmer says. "I want to let the users select a drawing color for my new program, *SuperDuperArtisticPro*, but I can't ask them to just type in new color values." "Why not use a color chooser?" you ask. "Good idea!" the NP says. "You write the code, and I'll watch."

You can let the user select a color with the Swing **JColorChooser** class, which is a prebuilt dialog box that presents the user with several ways of choosing colors. Here's the inheritance diagram for **JColorChooser**:

```
java.lang.Object
|____java.awt.Component
      |____java.awt.Container
            |____javax.swing.JComponent
                  |____javax.swing.JColorChooser
```

14. Swing: Combo Boxes, Progress Bars, Tooltips, Separators, And Choosers

You can find the fields of the **JColorChooser** class in Table 14.14, its constructors in Table 14.15, and its methods in Table 14.16.

Table 14.14   Fields of the JColorChooser class.

Field	Does This
protected AccessibleContext accessibleContext	The accessible context.
static String CHOOSER_PANELS _PROPERTY	The chooser panel array property name.
static String PREVIEW_PANEL _PROPERTY	The preview panel property name.
static String SELECTION_MODEL _PROPERTY	The selection model property name.

Table 14.15   Constructors of the JColorChooser class.

Constructor	Does This
JColorChooser( )	Constructs a color chooser pane.
JColorChooser(Color initialColor)	Constructs a color chooser pane with the indicated initial color.
JColorChooser(ColorSelection Model model)	Constructs a color chooser pane with the indicated color selection model.

Table 14.16   Methods of the JColorChooser class.

Method	Does This
void addChooserPanel(AbstractColor ChooserPanel panel)	Adds a color chooser panel.
static JDialog createDialog(Component c, String title, boolean modal, JColorChooser chooserPane, ActionListener okListener, Action Listener cancelListener)	Constructs and returns a new dialog with the indicated color chooser pane and with OK, Cancel, and Reset buttons.
AccessibleContext getAccessible Context( )	Get the accessible context.
AbstractColorChooserPanel[ ] get ChooserPanels( )	Gets the indicated color panels.

(continued)

*Table 14.16   Methods of the **JColorChooser** class* (continued).

Method	Does This
Color getColor( )	Gets the current color value from the color chooser.
JComponent getPreviewPanel( )	Gets the preview panel that shows a chosen color.
ColorSelectionModel getSelection Model( )	Gets the data model that handles color selections.
ColorChooserUI getUI( )	Gets the look and feel object that renders this component.
String getUIClassID( )	Gets the name of the look and feel class that renders this component.
protected String paramString( )	Gets a string representation of this **JColorChooser** object.
AbstractColorChooserPanel remove ChooserPanel(AbstractColorChooser Panel panel)	Removes the color panel indicated.
void setChooserPanels(AbstractColor ChooserPanel[ ] panels)	Specifies the color panels used to choose a color value.
void setColor(Color color)	Sets the current color of the color chooser to the indicated color.
void setColor(int c)	Sets the current color of the color chooser to the indicated color.
void setColor(int r, int g, int b)	Sets the current color of the color chooser to the indicated RGB color.
void setPreviewPanel(JComponent preview)	Sets the current preview panel.
void setSelectionModel(ColorSelection Model newModel)	Sets the model containing the selected color.
void setUI(ColorChooserUI ui)	Sets the look and feel object that renders this component.
static Color showDialog(Component component, String title, Color initialColor)	Shows a modal color chooser dialog box.
void updateUI( )	Called by the **UIManager** class when the look and feel has changed.

Using a color chooser is easy; all you have to do is show it with its **showDialog** method, and then passing that method a parent object, a caption, and a default color. This method returns the color selected by the user as a **Color** object (or the default color if the user didn't select a color).

Let's look at an example in which I place a button in a panel and let the user display a color chooser when he or she clicks the button. After the user selects a color, the code will set the background of the panel to that color. Here's what the code looks like:

```
import java.awt.*;
import javax.swing.*;
import java.awt.event.*;

/*
<APPLET
    CODE = colorchooser.class
    WIDTH = 200
    HEIGHT = 200 >
</APPLET>
*/

public class colorchooser extends JApplet implements ActionListener
{
    JPanel jpanel = new JPanel();
    JButton jbutton;

    public void init()
    {
        jbutton = new JButton("Click here to change colors.");
        jbutton.addActionListener(this);
        jpanel.add(jbutton);
        getContentPane().add(jpanel);
    }

    public void actionPerformed(ActionEvent e)
    {
        Color color = JColorChooser.showDialog(colorchooser.this,
            "Select a new color...", Color.white);

        jpanel.setBackground(color);
    }
}
```

As you can see, it's easy to use a color chooser; the color chooser, itself, appears in Figure 14.11.

When the user selects a color in the color chooser, the new color appears in the applet's panel, as shown in Figure 14.12. This example—colorchooser.java on the CD—is a success.

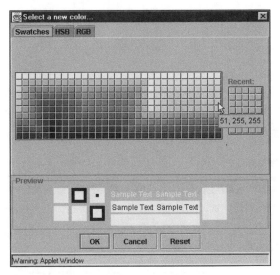

Figure 14.11   Using a color chooser.

Figure 14.12   Changing the color of a panel to a selected color.

Creating File Choosers

"Hmm," says the Novice Programmer, "I need to get the name of a file from the user—is there any quick way of doing that?" "Sure," you say, "a text field." "Well," the NP says, "I want to let the user browse for the correct field if needed." "Oh," you say, "then you want a file chooser."

File choosers are dialog boxes that let users specify the name and path of a file, letting them browse their disk storage if they need to. File choosers are supported by the **JFileChooser** class. Here's the inheritance diagram for that class:

```
java.lang.Object
|____java.awt.Component
     |____java.awt.Container
          |____javax.swing.JComponent
               |____javax.swing.JFileChooser
```

You'll find the fields of the **JFileChooser** class in Table 14.17, its constructors in Table 14.18, and its methods in Table 14.19.

Table 14.17   Fields of the *JFileChooser* class.

Field	Does This
protected AccessibleContext accessibleContext	The accessible context.
static String ACCESSORY_CHANGED _PROPERTY	Indicates that a different accessory component is in use.
static String APPROVE_BUTTON _MNEMONIC_CHANGED _PROPERTY	Indicates a change in the mnemonic for the approve button.
static String APPROVE_BUTTON _TEXT_CHANGED_PROPERTY	Indicates a change in the text on the approve/Yes/OK button.
static String APPROVE_BUTTON _TOOL_TIP_TEXT_CHANGED _PROPERTY	Indicates a change in the tooltip text for the approve/Yes/OK button.
static int APPROVE_OPTION	The return value if the approve/Yes/OK button is chosen.
static String APPROVE_SELECTION	Instruction to approve the current selection.
static int CANCEL_OPTION	The return value if the Cancel button is chosen.
static String CANCEL_SELECTION	Instruction to cancel the current selection.
static String CHOOSABLE_FILE _FILTER_CHANGED_PROPERTY	Indicates a change in the list of predefined file filters that the user can choose from.
static int CUSTOM_DIALOG	Type value indicating that the file chooser supports a developer-specified file operation.
static String DIALOG_TITLE _CHANGED_PROPERTY	Indicates a change in the dialog box's title.
static String DIALOG_TYPE _CHANGED_PROPERTY	Indicates a change in the type of files displayed (files only, directories only, or both files and directories).
static int DIRECTORIES_ONLY	Instruction to display only directories.

(continued)

Table 14.17   Fields of the *JFileChooser* class (continued).

Field	Does This
static String DIRECTORY_CHANGED _PROPERTY	Indicates a directory change.
static int ERROR_OPTION	The return value if an error occurred.
static String FILE_FILTER_CHANGED _PROPERTY	The user changed the kind of files to display.
static String FILE_HIDING_CHANGED _PROPERTY	Indicates a change in the "display hidden files" property.
static String FILE_SELECTION_MODE _CHANGED_PROPERTY	Indicates a change in the kind of selection (single, multiple, and so on).
static String FILE_SYSTEM_VIEW _CHANGED_PROPERTY	Indicates that a different object is being used to find available drives on the system.
static String FILE_VIEW_CHANGED _PROPERTY	Indicates that a different object is being used to retrieve file information.
static int FILES_AND_DIRECTORIES	Instruction to display both files and directories.
static int FILES_ONLY	Instruction to display only files.
static String MULTI_SELECTION _ENABLED_CHANGED_PROPERTY	Enables multiple-file selections.
static int OPEN_DIALOG	Indicates that the file chooser supports an Open file operation.
static int SAVE_DIALOG	Indicates that the file chooser supports a Save file operation.
static String SELECTED_FILE _CHANGED_PROPERTY	Indicates a change in the user's single-file selection.
static String SELECTED_FILES _CHANGED_PROPERTY	Indicates a change in the user's multiple-file selection.

Table 14.18   Constructors of the *JFileChooser* class.

Constructor	Does This
JFileChooser( )	Constructs a **JFileChooser** object.
JFileChooser(File currentDirectory)	Constructs a **JFileChooser** object using the given file as the path.
JFileChooser(File currentDirectory, FileSystemView fsv)	Constructs a **JFileChooser** object using the given current directory and file system view.
JFileChooser(FileSystemView fsv)	Constructs a **JFileChooser** object using the given file system view.
JFileChooser(String current DirectoryPath)	Constructs a **JFileChooser** object using the given path.
JFileChooser(String currentDirectory Path, FileSystemView fsv)	Constructs a **JFileChooser** object using the given current directory path and file system view.

Table 14.19   Methods of the _JFileChooser_ class.

Method	Does This
boolean accept(File f)	Returns True if the file should be displayed.
void addActionListener(ActionListener l)	Adds an action listener.
void addChoosableFileFilter (FileFilter filter)	Adds a filter to the list of choosable file filters.
void approveSelection( )	Called by the UI when the user clicks the Save or Open button.
void cancelSelection( )	Called by the UI when the user clicks the Cancel button.
void changeToParentDirectory( )	Changes the directory to be set to the parent of the current directory.
void ensureFileIsVisible(File f)	Makes sure that the indicated file is visible.
protected void fireActionPerformed (String command)	Notifies all listeners that have registered interest for notification on this event type.
FileFilter getAcceptAllFileFilter( )	Gets the **AcceptAll** file filter.
AccessibleContext getAccessible Context( )	Get the accessible context associated with this JFileChooser object.
JComponent getAccessory( )	Gets the accessory component.
int getApproveButtonMnemonic( )	Gets the approve button's mnemonic.
String getApproveButtonText( )	Gets the text used in the approve button in the **FileChooserUI**.
String getApproveButtonToolTipText( )	Gets the tooltip text used in the approve button.
FileFilter[ ] getChoosableFileFilters( )	Gets the list of user-choosable file filters.
File getCurrentDirectory( )	Gets the current directory.
String getDescription(File f)	Gets the file description.
String getDialogTitle( )	Gets the string that goes in the file chooser's title bar.
int getDialogType( )	Gets the type of this dialog box.
FileFilter getFileFilter( )	Gets the currently selected file filter.
int getFileSelectionMode( )	Gets the current file-selection mode.
FileSystemView getFileSystemView( )	Gets the file system view.
FileView getFileView( )	Gets the current file view.
Icon getIcon(File f)	Gets the icon for this file or type of file, depending on the system.
String getName(File f)	Gets the file name.
File getSelectedFile( )	Gets the selected file.

(continued)

Table 14.19   Methods of the JFileChooser class (continued).

Method	Does This
File[ ] getSelectedFiles( )	Gets a list of selected files if the file chooser is set to allow multiple selections.
String getTypeDescription(File f)	Gets the file type.
FileChooserUI getUI( )	Gets the UI object that implements the look and feel for this component.
String getUIClassID( )	Gets a string that specifies the name of the look and feel class that renders this component.
boolean isDirectorySelectionEnabled( )	A convenience method that determines whether directories are selectable.
boolean isFileHidingEnabled( )	Returns True if hidden files are not shown in the file chooser.
boolean isFileSelectionEnabled( )	A convenience method that determines whether files are selectable based on the current file selection mode.
boolean isMultiSelectionEnabled( )	Returns True if multiple files can be selected.
boolean isTraversable(File f)	Returns True if the file (directory) can be visited.
protected String paramString( )	Gets a string representation of this **JFileChooser** object.
void removeActionListener (ActionListener l)	Removes an action listener from the button.
boolean removeChoosableFileFilter (FileFilter f)	Removes a filter from the list of choosable file filters.
void rescanCurrentDirectory( )	Rescans the file list from the current directory.
void resetChoosableFileFilters( )	Resets the choosable file filter list to its starting state.
void setAccessory(JComponent new Accessory)	Sets the accessory component.
void setApproveButtonMnemonic (char mnemonic)	Sets the approve button's mnemonic using a character.
void setApproveButtonMnemonic (int mnemonic)	Sets the approve button's mnemonic using a numeric keycode.
void setApproveButtonText(String approveButtonText)	Sets the text used in the approve button.
void setApproveButtonToolTipText (String toolTipText)	Sets the Tooltip text used in the approve button.

(continued)

Table 14.19   Methods of the JFileChooser class (continued).

Method	Does This
void setCurrentDirectory(File dir)	Sets the current directory.
void setDialogTitle(String dialogTitle)	Sets the string that goes in the file chooser window's title bar.
void setDialogType(int dialogType)	Sets the type of this dialog box.
void setFileFilter(FileFilter filter)	Sets the current file filter.
void setFileHidingEnabled(boolean b)	Sets file hiding on or off.
void setFileSelectionMode(int mode)	Sets the file chooser to allow the user to just select files, just select directories, or select both files and directories.
void setFileSystemView (FileSystemView fsv)	Sets the file system view that the **JFileChooser** object uses.
void setFileView(FileView fileView)	Sets the file view used to retrieve UI information, such as the icon that represents a file or the type description of a file.
void setMultiSelectionEnabled (boolean b)	Sets the file chooser to allow multiple file selections.
void setSelectedFile(File file)	Sets the selected file.
void setSelectedFiles (File[ ] selectedFiles)	Sets the list of selected files if the file chooser is set to allow multiple selections.
protected void setup(FileSystem View view)	Performs constructor initialization and setup.
int showDialog(Component parent, String approveButtonText)	Displays a custom file chooser dialog box with a custom approve button.
int showOpenDialog(Component parent)	Displays an "Open File" file chooser dialog box.
int showSaveDialog(Component parent)	Displays a "Save File" file chooser dialog box.
void updateUI( )	Called by the **UIFactory** class when the look and feel has changed.

You can use the **JFileChooser** class's **showOpenDialog** method to show a file chooser for finding files to open, and you can use the **showSaveDialog** method to show a file chooser for specifying the file name and path to use to save a file. These methods return the following values:

- *APPROVE_OPTION*—Returned if the user clicks an approve button such as Save or Open.

- *CANCEL_OPTION*—Returned if the user clicks on Cancel.

- *ERROR_OPTION*—Returned if there was an error.

You can get the selected file as a **File** object with the file chooser's **getSelectedFile** method (you'll see the **File** class later in this book), and you can use the **File** class's **getPath**, **getName**, and other methods to return information about the file.

Let's look at an example that puts this to work. In this case, I display an Open File chooser when the user clicks a button. I let the user select a file and then I display that file's name and path in a text field. Because you usually don't open files from applets (for security reasons), I'll make this example an application. Here's the code (note that I check the return value from **showOpenDialog** to see whether the user clicked the Open button before displaying the file name in the text field):

```
import java.awt.*;
import java.io.File;
import javax.swing.*;
import java.awt.event.*;
import javax.swing.filechooser.*;

public class filechooser extends JFrame implements ActionListener
{
    JFileChooser chooser = new JFileChooser();
    JButton jbutton = new JButton("Display file chooser");
    JTextField jtextfield = new JTextField(30);

    public filechooser()
    {
        super();
        Container contentPane = getContentPane();

        contentPane.setLayout(new FlowLayout());
        contentPane.add(jbutton);
        contentPane.add(jtextfield);

        jbutton.addActionListener(this);
    }

    public void actionPerformed(ActionEvent e)
    {
        int result = chooser.showOpenDialog(null);
        File fileobj = chooser.getSelectedFile();

        if(result == JFileChooser.APPROVE_OPTION) {
            jtextfield.setText("You chose " + fileobj.getPath());
```

```
        } else if(result == JFileChooser.CANCEL_OPTION) {
            jtextfield.setText("You clicked Cancel");
        }
    }

    public static void main(String args[])
    {
        JFrame f = new filechooser();
        f.setBounds(200, 200, 400, 200);

        f.setVisible(true);

        f.setDefaultCloseOperation(WindowConstants.DISPOSE_ON_CLOSE);

        f.addWindowListener(new WindowAdapter() {
            public void windowClosing(WindowEvent e)
            {
                System.exit(0);
            }
        });
    }
}
```

The file chooser that this application displays appears in Figure 14.13. The user can browse and select a file. When he or she does, either by highlighting a file and clicking the Open button in the file chooser or by simply double-clicking the file in the file chooser, the file chooser closes and the name and path of the selected file appears in the text field in the application, as you can see in Figure 14.14. That's all there is to it. This example is in filechooser.java on the CD.

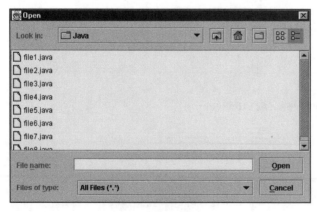

Figure 14.13   Creating a file chooser.

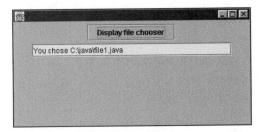

Figure 14.14   Determining the chosen file.

Creating File Chooser Filters

There are plenty of ways to customize file choosers, and one of them is to create file *filters*. You use filters to set the type of files—based on their extensions—that a file chooser will show. File filters are derived from the **FileFilter** class. To add a file filter to a file chooser, you use the **addChoosableFileFilter** method of **JFileChooser**.

Let's look at an example in which I add two new file filters to a file chooser—one filter for .gif files, and one for .java files. These two filters will be supported by the **filter1** and **filter2** classes, so I can use the **addChoosableFileFilter** method to add them to a file chooser, like this:

```
import java.io.*;
import java.awt.*;
import javax.swing.*;
import java.awt.event.*;

/*
<APPLET
    CODE = filechooserfilter.class
    WIDTH = 200
    HEIGHT = 200 >
</APPLET>
*/

public class filechooserfilter extends JFrame implements ActionListener
{
    JFileChooser jfilechooser = new JFileChooser();
    JButton jbutton = new JButton("Display file chooser");
    JTextField jtextfield = new JTextField(20);
```

```
public filechooserfilter()
{
    super();

    Container contentPane = getContentPane();

    contentPane.setLayout(new FlowLayout());

    contentPane.add(jbutton);
    contentPane.add(jtextfield);

    jbutton.addActionListener(this);

    jfilechooser.addChoosableFileFilter(new filter1());
    jfilechooser.addChoosableFileFilter(new filter2());
}

public void actionPerformed(ActionEvent e)
{
    int result = jfilechooser.showOpenDialog(null);

    if(result == JFileChooser.APPROVE_OPTION) {
        jtextfield.setText("You selected " +
            jfilechooser.getSelectedFile().getPath());
    }
}

public static void main(String a[])
{
    JFrame jframe = new filechooserfilter();

    jframe.setBounds(200, 200, 300, 300);

    jframe.setVisible(true);

    jframe.setDefaultCloseOperation(
        WindowConstants.DISPOSE_ON_CLOSE);

    jframe.addWindowListener(new WindowAdapter() {
        public void windowClosing(WindowEvent e)
        {
            System.exit(0);
        }
    });
}
}
```

Table 14.20   Methods of the JFileFilter class.

Method	Does This
abstract boolean accept(File f)	Returns True if the file is accepted by this filter.
abstract String getDescription( )	Returns the description of this filter.

Now I have to create the **filter1** and **filter2** classes. These classes are derived from the abstract **FileFilter** class, and you'll find the methods of this class in Table 14.20.

It's not difficult to implement the methods of the **FileFilter** class; the **accept** method is passed a **File** object (you'll see the **File** class later in this book). It returns True if the file should be displayed (that is, if its extension is one that the filter accepts, or, usually, if the file corresponds to a directory) and false otherwise. The **getDescription** method returns a string that will be displayed in the file chooser to indicate to the user what types of files the filter is for.

The **filter1** class will accept .gif files (described as "Gif Files (*.gif)" in this filter) and directories, and the **filter2** class will filter .java files (described as "Java Files (*.java)" in this filter) and directories. Here's what these classes look like in code:

```
class filter1 extends javax.swing.filechooser.FileFilter
{
    public boolean accept(File fileobj)
    {
        String extension = "";

        if(fileobj.getPath().lastIndexOf('.') > 0)
            extension = fileobj.getPath().substring(
                fileobj.getPath().lastIndexOf('.')
                + 1).toLowerCase();

        if(extension != "")
            return extension.equals("gif");
        else
            return fileobj.isDirectory();
    }

    public String getDescription()
    {
        return "Gif Files (*.gif)";
    }
}
```

```
class filter2 extends javax.swing.filechooser.FileFilter
{
    public boolean accept(File fileobj)
    {
        String extension = "";

        if(fileobj.getPath().lastIndexOf('.') > 0)
            extension = fileobj.getPath().substring(
                fileobj.getPath().lastIndexOf('.')
                + 1).toLowerCase();

        if(extension != "")
            return extension.equals("java");
        else
            return fileobj.isDirectory();
    }

    public String getDescription()
    {
        return "Java Files (*.java)";
    }
}
```

And that's it. The result of this code appears in Figure 14.15, where you can see the .java filter in action. Using filters like this, you can make it easy for the user to search for files of a particular type. This example is a success, and you'll find it in filechooserfilter.java on the CD.

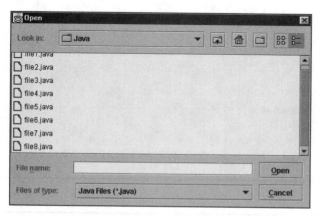

Figure 14.15   Using file filters in a file chooser.

Chapter 15

Swing: Layered Panes, Tabbed Panes, Split Panes, And Layouts

In Depth

In this chapter, we'll take a look at some of the Swing lightweight containers: layered panes, tabbed panes, and split panes. Swing provides a number of light-weight containers, including **JPanel** (which you've already seen), to let programmers manage components in simple ways. Layered panes, first discussed in Chapter 11, let you specify the *layer* of the components you add, making it easy to set the *ZOrder*, or stacking order in the Z axis (which points out of the screen) of components. Tabbed panes let you order components much like adding them to a collection of tabbed file folders, and you can click on the tabs to open each folder. Finally, split panes let you display two components side by side and adjust how much of each one is visible—a technique commonly used to support two views into the same model.

We'll also take a look at layouts in this chapter. You first saw the AWT layouts in Chapter 7. Swing supports all those layouts, and two more: box layouts and over-lay layouts. We'll take a look at these two new layouts in this chapter. Box layouts let you create rows or columns of components. Overlay layouts, as the name im-plies, let you draw overlapping components. Swing also defines the **Box** class, which lets you arrange components using visual constructs such as struts, rigid areas, and glue. We'll see all these in this chapter.

Layered Panes

Layered panes, themselves lightweight containers, are important panes of heavy-weight Swing containers such as **JApplet** and **JFrame**. Layered panes are di-vided into a number of vertical layers that you can work with and that Swing works with as well. This is one of the areas in which the implementation of Swing on top of AWT is not transparent to the programmer, because you can see the layers that Swing uses to display dialog boxes, drag components, pop-up menus, and so on. One of the most popular aspects of the layered pane is that it's home to the content pane.

Tabbed Panes

Dialog boxes that let users choose from many options have come to be organized by tabs as programs have gotten more complex and have offered more options. Setup dialog boxes are customarily implemented this way, organizing program settings into tabs such as Display, User Information, General, Files, and so on. Swing now supports tabbed panes to let you create dialog boxes and programs of this kind. As you might expect, all the Swing capabilities are available here, such as displaying images in the tabs.

Split Panes

Another popular GUI programming technique today is to let the user *split* a view into a model's data, thus creating a new view into that data. Word processors often let users split their presentations into two panes so they can move around in two areas of a document independently. Swing supports split panes to let programs present two components side by side. These components can represent views into the same or separate model data.

Layouts

You first saw the AWT layouts in Chapter 7, and Swing supports those layouts as well as two more: box layouts and overlay layouts. We'll take a look at these two new layouts in this chapter. Of the two, box layouts are the most popular, because they let you arrange components into vertical and horizontal rows and columns, called *boxes*. In fact, Swing also supports a **Box** class that goes further, letting you specify the spacing and arrangement of components, as you'll see. The overlay layout manager lets you overlap components in a well defined way, and although not as common as other layout managers, it has its uses.

That's it for the overview of what's in this chapter. As you can see, there's a lot coming up. It's time to turn to the "Immediate Solutions" section, starting with a look at stacking Swing components.

Immediate Solutions

Understanding Swing Components And ZOrder

"Java's gone all wacky again," says the Novice Programmer. "I drew some components in the same area of my program by mistake, and they actually appeared on top of each other!" You smile and say, "That's perfectly possible. In fact, in Swing, it's not uncommon to overlap or overlay components." The NP says, "Weird!"

When you add lightweight components to a content pane, those components are simply drawn on that pane, so there's nothing to stop you from making those components overlap. That is, as long as you don't use a layout manager—except the overlay layout manager—that would stop overlaying from taking place. When components overlap, their ZOrder becomes important; *ZOrder* represents the relative placement of components along the Z axis, which goes out of the screen. The lightweight components you add first will appear on top of those you add later. You can also add heavyweight AWT components to your program, and those components, which have their own operating system window, usually appear on top of Swing components.

Here's an example in which I remove the default border layout manager from a content pane and add a series of overlapping labels, showing that the first added label will appear on top of the rest. Here's what this looks like in code (note that I add a border to the labels to make the overlapping visible):

```
import java.awt.*;
import javax.swing.*;

/*
<APPLET
    CODE = layered.class
    WIDTH = 350
    HEIGHT = 280 >
</APPLET>
*/

public class layered extends JApplet
{
    JLabel labels[];
```

```
public void init()
{
    Container contentPane = getContentPane();
    contentPane.setLayout(null);

    labels = new JLabel[6];

    labels[0] = new JLabel("Label 0");
    labels[0].setOpaque(true);
    labels[0].setBorder(BorderFactory.createEtchedBorder());
    contentPane.add(labels[0]);

    labels[1] = new JLabel("Label 1");
    labels[1].setOpaque(true);
    labels[1].setBorder(BorderFactory.createEtchedBorder());
    contentPane.add(labels[1]);

    labels[2] = new JLabel("Label 2");
    labels[2].setOpaque(true);
    labels[2].setBorder(BorderFactory.createEtchedBorder());
    contentPane.add(labels[2]);

    labels[3] = new JLabel("Label 3");
    labels[3].setOpaque(true);
    labels[3].setBorder(BorderFactory.createEtchedBorder());
    contentPane.add(labels[3]);

    labels[4] = new JLabel("Label 4");
    labels[4].setOpaque(true);
    labels[4].setBorder(BorderFactory.createEtchedBorder());
    contentPane.add(labels[4]);

    labels[5] = new JLabel("Label 5");
    labels[5].setOpaque(true);
    labels[5].setBorder(BorderFactory.createEtchedBorder());
    contentPane.add(labels[5]);

    for(int loop_index = 0; loop_index < 6; loop_index++) {
        labels[loop_index].setBounds(40 * loop_index, 40
            * loop_index, 100, 60);
    }
}
}
```

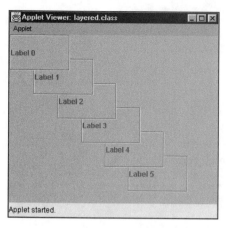

Figure 15.1   Overlapping controls.

The result appears in Figure 15.1. As you can see in the figure, the first label added appears on top of the others. The next added label appears on top of the ones added after it, and so on, thus defining a different ZOrder for each label. This example is in layered.java on the CD.

You might also notice that I used the **setOpaque** method for each label to make sure that the labels underneath it don't show through—take a look at the next topic for more details.

Making Swing Components Transparent

"I just saw the strangest program," the Novice Programmer says. "You could actually see through controls to the ones underneath!" "That's not so strange," you say. "In fact, many Swing programs do that intentionally." "Tell me more!" says the NP.

Because lightweight controls are just drawn in their containers, you can make them *transparent*. When you make a control transparent, it doesn't draw its background when drawn or redrawn, so the controls underneath it can show through. This is a widely used technique that enables you to make it appear as though you're drawing components that are irregular and nonrectangular.

In the previous topic, I wrote an example in which I overlapped opaque Swing labels, but I can also explicitly make those labels transparent. You can set the transparency of Swing components with the **setOpaque** method. Here's how I make the labels in the previous topic's example transparent (in fact, the calls to **setOpaque** are actually unnecessary here because the default setting for labels is to make them transparent):

```
import java.awt.*;
import javax.swing.*;

/*
<APPLET
    CODE = layered.class
    WIDTH = 350
    HEIGHT = 280 >
</APPLET>
*/

public class layered extends JApplet
{
    JLabel labels[];

    public void init()
    {
        Container contentPane = getContentPane();
        contentPane.setLayout(null);

        labels = new JLabel[6];

        labels[0] = new JLabel("Label 0");
        labels[0].setOpaque(false);
        labels[0].setBorder(BorderFactory.createEtchedBorder());
        contentPane.add(labels[0]);

        labels[1] = new JLabel("Label 1");
        labels[1].setOpaque(false);
        labels[1].setBorder(BorderFactory.createEtchedBorder());
        contentPane.add(labels[1]);

        labels[2] = new JLabel("Label 2");
        labels[2].setOpaque(false);
        labels[2].setBorder(BorderFactory.createEtchedBorder());
        contentPane.add(labels[2]);

        labels[3] = new JLabel("Label 3");
        labels[3].setOpaque(false);
        labels[3].setBorder(BorderFactory.createEtchedBorder());
        contentPane.add(labels[3]);
```

15. Swing: Layered Panes, Tabbed Panes, Split Panes, And Layouts

```
        labels[4] = new JLabel("Label 4");
        labels[4].setOpaque(false);
        labels[4].setBorder(BorderFactory.createEtchedBorder());
        contentPane.add(labels[4]);

        labels[5] = new JLabel("Label 5");
        labels[5].setOpaque(false);
        labels[5].setBorder(BorderFactory.createEtchedBorder());
        contentPane.add(labels[5]);

        for(int loop_index = 0; loop_index < 6; loop_index++) {
            labels[loop_index].setBounds(40 * loop_index, 40 *
                loop_index, 100, 60);
        }
    }
}
```

The result appears in Figure 15.2, where you can see the overlapping transparent labels.

Note that there's an explicit way of handling overlapping controls without setting up your own layout manager. This involves a layered pane, which you can use in most programs. See the next topic for the details.

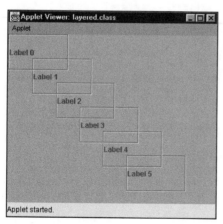

Figure 15.2   Making controls transparent.

Using Layered Panes

"I'm having some trouble," the Novice Programmer says. "I want to let the user drag components around in a Swing container, but when the components are dragged, they go over some other components and *under* others." You smile and say, "That's because you have to keep in mind that components are layered in Swing. You should put what you want to drag in the drag layer." "How's that?" the NP asks.

The layered pane inside the root pane holds the actual components that appear in applets and applications, including menu bars and the content pane. Here's the inheritance diagram for the layered pane class, **JLayeredPane**:

```
java.lang.Object
|____java.awt.Component
      |____java.awt.Container
            |____javax.swing.JComponent
                  |____javax.swing.JLayeredPane
```

JLayeredPane divides its depth range into several different layers. Putting a component into one of those layers makes it easy for you to ensure that components overlap properly, without having to worry about specifying numbers for specific depths:

- *DEFAULT_LAYER*—The standard, bottommost layer, where most components go.
- *PALETTE_LAYER*—The palette layer sits over the default layer and is useful for floating toolbars and palettes.
- *MODAL_LAYER*—The layer used for modal dialog boxes.
- *POPUP_LAYER*—The pop-up layer displays above the dialog layer.
- *DRAG_LAYER*—When you drag a component, assigning it to the drag layer makes sure it's positioned over all other components in the container.

You can use the **JLayeredPane** methods—**moveToFront**, **moveToBack**, and **setPosition**—to reposition a component within its layer. The **setLayer** method can also be used to change the component's current layer. I first covered **JLayeredPane** in Chapter 11, and you'll find the fields of the **JLayeredPane** class in Table 11.10, its constructor in Table 11.11, and its methods in Table 11.12.

Here's an example showing how to add components to a layered pane. In this case, I replace the content pane in an applet with a new layered pane, and I add a label to each standard layer. To set the current layer in the layered pane, I use the

setLayer method, and to specify what layer to use, I use the constants defined in the **JLayeredPane** class, such as **JLayeredPane.PALETTE_LAYER**. One Swing curiosity is that constants such as **JLayeredPane.PALETTE_LAYER** are actually **Integer** objects, not integers. However, methods such as **setLayer** need integers, so you must use the **Integer** class's **intValue** method to convert such constants to values you can use, like this:

```
JLayeredPane.PALETTE_LAYER.intValue()
```

Here's how I add labels to all the layers outlined in the preceding list:

```
import java.awt.*;
import javax.swing.*;

/*
<APPLET
    CODE = layeredpane.class
    WIDTH = 350
    HEIGHT = 280 >
</APPLET>
*/

public class layeredpane extends JApplet
{
    JLayeredPane jlayeredpane = new JLayeredPane();

    JLabel labels[];

    public void init()
    {
        setContentPane(jlayeredpane);
        jlayeredpane.setLayout(null);

        labels = new JLabel[6];

        labels[0] = new JLabel("Content layer");
        labels[0].setBorder(BorderFactory.createEtchedBorder());
        jlayeredpane.setLayer(labels[0],
            JLayeredPane.FRAME_CONTENT_LAYER.intValue());
        jlayeredpane.add(labels[0]);

        labels[1] = new JLabel("Default layer");
        labels[1].setBorder(BorderFactory.createEtchedBorder());
        jlayeredpane.setLayer(labels[1],
```

```
                  JLayeredPane.DEFAULT_LAYER.intValue());
        jlayeredpane.add(labels[1]);

        labels[2] = new JLabel("Palette layer");
        labels[2].setBorder(BorderFactory.createEtchedBorder());
        jlayeredpane.setLayer(labels[2],
            JLayeredPane.PALETTE_LAYER.intValue());
        jlayeredpane.add(labels[2]);

        labels[3] = new JLabel("Modal layer");
        labels[3].setBorder(BorderFactory.createEtchedBorder());
        jlayeredpane.setLayer(labels[3],
            JLayeredPane.MODAL_LAYER.intValue());
        jlayeredpane.add(labels[3]);

        labels[4] = new JLabel("Popup layer");
        labels[4].setBorder(BorderFactory.createEtchedBorder());
        jlayeredpane.setLayer(labels[4],
            JLayeredPane.POPUP_LAYER.intValue());
        jlayeredpane.add(labels[4]);

        labels[5] = new JLabel("Drag layer");
        labels[5].setBorder(BorderFactory.createEtchedBorder());
        jlayeredpane.setLayer(labels[5],
            JLayeredPane.DRAG_LAYER.intValue());
        jlayeredpane.add(labels[5]);


        for(int loop_index = 0; loop_index < 6; loop_index++) {
            labels[loop_index].setBounds(40 * loop_index, 40 *
                loop_index, 100, 60);
        }
    }
}
```

The result of this code appears in Figure 15.3, where you can see what layer is on top of what other layer. Now we've worked with all the standard layers in a layered pane (you can also define your own layers numerically). This example is in layeredpane.java on the CD.

In Figure 15.3, note that the drag layer appears on top, which makes sense because you want components that the user drags to ride above other components. To implement dragging using the drag layer, you add the component you want to

15. Swing: Layered Panes, Tabbed Panes, Split Panes, And Layouts

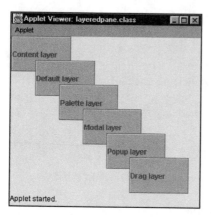

Figure 15.3   Adding components to a layered pane.

drag to the drag layer, make sure the layout manager has been set to null, and then use the component's **setLocation** method to position the component in response to the user's mouse actions.

Creating Tabbed Panes

"Darn," says the Novice Programmer. "My program has so many settings now that the setup dialog box is a little larger than the screen itself." "How much larger?" you ask. "About four times," the NP says. "Ah," you say, "it sounds like it's time to arrange those options using a tabbed pane."

Tabbed panes provide a handy way of arranging a lot of components in a little space. They present the user with a view based on tabbed file folders, and when the user clicks on the various tabs, the corresponding "folders" seems to open, showing a whole new pane of components. Tabbed panes are supported in Swing by the **JTabbedPane** class, and here's the inheritance diagram for that class:

```
java.lang.Object
|____java.awt.Component
        |____java.awt.Container
                |____javax.swing.JComponent
                        |____javax.swing.JTabbedPane
```

You'll find the fields for the **JTabbedPane** class in Table 15.1, its constructors in Table 15.2, and its methods in Table 15.3.

Table 15.1 Fields of the *JTabbedPane* class.

Field	Does This
protected ChangeEvent changeEvent	The **ChangeEvent**.
protected ChangeListener change Listener	The **ChangeListener** added to the model.
protected SingleSelectionModel model	The default selection model.
protected int tabPlacement	Where the tabs are placed.

Table 15.2 Constructors of the *JTabbedPane* class.

Constructor	Does This
JTabbedPane( )	Constructs an empty **TabbedPane**.
JTabbedPane(int tabPlacement)	Constructs an empty **TabbedPane** with the indicated tab placement of **TOP**, **BOTTOM**, **LEFT**, or **RIGHT**.

Table 15.3 Methods of the *JTabbedPane* class.

Method	Does This
Component add(Component component)	Adds a component.
Component add(Component component, int index)	Adds a component at the indicated tab index.
void add(Component component, Object constraints)	Adds a component to the tabbed pane.
void add(Component component, Object constraints, int index)	Adds a component at the indicated tab index.
Component add(String title, Component component)	Adds a component with the indicated tab title.
void addChangeListener(Change Listener l)	Adds a **ChangeListener** to this tabbed pane.
void addTab(String title, Component component)	Adds a tab represented by a title and no icon.
void addTab(String title, Icon icon, Component component)	Adds a tab represented by a title and/or icon, either of which can be null.
void addTab(String title, Icon icon, Component component, String tip)	Adds a tab and tip represented by a title and/or icon, either of which can be null.

(continued)

15. Swing: Layered Panes,
Tabbed Panes, Split Panes,
And Layouts

Table 15.3   Methods of the JTabbedPane class (continued).

Method	Does This
protected ChangeListener create ChangeListener( )	Overrides this method to return a subclass of **ModelListener** or another **ChangeListener** implementation.
protected void fireStateChanged( )	Sends a **ChangeEvent** to each listener.
AccessibleContext getAccessible Context( )	Gets the **AccessibleContext** associated with this **JComponent** .
Color getBackgroundAt(int index)	Gets the tab background color at **index**.
Rectangle getBoundsAt(int index)	Gets the tab bounds at **index**.
Component getComponentAt(int index)	Gets the component at **index**.
Icon getDisabledIconAt(int index)	Gets the tab disabled icon at **index**.
Color getForegroundAt(int index)	Gets the tab foreground color at **index**.
Icon getIconAt(int index)	Gets the tab icon at **index**.
SingleSelectionModel getModel( )	Gets the model associated with this tabbed pane.
Component getSelectedComponent( )	Gets the currently selected component for this tabbed pane.
int getSelectedIndex( )	Gets the currently selected index for this tabbed pane.
int getTabCount( )	Gets the number of tabs in this tabbed pane.
int getTabPlacement( )	Gets the placement of the tabs for this tabbed pane.
int getTabRunCount( )	Gets the number of tab runs currently used to display the tabs.
String getTitleAt(int index)	Gets the tab title at **index**.
String getToolTipText(MouseEvent event)	Gets the tooltip text for the component determined by the mouse event location.
TabbedPaneUI getUI( )	Gets the UI object that implements the look and feel for this component.
String getUIClassID( )	Gets the name of the UI class that implements the look and feel for this component.
int indexOfComponent(Component for the component)	Gets the index of the tab indicated component.
int indexOfTab(Icon icon)	Gets the first tab index with a given icon.
int indexOfTab(String title)	Gets the first tab index with a given title and gets -1 if no tab has this title.
void insertTab(String title, Icon icon, Component component, String tip, int index)	Inserts a component represented by a title and icon.

(continued)

Table 15.3   Methods of the *JTabbedPane* class (continued).

Method	Does This
boolean isEnabledAt(int index)	Gets whether the tab at **index** is currently enabled.
protected String paramString( )	Gets a string representation of this **JTabbedPane**.
void remove(Component component)	Removes the tab that corresponds to the indicated component.
void removeAll( )	Removes all the tabs from the tabbed pane.
void removeChangeListener (ChangeListener l)	Removes a **ChangeListener** from this tabbed pane.
void removeTabAt(int index)	Removes the tab at **index**.
void setBackgroundAt(int index, Color background)	Sets the background color.
void setComponentAt(int index, Component component)	Sets the component at **index** to **Component** .
void setDisabledIconAt(int index, Icon disabledIcon)	Sets the disabled icon at **index** to **Icon**, which can be null.
void setEnabledAt(int index, boolean enabled)	Sets whether the tab at **index** is enabled.
void setForegroundAt(int index, Color foreground)	Sets the foreground color.
void setIconAt(int index, Icon icon)	Sets the icon.
void setModel(SingleSelectionModel model)	Sets the model to be used with this tabbed pane.
void setSelectedComponent (Component c)	Sets the selected component for this tabbed pane.
void setSelectedIndex(int index)	Sets the selected index for this tabbed pane.
void setTabPlacement (int tabPlacement)	Sets the tab placement for this tabbed pane.
void setTitleAt(int index, String title)	Sets the title.
void setUI(TabbedPaneUI ui)	Sets the UI object that implements the look and feel for this component.
void updateUI( )	Called by **UIManager** when the look and feel has changed.

An example will make this clearer. In this case, I create a tabbed pane with three tabs and give each tab its own **JPanel** object with a label in it. The user will be able to move from tab to tab, seeing all the labels in turn. I start by creating the panels I'll use:

```
import java.awt.*;
import javax.swing.*;

/*
<APPLET
    CODE = tabbedpane.class
    WIDTH = 400
    HEIGHT = 200 >
</APPLET>
*/

public class tabbedpane extends JApplet
{
    public void init()
    {
        Container contentPane = getContentPane();

        JPanel jpanel1 = new JPanel();
        JPanel jpanel2 = new JPanel();
        JPanel jpanel3 = new JPanel();

        jpanel1.add(new JLabel("This is panel 1"));
        jpanel2.add(new JLabel("This is panel 2"));
        jpanel3.add(new JLabel("This is panel 3"));
            .
            .
            .
```

Now I'm ready to add these panels to a tabbed pane, so I create a new tabbed pane and use the **addTab** method to add three tabs to it. I pass to **addTab** the captions for each tab, the image icons to use in the tabs, the components to add to each tab (which are usually objects of the **JPanel** class), and a tooltip for each tab, like this:

```
public class tabbedpane extends JApplet
{
    public void init()
    {
        Container contentPane = getContentPane();
```

```
        JTabbedPane jtabbedpane = new JTabbedPane();

        JPanel jpanel1 = new JPanel();
        JPanel jpanel2 = new JPanel();
        JPanel jpanel3 = new JPanel();

        jpanel1.add(new JLabel("This is panel 1"));
        jpanel2.add(new JLabel("This is panel 2"));
        jpanel3.add(new JLabel("This is panel 3"));

        jtabbedpane.addTab("Tab 1",
                    new ImageIcon("tab.jpg"),
                    jpanel1, "This is tab 1");

        jtabbedpane.addTab("Tab 2",
                    new ImageIcon("tab.jpg"),
                    jpanel2, "This is tab 2");

        jtabbedpane.addTab("Tab three",
                    new ImageIcon("tab.jpg"),
                    jpanel3, "This is tab 3");

        contentPane.setLayout(new BorderLayout());
        contentPane.add(jtabbedpane);
    }
}
```

The result appears in Figure 15.4. As you can see in the figure, each tab has its own image and caption, as specified in the **addTab** method. Clicking in a new tab opens a new "folder" with a new label in it. That's all there is to it. This example is in tabbedpane.java on the CD.

You can do more with tabbed panes—you can also specify the placement you want for the tabs, for example. See the next topic for the details.

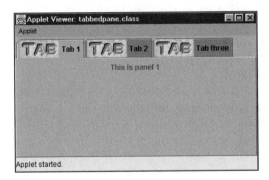

Figure 15.4   Creating a tabbed pane.

15. Swing: Layered Panes,
Tabbed Panes, Split Panes,
And Layouts

Specifying Tab Placement In Tabbed Panes

The Big Boss is looking over your shoulder and says, "No, no, that's all wrong—the tabs should go on the *left* side." "You keep changing your mind," you say. "Are you sure you want the tabs on the left?" "No, no," says the BB, "on the *right* side, like I said."

You can specify where the tabs appear in a tabbed pane—top, bottom, left, or right—using the **setTabPlacement** method. Here's an example showing how that works. In this case, I let the user select the orientation of the tabs in a tabbed pane—left, right, top, or bottom—by clicking a button. Here's the code:

```
import java.awt.*;
import javax.swing.*;
import java.awt.event.*;

/*
<APPLET
    CODE = tabbedpaneorientation.class
    WIDTH = 500
    HEIGHT = 200 >
</APPLET>
*/

public class tabbedpaneorientation extends JApplet implements
    ActionListener
{
    JTabbedPane jtabbedpane = new JTabbedPane(SwingConstants.BOTTOM);
    JButton button1, button2, button3, button4;

    public void init()
    {
        Container contentPane = getContentPane();

        JPanel buttonPanel = new JPanel();

        JPanel jpanel1 = new JPanel();
        JPanel jpanel2 = new JPanel();
        JPanel jpanel3 = new JPanel();

        jtabbedpane.setTabPlacement(JTabbedPane.TOP);

        jtabbedpane.addTab("Panel 1",
                new ImageIcon("tab.jpg"),
                jpanel1, "This is panel 1");
```

```
jtabbedpane.addTab("Panel 2",
            new ImageIcon("tab.jpg"),
            jpanel2, "This is panel 2");

jtabbedpane.addTab("Panel 3",
            new ImageIcon("tab.jpg"),
            jpanel3, "This is panel 3");

button1 = new JButton("Top");
button2 = new JButton("Left");
button3 = new JButton("Right");
button4 = new JButton("Bottom");

buttonPanel.add(button1);
buttonPanel.add(button2);
buttonPanel.add(button3);
buttonPanel.add(button4);

button1.addActionListener(this);
button2.addActionListener(this);
button3.addActionListener(this);
button4.addActionListener(this);

contentPane.setLayout(new BorderLayout());

contentPane.add(jtabbedpane, BorderLayout.CENTER);
contentPane.add(buttonPanel, BorderLayout.SOUTH);
}

public void actionPerformed(ActionEvent e)
{
    if(e.getSource() == button1) {
        jtabbedpane.setTabPlacement(JTabbedPane.TOP);
    }
    else if(e.getSource() == button2) {
        jtabbedpane.setTabPlacement(JTabbedPane.LEFT);
    }
    else if(e.getSource() == button3) {
        jtabbedpane.setTabPlacement(JTabbedPane.RIGHT);
    }
    else if(e.getSource() == button4) {
        jtabbedpane.setTabPlacement(JTabbedPane.BOTTOM);
    }
        jtabbedpane.validate();
    }
}
```

15. Swing: Layered Panes, Tabbed Panes, Split Panes, And Layouts

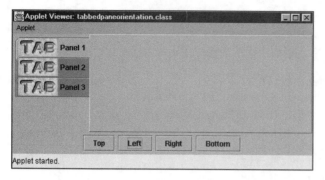

Figure 15.5   Creating a tabbed pane.

The result of this code appears in Figure 15.5. When the user clicks a button, the tabbed pane responds by displaying the tabs in the corresponding orientation, thus allowing the users to customize the tabbed pane as they like. The Big Boss would be proud. This example is in tabbedpaneorientation.java on the CD.

Using Split Panes

The Product Support Specialist is back and unhappy. "About your new word processor program," the PSS says, " users are complaining. When they edit a document more than a thousand pages long and have to refer to another part of the document, it can take a long time to scroll back and forth." "Who's editing documents more than a thousand pages long?" you ask. "How about adding a split pane to the word processor?" the PSS asks.

You can use split panes to display two components side by side, which can include two views into the same model. Using split panes, the user can manage two components, dragging the divider between the components to show more or less of each as needed. Split panes are supported by the **JSplitPane** class, and here's the inheritance diagram for that class:

```
java.lang.Object
|____java.awt.Component
     |____java.awt.Container
          |____javax.swing.JComponent
               |____javax.swing.JSplitPane
```

You'll find the fields of the **JSplitPane** class in Table 15.4, its constructors in Table 15.5, and its methods in Table 15.6.

Table 15.4   Fields of the JSplitPane class.

Field	Does This
static String BOTTOM	Used to add a component at the bottom.
static String CONTINUOUS_LAYOUT _PROPERTY	The bound property name for **continuousLayout**.
protected boolean continuousLayout	Returns True if views are continuously redisplayed while resizing.
static String DIVIDER	Used to add a component that will represent the divider.
static String DIVIDER_SIZE _PROPERTY	The bound property name for border.
protected int dividerSize	The size of the divider.
static int HORIZONTAL_SPLIT	A horizontal split indicates the components are split along the x axis.
static String LAST_DIVIDER _LOCATION_PROPERTY	The bound property for **lastLocation**.
protected int lastDividerLocation	The previous location of the split pane.
static String LEFT	Used to add a component to the left of the other component.
protected Component leftComponent	The left or top component.
static String ONE_TOUCH _EXPANDABLE_PROPERTY	The bound property for **oneTouchExpandable**.
protected boolean oneTouch Expandable	Returns True if the split pane is one-touch expandable.
protected int orientation	Indicates how the views are split.
static String ORIENTATION _PROPERTY	The bound property name for the orientation (horizontal or vertical).
static String RIGHT	Used to add a component to the right of the other component.
protected Component right Component	The right or bottom component.
static String TOP	Used to add a component above the other component.
static int VERTICAL_SPLIT	A vertical split indicates the components are split along the y axis.

Table 15.5   Constructors of the *JSplitPane* class.

Constructor	Does This
JSplitPane( )	Constructs a new **JSplitPane** with two buttons for the components.
JSplitPane(int newOrientation) orientation	Constructs a new **JSplitPane** configured with the indicated and no continuous layout.
JSplitPane(int newOrientation, boolean newContinuousLayout)	Constructs a new **JSplitPane** with the indicated orientation and redrawing style.
JSplitPane(int newOrientation, boolean newContinuousLayout, Component newLeftComponent, Component newRightComponent)	Constructs a new **JSplitPane** with the indicated orientation and redrawing style and with the indicated components.
JSplitPane(int newOrientation, with Component newLeftComponent,) Component newRightComponent	Constructs a new **JSplitPane**, with the indicated orientation and the specified components, that does not perform continuous redrawing.

Table 15.6   Methods of the *JSplitPane* class.

Method	Does This
protected void addImpl(Component comp, Object constraints, int index)	Adds *comp* with the given constraints.
AccessibleContext getAccessible Context( )	Get the **AccessibleContext**.
Component getBottomComponent( )	Gets the component below or to the right of the divider.
int getDividerLocation( )	Gets the location of the divider from the look and feel implementation.
int getDividerSize( )	Gets the size of the divider.
int getLastDividerLocation( )	Gets the last location of the divider.
Component getLeftComponent( )	Gets the component to the left of or above the divider.
int getMaximumDividerLocation( )	Gets the maximum location of the divider from the look and feel implementation.
int getMinimumDividerLocation( )	Gets the minimum location of the divider from the look and feel implementation.
int getOrientation( )	Gets the orientation.
Component getRightComponent( )	Gets the component to the right of or below the divider.
Component getTopComponent( )	Gets the component above or to the left of the divider.
SplitPaneUI getUI( )	Gets the **SplitPaneUI** that's providing the current look and feel.
String getUIClassID( )	Gets the name of the look and feel class that renders this component.

(continued)

Table 15.6   Methods of the *JSplitPane* class (continued).

Method	Does This
boolean isContinuousLayout( )	Returns True if the child components are continuously redisplayed and laid out during user intervention.
boolean isOneTouchExpandable( )	Returns True if the pane provides a UI widget to collapse/expand the divider.
boolean isValidateRoot( )	Returns True if the root validates.
protected void paintChildren (Graphics g)	Paints child components.
protected String paramString( )	Gets a string representation of this **JSplitPane**.
void remove(Component component)	Removes the child component from the pane.
void remove(int index)	Removes the component at the indicated index.
void removeAll( )	Removes all the child components from the receiver.
void resetToPreferredSizes( )	Repositions the **JSplitPane** based on the preferred size of the children.
void setBottomComponent (Component comp)	Sets the component below or to the right of the divider.
void setContinuousLayout(boolean newContinuousLayout)	Determines whether the child components are continuously redisplayed during user actions.
void setDividerLocation(double proportionalLocation)	Sets the divider location as a percentage of the **JSplitPane**'s size.
void setDividerLocation(int location)	Sets the location of the divider.
void setDividerSize(int newSize)	Sets the size of the divider.
void setLastDividerLocation(int new LastLocation)	Sets the last location the divider was at to **newLastLocation**.
void setLeftComponent (Component comp)	Sets the component to the left or above the divider.
void setOneTouchExpandable (boolean newValue)	Determines whether the **JSplitPane** provides a UI widget on the divider for quickly expanding/collapsing the divider.
void setOrientation(int orientation)	Sets the orientation or how the splitter is divided.
void setRightComponent (Component comp)	Sets the component to the right of or below the divider.
void setTopComponent (Component comp)	Sets the component above or to the left of the divider.
void setUI(SplitPaneUI ui)	Sets the look and feel object that draws this component.
void updateUI( )	Called by the **UIManager** when the look and feel has changed.

15. Swing: Layered Panes, Tabbed Panes, Split Panes, And Layouts

I'll put the **JSplitPane** class to use in an example here. In this case, I add two text fields to a split pane. That's easy enough to do—I just create two text fields and a split pane, like this:

```
import java.awt.*;
import javax.swing.*;
import java.awt.event.*;

/*
<APPLET
    CODE = splitpane.class
    WIDTH = 600
    HEIGHT = 200 >
</APPLET>
*/

public class splitpane extends JApplet implements ActionListener
{
    JTextField text1 = new JTextField("Text 1");
    JTextField text2 = new JTextField("Text 2");
    JSplitPane jsplitpane = new JSplitPane(JSplitPane.VERTICAL_SPLIT,
        text1, text2);
        .
        .
        .
```

TIP: If you don't explicitly add components to a split pane, it will display two buttons.

Now I just add the new split pane to the applet's content pane, like this:

```
public class splitpane extends JApplet implements ActionListener
{
    JTextField text1 = new JTextField("Text 1");
    JTextField text2 = new JTextField("Text 2");
    JSplitPane jsplitpane = new JSplitPane(JSplitPane.VERTICAL_SPLIT,
        text1, text2);

    public void init()
    {
        Container contentPane = getContentPane();

        contentPane.add(jsplitpane, BorderLayout.CENTER);
    }
}
```

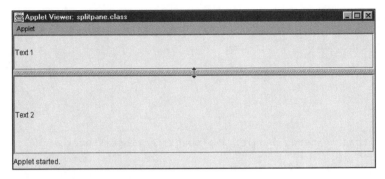

Figure 15.6   Creating a split pane.

That's all it takes. The result of this code appears in Figure 15.6. From now on, the user can adjust the divider between the text fields, showing more or less of each as needed. The split pane will manage the view of each text field from now on. This example is in splitpane.java on the CD.

Making Split Panes One-Touch Expandable

"Take a look at the new split pane I've put in my program," the Novice Programmer says. "That's a good one," you agree, "but why isn't it one-touch expandable?" The NP replies, "Huh?"

Making a split pane one-touch expandable adds small arrow buttons to its divider, which, when clicked, will expand one or the other pane to take up the full split pane. This is a useful mechanism if you want to maximize a component in a split pane, because split panes don't allow components to be reduced below a certain minimum otherwise.

You can make a split pane one-touch expandable with the split pane **setOneTouchExpandable** method. To show you how this works, I'll add a button to the split pane example in the previous topic that, when clicked, will make the split pane one-touch expandable. To add that button, I first create a new panel and add it to the layout of the applet, like this:

```
import java.awt.*;
import javax.swing.*;
import java.awt.event.*;
```

```
/*
<APPLET
    CODE = splitpane.class
    WIDTH = 600
    HEIGHT = 200 >
</APPLET>
*/

public class splitpane extends JApplet implements ActionListener
{
    JButton jbutton1;
    JTextField text1 = new JTextField("Text 1");
    JTextField text2 = new JTextField("Text 2");
    JSplitPane jsplitpane = new JSplitPane(JSplitPane.VERTICAL_SPLIT,
        text1, text2);

    public void init()
    {
        Container contentPane = getContentPane();
        JPanel jpanel = new JPanel();

        jbutton1 = new JButton("Make one-touch expandable");
        jbutton1.addActionListener(this);
        jpanel.add(jbutton1);

        contentPane.add(jsplitpane, BorderLayout.CENTER);
        contentPane.add(jpanel, BorderLayout.SOUTH);
    }

    public void actionPerformed(ActionEvent e)
    {
        if(e.getSource() == jbutton1) {
            jsplitpane.setOneTouchExpandable(true);
        }
    }
}
```

The result of this code appears in Figure 15.7. When the user clicks the button, two arrows appear in the split pane's divider, as you can see in the figure. Now the split pane is one-touch expandable; for example, when the user clicks the up arrow, the bottom text field expands to fill the split pane (except for the divider, which is still visible so the user can click the down arrow to restore the original appearance).

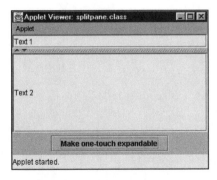

Figure 15.7   Making a split pane one-touch expandable.

Setting Split Pane Orientation

"No, no, no," says the Big Boss impatiently, "we don't want any horizontal splits in split panes. We want *vertical* splits." "OK," you say, "I can do that. When do you want it by?" "Is it done yet?" the BB asks.

You can set the orientation of the divider in a split pane by passing the **setOrientation** method the constant **JSplitPane.HORIZONTAL_SPLIT** or **JSplitPane.VERTICAL_SPLIT**. I'll add this capability to the split pane example from the previous topic with a new button that lets the user specify a horizontal split, like this:

```
import java.awt.*;
import javax.swing.*;
import java.awt.event.*;

/*
<APPLET
    CODE = splitpane.class
    WIDTH = 600
    HEIGHT = 200 >
</APPLET>
*/

public class splitpane extends JApplet implements ActionListener
{
    JButton jbutton1, jbutton2;
    JTextField text1 = new JTextField("Text 1");
    JTextField text2 = new JTextField("Text 2");
    JSplitPane jsplitpane = new JSplitPane(JSplitPane.VERTICAL_SPLIT,
        text1, text2);
```

```
public void init()
{
    Container contentPane = getContentPane();
    JPanel jpanel = new JPanel();

    jbutton1 = new JButton("Make one-touch expandable");
    jbutton1.addActionListener(this);
    jpanel.add(jbutton1);

    jbutton2 = new JButton("Make split horizontal");
    jbutton2.addActionListener(this);
    jpanel.add(jbutton2);

    contentPane.add(jsplitpane, BorderLayout.CENTER);
    contentPane.add(jpanel, BorderLayout.SOUTH);
}

public void actionPerformed(ActionEvent e)
{
    if(e.getSource() == jbutton1) {
        jsplitpane.setOneTouchExpandable(true);
    }
    if(e.getSource() == jbutton2) {
        jsplitpane.setOrientation(JSplitPane.HORIZONTAL_SPLIT);
    }
}
}
```

The result of this code appears in Figure 15.8, and you can see the new horizontally oriented split in the figure.

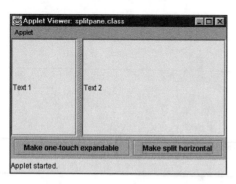

Figure 15.8   Setting split pane orientation.

Setting Split Pane Divider Size

You can set the size of the divider that appears in a split pane using the **setDividerSize** method and passing it a new divider width in pixels. Here's an example in which I add a new button to the example from the previous topic. When the user clicks this button, I get the current divider width with the **getDividerSize** method, add 10 pixels to it, and use the result as the new divider width. Here's what the code looks like:

```
import java.awt.*;
import javax.swing.*;
import java.awt.event.*;

/*
<APPLET
    CODE = splitpane.class
    WIDTH = 600
    HEIGHT = 200 >
</APPLET>
*/

public class splitpane extends JApplet implements ActionListener
{
    JButton jbutton1, jbutton2, jbutton3;
    JTextField text1 = new JTextField("Text 1");
    JTextField text2 = new JTextField("Text 2");
    JSplitPane jsplitpane = new JSplitPane(JSplitPane.VERTICAL_SPLIT,
        text1, text2);

    public void init()
    {
        Container contentPane = getContentPane();
        JPanel jpanel = new JPanel();

        jbutton1 = new JButton("Make one-touch expandable");
        jbutton1.addActionListener(this);
        jpanel.add(jbutton1);

        jbutton2 = new JButton("Make split horizontal");
        jbutton2.addActionListener(this);
        jpanel.add(jbutton2);

        jbutton3 = new JButton("Increase divider size");
        jbutton3.addActionListener(this);
        jpanel.add(jbutton3);
```

15. Swing: Layered Panes, Tabbed Panes, Split Panes, And Layouts

```
        contentPane.add(jsplitpane, BorderLayout.CENTER);
        contentPane.add(jpanel, BorderLayout.SOUTH);
    }

    public void actionPerformed(ActionEvent e)
    {
        if(e.getSource() == jbutton1) {
            jsplitpane.setOneTouchExpandable(true);
        }
        if(e.getSource() == jbutton2) {
            jsplitpane.setOrientation(JSplitPane.HORIZONTAL_SPLIT);
        }
        if(e.getSource() == jbutton3) {
            jsplitpane.setDividerSize(jsplitpane.getDividerSize() + 10);
        }
    }
}
```

The result appears in Figure 15.9. When the user clicks the Increase divider size button, the divider increases in size by 10 pixels each time.

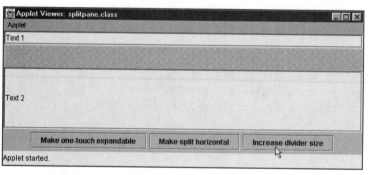

Figure 15.9   Setting a split pane divider's width.

Using The Box Layout Manager

"I've got a lot of drawing tools in my program," the Novice Programmer says, "and I want to arrange them vertically in one tall column. Any suggestions?" "Sure," you say, "use a box layout." "OK," says the NP, "but how?"

Swing introduces two new layouts: the box layout and the overlay layout. We'll take a look at the box layout in this topic and the overlay layout later in this chapter. You can use box layouts to lay components out along the x axis in a row or along the y axis in a column. Here's the inheritance diagram for the **BoxLayout** class, which supports the box layout:

```
java.lang.Object
|_____javax.swing.BoxLayout
```

You'll find the fields of the **BoxLayout** class in Table 15.7, its constructor in Table 15.8, and its methods in Table 15.9.

Table 15.7   Fields of the BoxLayout class.

Field	Does This
static int X_AXIS	Indicates that components should be arranged left to right.
static int Y_AXIS	Indicates that components should be arranged top to bottom.

Table 15.8   The constructor of the BoxLayout class.

Constructor	Does This
BoxLayout(Container target, int axis)	Constructs a box layout manager.

Table 15.9   Methods of the BoxLayout class.

Method	Does This
float getLayoutAlignmentX (Container target)	Gets the alignment along the x axis for the container.
float getLayoutAlignmentY (Container target)	Gets the alignment along the y axis for the container.
void invalidateLayout(Container target)	Indicates that a child has changed its layout information.
void layoutContainer(Container target)	Called by the AWT when the indicated container needs to be laid out.
Dimension maximumLayoutSize (Container target)	Gets the maximum dimensions the target container can use to lay out the components it contains.
Dimension minimumLayoutSize (Container target)	Gets the minimum dimensions needed to lay out the components contained in the indicated target container.
Dimension preferredLayoutSize (Container target)	Gets the preferred dimensions for this layout, given the components in the indicated target container.

Here's an example in which I arrange three panels using box layouts—two verti-cally and one horizontally—and add four text fields to each layout. This simply entails using a new box layout manager in each panel, like this:

```
import java.awt.*;
import javax.swing.*;

/*
<APPLET
    CODE = boxlayout.class
    WIDTH = 250
    HEIGHT = 200 >
</APPLET>
*/

public class boxlayout extends JApplet
{
    public void init()
    {
        Container contentPane = getContentPane();

        JPanel jpanel1, jpanel2, jpanel3;

        jpanel1 = new JPanel();
        jpanel2 = new JPanel();
        jpanel3 = new JPanel();

        jpanel1.setLayout(new BoxLayout(jpanel1, BoxLayout.Y_AXIS));
        jpanel2.setLayout(new BoxLayout(jpanel2, BoxLayout.X_AXIS));
        jpanel3.setLayout(new BoxLayout(jpanel3, BoxLayout.Y_AXIS));

        contentPane.setLayout(new FlowLayout());

        jpanel1.add(new JTextField("Text 1"));
        jpanel1.add(new JTextField("Text 2"));
        jpanel1.add(new JTextField("Text 3"));
        jpanel1.add(new JTextField("Text 4"));

        jpanel2.add(new JTextField("Text 1"));
        jpanel2.add(new JTextField("Text 2"));
        jpanel2.add(new JTextField("Text 3"));
        jpanel2.add(new JTextField("Text 4"));

        jpanel3.add(new JTextField("Text 1"));
        jpanel3.add(new JTextField("Text 2"));
```

```
        jpanel3.add(new JTextField("Text 3"));
        jpanel3.add(new JTextField("Text 4"));

        contentPane.add(jpanel1);
        contentPane.add(jpanel2);
        contentPane.add(jpanel3);
    }
}
```

The result appears in Figure 15.10, where you can see the three box layouts. This example was relatively easy to create and run. It appears in boxlayout.java on the CD.

However, there's more box layout power available—take a look at the **Box** class in the next topic.

Figure 15.10   Creating box layouts.

Using The **Box** Class

"Box layouts are OK," says the Novice Programmer, "but I need more control. For example, I want to space the controls in a row by myself, but I can't do that with a box layout." "Sure you can," you say, "if you use the **Box** class." "How's that?" the NP asks.

The **Box** class uses a box layout and adds methods to let you work with these constructs to extend that layout:

- *Glue*—expands to fill the empty region between components. You can use glue to space components evenly.

- *Struts*—are vertical or horizontal distances that you specify and add to the layout to space components as you want them. Struts are fixed in one dimension and fill the other dimension as needed.

- *Rigid areas*—are rectangular areas that do not resize themselves.

Here's the inheritance diagram for the **Box** class:

```
java.lang.Object
|____java.awt.Component
     |____java.awt.Container
          |____javax.swing.Box
```

You'll find the field of the **Box** class in Table 15.10, its constructor in Table 15.11, and its methods in Table 15.12.

*Table 15.10   The field of the **Box** class.*

Field	Does This
protected AccessibleContext accessibleContext	The **AccessibleContext** .

*Table 15.11   The Constructor of the **Box** class.*

Constructor	Does This
Box(int axis)	Constructs a box.

*Table 15.12   Methods of the **Box** class.*

Method	Does This
static Component createGlue( )	Constructs a glue component.
static Box createHorizontalBox( )	Constructs a box that displays its components from left to right.
static Component createHorizontal Glue( )	Constructs a horizontal glue component.
static Component createHorizontal Strut(int width)	Constructs an invisible, fixed-width strut.
static Component createRigidArea (Dimension d)	Constructs an invisible component that's always the indicated size.
static Box createVerticalBox( )	Constructs a box that displays its components from top to bottom.
static Component createVerticalGlue( )	Constructs a vertical glue component.
static Component createVerticalStrut (int height)	Constructs an invisible, fixed-height strut.
AccessibleContext getAccessible Context( )	Gets the **AccessibleContext**.
void setLayout(LayoutManager l)	Throws an **AWTError** (a **Box** object can only use **BoxLayout**).

Here's an example using the **Box** class. In this case, I use the **createGlue**, **createRigidArea**, **createHorizontalStrut**, and **createVerticalStrut** methods of the **Box** class to create glue, rigid areas, and struts. Those components can be added to box layouts, so I'll create six panels, each with a box layout, and add text areas to the panels using glue, struts, and rigid areas to show how all this works. Here's the code:

```
import java.awt.*;
import javax.swing.*;
import javax.swing.border.*;

/*
<APPLET
    CODE = box.class
    WIDTH = 450
    HEIGHT = 400 >
</APPLET>
*/

public class box extends JApplet
{
    public void init()
    {
        Container contentPane = getContentPane();
        contentPane.setLayout(new FlowLayout());

        JPanel jpanel1 = new JPanel();
        jpanel1.setBorder(
            BorderFactory.createTitledBorder(
                BorderFactory.createEtchedBorder(),
                "Glue"));
        jpanel1.setLayout(new BoxLayout(jpanel1, BoxLayout.X_AXIS));
        jpanel1.add(Box.createGlue());
        jpanel1.add(new JTextField("Text 1"));
        jpanel1.add(Box.createGlue());
        jpanel1.add(new JTextField("Text 2"));
        jpanel1.add(Box.createGlue());
        jpanel1.add(new JTextField("Text 3"));
        jpanel1.add(Box.createGlue());
        contentPane.add(jpanel1);

        JPanel jpanel2 = new JPanel();
        jpanel2.setBorder(
            BorderFactory.createTitledBorder(
                BorderFactory.createEtchedBorder(),
```

```
                "Struts"));
        jpanel2.setLayout(new BoxLayout(jpanel2, BoxLayout.X_AXIS));
        jpanel2.add(new JTextField("Text 1"));
        jpanel2.add(Box.createHorizontalStrut(20));
        jpanel2.add(new JTextField("Text 2"));
        jpanel2.add(Box.createHorizontalStrut(20));
        jpanel2.add(new JTextField("Text 3"));
        contentPane.add(jpanel2);


        JPanel jpanel3 = new JPanel();
        jpanel3.setBorder(
            BorderFactory.createTitledBorder(
                BorderFactory.createEtchedBorder(),
                "Rigid"));
        jpanel3.setLayout(new BoxLayout(jpanel3, BoxLayout.X_AXIS));
        jpanel3.add(Box.createRigidArea(new Dimension(10, 40)));
        jpanel3.add(new JTextField("Text 1"));
        jpanel3.add(Box.createRigidArea(new Dimension(10, 40)));
        jpanel3.add(new JTextField("Text 2"));
        jpanel3.add(Box.createRigidArea(new Dimension(10, 40)));
        jpanel3.add(new JTextField("Text 3"));
        contentPane.add(jpanel3);


        JPanel jpanel4 = new JPanel();
        jpanel4.setBorder(
            BorderFactory.createTitledBorder(
                BorderFactory.createEtchedBorder(),
                "Glue"));
        jpanel4.setLayout(new BoxLayout(jpanel4, BoxLayout.Y_AXIS));
        jpanel4.add(Box.createGlue());
        jpanel4.add(new JTextField("Text 1"));
        jpanel4.add(Box.createGlue());
        jpanel4.add(new JTextField("Text 2"));
        jpanel4.add(Box.createGlue());
        jpanel4.add(new JTextField("Text 3"));
        jpanel4.add(Box.createGlue());
        contentPane.add(jpanel4);

        JPanel jpanel5 = new JPanel();
        jpanel5.setBorder(
            BorderFactory.createTitledBorder(
                BorderFactory.createEtchedBorder(),
                "Struts"));
        jpanel5.setLayout(new BoxLayout(jpanel5, BoxLayout.Y_AXIS));
        jpanel5.add(new JTextField("Text 1"));
```

```
        jpanel5.add(Box.createVerticalStrut(30));
        jpanel5.add(new JTextField("Text 2"));
        jpanel5.add(Box.createVerticalStrut(30));
        jpanel5.add(new JTextField("Text 3"));
        contentPane.add(jpanel5);

        JPanel jpanel6 = new JPanel();
        jpanel6.setBorder(
            BorderFactory.createTitledBorder(
                BorderFactory.createEtchedBorder(),
                "Rigid"));
        jpanel6.setLayout(new BoxLayout(jpanel6, BoxLayout.Y_AXIS));
        jpanel6.add(Box.createRigidArea(new Dimension(40, 60)));
        jpanel6.add(new JTextField("Text 1"));
        jpanel6.add(Box.createRigidArea(new Dimension(40, 60)));
        jpanel6.add(new JTextField("Text 2"));
        jpanel6.add(Box.createRigidArea(new Dimension(40, 60)));
        jpanel6.add(new JTextField("Text 3"));
        contentPane.add(jpanel6);
    }
}
```

The result of this code appears in Figure 15.11. As you can see, using the **Box** class is an easy way to extend box layouts, allowing you to customize the spacing between those components. This example is in box.java on the CD.

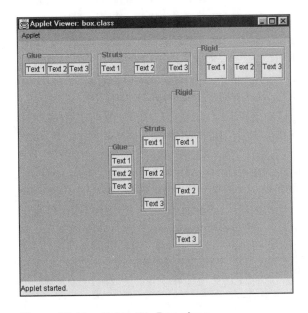

Figure 15.11   Using the **Box** class.

Using The Overlay Layout Manager

"My program is getting pretty cramped," says the Novice Programmer. "Is there any easy way I can overlap the controls?" "Are you sure you want to do that?" you ask. "Sure," says the NP. "Well," you say, "you can remove the layout manager and locate your controls yourself, or you can use the overlay manager." "There's an overlay manager?" the NP asks. "Tell me more!"

You can use the overlay manager to overlay components in Swing. This layout manager is supported by the **OverlayLayout** class. Here's the inheritance diagram for that class:

```
java.lang.Object
|____javax.swing.OverlayLayout
```

You'll find the constructor for this class in Table 15.13 and its methods in Table 15.14.

Table 15.13   The constructor of the _OverlayLayout_ class.

Constructor	Does This
OverlayLayout(Container target)	Constructs an overlay layout manager.

Table 15.14   Methods of the _OverlayLayout_ class.

Method	Does This
void addLayoutComponent (Component comp, Object constraints)	Adds the indicated component to the layout.
void addLayoutComponent(String name, Component comp)	Adds the indicated component to the layout.
float getLayoutAlignmentX (Container target)	Gets the alignment along the x axis for the container.
float getLayoutAlignmentY (Container target)	Gets the alignment along the y axis for the container.
void invalidateLayout(Container target)	Indicates a child has changed its layout-related information, which causes any cached calculations to be flushed.
void layoutContainer(Container target)	Called by the AWT when the indicated container needs to be laid out.
Dimension maximumLayoutSize (Container target)	Gets the maximum dimensions needed to lay out the components.
Dimension minimumLayoutSize (Container target)	Gets the minimum dimensions needed to lay out the components.

(continued)

Table 15.14   Methods of the *OverlayLayout* class (continued).

Method	Does This
Dimension preferredLayoutSize (Container target)	Gets the preferred dimensions for this layout given the components.
void removeLayoutComponent (Component comp)	Removes the indicated component from the layout.

Here's how you use an overlay layout: In this kind of a layout, you add components to a container so that their *alignment points* are at the same location. Each of these components also has an *alignment attribute* between 0.0 and 1.0, which you set with the **setAlignmentX** and **setAlignmentY** methods (the default value is 0.5). These specify where the alignment point is in each dimension. For example, an x alignment attribute of 0.5 refers to the center of the component in the x direction.

After you set the minimum, maximum, and preferred size of the components, the overlay layout manager attempts to resize the components so that their alignment points overlap, and it maintains that overlap, if possible, even when the container is resized.

Let's look at an example to make this clearer. In this case, I overlap two text fields, specify their minimum, maximum, and preferred sizes, and set their alignment points so one component will appear in the upper left and the other in the lower right. Here's the code:

```
import java.awt.*;
import javax.swing.*;

/*
<APPLET
    CODE = overlay.class
    WIDTH = 200
    HEIGHT = 200 >
</APPLET>
*/

public class overlay extends JApplet
{
    public void init()
    {
        Container contentPane = getContentPane();
```

```
         JPanel jpanel = new JPanel();
         jpanel.setLayout(new OverlayLayout(jpanel));
         jpanel.setBackground(Color.white);
         jpanel.setBorder(
             BorderFactory.createTitledBorder(
                 BorderFactory.createEtchedBorder(),
                 "Overlays"));
         JTextField text1 = new JTextField("Text 1");
         JTextField text2 = new JTextField("Text 2");
         text1.setMinimumSize(new Dimension(30, 30));
         text2.setMinimumSize(new Dimension(30, 30));
         text1.setPreferredSize(new Dimension(100, 100));
         text2.setPreferredSize(new Dimension(100, 100));
         text1.setMaximumSize(new Dimension(120, 120));
         text2.setMaximumSize(new Dimension(120, 120));

         text1.setAlignmentX(0.2f);
         text1.setAlignmentY(0.2f);

         text2.setAlignmentX(0.8f);
         text2.setAlignmentY(0.8f);

         jpanel.add(text1);
         jpanel.add(text2);

         contentPane.setLayout(new FlowLayout());
         contentPane.add(jpanel);
    }
}
```

The result appears in Figure 15.12, where you can see the two overlapped text fields. This example is a success, and you'll find it in overlay.java on the CD.

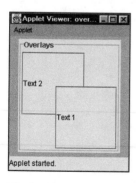

Figure 15.12   Using the overlay layout manager.

Chapter 16

Swing: Menus And Toolbars

In Depth

In this chapter, we'll cover two of the most important Swing components: menus and toolbars. Both of these components are familiar to all GUI users, and you'll see how to work with them in Swing. We'll take a look at what Swing has to offer here in overview first.

Menus

Swing menus provide some substantial improvements over AWT menus, such as the ability to display images, set a menu item's look and feel, and, notably, the ability to display menus in applet windows. Swing menus are supported by the **JMenuBar**, **JMenu**, and **JMenuItem** classes, which support menu bars, menus, and menu items, respectively. As in AWT, Swing menus are actually built using buttons behind the scenes, so you can use action listeners with them.

In this chapter, we'll take a look at what Swing menus have to offer, including creating basic menus, adding images to menus, creating check box and radio button menus and submenus, adding controls such as buttons to menus, creating menu accelerators and mnemonics, and more. We'll also take a look at creating pop-up menus here. Swing menus are more complex and powerful than their AWT counterparts, as you'll see.

Toolbars

Toolbars are popular GUI controls, and they're new in Swing. Like menus, toolbars are built using buttons in Swing. Toolbars provide a bar of buttons that are clickable just like menu items. In fact, toolbars and menus are closely related—you'll often add buttons to toolbars that represent popular menu items to save the user the trouble of opening a menu.

We'll take a look at Swing toolbars, which are supported by the **JToolBar** class, including adding images to toolbar buttons, letting the user align the toolbar against any edge of a window, and adding other controls such as combo boxes to toolbars.

That's it for the overview of what's in this chapter. As you can see, there's a lot coming up. It's time to turn to the "Immediate Solutions" section, which starts with a look at stacking Swing components.

Immediate Solutions

Creating A Menu Bar

The Novice Programmer appears and says, "The Big Boss says I need to add a menu system to my program. How the heck do I do that?" "With three components," you say, "menu bars, menus, and menu items. Get some coffee and we'll start with menu bars." "OK," the NP says.

To add a menu system to a Swing program, you must first create a menu bar, using the **JMenuBar** class. You can add the menu bar to applets or frame windows with the **setJMenuBar** method. Here's the inheritance diagram for the **JMenuBar** class:

```
java.lang.Object
|____java.awt.Component
        |____java.awt.Container
                |____javax.swing.JComponent
                        |____javax.swing.JMenuBar
```

You can find the constructor for **JMenuBar** in Table 16.1 and its methods in Table 16.2.

Table 16.1 The constructor of the JMenuBar class.

Constructor	Does This
JMenuBar( )	Constructs a new menu bar.

Table 16.2 Methods of the JMenuBar class.

Method	Does This
JMenu add(JMenu c)	Appends the indicated menu to the end of the menu bar.
void addNotify( )	Overrides **JComponent.addNotify** to register this menu bar.
AccessibleContext getAccessible Context( )	Gets the **AccessibleContext** associated with this **JComponent**.
Component getComponent( )	Implemented to be a **MenuElement**.

(continued)

Table 16.2   Methods of the *JMenuBar* class (continued).

Method	Does This
Component getComponentAtIndex(int i)	Gets the component at the indicated index.
int getComponentIndex(Component c)	Gets the index of the indicated component.
JMenu getHelpMenu( )	Gets the help menu for the menu bar.
Insets getMargin( )	Gets the margin between the menu bar's border and its menus.
JMenu getMenu(int index)	Gets the menu at the indicated position in the menu bar.
int getMenuCount( )	Gets the number of items in the menu bar.
SingleSelectionModel getSelection Model( )	Gets the model object that handles single selections.
MenuElement[ ] getSubElements( )	Returns the menus in this menu bar.
MenuBarUI getUI( )	Gets the menu bar's current UI.
String getUIClassID( )	Gets the name of the look and feel class that renders this component.
boolean isBorderPainted( )	Returns True if the menu bar's border should be painted.
boolean isManagingFocus( )	Returns True to indicate that this component manages focus events internally.
boolean isSelected( )	Returns True if the menu bar has a component selected.
void menuSelectionChanged(boolean isIncluded)	Implemented to be a **MenuElement** but does nothing currently.
protected void paintBorder(Graphics g)	Paints the menu bar's border.
protected String paramString( )	Gets a string representation of this **JMenuBar**.
void processKeyEvent(KeyEvent e, MenuElement[ ] path, MenuSelection Manager manager)	Implemented to be a **MenuElement** but does nothing.
void processMouseEvent(MouseEvent event, MenuElement[ ] path, Menu SelectionManager manager)	Implemented to be a **MenuElement** but does nothing.
void removeNotify( )	Overrides **JComponent.removeNotify** to unregister this menu bar.
void setBorderPainted(boolean b)	Sets whether the border should be painted.
void setHelpMenu(JMenu menu)	Sets the help menu that appears when the user selects the Help option in the menu bar.
void setMargin(Insets m)	Sets the margin between the menu bar's border and its menus.
void setSelected(Component sel)	Sets the selected component.
void setSelectionModel(Single SelectionModel model)	Sets the model object to handle single selections.

I'll put the **JMenuBar** class to work over the next few topics while creating a basic menu system. The next step is to create menus to add to the menu bar, and I'll do that in the next topic.

Creating A Menu

The Novice Programmer is back and says, "I've created a menu bar, but nothing appears in it—what's up?" You smile and say, "You've got to add menus to it explicitly." "Ah," says the NP, "now you can show me how that works."

You create the menus in a menu bar with the **JMenu** class. Here's the inheritance diagram for that class (note that **JMenu** is actually subclassed from **JMenuItem**, because **JMenuItem**, which is subclassed from **AbstractButton**, can respond to button clicks):

```
java.lang.Object
|____java.awt.Component
      |____java.awt.Container
            |____javax.swing.JComponent
                  |____javax.swing.AbstractButton
                        |____javax.swing.JMenuItem
                              |____javax.swing.JMenu
```

You'll find the field of the **JMenu** class in Table 16.3, its constructors in Table 16.4, and its methods in Table 16.5.

Table 16.3   The field of the JMenu class.

Field	Does This
protected JMenu.WinListener popupListener	The pop-up's window-closing listener.

Table 16.4   Constructors of the JMenu class.

Constructor	Does This
JMenu( )	Constructs a new **JMenu**.
JMenu(String s)	Constructs a new **JMenu** with the string as its text.
JMenu(String s, boolean b)	Constructs a new **JMenu** with the string as its text and specifies whether it has a tear-off menu, as indicated by the boolean value.

Table 16.5 *Methods of the* ***JMenu*** *class.*

Method	Does This
JMenuItem add(Action a)	Constructs a new menu item attached to the indicated **Action** object and appends it to the end of this menu.
Component add(Component c)	Appends a component to the end of this menu.
JMenuItem add(JMenuItem menuItem)	Appends a menu item to the end of this menu.
JMenuItem add(String s)	Constructs a new menu item with the indicated text and appends it to the end of this menu.
void addMenuListener(MenuListener l)	Adds a listener for menu events.
void addSeparator( )	Appends a new separator to the end of the menu.
protected PropertyChangeListener createActionChangeListener (JMenuItem b)	Creates an action change listener.
protected JMenu.WinListener create WinListener(JPopupMenu p)	Creates a window-closing listener.
void doClick(int pressTime)	Programmatically performs a click action.
protected void fireMenuCanceled( )	Notifies all listeners that have registered for this notification that this event occurred.
protected void fireMenuDeselected( )	Notifies all listeners that have registered for this notification.
protected void fireMenuSelected( )	Notifies all listeners that have registered for this notification.
AccessibleContext getAccessible Context( )	Gets the **AccessibleContext**.
Component getComponent( )	Returns the **java.awt.Component** used to paint this **MenuElement**.
int getDelay( )	Gets the suggested delay before the menu's **PopupMenu** is popped up or down.
JMenuItem getItem(int pos)	Gets the **JMenuItem** at the indicated position.
int getItemCount( )	Gets the number of items on the menu, including separators.
Component getMenuComponent(int n)	Gets the component at position **n**.
int getMenuComponentCount( )	Gets the number of components on the menu.
Component[ ] getMenuComponents( )	Gets an array of the menu's subcomponents.
JPopupMenu getPopupMenu( )	Gets the pop-up menu associated with this menu.
MenuElement[ ] getSubElements( )	Gets an array containing the submenu components for this menu component.
String getUIClassID( )	Gets the name of the look and feel class that renders this component.
JMenuItem insert(Action a, int pos)	Inserts a new menu item attached to the indicated **Action** object at a given position.

(continued)

Table 16.5   *Methods of the JMenu class* (continued).

Method	Does This
JMenuItem insert(JMenuItem mi, int pos)	Inserts the indicated **JMenuitem** at a given position.
void insert(String s, int pos)	Inserts a new menu item with the indicated text at a given position.
void insertSeparator(int index)	Inserts a separator at the indicated position.
boolean isMenuComponent (Component c)	Returns True if the indicated component exists in the submenu hierarchy.
boolean isPopupMenuVisible( )	Returns True if the menu's pop-up window is visible.
boolean isSelected( )	Returns True if the menu is currently selected (popped up).
boolean isTearOff( )	Returns True if the menu can be torn off.
boolean isTopLevelMenu( )	Returns True if the menu is a top-level menu.
void menuSelectionChanged (boolean isIncluded)	Called when the menu bar selection changes.
protected String paramString( )	Gets a string representation of this **JMenu**.
protected void processKeyEvent (KeyEvent e)	Overrides **processKeyEvent** to process events.
void remove(Component c)	Removes the component.
void remove(int pos)	Removes the menu item at the given position.
void remove(JMenuItem item)	Removes the indicated menu item.
void removeAll( )	Removes all menu items from this menu.
void removeMenuListener(MenuListener l)	Removes a listener for menu events.
void setAccelerator(KeyStroke key Stroke)	Not defined for **JMenu**.
void setDelay(int d)	Sets the suggested delay before the menu's **PopupMenu** is popped up or down.
void setMenuLocation(int x, int y)	Sets the location of the pop-up component.
void setModel(ButtonModel newModel)	Sets the data model for the menu button.
void setPopupMenuVisible(boolean b)	Sets the visibility of the menu's pop-up portion.
void setSelected(boolean b)	Sets the selection status of the menu.
void updateUI( )	Called by **UIFactory** when the look and feel has changed.

When you've created menus using the **JMenu** class, you populate those menus with menu items (see the next topic for the details).

16. Swing: Menus And Toolbars

Creating A Menu Item

"Alright," says the Novice Programmer, "I've created some menus. How do I add menu items to those menus—with the **JMenuItem** class?" "You've got it," you say.

The actual items in Swing menus are supported by the **JMenuItem** class. Here's the inheritance diagram for that class:

```
java.lang.Object
|____java.awt.Component
     |____java.awt.Container
          |____javax.swing.JComponent
               |____javax.swing.AbstractButton
                    |____javax.swing.JMenuItem
```

You'll find the constructors for the **JMenuItem** class in Table 16.6 and its methods in Table 16.7.

Table 16.6   Constructors of the *JMenuItem* class.

Constructor	Does This
JMenuItem( )	Constructs a **menuItem**.
JMenuItem(Icon icon)	Constructs a **menuItem** with an icon.
JMenuItem(String text)	Constructs a **menuItem** with text.
JMenuItem(String text, Icon icon)	Constructs a **menuItem** with the supplied text and icon.
JMenuItem(String text, int mnemonic)	Constructs a **menuItem** with the indicated text and keyboard mnemonic.

Table 16.7   Methods of the *JMenuItem* class.

Method	Does This
void addMenuDragMouseListener (MenuDragMouseListener l)	Adds a **MenuDragMouseListener**.
void addMenuKeyListener (MenuKeyListener l)	Adds a **MenuKeyListener** to the menu item.
protected void fireMenuDragMouse Dragged(MenuDragMouseEvent event)	Fires the "mouse dragged" event.
protected void fireMenuDragMouse Entered(MenuDragMouseEvent event)	Fires the "mouse entered" event.

(continued)

Table 16.7 Methods of the *JMenuItem* class (continued).

Method	Does This
protected void fireMenuDragMouse Exited(MenuDragMouseEvent event)	Fires the "mouse exited" event.
protected void fireMenuDragMouse Released(MenuDragMouseEvent event)	Fires the "mouse released" event.
protected void fireMenuKeyPressed (MenuKeyEvent event)	Fires the "key pressed" event.
protected void fireMenuKeyReleased (MenuKeyEvent event)	Fires the "key released" event.
protected void fireMenuKeyTyped (MenuKeyEvent event)	Fires the "key typed" event.
KeyStroke getAccelerator( )	Gets the **KeyStroke** that serves as an accelerator for the menu item.
AccessibleContext getAccessible Context( )	Gets the **AccessibleContext** associated with this **JComponent**.
Component getComponent( )	Returns the **java.awt.Component** used to paint this object.
MenuElement[ ] getSubElements( )	Returns an array containing the submenu components for this menu component.
String getUIClassID( )	Gets the name of the look and feel class that renders this component.
protected void init (String text, Icon icon)	Initializes the menu item with the indicated text and icon.
boolean isArmed( )	Determines whether the menu item is armed.
void menuSelectionChanged (boolean isIncluded)	Called by the **MenuSelectionManager** when the **MenuElement** is selected or unselected.
protected String paramString( )	Gets a string representation of this **JMenuItem**.
void processKeyEvent(KeyEvent e, MenuElement[ ] path, Menu Selection Manager manager)	Processes a key event forwarded from the **MenuSelectionManager**.
void processMenuDragMouseEvent (MenuDragMouseEvent e)	Handles mouse drag in a menu.
void processMenuKeyEvent(Menu KeyEvent e)	Handles a keystroke in a menu.
void processMouseEvent(Mouse, Event e, MenuElement[ ] path, Menu Selection Manager manager)	Processes a mouse event forwarded from the **MenuSelectionManager**.

(continued)

Table 16.7   Methods of the JMenuItem class (continued).

Method	Does This
void removeMenuDragMouseListener (MenuDragMouseListener l)	Removes a **MenuDragMouseListener**.
void removeMenuKeyListener (MenuKeyListener l)	Removes a **MenuKeyListener** from the menu item.
void setAccelerator(KeyStroke keyStroke)	Sets the key combination that invokes the menu item's action listeners without navigating the menu hierarchy.
void setArmed(boolean b)	Identifies the menu item as armed.
void setEnabled(boolean b)	Enables or disables the menu item.
void setUI(MenuItemUI ui)	Sets the look and feel object that renders this component.
void updateUI( )	Called by **UIFactory** when the look and feel has changed.

As you can see in Tables 16.6 and 16.7, the **JMenuItem** class has a lot to offer—for example, you can determine whether a menu item is "armed" (that is, it will be selected if the user releases the mouse) with the **isArmed** and **setArmed** methods.

This topic and the previous two have introduced menu bars, menus, and menu items in Swing; I'll put those elements together in the next topic to create a basic menu system.

Creating A Basic Menu System

"I've created a menu bar object, menu objects, and menu item objects," the Novice Programmer says, "but how the heck do I put them all together?" "Sit down and we'll go through it," you say. "It's not that hard."

The previous three topics have introduced the classes needed to create menus in Swing programming: **JMenuBar**, **JMenu**, and **JMenuItem**. I'll put these classes to work in an example that displays two menus—File and Edit—in a menu bar. When the user clicks a menu item, the code will display which item was clicked in the applet's status bar.

I start by creating a menu bar with the **JMenuBar** class. Then, I create the File menu with the **JMenu** class and three menu items for that menu—New, Open, and Exit—using the **JMenuItem** class:

```
import java.awt.*;
import javax.swing.*;
import java.awt.event.*;

/*
<APPLET
    CODE = menu.class
    WIDTH = 350
    HEIGHT = 280 >
</APPLET>
*/

public class menu extends JApplet implements ActionListener
{
    public void init()
    {
        JMenuBar jmenubar = new JMenuBar();

        JMenu jmenu1 = new JMenu("File");

        JMenuItem jmenuitem1 = new JMenuItem("New..."),
            jmenuitem2 = new JMenuItem("Open..."),
            jmenuitem3 = new JMenuItem("Exit");
               .
               .
               .
```

Now I can add the three menu items to the File menu using the **JMenu** class's **add** method. Action listeners are used with menu items, so I'll give each menu item an action command and add an action listener to each item (note menu separators can be added with the **addSeparator** method):

```
    public void init()
    {
        JMenuBar jmenubar = new JMenuBar();

        JMenu jmenu1 = new JMenu("File");

        JMenuItem jmenuitem1 = new JMenuItem("New..."),
            jmenuitem2 = new JMenuItem("Open..."),
            jmenuitem3 = new JMenuItem("Exit");

        jmenu1.add(jmenuitem1);
        jmenu1.add(jmenuitem2);
        jmenu1.addSeparator();
        jmenu1.add(jmenuitem3);
```

```
        jmenuitem1.setActionCommand("You selected New");
        jmenuitem2.setActionCommand("You selected Open");

        jmenuitem1.addActionListener(this);
        jmenuitem2.addActionListener(this);
        .
        .
        .
        .
```

I can create the Edit menu in the same way, giving it three items—Cut, Copy, and Paste:

```
public void init()
    {
        JMenuBar jmenubar = new JMenuBar();

        JMenu jmenu1 = new JMenu("File");

        JMenuItem jmenuitem1 = new JMenuItem("New..."),
            jmenuitem2 = new JMenuItem("Open..."),
            jmenuitem3 = new JMenuItem("Exit");

        jmenu1.add(jmenuitem1);
        jmenu1.add(jmenuitem2);
        jmenu1.addSeparator();
        jmenu1.add(jmenuitem3);

        jmenuitem1.setActionCommand("You selected New");
        jmenuitem2.setActionCommand("You selected Open");

        jmenuitem1.addActionListener(this);
        jmenuitem2.addActionListener(this);

        JMenu jmenu2 = new JMenu("Edit");
        JMenuItem jmenuitem4 = new JMenuItem("Cut"),
            jmenuitem5 = new JMenuItem("Copy"),
            jmenuitem6 = new JMenuItem("Paste");

        jmenu2.add(jmenuitem4);
        jmenu2.add(jmenuitem5);
        jmenu2.add(jmenuitem6);

        jmenuitem4.setActionCommand("You selected Cut");
        jmenuitem5.setActionCommand("You selected Copy");
        jmenuitem6.setActionCommand("You selected Paste");
```

```
        jmenuitem4.addActionListener(this);
        jmenuitem5.addActionListener(this);
        jmenuitem6.addActionListener(this);
            .
            .
            .
    }
```

All that's left is to use the **JMenuBar** class's **add** method to add the menu items to the menu bar and to add the menu bar, itself, to the applet with the **setJMenuBar** method:

```java
public void init()
    {
        JMenuBar jmenubar = new JMenuBar();

        JMenu jmenu1 = new JMenu("File");

        JMenuItem jmenuitem1 = new JMenuItem("New..."),
            jmenuitem2 = new JMenuItem("Open..."),
            jmenuitem3 = new JMenuItem("Exit");

        jmenu1.add(jmenuitem1);
        jmenu1.add(jmenuitem2);
        jmenu1.addSeparator();
        jmenu1.add(jmenuitem3);

        jmenuitem1.setActionCommand("You selected New");
        jmenuitem2.setActionCommand("You selected Open");

        jmenuitem1.addActionListener(this);
        jmenuitem2.addActionListener(this);

        JMenu jmenu2 = new JMenu("Edit");
        JMenuItem jmenuitem4 = new JMenuItem("Cut"),
            jmenuitem5 = new JMenuItem("Copy"),
            jmenuitem6 = new JMenuItem("Paste");

        jmenu2.add(jmenuitem4);
        jmenu2.add(jmenuitem5);
        jmenu2.add(jmenuitem6);

        jmenuitem4.setActionCommand("You selected Cut");
        jmenuitem5.setActionCommand("You selected Copy");
        jmenuitem6.setActionCommand("You selected Paste");
```

16. Swing: Menus And Toolbars

```
    jmenuitem4.addActionListener(this);
    jmenuitem5.addActionListener(this);
    jmenuitem6.addActionListener(this);

    jmenubar.add(jmenu1);
    jmenubar.add(jmenu2);

    setJMenuBar(jmenubar);
}
```

The menu system is now displayed to the user. When the user clicks a menu item, I'll get the item's **action** command and display it in the applet's status bar using the **actionPerformed** method. Here's the code:

```
public void actionPerformed(ActionEvent e)
{
    JMenuItem jmenuitem = (JMenuItem)e.getSource();

    showStatus(jmenuitem.getActionCommand());
}
```

That's all there is to creating a basic menu system. Working with menus in Swing is much like working with them in AWT, with the obvious difference that applet windows in AWT can't display menus. The result of this code appears in Figure 16.1, where you can see the menu system at work. This example—menu.java on the CD—works exactly as designed.

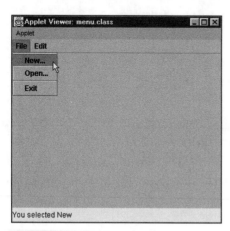

Figure 16.1   A basic menu system.

Adding Images To Menus

The Aesthetic Design Coordinator says, "Your menus are so bland—can't you jazz things up a bit?" "Well," you say, "I can add images to them." "Great!" says the ADC. "I'll send you the images I want to use—they're only 1024 by 1024 pixels." "Um," you say.

It's simple to add images to menus in Swing programming; you just add an icon to the appropriate constructor call. Here's how I add images to each menu item in the example from the previous topic:

```java
import java.awt.*;
import javax.swing.*;
import java.awt.event.*;

/*
<APPLET
    CODE = menuimages.class
    WIDTH = 350
    HEIGHT = 280 >
</APPLET>
*/

public class menuimages extends JApplet implements ActionListener
{

    ImageIcon icon = new ImageIcon("item.jpg");

    public void init()
    {
        JMenuBar jmenubar = new JMenuBar();

        JMenu jmenu1 = new JMenu("File");
        JMenuItem jmenuitem1 = new JMenuItem("New...", icon),
            jmenuitem2 = new JMenuItem("Open...", icon),
            jmenuitem3 = new JMenuItem("Exit", icon);

        jmenu1.add(jmenuitem1);
        jmenu1.add(jmenuitem2);
        jmenu1.addSeparator();
        jmenu1.add(jmenuitem3);
```

16. Swing: Menus And Toolbars

```
                    jmenuitem1.setActionCommand("You selected New");
                    jmenuitem2.setActionCommand("You selected Open");

                    jmenuitem1.addActionListener(this);
                    jmenuitem2.addActionListener(this);

                    JMenu jmenu2 = new JMenu("Edit");
                    JMenuItem jmenuitem4 = new JMenuItem("Cut", icon),
                        jmenuitem5 = new JMenuItem("Copy", icon),
                        jmenuitem6 = new JMenuItem("Paste", icon);

                    jmenu2.add(jmenuitem4);
                    jmenu2.add(jmenuitem5);
                    jmenu2.add(jmenuitem6);

                    jmenuitem4.setActionCommand("You selected Cut");
                    jmenuitem5.setActionCommand("You selected Copy");
                    jmenuitem6.setActionCommand("You selected Paste");

                    jmenuitem4.addActionListener(this);
                    jmenuitem5.addActionListener(this);
                    jmenuitem6.addActionListener(this);

                    jmenubar.add(jmenu1);
                    jmenubar.add(jmenu2);

                    setJMenuBar(jmenubar);
                }

                public void actionPerformed(ActionEvent e)
                {
                    JMenuItem jmenuitem = (JMenuItem)e.getSource();

                    showStatus(jmenuitem.getActionCommand());
                }
            }
```

The result appears in Figure 16.2. As you can see in the figure, each menu item now displays an image.

Figure 16.2   Adding images to menus.

Creating Check Box Menu Items

The Product Support Specialist appears and says, "Users are unhappy with your new program, especially the Make All Text Invisible menu item, because they never know whether that option is enabled until it's too late." "OK," you say, "I'll add a check mark in front of the item to show when it's active."

Swing menus support check box menu items just as AWT menus do. You use the **JCheckBoxMenuItem** class to create check box menu items in Swing programming. Here's the inheritance diagram for this class:

```
java.lang.Object
|____java.awt.Component
     |____java.awt.Container
          |____javax.swing.JComponent
               |____javax.swing.AbstractButton
                    |____javax.swing.JMenuItem
                         |____javax.swing.JCheckBoxMenuItem
```

You'll find the constructors for the **JCheckBoxMenuItem** class in Table 16.8 and its methods in Table 16.9.

Table 16.8   Constructors of the *JCheckBoxMenuItem* class.

Constructor	Does This
JCheckBoxMenuItem( )	Constructs an unselected **checkboxMenuItem**.
JCheckBoxMenuItem(Icon icon)	Constructs an initially unselected **checkboxMenuItem** with an icon.
JCheckBoxMenuItem(String text)	Constructs an initially unselected **checkboxMenuItem** with text.
JCheckBoxMenuItem(String text, selection boolean b)	Constructs a **checkboxMenuItem** with the indicated text and state.
JCheckBoxMenuItem(String text, Icon icon)	Constructs an initially unselected **checkboxMenuItem** with the indicated text and icon.
JCheckBoxMenuItem(String text, and Icon icon, boolean b)	Constructs a **checkboxMenuItem** with the indicated text, icon, selection state.

Table 16.9   Methods of the *JCheckBoxMenuItem* class.

Method	Does This
AccessibleContext getAccessible Context( )	Gets the **AccessibleContext**.
Object[ ] getSelectedObjects( )	Gets an array (length 1) containing the selected check box menu item's label.
boolean getState( )	Gets the selected state of the item.
String getUIClassID( )	Gets the name of the look and feel class that renders this component.
protected String paramString( )	Gets a string representation of this **JCheckBoxMenuItem**.
void requestFocus( )	Overrides **JComponent.requestFocus( )** to prevent grabbing the focus.
void setState(boolean b)	Sets the selected state of the item.

Let's look at an example. In this case, I add four check box items to a menu using the **JCheckBoxMenuItem** class. Here's how I create and add those items to a menu (note that action listeners can be used with check box menu items):

```
import java.awt.*;
import javax.swing.*;
import java.awt.event.*;

/*
<APPLET
    CODE = menucheckbox.class
    WIDTH = 350
    HEIGHT = 280 >
```

```
</APPLET>
*/

public class menucheckbox extends JApplet implements ActionListener
{
    ImageIcon icon = new ImageIcon("item.jpg");

    JCheckBoxMenuItem
        jcheckboxmenuitem1 = new JCheckBoxMenuItem("Item 1", icon),
        jcheckboxmenuitem2 = new JCheckBoxMenuItem("Item 2", icon),
        jcheckboxmenuitem3 = new JCheckBoxMenuItem("Item 3", icon),
        jcheckboxmenuitem4 = new JCheckBoxMenuItem("Item 4", icon);

    public void init()
    {
        Container contentPane = getContentPane();

        JMenuBar jmenubar = new JMenuBar();
        JMenu jmenu = new JMenu("Check Box Menu Items");

        jcheckboxmenuitem1.addActionListener(this);
        jcheckboxmenuitem2.addActionListener(this);
        jcheckboxmenuitem3.addActionListener(this);
        jcheckboxmenuitem4.addActionListener(this);

        jmenu.add(jcheckboxmenuitem1);
        jmenu.add(jcheckboxmenuitem2);
        jmenu.add(jcheckboxmenuitem3);
        jmenu.add(jcheckboxmenuitem4);

        jmenubar.add(jmenu);
        setJMenuBar(jmenubar);
    }
    .
    .
    .
}
```

When the user clicks a check box menu item, I list the state of all four items, like this:

```
public void actionPerformed(ActionEvent e)
{
    showStatus("Item 1:   " + jcheckboxmenuitem1.getState() +
        " Item 2:   " + jcheckboxmenuitem2.getState() +
```

```
            " Item 3:    " + jcheckboxmenuitem3.getState() +
            " Item 4:    " + jcheckboxmenuitem4.getState());
    }
```

That's all it takes. The result of this code appears in Figure 16.3. As you can see in the figure, the check boxes appear as they should in the menu. This example is in menucheckbox.java on the CD.

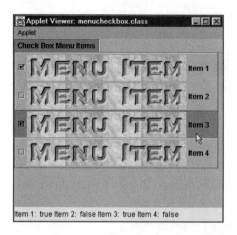

Figure 16.3   Creating check box menu items.

Creating Radio Button Menus

"OK," says the Novice Programmer, "I know you create check box menu items with the **JCheckBoxMenuItem** class. But what about radio buttons? Don't you have to add check box items to a group?" "Almost right," you say. "In fact, you add **JRadioButtonMenuItem** objects to a group."

You use the **JRadioButtonMenuItem** class to create radio button menu items in Swing. Here's the inheritance diagram for this class:

```
java.lang.Object
|____java.awt.Component
      |____java.awt.Container
            |____javax.swing.JComponent
                  |____javax.swing.AbstractButton
                        |____javax.swing.JMenuItem
                              |____javax.swing.JRadioButtonMenuItem
```

You'll find the constructors for the **JRadioButtonMenuItem** class in Table 16.10 and its methods in Table 16.11.

*Table 16.10   Constructors of the **JRadioButtonMenuItem** class.*

Constructor	Does This
JRadioButtonMenuItem( )	Constructs a **JRadioButtonMenuItem**.
JRadioButtonMenuItem(Icon icon)	Constructs a **JRadioButtonMenuItem** with an icon.
JRadioButtonMenuItem(Icon icon, and boolean selected)	Constructs a **JRadioButtonMenuItem** with the indicated image selection state, but no text.
JRadioButtonMenuItem(String text)	Constructs a **JRadioButtonMenuItem** with text.
JRadioButtonMenuItem(String text, boolean b)	Constructs a radio button menu item with the indicated text and selection state.
JRadioButtonMenuItem(String text, Icon icon)	Constructs a **JRadioButtonMenuItem** with the indicated text and icon.
JRadioButtonMenuItem(String text, icon, boolean selected)	Constructs a radio button menu item that has the indicated text, Icon image, and selection state.

*Table 16.11   Methods of the **JRadioButtonMenuItem** class.*

Method	Does This
AccessibleContext getAccessible Context( )	Gets the **AccessibleContext**.
String getUIClassID( )	Gets the name of the look and feel class that renders this component.
protected String paramString( )	Gets a string representation of this **JRadioButtonMenuItem**.
void requestFocus( )	Overrides **Component.requestFocus( )** to not grab focus.

Let's look at an example. In this case, I add four radio buttons to a menu and add an item listener to indicate when each radio button is selected or deselected. Here's what the code looks like:

```
import java.awt.*;
import javax.swing.*;
import java.awt.event.*;

/*
<APPLET
    CODE = menuradiobutton.class
    WIDTH = 350
    HEIGHT = 280 >
</APPLET>
*/
```

```java
public class menuradiobutton extends JApplet implements ItemListener
{
    ImageIcon icon = new ImageIcon("item.jpg");

    JRadioButtonMenuItem
        jradiobuttonmenuitem1 = new JRadioButtonMenuItem("Item 1", icon),
        jradiobuttonmenuitem2 = new JRadioButtonMenuItem("Item 2", icon),
        jradiobuttonmenuitem3 = new JRadioButtonMenuItem("Item 3", icon),
        jradiobuttonmenuitem4 = new JRadioButtonMenuItem("Item 4", icon);

    public void init()
    {
        Container contentPane = getContentPane();

        JMenuBar jmenubar = new JMenuBar();
        JMenu jmenu = new JMenu("Radio Button Menu Items");

        jmenu.add(jradiobuttonmenuitem1);
        jmenu.add(jradiobuttonmenuitem2);
        jmenu.add(jradiobuttonmenuitem3);
        jmenu.add(jradiobuttonmenuitem4);

        ButtonGroup group = new ButtonGroup();
        group.add(jradiobuttonmenuitem1);
        group.add(jradiobuttonmenuitem2);
        group.add(jradiobuttonmenuitem3);
        group.add(jradiobuttonmenuitem4);

        jradiobuttonmenuitem1.addItemListener(this);
        jradiobuttonmenuitem2.addItemListener(this);
        jradiobuttonmenuitem3.addItemListener(this);
        jradiobuttonmenuitem4.addItemListener(this);

        jmenubar.add(jmenu);
        setJMenuBar(jmenubar);
    }

    public void itemStateChanged(ItemEvent e)
    {
        JMenuItem jmenuitem = (JMenuItem) e.getSource();
        String itemtext = jmenuitem.getText();

        if(e.getStateChange() == ItemEvent.SELECTED)
            itemtext += " was selected";
```

16. Swing: Menus And Toolbars

```
        else
            itemtext += " was deselected";

        showStatus(itemtext);
    }
}
```

The result of this code appears in Figure 16.4, where you can see the radio buttons in the menu at work. When the user clicks on a radio button, this applet indicates which one was selected in the status bar. This example—menuradiobutton.java on the CD—is a success.

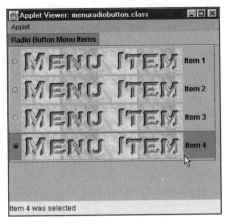

Figure 16.4   Creating radio button menu items.

Creating Submenus

"My menus are getting too big," the Novice Programmer says. "I want to let the user select the drawing color in my program by selecting menu items, but all the colors are crowding out the other items in the menu." "You should try putting all the colors into a submenu," you say. "How many colors do you want to display?" "About 3,000," says the NP. You say, "Uh-oh."

Submenus, also called *cascading menus*, are menus you open from other menus. Swing indicates that a menu item is actually a submenu by adding a clickable arrow to the right of the menu item; when the user clicks the arrow, the submenu opens.

You can create submenus menus easily in Swing. All you do is create a new menu, add items to the menu, and then add the menu, itself, as an item in another menu.

Here's an example to make this clearer. In this case, I add a submenu to a menu and give the submenu four items. Here's what this looks like in code:

```java
import java.awt.*;
import javax.swing.*;
import java.awt.event.*;

/*
<APPLET
    CODE = submenus.class
    WIDTH = 350
    HEIGHT = 280 >
</APPLET>
*/

public class submenus extends JApplet
{

    public void init()
    {
        JMenuBar jmenubar = new JMenuBar();

        JMenu jmenu = new JMenu("Sub Menus", true);
        JMenu jsubmenu = new JMenu("Cascading Menu", true);

        jmenu.add("Item 1");
        jmenu.add("Item 2");
        jmenu.add("Item 3");
        jmenu.add("Item 4");

        jsubmenu.add("Sub Item 1");
        jsubmenu.add("Sub Item 2");
        jsubmenu.add("Sub Item 3");
        jsubmenu.add("Sub Item 4");

        jmenu.add(jsubmenu);

        jmenubar.add(jmenu);

        setJMenuBar(jmenubar);
    }
}
```

The result of this code appears in Figure 16.5. As you can see, the submenu opens when the user selects the corresponding menu item. This example is in submenus.java on the CD.

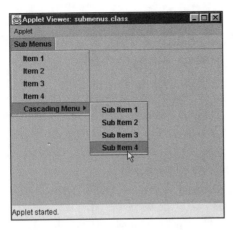

Figure 16.5   Creating submenus.

Creating Menu Accelerators And Mnemonics

"Say," says the Programming Correctness Czar, "what about those menu items I sometimes see that have keyboard shortcuts? Bet you can't do that in Java." "Sure can," you say, "with menu mnemonics and accelerators."

Menu *mnemonics* and *accelerators* both provide keyboard access to menu items. Mnemonics are represented by underlined characters in the caption of a menu or menu item. When the user presses the meta key for the system (such as the Alt key in Windows) and the mnemonic key, the menu item is triggered. You set a menu or menu item's mnemonic with the **setMnemonic** method.

Accelerators are much like mnemonics, except you specify the actual keystrokes involved to trigger a menu item, such as F1, Ctrl+X, and so on (the meta key isn't used in menu accelerators unless you specify that it should be). You can add an accelerator to a menu item (not menus) with the **setAccelerator** method, which takes an object of the **KeyStroke** class that defines the keystroke you want to use as the accelerator. Here's the inheritance diagram for the **KeyStroke** class:

```
java.lang.Object
|____javax.swing.KeyStroke
```

You can find the methods of the **KeyStroke** class in Table 16.12.

You can use the virtual key constants defined in the **KeyEvent** class—**KeyEvent.VK_A, KeyEvent.VK_ENTER,** and **KeyEvent.VK_TAB**—to specify

Table 16.12   Methods of the KeyStroke class.

Method	Does This
boolean equals(Object anObject)	Returns True if this object is identical to the indicated object.
char getKeyChar( )	Gets the character defined by this **KeyStroke** object.
int getKeyCode( )	Gets the numeric keycode defined by this **KeyStroke** object.
static KeyStroke getKeyStroke (char keyChar)	Returns a shared instance of a keystroke that's activated when the key is pressed.
static KeyStroke getKeyStroke(char keyChar, boolean onKeyRelease)	Deprecated. Use **getKeyStroke(char)**.
static KeyStroke getKeyStroke(int key Code, int modifiers)	Returns a shared instance of a keystroke given a char code and a set of modifiers. The key is activated when it's pressed.
static KeyStroke getKeyStroke(int key Code, int modifiers, boolean onKey Release)	Gets a shared instance of a keystroke given a numeric keycode and a set of modifiers.
static KeyStroke getKeyStroke (String s)	Parses a string and returns a **KeyStroke**.
static KeyStroke getKeyStrokeFor Event(KeyEvent anEvent)	Returns a keystroke from an event.
int getModifiers( )	Gets the modifier keys defined by this **KeyStroke** object.
int hashCode( )	Gets a numeric value for this object as the index value in a hashtable.
boolean isOnKeyRelease( )	Returns True if this keystroke is active upon key release.
String toString( )	Gets a string that displays and identifies this object's properties.

the key code when creating a **KeyStroke** object. The modifiers you can specify can be any combination of the following:

- **Event.SHIFT_MASK (= 1)**
- **Event.CTRL_MASK (= 2)**
- **Event.META_MASK (= 4)**
- **Event.ALT_MASK (= 8)**

I'll put this together in an example. In this case, I add a mnemonic, the letter *N*, to the New item in the File menu and give it the accelerator Ctrl+N. Here's how that looks in code:

```
import java.awt.*;
import javax.swing.*;
import java.awt.event.*;
```

```
/*
<APPLET
    CODE = menuaccelerator.class
    WIDTH = 350
    HEIGHT = 280 >
</APPLET>
*/

public class menuaccelerator extends JApplet implements ActionListener
{
    public void init()
    {
        Container contentPane = getContentPane();

        JMenuBar jmenubar = new JMenuBar();
        JMenu jmenu = new JMenu("File");
        JMenuItem jmenuitem = new JMenuItem("New...");

        jmenu.add(jmenuitem);
        jmenu.add("Open ...");
        jmenu.addSeparator();
        jmenu.add("Exit");

        jmenuitem.setMnemonic(KeyEvent.VK_N);

        KeyStroke keystroke = KeyStroke.getKeyStroke(KeyEvent.VK_N,
            Event.CTRL_MASK);
        jmenuitem.setAccelerator(keystroke);

        jmenuitem.addActionListener(this);

        jmenubar.add(jmenu);
        setJMenuBar(jmenubar);
    }

    public void actionPerformed(ActionEvent e)
    {
        showStatus("You selected the New item.");
    }
}
```

The result is shown in Figure 16.6, where you see both the mnemonic (the underlined *N* in the New menu item) and the accelerator (Ctrl+N). Providing mnemonics and accelerators like these can speed things up for users who don't want to switch from the keyboard to the mouse and back again. This example is in menuaccelerator.java on the CD.

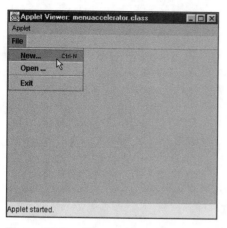

Figure 16.6   Menu mnemonics and accelerators.

Enabling/Disabling Menu Items And Changing Captions At Runtime

"That darn Johnson," the Novice Programmer says, "clicked the wrong option in my program at the wrong time, which made my code try to check email when it wasn't even connected to the Internet!" "Darn that Johnson," you say. "How about disabling menu items when they're not appropriate?" "Perfect!" says the NP.

You can enable and disable menu items with the **setEnabled** method; when a menu item is disabled, it appears dimmed and cannot be clicked. Here's a quick example in which I let the user disable a menu item in an applet's Edit menu. To do that, I add two items to the Edit menu: Disable bottom item and Enable bottom item. When the user clicks Disable bottom item, I disable a third menu item in the Edit menu and switch its caption to "Disabled item" with the **setText** method; when the user clicks Enable bottom item, I enable the third item and switch its caption to "Enabled item". Here's what this looks like in code:

```
import java.awt.*;
import javax.swing.*;
import java.awt.event.*;

/*
<APPLET
    CODE = menudisable.class
    WIDTH = 350
    HEIGHT = 280 >
</APPLET>
*/
```

```java
public class menudisable extends JApplet implements ActionListener
{
    JMenuBar jmenubar = new JMenuBar();

    JMenu jmenu1 = new JMenu("File");
    JMenu jmenu2 = new JMenu("Edit");

    JMenuItem jmenuitem1 = new JMenuItem("New..."),
        jmenuitem2 = new JMenuItem("Open..."),
        jmenuitem3 = new JMenuItem("Exit"),
        jmenuitem4 = new JMenuItem("Disable bottom item"),
        jmenuitem5 = new JMenuItem("Enable bottom item"),
        jmenuitem6 = new JMenuItem("Enabled item");

    public void init()
    {
        jmenu1.add(jmenuitem1);
        jmenu1.add(jmenuitem2);
        jmenu1.addSeparator();
        jmenu1.add(jmenuitem3);

        jmenuitem1.setActionCommand("You selected New");
        jmenuitem2.setActionCommand("You selected Open");

        jmenuitem1.addActionListener(this);
        jmenuitem2.addActionListener(this);

        jmenu2.add(jmenuitem4);
        jmenu2.add(jmenuitem5);
        jmenu2.add(jmenuitem6);

        jmenuitem4.setActionCommand("You selected Cut");
        jmenuitem5.setActionCommand("You selected Copy");

        jmenuitem4.addActionListener(this);
        jmenuitem5.addActionListener(this);

        jmenubar.add(jmenu1);
        jmenubar.add(jmenu2);

        setJMenuBar(jmenubar);
    }

    public void actionPerformed(ActionEvent e)
    {
```

16. Swing: Menus
And Toolbars

```
        JMenuItem jmenuitem = (JMenuItem)e.getSource();
        if(jmenuitem == jmenuitem4) {
            jmenuitem6.setText("Disabled item");
            jmenuitem6.setEnabled(false);
        }
        if(jmenuitem == jmenuitem5) {
            jmenuitem6.setText("Enabled item");
            jmenuitem6.setEnabled(true);
        }
    }
}
```

You can see the result of this code in Figure 16.7. When the user selects the items in the Edit menu, the bottom item in that menu is enabled or disabled accordingly, and its caption is changed to match. That's all there is to it. This example is in menudisabled.java on the CD.

TIP: You shouldn't disable too many menu items at once—doing so gives your program an inaccessible feel.

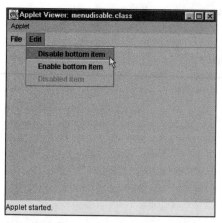

Figure 16.7   Disabling menu items.

Adding And Removing Menu Items At Runtime

The Big Boss says, "We're basing the options available in our new program on the user's ability to pay." You say, "What?" "After we've determined how much money the user has, we'll enable the appropriate number of menu items." You say, "What?"

You can add menu items to menus at runtime with the **add** method and remove them with the **remove** method. Here's an example in which I add a new menu item to a menu when the user clicks Add item, and I remove it when the user clicks Remove item. Here's what the code looks like:

```
import java.awt.*;
import javax.swing.*;
import java.awt.event.*;

/*
<APPLET
    CODE = menuupdate.class
    WIDTH = 350
    HEIGHT = 280 >
</APPLET>
*/

public class menuupdate extends JApplet implements ActionListener
{
    JMenuBar jmenubar = new JMenuBar();

    JMenu jmenu1 = new JMenu("File");
    JMenu jmenu2 = new JMenu("Edit");

    JMenuItem jmenuitem1 = new JMenuItem("New..."),
        jmenuitem2 = new JMenuItem("Open..."),
        jmenuitem3 = new JMenuItem("Exit"),
        jmenuitem4 = new JMenuItem("Add item"),
        jmenuitem5 = new JMenuItem("Remove item"),
        jmenuitem6 = new JMenuItem("New item");

    public void init()
    {
        jmenu1.add(jmenuitem1);
        jmenu1.add(jmenuitem2);
        jmenu1.addSeparator();
        jmenu1.add(jmenuitem3);

        jmenuitem1.setActionCommand("You selected New");
        jmenuitem2.setActionCommand("You selected Open");

        jmenuitem1.addActionListener(this);
        jmenuitem2.addActionListener(this);

        jmenu2.add(jmenuitem4);
        jmenu2.add(jmenuitem5);
```

```
            jmenuitem4.setActionCommand("You selected Cut");
            jmenuitem5.setActionCommand("You selected Copy");

            jmenuitem4.addActionListener(this);
            jmenuitem5.addActionListener(this);

            jmenubar.add(jmenu1);
            jmenubar.add(jmenu2);

            setJMenuBar(jmenubar);
        }

        public void actionPerformed(ActionEvent e)
        {
            JMenuItem jmenuitem = (JMenuItem)e.getSource();
            if(jmenuitem == jmenuitem4) {
                jmenu2.add(jmenuitem6);
            }
            if(jmenuitem == jmenuitem5) {
                jmenu2.remove(jmenuitem6);
            }
        }
    }
```

The result of this code appears in Figure 16.8, where you can see the new item added when the user clicks Add item. The user can remove the new item by clicking Remove item. Note that you can create new menu items on the fly with the **new** operator, and you can add as many menu items to your menus as you like at runtime. This example is in menuupdate.java on the CD.

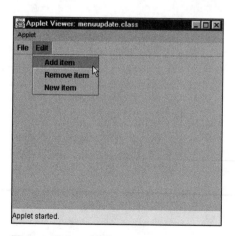

Figure 16.8   Adding and removing menu items at runtime.

Adding Buttons And Other Controls To Menus

You can add controls such as buttons to Swing menus. In fact, doing so is easy; you just use the **JMenu** class's **add** method. For example, here's how I add a **JButton** object to a menu, making the code display a message when the user clicks the button:

```java
import java.awt.*;
import javax.swing.*;
import java.awt.event.*;

/*
<APPLET
    CODE = menucontrols.class
    WIDTH = 350
    HEIGHT = 280 >
</APPLET>
*/

public class menucontrols extends JApplet implements ActionListener
{
    public void init()
    {
        JMenuBar jmenubar = new JMenuBar();

        JMenu jmenu1 = new JMenu("File");
        JMenuItem jmenuitem1 = new JMenuItem("New..."),
            jmenuitem2 = new JMenuItem("Open..."),
            jmenuitem3 = new JMenuItem("Exit");
        JButton jbutton = new JButton("Click Me!");
        jbutton.setActionCommand("You clicked the button");
        jbutton.addActionListener(this);

        jmenu1.add(jmenuitem1);
        jmenu1.add(jmenuitem2);
        jmenu1.addSeparator();
        jmenu1.add(jbutton);
        jmenu1.addSeparator();
        jmenu1.add(jmenuitem3);

        JMenu jmenu2 = new JMenu("Edit");
        JMenuItem jmenuitem4 = new JMenuItem("Cut"),
            jmenuitem5 = new JMenuItem("Copy"),
            jmenuitem6 = new JMenuItem("Paste");
```

```
                    jmenu2.add(jmenuitem4);
                    jmenu2.add(jmenuitem5);
                    jmenu2.add(jmenuitem6);

                    jmenubar.add(jmenu1);
                    jmenubar.add(jmenu2);

                    setJMenuBar(jmenubar);
        }

        public void actionPerformed(ActionEvent e)
        {
            JButton jbutton = (JButton)e.getSource();
            showStatus(jbutton.getActionCommand());
        }
}
```

The result of this code appears in Figure 16.9. As you can see in the figure, I've added a completely functional button to the File menu of the applet. This example is in menucontrols.java on the CD.

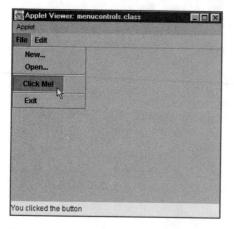

Figure 16.9   Adding a button to a menu.

Creating Pop-up Menus

The Big Boss is annoyed and says, "All these new features to keep up with, all these programmers to hire! The expense! Now it's pop-up menus, no less!" "That's OK," you say, "I can add those to our programs if I just put in a little overtime." The BB yells, "The expense! The expense!"

Pop-up menus are those menus the user can display by clicking the mouse (usually the right mouse button) when it's positioned over a component. In Swing, pop-up menus are supported by the (you guessed it) **JPopupMenu** class. Here's the inheritance diagram for that class:

```
java.lang.Object
|____java.awt.Component
      |____java.awt.Container
            |____javax.swing.JComponent
                  |____javax.swing.JPopupMenu
```

You'll find the constructors for the **JPopupMenu** class in Table 16.13 and its methods in Table 16.14.

Table 16.13   Constructors of the JPopupMenu class.

Constructor	Does This
JPopupMenu( )	Constructs a **JPopupMenu**.
JPopupMenu(String label)	Constructs a **JPopupMenu** with the indicated title.

Table 16.14   Methods of the JPopupMenu class.

Method	Does This
JMenuItem add(Action a)	Appends a new menu item to the end of the menu, which initiates the indicated action.
JMenuItem add(JMenuItem menuItem)	Appends the indicated menu item.
JMenuItem add(String s)	Constructs a new item with the indicated text and appends it to the end of the menu.
void addPopupMenuListener (PopupMenuListener l)	Adds a **PopupMenu** listener.
void addSeparator( )	Appends a new separator at the end of the menu.
protected PropertyChangeListener createActionChangeListener (JMenuItem b)	Creates an action-changed listener.
protected void firePopupMenu Canceled( )	Informs listeners that this pop-up menu is canceled.
protected void firePopupMenuWill BecomeInvisible( )	Informs **PopupMenuListeners** that this pop-up menu will become invisible.
protected void firePopupMenuWill BecomeVisible( )	Informs **PopupMenuListeners** that this pop-up menu will become visible.

(continued)

16. Swing: Menus And Toolbars

Table 16.14   Methods of the JPopupMenu class (continued).

Method	Does This
AccessibleContext getAccessible Context( )	Gets the **AccessibleContext**.
Component getComponent( )	Gets the **java.awt.Component** used to paint the receiving element.
Component getComponent AtIndex(int i)	Gets the component at the indicated index.
int getComponentIndex(Component c)	Gets the index of the indicated component.
static boolean getDefaultLightWeight PopupEnabled( )	Returns the default value for the **lightWeightPopupEnabled** property.
Component getInvoker( )	Gets the component that's the "invoker" of this pop-up menu (that is, the component in which the pop-up menu is to be displayed).
String getLabel( )	Gets the pop-up menu's label.
Insets getMargin( )	Gets the margin between the pop-up menu's border and its contained components.
SingleSelectionModel getSelection Model( )	Gets the model object that handles single selections.
MenuElement[ ] getSubElements( )	Should return an array containing the subelements.
PopupMenuUI getUI( )	Gets the look and feel object that renders this component.
String getUIClassID( )	Gets the name of the look and feel class that renders this component.
void insert(Action a, int index)	Inserts a menu item for the indicated **Action** object at a given position.
void insert(Component component, int index)	Inserts the indicated component into the menu at a given position.
boolean isBorderPainted( )	Checks whether the border should be painted.
boolean isLightWeightPopupEnabled( )	Returns True if lightweight pop-ups are in use and False if heavy weight pop-ups are in use.
boolean isVisible( )	Returns True if the pop-up menu is visible.
void menuSelectionChanged(boolean isIncluded)	Called when the menu selection is changed.
void pack( )	Lays out the container so that it uses the minimum space to display its contents.
protected void paintBorder(Graphics g)	Paints the pop-up menu's border.
protected String paramString( )	Gets a string representation of this **JPopupMenu**.

(continued)

Table 16.14   Methods of the *JPopupMenu* class (continued).

Method	Does This
void processKeyEvent(KeyEvent e, MenuElement[ ] path, MenuSelection Manager manager)	Processes a key event.
void processMouseEvent(MouseEvent event, MenuElement[ ] path, MenuSelectionManager manager)	Processes a mouse event.
void remove(Component comp)	Removes the indicated component.
void remove(int pos)	Removes the component at the indicated index.
void removePopupMenuListener (PopupMenuListener l)	Removes a **PopupMenu** listener.
void setBorderPainted(boolean b)	Sets whether the border should be painted.
static void setDefaultLightWeight PopupEnabled(boolean aFlag)	Sets the default value for the **lightWeightPopupEnabled** property.
void setInvoker(Component invoker)	Sets the invoker of this pop-up menu.
void setLabel(String label)	Sets the pop-up menu's label.
void setLightWeightPopupEnabled (boolean aFlag)	Chooses whether to use a lightweight pop-up if it fits.
void setLocation(int x, int y)	Sets the location of the upper-left corner of the pop-up menu.
void setPopupSize(Dimension d)	Sets the size of the pop-up using a **Dimension** object.
void setPopupSize(int width, int height)	Sets the size of the pop-up.
void setSelected(Component sel)	Sets the currently selected component.
void setSelectionModel(Single SelectionModel model)	Sets the model object to handle single selections.
void setUI(PopupMenuUI ui)	Sets the look and feel object that draws this component.
void setVisible(boolean b)	Sets the visibility of the menu.
void show(Component invoker, int x, int y)	Displays the pop-up menu.
void updateUI( )	Called by **UIFactory** when the look and feel has changed.

You create pop-up menus, add new items to them with the **add** method, and then display them with the **show** method.

Let's look at an example. In this case, I create a pop-up menu with three items in it—Cut, Copy, and Paste—which will appear when the user right-clicks the mouse. Pop-up menus need to be the child of some other component, so I'll add a label to an applet and cover the applet with the label. Here's what creating the label and the pop-up menu looks like in code:

```
import java.awt.*;
import javax.swing.*;
import java.awt.event.*;

/*
<APPLET
    CODE = popup.class
    WIDTH = 350
    HEIGHT = 280 >
</APPLET>
*/

public class popup extends JApplet implements MouseListener
{
    JLabel jlabel = new JLabel("Right click me!", JLabel.CENTER);
    JPopupMenu jpopupmenu = new JPopupMenu();

    public void init()
    {
        Container contentPane = getContentPane();

        jpopupmenu.add(new JMenuItem("Cut", new ImageIcon("item.jpg")));
        jpopupmenu.add(new JMenuItem("Copy", new ImageIcon("item.jpg")));
        jpopupmenu.add(new JMenuItem("Paste", new ImageIcon("item.jpg")));

        jlabel.addMouseListener(this);
        contentPane.add(jlabel);
    }
    .
    .
    .
}
```

Now when the user clicks a mouse button, I can check whether the right mouse button was clicked by using the **MouseEvent** class's **getModifiers** method and the mask for the right mouse button—**InputEvent.BUTTON3_MASK**. If the right mouse button was indeed clicked, I'll show the new pop-up menu at the mouse location, like this:

```
public void mousePressed (MouseEvent e)
{
    if((e.getModifiers() & InputEvent.BUTTON3_MASK) ==
        InputEvent.BUTTON3_MASK)
```

```
        jpopupmenu.show(jlabel, e.getX(), e.getY());
    }

    public void mouseClicked(MouseEvent e) {}
    public void mouseReleased(MouseEvent e) {}
    public void mouseEntered(MouseEvent e) {}
    public void mouseExited(MouseEvent e) {}
```

The result appears in Figure 16.10. When the user right-clicks the label in the applet, the pop-up menu appears at the mouse location, as shown in the figure. That's all there is to displaying pop-up menus. This example is in popup.java on the CD.

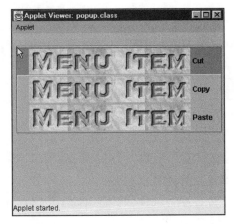

Figure 16.10   Displaying a pop-up menu.

Creating Toolbars

"Menus are OK," says the Novice Programmer, "but sometimes I'm working too fast to use them, so I've got a lot of menu accelerators in my program. But now I keep forgetting them." You smile and say, "Have you tried adding a toolbar?"

Toolbars display buttons and other controls that represent common actions in your program, such as saving a file or pasting the contents of the Clipboard. Buttons in a toolbar often represent frequently used menu items in your menu system. In Swing, you use the **JToolBar** class to create toolbars. Here's the inheritance diagram for the **JToolBar** class:

```
java.lang.Object
|____java.awt.Component
```

```
|____java.awt.Container
     |____javax.swing.JComponent
          |____javax.swing.JToolBar
```

You can find the constructors for the **JToolBar** class in Table 16.15 and its methods in Table 16.16.

Here's an example in which I add a toolbar with two buttons to a program. Note that in many ways, a toolbar just acts as a component that contains other components—you have to add it to the layout of your program where you want it. However, when you've done that, the user can grasp the toolbar handle, which appears on the left in toolbars, and realign the toolbar against any edge of the window the

Table 16.15   Constructors of the *JToolBar* class.

Constructor	Does This
JToolBar( )	Constructs a new toolbar.
JToolBar(int orientation)	Constructs a new toolbar with the given orientation.

Table 16.16   Methods of the *JToolBar* class.

Method	Does This
JButton add(Action a)	Adds a new **JButton** that initiates the action.
protected void addImpl(Component comp, Object constraints, int index)	Adds the indicated component to this container at the indicated index.
void addSeparator( )	Appends a toolbar separator.
void addSeparator(Dimension size)	Appends a toolbar separator with the given dimensions.
protected PropertyChangeListener createActionChangeListener (JButton b)	Creates an action changed listener.
AccessibleContext getAccessible Context( )	Gets the **AccessibleContext**.
Component getComponent AtIndex(int i)	Gets the component at the indicated index.
int getComponentIndex(Component c)	Gets the index of the indicated component.
Insets getMargin( )	Gets the margin between the toolbar's border and its buttons
int getOrientation( )	Gets the current orientation of the toolbar
ToolBarUI getUI( )	Gets the toolbar's current user interface

(continued)

*Table 16.16   Methods of the **JToolBar** class (continued).*

Method	Does This
String getUIClassID( )	Gets the name of the look and feel class that draws this component.
boolean isBorderPainted( )	Checks whether the border should be painted.
boolean isFloatable( )	Returns True if the toolbar can be dragged by the user.
protected void paintBorder(Graphics g)	Paints the toolbar's border.
protected String paramString( )	Gets a string representation of this **JToolBar**.
void remove(Component comp)	Removes the component from the toolbar.
void setBorderPainted(boolean b)	Sets whether the border should be painted.
void setFloatable(boolean b)	Sets whether the toolbar can be made to float.
void setMargin(Insets m)	Sets the margin between the toolbar's border and its buttons.
void setOrientation(int o)	Sets the orientation of the toolbar.
void setUI(ToolBarUI ui)	Sets the look and feel object that renders this component.
void updateUI( )	Called by **UIFactory** when the look and feel has changed.

toolbar appears in. In fact, the user can simply leave the toolbar floating in mid-space, not aligned against any edge of the window at all.

In the code for this example, I simply use the **JToolBar** class's **add** method to add two buttons to a toolbar, and I use its **addSeparator** method to add some space between the buttons. I also add code to make the applet display the toolbar buttons the user has clicked, and I add the toolbar to the north section of the content pane's border layout. Here's the code:

```
import java.awt.*;
import javax.swing.*;
import java.awt.event.*;

/*
<APPLET
    CODE = toolbar.class
    WIDTH = 500
    HEIGHT = 280 >
</APPLET>
*/

public class toolbar extends JApplet implements ActionListener
{
    JButton jbutton1 = new JButton("Button 1", new
        ImageIcon("button.jpg"));
```

16. Swing: Menus And Toolbars

```
JButton jbutton2 = new JButton("Button 2", new
    ImageIcon("button.jpg"));

public void init()
{
    Container contentPane = getContentPane();

    JToolBar jtoolbar = new JToolBar();

    jbutton1.addActionListener(this);
    jbutton2.addActionListener(this);

    jtoolbar.add(jbutton1);
    jtoolbar.addSeparator();
    jtoolbar.add(jbutton2);

    contentPane.add(jtoolbar, BorderLayout.NORTH);
}

public void actionPerformed(ActionEvent e)
{
    if(e.getSource() == jbutton1) {
        showStatus("You clicked button 1");
    } else if (e.getSource() == jbutton2) {
        showStatus("You clicked button 2");
    }
}
}
```

The result of this code appears in Figure 16.11, where you can see the two buttons in the toolbar. Note also the toolbar handle on the left of the toolbar, which

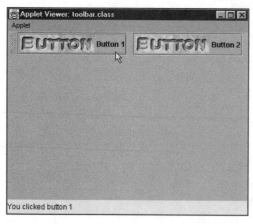

Figure 16.11   Displaying a toolbar with two buttons.

the user can use to move the toolbar around, aligning it as needed or leaving it free floating. This example—toolbar.java on the CD—is a success.

Adding Combo Boxes And Other Controls To Toolbars

The Product Support Specialist is in an unhappy mood and says, "Users are complaining again. You've got twenty buttons in your toolbar for selecting the font, and there isn't room for any other buttons." "Hmm," you say, "that could be a problem. I'll put the various font options into a combo box in the toolbar instead." The normally lugubrious PSS brightens momentarily.

You can add combo boxes and other controls to toolbars using the **JToolBar** class's **add** method. Here's an example in which I add a combo box to the toolbox example developed in the previous topic:

```java
import java.awt.*;
import javax.swing.*;
import java.awt.event.*;

/*
<APPLET
    CODE = toolbar.class
    WIDTH = 500
    HEIGHT = 280 >
</APPLET>
*/

public class toolbar extends JApplet implements ActionListener,
    ItemListener
{
    JButton jbutton1 = new JButton("Button 1", new
        ImageIcon("button.jpg"));
    JButton jbutton2 = new JButton("Button 2", new
        ImageIcon("button.jpg"));
    JComboBox jcombobox = new JComboBox();

    public void init()
    {
        Container contentPane = getContentPane();

        JToolBar jtoolbar = new JToolBar();

        jbutton1.addActionListener(this);
        jbutton2.addActionListener(this);
```

```
        jcombobox.addItem("Item 1");
        jcombobox.addItem("Item 2");
        jcombobox.addItem("Item 3");
        jcombobox.addItem("Item 4");
        jcombobox.addItemListener(this);

        jtoolbar.add(jbutton1);
        jtoolbar.addSeparator();
        jtoolbar.add(jbutton2);
        jtoolbar.addSeparator();
        jtoolbar.add(jcombobox);

        contentPane.add(jtoolbar, BorderLayout.NORTH);
    }
        .
        .
        .

}
```

When the user selects an item in the combo box, I display that item in the status bar:

```
    public void actionPerformed(ActionEvent e)
    {
        if(e.getSource() == jbutton1) {
            showStatus("You clicked button 1");
        } else if (e.getSource() == jbutton2) {
            showStatus("You clicked button 2");
        }
    }

    public void itemStateChanged(ItemEvent e)
    {
        String outString = "";

        if(e.getStateChange() == ItemEvent.SELECTED)
            outString += "Selected: " + (String)e.getItem();
        else
            outString += "Deselected: " + (String)e.getItem();

        showStatus(outString);
    }
```

The result of this code appears in Figure 16.12. When the user clicks an item in the combo box, the applet will display that item in the status bar. That's all there is to it. This example is in toolbar.java on the CD.

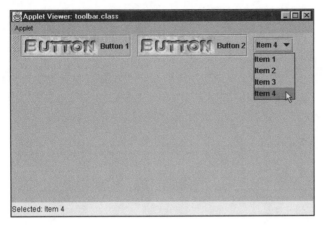

Figure 16.12   Adding a combo box to a toolbar.

Chapter 17

Swing: Windows, Desktop Panes, Inner Frames, And Dialog Boxes

In Depth

In this chapter, we'll take a look at handling all kinds of windows in Swing. We'll cover how to work with the **JWindow**, **JFrame**, **JDesktopPane**, **JInternalFrame**, **JOptionPane**, and **JDialog** classes. These classes can be conveniently broken down into two categories: windows and dialog boxes.

Windows

The **JWindow** and **JFrame** classes are the counterparts of the AWT **Window** and **Frame** classes, and they serve the same purpose. You can use the **JWindow** class to create a simple window—in fact, nothing more than a blank rectangle. Although you can add borders and controls to **JWindow** objects, you usually use the **JFrame** class to create windows that you present to the user.

The **JDesktopPane** and **JInternalFrame** classes are new in Swing, although together they represent something that's become common in GUIs—a multiple document interface. Objects of the **JDesktopPane** class present a space in which you can display multiple internal frames of the **JInternalFrame** class. For example, a word processor application may let the user open several views into the same document, or multiple documents, using a desktop with a number of internal frame windows. Internal frames are lightweight, drawn windows that appear inside other windows. In fact, desktop panes are lightweight components, too, derived from **JLayeredPane**. You can add internal frame windows to selected layers of a desktop pane.

Dialog Boxes

Swing provides a lot of support for dialog boxes with the **JOptionPane** class. Using the methods of this class, you can display all kinds of dialog boxes—message dialog boxes, confirmation dialog boxes, input dialog boxes, and more. As you'll see here, it's easy to create dialog boxes using **JOptionPane**.

In addition to **JOptionPane**, Swing also has the **JDialog** class, which you can use as the foundation of your own custom dialog box class. We'll cover how to use both **JOptionPane** and **JDialog** in this chapter in depth.

That's it for the overview of what's in this chapter. As you can see, there's a lot coming up. It's time to turn to the "Immediate Solutions" section, starting with a look at the **JWindow** class.

Immediate Solutions

Creating A Window

The Novice Programmer appears and says, "I want to create an entirely customized window in my program." "For that," you say, "you need the **JWindow** class, which displays an entirely blank window." "OK," says the NP, "can you code it for me?"

The **JWindow** class is much like the AWT **Window** class, because it displays a blank window that you can customize as you like. In fact, **JWindow** objects are so unadorned that you'll generally use the **JFrame** class instead. However, if you really need simplicity, **JWindow** is the place to start. Here's the inheritance diagram for this class:

```
java.lang.Object
|____java.awt.Component
      |____java.awt.Container
            |____java.awt.Window
                  |____javax.swing.JWindow
```

You can find the constructors for **JWindow** in Table 17.1 and its methods in Table 17.2.

Table 17.1   Constructors of the JWindow class.

Constructor	Does This
JWindow( )	Constructs a window.
JWindow(Frame owner)	Constructs a window with the indicated owner frame.
JWindow(Window owner)	Constructs a window with the indicated owner window.

Table 17.2   Methods of the JWindow class.

Method	Does This
protected void addImpl(Component comp, Object constraints, int index)	Adds components to the content pane instead.
protected JRootPane createRoot Pane( )	Called by the constructor methods to create the default root pane.

(continued)

Table 17.2   Methods of the *JWindow* class (continued).

Method	Does This
AccessibleContext getAccessible Context( )	Gets the **AccessibleContext**.
Container getContentPane( )	Gets the **contentPane** object for this window.
Component getGlassPane( )	Gets the **glassPane** object for this window.
JLayeredPane getLayeredPane( )	Gets the **layeredPane** object for this window.
JRootPane getRootPane( )	Gets the **rootPane** object for this window.
protected boolean isRootPane CheckingEnabled( )	Determines whether calls to **add** and **setLayout** cause an exception to be thrown.
protected String paramString( )	Gets a string representation of this **JWindow**.
void remove(Component comp)	Removes the indicated component from this container.
void setContentPane(Container contentPane)	Sets the **contentPane** property.
void setGlassPane(Component glass Pane)	Sets the **glassPane** property.
void setLayeredPane(JLayeredPane layeredPane)	Sets the **layeredPane** property.
void setLayout(LayoutManager manager)	By default, the layout of this component may not be set.
protected void setRootPane (JRootPane root)	Sets the **rootPane** property.
protected void setRootPaneChecking Enabled(boolean enabled)	Determines whether calls to **add** and **setLayout** cause an exception to be thrown.
protected void windowInit( )	Called by constructors to initialize the **JWindow** property.

When you create a **JWindow** object, you can add a border to it with the root pane's **setBorder** method, show the window with the **show** method, hide it with the **hide** method, and get rid of it with the **dispose** method. Note that the default layout in a **JWindow** is a border layout.

I'll create a **JWindow** object now in an example. In this case, I add a button to an applet and display the window when that button is clicked. I also add a border to the window and a button that, when clicked, will dispose of the window. Note that **JWindow** objects have content panes just like other windows, so I add the button to that pane. Also note that before a window can be displayed, it must be given a size, which I do here with the **setBounds** method. Here's the code:

```java
import java.awt.*;
import javax.swing.*;
import java.awt.event.*;

/*
<APPLET
    CODE = window.class
    WIDTH = 350
    HEIGHT = 280 >
</APPLET>
*/

public class window extends JApplet implements ActionListener
{
    JWindow jwindow = new JWindow();

    public void init()
    {
        Container contentPane = getContentPane();
        JButton jbutton = new JButton("Display window");
        JButton jwindowbutton = new JButton("Close");

        contentPane.setLayout(new FlowLayout());

        contentPane.add(jbutton);

        jwindow.getRootPane().setBorder(
            BorderFactory.createRaisedBevelBorder()
        );

        Container windowContentPane = jwindow.getContentPane();
        windowContentPane.setLayout(new FlowLayout());
        windowContentPane.add(jwindowbutton);

        jwindowbutton.addActionListener(new ActionListener() {
            public void actionPerformed(ActionEvent e)
            {
                jwindow.dispose();
            }
        });
```

```
        jbutton.addActionListener(this);

    }

    public void actionPerformed(ActionEvent e)
    {
        jwindow.setBounds(200, 200, 100, 100);

        jwindow.show();
    }
}
```

The result of this code appears in Figure 17.1, where you can see the new window that appears when the user clicks the Display window button. As you can see, the window has a border and a button (as well as a warning that Swing adds which indicates that the window is an applet window). That's all there is to it. This example is in window.java on the CD.

TIP: *Although in this example I pass numeric values to the window's **setBounds** method, you can also set the location of the window with respect to its parent window. First, you can get the location of the applet window's content pane like this: **Point loc = contentPane.getLocation()**. This point is in local coordinates, so you can convert it to screen coordinates, like this: **SwingUtilities.convertPointToScreen(loc, contentPane)**. Then you're free to use **loc** with **setBounds**.*

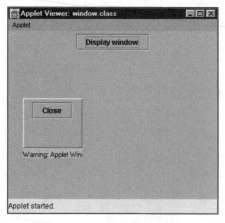

Figure 17.1   A basic **JWindow** window.

Creating A Frame Window

"OK," the Novice Programmer says, "so I was wrong. I don't want to start with just a basic window; I want to use a frame window that already supports resizing, minimizing, maximizing, and so on." "OK," you say. "It looks like you want the **JFrame** class."

We've been using the **JFrame** class as the foundation of Swing applications, so you're already familiar with this class. I'm including it in this chapter on windows and dialog boxes for completeness. In Chapter 11, you'll find the fields of the **JFrame** class in Table 11.15, its constructors in Table 11.16, and its methods in Table 11.17.

Here's a quick example using a **JFrame** window in which I add a panel to the window and then draw in the panel and add a text field to it. Because **JFrame** windows are used as the basis of Swing applications, I'll make this example an application. Here's the code:

```
import javax.swing.*;
import java.awt.*;
import java.awt.event.*;

public class jframe extends JFrame
{
    jpanel j;

    public jframe()
    {
        super("Swing application");

        Container contentPane = getContentPane();
        j = new jpanel();
        contentPane.add(j);
    }

    public static void main(String args[])
    {
        final JFrame f = new jframe();

        f.setBounds(100, 100, 300, 300);
        f.setVisible(true);
        f.setDefaultCloseOperation(DISPOSE_ON_CLOSE);

        f.addWindowListener(new WindowAdapter() {
```

```
                        public void windowClosing(WindowEvent e) {
                            System.exit(0);
                        }
                });
        }
}

class jpanel extends JPanel
{
    JTextField jtextfield = new JTextField("Hello from Swing!");

    jpanel()
    {
        setBackground(Color.white);
        add(jtextfield);
    }

    public void paintComponent (Graphics g)
    {
        super.paintComponent(g);
        g.drawString("Hello from Swing!", 0, 60);
    }
}
```

You can see the result of this code in Figure 17.2. As you see in the figure, the frame window already displays minimize, maximize, and close buttons. This example is in jframe.java on the CD. For more on using **JFrame**, such as the details on how to close these windows, see Chapter 11.

Figure 17.2   Using the JFrame class.

Creating A Desktop Pane

The Big Boss appears and says, "Our Java word processor isn't keeping pace with the competition. They can open five documents at once." "That's nothing," you say. "Using a desktop pane, I can open 10 documents at once and display them all." "You're hired," the BB says. You say, "I already work here."

The Swing desktop pane mimics a desktop and allows you to display multiple objects on it. In the next topic, I'll add inner frame windows to a desktop pane. Here's the inheritance diagram for the **JDesktopPane** class, which is the class Swing uses to support desktop panes:

```
java.lang.Object
|____java.awt.Component
    |____java.awt.Container
        |____javax.swing.JComponent
            |____javax.swing.JLayeredPane
                |____javax.swing.JDesktopPane
```

You'll find the constructor of the **JDesktopPane** class in Table 17.3 and its methods in Table 17.4.

Table 17.3   The constructor of the JDesktopPane class.

Constructor	Does This
JDesktopPane( )	Constructs a new **JDesktopPane**.

Table 17.4   Methods of the JDesktopPane class.

Method	Does This
AccessibleContext getAccessible Context( )	Gets the **AccessibleContext**.
JInternalFrame[ ] getAllFrames( )	Gets all **JInternalFrames** displayed in the desktop.
JInternalFrame[ ] getAllFramesInLayer (int layer)	Gets all **JInternalFrames** displayed in the given layer of the desktop.
DesktopManager getDesktop actions. Manager( )	Gets the **DesktopManager** that handles desktop-specific UI
DesktopPaneUI getUI( )	Gets the look and feel object that draws this component.
String getUIClassID( )	Gets the name of the look and feel class that draws this component.
boolean isOpaque( )	Returns True if this component paints every pixel in its range.

(continued)

Table 17.4   Methods of the *JDesktopPane* class (continued).

Method	Does This
protected String paramString( )	Gets a string representation of this **JdesktopPane**.
void setDesktopManager(Desktop Manager d)	Sets the **DesktopManger** that will handle desktop-specific UI actions.
void setUI(DesktopPaneUI ui)	Sets the look and feel object that draws this component.
void updateUI( )	Called by **UIManager** when the look and feel has changed.

Here's an example in which I just add a desktop pane to an applet's content pane. Here's what the code looks like:

```
import java.awt.*;
import javax.swing.*;
import java.awt.event.*;

/*
<APPLET
    CODE = desktopframe.class
    WIDTH = 350
    HEIGHT = 280>
</APPLET>
*/

public class desktopframe extends JApplet
{
    JDesktopPane jdesktoppane = new JDesktopPane();

    public void init()
    {
        Container contentPane = getContentPane();

        contentPane.add(jdesktoppane, BorderLayout.CENTER);
    }
}
```

The result of this code appears in Figure 17.3. You can see a blank desktop pane in the figure, but it's not much good to anyone—desktop panes are useful as containers, not components, so you need to add something to them. I'll do that in the next topic, where I cover internal frames.

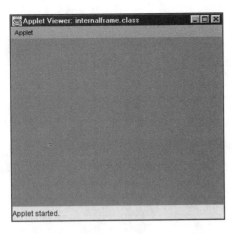

Figure 17.3   A basic desktop pane.

Creating Internal Frames

The Big Boss isn't impressed with the desktop pane in your program. "What's the point?" the BB asks. "The point," you say, "is that you can display windows inside the desktop pane." "Convince me," the BB says. "No problem," you say.

Internal frames, as supported by the **JInternalFrame** class, are lightweight frame windows that appear inside other windows. This is one of the biggest and most popular of all the Swing classes, and I'll put it to work here. Here's the inheritance diagram for the **JInternalFrame** class:

```
java.lang.Object
|____java.awt.Component
      |____java.awt.Container
            |____javax.swing.JComponent
                  |____javax.swing.JInternalFrame
```

You'll find the fields of the **JInternalFrame** class in Table 17.5, its constructors in Table 17.6, and its methods in Table 17.7.

Table 17.5   Fields of the JInternalFrame class.

Field	Does This
protected boolean closable	Indicates whether the frame can be closed.
static String CONTENT_PANE _PROPERTY	The bound property name.

(continued)

Table 17.5   Fields of the *JInternalFrame* class (continued).

Field	Does This
protected JInternalFrame.JDesktop Icon desktopIcon	The icon displayed when the frame is iconified.
static String FRAME_ICON_PROPERTY	The **FRAME_ICON_PROPERTY** bound property name.
protected Icon frameIcon	The icon shown in the top-left corner of the frame.
static String GLASS_PANE_PROPERTY	The **GLASS_PANE_PROPERTY** bound property name.
protected boolean iconable	Returns True if the frame can be minimized and displayed as an icon image.
static String IS_CLOSED_PROPERTY	The property indicating that the frame is closed.
static String IS_ICON_PROPERTY	The property indicating that the frame is iconified.
static String IS_MAXIMUM_PROPERTY	The property indicating that the frame is maximized.
static String IS_SELECTED_PROPERTY	The property indicated that this frame has selected status.
protected boolean isClosed	Returns True if the frame has been closed.
protected boolean isIcon	Returns True if the frame has been iconified.
protected boolean isMaximum	Returns True if the frame has been expanded to its maximum size.
protected boolean isSelected	Returns True if the frame is currently selected.
static String LAYERED_PANE _PROPERTY	The **LAYERED_PANE_PROPERTY** bound property name.
protected boolean maximizable	Returns True if the frame can be expanded to the size of the desktop pane.
static String MENU_BAR_PROPERTY	The bound **MENU_BAR_PROPERTY** property name.
protected boolean resizable	Returns True if the frame's size can be changed.
static String ROOT_PANE_PROPERTY	The bound **ROOT_PANE_PROPERTY** property name.
protected JRootPane rootPane	The **JRootPane** instance for this frame.
protected boolean rootPaneChecking to Enabled	Returns True when calls to **add** and **setLayout** cause an exception be thrown.
protected String title	The title to be displayed in the frame's title bar.
static String TITLE_PROPERTY	The bound **TITLE_PROPERTY** property name.

Table 17.6   Constructors of the *JInternalFrame* class.

Constructor	Does This
JInternalFrame( )	Constructs a nonresizable, nonclosable, nonmaximizable, noniconifiable **JInternalFrame**.
JInternalFrame(String title)	Constructs a nonresizable, nonclosable, nonmaximizable, noniconifiable **JInternalFrame** with the given title.

(continued)

Table 17.6   Constructors of the *JInternalFrame* class (continued).

Constructor	Does This
JInternalFrame(String title, boolean resizable)	Constructs a nonclosable, nonmaximizable, noniconifiable **JInternalFrame** with the given title, which can be resized if **resizeable** is True.
JInternalFrame(String title, boolean resizable, boolean closable)	Constructs a nonmaximizable, noniconifiable **JInternalFrame** with the given title and with the ability to be resized and closed.
JInternalFrame(String title, boolean resizable, boolean closable, boolean maximizable)	Constructs a noniconifiable **JInternalFrame** with the indicated title and with the ability to be resized, closed, and maximized, as given.
JInternalFrame(String title, boolean resizable, boolean closable, boolean maximizable, boolean iconifiable)	Constructs a **JInternalFrame** with the indicated title and with the ability to be resized, closed, maximized, and iconified, as given.

Table 17.7   Methods of the *JInternal Frame* class.

Method	Does This
protected void addImpl(Component comp, Object constraints, int index)	Adds child components to the **contentPane**.
void addInternalFrameListener(Internal FrameListener l)	Adds the given internal frame listener to receive internal frame events from this internal frame.
protected JRootPane createRoot Pane( )	Called by the constructor to set up the **JRootPane**.
void dispose( )	Disposes of this internal frame.
protected void fireInternalFrame Event(int id)	Fires an internal frame event.
AccessibleContext getAccessible Context( )	Gets the **AccessibleContext**.
Container getContentPane( )	Gets the **contentPane**.
int getDefaultCloseOperation( )	Gets the default operation that occurs when the user closes this window.
JInternalFrame.JDesktopIcon get DesktopIcon( )	Gets the **JDesktopIcon** used when this **JInternalFrame** is iconified.
JDesktopPane getDesktopPane( )	Searches the hierarchy for a **JDesktop** instance.
Icon getFrameIcon( )	Gets the image displayed in the title bar of the frame.
Component getGlassPane( )	Gets the **glassPane** object for this frame.

(continued)

Table 17.7   Methods of the *JInternal Frame* class (continued).

Method	Does This
JMenuBar getJMenuBar( )	Gets the current **JMenuBar** for this **JInternalFrame** or null if no menu bar has been set.
int getLayer( )	A convenience method for getting the layer attribute of this component.
JLayeredPane getLayeredPane( )	Gets the **layeredPane** object for this frame.
JMenuBar getMenuBar( )	Deprecated. Replaced by **getJMenuBar( )**.
JRootPane getRootPane( )	Gets the **rootPane** object for this frame.
String getTitle( )	Gets the title of the **JInternalFrame**.
InternalFrameUI getUI( )	Gets the look and feel object that draws this **JInternalFrame**.
String getUIClassID( )	Gets the name of the look and feel class that draws this component.
String getWarningString( )	Gets the warning string that's displayed with this window.
boolean isClosable( )	Gets whether this **JInternalFrame** can be closed by some user action.
boolean isClosed( )	Returns True if this **JInternalFrame** is currently closed.
boolean isIcon( )	Returns True if the **JInternalFrame** is currently iconified.
boolean isIconifiable( )	Returns True if the **JInternalFrame** can be iconified by some user action.
boolean isMaximizable( )	Returns True if the **JInternalFrame** can be maximized by some user action.
boolean isMaximum( )	Returns True if the **JInternalFrame** is currently maximized.
boolean isResizable( )	Returns True if the **JInternalFrame** can be resized by some user action.
protected boolean isRootPane be CheckingEnabled( )	Returns True if calls to **add** and **setLayout** cause an exception to thrown.
boolean isSelected( )	Returns True if the **JInternalFrame** is the currently selected frame.
void moveToBack( )	Moves this component to position -1 if its parent is a **JLayeredPane**.
void moveToFront( )	Moves this component to position 0 if its parent is a **JLayeredPane**.
void pack( )	Lays out children of this **JInternalFrame** to use their preferred size.
protected void paintComponent (Graphics g)	Calls the **paint** method.
protected String paramString( )	Gets a string representation of this **JInternalFrame**.
void remove(Component comp)	Removes the indicated component.
void removeInternalFrameListener (InternalFrameListener l)	Removes the indicated internal frame listener.

(continued)

Table 17.7   Methods of the *JInternal Frame* class (continued).

Method	Does This
void reshape(int x, int y, int width, int height)	Moves and resizes this component.
void setClosable(boolean b)	Determines whether this **JInternalFrame** can be closed by some user action.
void setClosed(boolean b)	Passing True to this method closes the frame.
void setContentPane(Container c)	Sets this **JInternalFrame**'s content pane.
void setDefaultCloseOperation (int operation)	Sets the operation that will occur by default when the user closes this window.
void setDesktopIcon(JInternalFrame.J DesktopIcon d)	Sets the **JDesktopIcon** associated with this **JInternalFrame**.
void setFrameIcon(Icon icon)	Sets an image to be displayed in the title bar of the frame (usually in the top-left corner).
void setGlassPane(Component glass)	Sets this **JInternalFrame**'s **glassPane** property.
void setIcon(boolean b)	Iconizes and deconizes the frame.
void setIconifiable(boolean b)	Specifies that the **JInternalFrame** can be made an icon by some user action.
void setJMenuBar(JMenuBar m)	Sets the **JMenuBar** for this **JInternalFrame**.
void setLayer(Integer layer)	Sets the layer attribute of this component.
void setLayeredPane(JLayeredPane layered)	Sets this **JInternalFrame**'s **layeredPane** property.
void setLayout(LayoutManager manager)	Sets the layout of the **contentPane**.
void setMaximizable(boolean b)	Specifies that the **JInternalFrame** can be maximized by some user action.
void setMaximum(boolean b)	Maximizes and restores the frame.
void setMenuBar(JMenuBar m)	Deprecated. Replaced by **setJMenuBar(JMenuBar m)**.
void setResizable(boolean b)	Specifies that the **JInternalFrame** can be resized by some user action.
protected void setRootPane (JRootPane root)	Sets the **rootPane** property.
protected void setRootPaneChecking Enabled(boolean enabled)	Determines whether calls to **add** and **setLayout** cause an exception to be thrown.

(continued)

Table 17.7   Methods of the *JInternal Frame* class (continued).

Method	Does This
void setSelected(boolean selected)	Selects and deselects the **JInternalFrame**.
void setTitle(String title)	Sets the **JInternalFrame** title.
void setUI(InternalFrameUI ui)	Sets the UI delegate for this **JInternalFrame**.
void setVisible(boolean b)	Sets the visible state of the object.
void show( )	Shows this internal frame and brings it to the front.
void toBack( )	Sends this internal frame to the back.
void toFront( )	Brings this internal frame to the front.
void updateUI( )	Called by **UIManager** when the look and feel has changed.

I'll now put together an example showing how to use internal frames in a desktop pane. I start by adding a desktop pane to an applet, and I add a **JPanel** object as well. I place a button with the caption "New internal frame" in the panel. When the user clicks that button, I display a new internal frame in the desktop pane. Each internal frame will enclose a text area object of the **JTextArea** class (which you'll see in a few chapters—for our purposes here, it acts like the AWT **TextArea** class), thus allowing the user to enter text.

Here's how I set up the applet with a desktop pane and the button New internal frame:

```
import java.awt.*;
import javax.swing.*;
import java.awt.event.*;

/*
<APPLET
    CODE = internalframe.class
    WIDTH = 350
    HEIGHT = 280>
</APPLET>
*/

public class internalframe extends JApplet implements ActionListener
{
    JDesktopPane jdesktoppane = new JDesktopPane();

    public void init()
    {
        JPanel jpanel = new JPanel();
        Container contentPane = getContentPane();
```

```
        JButton jbutton = new JButton("New internal frame");

        jpanel.add(jbutton);

        contentPane.add(jpanel, BorderLayout.SOUTH);
        contentPane.add(jdesktoppane, BorderLayout.CENTER);

        jbutton.addActionListener(this);
    }
    .
    .
    .
}
```

The real action takes place when the user clicks the button to display a new internal frame. I give each internal frame a new caption in its title bar, so I must keep track of the number of internal frames in a new variable:

```
public class internalframe extends JApplet implements ActionListener
{
    JDesktopPane jdesktoppane = new JDesktopPane();
    static int framenumber = 1;

    public void init()
    {
    .
    .
    .
    }
```

Next, I create, configure, and add new internal frames to the desktop pane. Here's how I create and configure the internal frames, setting their locations and titles. I enable them so that the user can close, resize, maximize, and minimize these frames, and I add a text area to the frames' content panes. Note, in particular, that internal frames must be made visible with the **setVisible** method. After components have been added to the content pane, the **pack** method is used to resize the frame window to match its contents. Note also that when internal frames are added to desktop panes using the **add** method, a layer must be specified. Here's what the code looks like:

```
    public void actionPerformed(ActionEvent event)
    {
        JInternalFrame jinternalframe = new JInternalFrame();
        Container contentPane = jinternalframe.getContentPane();
```

```
        jinternalframe.setLocation(20, 20);
        jinternalframe.setTitle("Internal Frame " + framenumber);
        framenumber++;

        jinternalframe.setClosable(true);
        jinternalframe.setResizable(true);
        jinternalframe.setMaximizable(true);
        jinternalframe.setIconifiable(true);

        jinternalframe.setVisible(true);

        contentPane.setLayout(new FlowLayout());
        contentPane.add(new JTextArea(5, 15), "Center");
        jinternalframe.pack();

        jdesktoppane.add(jinternalframe, 2);
    }
```

The result of this code appears in Figure 17.4. As you can see in the figure, you can create multiple internal frame windows in this applet, and you can resize and move them around. You can even minimize them, as you see in the figure. This applet works as designed, and you'll find it in internalframes.java on the CD.

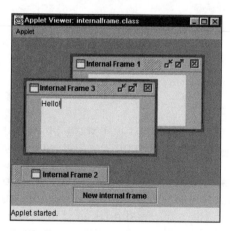

Figure 17.4   Creating internal frames in a desktop pane.

Using **JOptionPane** To Create Dialog Boxes

The Novice Programmer is distraught and says, "The Product Support Specialist wants me to add 12 new dialog boxes to my program! Isn't that a lot of coding?" "Probably not," you say, "when you are using the Swing **JOptionPane** class." "Oh," says the NP, calming down and beginning to smile.

The **JOptionPane** class supports a pane that you use in dialog boxes; in fact, it also provides convenience methods for creating dialog boxes that contain option panes. Here's the inheritance diagram for **JOptionPane**:

```
java.lang.Object
|____java.awt.Component
     |____java.awt.Container
          |____javax.swing.JComponent
               |____javax.swing.JOptionPane
```

You'll find the fields of the **JOptionPane** class in Table 17.8, its constructors in Table 17.9, and its methods in Table 17.10.

Table 17.8   Fields of the *JOptionPane* class.

Field	Does This
static int CANCEL_OPTION	The return value from the class method if **CANCEL** is chosen.
static int CLOSED_OPTION	The return value from the class method if the user closes the window without selecting anything.
static int DEFAULT_OPTION	The look and feel should not supply any options but only use the options from the **JOptionPane**.
static int ERROR_MESSAGE	Used for error messages.
protected Icon icon	The icon used in the pane.
static String ICON_PROPERTY	The bound property name for the icon.
static int INFORMATION_MESSAGE	Used for information messages.
static String INITIAL_SELECTION _VALUE_PROPERTY	The bound property name for **initialSelectionValue**.
static String INITIAL_VALUE _PROPERTY	The bound property name for **initialValue**.
protected Object initialSelectionValue	The initial value to select in **selectionValues**.
protected Object initialValue	The value that should be initially selected in the options.

(continued)

Table 17.8   Fields of the *JOptionPane* class (continued).

Field	Does This
static String INPUT_VALUE_PROPERTY	The bound property name for **inputValue**.
protected Object inputValue	The value the user has entered.
protected Object message	The message to display.
static String MESSAGE_PROPERTY	The bound property name for the message.
static String MESSAGE_TYPE _PROPERTY	The bound property name for the type.
protected int messageType	The message type.
static int NO_OPTION	The return value from the class method if the no button is clicked.
static int OK_CANCEL_OPTION	The type used for **showConfirmDialog**.
static int OK_OPTION	The return value from the class method if **OK** is chosen.
static String OPTION_TYPE _PROPERTY	The bound property name for **optionType**.
protected Object[ ] options	The options to display to the user.
static String OPTIONS_PROPERTY	The bound property name for the option.
protected int optionType	The option type (**DEFAULT_OPTION**, **YES_NO_OPTION**, **YES_NO_CANCEL_OPTION**, or **OK_CANCEL_OPTION**).
static int PLAIN_MESSAGE	Indicates that no icon should be used.
static int QUESTION_MESSAGE	Used for questions.
static String SELECTION_VALUES _PROPERTY	The bound property name for **selectionValues**.
protected Object[ ] selectionValues	The array of values the user can choose from.
static Object UNINITIALIZED_VALUE	Indicates that the user has not yet selected a value.
protected Object value	The currently selected value. It will be a valid option, **UNINITIALIZED_VALUE**, or null.
static String VALUE_PROPERTY	The bound property name for the value.
static String WANTS_INPUT _PROPERTY	The bound property name for **wantsInput**.
protected boolean wantsInput	If True, a UI widget will be provided to the user to get input.
static int WARNING_MESSAGE	Used for warning messages.
static int YES_NO_CANCEL_OPTION	The type used for **showConfirmDialog**.
static int YES_NO_OPTION	The type used for **showConfirmDialog**.
static int YES_OPTION	The return value from the class method if **YES** is chosen.

Table 17.9   Constructors of the *JOptionPane* class.

Constructor	Does This
JOptionPane( )	Constructs a **JOptionPane** with a test message.
JOptionPane(Object message)	Constructs an instance of **JOptionPane** to display a message using the plain-message message type and the default options delivered by the UI.
JOptionPane(Object message, int messageType)	Constructs an instance of **JOptionPane** to display a message with the indicated message type and the default options.
JOptionPane(Object message, int messageType, int optionType)	Constructs an instance of **JOptionPane** to display a message with the indicated message type and options.
JOptionPane(Object message, int messageType, int optionType, Icon icon)	Constructs an instance of **JOptionPane** to display a message with the indicated message type, options, and icon.
JOptionPane(Object message, int messageType, int optionType, Icon icon, Object[ ] options)	Constructs an instance of **JOptionPane** to display a message with the indicated message type, icon, and options.
JOptionPane(Object message, int messageType, int optionType, Icon icon, Object[ ] options, Object initial Value)	Constructs an instance of **JOptionPane** to display a message with the indicated message type, icon, and options, with the initially selected option indicated.

Table 17.10   Methods of the *JOptionPane* class.

Method	Does This
JDialog createDialog(Component parentComponent, String title)	Constructs and returns a new **JDialog**.
JInternalFrame createInternalFrame (Component parentComponent, String title)	Constructs and returns an instance of **JInternalFrame**.
AccessibleContext getAccessible Context( )	Get the **AccessibleContext**.
static JDesktopPane getDesktop PaneForComponent(Component parentComponent)	Gets the indicated component's desktop pane.
static Frame getFrameForComponent (Component parentComponent)	Gets the indicated component's frame.
Icon getIcon( )	Gets the icon this pane displays.

(continued)

Table 17.10   Methods of the *JOptionPane* class (continued).

Method	Does This
Object getInitialSelectionValue( )	Gets the initial selection value.
Object getInitialValue( )	Gets the initial value.
Object getInputValue( )	Gets the value the user has entered, if **wantsInput** is True.
int getMaxCharactersPerLineCount( )	Gets the maximum number of characters to place on a line in a message.
Object getMessage( )	Gets the message object this pane displays.
int getMessageType( )	Gets the message type.
Object[ ] getOptions( )	Gets the choices the user can make.
int getOptionType( )	Gets the type of options displayed.
static Frame getRootFrame( )	Gets the frame to use for the class methods in which a frame is not provided
Object[ ] getSelectionValues( )	Gets the selection values.
OptionPaneUI getUI( )	Gets the UI object that implements the look and feel for this component.
String getUIClassID( )	Gets the name of the UI class that implements the look and feel for this component.
Object getValue( )	Gets the value the user has selected
boolean getWantsInput( )	Returns True if a **parentComponent** will be provided for the user to input.
protected String paramString( )	Gets a string representation of this **JoptionPane**.
void selectInitialValue( )	Requests that the initial value be selected, which will set focus to the initial value.
void setIcon(Icon newIcon)	Sets the icon to display.
void setInitialSelectionValue (Object newValue)	Sets the initial selection value.
void setInitialValue (Object newInitialValue)	Sets the initial value that's to be enabled.
void setInputValue(Object newValue)	Sets the user's input value.
void setMessage(Object newMessage)	Sets the option pane's message object.
void setMessageType(int newType)	Sets the option pane's message type.
void setOptions(Object[ ] newOptions)	Sets the options this pane displays.
void setOptionType(int newType)	Sets the options to display.

(continued)

Table 17.10   Methods of the *JOptionPane* class (continued).

Method	Does This
static void setRootFrame(Frame newRootFrame)	Sets the frame to use for class methods in which a frame is not provided.
void setSelectionValues(Object[ ] newValues)	Sets the selection values for a pane that provides the user with a list of items to choose from.
void setUI(OptionPaneUI ui)	Sets the UI object that implements the look and feel for this component.
void setValue(Object newValue)	Sets the value the user has chosen.
void setWantsInput(boolean newValue)	If **newValue** is true, a component is added to allow the user to input a value.
static int showConfirmDialog (Component parentComponent, Object message)	Brings up a modal dialog box with the options Yes, No, and Cancel.
static int showConfirmDialog (Component parentComponent, Object message, String title, int optionType)	Brings up a modal dialog box where the number of choices is determined by the **optionType** parameter.
static int showConfirmDialog (Component parentComponent, message, String title, int optionType, int messageType)	Brings up a modal dialog box where the number of choices is determined by the **optionType** parameter and where the Object **messageType** parameter determines the icon to display.
static int showConfirmDialog (Component parentComponent, Object message, String title, int option Type, int messageType, Icon icon)	Brings up a modal dialog box with a indicated icon, where the number of choices is determined by the **optionType** parameter.
static String showInputDialog (Component parentComponent, Object message)	Shows a question message dialog box requesting input from the user parented to **parentComponent**.
static String showInputDialog (Component parentComponent, Object message, String title, int messageType)message type	Shows a dialog box requesting input from the user parented to **parentComponent** with the dialog box having the title **title** and **messageType**.
static Object showInputDialog (Component parentComponent, Object message, String title, int messageType, Icon icon, Object[ ] selectionValues, Object initialSelectionValue)	Prompts the user for input in a blocking dialog box where the initial selection, possible selections, and all other options can be indicated.

(continued)

Table 17.10   Methods of the JOptionPane class (continued).

Method	Does This
static String showInputDialog (Object message)	Shows a question message dialog box requesting input from the user.
static int showInternalConfirmDialog (Component parent Component, Object message)	Brings up an internal dialog box with the options Yes, No, and Cancel.
static int showInternalConfirmDialog (Component parentComponent, Object message, String title, int optionType)	Brings up an internal dialog box where the number of choices is determined by the **optionType** parameter.
static int showInternalConfirmDialog (Component parentComponent, Object String title, int optionType, int messageType)	Brings up an internal dialog box where the number of choices is determined by the **optionType** parameter and where the message, **messageType** parameter determines the icon to display.
static int showInternalConfirmDialog (Component parentComponent, Object message, String title, int optionType, int messageType, Icon icon)	Brings up an internal dialog box with a indicated icon, where the number of choices is determined by the **optionType** parameter.
static String showInternalInputDialog (Component parentComponent, Object message)	Shows an internal question message dialog box requesting input from the user parented to **parentComponent**.
static String showInternalInputDialog (Component parentComponent, Object message, String title, int messageType)	Shows an internal dialog box requesting input from the user parented to **parentComponent**, with the dialog box having the title **title** and the message type **messageType**.
static Object showInternalInputDialog (Component parentComponent, Object message, String title, int messageType, Icon icon, Object[ ] selectionValues, Object initialSelectionValue)	Prompts the user for input in a blocking internal dialog box where the initial selection, possible selections, and all other options can be indicated.
static void showInternalMessageDialog (Component parentComponent, Object message)	Brings up an internal confirmation dialog box.
static void showInternalMessageDialog (Component parentComponent, default Object message, String title, int messageType)	Brings up an internal dialog box that displays a message using an icon set by the **messageType** parameter.

(continued)

Table 17.10   Methods of the JOptionPane class (continued).

Method	Does This
static void showInternalMessage Dialog(Component parentComponent, Object message, String title, int messageType, Icon icon)	Brings up an internal dialog box displaying a message and specifying all parameters.
static int showInternalOptionDialog(Component parentComponent, Object message, String title, int option Type, int messageType, Icon icon, Object[ ] options, Object initialValue)	Brings up an internal dialog box with an indicated icon, where the initial choice is set by the **initialValue** parameter and the number of choices is determined by the **optionType** parameter.
static void showMessageDialog (Component parentComponent, Object message)	Brings up a confirmation dialog box.
static void showMessageDialog (Component parentComponent, Object message, String title, int messageType)	Brings up a dialog box that displays a message using a default icon set by the **messageType** parameter.
static void showMessageDialog (Component parentComponent, Object message, String title, int messageType, Icon icon)	Brings up a dialog box displaying a message and specifying all parameters.
static int showOptionDialog (Component parentComponent, Object message, String title, int optionType, int messageType, Icon icon, Object[ ] options, Object initialValue)	Brings up a modal dialog box with an indicated icon, where the initial choice is determined by the **initialValue** parameter and the number of choices is set by the **optionType** parameter.
void updateUI( )	Called by **UIManager** when the look and feel has changed.

You can use the **JOptionPane** static methods (that is, class methods which you invoke directly using the class, like this: **JOptionPane.showMessageDialog**) to display four types of dialog boxes. Here are those methods and the dialog boxes they create:

- *showMessageDialog*—Displays some message to the user.
- *showConfirmDialog*—Asks a confirming question and receives a yes/no/cancel response.
- *showInputDialog*—Prompts for input.
- *showOptionDialog*—A configurable dialog box.

For each of these methods, there's also an internal (lightweight) frame version, such as **showInternalMessageDialog**, **showInternalInputDialog**, and so on, in case you want to stick to internal frames to conserve system resources.

All these methods can return an integer indicating which button the user clicked on; the possible values are **YES_OPTION**, **NO_OPTION**, **CANCEL_OPTION**, **OK_OPTION**, and **CLOSED_OPTION**. These dialog boxes are *modal*, which means that the user must dismiss them before continuing with the rest of the program (clicking on any other window in the program just results in a beep).

All this is best understood through examples, so I'll dissect this class using several examples over the next few topics.

Creating Option Pane Confirmation Dialog Boxes

The Product Support Specialist says, "We need to make sure the users are OK with this." You ask, "We need to make sure they're OK with displaying the sum after they've clicked the Add button?" "Use a confirmation dialog box," the PSS says.

Confirmation dialog boxes let the user click buttons to confirm or stop an action. You use the **JOptionPane showConfirmDialog** static method to create this kind of dialog box. Here are the **JOptionPane** constants you can use with this method, indicating what buttons you want displayed: **DEFAULT_OPTION**, **YES_NO_OPTION**, **YES_NO_CANCEL_OPTION**, and **OK_CANCEL_OPTION**.

Here's an example in which I display a confirmation dialog box with a Yes and a No button. To display that dialog box, I place a button in an applet, giving the button the caption Display dialog. When that button is clicked, I use **showConfirmDialog** to display the new dialog box, and I use the return value from that method to indicate which button was clicked by displaying a message in the applet's status bar. Here's what this looks like in code:

```
import java.awt.*;
import javax.swing.*;
import java.awt.event.*;

/*
<APPLET
    CODE = dialogconfirm.class
    WIDTH = 350
    HEIGHT = 280>
```

```
</APPLET>
*/

public class dialogconfirm extends JApplet
{
    JWindow jwindow = new JWindow();

    public void init()
    {
        final Container contentPane = getContentPane();
        JButton jbutton = new JButton("Display dialog");

        contentPane.setLayout(new FlowLayout());
        contentPane.add(jbutton);

        jbutton.addActionListener(new ActionListener()
        {
            public void actionPerformed(ActionEvent e)
            {
                int result = JOptionPane.showConfirmDialog((Component)
                    null, "Choose yes or no", "Choose yes or no",
                    JOptionPane.YES_NO_OPTION);

                if (result == JOptionPane.YES_OPTION) {
                    showStatus("You clicked yes.");
                } else {
                    showStatus("You clicked no.");
                }
            }
        });
    }
}
```

The result of this code appears in Figure 17.5, where you can see the yes/no dialog box. Clicking a button will close the dialog box, and the applet will indicate which button was clicked with a message in the status area. This program is in dialogconfirm.java on the CD.

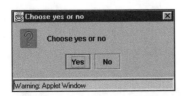

Figure 17.5   A confirmation dialog box.

Creating Option Pane Message Dialog Boxes

"No, no," says the Product Support Specialist. "I didn't mean you should use a confirmation dialog box there—it should be a message dialog box." "OK," you say, "if you're sure."

Message dialog boxes let you display a message to the user, and you use the **JOptionPane** class's **showMessageDialog** static method to create this kind of dialog box, passing the message you want to display to that method.

You can select the type of icon you want to display in these dialog boxes; here are the **JOptionPane** constants you can use with this method to indicate which icon you want displayed: **INFORMATION_MESSAGE**, **ERROR_MESSAGE**, **WARNING_MESSAGE**, **QUESTION_MESSAGE**, and **PLAIN_MESSAGE**.

Here's an example showing you how to use all of these types of message dialog boxes. In this case, I add a button for each type of dialog box, and clicking the button will display the corresponding dialog box:

```java
import java.awt.*;
import javax.swing.*;
import java.awt.event.*;

/*
<APPLET
    CODE = dialogmessage.class
    WIDTH = 350
    HEIGHT = 280 >
</APPLET>
*/

public class dialogmessage extends JApplet implements ActionListener
{
    JButton jbutton1 = new JButton("Display information dialog");
    JButton jbutton2 = new JButton("Display error dialog");
    JButton jbutton3 = new JButton("Display warning dialog");
    JButton jbutton4 = new JButton("Display question dialog");
    JButton jbutton5 = new JButton("Display plain dialog");

    public void init()
    {
        Container contentPane = getContentPane();

        contentPane.setLayout(new FlowLayout());
```

```
        contentPane.add(jbutton1);
        contentPane.add(jbutton2);
        contentPane.add(jbutton3);
        contentPane.add(jbutton4);
        contentPane.add(jbutton5);

        jbutton1.addActionListener(this);
        jbutton2.addActionListener(this);
        jbutton3.addActionListener(this);
        jbutton4.addActionListener(this);
        jbutton5.addActionListener(this);
    }

    public void actionPerformed(ActionEvent e)
    {
        String dialogtitle = "Dialog";
        String dialogmessage = "Hello from Swing!";
        int dialogtype = JOptionPane.PLAIN_MESSAGE;

        if(e.getSource() == jbutton1) {
            dialogtype = JOptionPane.INFORMATION_MESSAGE;
        } else if(e.getSource() == jbutton2) {
            dialogtype = JOptionPane.ERROR_MESSAGE;
        } else if(e.getSource() == jbutton3) {
            dialogtype = JOptionPane.WARNING_MESSAGE;
        } else if(e.getSource() == jbutton4) {
            dialogtype = JOptionPane.QUESTION_MESSAGE;
        } else if(e.getSource() == jbutton5) {
            dialogtype = JOptionPane.PLAIN_MESSAGE;
        }

        JOptionPane.showMessageDialog((Component) null,
            dialogmessage, dialogtitle, dialogtype);
    }
}
```

The result of this code appears in Figure 17.6, where you can see the buttons in the applet that represent the possible message dialog box types as well as an information dialog box. This example is in dialogmessage.java on the CD.

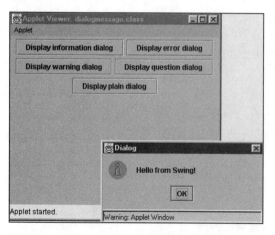

Figure 17.6   Creating different types of message dialog boxes.

Creating Option Pane Text Field Input Dialog Boxes

"No," says the Product Support Specialist, "that's not what I wanted at all. I didn't want a message dialog box; I wanted an input dialog box to let the user enter some text." "Hmm," you say.

You can use the **JOptionPane** class's **showInputDialog** method to display a dialog box with a text field that lets the user enter text. This method will return the text the user entered into the text field or null if the user clicks the Cancel button.

Here's an example in which I just read some text input from the user and display that text in an applet's status bar. The code itself is pretty simple. Here it is:

```
import java.awt.*;
import javax.swing.*;
import java.awt.event.*;

/*
<APPLET
    CODE = dialogtext.class
```

```
    WIDTH = 350
    HEIGHT = 280>
</APPLET>
*/

public class dialogtext extends JApplet implements ActionListener
{
    JButton jbutton = new JButton("Display dialog");
    String message = "Enter the text";

    public void init()
    {
        Container contentPane = getContentPane();

        contentPane.setLayout(new FlowLayout());

        contentPane.add(jbutton);

        jbutton.addActionListener(this);
    }

    public void actionPerformed(ActionEvent e)
    {
        String result = JOptionPane.showInputDialog(message);

        if(result == null)
            showStatus("You clicked Cancel");
        else
            showStatus("You typed: " + result);
    }
}
```

The result of this code appears in Figure 17.7, and you can see the input dialog box in the figure. When the user clicks the OK button, the dialog box disappears and the text from the text field in the dialog box appears in the applet's status bar. That's all there is to it. This example is in dialogtext.java on the CD.

Note that you can put **showInputDialog** to other uses as well—for example, you can display a combo box in a dialog box. See the next topic for the details.

17. Swing: Windows, Desktop Panes, Inner Frames, And Dialog Boxes

Figure 17.7   A basic text input dialog box.

Creating Option Pane Combo Box Input Dialog Boxes

"No, no," the Product Support Specialist says, "I didn't want a text field in that dialog box, I wanted a...." "Combo box?" you ask. "How did you know?" the PSS asks. "Telepathy," you say.

You can use the **JOptionPane** class's **showInputDialog** method to display a variety of controls; in this topic, I'll use a combo box. To do that, I pass a combo box to **showInputDialog** as well as an array holding the items I want in that combo box and the item I want selected by default. In this case, I list a variety of desserts and let the user select one. When the user clicks the OK button, I display the selection in the status bar of the applet. Here's the code:

```
import java.awt.*;
import javax.swing.*;
import java.awt.event.*;

/*
<APPLET
    CODE = dialogcombo.class
    WIDTH = 350
    HEIGHT = 280>
</APPLET>
*/
```

```
public class dialogcombo extends JApplet implements ActionListener
{
    JButton jbutton = new JButton("Display dialog");

    public void init()
    {
        Container contentPane = getContentPane();

        contentPane.setLayout(new FlowLayout());

        contentPane.add(jbutton);

        jbutton.addActionListener(this);
    }

    public void actionPerformed(ActionEvent e)
    {
        String dialogtitle = "Dialog";
        String dialogmessage = "Which one do you like best?";
        String[] desserts = {
            "cheesecake", "ice cream", "mousse", "carrot cake"
        };

        String dessert = (String)JOptionPane.showInputDialog(
            dialogcombo.this, dialogmessage, dialogtitle,
            JOptionPane.QUESTION_MESSAGE, null,
            desserts, desserts[0]);

        if(dessert == null)
            showStatus("You clicked Cancel");
        else
            showStatus("Your favorite: " + dessert);
    }
}
```

The result of this code appears in Figure 17.8, where you can see the combo box in the dialog box. When the user selects an item from the combo box and clicks OK, the dialog box closes and the selected item appears in the applet's status bar.

Figure 17.8   An input dialog box with a combo box.

Creating Option Pane Internal Frame Dialog Boxes

In addition to the heavyweight **JOptionPane** dialog boxes created in the previous few examples, you can create lightweight internal dialog boxes that appear inside a container. Here are the **JOptionPane** static methods you can use to create these types of dialog boxes:

- *showInternalMessageDialog*—Displays some message to the user.

- *showInternalConfirmDialog*—Asks a confirming question and receives a yes/no/cancel response.

- *showInternalInputDialog*—Prompts for input.

- *showInternalOptionDialog*—A configurable dialog box.

Here's an example in which I display an internal message dialog box in a desktop pane when the user clicks the button Display internal dialog. Here's what the code looks like:

```
import java.awt.*;
import javax.swing.*;
import java.awt.event.*;

/*
<APPLET
    CODE = optionpaneinternal.class
    WIDTH = 350
    HEIGHT = 280 >
```

```
</APPLET>
*/

public class optionpaneinternal extends JApplet implements ActionListener
{
    private JButton jbutton = new JButton("Display internal dialog");
    JDesktopPane jdesktoppane = new JDesktopPane();

    public void init()
    {
        Container contentPane = getContentPane();

        contentPane.add(jbutton, BorderLayout.SOUTH);
        contentPane.add(jdesktoppane);
        jbutton.addActionListener(this);
    }

    public void actionPerformed(ActionEvent e)
    {
        JOptionPane.showInternalMessageDialog(
            jdesktoppane, "Hello from Swing!", "Dialog",
            JOptionPane.INFORMATION_MESSAGE);
    }
}
```

The result appears in Figure 17.9, where you can see the internal message dialog box. This example is in optionpaneinternal.java on the CD.

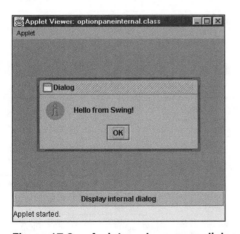

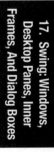

Figure 17.9   An internal message dialog.

Creating Dialog Boxes With **JDialog**

"Well," says the Novice Programmer, "the simple **JOptionPane** dialog boxes are very nice, but I want to build my own dialog boxes." "From scratch?" you ask. "From scratch," the NP says. "Then you want the **JDialog** class," you say.

The **JDialog** class is the foundation of dialog boxes you customize in Swing. Here's the inheritance diagram for this class:

```
java.lang.Object
|____java.awt.Component
     |____java.awt.Container
          |____java.awt.Window
               |____java.awt.Dialog
                    |____javax.swing.JDialog
```

You'll find the fields of the **JDialog** class in Table 17.11, its constructors in Table 17.12, and its methods in Table 17.13.

Table 17.11   Fields of the JDialog class.

Field	Does This
protected AccessibleContext accessibleContext	The accessible context.
protected JRootPane rootPane	The root pane.
protected boolean rootPaneChecking Enabled	Determines whether root pane checking is enabled.

Table 17.12   Constructors of the JDialog class.

Constructor	Does This
JDialog( )	Constructs a nonmodal dialog box.
JDialog(Dialog owner)	Constructs a nonmodal dialog box with the given dialog box as its owner.
JDialog(Dialog owner, boolean modal)	Constructs a modal or nonmodal dialog box without a title and with the indicated owner dialog box.
JDialog(Dialog owner, String title)	Constructs a nonmodal dialog box with the indicated title and with the indicated owner dialog box.
JDialog(Dialog owner, String title, boolean modal)	Constructs a modal or nonmodal dialog box with the indicated title and the indicated owner frame.

(continued)

*Table 17.12   Constructors of the **JDialog** class (continued).*

Constructor	Does This
JDialog(Frame owner)	Constructs a nonmodal dialog box without a title with the specified frame as its owner.
JDialog(Frame owner, boolean modal)	Constructs a modal or nonmodal dialog box without a title and with the indicated owner frame.
JDialog(Frame owner, String title)	Constructs a nonmodal dialog box with the indicated title and with the indicated owner frame.
JDialog(Frame owner, String title, boolean modal)	Constructs a modal or nonmodal dialog box with the indicated title and the indicated owner frame.

*Table 17.13   Methods of the **JDialog** class.*

Method	Does This
protected void addImpl(Component comp, Object constraints, int index)	Adds children to the **contentPane**.
protected JRootPane create RootPane( )	Called by the constructor methods to create the default **rootPane**.
protected void dialogInit( )	Called by the constructors to initialize the **JDialog** property.
AccessibleContext getAccessible Context( )	Gets the **AccessibleContext**.
Container getContentPane( )	Gets the **contentPane**.
int getDefaultCloseOperation( )	Gets the operation that occurs when the user initiates a close operation on this dialog box.
Component getGlassPane( )	Gets the **glassPane** object for this dialog box.
JMenuBar getJMenuBar( )	Gets the menu bar set on this dialog box.
JLayeredPane getLayeredPane( )	Gets the **layeredPane** object for this dialog box.
JRootPane getRootPane( )	Gets the **rootPane** object for this dialog box.
protected boolean isRootPane CheckingEnabled( )	Returns True if root pane checking is enabled.
protected String paramString( )	Gets a string representation of this **JDialog**.
protected void processKeyEvent(Key Event e)	Processes key events occurring on this **JDialog**.
protected void processWindowEvent (WindowEvent e)	Handles window events depending on the state of the **defaultCloseOperation** property.

17. Swing: Windows, Desktop Panes, Inner Frames, And Dialog Boxes

(continued)

Table 17.13   Methods of the JDialog class (continued).

Method	Does This
void remove(Component comp)	Removes the indicated component from this container.
void setContentPane(Container contentPane)	Sets the **contentPane** property.
void setDefaultCloseOperation (int operation)	Sets the operation that will occur by default when the user closes this dialog box.
void setGlassPane(Component glassPane)	Sets the **glassPane** property.
void setJMenuBar(JMenuBar menu)	Sets the menu bar for this dialog box.
void setLayeredPane(JLayeredPane layeredPane)	Sets the **layeredPane** property.
void setLayout(LayoutManager manager)	Sets the layout of the **contentPane**.
void setLocationRelativeTo (Component c)	Sets the location of the dialog box relative to the indicated component.
protected void setRootPane (JRootPane root)	Sets the **rootPane** property.
protected void setRootPaneChecking Enabled(boolean enabled)	Returns True if calls to **add( )** and **setLayout( )** will cause an exception to be thrown.
void update(Graphics g)	Simply calls **paint(g)**.

I'll create a dialog box example using the **JDialog** class here. In this case, I make the dialog box modal by passing a final parameter set to True to the **JDialog** constructor, and I add two buttons to the dialog box—OK and Cancel. By adding action listeners to those buttons, I can tell which button was clicked, and I can indicate that in the applet's status bar. After a button is clicked, I call the dialog box's **dispose** method to dispose of it. Here's what the code looks like (note that like other Swing windows, you add controls to a **JDialog** object using its content pane):

```
import java.awt.*;
import javax.swing.*;
import java.awt.event.*;

/*
<APPLET
    CODE = dialog.class
    WIDTH = 350
```

```
    HEIGHT = 280>
</APPLET>
*/

public class dialog extends JApplet implements ActionListener
{
    JLabel jlabel = new JLabel("Click the OK or Cancel button");

    JButton jbutton1 = new JButton("Display dialog"),
        jbutton2 = new JButton("OK"),
        jbutton3 = new JButton("Cancel");

    private JDialog dialog = new JDialog((Frame) null,
        "Dialog", true);

    public void init()
    {
        Container contentPane = getContentPane();
        Container dialogContentPane = dialog.getContentPane();

        contentPane.setLayout(new FlowLayout());
        contentPane.add(jbutton1);

        dialogContentPane.setLayout(new FlowLayout());

        dialogContentPane.add(jlabel);
        dialogContentPane.add(jbutton2);
        dialogContentPane.add(jbutton3);

        jbutton1.addActionListener(this);
        jbutton2.addActionListener(this);
        jbutton3.addActionListener(this);
    }

    public void actionPerformed(ActionEvent e)
    {
        if(e.getSource() == jbutton1) {
            dialog.setBounds(200, 200, 200, 120);
            dialog.show();
        } else if(e.getSource() == jbutton2) {
            showStatus("You clicked OK");
            dialog.dispose();
        } else if(e.getSource() == jbutton3) {
```

```
            showStatus("You clicked Cancel");
            dialog.dispose();
        }
    }
}
```

The result of this code appears in Figure 17.10. As you can see in the figure, the dialog box does indeed display OK and Cancel buttons. Clicking a button closes the dialog box and a message appears in the applet's status bar indicating which button was clicked. That's all there is to it. This example is in dialog.java on the CD.

Note that the dialog box in Figure 17.10 only accepts button input from the user; for a more advanced example, see the next topic.

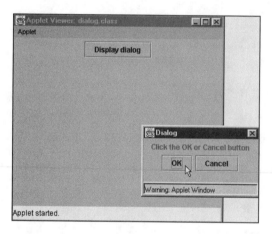

Figure 17.10   A basic JDialog dialog box.

Getting Input From Dialog Boxes Created With **JDialog**

You can configure dialog boxes created with the **JDialog** class as you like, and we'll take a look at an example in this topic. Here, I display a text field in which the user can enter text. If the dialog box is closed by clicking the OK button, the code will display the text the user entered into the text field in the applet's status bar; otherwise, if the user clicks the Cancel button, the code displays the message "You clicked Cancel." Here's what the code looks like:

```
import java.awt.*;
import javax.swing.*;
import java.awt.event.*;
```

```
/*
<APPLET
    CODE = dialoginput.class
    WIDTH = 350
    HEIGHT = 280>
</APPLET>
*/

public class dialoginput extends JApplet implements ActionListener
{
    JLabel jlabel = new JLabel("Enter the text:");

    JTextField jtextfield = new JTextField(15);

    JButton jbutton1 = new JButton("Display dialog"),
        jbutton2 = new JButton("OK"),
        jbutton3 = new JButton("Cancel");

    private JDialog dialog = new JDialog((Frame) null,
        "Dialog", true);

    public void init()
    {
        Container contentPane = getContentPane();
        Container dialogContentPane = dialog.getContentPane();

        contentPane.setLayout(new FlowLayout());
        contentPane.add(jbutton1);

        dialogContentPane.setLayout(new FlowLayout());

        dialogContentPane.add(jlabel);
        dialogContentPane.add(jtextfield);
        dialogContentPane.add(jbutton2);
        dialogContentPane.add(jbutton3);

        jbutton1.addActionListener(this);
        jbutton2.addActionListener(this);
        jbutton3.addActionListener(this);
    }

    public void actionPerformed(ActionEvent e)
    {
        if(e.getSource() == jbutton1) {
            dialog.setBounds(200, 200, 200, 150);
```

```
                    dialog.show();
            } else if(e.getSource() == jbutton2) {
                showStatus(jtextfield.getText());
                dialog.dispose();
            } else if(e.getSource() == jbutton3) {
                showStatus("You clicked Cancel");
                dialog.dispose();
            }
        }
    }
```

The result of this code appears in Figure 17.11, where you can see the dialog box
with the text field. When the user enters text and clicks OK, the text appears in the
status bar of the applet. That's all there is to it. This example is in dialoginput.java
on the CD.

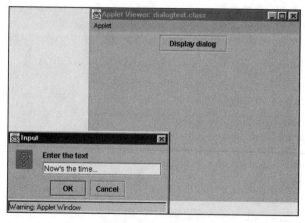

Figure 17.11   A **JDialog** dialog box with a text field.

Chapter 18
Swing: Tables And Trees

In Depth

In this chapter, we'll take a look at two of the biggest components of Swing: tables and trees. Both these topics are very large in scope and could take up an entire volume by themselves. You may guess their function from their names. Tables present the user with data in tabular form and trees display hierarchical data in a way that's become common—using expandable nodes. Before digging into these topics, we'll take an overview of each.

Tables

Tables may be the most complex component type in Swing. In fact, a whole package is devoted to them: **swing.table**. Tables present and let the user edit data arranged into rows and columns. In Swing, tables are, themselves, made up of column header and column objects. You can, of course, also address data by row and by individual cell, although those constructs are not objects.

Swing tables are very flexible, which accounts for some of their complexity. You can edit the data in a table directly and use a variety of selection modes (including column, row, and individual cell selection). You can use your own models for columns and column headers, decorate tables, draw your own cells by deriving a new cell renderer from the **TableCellRenderer** interface, handle cell editing by implementing the **CellEditor** interface, use keystroke actions, reorder columns, resize columns, and much more.

As with other Swing components, you can customize just about everything in a table, and because there are so many subcomponents here, the customization process can become very complex.

Trees

One of the new components in GUI programming that lets users handle data is the *tree*. If you've used Microsoft Windows Explorer, you know about trees already—this utility presents a directory structure using a tree. Trees use a "folder and leaf" analogy to present data; when you double-click a displayed folder, the pages (or *leaves*) inside that folder appear, as well as any subfolders. You can also close folders again by double-clicking them. Trees arrange their data into a vertical hierarchy, connected with lines, making an easily scrolled presentation. They're often used to display directories (as folders) and files (as leaves) in an easily manageable way.

Like tables, trees are complex enough to have their own package in Swing: **swing.tree**. In programming terms, trees are made up of *nodes*, and each node is either a folder or a leaf. Folders can have child nodes. All the nodes except for the root node have one single parent node. As you might guess, the appearance of folders and leaves is look-and-feel dependent. When you open a folder, it's considered *expanded*, and when you close it, it's *collapsed*. As with tables, you can customize trees with your own renderers and editors. You'll get a good introduction to the topic in this chapter.

That's it for the overview of what's in this chapter. There's a lot coming up here: Tables and trees represent a huge amount of programming depth. It's time to turn to the "Immediate Solutions" section, starting with a look at the **JTable** class.

Immediate Solutions

Creating Tables

The Big Boss appears and says, "About that new spreadsheet program you're writing...." "I didn't know I was writing anything like that," you say. "Don't interrupt," says the BB. "We need it yesterday. Is it done?" "Hmm," you say, "sounds like a job for the **JTable** class."

JTable is the Swing component that presents data in a two-dimensional table format. Here's the inheritance diagram for **JTable**:

```
java.lang.Object
|____java.awt.Component
     |____java.awt.Container
          |____javax.swing.JComponent
               |____javax.swing.JTable
```

You'll find the fields of the **JTable** class in Table 18.1, its constructors in Table 18.2, and its methods in Table 18.3 (note how extensive this class is).

Table 18.1   Fields of the JTable class.

Field	Does This
static int AUTO_RESIZE_ALL _COLUMNS	Resizes columns during resize operations.
static int AUTO_RESIZE_LAST _COLUMN	Resizes the last column only during all resize operations.
static int AUTO_RESIZE_NEXT _COLUMN	When a column is adjusted, this field adjusts the next column the opposite way.
static int AUTO_RESIZE_OFF	Uses a scroll bar to adjust column width.
static int AUTO_RESIZE _SUBSEQUENT_COLUMNS	Changes subsequent columns to preserve the total width upon resizing.
protected boolean autoCreate ColumnsFromModel	Queries the **TableModel** to build the default set of columns if this field is True.

(continued)

Table 18.1   Fields of the *JTable* class (continued).

Field	Does This
protected int autoResizeMode	Sets whether the table automatically resizes the width its columns to take up the entire width of the table.
protected TableCellEditor cellEditor	An object that overwrites the current cell and allows the user to change those contents.
protected boolean cellSelectionEnabled	If True, both a row selection and a column selection can be set at the same time.
protected TableColumnModel columnModel	The **TableColumnModel** of the table.
protected TableModel dataModel	The **TableModel** of the table.
protected Hashtable defaultEditorsByColumnClass	The table of objects that displays and edits the contents of a cell, indexed by class.
protected Hashtable defaultRenderersByColumnClass	The table of objects that displays the contents of a cell, indexed by class.
protected int editingColumn	The column of the cell being edited.
protected int editingRow	The row of the cell being edited.
protected Component editorComp	The component that handles editing.
protected Color gridColor	The color of the grid.
protected Dimension preferredViewportSize	Used by the **Scrollable** interface to determine the initial visible area.
protected int rowHeight	The height of rows in the table.
protected int rowMargin	The height margin between rows.
protected boolean rowSelectionAllowed	Returns True if row selection is allowed in this table.
protected Color selectionBackground	The background color of selected cells.
protected Color selectionForeground	The foreground color of selected cells.
protected ListSelectionModel selectionModel	The **ListSelectionModel** of the table; used to keep track of row selections.
protected boolean showHorizontalLines	Horizontal lines are drawn between cells if this field is True.
protected boolean showVerticalLines	Vertical lines are drawn between cells if this field is True.
protected JTableHeader tableHeader	The **TableHeader** working with the table.

18. Swing: Tables And Trees

Table 18.2   Constructors of the JTable class.

Constructor	Does This
JTable( )	Constructs a default **JTable**.
JTable(int numRows, int numColumns)	Constructs a **JTable** with **numRows** and **numColumns** of empty cells.
JTable(Object[ ][ ] rowData, Object[ ] columnNames)	Constructs a **JTable** to display the values in the two-dimensional array, **rowData**, with column names, **columnNames**.
JTable(TableModel dm)	Constructs a **JTable** that's initialized with **dm** as the data model, a default column model, and a default selection model.
JTable(TableModel dm, TableColumn Model cm)	Constructs a **JTable** that's initialized with **dm** as the data model, **cm** as the column model, and a default selection model.
JTable(TableModel dm, TableColumn Model cm, ListSelectionModel sm)	Constructs a **JTable** that's initialized with **dm** as the data model, **cm** as the column model, and **sm** as the selection model.
JTable(Vector rowData, Vector columnNames)	Constructs a **JTable** to display the values in the vector of **Vectors**, **rowData**, with column names as given in **columnNames**.

Table 18.3   Methods of the JTable class.

Method	Does This
void addColumn(TableColumn aColumn)	Appends a column to the end of the array of columns.
void addColumnSelectionInterval (int index0, int index1)	Adds the columns from **index0** to **index1**, inclusive, to the selection.
void addNotify( )	Calls **configureEnclosingScrollPane**.
void addRowSelectionInterval (int index0, int index1)	Adds the rows from **index0** to **index1**, inclusive, to the selection.
void clearSelection( )	Deselects all selected columns and rows.
void columnAdded(TableColumn ModelEvent e)	Indicates to listeners that a column was added to the model.
int columnAtPoint(Point point)	Gets the index of the column that **point** lies in (or -1 if it lies outside the receiver's bounds).
void columnMarginChanged (ChangeEvent e)	Notifies listeners that a column was moved because of a margin change.
void columnMoved(TableColumn ModelEvent e)	Notifies listeners that a column was repositioned.
void columnRemoved(TableColumn ModelEvent e)	Notifies listeners that a column was removed from the model.

(continued)

Table 18.3   Methods of the *JTable* class (continued).

Method	Does This
void columnSelectionChanged(List SelectionEvent e)	Notifies listeners that the selection model of the **TableColumnModel** changed.
protected void configureEnclosing ScrollPane( )	Configures the enclosing **ScrollPane** by installing the table's **tableHeader** as the **columnHeaderView** of the scroll pane, and so on.
int convertColumnIndexToModel (int viewColumnIndex)	Gets the index of the column in the model whose data is being displayed in the column **viewColumnIndex** in the display.
int convertColumnIndexToView (model intColumnIndex)	Gets the index of the column in the view that's displaying the data from the column **modelColumnIndex** in the model.
protected TableColumnModel create DefaultColumnModel( )	Gets the default column model object, which is a **DefaultTableColumnModel**.
void createDefaultColumnsFrom Model( )	Creates default columns for the table from the data model using the **getColumnCount( )** and **getColumnClass( )** methods defined in the **TableModel** interface.
protected TableModel createDefault DataModel( )	Gets the default table model object, which is a **DefaultTableModel**.
protected void createDefaultEditors( )	Creates default cell editors for objects, numbers, and Boolean values.
protected void createDefault Renderers( )	Creates the default renderers.
protected ListSelectionModel create DefaultSelectionModel( )	Gets the default selection model object, which is a **DefaultListSelectionModel**.
protected JTableHeader create DefaultTableHeader( )	Gets the default table header object, which is a **JTableHeader**.
static JScrollPane createScroll PaneForTable(JTable aTable)	Deprecated. Replaced by the new **JScrollPane(aTable)**.
boolean editCellAt(int row, int column)	Starts editing the cell at **row** and **column**, if the cell is editable.
boolean editCellAt(int row, int column, EventObject e)	Starts editing the cell at **row** and **column**, if the cell is editable.
void editingCanceled(ChangeEvent e)	Invoked when editing is canceled.
void editingStopped(ChangeEvent e)	Invoked when editing is finished.
AccessibleContext getAccessible Context( )	Gets the **AccessibleContext** associated with this **JComponent**.
boolean getAutoCreateColumns FromModel( )	Gets whether the table will create default columns from the model.

(continued)

Table 18.3   Methods of the JTable class (continued).

Method	Does This
int getAutoResizeMode( )	Gets the autoresize mode of the table.
TableCellEditor getCellEditor( )	Gets the **cellEditor**.
TableCellEditor getCellEditor(int row, int column)	Gets an appropriate editor for the cell given by this row and column.
Rectangle getCellRect(int row, int column, boolean includeSpacing)	Gets a rectangle locating the cell that lies at the intersection of **row** and **column**.
TableCellRenderer getCellRenderer (int row, int column)	Gets an appropriate renderer for the cell given by this row and column.
boolean getCellSelectionEnabled( )	Returns True if simultaneous row and column selections are allowed.
TableColumn getColumn (Object identifier)	Gets the **TableColumn** object for the column in the table whose identifier is equal to **identifier**, when compared using **equals( )**.
Class getColumnClass(int column)	Gets the type of the column at the given view position.
int getColumnCount( )	Gets the number of columns in the column model (note that this may be different from the number of columns in the table model).
TableColumnModel getColumnModel( )	Gets the **TableColumnModel** that contains all column information of this table.
String getColumnName(int column)	Gets the name of the column at the given view position.
boolean getColumnSelectionAllowed( )	Returns True if columns can be selected.
TableCellEditor getDefaultEditor (Class columnClass)	Gets the editor to be used when no editor has been set in a **TableColumn**.
TableCellRenderer getDefaultRenderer (Class columnClass)	Gets the renderer to be used when no renderer has been set in a **TableColumn**.
int getEditingColumn( )	Gets the index of the editing column.
int getEditingRow( )	Gets the index of the editing row.
Component getEditorComponent( )	Gets the component that was returned from the **CellEditor**.
Color getGridColor( )	Gets the color used to draw grid lines.
Dimension getIntercellSpacing( )	Gets the horizontal and vertical spacing between cells.
TableModel getModel( )	Gets the **TableModel** that provides the data displayed by the receiver.
Dimension getPreferredScrollable ViewportSize( )	Gets the preferred size of the viewport for this table.
int getRowCount( )	Gets the number of rows in the table.
int getRowHeight( )	Gets the height of a table row in the receiver.
int getRowMargin( )	Gets the amount of empty space between rows.

(continued)

Table 18.3   Methods of the JTable class (continued).

Method	Does This
boolean getRowSelectionAllowed( )	Returns True if rows can be selected.
int getScrollableBlockIncrement (Rectangle visibleRect, int orientation, int direction)	Gets **visibleRect.height** or **visibleRect.width**, depending on the table's orientation.
boolean getScrollableTracksViewport Height( )	Returns False if the height of the viewport does not determine the height of the table.
boolean getScrollableTracks ViewportWidth( )	Returns False if the width of the viewport does not determine the width of the table.
int getScrollableUnitIncrement (Rectangle visibleRect, int orientation, int direction)	Gets the scroll increment that completely exposes one new row or column.
int getSelectedColumn( )	Gets the index of the first selected column or -1 if no column is selected.
int getSelectedColumnCount( )	Gets the number of selected columns.
int[ ] getSelectedColumns( )	Gets the indexes of all selected columns.
int getSelectedRow( )	Gets the index of the first selected row or -1 if no row is selected.
int getSelectedRowCount( )	Gets the number of selected rows.
int[ ] getSelectedRows( )	Gets the indexes of all selected rows.
Color getSelectionBackground( )	Gets the background color for selected cells.
Color getSelectionForeground( )	Gets the foreground color for selected cells.
ListSelectionModel getSelectionModel( )	Gets the **ListSelectionModel** that's used to maintain row selection state.
boolean getShowHorizontalLines( )	Returns True if the receiver draws horizontal lines between cells and False if it doesn't.
boolean getShowVerticalLines( )	Returns True if the receiver draws vertical lines between cells and False if it doesn't.
JTableHeader getTableHeader( )	Gets the **tableHeader** working with this **JTable**.
String getToolTipText(Mouse the Event event)	Overrides **JComponent**'s **setToolTipText** method to allow use of renderer's tips (if the renderer has text set).
TableUI getUI( )	Gets the look and feel object that renders this component.
String getUIClassID( )	Gets the name of the look and feel class that renders this component.
Object getValueAt(int row, int column)	Gets the cell value at **row** and **column**.

(continued)

Table 18.3   Methods of the *JTable* class (continued).

Method	Does This
protected void initializeLocalVars( )	Initializes table properties to their default values.
boolean isCellEditable(int row, int column)	Returns True if the cell at **row** and **column** is editable.
boolean isCellSelected(int row, int column)	Returns True if the cell at the given position is selected.
boolean isColumnSelected(int column)	Returns True if the column at the given index is selected.
boolean isEditing( )	Returns True if the table is editing a cell.
boolean isManagingFocus( )	Overridden to return True.
boolean isRowSelected(int row)	Returns True if the row at the given index is selected.
void moveColumn(int column, int targetColumn)	Moves the column **column** to the position currently occupied by the column **targetColumn**.
protected String paramString( )	Gets a string representation of this **JTable**.
Component prepareEditor(TableCellEditor editor, int row, int column)	Prepares the given editor using the value at the given cell.
Component prepareRenderer(TableCellRenderer renderer, int row, int column)	Prepares the given renderer with an appropriate value from the **dataModel**.
void removeColumn(TableColumn aColumn)	Removes a column from the **JTable**'s array of columns.
void removeColumnSelectionInterval (int index0, int index1)	Deselects the columns from **index0** to **index1**, inclusive.
void removeEditor( )	Discards the editor object.
void removeRowSelectionInterval (int index0, int index1)	Deselects the rows from **index0** to **index1**, inclusive.
void reshape(int x, int y, int width, int height)	Calls **super.reshape( )** and is overridden to detect changes in the table's bounds.
protected void resizeAndRepaint( )	Equivalent to **revalidate( )** followed by **repaint( )**.
int rowAtPoint(Point point)	Gets the index of the row that **point** lies in.
void selectAll( )	Selects all rows, columns, and cells in the table.
void setAutoCreateColumnsFromModel(boolean createColumns)	Sets the table's **autoCreateColumnsFromModel** flag.
void setAutoResizeMode(int mode)	Sets the table's autoresize mode when the table is resized.

(continued)

Table 18.3   Methods of the *JTable* class (continued).

Method	Does This
void setCellEditor(TableCellEditor anEditor)	Sets the **cellEditor** variable.
void setCellSelectionEnabled (boolean flag)	Sets whether this table allows both a column selection and a row selection to exist at the same time.
void setColumnModel(TableColumn Model newModel)	Sets the column model for this table to **newModel** and registers for listener notifications from the new column model.
void setColumnSelectionAllowed (boolean flag)	Sets whether the columns in this model can be selected.
void setColumnSelectionInterval (int index0, int index1)	Selects the columns from **index0** to **index1**, inclusive.
void setDefaultEditor(Class column Class, TableCellEditor editor)	Sets a default editor to be used if no editor has been set in a **TableColumn**.
void setDefaultRenderer(Class column Class, TableCellRenderer renderer)	Sets a default renderer to be used if no renderer has been set in a **TableColumn**.
void setEditingColumn(int aColumn)	Sets the **editingColumn** variable.
void setEditingRow(int aRow)	Sets the **editingRow** variable.
void setGridColor(Color newColor)	Sets the color used to draw grid lines to **color** and redisplays the receiver.
void setIntercellSpacing (Dimension newSpacing)	Sets the width and height between cells to **newSpacing** and redisplays the receiver.
void setModel(TableModel newModel)	Sets the data model for this table to **newModel** and registers for listener notifications from the new data model.
void setPreferredScrollableViewport Size(Dimension size)	Sets the preferred size of the viewport for this table.
void setRowHeight(int newHeight)	Sets the height for rows.
void setRowMargin(int rowMargin)	Sets the amount of empty space between rows.
void setRowSelectionAllowed (boolean flag)	Sets whether the rows in this model can be selected.
void setRowSelectionInterval (int index0, int index1)	Selects the rows from **index0** to **index1**, inclusive.
void setSelectionBackground (Color selectionBackground)	Sets the background color for selected cells.
void setSelectionForeground (Color selectionForeground)	Sets the foreground color for selected cells.

(continued)

18. Swing: Tables And Trees

Table 18.3   Methods of the JTable class (continued).

Method	Does This
void setSelectionMode (int selectionMode)	Sets the table's selection mode to allow single selections, a single contiguous interval, or multiple intervals.
void setSelectionModel(ListSelection Model newModel)	Sets the row-selection model for this table to **newModel**.
void setShowGrid(boolean b)	Sets whether to draw grid lines around cells.
void setShowHorizontalLines(boolean b)	Sets whether to draw horizontal lines between cells.
void setShowVerticalLines(boolean b)	Sets whether to draw vertical lines between cells.
void setTableHeader(JTableHeader newHeader)	Sets the **tableHeader** working with this **JTable** to **newHeader**.
void setUI(TableUI ui)	Sets the look and feel object that draws this component.
void setValueAt(Object aValue, int row, int column)	Sets the value for the cell at **row** and **column**.
void sizeColumnsToFit(boolean last ColumnOnly)	Deprecated. Replaced by **sizeColumnsToFit(int)**.
void sizeColumnsToFit(int resizing Column)	Resizes one or more of the columns in the table so that the total width of all of **JTable**'s columns will be equal to the width of the table.
void tableChanged(TableModelEvent e)	Called when the table is changed.
void updateUI( )	Called by **UIManager** when the look and feel has changed.
void valueChanged(ListSelection Event e)	Invoked when the selection changes.

The model you use to hold the data in a table is derived from the **AbstractTableModel** class. The default table model is the **DefaultTableModel** class. Here's the inheritance diagram for this class:

```
java.lang.Object
|_____javax.swing.table.AbstractTableModel
     |_____javax.swing.table.DefaultTableModel
```

You'll find the fields of the **DefaultTableModel** class in Table 18.4, its constructors in Table 18.5, and its methods in Table 18.6.

*Table 18.4   Fields of the **DefaultTableModel** class.*

Field	Does This
protected Vector columnIdentifiers	A vector of column identifiers.
protected Vector dataVector	A Vector of Object values.

*Table 18.5   Constructors of the **DefaultTableModel** class.*

Constructor	Does This
DefaultTableModel( )	Constructs a **DefaultTableModel**.
DefaultTableModel(int numRows, numColumns)	Constructs a **DefaultTableModel** with **numRows** and int numColumns.
DefaultTableModel(Object[ ][ ] data, Object[ ] columnNames)	Constructs a **DefaultTableModel** and initializes the table by passing **data** and **columnNames** to the **setDataVector** method.
DefaultTableModel(Object[ ] column Names, int numRows)	Constructs a **DefaultTableModel** with as many columns as there are elements of null object values in **columnNames** and **numRows**.
DefaultTableModel(Vector column Names, int numRows)	Constructs a **DefaultTableModel** with as many columns as there are elements of null object values in **columnNames** and **numRows**.
DefaultTableModel(Vector data, Vector columnNames)	Constructs a **DefaultTableModel** and initializes the table by passing **data** and **columnNames** to the **setDataVector** method.

*Table 18.6   Methods of the **DefaultTableModel** class.*

Method	Does This
void addColumn(Object columnName)	Adds a column to the model.
void addColumn(Object columnName, Object[ ] columnData)	Adds a column to the model with name **columnName**.
void addColumn(Object columnName, Vector columnData)	Adds a column to the model.
void addRow(Object[ ] rowData)	Adds a row to the end of the model.
void addRow(Vector rowData)	Adds a row to the end of the model.
protected static Vector convertTo Vector(Object[ ] anArray)	Gets a Vector that contains the same objects as the array.
protected static Vector convertTo Vector(Object[ ][ ] anArray)	Gets a Vector of Vectors that contains the same objects as the array.
int getColumnCount( )	Gets the number of columns in this data table.

(continued)

Table 18.6   Methods of the *DefaultTableModel* class (continued).

Method	Does This
String getColumnName(int column)	Gets the column name.
Vector getDataVector( )	Returns the Vector of Vectors that contains the table's data values.
int getRowCount( )	Gets the number of rows in this data table.
Object getValueAt(int row, int column)	Gets an attribute value for the cell at **row** and **column**.
void insertRow(int row, Object[ ] rowData)	Inserts a row at **row** in the model.
void insertRow(int row, Vector rowData)	Inserts a row at **row** in the model.
boolean isCellEditable(int row, int column)	Returns True if the cell at **row** and **column** is editable.
void moveRow(int startIndex, int endIndex, int toIndex)	Moves one or more rows starting at **startIndex** to **endIndex** in the model to the **toIndex**.
void newDataAvailable(TableModel Event event)	Equivalent to **fireTableChanged**.
void newRowsAdded(TableModel Event event)	This method will make sure the new rows have the correct number of columns.
void removeRow(int row)	Removes the row at **row** from the model.
void rowsRemoved(TableModel Event event)	Equivalent to **fireTableChanged( )**.
void setColumnIdentifiers(Object[ ] newIdentifiers)	Replaces the column identifiers in the model.
void setColumnIdentifiers(Vector newIdentifiers)	Replaces the column identifiers in the model.
void setDataVector(Object[ ][ ] newData, Object[ ] columnNames)	Replaces the value in the **dataVector** instance variable with the values in the array **newData**.
void setDataVector(Vector newData, Vector columnNames)	Replaces the current **dataVector** instance variable with the new vector of rows, **newData**.
void setNumRows(int newSize)	Sets the number of rows in the model.
void setValueAt(Object aValue, int row, int column)	Sets the object value for the cell at **column** and **row**.

Although the **JTable** class is complex, it provides defaults for most aspects of table programming, which makes things easier. Here's an example in which I use the **DefaultTableModel** class to add data to a table, row by row. First, I create a new object of the **DefaultTableModel** class and a new **JTable** object that displays the data in that model object:

```
import java.awt.*;
import javax.swing.*;
import javax.swing.table.*;

/*
<APPLET
    CODE = table.class
    WIDTH = 350
    HEIGHT = 280 >
</APPLET>
*/

public class table extends JApplet
{
    DefaultTableModel defaulttablemodel = new DefaultTableModel();
    JTable jtable = new JTable(defaulttablemodel);
         .
         .
         .
}
```

Next, I use the default table model's **addColumn** method to add columns to the table, giving them the captions Column 0, Column 1, and so on:

```
public class table extends JApplet
{
    DefaultTableModel defaulttablemodel = new DefaultTableModel();
    JTable jtable = new JTable(defaulttablemodel);

    public void init()
    {
        for(int column = 0; column < 5; column++){
            defaulttablemodel.addColumn("Column " + column);
        }
         .
         .
         .
    }
}
```

Having added columns to the table, I'm ready to add the data the table will display in its rows, and I'll do that by constructing each row and then using the model's **addRow** method. Each row is an array of objects; in this case, I'll use **String** objects. Here's how I construct each row and then add it to the table:

```
public class table extends JApplet
{
    Object[] data = new Object[5];

    DefaultTableModel defaulttablemodel = new DefaultTableModel();
    JTable jtable = new JTable(defaulttablemodel);

    public void init()
    {
        for(int column = 0; column < 5; column++){
            defaulttablemodel.addColumn("Column " + column);
        }

        for(int row = 0; row < 10; row++) {
            for(int column = 0; column < 5; column++) {
                data[column] = "Cell " + row + "," + column;
            }
            defaulttablemodel.addRow(data);
        }
            .
            .
            .
    }
}
```

All that's left is to display the new table. Tables are usually displayed in scroll panes, and, in fact, you should do so to make sure column headers appear. Here's how I add the table to a **JScrollPane** and then display it:

```
public class table extends JApplet
{
    Object[] data = new Object[5];

    DefaultTableModel defaulttablemodel = new DefaultTableModel();
    JTable jtable = new JTable(defaulttablemodel);

    public void init()
    {
        for(int column = 0; column < 5; column++){
```

```
            defaulttablemodel.addColumn("Column " + column);
        }

        for(int row = 0; row < 10; row++) {
            for(int column = 0; column < 5; column++) {
                data[column] = "Cell " + row + "," + column;
            }
            defaulttablemodel.addRow(data);
        }
        getContentPane().add(new JScrollPane(jtable));
    }
}
```

And that's it; this table appears in Figure 18.1. You can see the table with the column headers in the figure. This example is in table.java on the CD.

You can already do a lot with this table; for example, you can resize columns simply by resizing the column headers. The default selection mode is by row, so you can select rows by double-clicking them or multiple rows by using the Ctrl and Shift keys. You can also edit the data in any cell by triple-clicking that cell, which makes it display a blinking text insertion caret and and which makes it turn into something much like a text field (you can create your own custom cell editors based on other controls). When you edit the text in a cell and press Enter, the new data appears in that cell. In fact, you can even rearrange the columns in the table just by dragging column headers. For example, in Figure 18.2, I've switched columns 2 and 3 around.

Column 0	Column 1	Column 3	Column 2	Column 4
Cell 0,0	Cell 0,1	Cell 0,3	Cell 0,2	Cell 0,4
Cell 1,0	Cell 1,1	Cell 1,3	Cell 1,2	Cell 1,4
Cell 2,0	Cell 2,1	Cell 2,3	Cell 2,2	Cell 2,4
Cell 3,0	Cell 3,1	Cell 3,3	Cell 3,2	Cell 3,4
Cell 4,0	Cell 4,1	Cell 4,3	Cell 4,2	Cell 4,4
Cell 5,0	Cell 5,1	Cell 5,3	Cell 5,2	Cell 5,4
Cell 6,0	Cell 6,1	Cell 6,3	Cell 6,2	Cell 6,4
Cell 7,0	Cell 7,1	Cell 7,3	Cell 7,2	Cell 7,4
Cell 8,0	Cell 8,1	Cell 8,3	Cell 8,2	Cell 8,4

Figure 18.1   A basic table.

18. Swing: Tables And Trees

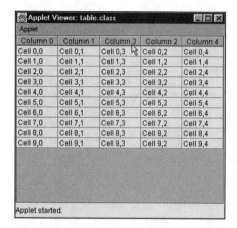

Figure 18.2   Switching column positions in a basic table.

Here's another way of constructing a table. In this case, I create a new table model derived from the **AbstractTableModel** class, overriding the **getColumnCount** method to indicate how many columns the table should have, the **getRowCount** method to indicate how many rows the table should have, and the **getValueAt** method to supply the data cell by cell. Here's the code:

```
TableModel newModel = new AbstractTableModel() {
    public int getColumnCount() {return 100;}
    public int getRowCount() {return 100;}
    public Object getValueAt(int row, int column) {return new
        String("Cell " + row + ", " + column);}
};


JTable jtable = new JTable(newModel);
getContentPane().add(new JScrollPane(jtable));
```

Adding Rows And Columns To Tables At Runtime

The Big Boss appears, aggrieved, and says, "Well, your new program does indeed have a spreadsheet in it, but it's pretty limited." "How limited?" you ask. "Well," the BB says, "for one thing, it can only use spreadsheets that have five columns and five rows." "That's a limitation?" you ask.

To add rows and columns to a table, you can use the table model's **addRow** and **addColumn** methods to add rows and columns at runtime (and you can use the

removeRow and **removeColumn** methods to remove them). This is a very useful feature, because tables cannot always remain static.

We'll take a look at an example here that lets the user add rows and columns to a table at runtime. I start by creating a table and a panel that has two buttons: Create a new row and Create a new column. Here's what this looks like in code:

```java
import java.awt.*;
import javax.swing.*;
import java.awt.event.*;
import javax.swing.table.*;

/*
<APPLET
    CODE = tableadd.class
    WIDTH = 350
    HEIGHT = 280 >
</APPLET>
*/

public class tableadd extends JApplet
{
    Object[] data = new Object[5];

    DefaultTableModel defaulttablemodel = new DefaultTableModel();
    JTable jtable = new JTable(defaulttablemodel);

    public void init()
    {
        for(int column = 0; column < 5; column++){
            defaulttablemodel.addColumn("Column " + column);
        }

        for(int row = 0; row < 5; row++) {
            for(int column = 0; column < 5; column++) {
                data[column] = "Cell " + row + "," + column;
            }
            defaulttablemodel.addRow(data);
        }

        getContentPane().add(new JScrollPane(jtable), BorderLayout.CENTER);
        getContentPane().add(new jpanel(), BorderLayout.SOUTH);
    }
        .
        .
        .
```

I'll add a new inner class to implement the button panel. Here's what creating the new buttons and connecting them looks like:

```
class jpanel extends JPanel implements ActionListener
{
    JButton jbutton1 = new JButton("Create new row"),
        jbutton2 = new JButton("Create new column");

    public jpanel()
    {
        add(jbutton1);
        add(jbutton2);

        jbutton1.addActionListener(this);
        jbutton2.addActionListener(this);

    }
    .
    .
    .
}
```

The real action takes place when the user clicks a button. When the user clicks the Create new row button, I use the **addRow** method to add a new row to the table after I fill it with data (note that I use the table model's **getRowCount** and **getColumnCount** methods to determine the current dimensions of the table):

```
public void actionPerformed(ActionEvent e)
{
    if(e.getSource() == jbutton1) {
        int numberrows = defaulttablemodel.getRowCount();
        int numbercolumns = defaulttablemodel.getColumnCount();

        Object[] data = new Object[numbercolumns];

        for(int column = 0; column < numbercolumns; column++) {
            data[column] = "Cell " + numberrows + "," + column;
        }
        defaulttablemodel.addRow(data);
        .
        .
        .
```

When the user clicks the Create new column button, on the other hand, I create a new column with the **addColumn** method and fill it with data using the **setValueAt** method:

```
public void actionPerformed(ActionEvent e)
{
    if(e.getSource() == jbutton1) {
        int numberrows = defaulttablemodel.getRowCount();
        int numbercolumns = defaulttablemodel.getColumnCount();

        Object[] data = new Object[numbercolumns];

        for(int column = 0; column < numbercolumns; column++) {
            data[column] = "Cell " + numberrows + "," + column;
        }
        defaulttablemodel.addRow(data);

    } else if(e.getSource() == jbutton2) {
        int numberrows = defaulttablemodel.getRowCount();
        int numbercolumns = defaulttablemodel.getColumnCount();
        defaulttablemodel.addColumn("Column " + numbercolumns);

        for(int row = 0; row < numberrows; row++) {
            defaulttablemodel.setValueAt("Cell " + row + "," +
                numbercolumns, row, numbercolumns);
        }

        jtable.sizeColumnsToFit(0);
    }
  }
}
```

Note the use of the **sizeColumnsToFit** method at the end of this code; calling this method resizes the columns in the table to fit into the scroll pane after I've added a new column. In fact, you can set the **JTable** resize mode like this:

```
jtable.setAutoResizeMode(JTable.AUTO_RESIZE_ALL_COLUMNS);
```

However, the table will still not be resized when you add a new column (although it should be), so you need to call **sizeColumnsToFit**.

The result of this code appears in Figure 18.3. In this figure, I've added one row and one column to the table—this example works just as it should. You'll find it in tableadd.java on the CD.

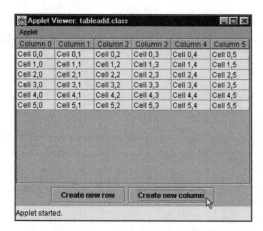

Figure 18.3   Adding rows and columns to tables at runtime.

Adding Controls And Images To Tables

"Hey," says the Novice Programmer, "I thought tables were Swing objects." "They are," you say. "Why?" "Well," says the NP, "what about adding images to them?" You smile and say, "No problem."

In this topic, we'll take a look at handling different data types in a table. Here, I create a table that manages data for a restaurant on various sandwich types, including string, floating-point, Boolean, date, and image data. Note that the Boolean data is automatically handled in tables by displaying a check box in the table cell.

The default table model won't let you use heterogeneous data types such as images, so I create a new model that extends **DefaultTableModel** in this example. That new model will be named, appropriately enough, **newModel**. Here's how I can fill a table with heterogeneous data using that model:

```
import java.awt.*;
import java.util.*;
import javax.swing.*;
import javax.swing.table.*;

/*
<APPLET
    CODE = tableimages.class
    WIDTH = 600
```

```
    HEIGHT = 280 >
</APPLET>
*/

public class tableimages extends JApplet
{
    String[] columns = {"Sandwich", "Available", "Price", "Date", "Image"};

    Date date = (new GregorianCalendar(2000, 9, 2)).getTime();

    Object[][] data = {
        {"Ham", new Boolean(false), new Float(4.99), date, new
            ImageIcon("table.jpg")},

        {"BBQ", new Boolean(true), new Float(5.99), date, new
            ImageIcon("table.jpg")},

        {"Turkey", new Boolean(false), new Float(4.99), date, new
            ImageIcon("table.jpg")},

        {"Watercress", new Boolean(true), new Float(4.99), date, new
            ImageIcon("table.jpg")},

        {"Cheese", new Boolean(false), new Float(4.99), date, new
            ImageIcon("table.jpg")},

        {"Beef", new Boolean(true), new Float(4.99), date, new
            ImageIcon("table.jpg")}
    };

    JTable jtable = new JTable(new newModel(data, columns));

    public void init()
    {
        getContentPane().add(new JScrollPane(jtable));
    }
}
```

All that's left is to derive **newModel** from **DefaultTableModel**. To do that, I override three methods: the **DefaultTableModel** constructor to install the data in the model, the **isCellEditable** method to indicate that all cells are not editable, and the **getColumnClass** method to return the class of the data in each cell (this is the method that you must implement to enable heterogeneous data handling).

18. Swing: Tables
And Trees

Here's what this looks like in code (note that I use the **getClass** method to get the class of the data in each cell, and I use the **elementAt** method to get the element at a particular location; **elementAt** returns an object of the **Vector** class, and we'll see that class later in this book):

```
class newModel extends DefaultTableModel
{
    public newModel(Object[][] data, Object[] columns)
    {
        super(data, columns);
    }

    public boolean isCellEditable(int row, int col)
    {
        return false;
    }

    public Class getColumnClass(int column)
    {
        Vector v = (Vector) dataVector.elementAt(0);

        return v.elementAt(column).getClass();
    }
}
```

The result of this code appears in Figure 18.4. As you can see in the figure, this new table supports various kinds of data, as represented by check boxes, numbers, and images. This example is in tableimages.java on the CD.

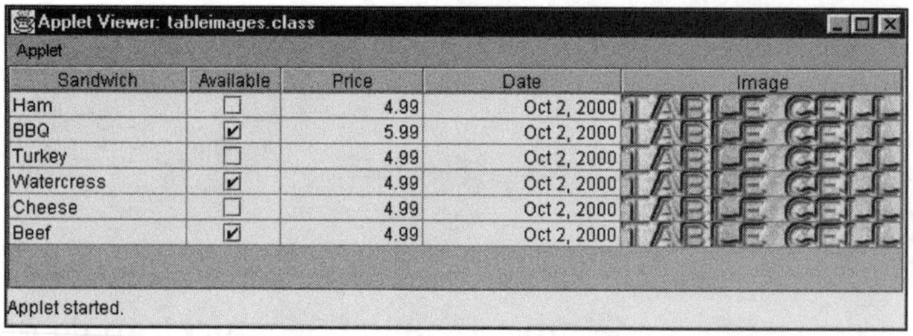

Figure 18.4   Adding images and check boxes to a table.

Creating Trees

"Uh-oh," says the Novice Programmer, "the Big Boss wants me to create a file directory utility that displays files and directories using a tree." "Well," you say, "you can use a *tree*." "Great," says the Novice Programmer. "Only, what's a tree?"

Trees are controls that display hierarchical data as an outline based on nodes. A specific node can be identified either by a **TreePath** (an object that encapsulates a node and all the nodes it's descended from—called its *ancestors*) or by its display row (the row in the display shows only one node). You can expand nodes to display all their children. A *collapsed node* is one that hides its children and a *hidden node* is one that's under a collapsed parent.

Trees are supported by the **JTree** class in Swing. Here's what the inheritance diagram for this class looks like:

```
java.lang.Object
|____java.awt.Component
     |____java.awt.Container
          |____javax.swing.JComponent
               |____javax.swing.JTree
```

You can find the fields of the **JTree** class in Table 18.7, its constructors in Table 18.8, and its methods in Table 18.9.

Table 18.7   Fields of the JTree class.

Field	Does This
static String CELL_EDITOR _PROPERTY	The bound property name for **cellEditor**.
static String CELL_RENDERER _PROPERTY	The bound property name for **cellRenderer**.
protected TreeCellEditor cellEditor	The editor for the entries.
protected TreeCellRenderer cellRenderer	The cell renderer used to draw nodes.
protected boolean editable	Returns True if the tree is editable.
static String EDITABLE_PROPERTY	The bound property name for editable.
static String INVOKES_STOP_CELL _EDITING_PROPERTY	The bound property name for **messagesStopCellEditing**.

(continued)

Table 18.7   Fields of the *JTree* class (continued).

Field	Does This
protected boolean invokesStop CellEditing	Returns True when editing is to be stopped.
static String LARGE_MODEL _PROPERTY	The bound property name for **largeModel**.
protected boolean largeModel	Returns True if the tree uses a large model.
static String ROOT_VISIBLE _PROPERTY	The bound property name for **rootVisible**.
protected boolean rootVisible	Returns True if the root node is displayed and false if its children are the highest visible nodes.
static String ROW_HEIGHT_PROPERTY	The bound property name for **rowHeight**.
protected int rowHeight	The height to use for each display row.
static String SCROLLS_ON_EXPAND _PROPERTY	The bound property name for **scrollsOnExpand**.
protected boolean scrollsOnExpand	Returns True if a node will scroll when expanded to show all descendants..
static String SELECTION_MODEL _PROPERTY	The bound property name for **selectionModel**.
protected TreeSelectionModel selectionModel	Models the set of selected nodes in this tree.
protected JTree.TreeSelection Redirector selectionRedirector	Creates a new event and passes it off the **selectionListeners**.
static String SHOWS_ROOT _HANDLES_PROPERTY	The bound property name for **showsRootHandles**.
protected boolean showsRootHandles	Returns True if handles are displayed at the topmost level of the tree.
protected int toggleClickCount	The number of mouse clicks before a node is expanded.
static String TREE_MODEL_PROPERTY	The bound property name for **treeModel**.
protected TreeModel treeModel	The model that defines the tree displayed by this object.
protected TreeModelListener tree ModelListener	Updates the **expandedState**.
static String VISIBLE_ROW_COUNT _PROPERTY	The bound property name for **visibleRowCount**.
protected int visibleRowCount	The number of rows to make visible at one time.

Table 18.8   Constructors of the *JTree* class.

Constructor	Does This
JTree( )	Constructs a **JTree** with a sample model.
JTree(Hashtable value)	Constructs a **JTree** created from a hashtable.
JTree(Object[ ] value)	Constructs a **JTree** with each element of the given array as the child of a new root node.
JTree(TreeModel newModel)	Constructs an instance of **JTree** that displays the root node using the given data model.
JTree(TreeNode root)	Constructs a **JTree** with the given **TreeNode** as its root, which displays the root node.
JTree(TreeNode root, boolean asks AllowsChildren)	Constructs a **JTree** with the given **TreeNode** as its root, which displays the root node and whether a node is a leaf node in the given manner.
JTree(Vector value)	Constructs a **JTree** with each element of the given **Vector** as the child of a new root node that is not displayed.

Table 18.9   Methods of the *JTree* class.

Method	Does This
void addSelectionInterval(int index0, int index1)	Adds the paths between **index0** and **index1**, inclusive, to the selection.
void addSelectionPath(TreePath path)	Adds the node identified by the given **TreePath** to the selection.
void addSelectionPaths (TreePath[ ] paths)	Adds each path in the array of paths to the selection.
void addSelectionRow(int row)	Adds the path at the given row to the selection.
void addSelectionRows(int[ ] rows)	Adds the paths at each of the given rows to the selection.
void addTreeExpansionListener (TreeExpansionListener tel)	Adds a listener for **TreeExpansion** events.
void addTreeSelectionListener (TreeSelectionListener tsl)	Adds a listener for **TreeSelection** events.
void addTreeWillExpandListener(TreeWillExpandListener tel)	Adds a listener for **TreeWillExpand** events.
void cancelEditing( )	Cancels the current editing session.
void clearSelection( )	Clears the selection.
protected void clearToggledPaths( )	Clears the cache of toggled paths.

(continued)

Table 18.9   Methods of the JTree class (continued).

Method	Does This
void collapsePath(TreePath path)	Makes sure that the node identified by the given path is collapsed and viewable.
void collapseRow(int row)	Makes sure that the node in the given row is collapsed.
String convertValueToText(Object value, boolean selected, boolean expanded, boolean leaf, int row, boolean hasFocus)	Called by the renderers to convert the given value to text.
protected static TreeModel create TreeModel(Object value)	Gets a **TreeModel** encapsulating the given object.
protected TreeModelListener create TreeModelListener( )	Creates and returns an instance of **TreeModelHandler**.
void expandPath(TreePath path)	Makes sure that the node identified by the given path is expanded.
void expandRow(int row)	Makes sure that the node in the given row is expanded.
void fireTreeCollapsed(TreePath path)	Notifies all listeners for this event.
void fireTreeExpanded(TreePath path)	Notifies all listeners for this event.
void fireTreeWillCollapse(TreePath path)	Notifies all listeners for this event.
void fireTreeWillExpand(TreePath path)	Notifies all listeners for this event.
protected void fireValueChanged (TreeSelectionEvent e)	Fires a "value changed" event.
AccessibleContext getAccessible Context( )	Gets the **AccessibleContext**.
TreeCellEditor getCellEditor( )	Gets the editor used to edit entries.
TreeCellRenderer getCellRenderer( )	Gets the current **TreeCellRenderer** that's rendering each cell.
TreePath getClosestPathFor Location(int x, int y)	Gets the path to the node that's closest to x,y.
int getClosestRowForLocation (int x, int y)	Gets the row of the node that's closest to x,y.
protected static TreeModel get DefaultTreeModel( )	Creates and returns a sample **TreeModel**.
protected Enumeration getDescendant are ToggledPaths(TreePath parent)	Gets an enumeration of **TreePaths** that have been expanded and descendants of **parent**.
TreePath getEditingPath( )	Gets the path to the element that's currently being edited.
Enumeration getExpanded Descendants(TreePath parent)	Gets an enumeration of the descendants of **path** that are currently expanded.

(continued)

Table 18.9   Methods of the JTree class (continued).

Method	Does This
boolean getInvokesStopCellEditing( )	Gets the indicator that tells what happens when editing is interrupted.
Object getLastSelectedPath Component( )	Gets the last path component in the first node of the current selection.
TreePath getLeadSelectionPath( )	Gets the path of the last node added to the selection.
int getLeadSelectionRow( )	Gets the row index of the last node added to the selection.
int getMaxSelectionRow( )	Gets the last selected row.
int getMinSelectionRow( )	Gets the first selected row.
TreeModel getModel( )	Gets the **TreeModel** that's providing the data.
protected TreePath[ ] getPathBetween and Rows(int index0, int index1)	Gets **JTreePath** instances representing the path between **index0 index1**, inclusive.
Rectangle getPathBounds (TreePath path)	Gets the rectangle that the given node will be drawn into.
TreePath getPathForLocation(int x, int y)	Gets the path for the node at the given location.
TreePath getPathForRow(int row)	Gets the path for the given row.
Dimension getPreferredScrollable ViewportSize( )	Gets the preferred display size of a **JTree**.
Rectangle getRowBounds(int row)	Gets the rectangle that the node at the given row is drawn in.
int getRowCount( )	Gets the total number of rows.
int getRowForLocation(int x, int y)	Gets the row for the given location.
int getRowForPath(TreePath path)	Gets the row that displays the node identified by the given path.
int getRowHeight( )	Gets the height of each row.
int getScrollableBlockIncrement(Rectangle visibleRect, int orientation, int direction)	Gets the block increment.
boolean getScrollableTracksViewport Height( )	False indicates that the height of the viewport does not determine the height of the table.
boolean getScrollableTracks ViewportWidth( )	False indicates that the width of the viewport does not determine the width of the table.
int getScrollableUnitIncrement (Rectangle visibleRect, int orientation, int direction)	Gets the amount to increment when scrolling.
boolean getScrollsOnExpand( )	Returns True if the tree will scroll to show previously hidden children.

(continued)

18. Swing: Tables And Trees

Table 18.9   Methods of the JTree class (continued).

Method	Does This
int getSelectionCount( )	Gets the number of nodes selected.
TreeSelectionModel getSelection Model( )	Gets the model for selections.
TreePath getSelectionPath( )	Gets the path to the first selected node.
TreePath[ ] getSelectionPaths( )	Gets the paths of all selected values.
int[ ] getSelectionRows( )	Gets all the currently selected rows.
boolean getShowsRootHandles( )	Returns True if handles for the root nodes are displayed.
String getToolTipText(Mouse the Event event)	Overrides **JComponent**'s **getToolTipText** method in order to allow renderer's tooltips to be used.
TreeUI getUI( )	Gets the look and feel object that draws this component.
String getUIClassID( )	Gets the name of the look and feel class that draws this component.
int getVisibleRowCount( )	Gets the number of rows that are displayed in the display area.
boolean hasBeenExpanded (TreePath path)	Returns True if the node identified by the path has ever been expanded.
boolean isCollapsed(int row)	Returns True if the node at the given display row is collapsed.
boolean isCollapsed(TreePath path)	Returns True if the value identified by **path** is currently collapsed.
boolean isEditable( )	Returns True if the tree is editable.
boolean isEditing( )	Returns True if the tree is being edited.
boolean isExpanded(int row)	Returns True if the node at the given display row is currently expanded.
boolean isExpanded(TreePath path)	Returns True if the node identified by the path is currently expanded.
boolean isFixedRowHeight( )	Returns True if the height of each display row is a fixed size.
boolean isLargeModel( )	Returns True if the tree is configured for a large model.
boolean isPathEditable(TreePath path)	Gets the value in **isEditable**.
boolean isPathSelected(TreePath path)	Returns True if the item identified by the path is currently selected.
boolean isRootVisible( )	Returns True if the root node of the tree is displayed.
boolean isRowSelected(int row)	Returns True if the node identified by **row** is selected.
boolean isSelectionEmpty( )	Returns True if the selection is currently empty.
boolean isVisible(TreePath path)	Returns True if the value identified by **path** is currently viewable.
void makeVisible(TreePath path)	Ensures that the node identified by **path** is currently viewable.
protected String paramString( )	Gets a string representation of this **JTree**.

(continued)

Table 18.9   Methods of the *JTree* class (continued).

Method	Does This
protected void removeDescendant ToggledPaths(Enumeration toRemove)	Removes any descendants of the **TreePaths** in **toRemove** that have been expanded.
void removeSelectionInterval(int the index0, int index1)	Removes the nodes between **index0** and **index1**, inclusive, from selection.
void removeSelectionPath (TreePath path)	Removes the node identified by the given path from the current selection.
void removeSelectionPaths (TreePath[ ] paths)	Removes the nodes identified by the given paths from the current selection.
void removeSelectionRow(int row)	Removes the path at the index row from the current selection.
void removeSelectionRows(int[ ] rows)	Removes the paths that are selected at each of the given rows.
void removeTreeExpansionListener (TreeExpansionListener tel)	Removes a listener for **TreeExpansion** events.
void removeTreeSelectionListener (TreeSelectionListener tsl)	Removes a **TreeSelection** listener.
void removeTreeWillExpandListener (TreeWillExpandListener tel)	Removes a listener for **TreeWillExpand** events.
void scrollPathToVisible(TreePath path)	Scrolls so that the node identified by **path** is displayed.
void scrollRowToVisible(int row)	Scrolls the item identified by **row** until it's displayed.
void setCellEditor(TreeCellEditor cellEditor)	Sets the cell editor.
void setCellRenderer(TreeCell Renderer x)	Sets the **TreeCellRenderer** that will be used to draw each cell.
void setEditable(boolean flag)	Determines whether the tree is editable.
protected void setExpandedState (TreePath path, boolean state)	Sets the expanded state of the receiver.
void setInvokesStopCellEditing (boolean newValue)	Determines what happens when editing is interrupted.
void setLargeModel(boolean newValue)	Specifies whether the user interface should use a large model.
void setModel(TreeModel newModel)	Sets the **TreeModel** that will provide the data.
void setRootVisible(boolean rootVisible)	Determines whether the root node from the **TreeModel** is visible.
void setRowHeight(int rowHeight)	Sets the height of each cell.
void setScrollsOnExpand(boolean newValue)	Determines whether the tree should scroll when a node is expanded.

(continued)

18. Swing: Tables And Trees

Table 18.9   Methods of the *JTree* class (continued).

Method	Does This
void setSelectionInterval(int index0, int index1)	Selects the nodes between **index0** and **index1**, inclusive.
void setSelectionModel(TreeSelection Model selectionModel)	Sets the tree's selection model.
void setSelectionPath(TreePath path)	Selects the node identified by the given path.
void setSelectionPaths (TreePath[ ] paths)	Selects the nodes identified by the given array of paths.
void setSelectionRow(int row)	Selects the node at the given row in the display.
void setSelectionRows(int[ ] rows)	Selects the nodes corresponding to each of the given rows in the display.
void setShowsRootHandles(boolean newValue)	Determines whether the node handles are to be displayed.
void setUI(TreeUI ui)	Sets the look and feel object that renders this component.
void setVisibleRowCount(int newCount)	Sets the number of rows that are to be displayed.
void startEditingAtPath(TreePath path)	Selects the given path and starts editing.
boolean stopEditing( )	Ends the editing session.
void treeDidChange( )	Called when the tree has changed enough that it needs to resize the bounds.
void updateUI( )	Called by **UIManager** when the look and feel has changed.

You can add data to a tree in a variety of ways; in this chapter, I'll use a popular technique: creating a hashtable, populating it with data, and adding that hash to the tree. You can use **JTree** to display compound nodes (for example, nodes containing both a graphic icon and text) by subclassing **TreeCellRenderer** and using **setTreeCellRenderer**. To edit nodes, you can subclass **TreeCellEditor** and use **setTreeCellEditor**.

Here's a quick example. In this case, I just create a default tree and add it to a scroll pane:

```
import java.awt.*;
import javax.swing.*;
import javax.swing.tree.*;
```

```
/*
<APPLET
    CODE = tree.class
    WIDTH = 350
    HEIGHT = 280>
</APPLET>
*/

public class tree extends JApplet
{
    public void init()
    {
        JTree jtree = new JTree();

        getContentPane().add(new JScrollPane(jtree));
    }
}
```

This code is all that's needed to display a basic tree—the result of this code appears in Figure 18.5, where you can see that Swing has added some default data to the tree. This example is in tree.java on the CD.

Note that trees aren't going to be much use unless you can add your own data to them—see the next topic for the details.

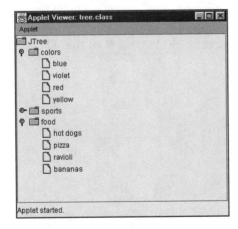

Figure 18.5   A basic tree.

Adding Data To Trees

"Just one problem," the Novice Programmer says. "I've created a Swing tree, but how can I add data to it?" "There are a number of ways to do it," you say. "Pull up a chair and we'll look at it." The NP goes to get some coffee.

There are a number of ways to populate trees with data. For example, here are the various possibilities using the **JTree** constructors:

- *JTree()*—Create a default tree with sample data.
- *JTree(Hashtable value)*—Create a tree from a hashtable.
- *JTree(Object[] value)*—Create a tree from an object array.
- *JTree(TreeModel newModel)*—Create a tree from a tree model.
- *JTree(TreeNode root)*—Create a tree with the given root node.
- *JTree(Vector value)*—Create a tree from a vector.

Using a hashtable is an easy way to create a tree with folders and leaves, and I'll use that technique here. You'll learn about hash tables in depth later in this book; hashes let you store data accessible with a text key, and you can populate them with the **put** method, which takes the key and value pair you want to store in the hash. Hashes are useful in constructing trees; they can, themselves, contain hashes, which is how you create nodes with subnodes.

An example will make this more clear. In this example, I create a hash with individual data items and subhashes, just by creating a single hash to represent the tree. When the hash has been built, all I have to do is pass it to the **JTree** constructor, like this:

```
import java.awt.*;
import java.util.*;
import javax.swing.*;
import javax.swing.tree.*;

/*
<APPLET·
    CODE = treedata.class
    WIDTH = 350
    HEIGHT = 280>
</APPLET>
*/
```

```
public class treedata extends JApplet
{
    Hashtable hashtable = new Hashtable();
    Hashtable subhashtable = new Hashtable();
    Hashtable subsubhashtable = new Hashtable();

    String[] strings = new String[] {"Item 1", "Item 2",
        "Item 3", "Item 4", "Item 5"};

    public void init()
    {
        Container contentPane = getContentPane();

        hashtable.put("Items", strings);
        hashtable.put("Subitems", subhashtable);

        subhashtable.put("Items", strings);
        subhashtable.put("Item 1", new Integer(1));
        subhashtable.put("Item 2", new Integer(2));
        subhashtable.put("Item 3", new Integer(3));
        subhashtable.put("Items with subitems", subsubhashtable);

        subsubhashtable.put("Yet more subitems", strings);
        subsubhashtable.put("Item 1", new Integer(1));
        subsubhashtable.put("Item 2", new Integer(2));
        subsubhashtable.put("Item 3", new Integer(3));

        JTree hashTree = new JTree(hashtable);

        JScrollPane hashPane = new JScrollPane(hashTree);

        hashTree.expandPath(new TreePath(hashTree.getModel().getRoot()));

        contentPane.add(hashPane);
    }
}
```

The **JTree** class interprets the hashes passed to it and creates the corresponding tree structure, as you can see in Figure 18.6. That's all it takes to add data to trees in a complex data hierarchy. This example is in treedata.java on the CD.

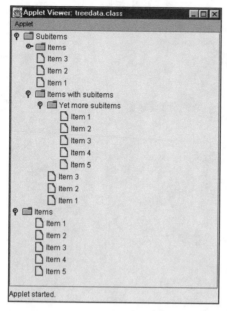

Figure 18.6   A tree populated with data.

Handling Tree Events

One of the important aspects of working with trees is handling tree events, such as when the user clicks or double-clicks a node. To handle mouse events, you can add a **MouseListener** to a tree. Here's an example in which I indicate which node in the tree was clicked or double-clicked.

When the user clicks a node, I find which row in the tree was clicked with the **getRowForLocation** method. To find the actual node, I use the **getPathForRow** and **getLastPathComponent** methods. Here's the code:

```
import java.awt.*;
import javax.swing.*;
import java.awt.event.*;
import javax.swing.tree.*;

/*
<APPLET
    CODE = treeevents.class
    WIDTH = 350
    HEIGHT = 280>
</APPLET>
*/
```

```
public class treeevents extends JApplet
{
    public void init()
    {
        JTree tree = new JTree();

        getContentPane().add(new JScrollPane(tree));

        tree.addMouseListener(new MouseAdapter() {
            public void mousePressed(MouseEvent e)
            {
                String outString = null;
                JTree jtree = (JTree)e.getSource();

                int clickedrow = jtree.getRowForLocation(e.getX(),
                    e.getY());

                if(clickedrow != -1) {
                    TreePath treepath = jtree.getPathForRow(clickedrow);
                    TreeNode treenode = (TreeNode)
                        treepath.getLastPathComponent();

                    outString = "Node " + treenode.toString();

                    if(e.getClickCount() == 1)
                    {
                        outString += " was single clicked.";
                    } else {
                        outString += " was double clicked.";
                    }

                    showStatus(outString);
                }
            }
        });
    }
}
```

You can see the results in Figure 18.7. When the user clicks or double-clicks any node, including folders, this applet will indicate in the status bar which node was clicked or double-clicked . Handling a tree event such as this makes tree controls come alive and allows users to organize their data as they like. This example is in treeevents.java on the CD.

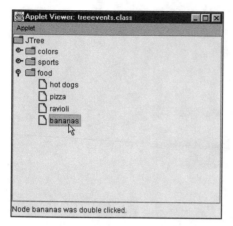

Figure 18.7   A tree populated with data.

Editing Tree Nodes

"Hmm," says the Novice Programmer, "I've created that file-managing program the Big Boss wanted using a tree, but there's a problem—users want to be able to change the names of files simply by editing a tree node. You can't do that, can you?" "Sure you can," you say. "Uh-oh," the NP says, "guess I've got some code to write."

To let the user edit the text in the nodes in a tree, you use the **setEditable** method. To allow the user to actually read the new text as edited, you can implement the **editingCanceled** and **editingStopped** methods of the **CellEditorListener** methods. If the user moves away from the edited node without pressing Enter, **editingCanceled** is called and the edit does not take effect; if the user does press Enter, the **editingStopped** method is called and the edit does take effect.

Here's an example in which I handle both the **editingCanceled** and **editingStopped** methods. When **editingCanceled** is called, I indicate that the editing was cancelled; when **editingStopped** is called, I display the new node text. Here's the code:

```
import java.awt.*;
import javax.swing.*;
import javax.swing.tree.*;
import javax.swing.event.*;
```

```
/*
<APPLET
    CODE = treeedit.class
    WIDTH = 350
    HEIGHT = 280>
</APPLET>
*/

public class treeedit extends JApplet implements CellEditorListener
{
    public void init()
    {
        JTree tree = new JTree();

        getContentPane().add(tree);

        tree.setEditable(true);

        tree.getCellEditor().addCellEditorListener(this);
    }

    public void editingCanceled(ChangeEvent e)
    {
        CellEditor editor = (CellEditor)e.getSource();

        showStatus("Change not made");
    }

    public void editingStopped(ChangeEvent e)
    {
        CellEditor editor = (CellEditor)e.getSource();

        showStatus("New text: " + (String)editor.getCellEditorValue());
    }
}
```

The result of this code appears in Figure 18.8, and you can see in the figure that I'm changing the text "basketball" to "basketballet". This applet works as it should, and it appears in treeedit.java on the CD.

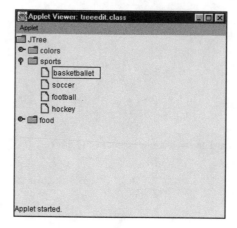

Figure 18.8   Editing a tree node.

Chapter 19

Swing: Text Components

In Depth

In this chapter, we'll take a look at the Swing text components: text fields, password fields, text areas, editor panes, and text panes. All these components are descendents of the **JTextComponent** class, which we'll also take a look at here.

Swing text components can get as complex and involved as you're ever likely to see. The **JTextPane** class is the top-of-the-line text component, and it's quite possible to get lost in a veritable forest of renderers and selection models when working with this class. The complete details on all the Swing text components would take many chapters, but you'll get a good introduction here.

Text Fields

Text fields are the old standby of text components, and we've used them as long as we've used Swing. Text fields, as supported by the **JTextField** class, let the user view, enter, and edit a single line of text. You can do more with Swing text fields than you can with AWT text fields—for example, you can scroll a Swing text field programmatically. You'll see the possibilities in this chapter. All in all, text fields are relatively simple Swing text components; the more complex ones are coming up.

Password Fields

Password fields are much like text fields where you've set the echo character so that each time the user types a character, the specified echo character appears instead of the actual typed character. Password fields mask what's really typed in case someone's looking over your shoulder as you type a password. Unlike AWT, in Swing, password fields get their own control and class: the **JPasswordField** class. We'll take a look at how to work with this class in this chapter.

Text Areas

Swing text areas constitute another relatively simple Swing text control. Text areas are much like text fields, except that they're two-dimensional and can display text in rows and columns. You can display the text with scroll bars as well as with word wrap—it's up to you. Text areas are popular controls when you have more than a single line of text to display; in fact, we've already used them in this book. We'll take an in-depth look at them here.

Editor Panes

Editor panes provide you with a way of working with three kinds of text: plain text, HTML, and rich-text format (RTF) text. You can load entire Web pages as well as RTF documents into editor panes (but note that the HTML support is by no means complete, at least not yet). We'll take a look at these options here.

Text Panes

Text panes are the most sophisticated of the Swing text components; they're derived from the **JEditorPane** class and extend editor panes by letting you mark up text with various style attributes. Using text panes, you can create entirely new styles and apply them to paragraphs or to individual runs of characters in your text. (Programming this component can get a little complex.) You can also embed other controls and images in text panes, thus creating complex documents.

That's it for the overview of what's in this chapter. There's a lot coming up—in fact, Swing text components could, themselves, take up an entire book. It's time to turn to the "Immediate Solutions" section, starting with a look at the **JTextComponent** class.

Immediate Solutions

Creating Swing Text Components: The **JTextComponent** Class

Swing text components are built on the **JTextComponent** class, and it's worth taking a look at the fields, constructor, and methods of this class because the Swing text components inherit them all. Here's the inheritance diagram for the **JTextComponent** class:

```
java.lang.Object
|____java.awt.Component
     |____java.awt.Container
          |____javax.swing.JComponent
               |____javax.swing.text.JTextComponent
```

You'll find the fields for the **JTextComponent** class in Table 19.1, its constructor in Table 19.2, and its methods in Table 19.3.

Table 19.1   Fields of the JTextComponent class.

Field	Does This
static String DEFAULT_KEYMAP	The default keymap.
static String FOCUS_ACCELERATOR _KEY	The bound property name for the focus accelerator.

Table 19.2   The constructor of the JTextComponent class.

Constructor	Does This
JTextComponent( )	Constructs a new **JTextComponent**.

Table 19.3   Methods of the JTextComponent class.

Method	Does This
void addCaretListener(CaretListener listener)	Adds a caret listener.
void addInputMethodListener(InputMe thodListener l)	Adds the given input method listener.

(continued)

Table 19.3   Methods of the *JTextComponent* class (continued).

Method	Does This
static Keymap addKeymap(String nm, Keymap parent)	Adds a new keymap into the keymap hierarchy.
void copy( )	Copies the currently selected range in the associated text model to the system Clipboard.
void cut( )	Copies the currently selected range in the associated text model to the system Clipboard, removing the contents from the model.
protected void fireCaretUpdate (CaretEvent e)	Notifies all listeners.
AccessibleContext getAccessible Context( )	Gets the **AccessibleContext**.
Action[ ] getActions( )	Gets the command list for the editor.
Caret getCaret( )	Gets the caret that allows text-oriented navigation over the view.
Color getCaretColor( )	Gets the current color used to draw the caret.
int getCaretPosition( )	Gets the position of the text-insertion caret for the text component.
Color getDisabledTextColor( )	Gets the current color used to render the selected text.
Document getDocument( )	Gets the model associated with the editor.
char getFocusAccelerator( )	Gets the key accelerator that will cause the receiving text component to get the focus.
Highlighter getHighlighter( )	Gets the object responsible for making highlights.
InputMethodRequests getInputMethod Requests( )	Gets the input method request handler that supports requests from input methods for this component.
Keymap getKeymap( )	Gets the keymap currently active in this text component.
static Keymap getKeymap(String nm)	Gets a named keymap previously added to the document.
Insets getMargin( )	Gets the margin between the text component's border and its text.
Dimension getPreferredScrollable ViewportSize( )	Gets the preferred size of the viewport for a view component.
int getScrollableBlockIncrement (Rectangle visibleRect, int orientation, int direction)	Gets the scroll increment that will completely expose one block of rows or columns.
boolean getScrollableTracks ViewportHeight( )	Returns True if a viewport should always force the height of this **Scrollable** object to match the height of the viewport.
boolean getScrollableTracksViewport Width( )	Returns True if a viewport should always force the width of this **Scrollable** object to match the width of the viewport.

(continued)

Table 19.3   Methods of the *JTextComponent* class (continued).

Method	Does This
int getScrollableUnitIncrement(Rectangle visibleRect, int orientation, int direction)	The scroll increment that will completely expose one new row or column, depending on the value of **orientation**.
String getSelectedText( )	Gets the selected text contained in this **TextComponent**.
Color getSelectedTextColor( )	Gets the current color used to render the selected text.
Color getSelectionColor( )	Gets the current color used to render the selection.
int getSelectionEnd( )	Gets the selected text's end position.
int getSelectionStart( )	Gets the selected text's start position.
String getText( )	Gets the text contained in this **TextComponent**.
String getText(int offs, int len)	Gets a portion of the text represented by the component.
TextUI getUI( )	Gets the user-interface factory for this text-oriented editor.
boolean isEditable( )	Gets the boolean value indicating whether this **TextComponent** is editable.
boolean isFocusTraversable( )	Returns True if the focus can be traversed.
boolean isOpaque( )	Returns True if this component is completely opaque.
static void loadKeymap(Keymap map, JTextComponent.KeyBinding[ ] bindings, Action[ ] actions)	Loads a keymap with bindings.
Rectangle modelToView(int pos)	Converts the given location in the model to the view coordinate system.
void moveCaretPosition(int pos)	Moves the caret to a new position.
protected String paramString( )	Gets a string representation of this **JTextComponent**.
void paste( )	Copies the contents of the system Clipboard into the associated text model.
protected void processComponent KeyEvent(KeyEvent e)	Processes any key events that the component, itself, recognizes.
protected void processInputMethod Event(InputMethodEvent e)	Processes input method events occurring in this component.
void read(Reader in, Object desc)	Initializes from a stream.
void removeCaretListener (CaretListener listener)	Removes a caret listener.
static Keymap removeKeymap(String nm)	Removes a named keymap previously added to the document.

(continued)

Table 19.3   *Methods of the JTextComponent class* (continued).

Method	Does This
void removeNotify( )	Notifies this component that it has been removed from its container.
void replaceSelection(String content)	Replaces the currently selected content with new content represented by the given string.
void select(int selectionStart, int selectionEnd)	Selects the text found between the given start and end locations.
void selectAll( )	Selects all the text in the **TextComponent**.
void setCaret(Caret c)	Sets the caret to be used.
void setCaretColor(Color c)	Sets the current color used to render the caret.
void setCaretPosition(int position)	Sets the position of the text-insertion caret for the **TextComponent**.
void setDisabledTextColor(Color c)	Sets the current color used to render the disabled text.
void setDocument(Document doc)	Associates the editor with a text document.
void setEditable(boolean b)	Sets the given boolean value to indicate whether this **TextComponent** should be editable.
void setEnabled(boolean b)	Enables or disables this component, depending on the value of the parameter **b**.
void setFocusAccelerator(char aKey)	Sets the key accelerator that will cause the receiving text component to get the focus.
void setHighlighter(Highlighter h)	Sets the highlighter to be used.
void setKeymap(Keymap map)	Sets the keymap to use for binding events to actions.
void setMargin(Insets m)	Sets margin space between the text component's border and its text.
void setOpaque(boolean o)	Sets whether the UI should draw a background.
void setSelectedTextColor(Color c)	Sets the current color used to draw the selected text.
void setSelectionColor(Color c)	Sets the current color used to draw the selection.
void setSelectionEnd(int selectionEnd)	Sets the selection end to the given position.
void setSelectionStart(int selectionStart)	Sets the selection start to the given position.
void setText(String t)	Sets the text of this **TextComponent** to the given text.
void setUI(TextUI ui)	Sets the user-interface factory for this text-oriented editor.
void updateUI( )	Reloads the UI object.
int viewToModel(Point pt)	Converts the given location in the view-coordinate system to the nearest location in the model.
void write(Writer out)	Stores the contents of the model using the given stream.

Creating Text Fields

The text field is the basic Swing text control. In fact, we've already put text fields to work as far back as Chapter 12. Here's the inheritance diagram for the **JTextField** class:

```
java.lang.Object
|____java.awt.Component
    |____java.awt.Container
        |____javax.swing.JComponent
            |____javax.swing.text.JTextComponent
                |____javax.swing.JTextField
```

In Chapter 12, you'll find the constructors of the **JTextField** class in Table 12.6 and its methods in Table 12.7. Here's a short example that puts a text field to work:

```java
import java.awt.*;
import javax.swing.*;

/*
<APPLET
    CODE=textfield.class
    WIDTH=300
    HEIGHT=200 >
</APPLET>
*/

public class textfield extends JApplet {
    JTextField text = new JTextField(20);

    public void init()
    {
        Container contentPane = getContentPane();

        contentPane.setLayout(new FlowLayout());
        contentPane.add(text);
        text.setText("Hello from Swing!");
    }
}
```

We'll take a look as some of the capabilities of Swing text fields over the next couple topics.

Setting Text Field Alignment

"Hmm," says the Novice Programmer, "I got a strange memo from the Big Boss. It says, 'We're trying something new. Left-align all your text.' Is it some political thing?" You smile and say, "No, it's all about your text fields."

You can set the alignment of text fields with the **setHorizontalAlignment** method (there is no **setVerticalAlignment** method for text fields). Here's an example that shows the possibilities—right, left, and center. In this case, I let the user click a button to set the alignment of the text in a text field; then, I use the **setHorizontalAlignment** method to justify the text to match. Here's the code:

```
import java.awt.*;
import javax.swing.*;
import java.awt.event.*;

/*
<APPLET
    CODE = textfieldalign.class
    WIDTH = 350
    HEIGHT = 280 >
</APPLET>
*/

public class textfieldalign extends JApplet
{
    JTextField jtextfield = new JTextField("Hello from Swing!");
    JButton jbutton1, jbutton2, jbutton3;

    public void init()
    {
        Container contentPane = getContentPane();

        jtextfield.setColumns(30);

        contentPane.setLayout(new FlowLayout());
        contentPane.add(new buttonpanel());
        contentPane.add(jtextfield);
    }

    class buttonpanel extends JPanel implements ActionListener
    {

        public buttonpanel()
        {
```

```
                    jbutton1 = new JButton("Left");
                    jbutton2 = new JButton("Right");
                    jbutton3 = new JButton("Center");

                    jbutton1.addActionListener(this);
                    jbutton2.addActionListener(this);
                    jbutton3.addActionListener(this);

                    setLayout(new FlowLayout());

                    add(new JLabel("Alignment"));
                    add(jbutton1);
                    add(jbutton2);
                    add(jbutton3);

                }

                public void actionPerformed(ActionEvent e)
                {
                    if(e.getSource() == jbutton1) {
                        jtextfield.setHorizontalAlignment(JTextField.LEFT);
                    } else if(e.getSource() == jbutton2) {
                        jtextfield.setHorizontalAlignment(JTextField.RIGHT);
                    } else if(e.getSource() == jbutton3) {
                        jtextfield.setHorizontalAlignment(JTextField.CENTER);
                    }
                }
            }
        }
```

You can see the result of this code in Figure 19.1, where the user can set the alignment of the text in the text field just by clicking a button. This example is in textfieldalign.java on the CD accompanying this book.

TIP: Note that I set the number of columns using **setColumns** in the text field in this example so that you can see horizontal space around the actual text. There are two things to note here: First, the size of a column in a text field is the width of the letter m, so **setColumn** does not actually set the number of characters visible. Second, **setColumn** sets only the text field's preferred size.

Figure 19.1   Aligning text in a text field.

Scrolling Text Fields

"I've got a problem," the Novice Programmer says. "I'm writing my novel in a text field, and I really hate having to move around in all that text using the keyboard." "OK," you say. "You can scroll the text field, but you really should be using a text area when working with a lot of text." The NP says, "Tell me more!"

Swing text fields implement the **Scrollable** interface, which means you can scroll them under programmatic command or inside scroll panes. Here's an example showing how that works. In this case, I use the text field's **getHorizontalVisibility** method to get an object that implements the **BoundedRangeModel** interface, and I pass that object to the constructor of a slider, implementing scrolling directly, without a scroll pane. When the user adjusts the slider, I use the text field's **setScrollOffset** method to scroll the text field. First, however, take a look at the methods of the **BoundedRangeModel** interface, which is specially designed to make scrolling controls easier, in Table 19.4.

*Table 19.4   Methods of the **BoundedRangeModel** interface.*

Method	Does This
void addChangeListener(ChangeListener x)	Adds a **ChangeListener**.
int getExtent( )	Gets the model's extent (that is, the length of the inner range that begins at the model's value).
int getMaximum( )	Gets the model's maximum value.

(continued)

Table 19.4   Methods of the *BoundedRangeModel* interface (continued).

Method	Does This
int getMinimum( )	Gets the model's minimum acceptable value.
int getValue( )	Gets the model's current value.
boolean getValueIsAdjusting( )	Returns True if the current changes to the **value** property are part of a sequence of changes.
void removeChangeListener (ChangeListener x)	Removes a **ChangeListener** from the model's listener list.
void setExtent(int newExtent)	Sets the model's extent.
void setMaximum(int newMaximum)	Sets the model's maximum value to **newMaximum**.
void setMinimum(int newMinimum)	Sets the model's minimum value to **newMinimum**.
void setRangeProperties(int value, int extent, int min, int max, boolean adjusting)	Sets the model's data with a single call.
void setValue(int newValue)	Sets the model's current value to **newValue** if **newValue** satisfies the model's constraints.
void setValueIsAdjusting(boolean b)	Indicates that changes to the value of the model should be considered a single event.

Here's the actual code. In this case, I cram a long string into a short text field, and I connect the text field to a slider, as outlined at the beginning of this topic:

```
import java.awt.*;
import javax.swing.*;
import javax.swing.event.*;

/*
<APPLET
    CODE = textfieldscroll.class
    WIDTH = 350
    HEIGHT = 280>
</APPLET>
*/

public class textfieldscroll extends JApplet
{
    private JTextField jtextfield = new JTextField(
        "Here is a pretty long string for one text field.", 12);

    public void init()
    {
        Container contentPane = getContentPane();
```

```
        contentPane.setLayout(new FlowLayout());
        contentPane.add(new jsliderpanel());
        contentPane.add(jtextfield);
    }

    class jsliderpanel extends JPanel
    {
        JSlider jslider = new
            JSlider(jtextfield.getHorizontalVisibility());

        public jsliderpanel() {
            add(new JLabel("Scroll the text field:"));

            add(jslider);

            jslider.addChangeListener(new ChangeListener() {
                public void stateChanged(ChangeEvent e) {
                    jtextfield.setScrollOffset(jslider.getValue());
                }
            });
        }
    }
}
```

You can see the result in Figure 19.2. As you see in the figure, a slider and a text field appear in this applet, and you can scroll the text in the text field using the slider. That's all there is to it—this applet is a success. You'll find it in textfieldscroll.java on the CD.

Figure 19.2   Scrolling a text field.

Creating Password Fields

"Help!" cries a voice over the phone, and you decide it must be the Novice Programmer. "What's wrong, NP?" you ask. "That darn Johnson was standing behind me, reading my password as I was typing!" the NP says. "Well," you say, "change your passwords to new ones—and switch to password fields instead of text fields." "Thanks," says the NP, relieved.

Swing includes a special control for entering passwords—the **JPasswordField** control. You can set the echo character that appears in this control each time the user types a character, so that the typed password is not actually visible. In addition, copying to the Clipboard is disabled for this control. This way, someone can't just copy and paste your password. Here's the inheritance diagram for **JPasswordField**:

```
java.lang.Object
|____java.awt.Component
     |____java.awt.Container
          |____javax.swing.JComponent
               |____javax.swing.text.JTextComponent
                    |____javax.swing.JTextField
                         |____javax.swing.JPasswordField
```

You'll find the constructors of the **JPasswordField** class in Table 19.5 and its methods in Table 19.6.

You use the **setEchoChar** method to set the echo character in a password field, and you can use the **getPassword** method to read the typed password. The **getPassword** method returns a character array, but you can transform that array into a **String** object by passing it to the **String** class's constructor.

Table 19.5   Constructors of the JPasswordField class.

Constructor	Does This
JPasswordField( )	Constructs a new **JPasswordField**.
JPasswordField(Document doc, String txt, int columns)	Constructs a new **JPasswordField** that uses the given text storage model and the given number of columns.
JPasswordField(int columns)	Constructs a new, empty **JPasswordField** with the given number of columns.
JPasswordField(String text)	Constructs a new **JPasswordField** initialized with the given text.
JPasswordField(String text, int and columns)	Constructs a new **JPasswordField** initialized with the given text columns.

Table 19.6   *Methods of the JPasswordField class.*

Method	Does This
void copy( )	Copies the selected range in the associated text model to the system Clipboard.
void cut( )	Copies the selected range in the associated text model to the system Clipboard, removing the contents from the model.
boolean echoCharIsSet( )	Returns True if this **JPasswordField** has a character set for echoing.
AccessibleContext getAccessible Context( )	Gets the **AccessibleContext**.
char getEchoChar( )	Gets the character to be used for echoing.
char[ ] getPassword( )	Gets the text contained in this **TextComponent**.
String getText( )	Deprecated. Replaced by **getPassword( )**.
String getText(int offs, int len)	Deprecated. Replaced by **getPassword( )**.
String getUIClassID( )	Gets the name of the look and feel class that renders this component.
protected String paramString( )	Gets a string representation of this **JPasswordField**.
void setEchoChar(char c)	Sets the echo character for this **JPasswordField**.

Here's an example in which the actual password is "open sesame," and if the user types this password and presses Enter, this applet will display "Correct" in its status bar; otherwise, it'll display "Incorrect." Here's the code (note that to capture Enter press events, I've add an action listener to the password control):

```
import java.awt.*;
import javax.swing.*;
import java.awt.event.*;

/*
<APPLET
    CODE = password.class
    WIDTH = 350
    HEIGHT = 280 >
</APPLET>
*/

public class password extends JApplet
{
    String correctpassword = "open sesame";
    JPasswordField jpasswordfield = new JPasswordField(10);
```

```
public void init()
{
    Container contentPane = getContentPane();

    contentPane.setLayout(new FlowLayout());
    contentPane.add(new JLabel("Type your password: "));
    contentPane.add(jpasswordfield);

    jpasswordfield.setEchoChar('*');

    jpasswordfield.addActionListener(new ActionListener() {
        public void actionPerformed(ActionEvent e) {
            String input = new String(jpasswordfield.getPassword());

            if(correctpassword.equals(input))
                showStatus("Correct");
            else
                showStatus("Incorrect");
        }
    });
}
}
```

The result of this code appears in Figure 19.3. As you can see in the figure, the password field displays the echo character and checks the password when the user presses Enter. This example is in password.java on the CD.

Figure 19.3   Using a password field.

Creating Text Areas

"Nope," the Novice Programmer says, "there's just no way I can write my novel in a Swing text field. I guess I'll have to use a word processor." "Or," you say, "you can use a Swing text area, which is perfect for longer documents." "Tell me more!" says the NP.

The text area control is a simple control that's really little more than a text field that lets you arrange text in both rows and columns (each column is the width of the letter m in the current font). Here's the inheritance diagram for the **JTextArea** class:

```
java.lang.Object
|____java.awt.Component
      |____java.awt.Container
            |____javax.swing.JComponent
                  |____javax.swing.text.JTextComponent
                        |____javax.swing.JTextArea
```

You'll find the constructors of the **JTextArea** class in Table 19.7 and its methods in Table 19.8.

Table 19.7   Constructors of the JTextArea class.

Constructor	Does This
JTextArea( )	Constructs a new **JTextArea**.
JTextArea(Document doc)	Constructs a new **JTextArea** with the given document model.
JTextArea(Document doc, String text, int rows, int columns)	Constructs a new **JTextArea** with the given number of rows and columns as well as the given model.
JTextArea(int rows, int columns)	Constructs a new **JTextArea** with the given number of rows and columns.
JTextArea(String text)	Constructs a new **JTextArea** with the given text displayed.
JTextArea(String text, int rows, int columns)	Constructs a new **JTextArea** with the given text and number of rows and columns.

Table 19.8   Methods of the JTextArea class.

Method	Does This
void append(String str)	Appends the given text to the end of the document.
protected Document createDefault Model( )	Constructs the default implementation of the model to be used at construction time.

(continued)

Table 19.8   Methods of the JTextArea class (continued).

Method	Does This
AccessibleContext getAccessible Context( )	Gets the **AccessibleContext**.
int getColumns( )	Gets the number of columns in the text area.
protected int getColumnWidth( )	Gets column width.
int getLineCount( )	Determines the number of lines contained in the area.
int getLineEndOffset(int line)	Determines the offset of the end of the given line.
int getLineOfOffset(int offset)	Translates an offset into the component's text into a line number.
int getLineStartOffset(int line)	Determines the offset of the start of the given line.
boolean getLineWrap( )	Gets the line-wrapping policy of the text area.
Dimension getPreferredScrollable ViewportSize( )	Gets the preferred size of the viewport if this text area is embedded in a **JScrollPane**.
Dimension getPreferredSize( )	Gets the preferred size of the text area.
protected int getRowHeight( )	Gets the height of a row.
int getRows( )	Gets the number of rows in the text area.
boolean getScrollableTracksViewport Width( )	Returns True if a viewport should always force the width of this **Scrollable** object to match the width of the viewport.
int getScrollableUnitIncrement (Rectangle visibleRect, int orientation, int direction)	The scroll increment that will completely expose one new row or column.
int getTabSize( )	Gets the number of characters used to expand tabs.
String getUIClassID( )	Gets the class ID for the UI.
boolean getWrapStyleWord( )	Gets the style of wrapping used if the text area wraps lines.
void insert(String str, int pos)	Inserts the given text at the given position.
boolean isManagingFocus( )	Turns off tab navigation when the focus is gained.
protected String paramString( )	Gets a string representation of this text area.
protected void processComponentKey Event(KeyEvent e)	Ensures that Tab and Shift+Tab events are acted upon.
void replaceRange(String str, int start, int end)	Replaces text from the indicated start-to-end position with the new text given.
void setColumns(int columns)	Sets the number of columns.
void setFont(Font f)	Sets the current font.
void setLineWrap(boolean wrap)	Sets the line-wrapping policy of the text area.

(continued)

Table 19.8   Methods of the *JTextArea* class (continued).

Method	Does This
void setRows(int rows)	Sets the number of rows.
void setTabSize(int size)	Sets the number of characters to expand tabs to.
void setWrapStyleWord(boolean word)	Sets the style of wrapping used if the text area wraps lines.

When you create a Swing text area, you can specify the number of rows and columns it has, and you can also use the **setRows** and **setColumns** methods to set its dimensions on the fly. The AWT text area control supports scrolling directly, but, like other Swing components, the **JTextArea** control does not. It instead implements the **Scrollable** interface, which means you can use text areas inside scroll panes. You can also specify how Swing text areas handle word wrap with methods such as **setWrapStyleWord** and **setLineWrap**. You can use the **setText** and **append** methods to place text in a text area. Here's one more thing to note—you can use **TextEvent** objects and the **TextListener** interface to handle editing in AWT text areas, but **JTextArea** adds another level of abstraction. This means you have to use **DocumentEvent** objects and the **DocumentListener** interface with the **JTextField**'s model if you want to handle editing events here.

Here's an example in which I create a new Swing text area with 5 rows and 20 columns, set the font, enable editing and word wrap, and place the text area into a scroll pane. To show off the text area's capabilities, I embed some newline (\n) characters into the displayed text to skip to the next lines:

```java
import java.awt.*;
import javax.swing.*;

/*
<APPLET
    CODE = textarea.class
    WIDTH = 350
    HEIGHT = 280>
</APPLET>
*/

public class textarea extends JApplet
{
    private JTextArea jtextarea = new JTextArea("Hello\nfrom\nSwing!",
        5, 20);

    public void init()
    {
        Container contentPane = getContentPane();
```

```
        jtextarea.setWrapStyleWord(true);
        jtextarea.setEditable(true);
        jtextarea.setFont(new Font("Times-Roman", Font.BOLD, 10));

        contentPane.setLayout(new FlowLayout());
        contentPane.add(new JScrollPane(jtextarea));
    }
}
```

The results of this code appear in Figure 19.4. You can see the text area with its text broken over three lines. That's all there is to it. This example works as it should—you'll find it in textarea.java on the CD.

Figure 19.4   A basic Swing text area.

Creating Editor Panes

"Jeez," says the Novice Programmer, "the Big Boss wants me to create an entire Web browser in Java! How the heck am I going to do that?" "Well," you smile, "a good start is to use the Swing editor pane, which already supports HTML 3.2 documents." "Wow!" says the NP. "I feel better already!"

Editor panes are text components that use implementations of the **EditorKit** class to allow sophisticated editing. You can create your own editor kits, but by default, the following types of MIME (Multipurpose Internet Mail Extension) content are known:

- *text/plain*—Plain text, which is the default type. The kit used in this case is an extension of **DefaultEditorKit**, which produces a wrapped plain text view.

- *text/html*—HTML text. The editor kit used in this case is the class **javax.swing.text.html.HTMLEditorKit**, which supports HTML 3.2.

- *text/rtf*—RTF text. The editor kit used in this case is the class **javax.swing.text.rtf.RTFEditorKit**, which provides a limited support of the rich-text format (RTF).

Here's the inheritance diagram for **JEditorPane**:

```
java.lang.Object
|____java.awt.Component
     |____java.awt.Container
          |____javax.swing.JComponent
               |____javax.swing.text.JTextComponent
                    |____javax.swing.JEditorPane
```

You'll find the constructors for **JEditorPane** in Table 19.9 and its methods in Table 19.10.

Although editor panes have a default editor kit, you can create your own editor kit and install it into an editor pane with the **setEditorKit** method. You'll find the constructor for the **EditorKit** class in Table 19.11 and its methods in Table 19.12.

Table 19.9   *Constructors of the JEditorPane class.*

Constructor	Does This
JEditorPane( )	Constructs a new **JEditorPane**.
JEditorPane(String url)	Constructs a **JEditorPane** based on a string containing data from a URL.
JEditorPane(String type, String text)	Constructs a **JEditorPane** initialized to the given text.
JEditorPane(URL initialPage)	Constructs a **JEditorPane** based on a given URL for input.

Table 19.10   *Methods of the JEditorPane class.*

Method	Does This
void addHyperlinkListener(Hyperlink Listener listener)	Adds a hyperlink listener.
protected EditorKit createDefault EditorKit( )	Constructs the default editor kit for use when the component is first created.
static EditorKit createEditorKitFor ContentType(String type)	Creates a handler for the given type from the default registry of editor kits.

(continued)

Table 19.10   Methods of the JEditorPane class.

Method	Does This
void fireHyperlinkUpdate(Hyperlink Event e)	Notifies all listeners about the "hyperlink update" event.
AccessibleContext getAccessible Context( )	Gets the **AccessibleContext**.
String getContentType( )	Gets the type of content that this editor is currently set to deal with.
EditorKit getEditorKit( )	Gets the currently installed kit for handling content.
EditorKit getEditorKitForContentType (String type)	Gets the editor kit to use for the given type of content.
URL getPage( )	Gets the current URL being displayed.
Dimension getPreferredSize( )	Gets the preferred size.
boolean getScrollableTracksViewport Height( )	Returns True if a viewport should always force the height of this **Scrollable** object to match the height of the viewport.
boolean getScrollableTracksViewport Width( )	Returns True if a viewport should always force the width of this **Scrollable** object to match the width of the viewport.
protected InputStream getStream (URL page)	Gets a stream for the given URL.
String getText( )	Gets the text contained in this editor pane.
String getUIClassID( )	Gets the class ID for the UI object.
boolean isManagingFocus( )	Turns off tab traversal once focus is gained.
protected String paramString( )	Gets a string representation of this **JeditorPane**.
protected void processComponent KeyEvent(KeyEvent e)	Makes sure that Tab and Shift+Tab events are acted upon.
void read(InputStream in, Object desc)	Reads data from a stream.
static void registerEditorKitForContent Type(String type, String classname)	Establishes the default bindings.
static void registerEditorKitForContent Type(String type, String classname, ClassLoader loader)	Establishes the default bindings of type to name.
void removeHyperlinkListener (HyperlinkListener listener)	Removes a hyperlink listener.
void replaceSelection(String content)	Replaces the currently selected content with new content.
protected void scrollToReference (String reference)	Scrolls the view to the given reference location.

(continued)

Table 19.10   Methods of the JEditorPane class (continued).

Method	Does This
void setContentType(String type)	Sets the type of content that this editor handles.
void setEditorKit(EditorKit kit)	Sets the currently installed kit for handling content.
void setEditorKitForContentType (String type, EditorKit k)	Directly sets the editor kit to use for the given type.
void setPage(String url)	Sets the URL being displayed.
void setPage(URL page)	Sets the URL being displayed.
void setText(String t)	Sets the text to the given **String**.

Table 19.11   The constructor of the EditorKit class.

Constructor	Does This
EditorKit( )	Constructs an **EditorKit**.

Table 19.12   Methods of the EditorKit class.

Method	Does This
abstract Object clone( )	Creates a copy of the editor kit.
abstract Caret createCaret( )	Gets a caret that can navigate through views.
abstract Document createDefault Document( )	Creates an uninitialized text-storage model.
void deinstall(JEditorPane c)	Called when the kit is being removed from the **JEditorPane**.
abstract Action[ ] getActions( ) produced by this kit.	Gets the set of commands that can be used in a model and view
abstract String getContentType( )	Gets the MIME type of the data that this kit represents support for.
abstract ViewFactory getViewFactory( )	Gets a factory that can produce views of any models that are produced by this kit.
void install(JEditorPane c)	Called when the kit is being installed into the **JEditorPane**.
abstract void read(InputStream in, Document doc, int pos)	Inserts content from the given stream.
abstract void read(Reader in, Document doc, int pos)	Inserts content from the given stream.
abstract void write(OutputStream out, Document doc, int pos, int len)	Writes content from a document to the given stream.
abstract void write(Writer out, Document doc, int pos, int len)	Writes content from a document to the given stream.

There are a number of ways to load text into editor panes. You can use the **setText** method to load text into an editor pane from a string. You can also use the **read** method to read data from a **Reader** object, which you'll see more about soon in this book. You can also use the **setPage** method to initialize a text pane from a URL (including URLs of plain text, HTML documents, and RTF documents). In this case, the content type will be determined from the URL, and the registered **EditorKit** for that content type will be used.

TIP: Note that if you're loading an HTML page with the **read** method, relative HTML references can't be resolved unless you use the **<BASE>** tag or set the **Base** property of the **HTMLDocument** object.

Here's a quick example in which I create an editor pane and place some text in it with the **setText** method—note that to enable scrolling, I enclose the text pane in a scroll pane:

```
import java.awt.*;
import javax.swing.*;

/*
<APPLET
    CODE = editorpane.class
    WIDTH = 350
    HEIGHT = 280>
</APPLET>
*/

public class editorpane extends JApplet
{
    JEditorPane jeditorpane = new JEditorPane();

    public editorpane()
    {
        Container contentPane = getContentPane();

        jeditorpane.setEditable(true);

        jeditorpane.setText("Hello from Swing!");

        contentPane.add(new JScrollPane(jeditorpane));
    }
}
```

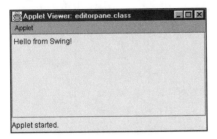

Figure 19.5   A basic text pane.

The result of this code appears in Figure 19.5. As you can see in the figure, the text I placed into the text pane is displayed. This example is editorpane.java on the CD.

However, this example treats its editor pane as a text area, which is much like using a backhoe to plant daisies—it works fine, but so much more is possible. See the next few topics for more details.

Using HTML In Editor Panes

The Novice Programmer is back and excited. "OK," says the NP putting a large lunch bag on your desk, "I'm ready to read an HTML document into an editor pane. Going to take a lot of programming, I expect." "Not at all," you say "You just use the **setPage** method." The NP pauses, sandwich in hand, and says, "Really?"

You can use the **JEditorPane setPage** method to read an HTML page by passing that method a URL. That page can include graphics, hyperlinks, and more.

Here's an example in which I open a Web page, which I call page.html, in an editor pane (note that I'm including an image in this Web page):

```
<HTML>
<BODY>

<H1>Here is some HTML</H1>

<CENTER>
<P>
This is an HTML page.
<P>
```

```
<B>Here's some bold text.</B>
<P>
<I>Here's some italic text.</I>
<P>
<U>Here's some underlined text.</U>
<P>
<IMG SRC = "image.jpg">

</CENTER>
</BODY>
</HTML>
```

To construct the URL of this page, which I'll store in the same directory as this example (editorpaneHTML.java), I use the **System.getProperty** method to get the current directory and the correct file separator (that is, \ or /) for the current system. When I've constructed the URL of the Web page to open, I use the **setPage** method, enclosed in a **try** block, to open that page. Note that for security reasons, Java will object, by default, if you try to open Web pages from applets; therefore, I've made this example an application. Here's the code:

```
import java.awt.*;
import javax.swing.*;
import java.awt.event.*;
import java.io.IOException;

public class editorpaneHTML extends JFrame
{
    JEditorPane jeditorpane = new JEditorPane();

    public editorpaneHTML()
    {
        super("JEditorPane application");

        Container contentPane = getContentPane();
        jeditorpane.setEditable(false);
        String urlstring = "file:" + System.getProperty("user.dir") +
                System.getProperty("file.separator") +
                "page.html";

        try {
            jeditorpane.setPage(urlstring);
        }
        catch(IOException e) {}
```

```
        contentPane.add(jeditorpane);
    }

    public static void main(String args[])
    {
        final JFrame jframe = new editorpaneHTML();

        jframe.setBounds(100, 100, 300, 300);
        jframe.setVisible(true);
        jframe.setBackground(Color.white);

        jframe.setDefaultCloseOperation(DISPOSE_ON_CLOSE);

        jframe.addWindowListener(new WindowAdapter() {
            public void windowClosing(WindowEvent e) {
                System.exit(0);
            }
        });
    }
}
```

The result appears in Figure 19.6. As you can see in the figure, the Web page appears in the editor pane in all its glory. This example is in editorpaneHTML.java on the CD.

Figure 19.6   Opening an HTML page in an editor pane.

Adding Hyperlinks To Editor Panes

You can handle hyperlinks in editor panes by using the **HyperLinkListener** interface. This interface has one method, called **hyperlinkUpdate**, which is passed an object of class **HyperlinkEvent**. You'll find the constructors of the **HyperlinkEvent** class in Table 19.13 and its methods in Table 19.14.

Here's an example in which I open a Web page, called page2.html, in an editor pane (note that this page has a hyperlink in it):

```
<HTML>
<BODY>

<H1>Here is some HTML</H1>

<CENTER>
<P>
This is an HTML page.
<P>
<B>Here's some bold text.</B>
<P>
<I>Here's some italic text.</I>
<P>
<U>Here's some underlined text.</U>
<P>
Here's a hyperlink to <A HREF = "page.html">page.html</A>.
<P>
<IMG SRC = "image.jpg">

</CENTER>
</BODY>
</HTML>
```

Table 19.13   *Constructors of the **HyperlinkEvent** class.*

Constructor	Does This
HyperlinkEvent(Object source, HyperlinkEvent.EventType type, URL u)	Constructs a new **HyperlinkEvent**.
HyperlinkEvent(Object source, HyperlinkEvent.EventType type, URL u, String desc)	Creates a new **HyperlinkEvent** with a description.

*Table 19.14   Methods of the **HyperlinkEvent** class.*

Method	Does This
String getDescription( )	Gets the description of the link as a string.
HyperlinkEvent.EventType get EventType( )	Gets the type of event.
URL getURL( )	Gets the URL that the link refers to.

This hyperlink points to the Web page (page.html) introduced in the previous topic. Here's how I load the new Web page and add a hyperlink listener to it:

```java
import java.awt.*;
import javax.swing.*;
import java.awt.event.*;
import javax.swing.event.*;
import java.io.IOException;

public class editorpaneURL extends JFrame
{
    JEditorPane jeditorpane = new JEditorPane();

    public editorpaneURL()
    {
        super("JEditorPane application");

        Container contentPane = getContentPane();

        jeditorpane.setEditable(false);

        String urlstring = "file:" + System.getProperty("user.dir") +
            System.getProperty("file.separator") +
            "page2.html";

        try {
            jeditorpane.setPage(urlstring);
        }
        catch(IOException e) {}

        jeditorpane.addHyperlinkListener(new HyperlinkListener(){
            public void hyperlinkUpdate(HyperlinkEvent e)
            {
                try {
                    jeditorpane.setPage(e.getURL());
                }
                catch(IOException e2) {}
            }
```

```
        });

        contentPane.add(jeditorpane);
    }

    public static void main(String args[])
    {
        final JFrame jframe = new editorpaneURL();

        jframe.setBounds(100, 100, 300, 300);
        jframe.setVisible(true);
        jframe.setBackground(Color.white);
        jframe.setDefaultCloseOperation(DISPOSE_ON_CLOSE);

        jframe.addWindowListener(new WindowAdapter() {
            public void windowClosing(WindowEvent e) {
                System.exit(0);
            }
        });
    }
}
```

TIP: *Hyperlinks are only active in noneditable editor panes.*

The result of this code appears in Figure 19.7, and you can see the hyperlink in the figure. As this code is written, when any hyperlink event occurs—including moving the mouse over the hyperlink—the editor pane loads the target of the hyperlink automatically. That's all there is to it. This example is in editorpaneURL.java on the CD.

Figure 19.7   A hyperlink in an editor pane.

Using RTF Files In Editor Panes

"Hmm," says the Novice Programmer, "I've got a file full of all kinds of codes that the Big Boss wants me to open—take a look." "That's an RTF file with formatting fields," you say, "and you should use an editor pane to open it." "Oh," says the NP.

Rich-text format (RTF) files can contain a great deal of text formatting, and many modern word processors, such as Microsoft Word, can store documents using this format. Editor panes can display RTF files, as I'll show with an example. In this case, I open an RTF file—document.rtf on the CD—in an editor pane using the **setPage** method:

```java
import java.awt.*;
import javax.swing.*;
import java.awt.event.*;
import java.io.IOException;

public class editorpaneRTF extends JFrame
{
    JEditorPane jeditorpane = new JEditorPane();

    public editorpaneRTF()
    {
        super("JEditorPane application");

        Container contentPane = getContentPane();
        jeditorpane.setEditable(false);
        String url = "file:" + System.getProperty("user.dir") +
            System.getProperty("file.separator") +
            "document.rtf";

        try {
            jeditorpane.setPage(url);
        }
        catch(IOException e) {}

        contentPane.add(jeditorpane);
    }

    public static void main(String args[])
    {
        final JFrame jframe = new editorpaneRTF();

        jframe.setBounds(100, 100, 300, 300);
        jframe.setVisible(true);
```

```
                jframe.setBackground(Color.white);
                jframe.setDefaultCloseOperation(DISPOSE_ON_CLOSE);

                jframe.addWindowListener(new WindowAdapter() {
                    public void windowClosing(WindowEvent e) {
                        System.exit(0);
                    }
                });
            }
        }
```

The result of this code appears in Figure 19.8, where you can see the RTF document inside the editor pane. This example is in editorpaneRTF.java on the CD.

Figure 19.8   An RTF document in an editor pane.

Creating Text Panes

The Novice Programmer is back and worried. "Now," says the NP, "I've got to display a button in a text area!" "That's tough," you say. "Why not do that in a text pane instead, where it's easy?"

The **JTextPane** class is derived from the **JEditorPane** class and adds quite a bit of functionality to **JEditorPane**—for example, you can insert controls into a text pane, and you can format text with style attributes. Here's the inheritance diagram for **JTextPane**:

```
java.lang.Object
|____java.awt.Component
      |____java.awt.Container
            |____javax.swing.JComponent
                  |____javax.swing.text.JTextComponent
                        |____javax.swing.JEditorPane
                              |____javax.swing.JTextPane
```

You'll find the constructors of the **JTextPane** class in Table 19.15 and its methods in Table 19.16.

Table 19.15   Constructors of the JTextPane class.

Constructor	Does This
JTextPane( )	Constructs a new **JTextPane**.
JTextPane(StyledDocument doc)	Constructs a new **JTextPane** with a given document model.

Table 19.16   Methods of the JTextPane class.

Method	Does This
Style addStyle(String nm, Style parent)	Adds a new style into the logical style hierarchy.
protected EditorKit createDefault EditorKit( )	Constructs the **EditorKit** to use by default.
AttributeSet getCharacterAttributes( )	Gets the character attributes in effect at the caret.
MutableAttributeSet getInputAttributes( )	Gets the input attributes for the pane.
Style getLogicalStyle( )	Gets the logical style assigned to the paragraph represented by the current position of the caret.
AttributeSet getParagraphAttributes( )	Gets the paragraph attributes in effect at the location of the caret.
boolean getScrollableTracksViewport Width( )	Returns True if a viewport should always force the width of this Width( ) **Scrollable** object to match the width of the viewport.
Style getStyle(String nm)	Gets a named style added previously.
StyledDocument getStyledDocument( )	Gets the model associated with the editor.
protected StyledEditorKit getStyled EditorKit( )	Gets the editor kit.
String getUIClassID( )	Gets the class ID for the UI.
void insertComponent(Component c)	Inserts a component into the document as a replacement for the currently selected content.
void insertIcon(Icon g)	Inserts an icon into the document.
protected String paramString( )	Gets a string representation of this **JtextPane**.
void removeStyle(String nm)	Removes a named non-null style previously added to the document.
void replaceSelection(String content)	Replaces the currently selected content.
void setCharacterAttributes(Attribute Set attr, boolean replace)	Applies the given attributes to character content.
void setDocument(Document doc)	Associates the editor with a text document.
void setEditorKit(EditorKit kit)	Sets the currently installed kit for handling content.
void setLogicalStyle(Style s)	Sets the logical style to use for the paragraph at the current caret position.

(continued)

Table 19.16   *Methods of the JTextPane class* (continued).

Method	Does This
void setParagraphAttributes(Attribute Set attr, boolean replace)	Applies the given attributes to paragraphs.
void setStyledDocument(Styled Document doc)	Associates the editor with a text document.

Here's an example in which I construct a text pane and add some text to it:

```
import java.awt.*;
import javax.swing.*;

/*
<APPLET
    CODE = textpane.class
    WIDTH = 350
    HEIGHT = 280>
</APPLET>
*/

public class textpane extends JApplet
{
    JTextPane jtextpane = new JTextPane();

    public void init()
    {
        Container contentPane = getContentPane();

        jtextpane.setFont(new Font("Times-Roman", Font.BOLD, 18));
        jtextpane.setText("Hello from Swing!");

        contentPane.add(jtextpane);
    }
}
```

You'll find the result of this code in Figure 19.9, where you can see the text pane with its displayed text. This example is in textpane.java on the CD.

Text panes are powerful controls, of course, and this example hasn't even scratched the surface. Take a look at the next couple topics for more details.

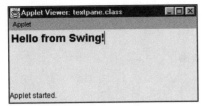

Figure 19.9   A basic text pane.

Inserting Images And Controls Into Text Panes

To insert images into text panes, you can use the **insertIcon** method; to insert other components into a text pane, you can use the **insertComponent** method. To show how this works, I use both methods in an example. In this case, I add a button and an image to a text pane, like this:

```
import java.awt.*;
import javax.swing.*;
import java.awt.event.*;

/*
<APPLET
    CODE = textpaneimages.class
    WIDTH = 350
    HEIGHT = 280>
</APPLET>
*/

public class textpaneimages extends JApplet implements ActionListener
{
    JTextPane jtextpane = new JTextPane();
    JButton jbutton = new JButton("Click Me");

    public void init()
    {
        Container contentPane = getContentPane();

        jtextpane.setFont(new Font("Times-Roman", Font.BOLD, 18));
        jtextpane.setText("Hello from Swing!");

        jbutton.addActionListener(this);
        jtextpane.insertComponent(jbutton);
        jtextpane.insertIcon(new ImageIcon("image.jpg"));
```

```
        contentPane.add(jtextpane);
    }

    public void actionPerformed(ActionEvent e)
    {
        showStatus("You clicked the button.");
    }
}
```

I've made the button active by adding an action listener to it. The result appears in Figure 19.10, where you can see the image and button in the text pane. This example—textpaneimages.java on the CD—is a success.

Figure 19.10   Adding components and images to a text pane.

Setting Text Pane Text Attributes

"OK," says the Novice Programmer, "I need to do a lot of text formatting—italics, bold, and colored fonts. Is there any way to do this in Java?" "There sure is," you say. "In fact, you can do it with text panes." "Great!" says the NP.

You can use the **setCharacterAttributes**, **setParagraphAttributes**, and **setLogicalStyle** methods of text panes to set and style the text attributes. These techniques are fairly involved. Here's an example in which I display several lines of text in a text pane, all with a different custom style.

I start by creating some new styles—normal, red, italic, bold, and big. To do that, I use the text pane's **getStyledDocument** method to get a **StyledDocument** object corresponding to the text pane; then I create the new styles with the **addStyle** method:

```
import java.awt.*;
import javax.swing.*;
import javax.swing.text.*;
```

```
/*
<APPLET
    CODE = textpaneattributes.class
    WIDTH = 350
    HEIGHT = 280>
</APPLET>
*/

public class textpaneattributes extends JApplet
{
    JTextPane jtextpane = new JTextPane();
    String string = new String("Hello from Swing!\r\n");
    int stringlength = string.length();
    int position = 0;

    public void init()
    {
        Container contentPane = getContentPane();

        jtextpane.setText(string);
        StyledDocument styleddocument = jtextpane.getStyledDocument();

        Style normal = styleddocument.addStyle("normal", null);
        StyleConstants.setFontFamily(normal, "SansSerif");

        Style red = styleddocument.addStyle("red", normal);
        StyleConstants.setForeground(red, Color.red);

        Style bold = styleddocument.addStyle("bold", normal);
        StyleConstants.setBold(bold, true);

        Style italic = styleddocument.addStyle("italic", normal);
        StyleConstants.setItalic(italic, true);

        Style big = styleddocument.addStyle("big", normal);
        StyleConstants.setFontSize(big, 24);
           .
           .
           .
```

Next, I add successive lines of text, applying one of the new styles to each line, by
moving the current location of the text-insertion caret in the text pane and using
setLogicalStyle:

```
public class textpaneattributes extends JApplet
{
    JTextPane jtextpane = new JTextPane();
    String string = new String("Hello from Swing!\r\n");
    int stringlength = string.length();
    int position = 0;

    public void init()
    {
        Container contentPane = getContentPane();

        jtextpane.setText(string);
        StyledDocument styleddocument = jtextpane.getStyledDocument();

        Style normal = styleddocument.addStyle("normal", null);
        StyleConstants.setFontFamily(normal, "SansSerif");

        Style red = styleddocument.addStyle("red", normal);
        StyleConstants.setForeground(red, Color.red);

        Style bold = styleddocument.addStyle("bold", normal);
        StyleConstants.setBold(bold, true);

        Style italic = styleddocument.addStyle("italic", normal);
        StyleConstants.setItalic(italic, true);

        Style big = styleddocument.addStyle("big", normal);
        StyleConstants.setFontSize(big, 24);

        styleddocument.setLogicalStyle(position, normal);

        position += stringlength;
        jtextpane.setCaretPosition(styleddocument.getLength());
        jtextpane.replaceSelection(string);
        styleddocument = jtextpane.getStyledDocument();
        styleddocument.setLogicalStyle(position, red);

        position += stringlength;
        jtextpane.setCaretPosition(styleddocument.getLength());
        jtextpane.replaceSelection(string);
        styleddocument = jtextpane.getStyledDocument();
        styleddocument.setLogicalStyle(position, bold);

        position += stringlength;
        jtextpane.setCaretPosition(styleddocument.getLength());
```

```
        jtextpane.replaceSelection(string);
        styleddocument = jtextpane.getStyledDocument();
        styleddocument.setLogicalStyle(position, italic);

        position += stringlength;
        jtextpane.setCaretPosition(styleddocument.getLength());
        jtextpane.replaceSelection(string);
        styleddocument = jtextpane.getStyledDocument();
        styleddocument.setLogicalStyle(position, big);

        contentPane.add(jtextpane);
    }
}
```

That's it. The result appears in Figure 19.11. You can see each styled line in the figure. Note, however, that this is only the beginning for style work in text panes—there's a tremendous amount of depth in this topic.

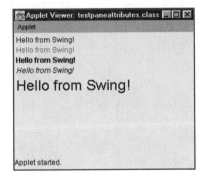

Figure 19.11   Styling text in a text pane.

Chapter 20

I/O Streams And Files

In Depth

In this chapter, we'll take a look at stream I/O and file handling in Java. Using streams is the way you handle I/O in languages such as Java. A stream is composed of bytes or characters (which used to be considered much the same in Java until Unicode and its two-byte characters arrived) that you can read from or write to, and you can connect them to various data sources and stores—even byte and character arrays.

Streams, Readers, And Writers

The concept of streams was introduced to make programming more uniform when handling disparate data sources or stores. When using streams, you use the **java.io** package, and you can handle input and output in much the same way, whether you're working with a disk file, a memory buffer, or a network.

In Java, stream I/O is based on the **InputStream**, **OutputStream**, **Reader**, and **Writer** classes. **InputStream** and **OutputStream** are for byte-oriented streams (such as when you work with binary files), and the **Reader** and **Writer** classes are for character-oriented streams (as when you work with text files). You don't use these classes directly; instead, you derive classes from them. In fact, Java has already done a lot of that for you—so much so that there are dozens of classes to work with.

In fact, the I/O stream classes have become somewhat of a thicket in Java—there seems to be at least one available for every possible use and some you probably haven't thought of. Some streams provide data buffering; some do not. Some are designed to work with data in memory buffers; some with files. I'll cover the important ones here.

Typically, you use a stream class's constructor to create a stream; the stream classes are usually divided into input and output streams, so you select the one that's appropriate. After you have a stream object, you can use its methods—typically **read** and **write**—to transfer data. When you're done with the stream object, you typically use its **close** method to close it and end your work with the data source or store.

After all this talk about streams, I'm going to start the chapter with a class that isn't a stream class at all—the **File** class. This class doesn't work with the contents of files but rather lets you determine a lot *about* files, such as their sizes, permissions, dates, and so on.

NOTE: Java objects when you try to read or write files from applets unless you make specific security arrangements, applet by applet. Therefore, for the sake of convenience, all the programs in this chapter are applications.

That's it for the overview of what's in this chapter. There's a lot coming up here: I/O is a huge topic in Java. It's time to turn to the "Immediate Solutions" section, starting with a look at the **File** class.

Immediate Solutions

Using The **File** Class

"Hmm," says the Novice Programmer, "little bit of an embarrassment—my program tried to open a file that didn't exist, right when I was running it for the Big Boss." "Well," you say, "why didn't you first test whether the file existed using the **File** class's **exists** method?" The NP says, "Now you tell me!"

You can use the **File** class to determine a lot about files, such as their sizes, whether you can write to them, whether an item is a file, directory, or named pipe, and more. Here's the inheritance diagram for the **File** class:

```
java.lang.Object
|____java.io.File
```

You'll find the fields for the **File** class in Table 20.1, its constructors in Table 20.2, and its methods in Table 20.3.

Table 20.1   Fields of the *File* class.

Field	Does This
static String pathSeparator	System-dependent path-separator string.
static char pathSeparatorChar	System-dependent path-separator character.
static String separator	System-dependent default name-separator character, represented as a string for convenience.
static char separatorChar	System-dependent default name-separator character.

Table 20.2   Constructors of the *File* class.

Constructor	Does This
File(File parent, String child)	Constructs a new **File** instance from a parent pathname and a child pathname string.
File(String pathname)	Constructs a new **File** instance by converting the given pathname string into an abstract pathname.
File(String parent, String child)	Constructs a new File instance from a parent pathname string and a child pathname string.

Table 20.3   Methods of the *File* class.

Method	Does This
boolean canRead( )	Returns True if the application can read the file given by this abstract pathname.
boolean canWrite( )	Returns True if the application can modify the file given by this abstract pathname.
int compareTo(File pathname)	Compares two abstract pathnames.
int compareTo(Object o)	Compares this abstract pathname to another object.
boolean createNewFile( )	Constructs a new, empty file.
static File createTempFile(String prefix, String suffix)	Constructs an empty file in the default temporary file directory.
static File createTempFile(String prefix, String suffix, File directory)	Constructs a new, empty file in the given directory.
boolean delete( )	Deletes the file or directory.
void deleteOnExit( )	Requests that the file or directory given by this pathname be deleted when the virtual machine exits.
boolean equals(Object obj)	Compares this pathname for equality with the given object.
boolean exists( )	Compares whether the file given by this abstract pathname exists.
File getAbsoluteFile( )	Gets the absolute form of this abstract pathname.
String getAbsolutePath( )	Gets the absolute pathname string of this abstract pathname.
File getCanonicalFile( )	Gets the canonical form of this abstract pathname.
String getCanonicalPath( )	Gets the canonical pathname string of this abstract pathname.
String getName( )	Gets the name of the file or directory given by this abstract pathname.
String getParent( )	Gets the pathname string of this abstract pathname's parent or gets null if this pathname does not name a parent directory.
File getParentFile( )	Gets the abstract pathname of this abstract pathname's parent or gets null if this pathname does not name a parent directory.
String getPath( )	Converts this abstract pathname into a pathname string.
int hashCode( )	Computes a hash code for this abstract pathname.
boolean isAbsolute( )	Returns True if this abstract pathname is absolute.
boolean isDirectory( )	Returns True if the file given by this abstract pathname is a directory.
boolean isFile( )	Returns True if the file given by this abstract pathname is a normal file.

(continued)

Table 20.3   Methods of the File class (continued).

Method	Does This
boolean isHidden( )	Returns True if the file named by this abstract pathname is a hidden file.
long lastModified( )	Gets the time that the file given by this abstract pathname was last modified.
long length( )	Gets the length of the file given by this abstract pathname.
String[ ] list( )	Gets an array of strings naming the files and directories in the directory given by this abstract pathname.
String[ ] list(FilenameFilter filter)	Gets an array of strings naming the files and directories in the directory given by this pathname that satisfy the given filter.
File[ ] listFiles( )	Gets an array of abstract pathnames indicating the files in the directory.
File[ ] listFiles(FileFilter filter)	Gets an array of abstract pathnames indicating the files and directories in the directory that fulfill the given filter.
File[ ] listFiles(FilenameFilter filter)	Gets an array of abstract pathnames indicating the files and directories in the directory that fulfill the given filter.
static File[ ] listRoots( )	Lists the available file system roots.
boolean mkdir( )	Constructs the directory named by this abstract pathname.
boolean mkdirs( )	Constructs the directory named by this pathname, including any necessary but nonexistent parent directories.
boolean renameTo(File dest)	Renames the file given by this pathname.
boolean setLastModified(long time)	Sets the last-modified time of the file or directory.
boolean setReadOnly( )	Marks the file or directory named by this pathname so that it can only be read.
String toString( )	Gets the pathname string of this abstract pathname.
URL toURL( )	Converts this abstract pathname into an URL.

Note that you can use **isFile** to determine whether an item is a true file or something else, such as a directory (which you can check with **isDirectory**) or a named pipe. Use **toURL** to convert a file's path to a URL, rename files, and more with the **File** class.

Let's look at an example. Here, I put several of the methods of the **File** class to work, getting some information about a file named file.txt. Here's what the code looks like:

```
import java.io.File;

class file
{
    public static void main(String args[])
    {
        File file1 = new File("file.txt");

        System.out.println("File: " + file1.getName() + (file1.isFile() ?
            " is a file" : " is a named pipe or directory"));
        System.out.println("Size: " + file1.length());
        System.out.println("Path: " + file1.getPath());
        System.out.println("Absolute Path: " + file1.getAbsolutePath());
        System.out.println("File was last modified: " +
            file1.lastModified());
        System.out.println(file1.exists() ? "File exists" :
            "File does not exist");
        System.out.println(file1.canRead() ? "File can be read from" :
            "File cannot be read from");
        System.out.println(file1.canWrite() ? "File can be written to" :
            "File cannot be written to");
        System.out.println(file1.isDirectory() ? "File is a directory" :
            "File is not a directory");
    }
}
```

Here are the results of this code (note that the time the file was last modified is returned in the usual fashion—in milliseconds since 1/1/70—which you can convert to a more readable date with the **Date** class):

```
C:\>java file
File: file.txt is a file
Size: 18
Path: file.txt
Absolute Path: C:\file.txt
File was last modified: 937406384000
File exists
File can be read from
File can be written to
File is not a directory
```

That's all there is to it. This example is in file.java on the CD accompanying this book. As you can see, using the **File** class, you can determine a great deal about files and directories.

Working With **InputStream**

The Novice Programmer appears and says, "I'm ready to start working with files. Where do I start?" "You start," you say, "with the **InputStream** and **OutputStream** classes."

The **InputStream** and **OutputStream** classes are the base classes for byte-oriented I/O in Java, so it's worth taking a look at the methods that these classes provide to all other byte-oriented stream classes. Here's the inheritance diagram for the **InputStream** class, on which you base input streams:

```
java.lang.Object
|____java.io.InputStream
```

You'll find the constructor of the **InputStream** class in Table 20.4 and its methods in Table 20.5.

We'll take a look at the **OutputStream** class in the next topic.

Table 20.4   The constructor of the InputStream class.

Field	Does This
InputStream( )	Constructs an **InputStream**.

Table 20.5   Methods of the InputStream class.

Method	Does This
int available( )	Gets the number of bytes that can be read from this input stream.
void close( )	Closes this input stream.
void mark(int readlimit)	Marks the current position in this input stream.
boolean markSupported( )	Returns True if this input stream supports the **mark** and **reset** methods.
abstract int read( )	Reads the next byte of data from the input stream.
int read(byte[ ] b)	Reads some number of bytes from the input stream and stores them into the buffer array **b**.
int read(byte[ ] b, int off, int len)	Reads up to **len** bytes of data from the input stream into an array of bytes.
void reset( )	Repositions this stream to the position where the mark method was last called on this input stream.
long skip(long n)	Skips over **n** bytes of data from this input stream.

Working With **OutputStream**

The counterpart to the **InputStream** class, introduced in the previous topic, is the **OutputStream** class, on which you base output streams. Here's the inheritance diagram for **OutputStream**:

```
java.lang.Object
|____java.io.OutputStream
```

You'll find the constructor of the **OutputStream** class in Table 20.6 and its methods in Table 20.7.

Now that you've seen **InputStream** and **OutputStream**, it's time to put these classes to work, starting in the next topic.

Table 20.6   The constructor of the OutputStream class.

Constructor	Does This
OutputStream( )	Constructs an **OutputStream**.

Table 20.7   Methods of the OutputStream class.

Method	Does This
void close( )	Closes this output stream.
void flush( )	Flushes this output stream and writes any waiting buffered output bytes.
void write(byte[ ] b)	Writes **b.length** bytes from the given byte array to this output stream.
void write(byte[ ] b, int off, int len)	Writes **len** bytes from the given byte array, starting at offset **off**, to this output stream.
abstract void write(int b)	Writes the given byte to this output stream.

Working With **FileInputStream**

"I need to open an image file and work with its individual bytes," the Novice Programmer says. "How can I do that?" "You can use the **FileInputStream** class to work with the bytes in a file," you say. The NP says, "Tell me more!"

The **FileInputStream** class is specially designed to work with byte-oriented input from files, and it's derived from **InputStream**, as you see here:

```
java.lang.Object
|____java.io.InputStream
     |____java.io.FileInputStream
```

You'll find the constructors of the **FileInputStream** class in Table 20.8 and its methods in Table 20.9.

To create a file input stream, you use the **FileInputStream** class's constructor. Here are the reading methods you use with this class:

• *int read()*—Reads a byte of data from this input stream and returns it.

• *int read(byte[] b)*—Reads up to **b.length** bytes of data from this input stream into an array of bytes and returns the number of bytes read.

Table 20.8   Constructors of the *FileInputStream* class.

Constructor	Does This
FileInputStream(File file)	Constructs a **FileInputStream** by opening a connection to an actual file.
FileInputStream(FileDescriptor fdObj)	Constructs a **FileInputStream** by using the file descriptor **fdObj**.
FileInputStream(String name)	Constructs a **FileInputStream** by opening a connection to an actual file given by the file named by **name**.

Table 20.9   Methods of the *FileInputStream* class.

Method	Does This
int available( )	Gets the number of bytes that can be read from this file input.
void close( )	Closes this file input stream.
protected void finalize( )	Makes sure that the **close** method of this file input stream is called when there are no more references to it.
FileDescriptor getFD( )	Gets the **FileDescriptor** object.
int read( )	Reads a byte of data from this input stream.
int read(byte[ ] b)	Reads up to **b.length** bytes of data from this input stream into an array of bytes.
int read(byte[ ] b, int off, int len)	Reads up to **len** bytes of data from this input stream into an array of bytes.
long skip(long n)	Skips over and discards **n** bytes.

- *int read(byte[] b, int off, int len)*—Reads up to **len** bytes of data from this input stream into an array of bytes and returns the number of bytes read.

Let's look at an example. In this case, I open this application's own source code file, read and display 50 bytes of code, skip 50 bytes with the **skip** method, and then read and display 50 more bytes (note that I can also determine how many bytes there are waiting to be read using the **available** method, and I can close the stream at the end of the code):

```java
import java.io.*;

class fileinputstream
{
    public static void main(String args[]) throws Exception
    {
        int size;
        FileInputStream fileinputstream = new
            FileInputStream("fileinputstream.java");

        System.out.println("Available bytes: " + (size =
            fileinputstream.available()));
        System.out.println("Reading 50 bytes....");

        byte bytearray[] = new byte[50];
        if (fileinputstream.read(bytearray) != 50) {
          System.out.println("Could not get 50 bytes");
        }

        System.out.println(new String(bytearray, 0, 50));

        System.out.println("Skipping 50 bytes...");

        fileinputstream.skip(50);

        System.out.println("Reading 50 bytes....");
        if (fileinputstream.read(bytearray) != 50) {
          System.out.println("Could not get 50 bytes");
        }
        System.out.println(new String(bytearray, 0, 50));

        fileinputstream.close();
    }
}
```

Here's the output from this code:

```
C:\>java fileinputstream
Available bytes: 966
Reading 50 bytes....
import java.io.*;

class fileinputstream
{

Skipping 50 bytes...
Reading 50 bytes....
ception
    {
        int size;
        InputS
```

That's all there is to it. This example is in fileinputstream.java on the CD.

Working With **FileOutputStream**

"OK," says the Novice Programmer, "I know you use **FileInputStream** to read from files, but what class do you use if you want to write to a file?" You smile and say, "I bet you can guess."

You can use the **FileOutputStream** class to write data, byte by byte, to a file. Here's the inheritance diagram for that class, which is derived from the **OutputStream** class:

```
java.lang.Object
|____java.io.OutputStream
     |____java.io.FileOutputStream
```

You'll find the constructors of the **FileOutputStream** class in Table 20.10 and its methods in Table 20.11.

Table 20.10   Constructors of the FileOutputStream class.

Constructor	Does This
FileOutputStream(File file)	Constructs a file output stream to write to the given **File** object.
FileOutputStream(FileDescriptor fdObj)	Constructs an output file stream to write to the given file descriptor.

(continued)

Table 20.10   Constructors of the *FileOutputStream* class (continued).

Constructor	Does This
FileOutputStream(String name)	Constructs an output file stream to write to the file with the given name.
FileOutputStream(String name, boolean append)	Constructs an output file stream to append to the file with the given name.

Table 20.11   Methods of the *FileOutputStream* class.

Method	Does This
void close( )	Closes this file output stream.
protected void finalize( )	Makes sure that the **close** method of this file output stream is called when there are no more references to this stream.
FileDescriptor getFD( )	Gets the file descriptor associated with this stream.
void write(byte[ ] b)	Writes **b.length** bytes from the given byte array to this file output stream.
void write(byte[ ] b, int off, int len)	Writes **len** bytes from the given byte array starting at offset **off**, to this file output stream.
void write(int b)	Writes the given byte to this file output stream.

Here are the writing methods you use with this class:

- *void write(byte[] b)*—Writes **b.length** bytes from the given byte array to this file output stream.
- *void write(byte[] b, int off, int len)*—Writes **len** bytes from the given byte array, starting at offset **off**, to this file output stream.
- *void write(int b)*—Writes the given byte to this file output stream.

Here's an example in which I write the string of text "This is a string of text." to a file in three ways—byte by byte, all at once, and in part. Here's what the code looks like:

```
import java.io.*;

class fileoutputstream
{
    public static void main(String args[]) throws Exception
    {
        byte data[] = "This is a string of text.".getBytes();
```

```
        FileOutputStream fileoutputstream1 = new
            FileOutputStream("file1.txt");
        for (int loop_index = 0; loop_index < data.length; loop_index++) {
            fileoutputstream1.write(data[loop_index]);
        }

        FileOutputStream fileoutputstream2 = new
            FileOutputStream("file2.txt");
        fileoutputstream2.write(data);

        FileOutputStream fileoutputstream3 = new
            FileOutputStream("file3.txt");
        fileoutputstream3.write(data, 5, 10);

        fileoutputstream1.close();
        fileoutputstream2.close();
        fileoutputstream3.close();
    }
}
```

That's all there is to it. This example is in fileoutputstream.java on the CD.

Working With **ByteArrayInputStream**

"I've got a huge array of bytes in my program," the Novice Programmer says, "and I'm always losing my place in it. Too bad you can't treat an array of bytes like a file and open an input stream from it!" "But you can," you say. The NP is astounded.

You can use the **ByteArrayInputStream** class to open an input stream from an array of bytes in memory. Here's the inheritance diagram for this class:

```
java.lang.Object
|____java.io.InputStream
     |____java.io.ByteArrayInputStream
```

You'll find the fields of the **ByteArrayInputStream** class in Table 20.12, its constructors in Table 20.13, and its methods in Table 20.14.

*Table 20.12   Fields of the **ByteArrayInputStream** class.*

Field	Does This
protected byte[ ] buf	An array of bytes that was supplied by the creator of the stream.
protected int count	The number of characters in the input stream buffer.
protected int mark	The currently marked position in the stream.
protected int pos	The index of the next character to read from the input stream.

*Table 20.13   Constructors of the **ByteArrayInputStream** class.*

Constructor	Does This
ByteArrayInputStream(byte[ ] buf)	Constructs a **ByteArrayInputStream**.
ByteArrayInputStream(byte[ ] buf, int offset, int length)	Constructs a **ByteArrayInputStream** that uses **buf** as its buffer array.

*Table 20.14   Methods of the **ByteArrayInputStream** class.*

Method	Does This
int available( )	Gets the number of bytes that can be read from this input.
void close( )	Closes this input stream.
void mark(int readAheadLimit)	Sets the current marked position in the stream.
boolean markSupported( )	Returns True if this **ByteArrayInputStream** object supports **mark/reset**.
int read( )	Reads the next byte of data.
int read(byte[ ] b, int off, int len)	Reads up to **len** bytes of data into an array of bytes from this input stream.
void reset( )	Resets the buffer to the marked position.
long skip(long n)	Skips **n** bytes of input from this input stream.

Here's an example. In this case, I'm just creating a memory buffer with the text "Here is a string" in it and then opening a **ByteArrayInputStream** to that buffer, reading and displaying that text byte by byte:

```
import java.io.*;

class bytearrayinputstream
{
    public static void main(String args[]) throws IOException
    {
```

```
        byte data[] = "Here is a string".getBytes();
        ByteArrayInputStream in = new ByteArrayInputStream(data);

        int character;
        while((character = in.read()) != -1){
            System.out.print((char) character);
        }
    }
}
```

Here's the output from this code:

```
C:\>java bytearrayinputstream
Here is a string
```

That's all it takes. This example is in bytearrayinputstream.java on the CD.

Working With **ByteArrayOutputStream**

"So you can read bytes with **ByteArrayInputStream**," says the Novice Programmer. "Can you also write them?" "Sure," you say, "with **ByteArrayOutputStream**."

The **ByteArrayOutputStream** class lets you write streams of bytes to buffers. Here's the inheritance diagram for this class:

```
java.lang.Object
|____java.io.OutputStream
     |____java.io.ByteArrayOutputStream
```

You'll find the fields of the **ByteArrayOutputStream** class in Table 20.15, its constructors in Table 20.16, and its methods in Table 20.17.

Table 20.15   Fields of the ByteArrayOutputStream class.

Field	Does This
protected byte[ ] buf	The buffer where data is stored.
protected int count	The number of bytes in the buffer.

Table 20.16 **Constructors of the *ByteArrayOutputStream* class.**

Constructor	Does This
ByteArrayOutputStream( )	Constructs a new byte array output stream.
ByteArrayOutputStream(int size)	Constructs a new byte array output stream, with a buffer of the given size.

Table 20.17 **Methods of the *ByteArrayOutputStream* class.**

Method	Does This
void close( )	Closes this output stream.
void reset( )	Resets the count field of this byte array output stream to zero.
int size( )	Gets the current size of the buffer.
byte[ ] toByteArray( )	Constructs a newly allocated byte array.
String toString( )	Converts the buffer's contents into a string.
String toString(int hibyte)	Deprecated. Use the **toString** method.
String toString(String enc)	Converts the buffer's contents into a string.
void write(byte[ ] b, int off, int len)	Writes **len** bytes from the given byte array starting at offset **off**.
void write(int b)	Writes the given byte to this byte array output stream.
void writeTo(OutputStream out)	Writes the complete contents of this byte array output stream to the given output stream argument.

Here's an example. In this case, I'm writing bytes to a **ByteOutputStream**, writing bytes to a memory buffer, and sending bytes to a file output stream:

```
import java.io.*;

class bytearrayoutputstream
{
    public static void main(String args[]) throws IOException
    {
        ByteArrayOutputStream bytearrayoutputstream = new
            ByteArrayOutputStream();
        byte data[] = "Here is a string".getBytes();

        bytearrayoutputstream.write(data);

        System.out.println(bytearrayoutputstream.toString());
```

```
        byte buffer[] = bytearrayoutputstream.toByteArray();
        for (int loop_index = 0; loop_index < data.length; loop_index++) {
            System.out.print((char) buffer[loop_index]);
        }

        OutputStream fileoutputstream = new FileOutputStream("file.txt");
        bytearrayoutputstream.writeTo(fileoutputstream);
        fileoutputstream.close();
    }
}
```

This example is in bytearrayoutputstream.java on the CD. Here's the output from this code:

```
C:\>java bytearrayoutputstream
Here is a string
Here is a string
```

Working With **BufferedInputStream**

"Jeez," says the Novice Programmer, "my code interprets data from an input stream, and sometimes it'd be handy to be able to reset the stream and go back to an earlier position." "You can do that with buffered streams," you say. "Wow!" the NP says.

Using the **BufferedInputStream** class, you can use the **mark** and **reset** methods to actually move backward in a buffered input stream. Here's the inheritance diagram for this class:

```
java.lang.Object
|____java.io.InputStream
     |____java.io.FilterInputStream
          |____java.io.BufferedInputStream
```

You'll find the fields of the **BufferedInputStream** class in Table 20.18, its constructors in Table 20.19, and its methods in Table 20.20.

Table 20.18   Fields of the BufferedInputStream class.

Field	Does This
protected byte[ ] buf	The internal buffer where the data is stored.
protected int count	The count of bytes in the buffer.
protected int marklimit	The maximum read-ahead allowed after a call to the **mark** method.
protected int markpos	The value of the **pos** field at the time the last **mark** method was called.
protected int pos	The position in the buffer.

Table 20.19   Constructors of the BufferedInputStream class.

Constructor	Does This
BufferedInputStream(InputStream in)	Constructs a **BufferedInputStream**.
BufferedInputStream(InputStream in, int size)	Constructs a **BufferedInputStream** with the given buffer size.

Table 20.20   Methods of the BufferedInputStream class.

Method	Does This
int available( )	Gets the number of bytes that can be read from this input.
void close( )	Closes this input stream.
void mark(int readAheadLimit)	Sets the current marked position in the stream.
boolean markSupported( )	Tests whether this input stream supports the **mark** and **reset** methods.
int read( )	Reads the next byte of data.
int read(byte[ ] b, int off, int len)	Reads bytes from this byte-input stream into the given byte array, starting at the given offset.
void reset( )	Resets the buffer to the marked position.
long skip(long n)	Skips **n** bytes of input from this input stream.

Here's an example. In this case, I'll remove comments from a **ByteArrayInputStream** that are delimited with the # character. That means when I encounter a # character, I'll just stop displaying bytes until I encounter a closing #.

For the purpose of this example, I'll only use comments that don't include spaces. Note that sometimes the # character is a valid character in text, so if I encounter a # and stop displaying text and then encounter a space before seeing a closing #, the text was not a comment. Therefore, I have to move back to the first # and redisplay the text up to the space.

I'll write this example using the **mark** and **reset** methods; I mark a location, then, if needed, use the **reset** method to go back to that location. Here's what the code looks like (note that you pass a length, in bytes, to the **mark** method that indicates the maximum number of bytes you'll read before possibly using **reset**):

```java
import java.io.*;

class bufferedinputstream
{
    public static void main(String args[]) throws IOException
    {

        byte data[] = "The specimen was #5 in the " +
            "series.#comment_goes_here#".getBytes();

        ByteArrayInputStream in = new ByteArrayInputStream(data);
        BufferedInputStream bufferedinputstream = new
            BufferedInputStream(in);

        int character;
        boolean silentflag = false;

        while ((character = bufferedinputstream.read()) != -1) {

            switch(character) {
            case '#':
                if (silentflag) {
                    silentflag = false;
                } else {
                    silentflag = true;
                    bufferedinputstream.mark(100);
                }
                break;
            case ' ':
                if (silentflag) {
                    silentflag = false;
                    System.out.print("#");
                    bufferedinputstream.reset();
                } else
                    System.out.print((char) character);
                break;
            default:
```

```
            if (!silentflag) System.out.print((char) character);
        }
      }
    }
}
```

Here's the output of this code (bufferedinputstream.java on the CD) when it strips the comment "The specimen was #5 in the series.#comment_goes_here#" out of the text:

```
C:\>java bufferedinputstream
The specimen was #5 in the series.
```

Working With **BufferedOutputStream**

The **BufferedOutputStream** class is the output counterpart of the **BufferedInputStream** class (see the previous topic). Here's the inheritance diagram for the **BufferedOutputStream** class:

```
java.lang.Object
|____java.io.OutputStream
      |____java.io.FilterOutputStream
            |____java.io.BufferedOutputStream
```

You'll find the fields of the **BufferedInputStream** class in Table 20.21, its constructors in Table 20.22, and its methods in Table 20.23.

Table 20.21   Fields of the BufferedOutputStream class.

Field	Does This
protected byte[ ] buf	The internal buffer where data is stored.
protected int count	The number of bytes in the buffer.

Table 20.22   Constructors of the BufferedOutputStream class.

Constructor	Does This
BufferedOutputStream(Output Stream out)	Constructs a new buffered output stream.
BufferedOutputStream(OutputStream out, int size)	Constructs a new buffered output stream to write data with the given buffer size.

Table 20.23   Methods of the BufferedOutputStream class.

Method	Does This
void flush( )	Flushes this buffered output stream.
void write(byte[ ] b, int off, int len)	Writes **len** bytes from the given byte array, starting at offset **off**, to this buffered output stream.
void write(int b)	Writes the given byte to this buffered output stream.

The idea behind **BufferedOutputStream** is that you don't have to write data to disk every time a byte is written, because output is buffered. To force a write operation, you can use the **flush** method.

Working With **RandomAccessFile**

Using the **RandomAccessFile** class, you can move around in a file using the **seek** method. That's what random access is all about—being able to move around in a file at random. Here's the inheritance diagram for **RandomAccessFile**:

```
java.lang.Object
|____java.io.RandomAccessFile
```

You'll find the constructors of the **RandomAccessFile** class in Table 20.24, and its methods in Table 20.25.

Table 20.24   Constructors of the RandomAccessFile class.

Constructor	Does This
RandomAccessFile(File file, String mode)	Constructs a random-access file stream to read from, and optionally to write to, the file given by the **File** argument.
RandomAccessFile(String name, String mode)	Constructs a random-access file stream to read from, and optionally to write to, a file with the given name.

Table 20.25   Methods of the RandomAccessFile class.

Method	Does This
void close( )	Closes this random-access file stream.
FileDescriptor getFD( )	Gets the file descriptor object associated with this stream.
long getFilePointer( )	Gets the current offset in this file.

(continued)

Table 20.25   Methods of the *RandomAccessFile* class (continued).

Method	Does This
long length( )	Gets the length of this file.
int read( )	Gets a byte of data from this file.
int read(byte[ ] b)	Gets up to **b.length** bytes of data from this file into an array of bytes.
int read(byte[ ] b, int off, int len)	Gets up to **len** bytes of data from this file into an array of bytes.
boolean readBoolean( )	Gets a boolean from this file.
byte readByte( )	Gets a signed eight-bit value from this file.
char readChar( )	Gets a Unicode character from this file.
double readDouble( )	Gets a double from this file.
float readFloat( )	Gets a float from this file.
void readFully(byte[ ] b)	Gets **b.length** bytes from this file into the byte array, starting at the current file pointer.
void readFully(byte[ ] b, int off, int len)	Gets exactly **len** bytes from this file into the byte array, starting at the current file pointer.
int readInt( )	Gets a signed 32-bit integer from this file.
String readLine( )	Gets the next line of text from this file.
long readLong( )	Gets a signed 64-bit integer from this file.
short Getshort( )	Gets a signed 16-bit number from this file.
int readUnsignedByte( )	Gets an unsigned eight-bit number from this file.
int readUnsignedShort( )	Gets an unsigned 16-bit number from this file.
String readUTF( )	Gets a string from this file.
void seek(long pos)	Sets the file-pointer offset at which the next read or write happens.
void setLength(long newLength)	Sets the length of this file.
int skipBytes(int n)	Attempts to skip over **n** bytes of input.
void write(byte[ ] b)	Writes **b.length** bytes from the given byte array to this file, starting at the file pointer.
void write(byte[ ] b, int off, int len)	Writes **len** bytes from the given byte array starting at offset **off** to this file.
void write(int b)	Writes the given byte to this file.
void writeBoolean(boolean v)	Writes a boolean to the file as a one-byte value.
void writeByte(int v)	Writes a byte to the file as a one-byte value.
void writeBytes(String s)	Writes the string to the file as a sequence of bytes.

(continued)

20. I/O Streams
And Files

Table 20.25   Methods of the RandomAccessFile class (continued).

Method	Does This
void writeChar(int v)	Writes a char to the file as a two-byte value, high byte first.
void writeChars(String s)	Writes a string to the file as a sequence of characters.
void writeDouble(double v)	Converts the double argument to a long and then writes that long value to the file.
void writeFloat(float v)	Converts the float argument to an int and then writes that int value to the file.
void writeInt(int v)	Writes an int to the file as four bytes, high byte first.
void writeLong(long v)	Writes a long to the file as eight bytes, high byte first.
void writeShort(int v)	Writes a short to the file as two bytes, high byte first.
void writeUTF(String str)	Writes a string to the file using UTF-8 encoding.

NOTE: One of the attractions of RandomAccessFile is that you can both read and write using this class, without having to break things up into input and output objects.

Working With **Reader**

"OK," says the Novice Programmer, "I'm going to be working with characters instead of just bytes, including Unicode. How do I handle that?" "With the **Reader** and **Writer** classes," you say. "Tell me more!" says the NP.

You use the **Reader** and **Writer** classes to read and write character streams. As with **InputStream** and **OutputStream**, you base classes on **Reader** and **Writer** instead of using them directly. Here's the inheritance diagram for **Reader**:

```
java.lang.Object
|____java.io.Reader
```

You'll find the field of the **Reader** class in Table 20.26, its constructors in Table 20.27, and its methods in Table 20.28.

Table 20.26   The field of the Reader class.

Field	Does This
protected Object lock	The lock used to synchronize operations.

*Table 20.27   Constructors of the **Reader** class.*

Constructor	Does This
protected Reader( )	Constructs a new character stream.
protected Reader(Object lock)	Constructs a new character-stream reader whose critical sections will synchronize on the given lock.

*Table 20.28   Methods of the **Reader** class.*

Method	Does This
abstract void close( )	Closes the stream.
void mark(int readAheadLimit)	Marks the present position in the stream.
boolean markSupported( )	Tells whether this stream supports the **mark( )** operation.
int read( )	Reads a single character.
int read(char[ ] cbuf)	Reads characters into an array.
abstract int read(char[ ] cbuf, int off, int len)	Reads characters into a portion of an array.
boolean ready( )	Tells whether this stream is ready to be read.
void reset( )	Resets the stream.
long skip(long n)	Skips characters.

Working With **Writer**

The **Writer** class is the character-based counterpart of the **Reader** class (see the previous topic). Here's the inheritance diagram for **Writer**:

```
java.lang.Object
|____java.io.Writer
```

You'll find the field of the **Writer** class in Table 20.29, its constructors in Table 20.30, and its methods in Table 20.31.

*Table 20.29   The field of the **Writer** class.*

Field	Does this
protected Object lock	The lock used to synchronize operations on this stream.

Table 20.30   Constructors of the Writer class.

Constructor	Does This
protected Writer( )	Creates a new character-stream writer.
protected Writer(Object lock)	Creates a new character-stream writer whose critical sections will synchronize on the given lock.

Table 20.31   Methods of the Writer class.

Method	Does This
abstract void close( )	Closes the stream, flushing it first.
abstract void flush( )	Flushes the stream.
void write(char[ ] cbuf)	Writes an array of characters.
abstract void write(char[ ] cbuf, int off, int len)	Writes a portion of an array of characters.
void write(int c)	Writes a single character.
void write(String str)	Writes a string.
void write(String str, int off, int len)	Writes a portion of a string.

Keyboard Input: Working With **InputStreamReader**

"Well," says the Novice Programmer, "all I want to do is read input from the keyboard. Can I use **System.in**?" "Yes," you say, "but construct an **InputStreamReader** stream from it first." "Oh," the NP says.

To read keys from the keyboard, you usually construct an **InputStreamReader** stream from **System.in** and then use the **InputStreamReader** class's **read** method to read what the user has typed. Here's the inheritance diagram for **InputStreamReader**:

```
java.lang.Object
|____java.io.Reader
     |____java.io.InputStreamReader
```

You'll find the constructors of the **InputStreamReader** class in Table 20.32 and its methods in Table 20.33.

Table 20.32   **Constructors of the InputStreamReader class.**

Constructor	Does This
InputStreamReader(InputStream in)	Creates an **InputStreamReader**.
InputStreamReader(InputStream in, enc)	Creates an **InputStreamReader** that uses the named character String encoding.

Table 20.33   **Methods of the InputStreamReader class.**

Method	Does This
void close( )	Closes the stream.
String getEncoding( )	Gets the name of the character encoding.
int read( )	Reads a single character.
int read(char[ ] cbuf, int off, int len)	Reads characters into a portion of an array.
boolean ready( )	Returns True if this stream is ready to be read.

Here's an example. In this case, I'll just read keys from the keyboard and echo them. Note that the input stream does not become available until the user presses the Enter key. Here's what the code looks like:

```
import java.io.*;

class inputstreamreader
{
    public static void main(String args[]) {
        try {
            int character;
            InputStreamReader inputstreamreader = new
                InputStreamReader(System.in);
            while ((character = inputstreamreader.read()) != -1) {
                System.out.print((char) character);
            }
        }
        catch (IOException e) {}
    }
}
```

Here's the output of this code (inputstreamreader.java on the CD). Note that the echoed line appears after the user enters text and presses the Enter key:

```
C:\>java inputstreamreader
Hello there!
Hello there!
```

Working With **OutputStreamWriter**

The **OutputStreamWriter** class is the output counterpart to the **InputStreamWriter** class (see the previous topic). Here's the inheritance diagram for **OutputStreamWriter**:

```
java.lang.Object
|____java.io.Writer
     |____java.io.OutputStreamWriter
```

You'll find the constructors of the **OutputStreamReader** class in Table 20.34 and its methods in Table 20.35.

*Table 20.34   Constructors of the **OutputStreamWriter** class.*

Constructor	Does This
OutputStreamWriter(OutputStream out)	Construct an **OutputStreamWriter.**
OutputStreamWriter(OutputStream out, String enc)	Construct an **OutputStreamWriter** that uses the named character encoding.

*Table 20.35   Methods of the **OutputStreamWriter** class.*

Method	Does This
void close( )	Closes the stream.
void flush( )	Flushes the stream.
String getEncoding( )	Gets the name of the character encoding being used by this stream.
void write(char[ ] cbuf, int off, int len)	Writes a section of an array of characters.
void write(int c)	Writes a single character.
void write(String str, int off, int len)	Writes a portion of a string.

Working With **FileReader**

"How can I read a character-based file?" the Novice Programmer asks. "Well," you say, "probably the best way is with the **FileReader** class." "Great," says the NP. "Let's write some code!"

You use the **FileReader** class to create a character-based stream that reads from a file. Here's the inheritance diagram for this class:

```
java.lang.Object
|____java.io.Reader
      |____java.io.InputStreamReader
            |____java.io.FileReader
```

This class only defines constructors in addition to the functionality it inherits from **InputStreamReader**, and you'll find them in Table 20.36.

Here's an example. In this case, I'll open a file, file.txt, that has the contents "Here is a string", read that file's data into a buffer, and then display the data:

```java
import java.io.*;

class filereader
{
    public static void main(String args[]) throws Exception
    {
        FileReader filereader = new FileReader("file.txt");
        char data[] = new char[1024];

        int charsread = filereader.read(data);
        System.out.println(new String(data, 0 , charsread));

        filereader.close();
    }
}
```

Table 20.36   Constructors of the *FileReader* class.

Constructor	Does This
FileReader(File file)	Constructs a **FileReader**.
FileReader(FileDescriptor fd)	Constructs a **FileReader** from a file descriptor.
FileReader(String fileName)	Constructs a **FileReader** from a file name.

Here's the output of this program (filereader.java on the CD):

```
C:\>java filereader
Here is a string
```

As you can see, working with **FileReader** is a relatively simple process.

Working With **FileWriter**

The **FileWriter** class is the character-based **Writer** counterpart of **FileReader** (see the previous topic for more details). Here's the inheritance diagram for **FileWriter**:

```
java.lang.Object
|____java.io.Writer
     |____java.io.OutputStreamWriter
          |____java.io.FileWriter
```

This class only defines constructors in addition to the functionality it inherits from **OutputStreamReader**, and you'll find them in Table 20.37.

Here's an example. In this case, I'll write data from a character buffer to a file, character by character, all at once, and in part, using **FileWriter**:

```
import java.io.*;

class filewriter
{
    public static void main(String args[]) throws Exception
    {
        char data[] = {'T','h','i','s',' ','i','s',' ','a',
            ' ','s','t','r','i','n','g',' ','o','f',
            ' ','t','e','x','t','.'};

        FileWriter filewriter1 = new FileWriter("file1.txt");
        for (int loop_index = 0; loop_index < data.length; loop_index++) {
            filewriter1.write(data[loop_index]);
        }

        FileWriter filewriter2 = new FileWriter("file2.txt");
        filewriter2.write(data);

        FileWriter filewriter3 = new FileWriter("file3.txt");
```

```
        filewriter3.write(data, 5, 10);

        filewriter1.close();
        filewriter2.close();
        filewriter3.close();
    }
}
```

That's all there is to it. This example is in filewriter.java on the CD.

Table 20.37   *Constructors of the FileWriter class.*

Constructor	Does This
FileWriter(File file)	Constructs a **FileWriter** from a **File** object.
FileWriter(FileDescriptor fd)	Constructs a **FileWriter** from a file descriptor.
FileWriter(String fileName)	Constructs a **FileWriter** from a file name.
FileWriter(String fileName, boolean append)	Constructs a **FileWriter** for appending.

Working With **CharArrayReader**

"You can use **ByteArrayInputStream** and **ByteArrayOutputStream** to read and write bytes from an array," the Novice Programmer says, "but what about characters? Are there **CharArrayInputStream** and **CharArrayOutputStream** classes?" "No," you say, "remember that you use readers and writers with character streams, which means you should use **CharArrayReader** and **CharArrayWriter** instead."

You use **CharArrayReader** to read from a character array. Here's the inheritance diagram for this class:

```
java.lang.Object
|____java.io.Reader
     |____java.io.CharArrayReader
```

You'll find the fields of the **CharArrayReader** class in Table 20.38, its constructors in Table 20.39, and its methods in Table 20.40.

Table 20.38   Fields of the *CharArrayReader* class.

Field	Does This
protected char[ ] buf	The character buffer.
protected int count	The number of characters in the buffer.
protected int markedPos	The position of the current mark in the buffer.
protected int pos	The current buffer position.

Table 20.39   Constructors of the *CharArrayReader* class.

Constructor	Does This
CharArrayReader(char[ ] buf)	Constructs a **CharArrayReader** from the given array of characters.
CharArrayReader(char[ ] buf, int offset, int length)	Constructs a **CharArrayReader** from the given array of characters.

Table 20.40   Methods of the *CharArrayReader* class.

Method	Does This
void close( )	Closes the stream.
void mark(int readAheadLimit)	Marks the present position in the stream.
boolean markSupported( )	Returns True if this stream supports the **mark** operation.
int read( )	Reads a single character.
int read(char[ ] b, int off, int len)	Reads characters into a portion of an array.
boolean ready( )	Tells whether this stream is ready to be read.
void reset( )	Resets the stream to the most recent mark.
long skip(long n)	Skips characters.

Here's an example. In this case, I just read characters from an array and print them out:

```
import java.io.*;

public class chararrayreader
{
    public static void main(String args[]) throws IOException
    {
        char data[] = {'T','h','i','s',' ','i','s',' ','a',
            ' ','s','t','r','i','n','g',' ','o','f',
            ' ','t','e','x','t','.'};
```

```
        CharArrayReader chararrayreader = new CharArrayReader(data);

        int character;

        while((character = chararrayreader.read()) != -1) {
            System.out.print((char)character);
        }
    }
}
```

Here's the output of this code (chararrayreader.java on the CD):

```
C:\>java chararrayreader
This is a string of text.
```

Working With **CharArrayWriter**

The **CharArrayWriter** class is the **Writer** counterpart of the **CharArrayReader** class (see the previous topic). You use this class to write to character arrays. Here's the inheritance diagram for this class:

```
java.lang.Object
|____java.io.Writer
     |____java.io.CharArrayWriter
```

You'll find the fields of the **CharArrayWriter** class in Table 20.41, its constructors in Table 20.42, and its methods in Table 20.43.

Table 20.41   Fields of the CharArrayWriter class.

Field	Does This
protected char[ ] buf	The buffer where data is stored.
protected int count	The number of characters in the buffer.

Table 20.42   Constructors of the CharArrayWriter class.

Constructor	Does This
CharArrayWriter( )	Constructs a new **CharArrayWriter**.
CharArrayWriter(int initialSize)	Constructs a new **CharArrayWriter** with the given initial size.

Table 20.43   Methods of the _CharArrayWriter_ class.

Method	Does This
void close( )	Closes the stream.
void flush( )	Flushes the stream.
void reset( )	Resets the buffer.
int size( )	Gets the current size of the buffer.
char[ ] toCharArray( )	Gets a copy of the input data.
String toString( )	Converts input data to a string.
void write(char[ ] c, int off, int len)	Writes characters to the buffer.
void write(int c)	Writes a character to the buffer.
void write(String str, int off, int len)	Writes a portion of a string to the buffer.
void writeTo(Writer out)	Writes the contents of the buffer to another character stream.

Working With **BufferedReader**

"My files are line-oriented," says the Novice Programmer. "Is there some easy way to read them in line by line instead of character by character?" "Certainly," you say, "you can use the **readLine** method of the **BufferedReader** class." "Great," says the NP. "You write the code, and I'll watch."

The **BufferedReader** class provides a buffered character reader class. One of its advantages is that **BufferedReader** provides a **readLine** method. Here's the inheritance diagram for **BufferedReader**:

```
java.lang.Object
|____java.io.Reader
      |____java.io.BufferedReader
```

You'll find the constructors of the **BufferedReader** class in Table 20.44 and its methods in Table 20.45.

Table 20.44   Constructors of the _BufferedReader_ class.

Constructor	Does This
BufferedReader(Reader in)	Constructs a buffering character-input stream.
BufferedReader(Reader in, int sz)	Construct a buffering character-input stream that uses an input buffer of the given size.

*Table 20.45   Methods of the **BufferedReader** class.*

Method	Does This
void close( )	Closes the stream.
void mark(int readAheadLimit)	Marks the present position in the stream.
boolean markSupported( )	Returns True if this stream supports the **mark** operation.
int read( )	Reads a single character.
int read(char[ ] cbuf, int off, int len)	Reads characters into a portion of an array.
String readLine( )	Reads a line of text.
boolean ready( )	Tells whether this stream is ready to be read.
void reset( )	Resets the stream to the most recent mark.
long skip(long n)	Skips characters.

Here's an example using the **BufferedReader** class. In this case, I read the file file.txt line by line with the **readLine** method. Here's the contents of that file:

```
Here is a string
Here is a string
Here is a string
Here is a string
Here is a string
```

Here's the code:

```java
import java.io.*;

class bufferedreader
{
    public static void main(String args[]) throws Exception
    {
        FileReader filereader = new FileReader("file.txt");
        BufferedReader bufferedreader = new BufferedReader(filereader);
        String instring;

        while((instring = bufferedreader.readLine()) != null) {
            System.out.println(instring);
        }

        filereader.close();
    }
}
```

Here's the output of the code (filereader.java on the CD) when it's run:

```
C:\>java bufferedreader
Here is a string
Here is a string
Here is a string
Here is a string
Here is a string
```

Working With **BufferedWriter**

The **BufferedWriter** class is the **Writer** counterpart of **BufferedReader** (see the previous topic). Here's the inheritance diagram for **BufferedWriter**:

```
java.lang.Object
|____java.io.Writer
     |____java.io.BufferedWriter
```

You'll find the constructors of the **BufferedWriter** class in Table 20.46 and its methods in Table 20.47.

*Table 20.46   Constructors of the **BufferedWriter** class.*

Constructor	Does This
BufferedWriter(Writer out)	Constructs a buffered character-output stream.
BufferedWriter(Writer out, int sz)	Constructs a new, buffered character-output stream that uses an output buffer of the given size.

*Table 20.47   Methods of the **BufferedWriter** class.*

Method	Does This
void close( )	Closes the stream.
void flush( )	Flushes the stream.
void newLine( )	Writes a line separator.
void write(char[ ] cbuf, int off, int len)	Writes a section of an array of characters.
void write(int c)	Writes a single character.
void write(String s, int off, int len)	Writes a portion of a **String**.

Working With **PushbackReader**

You can use the **PushbackReader** class when you want to look ahead in a stream to check what's coming. When you use this class's **unread** method, you can return one or more characters to the stream. Here's the inheritance diagram for **PushbackReader**:

```
java.lang.Object
|____java.io.Reader
     |____java.io.FilterReader
          |____java.io.PushbackReader
```

You'll find the constructors of the **PushbackReader** class in Table 20.48 and its methods in Table 20.49.

Table 20.48   Constructors of the PushbackReader class.

Constructor	Does This
PushbackReader(Reader in)	Creates a new pushback reader.
PushbackReader(Reader in, int size)	Creates a new pushback reader with a pushback buffer of the given size.

Table 20.49   Methods of the PushbackReader class.

Method	Does This
void close( )	Closes the stream.
void mark(int readAheadLimit)	Marks the present position in the stream.
boolean markSupported( )	Returns True if this stream supports the **mark** operation.
int read( )	Reads a single character.
int read(char[ ] cbuf, int off, int len)	Reads characters into a portion of an array.
boolean ready( )	Tells whether this stream is ready to be read.
void reset( )	Resets the stream.
void unread(char[ ] cbuf)	Pushes back an array of characters.
void unread(char[ ] cbuf, int off, int len)	Pushes back a section of an array of characters.
void unread(int c)	Pushes back a single character.

Working With **StreamTokenizer**

"What are you doing?" you ask the Novice Programmer. "I'm writing the code to break a character input stream up into words." "Why not use a stream tokenizer?" you ask. "OK," says the NP. "What's that?"

You can use a stream tokenizer to break an input stream into tokens, such as words. Here's the inheritance diagram for the **StreamTokenizer** class:

```
java.lang.Object
|____java.io.StreamTokenizer
```

You'll find the fields of the **StreamTokenizer** class in Table 20.50, its constructors in Table 20.51, and its methods in Table 20.52.

*Table 20.50   Fields of the **StreamTokenizer** class.*

Field	Does This
double nval	The value of a number token.
String sval	The string giving the characters of a word token.
static int TT_EOF	A constant indicating that the end of the stream has been read.
static int TT_EOL	A constant indicating that the end of the line has been read.
static int TT_NUMBER	A constant indicating that a number token has been read.
static int TT_WORD	A constant indicating that a word token has been read.
int ttype	Contains the type of the token just read.

*Table 20.51   Constructors of the **StreamTokenizer** class.*

Constructor	Does This
StreamTokenizer(InputStream is)	Deprecated. You should tokenize a stream by converting it into a character stream first; use the other constructor after converting the stream into a reader.
StreamTokenizer(Reader r)	Constructs a tokenizer that parses the given character stream.

*Table 20.52   Methods of the **StreamTokenizer** class.*

Method	Does This
void commentChar(int ch)	The character argument starts a single-line comment.
void eollsSignificant(boolean flag)	Returns True if the ends of lines are treated as tokens.
int lineno( )	Gets the current line number.

(continued)

Table 20.52   Methods of the *StreamTokenizer* class (continued).

Method	Does This
void lowerCaseMode(boolean fl)	Determines whether word tokens are automatically lowercased.
int nextToken( )	Parses the next token from the input stream of this tokenizer.
void ordinaryChar(int ch)	Specifies that the character argument is ordinary in this tokenizer.
void ordinaryChars(int low, int hi)	Specifies that all characters in the range **low** to **high** are considered ordinary in this tokenizer.
void parseNumbers( )	Specifies that numbers should be parsed by this tokenizer.
void pushBack( )	Pushes back a token.
void quoteChar(int ch)	Indicates that matching pairs of this character delimit string constants.
void resetSyntax( )	Resets this tokenizer's syntax table so that all characters are "ordinary."
void slashSlashComments (boolean flag)	Sets whether the tokenizer recognizes C++-style comments.
void slashStarComments(boolean flag)	Sets whether the tokenizer recognizes C-style comments.
String toString( )	Gets the string representation of the current stream token.
void whitespaceChars(int low, int hi)	Makes all characters in the range **low** to **high** white space characters.
void wordChars(int low, int hi)	Specifies that all characters in the range **low** to **high** are word characters.

Here's an example in which I use a **FileReader** to read from a file, file.txt, whose content is the string "Here is a string". I break that text up into words, check for words with the **TT_WORD** field, and get the current token's value as a string using **sval**, like this:

```
import java.io.*;

class streamtokenizer
{
    public static void main(String args[]) throws Exception
    {
        FileReader filereader = new FileReader("file.txt");
        StreamTokenizer streamtokenizer = new StreamTokenizer(filereader);

        String instring;

        while(streamtokenizer.nextToken() != StreamTokenizer.TT_EOF) {
```

```
                    if(streamtokenizer.ttype == StreamTokenizer.TT_WORD)
                        System.out.println(streamtokenizer.sval);
                }

            filereader.close();
        }
    }
```

Here's the output if this example (streamtokenizer.java on the CD):

```
C:\>java streamtokenizer
Here
is
a
string
```

Working With Serialization

"Uh-oh," says the Novice Programmer, "now I really have a problem. I want to write objects out to a file and read them back in. No way, right?" "Of course there's a way," you say. "You can *serialize* your objects."

Serialization is the process of writing objects to a stream and reading them back. To be serialized, your objects must implement the **Serializable** interface. This interface has no fields, constructors, or methods—it just shows that an object is serializable.

To work with serializable objects, you use the **ObjectInputStream** and **ObjectOutputStream** classes, which are derived from **InputStream** and **OutputStream**, respectively. Here's the inheritance diagram for **ObjectInputStream**:

```
java.lang.Object
|____java.io.InputStream
     |____java.io.ObjectInputStream
```

Here's the inheritance diagram for **ObjectOutputStream**:

```
java.lang.Object
|____java.io.OutputStream
     |____java.io.ObjectOutputStream
```

You'll find the constructors of the **ObjectOutputStream** class in Table 20.53 and its methods in Table 20.54. You'll find the constructors of the **ObjectInputStream** class in Table 20.55 and its methods in Table 20.56.

Table 20.53   Constructors of the *ObjectOutputStream* class.

Constructor	Does This
protected ObjectOutputStream( )	Creates an **ObjectOutputStream**.
ObjectOutputStream(OutputStream out)	Constructs an **ObjectOutputStream** that writes to the given **OutputStream**.

Table 20.54   Methods of the *ObjectOutputStream* class.

Method	Does This
protected void annotateClass(Class cl)	Implements this method to allow class data to be stored in the stream.
void close( )	Closes the stream.
void defaultWriteObject( )	Writes the nonstatic and nontransient fields of the current class to this stream.
protected void drain( )	Clears any buffered data in **ObjectOutputStream**.
protected boolean enableReplace Object(boolean enable)	Enables the stream to replace objects in the stream.
void flush( )	Flushes the stream.
ObjectOutputStream.PutField putFields( )	Retrieves the object used to buffer persistent fields.
protected Object replaceObject (Object obj)	Allows trusted subclasses of **ObjectOutputStream** to substitute one object for another.
void reset( )	Disregards the state of any objects already written to the stream.
void useProtocolVersion(int version)	Specifies the stream protocol version to use when writing the stream.
void write(byte[ ] b)	Writes an array of bytes.
void write(byte[ ] b, int off, int len)	Writes a subarray of bytes.
void write(int data)	Writes a byte.
void writeBoolean(boolean data)	Writes a boolean.
void writeByte(int data)	Writes an eight-bit byte.
void writeBytes(String data)	Writes a **String** as a sequence of bytes.
void writeChar(int data)	Writes a 16-bit char.
void writeChars(String data)	Writes a **String** as a sequence of chars.

(continued)

Table 20.54   Methods of the *ObjectOutputStream* class (continued).

Method	Does This
void writeDouble(double data)	Writes a 64-bit double.
void writeFields( )	Writes the buffered fields to the stream.
void writeFloat(float data)	Writes a 32-bit float.
void writeInt(int data)	Writes a 32-bit int.
void writeLong(long data)	Writes a 64-bit long.
void writeObject(Object obj)	Writes the given object to the **ObjectOutputStream**.
protected void writeObjectOverride (Object obj)	Called by trusted subclasses of **ObjectInputStream**.
void writeShort(int data)	Writes a 16-bit short.
protected void writeStreamHeader( )	Provided so subclasses can append or prepend their own header to the stream.
void writeUTF(String data)	Primitive data write operation of the given **String**.

Table 20.55   Constructors of the *ObjectInputStream* class.

Constructor	Does This
protected ObjectInputStream( )	Constructs an **ObjectInputStream**.
ObjectInputStream(InputStream in)	Creates an **ObjectInputStream** that reads from the given **InputStream**.

Table 20.56   Methods of the *ObjectInputStream* class.

Method	Does This
int available( )	Gets the number of bytes that can be read.
void close( )	Closes the input stream.
void defaultReadObject( )	Reads the nonstatic and nontransient fields of the current class from this stream.
protected boolean enableResolve Object(boolean enable)	Enables the stream to allow objects read from the stream to be replaced.
int read( )	Reads a byte of data.
int read(byte[ ] b, int off, int len)	Reads into an array of bytes.
boolean readBoolean( )	Reads in a boolean.
byte readByte( )	Reads an eight-bit byte.

(continued)

Table 20.56   *Methods of the ObjectInputStream class* (continued).

Method	Does This
char readChar( )	Reads a 16-bit char.
double readDouble( )	Reads a 64-bit double.
ObjectInputStream.GetField read Fields( )	Reads the persistent fields from the stream and makes them available by name.
float readFloat( )	Reads a 32-bit float.
void readFully(byte[ ] data)	Reads bytes, blocking until all bytes are read.
void readFully(byte[ ] data, int offset, int size)	Reads bytes, blocking until all bytes are read.
int readInt( )	Reads a 32-bit int.
String readLine( )	Deprecated. Use a buffered stream instead.
long readLong( )	Reads a 64-bit long.
Object readObject( )	Reads an object from the **ObjectInputStream**.
protected Object readObjectOverride( )	Called by trusted subclasses of **ObjectOutputStream**.
short readShort( )	Reads a 16-bit short.
protected void readStreamHeader( )	Allows subclasses to read and verify their own stream headers.
int readUnsignedByte( )	Reads an unsigned eight-bit byte.
int readUnsignedShort( )	Reads an unsigned 16-bit short.
String readUTF( )	Reads a UTF format **String**.
void registerValidation (ObjectInputValidation obj, int prio)	Registers an object to be validated before the graph is returned.
protected Class resolveClass (ObjectStreamClass v)	Loads the local class equivalent of the given stream class description.
protected Object resolveObject(Object obj)	Allows trusted subclasses of **ObjectInputStream** to substitute one object for another.
int skipBytes(int len)	Skips bytes.

Here's an example showing how serialization works. In this case, I create a new serializable class named **NewString**. This class has a constructor that takes a **String** and one method, **toString**, which returns that string (note that I implement the **Serializable** interface here):

```
class NewString implements Serializable
{
    String data;
```

```
        public NewString(String instring)
        {
            data = instring;
        }
        public String toString()
        {
            return data;
        }
    }
```

After creating a new object of the **NewString** class containing the text "Hello from Java!", I use a **FileOutputStream** stream as encapsulated by an **ObjectOutputStream** stream to write that object out to a file—serialized.dat. Next, I use a **FileInputStream** stream encapsulated in an **ObjectInputStream** stream to read that object back from the file and display its text. Here's the code:

```
import java.io.*;

public class serialization
{
    public static void main(String args[])
    {
        NewString inobject, outobject;
        inobject = new NewString("");
        outobject = new NewString("Hello from Java!");

        try {
            FileOutputStream fileoutputstring = new
                FileOutputStream("serialized.dat");
            ObjectOutputStream objectoutputstream = new
                ObjectOutputStream(fileoutputstring);
            objectoutputstream.writeObject(outobject);
            objectoutputstream.flush();
            objectoutputstream.close();

            FileInputStream fileinputstring = new
                FileInputStream("serialized.dat");
            ObjectInputStream objectinputstream = new
                ObjectInputStream(fileinputstring);
            inobject = (NewString)objectinputstream.readObject();
            objectinputstream.close();
        }
        catch(Exception e) {}
```

```
        System.out.println(inobject);
    }
}
```

Here's the output of this code (serialization.java on the CD):

```
C:\>java serialization
Hello from Java!
```

That's it. Now we're working with serialization.

Working With The Clipboard

You can use the Java toolkit's **getSystemClipboard** method and **ClipboardOwner** interface to place data into the Clipboard and retrieve it from the Clipboard. Here's an example. This code places the text "Hello from Java!" into the Clipboard (note that I have to create an object that has a toolkit—a **Frame** object here—to use **getSystemClipboard**):

```
import java.awt.*;
import java.awt.datatransfer.*;

public class clipboard
{
    public static void main(String[] argv)
    {
        useClipboard useclipboard = new useClipboard();
    }

}

class useClipboard extends Frame implements ClipboardOwner
{
    useClipboard()
    {
        Clipboard clipboard = getToolkit().getSystemClipboard();
        StringSelection contents = new StringSelection("Hello from Java!");
        clipboard.setContents(contents, this);
        System.exit(0);
    }

    public void lostOwnership(Clipboard clipboard, Transferable contents)
```

```
    {
        System.out.println("Clipboard contents replaced");
    }
}
```

That's all it takes; this example is in clipboard.java on the CD.

Working With The Printer

You can use the Java toolkit's **getPrintJob** method to create a new print job for
the printer, and you can use the print job's **getGraphics** method to get a **Graphics** object that you can use to draw on the printed page. Here's an example that
draws a small graphics figure on a page and then prints it (note that I have to
create an object that has a toolkit—a **Frame** object here—to use **getPrintJob**):

```
import java.awt.*;
import java.awt.event.*;

public class printer
{
    public static void main(String[] argv) {
        usePrinter useprinter = new usePrinter();
    }
}

class usePrinter extends Frame
{
    usePrinter()
    {
        PrintJob printjob = getToolkit().getPrintJob(this,
            "Print graphics", null);
        Graphics g = printjob.getGraphics();
        g.drawRect(2, 2, 100, 100);
        g.drawLine(2, 2, 100, 100);
        g.dispose();
        printjob.end();
        System.exit(0);
    }
}
```

Being able to use the printer this way is a very powerful aspect of Java I/O. This
example is in printer.java on the CD.

Chapter 21

Collections

In Depth

In this chapter, we'll take a look at the collection classes in Java, which are supported by java.util. As you can infer from their names, the collection classes let you group elements in various ways. The collection classes also define various methods that make working with those items easier. These classes are important, not just for their utility, but because many other Java methods use or return objects of these classes, such as the **Vector** and **Properties** classes.

The Collection Interfaces

Here are the four collection interfaces:

- *Collection*—The top of the collections hierarchy. Supports basic grouping of elements.
- *List*—Extends **Collection** to implement lists of objects.
- *Set*—Extends **Collection** to implement sets, in which all elements must be unique.
- *SortedSet*—Extends **Set** to implement a sorted set.

Sets manage unique collections of objects, and they're handy if you want to see if some object is in a particular set (such as when you categorize products you have for sale and want to see what category a specific product is in). In this case, you can use the **contains** method. You'll see the details in this chapter; in particular, there's a standard set of classes that implement the collection interfaces—the collection classes.

The Collection Classes

Here are the standard collection classes that implement the collection interfaces:

- *AbstractCollection*—Implements the **Collection** interface.
- *AbstractList*—Extends **AbstractCollection** and implements the **List** interface.
- *AbstractSequentialList*—Extends **AbstractList** into a sequential (not random access) list.
- *LinkedList*—Extends **AbstractSequentialList** into a linked list, where each element knows where the next element is.
- *ArrayList*—Implements a dynamic (resizable) array.

- *AbstractSet*—Extends **AbstractCollection** and implements the **Set** interface.
- *HashSet*—Extends **AbstractSet** to be used with a hash.
- *TreeSet*—Extends **AbstractSet** to implement a set stored in tree form.

Note the **HashSet** class, which implements a set using a hash internally. In Java, a *hash* stores information using hashing, which converts a key to a *hash code* that's then used to access the corresponding value. You don't deal with the hash code yourself—it's generated internally in Java.

The Map Interfaces

You can also use maps in Java. A *map* stores data in key/value pairs, much like an array where the indexes are, themselves, objects. Typically, keys are strings, and you can look up an object in a map by using that object. Here are the map interfaces:

- *Map*—Implements a map.
- *Map.Entry*—The inner class of **Map** that describes a key/value pair in a map.
- *SortedMap*—Extends **Map** to keep the keys in ascending order.

Java also derives some standard classes from these interfaces—the **Map** classes.

The Map Classes

Here are the standard map classes defined by Java:

- *AbstractMap*—Implements the **Map** interface.
- *HashMap*—Extends **AbstractMap** using a hash.
- *TreeMap*—Extends **AbstractMap** using a tree.
- *WeakHashMap*—Extends **AbstractMap** using a hash with weak keys, which means that elements whose keys are no longer in use will be discarded.

You'll also see other classes here that are not technically members of the collections framework—**Arrays**, **Vector**, **Stack, HashTable**, and others. These older collections have been rebuilt on collection framework functionality. In fact, most standard computing collections are implemented in Java in various ways; for example, the **TreeSet** class implements a set using a tree internally, which means access times are quick. **HashSet** implements a set using a hash internally, which means that adding and removing elements from such a set should always take the same amount of time, no matter how large the set grows.

That's it for the overview of what's in this chapter. There's a lot coming up here—the collections framework is very large. It's time to turn to the "Immediate Solutions" section.

Immediate Solutions

Using The **Collection** Interface

The foundation of the collections framework is the **Collection** interface, and because the collection classes implement this interface, we'll take a look at its methods here for reference. You'll find the methods for the **Collection** interface in Table 21.1.

Table 21.1   Methods of the Collection interface.

Method	Does This
boolean add(Object o)	Adds the given element.
boolean addAll(Collection c)	Adds all the elements in the given collection.
void clear( )	Removes all the elements from this collection.
boolean contains(Object o)	Returns True if this collection contains the given element.
boolean containsAll(Collection c)	Returns True if this collection contains all the elements in the given collection.
boolean equals(Object o)	Compares the given object with this collection for equality.
int hashCode( )	Gets the hashcode value for this collection.
boolean isEmpty( )	Returns True if this collection has no elements.
Iterator iterator( )	Gets an iterator over the elements in this collection.
boolean remove(Object o)	Removes a single instance of the given element.
boolean removeAll(Collection c)	Removes all this collection's elements that are also contained in the given collection.
boolean retainAll(Collection c)	Keeps only the elements in this collection that are contained in the given collection.
int size( )	Gets the number of elements in this collection.
Object[ ] toArray( )	Gets an array containing all the elements in this collection.
Object[ ] toArray(Object[ ] a)	Gets an array containing all the elements in this collection whose type is that of the given array.

Using The **List** Interface

The **List** interface is the foundation of classes such as **LinkedList** and **ArrayList**, so we'll take a look at the methods of this interface for reference. You'll find the methods of the **List** interface in Table 21.2.

*Table 21.2 Methods of the **List** interface.*

Method	Does This
void add(int index, Object element)	Inserts the given element at the given position in this list.
boolean add(Object o)	Adds the given element to the end of this list.
boolean addAll(Collection c)	Adds all the elements in the given collection to the end of this list.
boolean addAll(int index, Collection c)	Inserts all the elements in the given collection into this list.
void clear( )	Removes all the elements from this list.
boolean contains(Object o)	Returns True if this list contains the given element.
boolean containsAll(Collection c)	Returns True if this list contains all the elements of the given collection.
boolean equals(Object o)	Compares the given object with this list for equality.
Object get(int index)	Gets the element at the given position in this list.
int hashCode( )	Gets the hashcode value for this list.
int indexOf(Object o)	Gets the index in this list of the first occurrence of the given element or -1 if this list does not contain the element.
boolean isEmpty( )	Returns True if this list contains no elements.
Iterator iterator( )	Gets an iterator over the elements in this list in proper sequence.
int lastIndexOf(Object o)	Gets the index in this list of the last occurrence of the given element or -1 if this list does not contain the element.
ListIterator listIterator( )	Gets a list iterator of the elements in this list.
ListIterator listIterator(int index)	Gets a list iterator of the elements in this list, starting at the given position in this list.
Object remove(int index)	Removes the element at the given position in this list.
boolean remove(Object o)	Removes the first occurrence in this list of the given element.
boolean removeAll(Collection c)	Removes from this list all the elements that are contained in the given collection.
boolean retainAll(Collection c)	Keeps only the elements in this list that are contained in the given collection.

(continued)

Table 21.2   Methods of the List interface (continued).

Method	Does This
Object set(int index, Object element)	Replaces the element at the given position list with the new element.
int size( )	Gets the number of elements in this list.
List subList(int fromIndex, int toIndex)	Gets a view of the section between the given **fromIndex** (inclusive) and **toIndex**.
Object[ ] toArray( )	Gets an array containing all the elements.
Object[ ] toArray(Object[ ] a)	Gets an array containing all the elements in this list in proper sequence.

Using The **Set** Interface

The **Set** interface is the foundation of classes such as **HashSet** and **TreeSet**, and it's used by the collections framework to implement sets. Therefore, we'll take a look at this interface for reference. You'll find the methods of the **Set** interface in Table 21.3.

Table 21.3   Methods of the Set class.

Method	Does This
boolean add(Object o)	Adds the given element to this set.
boolean addAll(Collection c)	Adds all the elements in the given collection.
void clear( )	Removes all the elements from this set.
boolean contains(Object o)	Returns True if this set contains the given element.
boolean containsAll(Collection c)	Returns True if this set contains all the elements of the given collection.
boolean equals(Object o)	Compares the given object with this set for equality.
int hashCode( )	Gets the hashcode value for this set.
boolean isEmpty( )	Returns True if this set contains no elements.
Iterator iterator( )	Gets an iterator over the elements in this set.
boolean remove(Object o)	Removes the given element from this set if it is present.
boolean removeAll(Collection c)	Removes all elements contained in the given collection.
boolean retainAll(Collection c)	Keeps only the elements in this set that are contained in the given collection.
int size( )	Gets the number of elements in this set.

(continued)

Table 21.3   Methods of the Set class (continued).

Method	Does This
Object[ ] toArray( )	Gets an array containing all the elements in this set.
Object[ ] toArray(Object[ ] a)	Gets an array containing all the elements in this set whose runtime type is that of the given array.

Using The **SortedSet** Interface

The **SortedSet** interface maintains a sorted set, and you'll find the methods of this interface in Table 21.4.

Table 21.4   Methods of the SortedSet class.

Method	Does This
Comparator comparator( )	Gets the comparator associated with this sorted set.
Object first( )	Gets the first element currently in this sorted set.
SortedSet headSet(Object toElement)	Gets a view of the section of this sorted set whose elements are less than **toElement**.
Object last( )	Gets the last (highest) element currently in this sorted set.
SortedSet subSet(Object from Element, Object toElement)	Gets a view of the portion of this set whose elements range from **fromElement** to **toElement**.
SortedSet tailSet(Object fromElement)	Gets a view of the portion of this set whose elements are greater than or equal to **fromElement**.

Using The **AbstractCollection** Class

The **AbstractCollection** class is the implementation of the **Collection** interface upon which many Java collection classes are built, so we'll take a look at **AbstractCollection** for reference. Here's the inheritance diagram for this class:

```
java.lang.Object
|____java.util.AbstractCollection
```

You'll find the constructor for the **AbstractCollection** class in Table 21.5 and its methods in Table 21.6.

Table 21.5 *The constructor of the **AbstractCollection** class.*

Constructor	Does This
protected AbstractCollection( )	Constructs an **AbstractCollection**.

Table 21.6 *Methods of the **AbstractCollection** class.*

Method	Does this
boolean add(Object o)	Ensures that this collection contains the given element.
boolean addAll(Collection c)	Adds all the elements in the given collection to this collection.
void clear( )	Removes all the elements from this collection.
boolean contains(Object o)	Returns True if this collection contains the given element.
boolean containsAll(Collection c)	Returns True if this collection contains all the elements in the given collection.
boolean isEmpty( )	Returns True if this collection contains no elements.
abstract Iterator iterator( )	Gets an iterator over the elements contained in this collection.
boolean remove(Object o)	Removes the given element from this collection.
boolean removeAll(Collection c)	Removes all elements that are contained in the given collection.
boolean retainAll(Collection c)	Keeps only the elements contained in the given collection.
abstract int size( )	Gets the number of elements in this collection.
Object[ ] toArray( )	Gets an array containing all the elements in this collection.
Object[ ] toArray(Object[ ] a)	Gets an array that contains all the elements in this collection.
String toString( )	Gets a string representation of this collection.

Using The **AbstractList** Class

The **AbstractList** class extends the **AbstractCollection** class. **AbstractList** is an important class because it's the foundation of classes such as **ArrayList**, which supports dynamic arrays. Therefore, I'll include **AbstractList** here for reference. Here's the inheritance diagram for this class:

```
java.lang.Object
|____java.util.AbstractCollection
    |____java.util.AbstractList
```

You'll find the field of the **AbstractList** class in Table 21.7, its constructor in Table 21.8, and its methods in Table 21.9.

Table 21.7   **The field of the *AbstractList* class.**

Field	Does This
protected int modCount	Indicates the number of times this list has been modified.

Table 21.8   **The constructor of the *AbstractList* class.**

Constructor	Does This
protected AbstractList( )	Constructs an **AbstractList**.

Table 21.9   **Methods of the *AbstractList* class.**

Method	Does This
void add(int index, Object element)	Inserts the given element into this list.
boolean add(Object o)	Adds the given element to the end of this list.
boolean addAll(int index, Collection c)	Inserts the elements in the given collection into this list.
void clear( )	Removes all the elements from this collection.
boolean equals(Object o)	Compares the given object with this list for equality.
abstract Object get(int index)	Gets the element at the given position in this list.
int hashCode( )	Gets the hashcode value for this list.
int indexOf(Object o)	Gets the index in this list of the first occurrence of the given element or -1 if this element is not present.
Iterator iterator( )	Gets an iterator over the elements in this list in proper sequence.
int lastIndexOf(Object o)	Gets the index in this list of the last occurrence of the given element or -1 if this element is not present.
ListIterator listIterator( )	Gets an iterator of the elements in this list (in proper sequence).
ListIterator listIterator(int index)	Gets a list iterator of the elements in this list (in proper sequence), starting at the given position in the list.
Object remove(int index)	Removes the element at the given position in this list.
protected void removeRange (int fromIndex, int toIndex)	Removes from this list all the elements whose indexes are between **fromIndex** and **toIndex**.
Object set(int index, Object element)	Replaces the element at the given position in this list with the new element.
List subList(int fromIndex, int toIndex)	Gets a view of the portion of this list between **fromIndex** (inclusive) and **toIndex** (exclusive).

21. Collections

Using The **AbstractSequentialList** Class

The **AbstractSequentialList** class is extended from the **AbstractList** class (see the previous topic) and is the foundation of classes such as **LinkedList**. Here's the inheritance diagram for the **AbstractSequentialList** class:

```
java.lang.Object
|____java.util.AbstractCollection
    |____java.util.AbstractList
        |____java.util.AbstractSequentialList
```

You'll find the constructor of the **AbstractSequentialList** class in Table 21.10 and its methods in Table 21.11.

Table 21.10   The constructor of the *AbstractSequentialList* class.

Constructor	Does This
protected AbstractSequentialList( )	Constructs an **AbstractSequentialList**.

Table 21.11   Methods of the *AbstractSequentialList* class.

Method	Does This
void add(int index, Object element)	Inserts the given element at the given position in this list.
boolean addAll(int index, Collection c)	Inserts all the elements in the given collection.
Object get(int index)	Gets the element at the given position in this list.
Iterator iterator( )	Gets an iterator over the elements in this list.
abstract ListIterator listIterator(int index)	Gets a list iterator over the elements in this list.
Object remove(int index)	Removes the element at the given position in this list.
Object set(int index, Object element)	Replaces the element at the given position in this list.

Using The **ArrayList** Class

The Novice Programmer appears and says, "Jeez! My code stores phone numbers in an array, but I'm never sure whether the user will store three phone numbers there or 10,000, so I have to set up an array with enough space for 10,000 numbers." "Unless," you say, "you use an **ArrayList** object, which is a dynamic array that can grow at runtime." The NP says, "Wow!"

The **ArrayList** class is an array class that can grow or shrink at runtime. Note that arrays of this class must hold objects, not just simple data types. Here's the inheritance diagram for this class:

```
java.lang.Object
|____java.util.AbstractCollection
        |____java.util.AbstractList
                |____java.util.ArrayList
```

You'll find the constructors of the **ArrayList** class in Table 21.12 and its methods in Table 21.13.

Table 21.12   Constructors of the ArrayList class.

Constructor	Does This
ArrayList( )	Constructs an **ArrayList**.
ArrayList(Collection c)	Constructs a list containing the elements of the given collection.
ArrayList(int initialCapacity)	Constructs an empty list with the given initial capacity.

Table 21.13   Methods of the ArrayList class.

Method	Does This
void add(int index, Object element)	Inserts the given element at the given position in this list.
boolean add(Object o)	Adds the given element to the end of this list.
boolean addAll(Collection c)	Adds all the elements in the given collection to the end of this list.
boolean addAll(int index, Collection c)	Inserts all the elements in the given collection into this list, starting at the given position.
void clear( )	Removes all the elements from this list.
Object clone( )	Gets a copy of this **ArrayList** instance.
boolean contains(Object elem)	Returns True if this list contains the given element.
void ensureCapacity(int minCapacity)	Increases the capacity of this **ArrayList** instance.
Object get(int index)	Gets the element at the given position in this list.
int indexOf(Object elem)	Searches for the first occurrence of the given argument.
boolean isEmpty( )	Tests whether this list has no elements.
int lastIndexOf(Object elem)	Gets the index of the last occurrence of the given object in this list.
Object remove(int index)	Removes the element at the given position in this list.

(continued)

Table 21.13   *Methods of the ArrayList class* (continued).

Method	Does This
protected void removeRange (int fromIndex, int toIndex)	Removes from this list all the elements whose indexes are between **fromIndex** and **toIndex**.
Object set(int index, Object element)	Replaces the element at the given position in this list with the given element.
int size( )	Gets the number of elements in this list.
Object[ ] toArray( )	Gets an array containing all the elements.
Object[ ] toArray(Object[ ] a)	Gets an array containing all the elements.
void trimToSize( )	Trims the capacity to be the list's current size.

You can add elements to an **ArrayList** object with the **add** method, get an element at a certain index with the **get** method, and remove elements with the **remove** method.

Here's an example in which I add elements to an array at runtime. Note that I'm using two forms of the **add** method—the general form and the form that lets me add an element at a specific index. I'm also using the **remove** method to remove one element, as you see here:

```
import java.util.*;

class arraylist
{
    public static void main(String args[])
    {
        ArrayList arraylist = new ArrayList();

        arraylist.add("Item 0");
        arraylist.add("Item 2");
        arraylist.add("Item 3");
        arraylist.add("Item 4");
        arraylist.add("Item 5");
        arraylist.add("Item 6");
        arraylist.add(1, "Item 1");

        System.out.println(arraylist);

        arraylist.remove("Item 5");

        System.out.println(arraylist);
    }
}
```

Here's the output of this code (arraylist.java on the CD accompanying this book):

```
C:\>java arraylist
[Item 0, Item 1, Item 2, Item 3, Item 4, Item 5, Item 6]
[Item 0, Item 1, Item 2, Item 3, Item 4, Item 6]
```

Using The **LinkedList** Class

The Programming Correctness Czar appears and says, "Well, Java has many aspects of C++, but what about support for programming constructs such as linked lists?" "No problem," you say.

The **LinkedList** class supports linked lists in which you keep track of items in these lists. Using such a list, you can move from one element to the next using a *list iterator*, as you'll see in this chapter. Here's the inheritance diagram for the **LinkedList** class:

```
java.lang.Object
|____java.util.AbstractCollection
     |____java.util.AbstractList
          |____java.util.AbstractSequentialList
               |____java.util.LinkedList
```

You'll find the constructors of the **LinkedList** class in Table 21.14 and its methods in Table 21.15.

Table 21.14   Constructors of the *LinkedList* class.

Constructor	Does This
LinkedList( )	Constructs a **LinkedList**.
LinkedList(Collection c)	Constructs a list containing the elements of the given collection.

Table 21.15   Methods of the *LinkedList* class.

Method	Does This
void add(int index, Object element)	Inserts the given element at the given position.
boolean add(Object o)	Adds the given element to the end of this list.
boolean addAll(Collection c)	Adds all the elements in the given collection to the end of this list.
boolean addAll(int index, Collection c)	Inserts all the elements in the given collection into this list.

(continued)

Table 21.15   Methods of the *LinkedList* class (continued).

Method	Does This
void addFirst(Object o)	Inserts the given element at the beginning of this list.
void addLast(Object o)	Adds the given element to the end of this list.
void clear( )	Removes all the elements from this list.
Object clone( )	Gets a copy of this **LinkedList**.
boolean contains(Object o)	Returns True if this list contains the given element.
Object get(int index)	Gets the element at the given position in this list.
Object getFirst( )	Gets the first element in this list.
Object getLast( )	Gets the last element in this list.
int indexOf(Object o)	Gets the index in this list of the first occurrence of the given element.
int lastIndexOf(Object o)	Gets the index in this list of the last occurrence of the given element.
ListIterator listIterator(int index)	Gets a list iterator of the elements in this list, starting at the given position in the list.
Object remove(int index)	Removes the element at the given position in this list.
boolean remove(Object o)	Removes the first occurrence of the given element in this list.
Object removeFirst( )	Removes and returns the first element from this list.
Object removeLast( )	Removes and returns the last element from this list.
Object set(int index, Object element)	Replaces the element at the given position in this list with the given element.
int size( )	Gets the number of elements in this list.
Object[ ] toArray( )	Gets an array containing all the elements in this list in the correct order.
Object[ ] toArray(Object[ ] a)	Gets an array containing all the elements in this list in the correct order.

To build a linked list, you can use the **add**, **addFirst**, and **addLast** methods; to get an element at a certain index, you can use the **get**, **getFirst**, and **getLast** methods; to set an element's value, you can use the **set** method, and to remove an element, you can use the **remove**, **removeFirst**, and **removeLast** methods.

Here's an example. In this case, I'm simply building a linked list, adding some elements, and then removing some elements:

```
import java.util.*;

class linkedlist
{
```

```
public static void main(String args[])
{
    LinkedList linkedlist1 = new LinkedList();

    linkedlist1.add("Item 2");
    linkedlist1.add("Item 3");
    linkedlist1.add("Item 4");
    linkedlist1.add("Item 5");

    linkedlist1.addFirst("Item 0");
    linkedlist1.addLast("Item 6");

    linkedlist1.add(1, "Item 1");

    System.out.println(linkedlist1);

    linkedlist1.remove("Item 6");

    System.out.println(linkedlist1);

    linkedlist1.removeLast();

    System.out.println(linkedlist1);

    linkedlist1.set(3, "New Item");

    System.out.println(linkedlist1);
}
}
```

Here's the output of this code (linkedlist.java on the CD):

```
[Item 0, Item 1, Item 2, Item 3, Item 4, Item 5, Item 6]
[Item 0, Item 1, Item 2, Item 3, Item 4, Item 5]
[Item 0, Item 1, Item 2, Item 3, Item 4]
[Item 0, Item 1, Item 2, New Item, Item 4]
```

Using The **HashSet** Class

A *set* is a collection of unique elements, and the **HashSet** class supports sets using a hash internally for storage. Because this class uses a hash internally, methods such as **contains**, **remove**, **add**, and **size** always take the same amount of time to execute. Here's the inheritance diagram for this class:

```
java.lang.Object
|____java.util.AbstractCollection
     |____java.util.AbstractSet
          |____java.util.HashSet
```

You'll find the constructors of the **HashSet** class in Table 21.16 and its methods in Table 21.17.

*Table 21.16   Constructors of the **HashSet** class.*

Constructor	Does This
HashSet( )	Constructs a new, empty set.
HashSet(Collection c)	Constructs a new set containing the elements in the given collection.
HashSet(int initialCapacity)	Constructs a new, empty set with the given initial capacity.
HashSet(int initialCapacity, float loadFactor)	Constructs a new, empty set with the given initial capacity and the given load factor.

*Table 21.17   Methods of the **HashSet** class.*

Method	Does This
boolean add(Object o)	Adds the given element to this set if it's not already present.
void clear( )	Removes all the elements from this set.
Object clone( )	Gets a copy of this **HashSet** instance.
boolean contains(Object o)	Returns True if this set contains the given element.
boolean isEmpty( )	Returns True if this set contains no elements.
Iterator iterator( )	Gets an iterator over the elements in this set.
boolean remove(Object o)	Removes the given element from this set if it's present.
int size( )	Gets the number of elements in this set.

Here's an example in which I add elements to a set and then print out that set:

```
import java.util.*;

class hashset
{
    public static void main(String args[])
    {
        HashSet hashset1 = new HashSet();

        hashset1.add("Item 0");
        hashset1.add("Item 1");
        hashset1.add("Item 2");
        hashset1.add("Item 3");
        hashset1.add("Item 4");
        hashset1.add("Item 5");
        hashset1.add("Item 6");

        System.out.println(hashset1);
    }
}
```

One thing to note about hashes is that you can't guarantee the order in which elements are stored internally. In fact, when you print out this set, you can see that all elements are stored in exactly reverse order:

```
C:\>java hashset
[Item 6, Item 5, Item 4, Item 3, Item 2, Item 1, Item 0]
```

This example is in hashset.java on the CD.

Using The **TreeSet** Class

The **TreeSet** class uses a tree construct for internal storage to implement a set, which means that access times are fast. The elements of a **TreeSet** are stored in sorted order. Here's the inheritance diagram for this class:

```
java.lang.Object
|____java.util.AbstractCollection
     |____java.util.AbstractSet
          |____java.util.TreeSet
```

21. Collections

You'll find the constructors for the **TreeSet** class in Table 21.18 and its methods in Table 21.19.

Table 21.18   Constructors of the TreeSet class.

Constructor	Does This
TreeSet( )	Constructs a new, empty set.
TreeSet(Collection c)	Constructs a new set containing the elements in the given collection.
TreeSet(Comparator c)	Constructs a new, empty set, sorted according to the given comparator.
TreeSet(SortedSet s)	Constructs a new set containing the same elements as the given sorted set.

Table 21.19   Methods of the TreeSet class.

Method	Does This
boolean add(Object o)	Adds the given element to this set.
boolean addAll(Collection c)	Adds all the elements in the given collection.
void clear( )	Removes all the elements from this set.
Object clone( )	Gets a shallow copy of this **TreeSet** instance.
Comparator comparator( )	Gets the comparator used to order this sorted set.
boolean contains(Object o)	Returns True if this set contains the given element.
Object first( )	Gets the first element currently in this sorted set.
SortedSet headSet(Object toElement)	Gets a view of the portion of this set whose elements are less than **toElement**.
boolean isEmpty( )	Returns True if this set contains no elements.
Iterator iterator( )	Gets an iterator over the elements in this set.
Object last( )	Gets the last element currently in this sorted set.
boolean remove(Object o)	Removes the given element from this set if it's present.
int size( )	Gets the number of elements in this set.
SortedSet subSet(Object fromElement, Object toElement)	Gets a view of the portion of this set whose elements range from **fromElement** to **toElement**.
SortedSet tailSet(Object fromElement)	Gets a view of the portion of this set whose elements are greater than or equal to **fromElement**.

The **TreeSet** class just implements a set using a tree for storage internally. One big difference from the **HashSet** class is that elements in a **TreeSet** object are stored in sorted order. Here's the same example as the previous one, where I stored elements in a **HashSet**; however, this time I'm using a **TreeSet**:

```
import java.util.*;

class treeset
{
    public static void main(String args[])
    {
        TreeSet treeset1 = new TreeSet();

        treeset1.add("Item 0");
        treeset1.add("Item 1");
        treeset1.add("Item 2");
        treeset1.add("Item 3");
        treeset1.add("Item 4");
        treeset1.add("Item 6");
        treeset1.add("Item 5");

        System.out.println(treeset1);
    }
}
```

Here's the output of this code (note that, unlike the **HashSet** example in the previous topic, the **TreeSet** elements are sorted in ascending order):

```
C:\>java treeset
[Item 0, Item 1, Item 2, Item 3, Item 4, Item 5, Item 6]
```

In fact, you can specify the sorting order for **TreeSet** objects—see the next topic for the details.

Using The **Comparator** Interface

The Novice Programmer appears and says, "I like the speed of **TreeSet** objects. On the other hand, sometimes I want to print out what's in those objects, and I want to sort the elements in a particular order." "No problem," you say. "Just set up a **Comparator** class." "How's that?" the NP asks.

You can use a comparator to determine the sorting order used in **TreeSet** objects, for example, by implementing the **Comparator** interface. The methods of this interface appear in Table 21.20.

The **compare** method compares two objects, **obj1** and **obj2**, and returns -1 if **obj1** is less than **obj2**, 0 if they are equal, and 1 if **obj1** is greater than **obj2**. By overriding this method, you can support a custom sorting order.

Here's an example in which I sort a **TreeSet** object in ascending order—except for one element, Item 3, which I always want to appear at the beginning of the set. Here's what this looks like in code:

```java
import java.util.*;

class comparator
{
    public static void main(String args[])
    {
        TreeSet treeset = new TreeSet(new NewComparator());

        treeset.add("Item 0");
        treeset.add("Item 1");
        treeset.add("Item 2");
        treeset.add("Item 3");
        treeset.add("Item 4");
        treeset.add("Item 5");
        treeset.add("Item 6");

        Iterator iterator = treeset.iterator();

        while(iterator.hasNext()) {
            System.out.println(iterator.next());
        }
    }
}


class NewComparator implements Comparator
{
    public int compare(Object obj1, Object obj2)
    {
        if (((String) obj1).equals("Item 3")) return -1;
        return ((String) obj1).compareTo((String) obj2);
    }
}
```

*Table 21.20   Methods of the **Comparator** interface.*

Method	Does This
int compare(Object obj1, Object obj2)	Compares its two arguments.
boolean equals(Object obj)	Specifies whether another object is equal to this comparator.

Here's the output of this code (comparator.java on the CD). Note that Item 3 comes first:

```
C:\>java comparator
Item 3
Item 0
Item 1
Item 2
Item 4
Item 5
Item 6
```

Using The **Iterator** Interface

"Hmm," says the Novice Programmer, "I want to loop over all the elements in a list. How the heck do I do that?" "With an iterator," you say. "OK," says the NP, "but what's an iterator?"

You can use the methods of the **Iterator** interface to move through a collection using the **next** method, thus enabling you to iterate (or *cycle through*) the elements of the collection. The methods of the **Iterator** interface appear in Table 21.21.

*Table 21.21   Methods of the **Iterator** class.*

Methods	Does This
boolean hasNext( )	Returns True if the iteration has more elements.
Object next( )	Gets the next element in the iteration.
void remove( )	Removes the last element returned.

Here's an example in which I print out each element in a linked list from first to last, using an iterator and the methods **next** and **hasNext** (which returns True if the collection has a next element):

```java
import java.util.*;

class iterator
{
    public static void main(String args[])
    {
        LinkedList linkedlist = new LinkedList();

        linkedlist.add("Item 0");
        linkedlist.add("Item 1");
        linkedlist.add("Item 2");
        linkedlist.add("Item 3");
        linkedlist.add("Item 4");
        linkedlist.add("Item 5");
        linkedlist.add("Item 6");

        Iterator iterator = linkedlist.iterator();

        while(iterator.hasNext()) {
            System.out.println(iterator.next());
        }
    }
}
```

Here's the output of this code (iterator.java on the CD):

```
C:\>java iterator
Item 0
Item 1
Item 2
Item 3
Item 4
Item 5
Item 6
```

Besides iterators, you can also use *list iterators*. See the next topic.

Using The **ListIterator** Interface

"Well," says the Novice Programmer, "iterators are fine, but I want to work through a collection backwards. No way, huh?" "No problem," you say. "Just use a list iterator." The NP says, "Tell me more!"

Whereas iterators can only work forward through a list using the **next** method, list iterators also support the **previous** method, so they can work backward through lists. This is particularly useful for linked lists, where each element often must know about the next and previous elements (called a bidirectional linked list). This is handy, for example, when you're implementing a buffer that can grow or shrink.

You'll find the methods of the **ListIterator** interface in Table 21.22.

Table 21.22   *Methods of the* **ListIterator** *interface.*

Method	Does This
void add(Object o)	Inserts the given element into the list.
boolean hasNext( )	Returns True if this list iterator has more elements in the forward direction.
boolean hasPrevious( )	Returns True if this list iterator has more elements in the reverse direction.
Object next( )	Gets the next element in the list.
int nextIndex( )	Gets the index of the element that would be returned by a subsequent call to **next**.
Object previous( )	Gets the previous element in the list.
int previousIndex( )	Gets the index of the element that would be returned by a subsequent call to **previous**.
void remove( )	Removes from the list the last element that was returned by **next** or **previous**.
void set(Object o)	Replaces the last element returned by next or **previous** with the given element.

Here's an example in which I print out a linked list backwards:

```java
import java.util.*;

class listiterator
{
    public static void main(String args[])
    {
        LinkedList linkedlist = new LinkedList();

        linkedlist.add("Item 0");
        linkedlist.add("Item 1");
        linkedlist.add("Item 2");
        linkedlist.add("Item 3");
        linkedlist.add("Item 4");
        linkedlist.add("Item 5");
        linkedlist.add("Item 6");

        ListIterator listiterator = linkedlist.listIterator();

        while(listiterator.hasNext()) {
            listiterator.set("This is " + listiterator.next());
        }

        while(listiterator.hasPrevious()) {
            System.out.println(listiterator.previous());
        }
    }
}
```

Here's the output of this code (linkedlist.java on the CD):

```
C:\>java listiterator
This is Item 6
This is Item 5
This is Item 4
This is Item 3
This is Item 2
This is Item 1
This is Item 0
```

Using The **AbstractMap** Class

The **AbstractMap** class forms the foundation of the map classes in Java, so we'll take a look at this class here for reference. Here's the inheritance diagram for the **AbstractMap** class:

```
java.lang.Object
|____java.util.AbstractMap
```

You'll find the constructor of the **AbstractMap** interface in Table 21.23 and its methods in Table 21.24.

Table 21.23   The constructor of the AbstractMap class.

Constructor	Does This
protected AbstractMap( )	Constructs an **AbstractMap**.

Table 21.24   Methods of the AbstractMap class.

Method	Does This
void clear( )	Removes all mappings.
boolean containsKey(Object key)	Returns True if this map contains a mapping for the given key.
boolean containsValue(Object value)	Returns True if this map maps one or more keys to this value.
abstract Set entrySet( )	Gets a set view of the mappings contained in this map.
boolean equals(Object o)	Compares the given object with this map for equality.
Object get(Object key)	Gets the value to which this map maps the given key.
int hashCode( )	Gets the hashcode value for this map.
boolean isEmpty( )	Returns True if this map contains no key/value mappings.
Set keySet( )	Gets a set view of the keys contained in this map.
Object put(Object key, Object value)	Associates the given value with the given key in this map.
void putAll(Map t)	Copies all the mappings from the given map to this map.
Object remove(Object key)	Removes the mapping for this key from this map, if present.
int size( )	Gets the number of key/value mappings in this map.
String toString( )	Gets a string representation of this map.
Collection values( )	Gets a collection view of the values contained in this map.

Using The **HashMap** Class

"I'm writing a phonebook application," the Novice Programmer says, "and it's hard to keep track of the people in it by converting them to indexes in an array. Wouldn't it be great if I could access an array using strings such as people's names instead of numeric indexes?" "You can," you say. "Just use a map."

Maps let you store data as key/value pairs, where both the key and the value are objects. For example, you can create a map that's indexed with strings instead of numbers. Here's the inheritance diagram for the **HashMap** class:

```
java.lang.Object
|____java.util.AbstractMap
     |____java.util.HashMap
```

You'll find the constructors for the **HashMap** class in Table 21.25 and its methods in Table 21.26.

*Table 21.25   Constructors of the **HashMap** class.*

Constructor	Does This
HashMap( )	Constructs a new, empty map.
HashMap(int initialCapacity)	Constructs a new, empty map with the given initial capacity.
HashMap(int initialCapacity, float loadFactor)	Constructs a new, empty map with the given initial capacity and the given load factor.
HashMap(Map m)	Constructs a new map with the same mappings as the given map.

*Table 21.26   Methods of the **HashMap** class.*

Method	Does This
void clear( )	Removes all mappings.
Object clone( )	Gets a copy of this **HashMap** instance.
boolean containsKey(Object key)	Returns True if this map contains a mapping for the given key.
boolean containsValue(Object value)	Returns True if this map maps one or more keys to the given value.
Set entrySet( )	Gets a collection view of the mappings contained in this map.
Object get(Object key)	Gets the value to which this map maps the given key.
boolean isEmpty( )	Returns True if this map contains no key/value mappings.
Set keySet( )	Gets a set view of the keys contained in this map.

(continued)

*Table 21.26   Methods of the **HashMap** class* (continued).

Method	Does This
Object put(Object key, Object value)	Associates the given value with the given key in this map.
void putAll(Map t)	Copies all the mappings from the given map to this one.
Object remove(Object key)	Removes the mapping for this key from this map.
int size( )	Gets the number of key/value mappings in this map.
Collection values( )	Gets a collection view of the values in this map.

The **put** method is used to add a key/value pair to a map and the **get** method is used to retrieve a value, given a key. For example, the string **drink** will be left holding the text "root beer" after this code executes:

```
hashmap.put("drink", "root beer");
String drink = hashmap.get("drink");
```

You can also get a set corresponding to the map with the **entrySet** method, and you can iterate over that set using the **Map.Entry** class. Here's an example in which I create a map and then print out all the key/value pairs in the map:

```
import java.util.*;

class hashmap
{
    public static void main(String args[])
    {
        HashMap hashmap1 = new HashMap();

        hashmap1.put("Item 0", "Value 0");
        hashmap1.put("Item 1", "Value 1");
        hashmap1.put("Item 2", "Value 2");
        hashmap1.put("Item 3", "Value 3");
        hashmap1.put("Item 4", "Value 4");
        hashmap1.put("Item 5", "Value 5");
        hashmap1.put("Item 6", "Value 6");

        Set set = hashmap1.entrySet();

        Iterator iterator = set.iterator();

        while(iterator.hasNext()) {
```

```
                    Map.Entry mapentry = (Map.Entry) iterator.next();
                    System.out.println(mapentry.getKey() + "/" +
                        mapentry.getValue());
            }
        }
    }
```

Here's the output of this code (hashmap.java on the CD):

```
C:\>java hashmap
Item 6/Value 6
Item 5/Value 5
Item 4/Value 4
Item 3/Value 3
Item 2/Value 2
Item 1/Value 1
Item 0/Value 0
```

Using The **TreeMap** Class

The **TreeMap** class implements a map using a tree internally to store data. Here's the inheritance diagram for this class:

```
java.lang.Object
|____java.util.AbstractMap
        |____java.util.TreeMap
```

You'll find the constructors for the **TreeMap** class in Table 21.27 and its methods in Table 21.28.

Table 21.27   Constructors of the TreeMap class.

Constructor	Does This
TreeMap( )	Constructs a new, empty map.
TreeMap(Comparator c)	Constructs a new, empty map, sorted according to the given comparator.
TreeMap(Map m)	Constructs a new map containing the same mappings as the given map.
TreeMap(SortedMap m)	Constructs a new map containing the same mappings as the given **SortedMap**.

Table 21.28   Methods of the TreeMap class.

Method	Does This
void clear( )	Removes all mappings.
Object clone( )	Gets a copy of this **TreeMap** instance.
Comparator comparator( )	Gets the comparator used to order this map.
boolean containsKey(Object key)	Returns True if this map contains a mapping for the specified key.
boolean containsValue(Object value)	Returns True if this map maps one or more keys to the specified value.
Set entrySet( )	Gets a set view of the mappings contained in this map.
Object firstKey( )	Gets the first key currently in this sorted map.
Object get(Object key)	Gets the value to which this map maps the specified key.
SortedMap headMap(Object toKey)	Gets a view of the portion of this map whose keys are strictly less than **toKey**.
Set keySet( )	Gets a set view of the keys contained in this map.
Object lastKey( )	Gets the last key currently in this sorted map.
Object put(Object key, Object value)	Associates the specified value with the specified key in this map.
void putAll(Map map)	Copies all the mappings from the specified map to this map.
Object remove(Object key)	Removes the mapping for this key.
int size( )	Gets the number of key/value mappings.
SortedMap subMap(Object fromKey, toKey)	Gets a view of the portion of this map whose keys range from Object **fromKey** to **toKey**.
SortedMap tailMap(Object fromKey)	Gets a view of the portion of this map whose keys are greater than or equal to **fromKey**.
Collection values( )	Gets a collection view of the values.

Using The **Arrays** Class

"What are you doing?" you ask the Novice Programmer. "I'm writing code to sort an array," says the NP. "Why don't you just use the **Arrays** class?" you ask. "How's that?" the NP asks.

You can use the **Arrays** class to work with arrays, including sorting and searching arrays. Here's the inheritance diagram for this class:

```
java.lang.Object
|_____java.util.Arrays
```

You'll find the methods for the **Arrays** class in Table 21.29. Note that these are static methods that you can use without instantiating an object of this class.

Table 21.29   Methods of the Arrays class.

Method	Does This
static List asList(Object[ ] a)	Gets a fixed-size list.
static int binarySearch(byte[ ] a, byte key)	Searches the given array of bytes for the given value.
static int binarySearch(char[ ] a, char key)	Searches the given array of characters for the given value.
static int binarySearch(double[ ] a, double key)	Searches the given array of doubles for the given value.
static int binarySearch(float[ ] a, float key)	Searches the given array of floats for the given value.
static int binarySearch(int[ ] a, int key)	Searches the given array of ints for the given value.
static int binarySearch(long[ ] a, long key)	Searches the given array of longs for the given value.
static int binarySearch(Object[ ] a, Object key)	Searches the given array for the given object.
static int binarySearch(Object[ ] a, Object key, Comparator c)	Searches the given array for the given object using a comparator.
static int binarySearch(short[ ] a, short key)	Searches the given array of shorts for the given value.
static boolean equals(boolean[ ] a, boolean[ ] a2)	Returns True if the two given arrays of booleans are equal.
static boolean equals(byte[ ] a, byte[ ] a2)	Returns True if the two given arrays of bytes are equal to one another.
static boolean equals(char[ ] a, char[ ] a2)	Returns True if the two given arrays of characters are equal to one another.
static boolean equals(double[ ] a, double[ ] a2)	Returns True if the two given arrays of doubles are equal.
static boolean equals(float[ ] a, float[ ] a2)	Returns True if the two given arrays of floats are equal.
static boolean equals(int[ ] a, int[ ] a2)	Returns True if the two given arrays of ints are equal.
static boolean equals(long[ ] a, long[ ] a2)	Returns True if the two given arrays of longs are equal.

(continued)

*Table 21.29   Methods of the **Arrays** class (continued).*

Method	Does This
static boolean equals(Object[ ] a, Object[ ] a2)	Returns True if the two given arrays of objects are equal.
static boolean equals(short[ ] a, short[ ] a2)	Returns True if the two given arrays of shorts are equal to one another.
static void fill(boolean[ ] a, boolean val)	Assigns the given boolean value to each element of the given array of booleans.
static void fill(boolean[ ] a, int from Index, int toIndex, boolean val)	Assigns the given boolean value to each element of the given range of the given array of booleans.
static void fill(byte[ ] a, byte val)	Assigns the given byte value to each element of the given array of bytes.
static void fill(byte[ ] a, int fromIndex, int toIndex, byte val)	Assigns the given byte value to each element of the given range of the given array of bytes.
static void fill(char[ ] a, char val)	Assigns the given character value to each element of the given array of characters.
static void fill(char[ ] a, int fromIndex, int toIndex, char val)	Assigns the given character value to each element of the given range of the given array of characters.
static void fill(double[ ] a, double val)	Assigns the given double value to each element of the given array of doubles.
static void fill(double[ ] a, int from Index, int toIndex, double val)	Assigns the given double value to each element of the given range of the given array of doubles.
static void fill(float[ ] a, float val)	Assigns the given float value to each element of the given array of floats.
static void fill(float[ ] a, int fromIndex, int toIndex, float val)	Assigns the given float value to each element of the given range of the given array of floats.
static void fill(int[ ] a, int val)	Assigns the given int value to each element of the given array of ints.
static void fill(int[ ] a, int fromIndex, int toIndex, int val)	Assigns the given int value to each element of the given range of the given array of ints.
static void fill(long[ ] a, int fromIndex, int toIndex, long val)	Assigns the given long value to each element of the given range of the given array of longs.
static void fill(long[ ] a, long val)	Assigns the given long value to each element of the given array of longs.
static void fill(Object[ ] a, int from Index, int toIndex, Object val)	Assigns the given object reference to each element of the given range of the given array of objects.

(continued)

Table 21.29   Methods of the Arrays class (continued).

Method	Does This
static void fill(Object[ ] a, Object val)	Assigns the given object reference to each element of the given array of objects.
static void fill(short[ ] a, int fromIndex, int toIndex, short val)	Assigns the given short value to each element of the given range of the given array of shorts.
static void fill(short[ ] a, short val)	Assigns the given short value to each element of the given array of shorts.
static void sort(byte[ ] a)	Sorts the given array of bytes into ascending numerical order.
static void sort(byte[ ] a, int from Index, int toIndex)	Sorts the given range of the given array of bytes into ascending numerical order.
static void sort(char[ ] a)	Sorts the given array of characters into ascending numerical order.
static void sort(char[ ] a, int from Index, int toIndex)	Sorts the given range of the given array of characters into ascending numerical order.
static void sort(double[ ] a)	Sorts the given array of doubles into ascending numerical order.
static void sort(double[ ] a, int from Index, int toIndex)	Sorts the given range of the given array of doubles into ascending numerical order.
static void sort(float[ ] a)	Sorts the given array of floats into ascending numerical order.
static void sort(float[ ] a, int from Index, int toIndex)	Sorts the given range of the given array of floats into ascending numerical order.
static void sort(int[ ] a)	Sorts the given array of ints into ascending numerical order.
static void sort(int[ ] a, int from Index, int toIndex)	Sorts the given range of the given array of ints into ascending numerical order.
static void sort(long[ ] a)	Sorts the given array of longs into ascending numerical order.
static void sort(long[ ] a, int from Index, int toIndex)	Sorts the given range of the given array of longs into ascending numerical order.
static void sort(Object[ ] a)	Sorts the given array of objects into ascending order, according to the natural ordering of its elements.
static void sort(Object[ ] a, Comparator c)	Sorts the given array of objects according to the order induced by the given comparator.
static void sort(Object[ ] a, int from Index, int toIndex)	Sorts the given range of the given array of objects into ascending order, according to the natural ordering of its elements.
static void sort(Object[ ] a, int from Index, int toIndex, Comparator c)	Sorts the given range of the given array of objects according to the order induced by the given comparator.
static void sort(short[ ] a)	Sorts the given array of shorts into ascending numerical order.
static void sort(short[ ] a, int from Index, int toIndex)	Sorts the given range of the given array of shorts into ascending numerical order.

Here's an example in which I create an array, print it out, sort it, and then search for a particular element:

```java
import java.util.*;

class arrays
{
    public static void main(String args[])
    {
        int array[] = new int[10];
        for(int loop_index = 9; loop_index > 0; loop_index--)
            array[loop_index] = -loop_index;

        for(int loop_index = 0; loop_index < array.length; loop_index++)
            System.out.print(array[loop_index] + " ");
        System.out.println();

        Arrays.sort(array);

        for(int loop_index = 0; loop_index < array.length; loop_index++)
            System.out.print(array[loop_index] + " ");
        System.out.println();

        System.out.print("Found -5 at position " +
            Arrays.binarySearch(array, -5));
    }
}
```

Here's the output of this code:

```
C:\>java arrays
0 -1 -2 -3 -4 -5 -6 -7 -8 -9
-9 -8 -7 -6 -5 -4 -3 -2 -1 0
Found -5 at position 4
```

Using The **Enumeration** Interface

You use the **Enumeration** interface's methods to loop over elements in classes such as **HashTable**. This interface is a useful one, and I'll put it to work later in this chapter. For now, I'll list its methods for reference. You'll find the methods for the **Enumeration** interface in Table 21.30.

*Table 21.30   Methods of the **Enumeration** class.*

Method	Does This
boolean hasMoreElements( )	Returns True if this enumeration contains more elements.
Object nextElement( )	Gets the next element of this enumeration.

Using The **Vector** Class

The **Vector** class predates the collections framework, and it implements a dynamic array. Since the appearance of the collections framework, **Vector** has been rewritten to be compatible with it. Here's the inheritance diagram for **Vector**:

```
java.lang.Object
|____java.util.AbstractCollection
     |____java.util.AbstractList
          |____java.util.Vector
```

You'll find the fields of the **Vector** class in Table 21.31, its constructors in Table 21.32, and its methods in Table 21.33.

*Table 21.31   Fields of the **Vector** class.*

Field	Does This
protected int capacityIncrement	The amount by which the capacity of the vector is increased when its size exceeds its capacity.
protected int elementCount	The number of components in this **Vector** object.
protected Object[ ] elementData	The array buffer where the components of the vector are stored.

*Table 21.32   Constructors of the **Vector** class.*

Constructor	Does This
Vector( )	Constructs an empty vector.
Vector(Collection c)	Constructs a vector containing the elements of the given collection.
Vector(int initialCapacity)	Constructs an empty vector with the given initial capacity.
Vector(int initialCapacity, int capacity Increment)	Constructs an empty vector with the given initial capacity and capacity increment.

Table 21.33 **Methods of the *Vector* class.**

Method	Does This
void add(int index, Object element)	Inserts the given element.
boolean add(Object o)	Adds the given element to the end of this vector.
boolean addAll(Collection c)	Adds all the elements in the given collection to the end of this vector in the order that they're returned by the given collection's iterator.
boolean addAll(int index, Collection c)	Inserts all the elements in the given collection into this vector at the given position.
void addElement(Object obj)	Adds the given component to the end of this vector, increasing its size by one.
int capacity( )	Gets the current capacity of this vector.
void clear( )	Removes all the elements from this vector.
Object clone( )	Gets a clone of this vector.
boolean contains(Object elem)	Returns True if the object is in this vector.
boolean containsAll(Collection c)	Returns True if this vector contains all the elements in the given collection.
void copyInto(Object[ ] anArray)	Copies the components of this vector into the given array.
Object elementAt(int index)	Gets the component at the given index.
Enumeration elements( )	Gets an enumeration of the components of this vector.
void ensureCapacity(int minCapacity)	Increases the capacity of this vector, if necessary.
boolean equals(Object o)	Compares the given object with this vector for equality.
Object firstElement( )	Gets the first component of this vector.
Object get(int index)	Gets the element at the given position in this vector.
int hashCode( )	Gets the hashcode value for this vector.
int indexOf(Object elem)	Searches for the first occurrence of the given argument.
int indexOf(Object elem, int index)	Searches for the first occurrence of the given argument, beginning the search at **index**.
void insertElementAt(Object obj, int index)	Inserts the given object as a component in this vector at the given index.
boolean isEmpty( )	Tests whether this vector has no components.
Object lastElement( )	Gets the last component of the vector.
int lastIndexOf(Object elem)	Gets the index of the last occurrence of the given object in this vector.

(continued)

Table 21.33   Methods of the Vector class (continued).

Method	Does This
int lastIndexOf(Object elem, int index)	Searches backwards for the given object and returns an index to it.
Object remove(int index)	Removes the element at the given position in this vector.
boolean remove(Object o)	Removes the first occurrence of the given element.
boolean removeAll(Collection c)	Removes from this vector all its elements that are contained in the given collection.
void removeAllElements( )	Removes all components from this vector and sets its **size** to zero.
boolean removeElement(Object obj)	Removes the first occurrence of the argument from this vector.
void removeElementAt(int index)	Deletes the component at the given index.
protected void removeRange(int fromIndex, int toIndex)	Removes from this list all the elements whose indexes are between **fromIndex** and **toIndex**.
boolean retainAll(Collection c)	Keeps only the elements in this vector that are contained in the given collection.
Object set(int index, Object element)	Replaces the element at the given position in this vector with the given element.
void setElementAt(Object obj, int index)	Sets the component at the given index of this vector to be the given object.
void setSize(int newSize)	Sets the size of this vector.
int size( )	Gets the number of components in this vector.
List subList(int fromIndex, int toIndex)	Gets a view of the portion of this list between **fromIndex** and **toIndex**.
Object[ ] toArray( )	Gets an array containing all the elements in this vector.
Object[ ] toArray(Object[ ] a)	Gets an array containing all the elements in this vector.
String toString( )	Gets a string representation of this vector.
void trimToSize( )	Trims the capacity of this vector to the current size.

Each vector has a *capacity*, which is the maximum size it can grow to. When you exceed that size, the capacity is automatically increased. You can use the **add** and **addElement** methods to add elements to a vector, the **remove** and **removeElement** methods to remove elements, and the **contains** method to do a search. Here's an example using the **Vector** class in which I create a vector, check its size and capacity, and search for an element:

```
import java.util.*;

class vector
{
```

```
    public static void main(String args[])
    {
        Vector vector = new Vector(5);

        System.out.println("Capacity: " + vector.capacity());

        vector.addElement(new Integer(0));
        vector.addElement(new Integer(1));
        vector.addElement(new Integer(2));
        vector.addElement(new Integer(3));
        vector.addElement(new Integer(4));
        vector.addElement(new Integer(5));
        vector.addElement(new Integer(6));
        vector.addElement(new Double(3.14159));
        vector.addElement(new Float(3.14159));

        System.out.println("Capacity: " + vector.capacity());

        System.out.println("Size: " + vector.size());

        System.out.println("First item: " + (Integer)
            vector.firstElement());
        System.out.println("Last item: " + (Float) vector.lastElement());

        if(vector.contains(new Integer(3)))
            System.out.println("Found a 3.");
    }
}
```

Here's the output of this code (vector.java on the CD):

```
C:\>java vector
Capacity: 5
Capacity: 10
Size: 9
First item: 0
Last item: 3.14159
Found a 3.
```

Using The **Stack** Class

The Novice Programmer is back and says, "I wish I could reverse the elements of a list—I'm converting a number to base 20, and each time I divide by 20, the new digits come off in reverse order." "No problem," you say, "just put them on a stack and pop them to reverse the order." "Great!" says the NP.

The **Stack** class is built on the **Vector** class, and it implements a stack construct. Here's the inheritance diagram for the **Stack** class:

```
java.lang.Object
|____java.util.AbstractCollection
     |____java.util.AbstractList
          |____java.util.Vector
               |____java.util.Stack
```

You'll find the constructor for the **Stack** class in Table 21.34 and its method in Table 21.35.

You use the **push** method to add an element to a stack and the **pop** method to retrieve it; note that elements come off a stack in the reverse order in which

Table 21.34   The constructor of the Stack class.

Constructor	Does This
Stack( )	Creates an empty stack.

Table 21.35   Methods of the Stack class.

Method	Does This
boolean empty( )	Returns True if this stack is empty.
Object peek( )	Gets the object at the top of this stack without removing it.
Object pop( )	Removes the object at the top of this stack and returns that object.
Object push(Object item)	Adds an item onto the top of this stack.
int search(Object o)	Gets the position of an object on this stack.

they were added to it. Here's an example in which I push and then pop elements on a stack:

```java
import java.util.*;

class stack
{
    public static void main(String args[])
    {
        Stack stack1 = new Stack();

        try {
            stack1.push(new Integer(0));
            stack1.push(new Integer(1));
            stack1.push(new Integer(2));
            stack1.push(new Integer(3));
            stack1.push(new Integer(4));
            stack1.push(new Integer(5));
            stack1.push(new Integer(6));

            System.out.println((Integer) stack1.pop());
            System.out.println((Integer) stack1.pop());
            System.out.println((Integer) stack1.pop());
            System.out.println((Integer) stack1.pop());
            System.out.println((Integer) stack1.pop());
            System.out.println((Integer) stack1.pop());
            System.out.println((Integer) stack1.pop());
        }
        catch (EmptyStackException e) {}
    }
}
```

Here's the output of this code (stack.java on the CD):

```
C:\>java stack
6
5
4
3
2
1
0
```

Using The **Dictionary** Class

The **Dictionary** class is a class used by classes such as **Hashtable**, and it stores elements much like a map does, although it was introduced before the collections framework appeared. Because it forms the foundation of the **Hashtable** class, I'll include **Dictionary** here for reference. Here's the inheritance diagram for **Dictionary**:

```
java.lang.Object
|____java.util.Dictionary
```

You'll find the constructor for **Dictionary** in Table 21.36 and its methods in Table 21.37.

Table 21.36   The constructor of the Dictionary class.

Constructor	Does This
Dictionary( )	Creates a dictionary.

Table 21.37   Methods of the Dictionary class.

Method	Does This
abstract Enumeration elements( )	Gets an enumeration of the values in this dictionary.
abstract Object get(Object key)	Gets the value for this key.
abstract boolean isEmpty( )	Returns True if this dictionary has no keys.
abstract Enumeration keys( )	Gets an enumeration of the keys in this dictionary.
abstract Object put(Object key, Object value)	Maps the given key to the given value in this dictionary.
abstract Object remove(Object key)	Removes the key and its value from this dictionary.
abstract int size( )	Gets the number of entries in this dictionary.

Using The **Hashtable** Class

The **Hashtable** class implements the **Map** interface, and it was how you used to implement maps before the collections framework appeared. Here's the inheritance diagram for **Hashtable**:

```
java.lang.Object
|____java.util.Dictionary
     |____java.util.Hashtable
```

You'll find the constructors for the **Hashtable** class in Table 21.38 and its methods in Table 21.39.

Table 21.38   Constructors of the *Hashtable* class.

Constructor	Does This
Hashtable( )	Constructs a new, empty hash table.
Hashtable(int initialCapacity)	Constructs a new, empty hash table with the given initial capacity.
Hashtable(int initialCapacity, float loadFactor)	Constructs a new, empty hash table with the given initial capacity and the given load factor.
Hashtable(Map t)	Constructs a new hash table with the same mappings as the given map.

Table 21.39   Methods of the *Hashtable* class.

Method	Does This
void clear( )	Clears this hash table so that it contains no keys.
Object clone( )	Creates a copy of this hash table.
boolean contains(Object value)	Returns True if some key maps into the given value in this hash table.
boolean containsKey(Object key)	Returns True if the given object is a key in this hash table.
boolean containsValue(Object value)	Returns True if this hash table maps one or more keys to this value.
Enumeration elements( )	Gets an enumeration of the values in this hash table.
Set entrySet( )	Gets a set view of the entries contained in this hash table.
boolean equals(Object o)	Compares the given object with this map for equality.
Object get(Object key)	Gets the value to which the given key is mapped in this hash table.
int hashCode( )	Gets the hashcode value for this map, as per the definition in the **Map** interface.
boolean isEmpty( )	Tests whether this hash table maps no keys to values.
Enumeration keys( )	Gets an enumeration of the keys in this hash table.
Set keySet( )	Gets a set view of the keys contained in this hash table.
Object put(Object key, Object value)	Maps the given key to the given value in this hash table.
void putAll(Map t)	Copies all the mappings from the given map to this hash table.
protected void rehash( )	Increases the capacity of and internally reorganizes this hash table.
Object remove(Object key)	Removes the key (and its corresponding value) from this hash table.
int size( )	Gets the number of keys in this hash table.
String toString( )	Gets a string representation of this **Hashtable** object in the form of a set of entries.
Collection values( )	Gets a collection view of the values contained in this hash table.

21. Collections

You store and retrieve key/value pairs in a hash table using the **put** and **get** methods. You can get an **Enumeration** object for the keys in a hash table using the **keys** method, and you can use that object to loop over the elements of the hash. Here's an example in which I create a hash table and then print out its key/value pairs:

```java
import java.util.*;

class hashtable
{
    public static void main(String args[])
    {
        Hashtable hashtable1 = new Hashtable();

        hashtable1.put("Item 0", "Value 0");
        hashtable1.put("Item 1", "Value 1");
        hashtable1.put("Item 2", "Value 2");
        hashtable1.put("Item 3", "Value 3");
        hashtable1.put("Item 4", "Value 4");
        hashtable1.put("Item 5", "Value 5");
        hashtable1.put("Item 6", "Value 6");

        Enumeration keys = hashtable1.keys();

        while(keys.hasMoreElements()) {
            String key = (String) keys.nextElement();
            System.out.println(key + "/" + hashtable1.get(key));
        }
    }
}
```

Here's the output of this code (hashtable.java on the CD). Note that the order in which elements are stored in a hash is determined by the hash, and you can't count on any specific order:

```
C:\>java hashtable
Item 6/Value 6
Item 5/Value 5
Item 4/Value 4
Item 3/Value 3
Item 2/Value 2
Item 1/Value 1
Item 0/Value 0
```

Using The **Properties** Class

The **Properties** class is derived from the **Hashtable** class (see the previous topic) and uses string keys and values. This class maintains the properties of various other classes, and an object of the **Properties** class is returned by those class' **getProperties** method.

Here's the inheritance diagram for the **Properties** class:

```
java.lang.Object
|____java.util.Dictionary
     |____java.util.Hashtable
          |____java.util.Properties
```

You'll find the field of the **Properties** class in Table 21.40, its constructors in Table 21.41, and its methods in Table 21.42.

Table 21.40   The field of the Properties class.

Field	Does This
protected Properties defaults	A property list that contains default values for keys.

Table 21.41   Constructors of the Properties class.

Constructor	Does This
Properties( )	Constructs a property list.
Properties(Properties defaults)	Constructs a property list with the given defaults.

Table 21.42   Methods of the Properties class.

Method	Does This
String getProperty(String key)	Searches for the property with the given key.
String getProperty(String key, String defaultValue)	Searches for the property with the given key and returns the default value if the key is not found.
void list(PrintStream out)	Prints this property list to the given output stream.
void list(PrintWriter out)	Prints this property list to the given writer stream.
void load(InputStream inStream)	Reads a property list from the input stream.
Enumeration propertyNames( )	Gets an enumeration of all the keys in this property list.
void save(OutputStream out, String header)	Deprecated. Use the **store** method instead.

(continued)

Table 21.42   Methods of the Properties class (continued).

Method	Does This
Object setProperty(String key, String value)	Calls the hash table method **put**.
void store(OutputStream out, String header)	Writes this property list in this Properties table to the output stream in a format acceptable for use with the **load** method.

You can put property values into a **Properties** object with the **setProperty** method, and you can get property values with the **getProperty** method. Here's an example in which I create a **Properties** object, add property values to it, and then retrieve a property value. Note, in particular, that you can supply a default value to **getProperty** that it will return if there's no property value matching the property you've requested:

```
import java.util.*;

class properties
{
    public static void main(String args[])
    {
        Properties properties1 = new Properties();
        Set states;
        String outString;

        properties1.setProperty("Property 0", "Value 0");
        properties1.setProperty("Property 1", "Value 1");
        properties1.setProperty("Property 2", "Value 2");
        properties1.setProperty("Property 3", "Value 3");
        properties1.setProperty("Property 4", "Value 4");
        properties1.setProperty("Property 5", "Value 5");
        properties1.setProperty("Property 6", "Value 6");

        outString = properties1.getProperty("Property 3", "Missing");
        System.out.println(outString);

        outString = properties1.getProperty("Property 7", "Missing");
        System.out.println(outString);
    }
}
```

Here's the output of this code (properties.java on the CD):

```
C:\>java properties
Value 3
Missing
```

Chapter 22

Multithreaded Programming And Animation

In Depth

In this chapter, we're going to take a look at multithreaded programming in Java and how it lets you support graphics animation. A *thread* is a stream of code execution, and using threads, you can have your programs seemingly do several things at once. For example, your code might be interacting with the user while also performing time-consuming tasks in the background. Separate threads don't actually run at the same time, of course (unless you have a multiprocessor machine); in reality, each thread gets time slices on the same processor. The apparent result, however, is that various threads are executing at the same time, and that can be very impressive. In fact, Java is one of the few programming languages that explicitly supports multithreading.

> **TIP:**   *Many components in Java, notably most Swing components, are not thread-safe—that is, they're not safe to use in a multithreaded manner.*

Using Threads In Java

When a Java program starts, it has one thread—the main thread. You can interact with the main thread in various ways, as you'll see in this chapter, such as getting or setting its name, pausing it, and more. However, you can also start other threads as well. You start the code in such threads by calling the object's **start** method, and you place the code you want the thread to use in the **run** method.

There are two ways to create new threads. One is to declare a class to be a subclass of **Thread**. This subclass should override the **run** method of class **Thread**, and you can then allocate and start an instance of that class. For example, here's how you can define a new **Thread** class that starts when you create an instance of it:

```
class CustomThread extends Thread
{
    CustomThread()
    {
        //Do standard constructor initialization
        start();
    }
```

```
        public void run()
        {
            //Do the work this thread was created for
        }
    }
```

You can then create and start a thread of this type like this:

```
CustomThread thread1 = new CustomThread();
```

The other way to create a thread is to declare a class that implements the **Runnable** interface. That class then implements the **run** method. An instance of the class can then be allocated (passed as an argument when you're creating a **Thread** object). Here's how this looks in code:

```
class CustomThread implements Runnable
{
    Thread thread;

    CustomThread()
    {
        //Do standard constructor initialization
        thread = new Thread(this, "second");
        thread.start();
    }

    public void run()
    {
        //Do the work this thread was created for
    }
}
```

This code would then create a thread of this type and start it running:

```
CustomThread thread1 = new CustomThread();
```

It's also worth noting that every thread has a name for identification purposes (in fact, more than one thread may have the same name). Every thread also has a priority, and threads with higher priorities are executed in preference to threads with lower priorities.

That's it for the overview of what's in this chapter. Let's put multithreaded programming to work. It's time to turn to the "Immediate Solutions" section.

Immediate Solutions

Getting The Main Thread

The Novice Programmer appears and says, "Threads? I've been programming Java for a while now and I can't see any threads." You smile and say, "Every Java program has at least one thread, called the *main* thread, and you can take a look at it with the **currentThread** method."

The **currentThread** method of the **Thread** class gets the current thread; if you're executing in the main thread, **currentThread** gets the main thread. Here's an example in which I'm getting the main thread of an application and printing out its name using the **getName** method (note that you can set a thread's name with **setName**—see the next topic):

```
class mainthread
{
    public static void main(String args[])
    {
        Thread thread = Thread.currentThread();

        System.out.println("Main thread is named " + thread.getName());
    }
}
```

Here's the output of this code (mainthread.java on the CD accompanying this book):

```
C:\>java mainthread
Main thread is named main
```

Naming A Thread

One way to distinguish threads is by name, and you can set the name of a thread with the **setName** method. Here's an example in which I rename the main thread in an application and display that name:

```
class setname
{
    public static void main(String args[])
    {
        Thread thread = Thread.currentThread();

        System.out.println("Main thread's original name is " +
            thread.getName());

        thread.setName("The Main Thread");

        System.out.println("Main thread's name is now " +
            thread.getName());
    }
}
```

Here's the output of this code (setname.java on the CD):

```
C:\>java setname
Main thread's original name is main
Main thread's name is now The Main Thread
```

After you've given a thread a name, you can use the **getName** method to check the name and so determine what thread you're working with in a section of code that many threads execute (such as the code in a **Thread** class's **run** method).

Pausing A Thread

Sometimes, you want to pause a thread's execution, and you can do that with the **sleep** method. You pass this method the amount of time to pause, in milliseconds (a millisecond is *one-thousandth* of a second), and the thread will wait that amount of time before continuing. Here's an example in which I print out a message, pausing for a second between words:

```
class sleep
{
    public static void main(String args[])
    {
        try {
            System.out.println("Hello");
            Thread.sleep(1000);
            System.out.println("from");
```

```
              Thread.sleep(1000);
              System.out.println("Java.");
              Thread.sleep(1000);
          } catch (InterruptedException e) {}
      }
}
```

Here's the result. When you run this code (wait.java on the CD), you'll see the words appear with a one-second pause between them:

```
C:\>java sleep
Hello
from
Java!
```

Creating A Thread With The **Runnable** Interface

"I want to create a new thread to spell-check a document while the user is doing other things," the Novice Programmer says. "How do I do that?" "Well," you say, "there are two ways to create your own threads—implementing the **Runnable** interface and extending the **Thread** class." "Hmm," says the NP, "let's start with **Runnable**."

Overriding the **Runnable** interface is one of two ways to create your own threads in Java. This interface has only one method: **run**. You place the code you want to have the new thread execute in that method. When you create a new **Runnable** object, you can pass that object to the constructor of the **Thread** class to create the new thread.

Here's an example in which I create a new class that implements the **Runnable** interface. It passes itself to a **Thread** class constructor and starts itself when an object of this class is created. When it runs, it prints out its name once a second for 10 seconds and then quits. Here's the code for this new **Runnable** class, which I call **SecondThread** (note that the actual work is done in the **run** method and that the code is executed with the **Thread** class's **start** method):

```
class SecondThread implements Runnable
{
    Thread thread;

    SecondThread()
    {
```

```
        thread = new Thread(this, "second");
        System.out.println("Starting second thread");
        thread.start();
    }

    public void run()
    {
        try {
            for(int loop_index = 0; loop_index < 10; loop_index++) {
                System.out.println((Thread.currentThread()).getName()
                    + " thread here...");
                Thread.sleep(1000);
            }
        } catch (InterruptedException e) {}

        System.out.println("Second thread ending.");
    }
}
```

Here's the application that will create a new thread of the **SecondThread** class and run it; note that I'm also having the main thread print out its name so that you can see the two threads alternate:

```
class runnable
{
    public static void main(String args[])
    {
        SecondThread secondthread = new SecondThread();

        try {
            for(int loop_index = 0; loop_index < 10; loop_index++) {
                System.out.println((Thread.currentThread()).getName()
                    + " thread here...");
                Thread.sleep(1000);
            }
        } catch (InterruptedException e) {}
    }
}
```

Here's the result of these code (runnable.java on the CD). Note that the two threads alternate printing out their names (note also that you can't guarantee that they'll alternate—that's up to the operating system):

```
C:\>java runnable
Starting second thread
```

```
main thread here...
second thread here...
main thread here...
second thread here...
main thread here...
second thread here...
main thread here...
second thread here...
main thread here...
second thread here...
main thread here...
second thread here...
main thread here...
second thread here...
main thread here...
second thread here...
main thread here...
second thread here...
second thread here...
main thread here...
Second thread ending.
```

Creating A Thread With The **Thread** Class

"OK," says the Novice Programmer, "I know I can create a new thread using the **Runnable** interface...." "Or," you say, "using the **Thread** class." "Tell me more!" says the NP.

The **Thread** class supports new threads. It also implements the **Runnable** interface, so you don't have to. Here's the inheritance diagram for **Thread**:

```
java.lang.Object
|  +--java.lang.Thread
```

You'll find the fields for the **Thread** class in Table 22.1, its constructors in Table 22.2, and its methods in Table 22.3.

Table 22.1   Fields of the Thread class.

Field	Does This
static int MAX_PRIORITY	The maximum priority a thread can have.
static int MIN_PRIORITY	The minimum priority a thread can have.
static int NORM_PRIORITY	The default priority assigned to a thread.

Table 22.2   Constructors of the *Thread* class.

Constructor	Does This
Thread( )	Constructs a new **Thread** object.
Thread(Runnable target)	Constructs a new **Thread** object using a **Runnable** object.
Thread(Runnable target, String name)	Constructs a new **Thread** object with a **Runnable** object and a name.
Thread(String name)	Constructs a new **Thread** object with a name.
Thread(ThreadGroup group, Runnable target)	Constructs a new **Thread** object as part of a group.
Thread(ThreadGroup group, Runnable target, String name)	Constructs a new **Thread** object with a **Runnable** object. This **Thread** object has the specified name as its name and belongs to the thread group referred to by **group**.
Thread(ThreadGroup group, String name)	Constructs a new **Thread** object that's part of a group and has a name.

Table 22.3   Methods of the Thread class.

Method	Does This
static int activeCount( )	Gets the current number of active threads in this thread's thread group.
void checkAccess( )	Determines whether the currently running thread has permission to modify this thread.
int countStackFrames( )	Deprecated. The definition of this call depends on **suspend**, which is deprecated.
static Thread currentThread( )	Gets a reference to the currently executing **Thread** object.
void destroy( )	Destroys this thread.
static void dumpStack( )	Prints a stack trace of the current thread.
static int enumerate(Thread[ ] tarray)	Copies to the indicated array every active thread in this thread's thread group.
ClassLoader getContextClassLoader( )	Gets the context **ClassLoader** for this thread.
String getName( )	Gets this thread's name.
int getPriority( )	Gets this thread's priority.
ThreadGroup getThreadGroup( )	Gets the thread group to which this thread belongs.
void interrupt( )	Interrupts this thread.
static boolean interrupted( )	Returns True if the current thread has been interrupted.
boolean isAlive( )	Returns True if this thread is alive.

(continued)

Table 22.3   Methods of the *Thread* class (continued).

Method	Does This
boolean isDaemon( )	Returns True if this thread is a daemon thread.
boolean isInterrupted( )	Returns True if this thread has been interrupted.
void join( )	Waits for this thread to die.
void join(long millis)	Waits at most **millis** milliseconds for this thread to die.
void join(long millis, int nanos)	Waits at most **millis** milliseconds plus **nanos** nanoseconds for this thread to die.
void resume( )	Deprecated. This method exists solely for use with **suspend**, which is deprecated.
void run( )	If this thread was constructed using a separate **Runnable** interface **run** object, that **Runnable** object's **run** method is called.
void setContextClassLoader (ClassLoader cl)	Sets the context **ClassLoader** for this thread.
void setDaemon(boolean on)	Marks this thread as either a daemon thread or a user thread.
void setName(String name)	Changes the name of this thread to be equal to the argument name.
void setPriority(int newPriority)	Changes the priority of this thread.
static void sleep(long millis)	Causes the currently executing thread to sleep for the indicated number of milliseconds.
static void sleep(long millis, int nanos)	Causes the currently executing thread to sleep for the indicated number of milliseconds plus the indicated number of nanoseconds.
void start( )	Causes this thread to begin execution, which means that the Java Virtual Machine will call the **run** method of this thread.
void stop( )	Deprecated. This method is considered inherently unsafe.
void stop(Throwable obj)	Deprecated. This method is considered inherently unsafe.
void suspend( )	Deprecated. This method has been deprecated because it's considered inherently deadlock prone.
String toString( )	Gets a string representation of this thread.
static void yield( )	Causes the currently executing **Thread** object to temporarily pause, which can allow other threads to execute.

Here's an example in which I create a second thread and have it print out its name 10 times, once a second. Note that in this case, I'm calling the thread's constructor and passing it a name for this second thread, and then I'm calling the thread's **start** method to start execution of the code in the **run** method. The action takes place in the **run** method; that's where I have the thread print out its name every second. Here's the code:

```java
class SecondThread extends Thread
{
    SecondThread()
    {
        super("second");
        start();
    }

    public void run()
    {
        try {
            for(int loop_index = 0; loop_index < 10; loop_index++) {
                System.out.println((Thread.currentThread()).getName()
                    + " thread here...");
                Thread.sleep(1000);
            }
        } catch (InterruptedException e) {}

        System.out.println("Second thread ending.");
    }
}
```

Here's an application in which I use the **SecondThread** class and also print out the name of the main thread every second:

```java
class thread
{
    public static void main(String args[])
    {
        SecondThread secondthread = new SecondThread();

        try {
            for(int loop_index = 0; loop_index < 10; loop_index++) {
                System.out.println((Thread.currentThread()).getName()
                    + " thread here...");
                Thread.sleep(1000);
            }
        } catch (InterruptedException e) {}
    }
}
```

Here's the results of this code (thread.java on the CD). Note that both threads are running and displaying their names, once a second:

```
C:\>java runnable
Starting second thread
main thread here...
second thread here...
main thread here...
second thread here...
main thread here...
second thread here...
main thread here...
second thread here...
main thread here...
second thread here...
main thread here...
second thread here...
main thread here...
second thread here...
main thread here...
second thread here...
main thread here...
second thread here...
second thread here...
main thread here...
Second thread ending.
```

Creating Multiple Threads

"I know I can start a second thread," the Novice Programmer says, "but what about starting *four* new threads?" You smile and say, "No problem."

You can create and run multiple threads in a program—just give each thread a new object. Here's an example in which I create four new threads and have each one print out its name once a second:

```
class CustomThread extends Thread
{
    CustomThread(String name)
    {
        super(name);
        start();
    }
}
```

```
    public void run()
    {
        try {
            for(int loop_index = 0; loop_index < 4; loop_index++) {
                System.out.println((Thread.currentThread()).getName()
                    + " thread here...");
                Thread.sleep(1000);
            }
        } catch (InterruptedException e) {}

        System.out.println((Thread.currentThread()).getName() +
            " ending.");
    }
}


class multithread
{
    public static void main(String args[])
    {
        CustomThread thread1 = new CustomThread("first");
        CustomThread thread2 = new CustomThread("second");
        CustomThread thread3 = new CustomThread("third");
        CustomThread thread4 = new CustomThread("fourth");

        try {
            for(int loop_index = 0; loop_index < 10; loop_index++) {
                System.out.println((Thread.currentThread()).getName()
                    + " thread here...");
                Thread.sleep(1000);
            }
        } catch (InterruptedException e) {}
    }
}
```

Here's the result of this code (multithread.java on the CD):

```
C:\>java multithread
main thread here...
first thread here...
second thread here...
third thread here...
fourth thread here...
main thread here...
first thread here...
```

```
second thread here...
third thread here...
fourth thread here...
main thread here...
first thread here...
second thread here...
third thread here...
fourth thread here...
```

.

.

.

Waiting For (Joining) Threads

"I need more control over threads," the Novice Programmer says. "For example, I need to be able to wait until a thread is done executing before going on with the rest of the program. Any way to check that?" "Certainly," you say, "you can use the **join** method to wait until a thread is done." "Really?" the NP asks excitedly.

The **Thread** class's **join** method waits until a thread is finished executing (also called *waiting for a thread to die*) before returning. Here's an example in which I create four new threads and wait for each one to finish executing before ending the main application:

```java
class CustomThread extends Thread
{
    CustomThread(String name)
    {
        super(name);
        start();
    }

    public void run()
    {
        try {
            for(int loop_index = 0; loop_index < 4; loop_index++) {
                System.out.println((Thread.currentThread()).getName()
                    + " thread here...");
                Thread.sleep(1000);
            }
        } catch (InterruptedException e) {}
```

```
        System.out.println((Thread.currentThread()).getName() +
            " ending.");
    }
}

class join
{
    public static void main(String args[])
    {
        CustomThread thread1 = new CustomThread("first");
        CustomThread thread2 = new CustomThread("second");
        CustomThread thread3 = new CustomThread("third");
        CustomThread thread4 = new CustomThread("fourth");

        try {
            thread1.join();
            thread2.join();
            thread3.join();
            thread3.join();
        } catch (InterruptedException e) {}
    }
}
```

Here's the output of this code (join.java on the CD):

```
C:\>java join
first thread here...
second thread here...
third thread here...
fourth thread here...
first thread here...
third thread here...
second thread here...
fourth thread here...
first thread here...
third thread here...
second thread here...
fourth thread here...
first thread here...
second thread here...
fourth thread here...
third thread here...
first ending.
fourth ending.
second ending.
third ending.
```

Checking Whether A Thread Is Alive

"Uh-oh," says the Novice Programmer, "I've lost a thread. How do I know if it's still doing anything?" "No problem at all," you say. "To check on a thread, you can use the **isAlive** method to see whether the thread is still active." "How does it work?" the NP asks.

Here's an example in which I create and run four new threads. As the threads are executing, I use the **isAlive** method on the first new thread, and when all threads are done (which I verify with the **join** method), I check that thread again with **isAlive**. Here's the code:

```
class CustomThread extends Thread
{
    CustomThread(String name)
    {
        super(name);
        start();
    }

    public void run()
    {
        try {
            for(int loop_index = 0; loop_index < 4; loop_index++) {
                System.out.println((Thread.currentThread()).getName()
                    + " thread here...");
                Thread.sleep(1000);
            }
        } catch (InterruptedException e) {}

        System.out.println((Thread.currentThread()).getName() +
            " ending.");
    }
}

class isalive
{
    public static void main(String args[])
    {
        CustomThread thread1 = new CustomThread("first");
        CustomThread thread2 = new CustomThread("second");
        CustomThread thread3 = new CustomThread("third");
        CustomThread thread4 = new CustomThread("fourth");
```

```
        System.out.println(thread1.isAlive());

    try {
        thread1.join();
        thread2.join();
        thread3.join();
        thread3.join();
    } catch (InterruptedException e) {}

        System.out.println(thread1.isAlive());
    }
}
```

Here's the output of this code (isalive.java on the CD). Note the reported value of **isAlive**, which is true when **thread1** is running and false after that thread has quit:

```
C:\>java isalive
true
first thread here...
second thread here...
fourth thread here...
third thread here...
first thread here...
second thread here...
fourth thread here...
third thread here...
first thread here...
second thread here...
fourth thread here...
third thread here...
first thread here...
second thread here...
fourth thread here...
third thread here...
first ending.
second ending.
third ending.
fourth ending.
false
```

Setting Thread Priority And Stopping Threads

"Hmm," says the Novice Programmer, "I'm getting the hang of threads, but there's a problem. I'm working on my new program, *SuperDuperMultiThreadedDataCrunch*, and some tasks are more important than others. For example, I want to download images the user has asked for before doing a background spelling check." "Well," you say, "you can give threads different *priorities*." The NP says, "Tell me more!"

Each thread in Java has a priority, which is between **Thread.MAX_PRIORITY** and **Thread.MIN_PRIORITY**. Here are the priorities that are currently defined:

- *MAX_PRIORITY*—The maximum priority that a thread can have.

- *MIN_PRIORITY*—The minimum priority that a thread can have.

- *NORM_PRIORITY*—The default priority assigned to a thread.

The value of **Thread.MAX_PRIORITY** is 10, **Thread.MIN_PRIORITY** is 1, and **NORM_PRIORITY** is 5.

Setting priorities is a very tricky business because it's operating system dependent, and the actual results depend very much on what else is running at the same time. Nonetheless, you can set the relative priorities of threads. Here's an example in which I give four threads different priorities and just have them count for five seconds. Then I end them and display their results to get an indication of their relative execution speeds. Here's the code (note that to stop the threads, I'm using a flag that's checked in the **run** method and is defined as **volatile**, which means its value can be changed by another thread):

```
class Counter implements Runnable
{
    Thread thread;
    int counter = 0;
    volatile boolean goflag;

    public Counter(int p)
    {
        thread = new Thread(this);
        thread.setPriority(p);
    }

    public void start()
    {
        goflag = true;
        thread.start();
    }
```

```
    public void run()
    {
        while (goflag) counter++;
    }

    public void end() {
        goflag = false;
    }
}

class priority
{
    public static void main(String args[])
    {
        Counter thread1 = new Counter(Thread.NORM_PRIORITY + 2);
        Counter thread2 = new Counter(Thread.NORM_PRIORITY + 1);
        Counter thread3 = new Counter(Thread.NORM_PRIORITY - 1);
        Counter thread4 = new Counter(Thread.NORM_PRIORITY - 2);

        thread1.start();
        thread2.start();
        thread3.start();
        thread4.start();

        try {
            Thread.sleep(5000);
        } catch (InterruptedException e) {}

        thread1.end();
        thread2.end();
        thread3.end();
        thread4.end();

        System.out.println("Thread 1 counted: " + thread1.counter);
        System.out.println("Thread 2 counted: " + thread2.counter);
        System.out.println("Thread 3 counted: " + thread3.counter);
        System.out.println("Thread 4 counted: " + thread4.counter);
    }
}
```

To stop the threads, I call the custom **end** method, which sets a flag named **goflag** to False, which in turn stops the code in the **run** method. In the early days of Java, you could stop a thread with a built-in **stop** method, but that method is now deprecated because it's unsafe—it can leave operating system access monitors in an unstable state. Instead, to stop a thread, you now use the preceding method—that is, checking some flag that you can set from outside the thread.

Here's the output of this code (priority.java on the CD). Note the different number of counts from the threads with different priorities (your results may vary, of course, depending on your operating system and machine speed):

```
C:\>java priority
Thread 1 counted: 145565315
Thread 2 counted: 123477095
Thread 3 counted: 6936384
Thread 4 counted: 6057269
```

Why Use Synchronization?

"Well," says the Novice Programmer, "I guess I can't use threads anymore. I have one object that stores the data in my program, and I can't have many different threads working with that same object at the same time—what if one thread changes part of the data object and then another thread changes the same part of the data object before the first thread is finished? Chaos!" "Well," you smile, "you can prevent new threads from working with objects like that until the current thread is finished by synchronizing your threads." "Wow!" says the NP.

Excluding other threads from an operation until that operation has completed is called *synchronization*. Here's an example that shows why synchronization is useful. In this case, I have four new threads all working with one shared data object. This object prints out a start message and an end message, and it completes a half-second task between the messages. Ideally, the data object should start, perform its task, and end before the next thread starts a new task, but that's not the way it works here—each thread grabs the data object for itself. Here's the code:

```
class synchronize1
{
    public static void main(String args[])
    {
        Shared shared = new Shared();

        CustomThread thread1 = new CustomThread(shared, "one");
        CustomThread thread2 = new CustomThread(shared, "two");
        CustomThread thread3 = new CustomThread(shared, "three");
        CustomThread thread4 = new CustomThread(shared, "four");
```

```
        try {
            thread1.join();
            thread2.join();
            thread3.join();
            thread4.join();
        } catch(InterruptedException e) {}
    }
}

class CustomThread extends Thread
{
    Shared shared;

    public CustomThread(Shared shared, String string)
    {
        super(string);
        this.shared = shared;
        start();
    }

    public void run() {
        shared.doWork(Thread.currentThread().getName());
    }
}

class Shared
{
    void doWork(String string)
    {
        System.out.println("Starting " + string);

        try {
            Thread.sleep((long) (Math.random() * 500));
        } catch (InterruptedException e) {}

        System.out.println("Ending " + string);
    }
}
```

Here's the output of this code (synchronize1.java on the CD). Note that each task overlaps the others:

```
C:\>java synchronize1
Starting one
Starting two
```

```
Starting three
Starting four
Ending four        no guaranteed order
Ending one
Ending two
Ending three
```

This is a problem if you're working with actual data—what if you read some data from the data object, worked on it, and were about to rewrite it, but another thread has already done the same thing? When you rewrite the data, the changes from the other thread will be lost. As you can see, it's important to be able to block access to other threads to critical resources at times. Take a look at the next two topics to see how this works.

Synchronizing Code Blocks

"OK," says the Novice Programmer, "I know there can be a problem when multiple threads access the same object or resource, but how do I block the threads' access to new threads until the current one is done with that object or resource?" "There are two ways," you say. "OK," the NP says, "what's the first way?"

There are two ways to synchronize thread code execution—synchronizing blocks of code and synchronizing methods. We'll take a look at synchronizing blocks of code in this topic and synchronizing methods in the next. To synchronize a block of code, you use the **synchronize** keyword, indicating the object you want to restrict access to. Extending the example from the previous topic, the process looks like this:

```
class synchronize2
{
    public static void main(String args[])
    {
        Shared shared = new Shared();

        CustomThread thread1 = new CustomThread(shared, "one");
        CustomThread thread2 = new CustomThread(shared, "two");
        CustomThread thread3 = new CustomThread(shared, "three");
        CustomThread thread4 = new CustomThread(shared, "four");

        try {
            thread1.join();
            thread2.join();
```

```
                  thread3.join();
                  thread4.join();
              } catch(InterruptedException e) {}
        }
}

class CustomThread extends Thread
{
      Shared shared;

      public CustomThread(Shared shared, String string)
      {
          super(string);
          this.shared = shared;
          start();
      }

      public void run() {
          synchronized(shared) {
              shared.doWork(Thread.currentThread().getName());
          }
      }
}

class Shared
{
      void doWork(String string)
      {
          System.out.println("Starting " + string);

          try {
              Thread.sleep((long) (Math.random() * 500));
          } catch (InterruptedException e) {}

          System.out.println("Ending " + string);
      }
}
```

object to make exclusive occen

Here's the output of this code (synchronize2.java on the CD). Note that each task starts and ends before any other thread starts a new task:

```
C:\>java synchronize2
Starting one
Ending one
```

```
Starting two
Ending two
Starting three
Ending three
Starting four
Ending four
```

Synchronizing Methods

Besides synchronizing code blocks (see the previous topic), you can also block access to other threads by synchronizing methods. In this case, you use the **synchronize** keyword when defining a method. Here's how I modify the **doWork** method in the **shared** object from the example in the topic before the previous one to synchronize the threads in that example:

```
class synchronize3
{
    public static void main(String args[])
    {
        Shared shared = new Shared();

        CustomThread thread1 = new CustomThread(shared, "one");
        CustomThread thread2 = new CustomThread(shared, "two");
        CustomThread thread3 = new CustomThread(shared, "three");
        CustomThread thread4 = new CustomThread(shared, "four");

        try {
            thread1.join();
            thread2.join();
            thread3.join();
            thread4.join();
        } catch(InterruptedException e) {}
    }
}

class CustomThread extends Thread
{
    Shared shared;

    public CustomThread(Shared shared, String string)
    {
        super(string);
```

```
            this.shared = shared;
            start();
    }

    public void run() {
        shared.doWork(Thread.currentThread().getName());
    }
}

class Shared
{
    synchronized void doWork(String string)
    {
        System.out.println("Starting " + string);

        try {
            Thread.sleep((long) (Math.random() * 500));
        } catch (InterruptedException e) {}

        System.out.println("Ending " + string);
    }
}
```

Now only one thread at a time can enter the **doWork** method. Here's the output of this code (synchronize3.java on the CD):

```
C:\>java synchronize3
Starting one
Ending one
Starting two
Ending two
Starting three
Ending three
Starting four
Ending four
```

Communicating Between Threads

"Darn," says the Novice Programmer, "I've got a threading problem. Part of my program is writing data and part of it is reading data—but sometimes the reading part gets ahead of the writing part!" "That's a classic producer/consumer problem," you say, "and you can fix it with the **wait** and **notify** methods." The NP smiles and says, "You can?"

Often, threads will need to coordinate between themselves, especially when the output of one thread is used by another thread. One way of coordinating between threads is to use the **wait**, **notify**, and **notifyAll** methods:

- *wait*—Makes a thread sleep until **notify** or **notifyAll** is called on the same object.

- *notify*—Starts the first thread that called **wait** on the same object.

- *notifyAll*—Starts all the threads that called **wait** on the same object.

The usual process is for the reader thread to call **wait** and the writer thread to call **notify** when the data the reader wants to read is ready. Here's an example. In this case, a writer thread will call an object's **doWork** method, which is a time-consuming method, to write some data, and a reader thread will call the same object's **getResult** method to read the results. Clearly, we want the reader thread to have to wait until **doWork** is done. Therefore, all I have to do is call **wait** in **getResult** to make the reader thread wait and call **notify** in **doWork** when the writer thread is done and the data is ready to be read. Here's what the code looks like:

```
class Shared
{
    int data = 0;

    synchronized void doWork()
    {
        try {
            Thread.sleep(1000);
        } catch(InterruptedException e) {}

        data = 1;          → write (or talk)
        notify();
    }

    synchronized int getResult() {
        try {
            wait();
        } catch(InterruptedException e) {}

        return data;          → activate read (or hear)
    }
}

class CustomThread1 extends Thread
{
```

```
    Shared shared;

    public CustomThread1 (Shared shared, String string)
    {
        super(string);
        this.shared = shared;
        start();
    }

    public void run() {
        System.out.println("The result is " + shared.getResult());
    }
}

class CustomThread2 extends Thread
{
    Shared shared;

    public CustomThread2 (Shared shared, String string)
    {
        super(string);
        this.shared = shared;
        start();
    }

    public void run() {
        shared.doWork();
    }
}


class wait
{
    public static void main(String args[])
    {
        Shared shared = new Shared();
        CustomThread1 thread1 = new CustomThread1(shared, "one");
        CustomThread2 thread2 = new CustomThread2(shared, "two");
    }
}
```

Here's the output of this code (wait.java on the CD). Note that the reader thread did indeed wait until the writer thread was through:

```
C:\>java wait
The result is 1
```

Suspending And Resuming Threads

In the early days of Java, threads supported both a **suspend** and a **resume** method, which you could use to temporarily halt and start a thread again. Unfortunately, like the **stop** method, both **suspend** and **resume** have been deprecated. In this case, these methods are deprecated because they're deadlock prone and can block access to other threads. However, you can create your own **suspend** and **resume** methods, and I'll show how to do that here.

Note that when subclassing the **Thread** class, you can't call your new suspend and resume methods **suspend** and **resume**, because Java will complain that you're trying to override deprecated methods. Therefore, in this example, I'll call these methods **newSuspend** and **newResume** (this isn't a problem when working with an object that implements the **Runnable** class instead). As is the case when you implement a new **stop** method (see the topic "Setting Thread Priority And Stopping Threads" earlier in this chapter), these methods work by setting a flag that's checked in the **run** method. When you set that flag to True in **newSuspend**, you use the **wait** method in the **run** method to suspend the thread, and you wake the thread up again with the **notify** method in the **newResume** method. Here's how this looks in code:

```
class CustomThread extends Thread
{
    volatile boolean goFlag = true;

    CustomThread(String name)
    {
        super(name);
        start();
    }

    public void run()
    {
        try {
            for(int loop_index = 0; loop_index <= 5; loop_index++) {
                System.out.println(Thread.currentThread().getName() + "
                    here...");
                Thread.sleep(500);
                synchronized(this) {
                    while(!goFlag) {
                        wait();
                    }
                }
            }
```

```
            }
        } catch (InterruptedException e) {}
    }

    public void newSuspend()
    {
        goFlag = false;
    }

    synchronized public void newResume()
    {
        goFlag = true;
        notify();
    }
}

class suspend
{
    public static void main(String args[])
    {
        CustomThread thread1 = new CustomThread("one");
        CustomThread thread2 = new CustomThread("two");

        try {
            Thread.sleep(1000);
            System.out.println("Suspending thread one...");
            thread1.newSuspend();
            Thread.sleep(1000);
            System.out.println("Resuming thread one...");
            thread1.newResume();
        } catch (InterruptedException e) {}

        try {
            thread1.join();
            thread2.join();
        } catch (InterruptedException e) {}
    }
}
```

Here's the output of this code (suspend.java on the CD). Note that threads one and two run until the code suspends thread one; then when the code starts thread one again, they alternate again:

```
C:\>java suspend
one here...
two here...
```

```
one here...
two here...
Suspending thread one
two here...
two here...
Resuming thread one
one here...
two here...
one here...
two here...
one here...
one here...
```

Creating Graphics Animation With Threads

"Say," says the Novice Programmer, "I just thought of something—using threads is ideal when you want to support graphics animation, isn't it?" "Sure is," you say. "Great," says the NP. "You write the code, I'll watch."

Here's an example showing how graphics animation using threads can work. In this applet, I load four images into an image array and then I cycle through them in the **paint** method, making Java call that method repeatedly by calling **repaint** in a new thread.

There's one interesting point here—although the **Thread** class's **stop** method has been deprecated, Web browsers and the Sun appletviewer still call this method when the page containing the applet is no longer the current page. To stop the applet's animation thread so that it doesn't keep taking up system resources until the browser decides to unload it, you can place code in the **stop** method yourself—but that means you can't base your code on the **Thread** class, because **stop** has been deprecated there. Therefore, I'll write an example using the **Runnable** interface, which doesn't have a deprecated **stop** method. Here's the code:

```
import java.awt.*;
import java.applet.Applet;

/*
<APPLET
    CODE = whirl1.class
    WIDTH = 300
    HEIGHT = 300>
</APPLET>
*/
```

```
public class whirl1 extends Applet implements Runnable
{
    Image whirlImages[] = new Image[4];
    Image nowImage;
    int whirlIndex = 0;
    Thread whirlThread;
    boolean animateFlag = true;

    public void init()
    {
        whirlImages[0] = getImage(getCodeBase(), "whirl1.gif");
        whirlImages[1] = getImage(getCodeBase(), "whirl2.gif");
        whirlImages[2] = getImage(getCodeBase(), "whirl3.gif");
        whirlImages[3] = getImage(getCodeBase(), "whirl4.gif");
    }

    public void start()
    {
        whirlThread = new Thread(this);
        whirlThread.start();
    }

    public void stop()
    {
        animateFlag = false;
    }

    public void run()
    {
        while(animateFlag){
            nowImage = whirlImages[whirlIndex++];
            if(whirlIndex > 3)whirlIndex = 0;
            repaint();
            try {Thread.sleep(200);}
            catch(InterruptedException e) { }
        }
    }

    public void paint (Graphics g)
    {
        if(nowImage != null) g.drawImage(nowImage, 10, 10, this);
    }
}
```

how to display gif .jpeg images

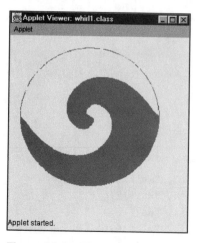

Figure 22.1   Displaying graphics animation.

You can see the result of this code in Figure 22.1. This applet makes the image you see in that figure appear to whirl around, and the code is in whirl1.java on the CD.

However, there's one problem here—I've implemented this example as an AWT applet, and each time the image is redrawn, the background behind the image is also redrawn, so the animation flickers a lot. To fix this problem, see the next topic.

Eliminating Flicker In Graphics Animation

"Hmm," says the Novice Programmer, "I can create graphics animation using threads now, but it sure flickers a lot." "No problem," you say. "Just override the **update** method." The NP asks, "How's that?"

In AWT programming, when you redraw an image, its background is redrawn first, which can make for a lot of flickering in graphics animation. The way to fix this is to override the **update** method, which is what does the redrawing. When you override **update**, the image's background is not redrawn. In fact, you can do more—you can make the **paint** method redraw only the area covered by the image you want to redraw by using the **Graphics** class's **clipRect** method, like this:

```
import java.awt.*;
import java.applet.Applet;
```

```
/*
<APPLET
    CODE = whirl2.class
    WIDTH = 300
    HEIGHT = 300 >
</APPLET>
*/

public class whirl2 extends Applet implements Runnable
{
    Image whirlImages[] = new Image[4];
    Image nowImage;
    int whirlIndex = 0;
    Thread whirlThread;
    boolean animateFlag = true;

    public void init()
    {
        whirlImages[0] = getImage(getCodeBase(), "whirl1.gif");
        whirlImages[1] = getImage(getCodeBase(), "whirl2.gif");
        whirlImages[2] = getImage(getCodeBase(), "whirl3.gif");
        whirlImages[3] = getImage(getCodeBase(), "whirl4.gif");
    }

    public void start()
    {
        whirlThread = new Thread(this);
        whirlThread.start();
    }

    public void stop()
    {
        animateFlag = false;
    }

    public void run()
    {
        while(animateFlag){
            nowImage = whirlImages[whirlIndex++];
            if(whirlIndex > 3)whirlIndex = 0;
            repaint();
            try {Thread.sleep(200);}
            catch(InterruptedException e) { }
        }
    }
```

```
public void paint (Graphics g)
{
    if(nowImage != null) g.drawImage(nowImage, 10, 10, this);
}

public void update(Graphics g)
{
    g.clipRect(10, 10, 280, 280);
    paint(g);
}
}
```

Now the image in Figure 22.1 will rotate practically flicker free. This example is in whirl2.java on the CD.

Suspending And Resuming Graphics Animation

"What," the Novice Programmer says, "if I want to suspend and resume graphics animation? Can I do that?" "Sure," you say, "no problem. Just use the standard suspend and resume techniques." "Great," says the NP. "Show me how."

Here's an example that adds buttons to suspend and resume the animation developed over the previous two topics. This puts to work the thread suspend and resume techniques discussed in the topic "Suspending And Resuming Threads" earlier in this chapter (that is, using a boolean flag and the **wait** and **notify** methods):

```
import java.awt.*;
import java.awt.event.*;
import java.applet.Applet;

/*
<APPLET
    CODE = whirl3.class
    WIDTH = 300
    HEIGHT = 300 >
</APPLET>
*/

public class whirl3 extends Applet implements ActionListener, Runnable
{
    Image whirlImages[] = new Image[4];
    Image nowImage;
```

```
    int whirlIndex = 0;
    Thread whirlThread;
    Button suspendButton, resumeButton;
    boolean animateFlag = true;
    boolean goFlag = true;

    public void init()
    {
        whirlImages[0] = getImage(getCodeBase(), "whirl1.gif");
        whirlImages[1] = getImage(getCodeBase(), "whirl2.gif");
        whirlImages[2] = getImage(getCodeBase(), "whirl3.gif");
        whirlImages[3] = getImage(getCodeBase(), "whirl4.gif");
        suspendButton = new Button("Suspend");
        add(suspendButton);
        suspendButton.addActionListener(this);
        resumeButton = new Button("Resume");
        add(resumeButton);
        resumeButton.addActionListener(this);
    }

    public synchronized void actionPerformed(ActionEvent e)
    {
        if(e.getSource() == suspendButton){
            goFlag = false;
        }
        if(e.getSource() == resumeButton){
            goFlag = true;
            notify();
        }
    }

    public void start()
    {
        whirlThread = new Thread(this);
        whirlThread.start();
    }

    public void stop()
    {
        animateFlag = false;
    }

    public void run()
    {
        while(animateFlag){
```

```
                nowImage = whirlImages[whirlIndex++];
                if(whirlIndex > 3)whirlIndex = 0;
                repaint();
                try {
                    Thread.sleep(200);
                    synchronized(this){
                    while(!goFlag)
                        wait();
                    }
                }
                catch(InterruptedException e) { }
            }
        }

        public void paint (Graphics g)
        {
            if(nowImage != null) g.drawImage(nowImage, 10, 10, this);
        }

        public void update(Graphics g)
        {
            g.clipRect(10, 10, 280, 280);
            paint(g);
        }
    }
```

The result of this code—whirl3.java on the CD—appears in Figure 22.2.

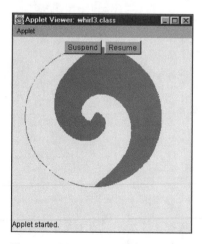

Figure 22.2   Displaying graphics animation with suspend and resume buttons.

Double Buffering

Double buffering is the process of creating images offscreen and flashing them onscreen as required, which means you don't have to create the image while the user watches. You can create a graphics buffer by creating an **Image** object and then using that object's **getGraphics** method to get a **Graphics** object for the image that you can use to draw in. Here's an example showing how double buffering works. This example draws a succession of boxes offscreen and then displays them, thus creating an animation:

```java
import java.awt.*;
import java.applet.Applet;

/*
  <APPLET
      CODE=dbuffer.class
      WIDTH=200
      HEIGHT=200>
  </APPLET>
*/

public class dbuffer extends Applet implements Runnable
{
    Image image1;
    Thread thread1;
    Graphics graphics;
    int loop_index = 0;
    boolean goFlag = true;

    public void init()
    {
        image1 = createImage(100, 100);
        graphics = image1.getGraphics();
    }

    public void start()
    {
        thread1 = new Thread(this);
        thread1.start();
    }

    public void stop()
    {
        goFlag = false;
    }
```

```
public void run()
{
    while(goFlag){
        repaint();
        try {Thread.sleep(100);}
        catch(InterruptedException e) {}
    }
}

public void paint (Graphics g)
{
    loop_index += 5;
    if(loop_index >= 100) loop_index = 5;

    graphics.setColor(new Color(255, 255, 255));
    graphics.fillRect(0, 0, 100, 100);
    graphics.setColor(new Color(0, 0, 0));
    graphics.drawRect(0, 0, loop_index, loop_index);

    g.drawImage(image1, 10, 10, this);
}
}
```

Chapter 23

Creating Packages, Interfaces, JAR Files, And Java Beans

In Depth

In this chapter, we're going to take a look at several important Java topics—creating packages, interfaces, JAR files, and Java beans. All these topics are popular, and they're good ones to have under your belt.

Creating Packages And Interfaces

We've been using packages and interfaces throughout the book, and in this chapter, we'll look at how to create them. Being able to create your own packages is a useful skill—one that allows you to divide class libraries into smaller units, much as Sun has done with the Java packages. You'll see how to create packages in code and how to arrange class files on disk to match package structure. We'll also take a look at how to create interfaces, which is Java's answer to multiple inheritance.

JAR Files

To make it easier to download class files from the Web, Java supports Java Archive (JAR) files. The archives pack files using the ZIP format, and you'll see how to create JAR files and use them with the JAR tool that comes with Java. In addition, JAR files are the foundation of other parts of Java, such as Java beans.

Java Beans

Java beans are Sun's answer to Microsoft's ActiveX controls. Beans are reusable code components written in Java that you can use in a variety of programming environments, including third-party programming environments. In fact, they work much like ActiveX controls, exposing properties, methods, and events to other code components. Using beans, you can create your own new Java "controls," such as buttons that turn colors when you click them or stock tickers that download information from the Internet.

Java beans are designed to be used in application builder tools, which are programming environments that let you configure beans. One such tool, the *beanbox*, comes with the Sun Bean Development Kit (BDK), which you can download and install from java.sun.com. I'll use the BDK in this chapter to construct and use beans. As reusable code components that you can create applications from, beans represent a powerful new way of looking at programming—you can create your own applications on the fly from prewritten components by adding just what you need—and nothing more.

Sun supports Java beans in the java.beans package. Here's an overview of the interfaces in that package:

- *AppletInitializer*—Initializes applets and is designed to work with **java.beans.Beans.instantiate**.

- *BeanInfo*—This interface provides explicit information about the methods, properties, events, and so on of a bean.

- *Customizer*—A customizer class provides a complete custom GUI for customizing a target Java bean.

- *DesignMode*—This interface is intended to be implemented by or delegated from instances of **java.beans.BeanContext** in order to determine whether a bean is under design using the **designTime** property.

- *PropertyChangeListener*—Handles **PropertyChange** events when a bean changes a bound property.

- *PropertyEditor*—Provides support for GUIs that allow users to edit a property value of a given type.

- *VetoableChangeListener*—Handles events that are fired when a bean changes a constrained property.

- *Visibility*—Indicates whether a bean is visible (under some circumstances a bean may be run on servers where a GUI is not available).

Here's an overview of the classes in java.beans:

- *BeanDescriptor*—Provides global information about a bean, including its Java class, its name, and so on.

- *Beans*—Provides some general-purpose bean control methods.

- *EventSetDescriptor*—Describes a group of events that a given Java bean fires.

- *FeatureDescriptor*—The common base class for **PropertyDescriptor**, **EventSetDescriptor**, and **MethodDescriptor**.

- *IndexedPropertyDescriptor*—Describes a property that acts like an array.

- *Introspector*—Provides a standard way for tools to learn about the properties, events, and methods supported by a Java bean.

- *MethodDescriptor*—Describes a particular method that a Java bean supports for external access from other components.

23. Creating Packages, Interfaces, JAR Files, And Java Beans

- *ParameterDescriptor*—Provides information on each of a method's parameters, beyond the low-level information provided by the **java.lang.reflect.Method** class.

- *PropertyChangeEvent*—Listens for **PropertyChange** events that are fired when a bean changes a bound or constrained property.

- *PropertyChangeSupport*—A utility class that can be used by beans that support bound properties.

- *PropertyDescriptor*—Describes one property that a Java bean exports.

- *PropertyEditorManager*—Can be used to locate a property editor for any given type name.

- *PropertyEditorSupport*—A support class that helps build property editors.

- *SimpleBeanInfo*—A class that makes it easier for users to provide **BeanInfo** data.

- *VetoableChangeSupport*—A utility class that can be used by beans that support constrained properties.

In this chapter, I'll create a number of Java beans—from simple ones to ones that support properties and methods and let users embed other controls inside them.

TIP: *The way you create beans varies a little among operating systems because the BDK differs a little among operating systems. I use the BDK for Windows in this chapter.*

That's it for the overview of what's in this chapter. There's a great deal coming up, so it's time to turn to the "Immediate Solutions" section.

Immediate Solutions

Creating A Package

"Jeez," says the Novice Programmer, "I have so many classes that things are getting pretty cluttered now. How can I wade through all that mess?" "Well," you say, "why not divide your classes into packages? That will let you arrange your class files in a directory structure much like you'd arrange files when you have too many of them. Problem solved." "Great," says the NP. "Tell me how it works."

When you have a number of class files, it's often a good idea to arrange them on disk using a directory hierarchy. In fact, Java packages were originally designed to reflect such file organization. You can arrange class files into a directory hierarchy and let Java know what's going on with the packages.

For example, if you have a package named **package1** with one class in it, **app.class**, the class file would go into a directory named package1, like this:

```
package1
|____app
```

Multiple class files in the same package go into the same directory:

```
package1
|____app1
|____app2
|____app3
```

As long as the package1 directory is in a location that Java will search (see Chapter 1 for more information on where Java will search for class files and how to use the **ClassPath** environment variable), Java will look for the class files you list as part of that package in that directory.

You need to indicate what package a class file is part of by using the **package** statement in your code. Here's an example where I'm creating **app.class** and indicating that it's part of **package1** using the **package** statement:

```
package package1;
```

```
public class app
{
    public static void main(String[] args)
    {
        System.out.println("Hello from Java!");
    }
}
```

After I've compiled **app.class** and stored it in the package1 directory, I can then import the **app** class into my code with statements such as the following, just as I would with any other Java package:

```
import package1.*;
import package1.app;
```

The java runtime tool also knows about packages; therefore, because **app.class** is itself an application, I can run this class with a command line that specifies the **app** class's package using a dot (.) for the directory separator:

```
C:\>java package1.app
Hello from Java!
```

In fact, the dot package separator comes in handy when you create subpackages of packages—take a look at the next topic for the details.

Creating Packages That Have Subpackages

"Hmm," says the Novice Programmer, "I understand that you can put class files into a package by setting up the correct directory structure and using the **package** statement, but what if the packages have subpackages? How deep can I nest the package structure?" "As deep as you want," you say, "that is, as deep as your operating system supports nested directories."

When you have a lot of class files, you may want to organize them into quite a complex package structure, and you do that by creating the corresponding directory structure on disk, including giving directories subdirectories. For example, if you wanted the **app** class to be in **package2**, which itself was a subpackage of **package1**, this is the directory structure you'd use:

```
package1
|____package2
     |____app
```

To create this package structure in code, you just use the dot package separator. Here's an example:

```
package package1.package2;
```

```
public class app
{
    public static void main(String[] args)
    {
        System.out.println("Hello from Java!");
    }
}
```

Now you can import the **app** class into your code with statements such as these:

```
import package1.package2.*;
import package1.package2.app;
```

Because in this case **app** is already an application class, you can also run it like this, specifying the package structure:

```
C:\>java package1.package2.app
Hello from Java!
```

Creating An Interface

"Well," the Novice Programmer says, "I want to derive a new class from two base classes, but I know that Java doesn't support multiple inheritance, so...." "So you have to use interfaces," you say.

We've used interfaces throughout the book, and we'll take a look at how to create one here. When you create an interface, you specify the methods for the interface, and when you implement the interface, you provide code for those methods.

Here's an example in which I create an interface named **Printem** that has one method: **printText**. I implement this interface in a class named **class1**. To create an interface, I simply use the **interface** statement and list the prototypes (declarations without bodies) of the methods I want in the interface, like this:

```
interface Printem
{
    void printText();
}
```

Now I can implement this interface in **class1**:

```
interface Printem
{
    void printText();
}

public class interfaces
{
    public static void main(String[] args)
    {
        class1 object1 = new class1();
        object1.printText();
    }
}

class class1 implements Printem
{
    public void printText()
    {
        System.out.println("Hello from Java!");
    }
}
```

Here's the output of the code (interfaces.java on the CD accompanying this book):

```
C:\>java interfaces
Hello from Java!
```

Partially Implementing An Interface

You can create classes that partly implement an interface, but these classes must be declared abstract because they're only partial implementations and therefore cannot be instantiated into objects.

Here's an example in which I create an interface with two methods, **printText1** and **printText2**:

```
interface Printem
{
    void printText1();
    void printText2();
}
```

Next, I create a new class, **class2**, that implements the interface but only defines one method, **printText2** (note that because this class is not a full implementation of the interface, I must declare it abstract):

```
interface Printem
{
    void printText1();
    void printText2();
}

abstract class class1 implements Printem
{
    public void printText1()
    {
        System.out.println("Hello from Java!");
    }
}
```

Finally, I can create a new class, **class2**, that extends **class1** and implements **printText2**, which means I can instantiate objects of **class2**, as shown here:

```
interface Printem
{
    void printText1();
    void printText2();
}

abstract class class1 implements Printem
{
    public void printText1()
    {
        System.out.println("Hello from Java!");
    }
}

class class2 extends class1
{
    public void printText2()
    {
        System.out.println("Hello from Java interfaces!");
    }
}

public class interfaces2
{
```

```
        public static void main(String[] args)
        {
            class2 object2 = new class2();
            object2.printText2();
        }
    }
}
```

Here's the output of this code (interfaces2.java on the CD):

```
C:\>java interfaces2
Hello from Java interfaces!
```

Note that partial implementations can be useful, such as when you want to specify how some, but not all, of an interface's methods should work in a series of subclasses.

Creating A JAR File

"Wow," says the Novice Programmer, "my class files are getting huge and there's a lot of them. Do you have any idea what that does to the download times for my applets?" You smile and say, "I sure do—which is why you should be using JAR files." "*What* files?" the NP asks.

A Java archive (JAR) file enables you to enclose a number of files into one. In fact, JAR files compress their contents using a ZIP format, so if your applet needs a lot of large files, it makes sense to create and download a JAR file. Web browsers only need one connection rather than new connections for each subfile, which can improve download times. You can also digitally *sign* the files in a JAR file to prove their origin.

You create JAR files with the jar tool, and we'll take a look at that tool in this and the next few sections. This tool comes with Java, and here's how you use it:

```
jar [options] [manifest] destination input-file [additional input files]
```

Here, **options** are the options you can use with the jar tool, and they're much like the options you can use with the Unix tar tool. The optional **manifest** argument consists of the name of a manifest file, which supports digital signing and lists the contents of the JAR file. When you create a Java bean, you use the manifest file to indicate which classes are beans, as I'll do later in this chapter.

Here are the possible options you can use when using the jar tool:

- *c*—Creates a new or empty archive on the standard output.

- *t*—Lists the table of contents from standard output.

- *x file*—Extracts all files or just the named files. If **file** is omitted, all files are extracted; otherwise, only the specified files are extracted.

- *f*—The second argument specifies a JAR file to work with.

- *v*—Generates "verbose" output on **stderr**.

- *m*—Includes manifest information from a specified manifest file.

- *0*—Indicates "store only," without using ZIP compression.

- *M*—Specifies that a manifest file should not be created for the entries.

- *u*—Updates an existing JAR file by adding files or changing the manifest.

- *-C*—Changes directories during execution of **jar** command. For example, **jar uf jarfile.jar -C classes** would add all files within the classes directory, but not the classes directory itself, to jarfile.jar.

TIP: *You can use an argument beginning with the character "@" to specify a file containing additional arguments, one argument per line. These arguments are inserted into the command line at the position of the @filename argument.*

Here's a typical usage of the jar tool:

```
C:\>jar cf jarfile.jar *.class
```

In this case, all the class files in the current directory are placed in the file named jarfile.jar. A default manifest file is automatically generated by the jar tool and is always the first entry in the jar file (by default, it's named META-INF/MANIFEST.MF).

If you have a manifest file that you want the jar tool to use for a new JAR archive, you can use the **-m** option and specify it like this (we'll create manifest files later in this chapter):

```
C:\>jar cmf manifest.mft jarfile.jar *.class
```

Note that when you specify the options **cfm** instead of **cmf**, you need to specify the name of the JAR archive first, followed by the name of the manifest file:

```
C:\>jar cfm jarfile.jar manifest.mft *.class
```

Note also that JAR files are not just for class files; they can store any type of files. Here's how to pack all the files in a directory into a JAR file:

```
C:\>jar cfm jarfile.jar manifest.mft *.*
```

If the file names you want to pack include any directories, those directories are searched recursively and the files in them are stored. When the JAR file is unpacked, the directory structure will be re-created.

23. Creating Packages, Interfaces, JAR Files, And Java Beans

Getting The Contents Of A JAR File

"Uh-oh," says the Novice Programmer, "I have a JAR file and I've forgotten what's in it. I guess I'll have to rebuild it." "Not at all," you say, "just use the **tf** options." "How's that?" the NP asks.

You can determine what's in a JAR file with the **tf** options, as in this case, where the JAR file contains a default manifest in the META-INF internal directory and a number of class files:

```
C:\>jar tf jarfile.jar
META-INF/
META-INF/MANIFEST.MF
applet.class
jpanel.class
newButton.class
textPanel.class
```

Extracting Files From A JAR File

"OK," says the Novice Programmer, "I've been using JAR files to archive my files—but how do I get those files out of a JAR file?" You say, "With the **xf** options." "Great!" says the NP.

You can extract files from a JAR file using the **xf** options. For example, here's how to extract all the files in the file jarfile.jar introduced in the previous topic:

```
C:\>jar xf jarfile.jar
```

Unpacking all the files in a JAR file this way will also re-create their directory structures. In this case, the jar tool unpacks the class files, and it also makes a directory named META-INF and places the default manifest file MANIFEST.MF in it.

You can also extract files by specifying their names. Here's an example in which I'm extracting applet.class:

```
C:\>jar xf jarfile.jar applet.class
```

Updating JAR Files

Here's how to update a JAR file with a new version of one of the files stored in it, class1.class, using the **-uf** options:

```
C:\>jar -uf jarfile.jar class1.class
```

Reading From JAR Files In Code

"Say," the Novice Programmer says, "now that I've created JAR files, how can I unpack them at runtime from my code? Is there any way?" "Yes," you say, "you can use the **JarFile** class." "Tell me more!" says the NP.

You can use the **JarFile** class to read the contents of a JAR file from any file that can be opened with **java.io.RandomAccessFile**. The **JarFile** class extends the java.util **ZipFile** class with support for reading an optional manifest entry. Here's the inheritance diagram for the **ZipFile** class:

```
java.lang.Object
|____java.util.zip.ZipFile
```

You'll find the constructors for the **ZipFile** class in Table 23.1 and its methods in Table 23.2.

Table 23.1   Constructors of the ZipFile class.

Constructor	Does This
ZipFile(File file)	Opens a ZIP file for reading from the indicated **File** object.
ZipFile(String name)	Opens a ZIP file for reading.

Table 23.2   Methods of the *ZipFile* class.

Method	Does This
void close( )	Closes the ZIP file.
Enumeration entries( )	Gets an enumeration of the ZIP file entries.
ZipEntry getEntry(String name)	Gets the ZIP file entry for the indicated name (or null if not found).
InputStream getInputStream(ZipEntry entry)	Gets an input stream for reading the contents of the indicated ZIP file entry.
String getName( )	Gets the pathname of the ZIP file.
int size( )	Gets the number of entries in the ZIP file.

The **JarFile** class is built on the **ZipFile** class. Here's the inheritance diagram for the **JarFile** class:

```
java.lang.Object
|____java.util.zip.ZipFile
     |____java.util.jar.JarFile
```

You'll find the field of the **JarFile** class in Table 23.3, its constructors in Table 23.4, and its methods in Table 23.5.

Table 23.3   The field of the *JarFile* class.

Field	Does This
static String MANIFEST_NAME	Holds the name of the manifest.

Table 23.4   Constructors of the *JarFile* class.

Constructor	Does This
JarFile(File file)	Constructs a new **JarFile** to read from the indicated **File** object.
JarFile(File file, boolean verify)	Constructs a new **JarFile** to read from the indicated **File** object and allows for verification.
JarFile(String name)	Constructs a new **JarFile** to read from the indicated file name.
JarFile(String name, boolean verify)	Constructs a new **JarFile** to read from the indicated file name and allows for verification.

Table 23.5   Methods of the *JarFile* class.

Method	Does This
Enumeration entries( )	Gets an enumeration of the ZIP file entries.
ZipEntry getEntry(String name)	Gets the ZIP file entry for the indicated name (or null if not found).
InputStream getInputStream (ZipEntry ze)	Gets an input stream for reading the contents of the indicated ZIP file entry.
JarEntry getJarEntry(String name)	Gets the **JarEntry** for the given entry name (or null if not found).
Manifest getManifest( )	Gets the JAR file manifest (or null if none).

You actually handle the items in a JAR file as **JarEntry** objects, and the **JarEntry** class is derived from the **ZipEntry** class. Here's the inheritance diagram for **ZipEntry**:

```
java.lang.Object
|____java.util.zip.ZipEntry
```

You'll find the fields of the **ZipEntry** class in Table 23.6, its constructors in Table 23.7, and its methods in Table 23.8.

Table 23.6   Fields of the *ZipEntry* class.

Field	Does This
static int DEFLATED	Specifies the compression method for compressed entries.
static int STORED	Specifies the compression method for uncompressed entries.

Table 23.7   Constructors of the *ZipEntry* class.

Constructor	Does This
ZipEntry(String name)	Constructs a new ZIP entry with the indicated name.
ZipEntry(ZipEntry e)	Constructs a new ZIP entry with fields taken from the indicated ZIP entry.

Table 23.8   Methods of the *ZipEntry* class.

Method	Does This
Object clone( )	Gets a copy of this entry.
String getComment( )	Gets the comment string for the entry (or null if none).
long getCompressedSize( )	Gets the size of the compressed entry data (or -1 if not known).

(continued)

Table 23.8   Methods of the ZipEntry class (continued).

Method	Does This
long getCrc( )	Gets the CRC-32 checksum of the uncompressed entry data (or -1 if not known).
byte[ ] getExtra( )	Gets the extra field data for the entry (or null if none).
int getMethod( )	Gets the compression method of the entry (or -1 if not indicated).
String getName( )	Gets the name of the entry.
long getSize( )	Gets the uncompressed size of the entry data (or -1 if not known).
long getTime( )	Gets the modification time of the entry (or -1 if not indicated).
int hashCode( )	Gets the hashcode value for this entry.
boolean isDirectory( )	Returns True if this is a directory entry.
void setComment(String comment)	Sets the optional comment string for the entry.
void setCompressedSize(long csize)	Sets the size of the compressed entry data.
void setCrc(long crc)	Sets the CRC-32 checksum of the uncompressed entry data.
void setExtra(byte[ ] extra)	Sets the optional extra field data for the entry.
void setMethod(int method)	Sets the compression method for the entry.
void setSize(long size)	Sets the uncompressed size of the entry data.
void setTime(long time)	Sets the modification time of the entry.
String toString( )	Gets a string representation of the ZIP entry.

Here's the inheritance diagram for the **JarEntry** class:

```
java.lang.Object
|____java.util.zip.ZipEntry
     |____java.util.jar.JarEntry
```

You'll find the constructors for the **JarEntry** class in Table 23.9 and its methods in Table 23.10.

Table 23.9   Constructors of the JarEntry class.

Constructor	Does This
JarEntry(JarEntry je)	Constructs a new **JarEntry** from the given **JarEntry** object.
JarEntry(String name)	Constructs a new **JarEntry** for the given JAR file entry name.
JarEntry(ZipEntry ze)	Constructs a new **JarEntry** from the given **ZipEntry** object.

Table 23.10 *Methods of the **JarEntry** class.*

Method	Does This
Attributes getAttributes( )	Gets the manifest attributes for this entry (or null if none).
Certificate[ ] getCertificates( )	Gets the certificate objects for this entry (or null if none).

Using javac To Get Classes From JAR Files

As a convenience, you can use the Java compiler, javac, to unpack class files from JAR files as needed. Here's an example in which I have a class named **display** with one method, **displayText**, which displays a message:

```
public class display
{
    public void displayText()
    {
        System.out.println("Hello from Java!");
    }
}
```

Here's how I make a JAR file from this class:

```
C:\>jar cf display.jar display.class
```

Next, I delete the display.class file, so all that's left is the JAR file, display.jar. Now I can make use of the **display** class in an application, like this:

```
import display.*;

public class useDisplay
{
    public static void main(String[] args)
    {
        display display1 = new display();
        display1.displayText();
    }
}
```

When I compile this application, javac will search the JAR file for display.class and unpack that class. Because display.class is now unpacked, it's available when I run the application that uses it:

```
C:\>java useDisplay
Hello from Java!
```

Letting Applets Get Classes From JAR Files

The Novice Programmer is back and says, "Now I've put my applet into a JAR file, as well as all the support files it needs. But there's one problem." What's that? you ask. The NP says, "How the heck do I tell the browser about JAR files?"

You can tell Web browsers and the Sun appletviewer that you're storing files in a JAR file with the **archive** parameter in the **<APPLET>** tag. Here's an example. In this case, I'm creating an applet that will be stored in a JAR file named applet.jar. Here's the code for this applet, including the **<APPLET>** tag:

```
import java.awt.*;
import java.applet.Applet;

/*
<APPLET
    CODE=applet.class
    WIDTH=200
    HEIGHT=200>
    <PARAM NAME=archive VALUE="applet.jar">
</APPLET>
*/

public class applet extends Applet
{
    public void paint(Graphics g)
    {
        g.drawString("Hello from Java!", 60, 100);
    }
}
```

After compiling this applet to applet.class, I create the applet.jar file:

```
C:\>jar cf applet.jar applet.class
```

Next, I delete applet.class and open applet.java using the Sun appletviewer:

```
C:>appletviewer applet.java
```

The result appears in Figure 23.1. As you can see, the appletviewer has opened the applet from the JAR file.

This example is applet.java on the CD.

Figure 23.1   Opening an applet from a JAR file.

Designing Programs Using Java Beans

"So how do I use Java beans anyway?" the Novice Programmer wants to know. "You use them in application builder tools," you say, "such as the beanbox tool that comes with the Bean Development Kit." "Show me," the NP says.

After you've downloaded and installed the Bean Development Kit (BDK), you can work with beans in the beanbox tool that comes with the BDK. Assuming you've installed the BDK to its default path, C:\BDK, you can open the beanbox with the run.bat file in C:\BDK\beanbox. When you run this batch file, the beanbox opens, as shown in Figure 23.2.

You can see the available beans in the toolbox on the left part of the figure. When you add beans to an application, they'll appear in the beanbox window next to the toolbox. You can also use the Properties window to set the properties that have been designed into a bean, and you can use the Method Tracer window to handle method execution.

Look at Figure 23.3. It's an example showing how to work with some beans. Click on the Juggler bean in the toolbox, which changes your cursor to a cross. Next,

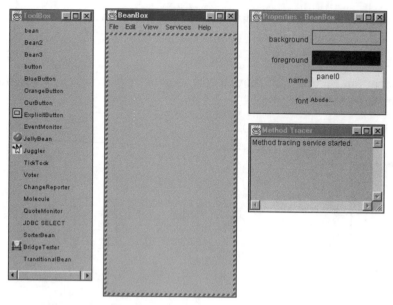

Figure 23.2   Using the beanbox.

"draw" a Juggler bean in the beanbox by dragging the mouse (this bean displays the Java mascot image "juggling" coffee beans). Do the same for the bean named OurButton. This results in the application under design you see in Figure 23.3.

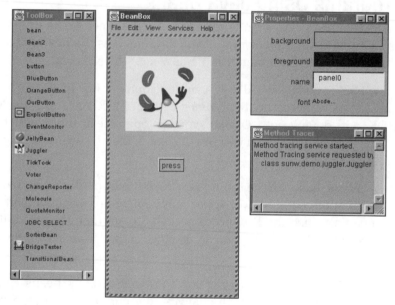

Figure 23.3   Creating an application.

You can connect the beans in a beanbox, thus creating a single application from several beans. For example, you can connect the button to the Juggler bean so when you click on the button, the juggler will stop juggling.

First, click the button bean in the beanbox. The Properties window will display the properties you can set for this bean, including its label—if you want to enter a new label for this button (such as "Click Me"), you can do so in the Properties window (you'll see how to set the properties of your own beans this way later).

To make the button do something when you click it, select the Edit|Events|action|actionPerformed menu item now. When you do, a red line appears between the mouse location and the button. Stretch that line to the Juggler bean now and click the Juggler bean, as shown in Figure 23.4. This connects the button and the Juggler bean.

When you click the Juggler bean, the Event Target dialog box appears as shown in Figure 23.5, displaying the available methods you can call in the Juggler bean when the button is clicked. For this example, choose the **stopJuggling** method to make the juggler stop juggling; then click OK to close the Event Target dialog box.

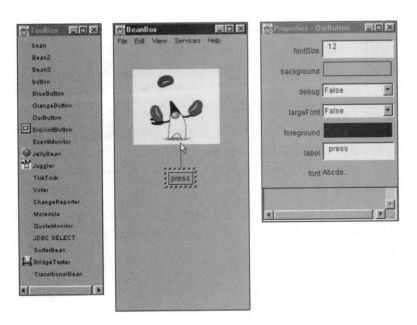

Figure 23.4   Connecting one bean to another.

Figure 23.5   The Event Target dialog box.

That's all there is to it. Now when you click the button in the beanbox, the juggler will stop juggling. Congratulations, you've connected two beans together, thus creating a new program.

How do you actually run this program outside the beanbox? Take a look at the next topic.

Creating Applets That Use Java Beans

"OK," says the Novice Programmer, "I've designed an applet with plenty of beans in it and I want to create a JAR file that I can let people use. How do I do that?" "Simple," you say. "Maybe," the NP says, "but *how*?"

After you've designed an applet using the beanbox, you can use the MakeApplet item in the File menu to create a JAR file containing your new applet and all the beans it uses. When you select this menu item, it opens the Make an Applet dialog box you see in Figure 23.6.

In this example, I'll use the applet we developed in the previous topic. I'll stick to the default JAR file name, myApplet.jar, and applet class, **MyApplet**. When I click OK, the myApplet.jar file is created.

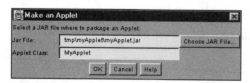

Figure 23.6   The Make an Applet dialog box.

The myApplet.jar file can be used with Web browsers and the Sun appletviewer (see the topic "Letting Applets Get Classes From JAR Files" for more information). Here's the HTML page I'll use with myApplet.jar:

```html
<HTML>

<HEAD>
<TITLE>Beans applet example</TITLE>
</HEAD>

<BODY>
<APPLET
    CODE=MyApplet.class
    WIDTH=200
    HEIGHT=200>
    <PARAM NAME=archive VALUE="myApplet.jar">
</APPLET>
</BODY>

</HTML>
```

The result appears in Figure 23.7, where you can see the applet in the appletviewer. Now you know how to use Java beans in applets.

Figure 23.7   An applet that uses beans.

Creating A Java Bean

The Novice Programmer appears and says, "I've used Java beans now—but how do I actually create my own beans?" "Well," you say, "it's not too hard, but it does take a little work." "Uh-oh," says the NP.

I'll create a simple Java bean in this topic to show how beans work, and I'll elaborate on this bean in the rest of the chapter. This bean will just draw itself in red, and when you click on it, it'll display a count of the number of times it's been clicked.

I'll place this bean in the BDK's demo directories, so I create a directory named bean—C:\BDK\demo\sunw\demo\bean—and store the class files for this bean in that directory. I'll start the code, bean.java, by indicating that this bean is part of a package named sunw.demo.bean:

```
package sunw.demo.bean;
import java.awt.*;
import java.awt.event.*;
        .
        .
        .
```

As far as the actual bean class goes, I use the **Canvas** class to draw the bean itself (you can also use other classes, such as the **Panel** class, which we'll do in this chapter). The rest of the code is pretty ordinary; I just add a mouse listener to the canvas to record mouse clicks, and I set the size of the canvas (and therefore set the size of the bean):

```
package sunw.demo.bean;
import java.awt.*;
import java.awt.event.*;

public class bean extends Canvas
{
    int count;

    public bean()
    {
        addMouseListener(new MouseAdapter() {
            public void mousePressed(MouseEvent me) {
                clicked();
            }
        });
```

```
        count = 0;
        setSize(200, 100);
    }
    .
    .
    .
    .
}
```

Finally, I implement the method that handles mouse clicks, and I draw the bean, including the click count, in the **paint** method:

```java
package sunw.demo.bean;
import java.awt.*;
import java.awt.event.*;

public class bean extends Canvas
{
    int count;

    public bean()
    {
        addMouseListener(new MouseAdapter() {
            public void mousePressed(MouseEvent me) {
                clicked();
            }
        });
        count = 0;
        setSize(200, 100);
    }

    public void clicked()
    {
        count++;
        repaint();
    }

    public void paint(Graphics g)
    {
        Dimension dimension = getSize();
        int height = dimension.height;
        int width = dimension.width;

        g.setColor(new Color(255, 0, 0));
        g.fillRect(0, 0, --width, --height);
```

```
        g.setColor(new Color(0, 0, 0));
        g.drawString("Click count = " + count, 50, 50);
    }
}
```

This example is in bean.java on the CD. As you can see, the code for a new Java bean is pretty simple—essentially, you just draw a component. However, it's not a bean yet—I still have to put it into a JAR file and label it in that JAR file as a bean. To see more about how this works, see the next topic.

Creating A Bean Manifest File

The Novice Programmer appears and says, "Well, I've written the code for my new Java bean, but now what?" You smile and say, "You have to pack the bean into a JAR file and indicate that it's a bean in the JAR file's manifest file." "Tell me more!" says the NP.

To make a bean into a bean, you have to store the class file(s) to use in a JAR file, and you use a manifest to indicate which classes are beans. To show you how this works, I'll use the bean we started developing in the previous topic and create a manifest file, bean.mft, for it here. I'll place this manifest file in C:\BDK\demo to make creating the JAR file easier (see the next topic).

To indicate that a class in a JAR file is a Java bean, you have to set its **Java-Bean** attribute to True. Here's how that works with the bean introduced in the previous topic, bean.class. That class file is in the sunw.demo.bean package, which means it'll be stored in the JAR file as sunw/demo/bean/bean.class (like Unix, JAR files use forward slashes as directory separators). To indicate that this class file is a bean, here's what I put in the manifest file, bean.mft:

```
Name: sunw/demo/bean/bean.class
Java-Bean: True
```

This example is bean.mft on the CD. We'll put this manifest to work in the next topic when we create the JAR file for this bean.

Creating A Bean Jar File

The Novice Programmer appears and says, "OK, I've got the class files for my new bean, and I've got the manifest file I want to use. Now what?" "Now," you say, "you're ready to use the jar tool." "You do it," the NP says. "I'll watch."

In this topic, we'll create the JAR file for the bean we've been developing over the previous two topics. First, compile bean.java, which will create two class files: bean.class and bean$1.class. Copy these files to C:\BDK\demo\sunw\demo\bean. Next, place the manifest file developed in the previous topic, bean.mft, into C:\BDK\demo. Now we're ready to go. Make sure you're in the C:\BDK\demo directory and use the jar tool, like this:

```
C:\BDK\demo>jar cfm ..\jars\bean.jar bean.mft sunw\demo\bean\*.class
```

This creates the new JAR file for this bean, bean.jar, and stores it in the C:\BDK\demo\jars directory, which is where the beanbox will look for it. That's how you install a bean—by placing its JAR file in that directory.

The new bean is ready to go, and it's put to work in the next topic.

Using A New Bean

We've developed a new Java bean over the previous few topics and installed it in the C:\BDK\demo\jars directory. When you open the beanbox, you'll see this bean (which we've just called "bean") listed in the toolbox, as shown in Figure 23.8. You can draw a bean of this new type in the beanbox, also shown in Figure 23.8. This new bean is already active in the beanbox, as you can see by clicking it, because it shows the number of times it's been clicked.

This new Java bean is a good start, but what about doing more, such as adding other Java controls to it? Take a look at the next topic.

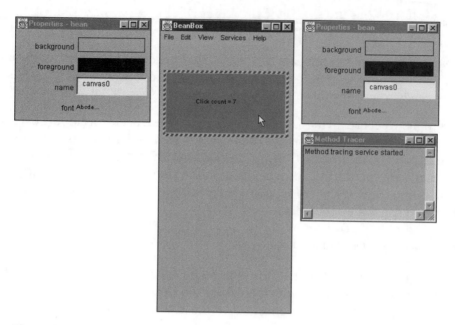

Figure 23.8   A new bean.

Adding Controls To Beans

"I don't want to have to reinvent the wheel," says the Novice Programmer. "Which means what?" you ask. "Well, it means that if I want a button in my new Java bean, why do I have to draw and support it myself—why can't I just use a standard Java button?" "You can," you say.

You can add Java controls such as buttons to your beans—you just have to make sure you base your bean on a class that's a container, such as the **Panel** class. Here's an example in which I add a button to a bean and have the bean display the number of times it has been clicked. I start by basing this bean, which I'll call "button," on the **Panel** class and adding it to the sunw.demo.button package (which means I'll store its class files in C:\BDK\demo\sunw\button). Here's how I create the panel, size it, and add a button to it:

```
package sunw.demo.button;
import java.awt.*;
import java.awt.event.*;

public class button extends Panel implements ActionListener
{
```

```
    int count;
    Button button1;

    public button()
    {
        count = 0;
        setSize(200, 100);

        button1 = new Button("Click me");

        button1.addActionListener(this);

        add(button1);
    }
```

All that's left now is to make the button active by incrementing the click count
when the button is clicked, repainting the bean to display the click count, and
creating the **paint** method:

```
package sunw.demo.button;
import java.awt.*;
import java.awt.event.*;

public class button extends Panel implements ActionListener
{
    int count;
    Button button1;

    public button()
    {
        count = 0;
        setSize(200, 100);

        button1 = new Button("Click me");

        button1.addActionListener(this);

        add(button1);
    }

    public void actionPerformed(ActionEvent e)
    {
        count++;
        repaint();
    }
```

```
public void paint(Graphics g)
{
    Dimension dimension = getSize();
    int height = dimension.height;
    int w = d.width;
    g.setColor(new Color(255, 0, 0));
    g.fillRect(0, 0, w-1, h-1);

    g.setColor(new Color(0, 0, 0));
    g.drawString("Click count = " + count, 50, 50);
}
}
```

The result of this code (button.java and button.mft on the CD) appears in Figure 23.9.

As you can see, it's easy to add Java controls to a bean.

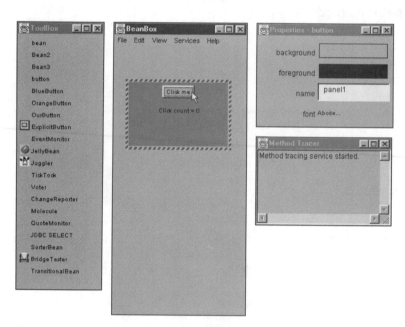

Figure 23.9 Creating a new bean with a Java button.

Giving A Bean Properties

"I notice," the Novice Programmer says, "that you can set the properties of a bean in the beanbox using the properties window. Can I do that with the beans I create?" "You certainly can," you say. The NP says, "Wow!"

The properties of a bean let you configure it, setting its caption, size, color, and any other aspect of the bean for which properties are defined. Although any public data member of a bean class can be treated as a property, there's a formal procedure you should follow to inform the Java framework about the properties of your beans: implementing the **BeanInfo** interface. The fields of the **BeanInfo** interface appear in Table 23.11 and its methods in Table 23.12.

Table 23.11   *Fields of the **BeanInfo** interface.*

Field	Does This
static int ICON_COLOR_16x16	Indicates a 16 x 16 color icon.
static int ICON_COLOR_32x32	Indicates a 32 x 32 color icon.
static int ICON_MONO_16x16	Indicates a 16 x 16 monochrome icon.
static int ICON_MONO_32x32	Indicates a 32 x 32 monochrome icon

Table 23.12   *Methods of the **BeanInfo** interface.*

Method	Does This
BeanInfo[ ] getAdditionalBeanInfo( )	Allows a **BeanInfo** object to return an arbitrary collection of other **BeanInfo** objects.
BeanDescriptor getBeanDescriptor( )	Gets the bean's **BeanDescriptor**.
int getDefaultEventIndex( )	Gets the default event. A bean may have a default event that's the event that will mostly commonly be used.
int getDefaultPropertyIndex( )	Gets the default property index. A bean may have a default property that's the property that will mostly commonly be initially chosen for update.
EventSetDescriptor[ ] getEventSet Descriptors( )	Gets the bean's **EventSetDescriptors**.
Image getIcon(int iconKind)	Gets an image object that can be used to represent the bean in tool boxes, toolbars, and so on.
MethodDescriptor[ ] getMethod Descriptors( )	Gets the bean's **MethodDescriptors**.
PropertyDescriptor[ ] getProperty Descriptors( )	Gets the bean's **PropertyDescriptors**.

In fact, most beans don't implement the **BeanInfo** interface directly. Instead, they extend the **SimpleBeanInfo** class, which implements **BeanInfo**. Here's the inheritance diagram for **SimpleBeanInfo**:

```
java.lang.Object
|____java.beans.SimpleBeanInfo
```

You'll find the constructor of the **SimpleBeanInfo** class in Table 23.13 and its methods in Table 23.14.

To actually describe a property, you use the **PropertyDescriptor** class, which in turn is derived from the **FeatureDescriptor** class. Here's the inheritance diagram for the **FeatureDescriptor** class:

```
java.lang.Object
|____java.beans.FeatureDescriptor
```

You'll find the constructor of the **FeatureDescriptor** class in Table 23.15 and its methods in Table 23.16.

Table 23.13   The constructor of the *SimpleBeanInfo* class.

Constructor	Does This
SimpleBeanInfo( )	Constructs a **BeanInfo** object.

Table 23.14   Methods of the *SimpleBeanInfo* class.

Method	Does This
BeanInfo[ ] getAdditionalBeanInfo( )	Implemented to indicate that there are no other relevant **BeanInfo** objects.
BeanDescriptor getBeanDescriptor( )	Implemented to indicated that there is no descriptor.
int getDefaultEventIndex( )	Implemented to deny knowledge of a default event.
int getDefaultPropertyIndex( )	Implemented to deny knowledge of a default property.
EventSetDescriptor[ ] getEventSet Descriptors( )	Implemented to deny knowledge of event sets.
Image getIcon(int iconKind)	Implemented to deny that there are no icons available.
MethodDescriptor[ ] getMethod Descriptors( )	Implemented to deny knowledge of methods.
PropertyDescriptor[ ] getProperty Descriptors( )	Implemented to deny knowledge of properties.
Image loadImage(String resourceName)	The utility method used to help in loading icon images.

Table 23.15   The constructor of the FeatureDescriptor class.

Constructor	Does This
FeatureDescriptor( )	Constructs a FeatureDescriptor.

Table 23.16   Methods of the FeatureDescriptor class.

Method	Does This
Enumeration attributeNames( )	Gets an enumeration of the locale-independent names of this feature.
String getDisplayName( )	Gets the localized display name of this feature.
String getName( )	Gets the programmatic name of this feature.
String getShortDescription( )	Gets the short description of this feature.
Object getValue(String attributeName)	Retrieves a named attribute with this feature.
boolean isExpert( )	Returns True for features that are intended for expert users.
boolean isHidden( )	Returns True for features that are intended only for tool use.
boolean isPreferred( )	Returns True for features that are particularly important for presenting to people.
void setDisplayName(String displayName)	Sets the localized display name of this feature.
void setExpert(boolean expert)	Sets the expert flag for features that are intended for expert users.
void setHidden(boolean hidden)	Sets the hidden flag for features intended only for tool use.
void setName(String name)	Sets the name of this feature.
void setPreferred(boolean preferred)	Sets the preferred flag, used to identify features that are particularly important for presenting to people.
void setShortDescription(String text)	You can associate a short descriptive string with a feature.
void setValue(String attributeName, Object value)	You can associate a named attribute with this feature.

Here's the inheritance diagram for the **PropertyDescriptor** class:

```
java.lang.Object
|____java.beans.FeatureDescriptor
      |____java.beans.PropertyDescriptor
```

You'll find the constructors of the **PropertyDescriptor** class in Table 23.17 and its methods in Table 23.18.

Table 23.17   Constructors of the *PropertyDescriptor* class.

Constructor	Does This
PropertyDescriptor(String property Name, Class beanClass)	Constructs a **PropertyDescriptor**.
PropertyDescriptor(String property Name, Class beanClass, String getter Name, String setterName)	Takes the name of a simple property as well as method names for reading and writing the property.
PropertyDescriptor(String property Name, Method getter, Method setter)	Takes the name of a simple property as well as **Method** objects for reading and writing the property.

Table 23.18   Methods of the *PropertyDescriptor* class.

Method	Does This
Class getPropertyEditorClass( )	Gets any explicit **PropertyEditor** class that has been registered for this property.
Class getPropertyType( )	Gets the **Class** object for the property.
Method getReadMethod( )	Gets the method that should be used to read the property value.
Method getWriteMethod( )	Gets the method that should be used to write the property value.
boolean isBound( )	Updates to bound properties will cause a **PropertyChange** event to be fired when the property is changed.
boolean isConstrained( )	Attempted updates to constrained properties will cause a **VetoableChange** event to be fired when the property is changed.
void setBound(boolean bound)	Updates to bound properties will cause a **PropertyChange** event to be fired when the property is changed.
void setConstrained(boolean constrained)	Attempted updates to constrained properties will cause a **VetoableChange** event to be fired when the property is changed.
void setPropertyEditorClass (Class propertyEditorClass)	Normally **PropertyEditors** will be found using the **PropertyEditorManager**.
void setReadMethod(Method getter)	Sets the method that should be used to read the property value.
void setWriteMethod(Method setter)	Sets the method that should be used to write the property value.

Let's look at an example that implements a property in a Java bean. In this case, I'll add a property named **filled** to the click-counting operation developed in this chapter. This property is a boolean property that, when True, makes sure the bean will be filled in with color. I'll call this new bean **Bean2**.

To keep track of the new **filled** property, I'll add a private boolean variable of that name to the **Bean2** class:

```
package sunw.demo.bean2;
import java.awt.*;
import java.awt.event.*;

public class Bean2 extends Canvas
{
    private boolean filled;
    .
    .
    .
```

I initialize this property to False when the bean is created:

```
package sunw.demo.bean2;
import java.awt.*;
import java.awt.event.*;

public class Bean2 extends Canvas
{
    private boolean filled;
    int count;

    public Bean2()
    {
        addMouseListener(new MouseAdapter() {
            public void mousePressed(MouseEvent me)
            {
                clicked();
            }
        });

        count = 0;
        filled = false;
        setSize(200, 100);
    }
    .
    .
    .
}
```

When you implement a property, Java will look for two methods: **get***PropertyName* and **set***PropertyName*, where ***PropertyName*** is the name of the property. The **get** method returns the current value of the property, which can be any supported type, and the **set** method takes an argument of that type, which you're supposed to set that property to. Here's how I implement the **getfilled** and **setfilled** methods:

```java
package sunw.demo.bean2;
import java.awt.*;
import java.awt.event.*;

public class Bean2 extends Canvas
{
    private boolean filled;
    int count;

    public Bean2()
    {
        addMouseListener(new MouseAdapter() {
            public void mousePressed(MouseEvent me)
            {
                clicked();
            }
        });

        count = 0;
        filled = false;
        setSize(200, 100);
    }

    public void clicked()
    {
        count++;
        repaint();
    }

    public boolean getfilled()
    {
        return filled;
    }

    public void setfilled(boolean flag)
    {
        this.filled = flag;
        repaint();
```

```
    }
    .
    .
    .
}
```

All that's left is to put the **filled** property to use. If it's True, the bean should be filled in with color, so here's the code I add to the **paint** method:

```
public void paint(Graphics g)
{
    Dimension dimension = getSize();
    int height = dimension.height;
    int width = dimension.width;

    if(filled){
        g.setColor(new Color(255, 0, 0));
        g.fillRect(0, 0, --width, --height);
    }

    g.setColor(new Color(0, 0, 0));
    g.drawString("Click count = " + count, 50, 50);
}
```

Now I have to create a new class, **Bean2BeanInfo**, which will return information about this new bean property. This class will go into the same package as the bean, itself, but it's based on the **SimpleBeanInfo** class:

```
package sunw.demo.bean2;
import java.beans.*;

public class Bean2BeanInfo extends SimpleBeanInfo
{
    .
    .
    .
}
```

To let Java know about properties, you implement the **getPropertyDescriptors** method, which returns an array of **PropertyDescriptor** objects. Each **PropertyDescriptor** object holds the name of a property and points to the class that supports that property. Here's how I create a **PropertyDescriptor** object for the **filled** property:

```
package sunw.demo.bean2;
import java.beans.*;

public class Bean2BeanInfo extends SimpleBeanInfo
{
    public PropertyDescriptor[] getPropertyDescriptors()
    {
        try {
            PropertyDescriptor filled = new
                PropertyDescriptor("filled", Bean2.class);
                    .
                    .
                    .
        }
        catch(Exception e) {}

        return null;
    }
}
```

This is the only property in **Bean2**, so I add the new **PropertyDescriptor** object to an array and return it, like this:

```
package sunw.demo.bean2;
import java.beans.*;

public class Bean2BeanInfo extends SimpleBeanInfo
{
    public PropertyDescriptor[] getPropertyDescriptors()
    {
        try {
            PropertyDescriptor filled = new
                PropertyDescriptor("filled", Bean2.class);
            PropertyDescriptor propertydescriptor[] = {filled};
            return propertydescriptor;
        }
        catch(Exception e) {}

        return null;
    }
}
```

After compiling this new class (bean2BeanInfo.java), I place bean2BeanInfo.class in C:\BDK\demo\sunw\demo\bean2, along with the classes that were created when I compiled Bean2.java. I'll need a new manifest file that includes the Bean2BeanInfo class. Here's what bean2.mft looks like:

```
Name: sunw/demo/bean2/Bean2BeanInfo.class
Name: sunw/demo/bean2/Bean2.class
Java-Bean: True
```

I place this new manifest file in C:\BDK\demo. Finally, here's how I create the new Bean2.jar file and install it:

```
C:\BDK\demo>jar cfm ..\jars\bean2.jar bean2.mft sunw\demo\bean2\*.class
```

Now when I run the beanbox and add a new Bean2 bean to the beanbox, the new **filled** property will appear in the Properties window, as you can see in Figure 23.10. Setting **filled** to true causes the bean to be filled with color, which is also shown in the figure.

You'll find this example in Bean2.java and bean2.mft on the CD.

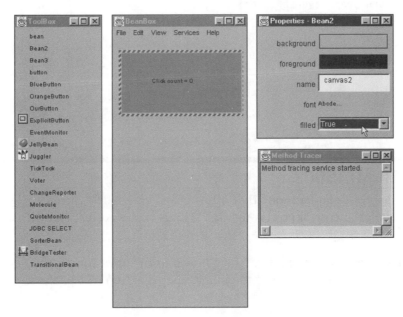

Figure 23.10　Setting a bean's properties in the beanbox.

Creating Bound Properties

You can also create *bound* properties in Java beans. Bound properties generate an event when their values change. This event is of type **PropertyChangeEvent** and is sent to all registered event listeners of this type. To make a property a bound property, you can use the **setBound** method like this (note that I'm adapting code from the previous topic):

```
package sunw.demo.bean2;
import java.beans.*;

public class Bean2BeanInfo extends SimpleBeanInfo
{
    public PropertyDescriptor[] getPropertyDescriptors()
    {
        try {
            PropertyDescriptor filled = new
                PropertyDescriptor("filled", Bean2.class);
            filled.setBound(true);
            PropertyDescriptor propertydescriptor[] = {filled};
            return propertydescriptor;
        }
        catch(Exception e) {}

        return null;
    }
}
```

Giving A Bean Methods

"Can you give a Java bean methods that other beans can call?" "Sure can," you say. "Pull up a chair and we'll go through it." "I'll get some coffee," the NP says while running off.

You can formally describe methods of Java beans to the Java framework using the **MethodDescriptor** class. Here's the inheritance diagram of this class:

```
java.lang.Object
|____java.beans.FeatureDescriptor
    |____java.beans.MethodDescriptor
```

You'll find the constructors of the **MethodDescriptor** class in Table 23.19 and its methods in Table 23.20.

Table 23.19   Constructors of the MethodDescriptor class.

Constructor	Does This
MethodDescriptor(Method method)	Constructs a **MethodDescriptor**.
MethodDescriptor(Method method, ParameterDescriptor[ ] parameterDescriptors)	Constructs a **MethodDescriptor** from a method, providing descriptive information for each of the method's parameters.

Table 23.20   Methods of the MethodDescriptor class.

Method	Does This
Method getMethod( )	Gets the method that this **MethodDescriptor** encapsulates.
ParameterDescriptor[ ] getParameter Descriptors( )	Gets the **ParameterDescriptor** for each of the parameters of this **MethodDescriptor**'s methods.

Many beans, however, don't bother to use **MethodDescriptor** objects, because any public bean method is accessible from other beans. Here's an example in which I create a new bean based on the ones we've developed in this chapter. This bean, **Bean3**, will count the number of times it's been clicked and will also support a method named **increment** that, when invoked, will increment the click count.

Here's the code for **Bean3**, including the public **increment** method:

```
package sunw.demo.bean3;
import java.awt.*;
import java.awt.event.*;

public class Bean3 extends Canvas
{
    int count;

    public Bean3()
    {
        addMouseListener(new MouseAdapter() {
            public void mousePressed(MouseEvent me)
            {
                clicked();
            }
        });

        count = 0;
        setSize(200, 100);
    }
```

```
public void clicked()
{
    count++;
    repaint();
}

public void increment()
{
    count++;
    repaint();
}

public void paint(Graphics g)
{
    Dimension dimension = getSize();
    int height = dimension.height;
    int width = dimension.width;

    g.setColor(new Color(255, 0, 0));
    g.fillRect(0, 0, --width, --height);

    g.setColor(new Color(0, 0, 0));
    g.drawString("Click count = " + count, 50, 50);
}
}
```

After creating **Bean3** and adding it to the beanbox, as shown in Figure 23.11, I can connect other beans to the **increment** method. I've connected a button to that method in Figure 23.11, and each time the button is clicked, the click count in the **Bean3** bean is incremented and displayed. That's it.

You'll find this example in Bean3.java and bean3.mft on the CD.

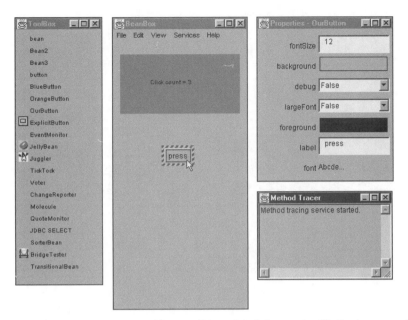

Figure 23.11   Incrementing a test bean's click count with the increment method.

Giving A Bean An Icon

You may have noticed that some beans have icons in the beanbox. You can add your own icons to your beans—all you have to do is add a **getIcon** method to the **BeanInfo** class. Here's how to implement this method and handle all possibilities—monochrome or color icons of either 16×16 or 32×32 pixels:

```java
public java.awt.Image getIcon(int iconKind)
{
    if (iconKind == BeanInfo.ICON_MONO_16x16 ||
            iconKind == BeanInfo.ICON_COLOR_16x16 ) {
        java.awt.Image image = loadImage("Icon16.gif");
        return image;
    }

    if (iconKind == BeanInfo.ICON_MONO_32x32 ||
            iconKind == BeanInfo.ICON_COLOR_32x32 ) {
        java.awt.Image image = loadImage("Icon32.gif");
        return image;
    }

    return null;
}
```

Chapter 24

Exception Handling, Debugging, And Networking

In Depth

In this chapter, we're going to take a look at some unusually powerful aspects of Java: exception handling, debugging, and networking. Each of these topics are important, and we'll take a look at them in overview now.

Exception Handling

Exception handling is the way that Java handles runtime errors. The basis of exception handling is the **try** block, in which you place code that can cause exceptions. In fact, you've see this throughout the book, such as in this example, where an operation using an **InputStreamReader** can generate an exception (called *throwing* an exception), which is then caught and handled in a **catch** block:

```
import java.io.*;

class inputstreamreader
{
    public static void main(String args[]) {
        try {
            int character;
            InputStreamReader inputstreamreader = new
                InputStreamReader(System.in);
            while ((character = inputstreamreader.read()) != -1) {
                System.out.print((char) character);
            }
        }
        catch (IOException e) {System.out.println("Error!");}
    }
}
```

I/O operations are typically placed in **try** blocks, because they're error prone—Java will usually insist that you use a **try/catch** block (and if you don't, it'll ask you to do so when you try to compile your code). Here, the sensitive operation is enclosed in a **try** block, and if an exception occurs, it's caught in the **catch** block. You can do various things in the **catch** block, such as attempt to recover from the exception, ignore it, inform the user, and so on. You'll see the options in this chapter.

TIP: *It's a good idea to handle exceptions yourself in any program you release for general use, because if you don't, Java passes the exception on to the default exception handler, which prints out its internal stack and terminates your program.*

Debugging

Exception handling lets you work with runtime errors, but there's another kind of error: logic errors in your code (also know as *bugs*). Java provides a debugging tool, the jdb tool, that lets you single step through your code, set *breakpoints* in your code that halt execution when you reach them, examine the variables of a program while it's executing, and more. We'll take a look at the jdb tool in this chapter.

Networking

Networking is a particularly important topic in Java because of Java's association with the Web. In this chapter, we'll take a look at the **URL** class, which is how Java handles URLs, the **URLConnection** class, which allows you to get information about Web pages (including their content), and the **Socket** class, which you use to create sockets for communication across the Internet and intranets. The **Socket** class is particularly powerful—using it, you can write client/server Internet programs in which the client is on one machine and the server is on another. You'll see how to do this in this chapter.

We'll also take a look at the Java Database Connectivity (JDBC) package in this chapter. This package lets you connect to standard data sources, usually Open Database Connectivity (ODBC) data sources, which we'll do in this chapter as well.

In addition, we'll take a look at Java *servlets*. The programs in this book that use the Internet have been client programs that are installed on the user's machine; however, servlets are installed on the server machine, such as an Internet Service Provider (ISP). Servlets are Java's answer to Common Gateway Interface (CGI) scripts that generate Web pages, and you'll see how to generate Web pages using servlets in this chapter.

We'll also take a look at another networking issue here. Novice Java programmers are frequently surprised to find that Java has no built-in way to submit an HTML form. In other words, Java lets you fill your Web pages with controls—as long as none of them is a Submit button, because you can't easily send data to CGI scripts from Java. I'll show how to submit data to HTML forms in this chapter.

There's one more issue to take a look at as well: security. As you know, you can't write files from an applet unless you make some special security arrangements, and we'll cover how that works in this chapter.

That's it for the overview of what's in this chapter. There's a great deal of material here, and it's time to turn to the "Immediate Solutions" section.

Immediate Solutions

Catching An Exception

"Darn," says the Novice Programmer, "my program just crashes when I divide by zero." "Well," you say, "it's pretty hard for Java to know what to do when you do that. Why not catch **ArithmeticException** exceptions and handle divisions by zero yourself?" The NP says, "Tell me more!"

You can use **try/catch** blocks to handle runtime errors, called *exceptions*. Exceptions are encapsulated into objects that extend the **Throwable** class. In fact, there's another kind of runtime error in Java that's built on the **Throwable** class—it's called **Error**. However, this type of error is serious and cannot be caught in code.

Here's the inheritance diagram for the **Throwable** class:

```
java.lang.Object
|____java.lang.Throwable
```

You'll find the constructors of the **Throwable** class in Table 24.1 and its methods in Table 24.2. Note, in particular, the **getMessage** method, which returns an error message you can display to the user, and the **toString** method, which lets you print out an exception object as part of a string, like this:

```
System.out.println("Exception: " + e)
```

Here, **e** is an exception object.

Table 24.1   Constructors of the *Throwable* class.

Constructor	Does This
Throwable( )	Constructs a new **Throwable** object.
Throwable(String message)	Constructs a new **Throwable** object with the indicated error message.

Table 24.2   Methods of the Throwable class.

Method	Does This
Throwable fillInStackTrace( )	Fills in the execution stack trace.
String getLocalizedMessage( )	Gets a localized description of this throwable object.
String getMessage( )	Gets the error message string of this throwable object.
void printStackTrace( )	Prints the stack trace to the standard error stream.
void printStackTrace(PrintStream s)	Prints the stack trace to the indicated print stream.
void printStackTrace(PrintWriter s)	Prints the stack trace to the indicated print writer.
String toString( )	Gets a short description of this throwable object.

Here's the inheritance diagram for the **Exception** class:

```
java.lang.Object
|____java.lang.Throwable
    |____java.lang.Exception
```

You'll find the constructors of the **Exception** class in Table 24.3.

Here's how you use a **try/catch** block in general:

```
try {
    // Sensitive code
}
catch (Exception1Type e1) {
    // Handle exception1 type
}
catch (Exception1Type e1) {
    // Handle exception1 type
}
    .
    .
    .
finally {
    // Code to be executed before try block ends
}
```

Table 24.3   Constructors of the Exception class.

Constructor	Does This
Exception( )	Constructs an **Exception** object.
Exception(String s)	Constructs an **Exception** object with the indicated detail message.

24. Exception Handling, Debugging, And Networking

When some sensitive code inside a **try** block throws an exception, you can catch it with a **catch** block. You can also use a **finally** block to execute code after the **try/catch** block is complete, and the code in the **finally** block will be executed whether or not an exception occurred. You can use a **finally** block to handle exceptions not explicitly caught in a **catch** block. There are many, many different types of exceptions in Java, and you'll find some of the exception classes in Table 24.4.

Here's one example of catching an exception. In this case, I'm catching an "array out of bounds" exception:

```java
class excep
{
    public static void main(String args[])
    {
        try {
            int array[] = new int[100];
            array[100] = 100;
        } catch (ArrayIndexOutOfBoundsException e) {
            System.out.println("Exception: " + e.getMessage());
            e.printStackTrace();
        }
    }
}
```

Table 24.4   Some Java exception classes.

AclNotFoundException	ActivationException	AlreadyBoundException
ApplicationException	ArithmeticException	ArrayIndexOutOfBoundsException
AWTException	BadLocationException	ClassNotFoundException
CloneNotSupportedException	DataFormatException	ExpandVetoException
FileException	GeneralSecurityException	IllegalAccessException
InstantiationException	InterruptedException	IntrospectionException
InvocationTargetException	IOException	LastOwnerException
NoninvertibleTransformException	NoSuchFieldException	NoSuchMethodException
NotBoundException	NotOwnerException	ParseException
PrinterException RemarshalException	PrivilegedActionException RuntimeException	PropertyVetoException ServerNotActiveException
SQLException	TooManyListenersException	UnsupportedFlavorException
UnsupportedLookAndFeelException	UserException	

When you run this example (excep.java on the CD accompanying this book), here's the result you get, which includes an error message and a stack trace that indicates where the exception occurred:

```
C:\>java excep
Exception: 100
java.lang.ArrayIndexOutOfBoundsException: 100
        at excep.main(excep.java:7)
```

You can also pass exceptions back to methods that called the current method by using the **throw** keyword. Here's an example in which I indicate that the **doWork** method can throw an exception of class **ArithmeticException**, which will be caught in the calling method (or, if not, by the default exception handler in Java), by specifying the **throw** keyword in the method's definition (note that if you use the **throw** keyword like this, you don't need a **try/catch** block in the method's body):

```
class excep2
{
    public static void main(String args[])
    {
        try {
            doWork();
        } catch (ArrayIndexOutOfBoundsException e) {
            System.out.println("Exception: " + e.getMessage());
            e.printStackTrace();
        }
    }

    static void doWork() throws ArithmeticException
    {
        int array[] = new int[100];
        array[100] = 100;
    }
}
```

Here's the result of this code (excep2.java on the CD). Note that the stack trace indicates that the exception occurred in the **doWork** method:

```
C:\>java excep2
Exception: 100
java.lang.ArrayIndexOutOfBoundsException: 100
        at excep2.doWork(excep2.java:16)
        at excep2.main(excep2.java:6)
```

Nesting **try** Statements

You can nest **try** blocks inside other **try** blocks. If one **try** block doesn't have a corresponding **catch** block that handles an exception, Java searches the next outer **try** block for a **catch** block that will handle the exception (and so on, back through the successive nestings). If Java can't find a **catch** block for the exception, it will pass the exception to its default exception handler. Here's an example of nested **try** blocks:

```
class nested
{
    public static void main(String args[])
    {
        try {
            try {
                int c[] = {0, 1, 2, 3};
                c[4] = 4;
            } catch(ArrayIndexOutOfBoundsException e) {
                System.out.println("Array index out of bounds: " + e);
            }

        } catch(ArithmeticException e) {
            System.out.println("Divide by zero: " + e);
        }
    }
}
```

Here's the result of this code (nested.java on the CD):

```
C:\>java nested
Array index out of bounds: java.lang.ArrayIndexOutOfBoundsException: 4
```

Throwing Exceptions

"That darn Johnson is at it again," says the Novice Programmer, "he's abusing my code." "Well," you say, "you can throw exceptions yourself in code if you want to." "Yes?" asks the NP. "Tell me more!"

You can throw your own exceptions with the **throw** statement. Here's an example in which I throw an exception that will be caught in a **catch** block that, in turn, throws the exception again to be caught in the calling method:

```
class thrower
{
    public static void main(String args[])
    {
        try {
            doWork();
        } catch(ArithmeticException e) {
            System.out.println("Caught in main" + e);
        }
    }

    static void doWork()
    {
        try {
            throw new ArithmeticException("exception!");
        } catch(ArithmeticException e) {
            System.out.println("Caught inside doWork " + e);
            throw e;
        }
    }
}
```

Here's the output of this code (thrower.java on the CD):

```
C:\>java thrower
Caught inside doWork java.lang.ArithmeticException: exception!
Caught in mainjava.lang.ArithmeticException: exception!
```

Note that you don't have to throw any of the predefined Java exceptions—you can define your own exceptions. See the next topic for the details.

Creating A Custom Exception

"Darn," says the Novice Programmer, "Java just doesn't have the exception I need to use." "What is it?" you ask. "The temperature-too-high exception," the NP says. "Hmm," you say, "how thoughtless of Java not to include that. However, you can create your own exception classes, so you're OK." "Great!" says the NP.

You can create your own exception classes by extending the **Exception** class—just provide a constructor and override the methods you plan to use, such as **getMessage** and **toString**. Here's an example:

```
class NewException extends Exception
{
    int value;

    NewException(int v)
    {
        value = v;
    }

    public String toString()
    {
        return "NewException " + value;
    }
}

class customexception
{
    public static void main(String args[])
    {
        try {
            doWork(3);
            doWork(2);
            doWork(1);
            doWork(0);
        }
        catch (NewException e) {
            System.out.println("Exception: " + e);
        }
    }

    static void doWork(int value) throws NewException
    {
        if(value == 0){
            throw new NewException(value);
        } else {
            System.out.println("No problem.");
        }
    }
}
```

24. Exception Handling, Debugging, And Networking

Here's the output of this example (customexception.java on the CD):

```
C:\>java customexception
No problem.
No problem.
No problem.
Exception: NewException 0
```

Debugging Java Programs

"Uh-oh," says the Novice Programmer, "I've got a logic problem in my code." "You mean a bug," you say. "I prefer to think of it as a logic problem," says the NP. "OK," you say, "either way, it's time to use the Java debugger."

The Java debugging tool is jdb, and you can use it much like you use the java tool, except jdb lets you single-step through your code, install breakpoints to stop execution at a particular line, and more. Here's an example in which I use the debugger on an application:

```java
public class app
{
    public static void main(String[] args)
    {
        int a = 1, b = 2, c = 3, d = 4;

        System.out.println("a = " + a);
        System.out.println("b = " + b);
        System.out.println("c = " + c);
        System.out.println("d = " + d);
    }
}
```

To start, I compile the application with the **-g** option, which makes Java include debugging information (it's not necessary to use **-g**, but the debugger will often suggest it if you don't use it):

```
C:\>javac -g -deprecation app.java
```

Now I start jdb just as I would the java tool. One of the best ways to see what's available in the Java debugger is to ask it to explain itself, which I do with the **help** command at the jbd prompt (see the highlighted line of code):

```
C:\>jdb app
Initializing jdb...
0xae:class(app)
> help
** command list **
threads [threadgroup]     -- list threads
thread <thread id>        -- set default thread
suspend [thread id(s)]    -- suspend threads (default: all)
resume [thread id(s)]     -- resume threads (default: all)
```

```
where [thread id] | all      -- dump a thread's stack
wherei [thread id] | all     -- dump a thread's stack, with pc info
threadgroups                 -- list threadgroups
threadgroup <name>           -- set current threadgroup
print <id> [id(s)]           -- print object or field
dump <id> [id(s)]            -- print all object information
locals                       -- print all local variables in current stack
classes                      -- list currently known classes
methods <class id>           -- list a class's methods
stop in <class id>.<method>[(argument_type,...)] -- set a breakpoint in
                                a method
stop at <class id>:<line>    -- set a breakpoint at a line
up [n frames]                -- move up a thread's stack
down [n frames]              -- move down a thread's stack
clear <class id>.<method>[(argument_type,...)]   -- clear a breakpoint
                                in a method
clear <class id>:<line>      -- clear a breakpoint at a line
step                         -- execute current line
step up                      -- execute until the current method returns
                                to its caller
stepi                        -- execute current instruction
next                         -- step one line (step OVER calls)
cont                         -- continue execution from breakpoint
catch <class id>             -- break for the specified exception
ignore <class id>            -- ignore when the specified exception
list [line number|method]    -- print source code
use [source file path]       -- display or change the source path
memory                       -- report memory usage
gc                           -- free unused objects
load classname               -- load Java class to be debugged
run <class> [args]           -- start execution of a loaded Java class
!!                           -- repeat last command
help (or ?)                  -- list commands
exit (or quit)               -- exit debugger
```

To debug, I first select a thread to work with. The **threads** command lists all available threads:

```
> threads
Group system:
 1.(java.lang.Thread)0xb1                                  Sig dispatcher    running
 2.(java.lang.ref.Reference$ReferenceHandler)0xb2 Ref Handler       cond. wait
 3.(java.lang.ref.Finalizer$FinalizerThread)0xb3  Finalizer         cond. wait
 4.(java.lang.Thread)0xb4                                  Debugger agent    running
 5.(sun.tools.agent.Handler)0xb5                           Breakpt handler   cond. wait
```

24. Exception Handling, Debugging, And Networking

```
6.(sun.tools.agent.StepHandler)0xb6              Step handler    cond. wait
Group main:
7.(java.lang.Thread)0xb7 main cond. waiting
```

I'll work with the main thread here, thread 7, which I specify with the thread command:

```
> thread 7
main[1]
```

The jdb prompt changes to **main[1]**, which indicates the current method and line. I then set a breakpoint in the main method like this:

```
main[1] stop in app.main
Breakpoint set in app.main
```

Now I can run the code with the **run** command, which will run and stop immediately because of the breakpoint. To find out where I am, I use the **list** command to list the code:

```
main[1] run
run app
running ...
main[1]
Breakpoint hit: app.main (app:5)
main[1] list
1          public class app
2          {
3              public static void main(String[] args)
4              {
5          =>         int a = 1, b = 2, c = 3, d = 4;
6
7                  System.out.println("a = " + a);
8                  System.out.println("b = " + b);
9                  System.out.println("c = " + c);
```

Now I can use the **next** command to single-step through the code, like this:

```
main[1] next
main[1] a = 1

Breakpoint hit: app.main (app:8)
main[1] next
main[1] b = 2
```

```
Breakpoint hit: app.main (app:9)
main[1] next
main[1] c = 3
```

As you can see, there are all kinds of debugging options. Try it yourself. The best way to learn how to use jdb is to put it to work.

Setting Applet Security Policies

"Hey," says the Novice Programmer, "why can't I write a file from an applet?" "Because of security," you say. "But you can change that if you really want to." "I do," says the NP, "but how do I do it?"

You can use the Java policy tool to change security settings. For example, you can allow applets to read and write files (normally they don't have access to files because when a user opens an applet in a browser, he or she might not expect you to start working with files on the system). Here's an example of an applet called writer.java that tries to write a file:

```java
import java.applet.Applet;
import java.awt.*;
import java.io.*;

/*
<APPLET
    CODE=writer.class
    WIDTH=300
    HEIGHT=200 >
</APPLET>
*/

public class writer extends Applet
{
    public void init()
    {
        byte data[] = "This is a string of text.".getBytes();

        try {
            FileOutputStream fileoutputstream = new
                FileOutputStream("file.txt");
            fileoutputstream.write(data);
            fileoutputstream.close();
```

```
        } catch (Exception e) {
            System.out.println("Error: " + e);
        }
    }
}
```

If you try to run this applet as it stands, you'll get a security violation error in the console window, and the applet won't start. However, you can change that with the policy tool, which lets you set security settings on an applet-by-applet and application-by-application basis.

NOTE: *You must be very careful when adjusting Java's security settings—don't leave yourself open to security problems.*

Start the policy tool now by typing "policytool" in the console window. The policy tool appears in Figure 24.1.

To add a new policy entry for writer.class, click the Add Policy Entry button in the policy tool, which opens the Policy Entry dialog box you see in Figure 24.2.

Enter the URL of the applet or application you want to set the security settings for (I'll use a file:// URL here, but of course you can specify HTTP:// URLs as well), and click the Add Permission button, which opens the Permissions dialog box you see in Figure 24.3.

In this case, we want to set the file-writing permission for writer.class, so select FilePermission, <<ALL FILES>>, and write, as shown in Figure 24.3 (you don't have to fill in the Signed By line unless the code has been digitally signed).

Now click OK to close the Permissions dialog box and click Done to close the Policy Entry dialog box. You'll see the new policy entry in the policy tool, as shown

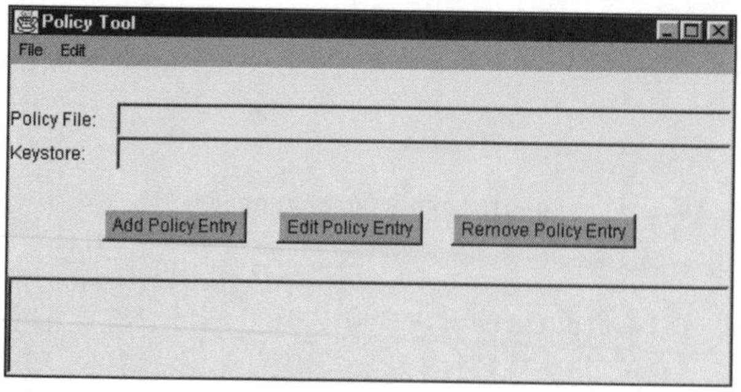

Figure 24.1   The policy tool.

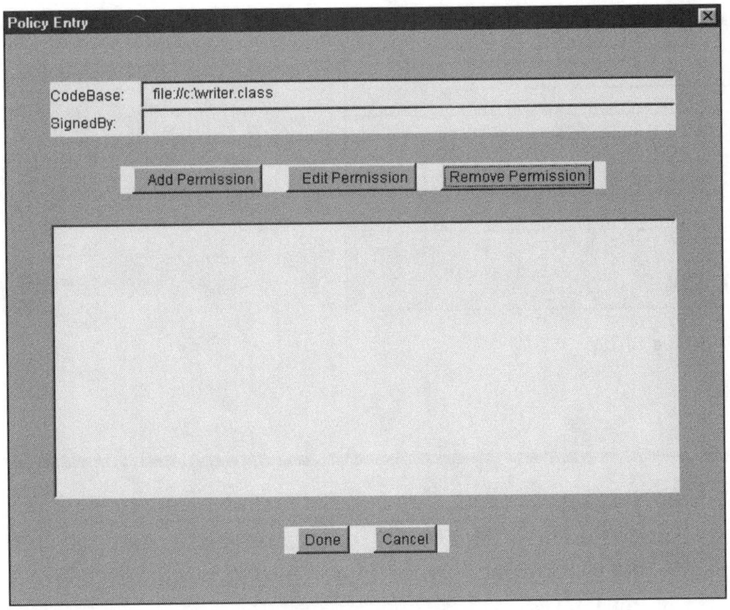

Figure 24.2   The Policy Entry dialog box.

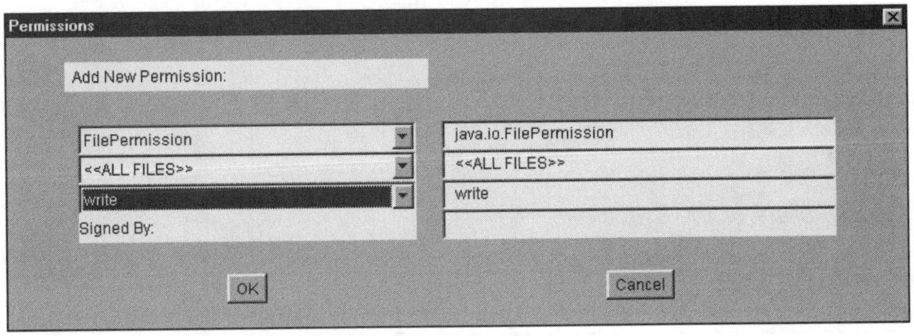

Figure 24.3   The Permissions dialog box.

in Figure 24.4. In addition, you must save the new policy entry in a file, and you do that with the Save As menu item in the File menu. I'll save the policy entry in the file c:\windows\.java.policy, as you can see in Figure 24.4.

That's all it takes. When you set the security policy for a program by providing that program's URL, you can grant all kinds of permissions to the program. In this case, the writer applet can now create file.txt and write this text to it:

```
This is a string of text.
```

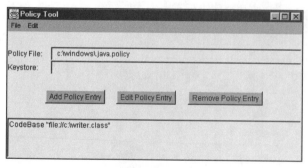

Figure 24.4   A new policy entry.

Using **URL** Objects

In Java, you handle URLs with the **URL** class—for example, you can pass a **URL** object to the **getImage** method of the **Applet** class to load in images. Here's the inheritance diagram for the **URL** class:

```
java.lang.Object
|____java.net.URL
```

You'll find the constructors of the **URL** class in Table 24.5 and its methods in Table 24.6.

Table 24.5   Constructors of the URL class.

Constructor	Does This
URL(String spec)	Constructs a **URL** object from a **String** object.
URL(String protocol, String host, int port, String file)	Constructs a **URL** object from the indicated protocol, host, port number, and file.
URL(String protocol, String host, int port, String file, URLStreamHandler handler)	Constructs a **URL** object from the indicated protocol, host, port number, file, and handler.
URL(String protocol, String host, String file)	Constructs an absolute URL from the indicated protocol name, host name, and file name.
URL(URL context, String spec)	Constructs a URL by parsing the specification **spec** within an indicated context.
URL(URL context, String spec, URL StreamHandler handler)	Constructs a URL by parsing the specification **spec** within an indicated context.

Table 24.6   Methods of the URL class.

Method	Does This
boolean equals(Object obj)	Compares two URLs.
Object getContent( )	Gets the contents of this URL.
String getFile( )	Gets the file name of this URL.
String getHost( )	Gets the host name of this URL, if applicable.
int getPort( )	Gets the port number of this URL.
String getProtocol( )	Gets the protocol name of this URL.
String getRef( )	Gets the anchor (also known as the *reference*) of this URL.
int hashCode( )	Constructs an integer suitable for hash table indexing.
URLConnection openConnection( )	Gets a **URLConnection** object that represents a connection to the remote object referred to by the URL.
InputStream openStream( )	Opens a connection to this URL and returns an **InputStream** for reading from that connection.
boolean sameFile(URL other)	Compares two URLs, excluding the "ref" fields.
protected void set(String protocol, String host, int port, String file, String ref)	Sets the fields of the URL.
static void setURLStreamHandler Factory(URLStreamHandlerFactory fac)	Sets an application's **URLStreamHandlerFactory**.
String toExternalForm( )	Constructs a string representation of this URL in standard URL form.
String toString( )	Constructs a string representation of this URL.

Here's an example that puts the **URL** class to work. In this case, I create a **URL** object for the Web page http://www.sun.com/worldwide/, and then use the **URL** class's methods to get various parts of the URL:

```
import java.net.*;

class URLs
{
    public static void main(String args[]) throws MalformedURLException
    {
        URL url = new URL("http://www.sun.com/worldwide/");

        System.out.println("URL protocol: " + url.getProtocol());
        System.out.println("Host name: " + url.getHost());
```

```
            System.out.println("File name: " + url.getFile());
            System.out.println("Ext:" + url.toExternalForm());
    }
}
```

Here's the output of this code (URLs.java on the CD):

```
C:\>java URLs
URL protocol: http
Host name: www.sun.com
File name: /worldwide/
Ext:http://www.sun.com/worldwide/
```

Using **URLConnection** Objects

"Hey," says the Novice Programmer, "why can't I download Web pages using the **URL** class?" You smile and say, "For that, you can use the **URLConnection** class."

You can use the **URLConnection** class to get a great deal of information about Web pages. Here's the inheritance diagram for this class:

```
java.lang.Object
|_____java.net.URLConnection
```

You'll find the fields of the **URLConnection** class in Table 24.7, its constructor in Table 24.8, and its methods in Table 24.9.

Table 24.7   Fields of the _URLConnection_ class.

Field	Does This
protected boolean allowUserInteraction	Returns True if this URL is being examined in a context in which it can support user interactions.
protected boolean connected	Returns False if this connection object has not created a link to the indicated URL.
protected boolean doInput	Set by the **setDoInput** method.
protected boolean doOutput	Set by the **setDoOutput** method.
protected long ifModifiedSince	Some protocols skip the fetching of the object unless the object has been modified recently.
protected URL url	Represents the remote object on the World Wide Web to which this connection is opened.
protected boolean useCaches	Returns True if the protocol is allowed to use caching.

Table 24.8   The constructor of the URLConnection class.

Constructor	Does This
protected URLConnection(URL url)	Constructs a URL connection to the indicated URL.

Table 24.9   Methods of the URLConnection class.

Method	Does This
abstract void connect( )	Opens a link to the resource referenced by this URL.
boolean getAllowUserInteraction( )	Gets the value of the **allowUserInteraction** field for this object.
Object getContent( )	Gets the contents of this URL connection.
String getContentEncoding( )	Gets the value of the content-encoding header field.
int getContentLength( )	Gets the value of the content-length header field.
String getContentType( )	Gets the value of the content-type header field.
long getDate( )	Gets the value of the date header field.
static boolean getDefaultAllow UserInteraction( )	Gets the default value of the **allowUserInteraction** field.
static String getDefaultRequest Property(String key)	Gets the value of the default request property.
boolean getDefaultUseCaches( )	Gets the default value of a **URLConnection**'s **useCaches** flag.
boolean getDoInput( )	Gets the value of this **URLConnection**'s **doInput** flag.
boolean getDoOutput( )	Gets the value of this **URLConnection**'s **doOutput** flag.
long getExpiration( )	Gets the value of the expires header field.
static FileNameMap getFileNameMap( )	Gets the **FileNameMap**.
String getHeaderField(int n)	Gets the value for the *n*th header field.
String getHeaderField(String name)	Gets the name of the indicated header field.
long getHeaderFieldDate(String name, long Default)	Gets the value of the named field parsed as a date.
int getHeaderFieldInt(String name, int Default)	Gets the value of the named field parsed as a number.
String getHeaderFieldKey(int n)	Gets the key for the *n*th header field.
long getIfModifiedSince( )	Gets the value of this object's **ifModifiedSince** field.
InputStream getInputStream( )	Gets an input stream that reads from this open connection.
long getLastModified( )	Gets the value of the last-modified header field.
OutputStream getOutputStream( )	Gets an output stream that writes to this connection.

(continued)

Table 24.9   Methods of the URLConnection class (continued).

Method	Does This
Permission getPermission( )	Gets a permission object representing the permission necessary to make the connection represented by this object.
String getRequestProperty(String key)	Gets the value of the named general request property for this connection.
URL getURL( )	Gets the value of this **URLConnection**'s **URL** field.
boolean getUseCaches( )	Gets the value of this **URLConnection**'s **useCaches** field.
protected static String guessContent TypeFromName(String fname)	Determines the content type of an object.
static String guessContentTypeFrom Stream(InputStream is)	Determines the type of an input stream.
void setAllowUserInteraction(boolean allowuserinteraction)	Sets the value of the **allowUserInteraction** field of this **URLConnection**.
static void setContentHandlerFactory (ContentHandlerFactory fac)	Sets the **ContentHandlerFactory** of an application.
static void setDefaultAllowUser Interaction(boolean defaultallowuserinteraction)	Sets the default value of the **allowUserInteraction** field.
static void setDefaultRequestProperty (String key, String value)	Sets the default value of a general request property.
void setDefaultUseCaches(boolean defaultusecaches)	Sets the default value of the **useCaches** field.
void setDoInput(boolean doinput)	Sets the value of the **doInput** field for this **URLConnection**.
void setDoOutput(boolean dooutput)	Sets the value of the **doOutput** field for this **URLConnection**.
static void setFileNameMap(File NameMap map)	Sets the **FileNameMap**.
void setIfModifiedSince(long ifmodifiedsince)	Sets the value of the **ifModifiedSince** field.
void setRequestProperty(String key, String value)	Sets the general request property.
void setUseCaches(boolean usecaches)	Sets the value of the **useCaches** field.
String toString( )	Gets a **String** representation of this object.

Here's an example in which I check on a fictitious URL: **http://www.yourserver.com/user/index.html**. Here's the code (note that I can use the **getInputStream** method to actually get the Web page content):

```
import java.io.*;
import java.net.*;
import java.util.Date;

class URLConnections
{
    public static void main(String args[]) throws Exception
    {
        int character;
        URL url = new URL("http://www.yourserver.com/user/index.html");
        URLConnection urlconnection = url.openConnection();

        System.out.println("Content type: " +
            urlconnection.getContentType());
        System.out.println("Document date: " +
            new Date(urlconnection.getDate()));
        System.out.println("Last modified: " +
            new Date(urlconnection.getLastModified()));
        System.out.println("Document expires: " +
            urlconnection.getExpiration());

        int contentlength = urlconnection.getContentLength();

        System.out.println("Content length: " + contentlength);

        if (contentlength > 0) {
            InputStream in = urlconnection.getInputStream();

            while ((character = in.read()) != -1) {
                System.out.print((char) character);
            }

            in.close();
        }
    }
}
```

This example is in URLConnections.java on the CD. If you use it, make sure you specify a URL in the code.

Creating And Using Sockets

"OK," says the Novice Programmer, "I want to start working with the Internet up close and personal." "Are you sure?" you ask. "Sure I'm sure," says the NP. "In that case," you say, "check out the **Socket** class."

Communication over the Internet involves *sockets* for creating connections. Sockets connect to numbered communication ports. The bottom 1,024 ports are reserved for system use (for example, port 21 is for FTP, 23 is for telnet, 25 is for email, 80 is for HTTP connections, and 119 is for Usenet connections). Java supports sockets with the **Socket** class. Here's the inheritance diagram for the **Socket** class:

```
java.lang.Object
|____java.net.Socket
```

You'll find the constructors of the **Socket** class in Table 24.10 and its methods in Table 24.11.

Table 24.10   Constructors of the *Socket* class.

Constructor	Does This
protected Socket( )	Constructs an unconnected socket.
Socket(InetAddress address, int port)	Constructs a stream socket and connects it to the indicated port number at the indicated IP address.
Socket(InetAddress host, int port, boolean stream)	Deprecated. Use **DatagramSocket** instead.
Socket(InetAddress address, int port, InetAddress localAddr, int localPort)	Constructs a socket and connects it to the indicated remote address on the indicated remote port.
protected Socket(SocketImpl impl)	Constructs an unconnected socket using the abstract **SocketImpl** class.
Socket(String host, int port)	Constructs a stream socket and connects it to the indicated port number on the named host.
Socket(String host, int port, boolean stream)	Deprecated. Use **DatagramSocket** instead.
Socket(String host, int port, InetAddress localAddr, int localPort)	Constructs a socket and connects it to the indicated remote host on the indicated remote port.

Table 24.11   Methods of the *Socket* class.

Method	Does This
void close( )	Closes this socket.
InetAddress getInetAddress( )	Gets the address to which the socket is connected.
InputStream getInputStream( )	Gets an input stream for this socket.
InetAddress getLocalAddress( )	Gets the local address to which the socket is bound.
int getLocalPort( )	Gets the local port to which this socket is bound.
OutputStream getOutputStream( )	Gets an output stream for this socket.
int getPort( )	Gets the remote port to which this socket is connected.
int getReceiveBufferSize( )	Gets value of the **SO_RCVBUF** option for this socket (the buffer size used for input).
int getSendBufferSize( )	Gets value of the **SO_SNDBUF** option for this socket (the buffer size used for output).
int getSoLinger( )	Gets setting for **SO_LINGER**.
int getSoTimeout( )	Gets setting for **SO_TIMEOUT**.
boolean getTcpNoDelay( )	Tests whether **TCP_NODELAY** is enabled.
void setReceiveBufferSize(int size)	Sets the **SO_RCVBUF** option to the indicated value.
void setSendBufferSize(int size)	Sets the **SO_SNDBUF** option to the indicated value.
static void setSocketImplFactory (SocketImplFactory fac)	Sets the client socket implementation factory.
void setSoLinger(boolean on, int linger)	Enables/disables **SO_LINGER** with the indicated time in seconds.
void setSoTimeout(int timeout)	Enables/disables **SO_TIMEOUT** with the indicated timeout, in milliseconds.
void setTcpNoDelay(boolean on)	Enables/disables **TCP_NODELAY**.
String toString( )	Converts this socket to a String.

24. Exception Handling, Debugging, And Networking

Here's an example. In this case, I'll connect to port 80 at sun.com, the HTTP port, and get the main Web page at www.sun.com, index.html, by writing an HTTP **GET** request to that port. To write to a socket, you can use a **PrintWriter** object, and to read from it, you use a **BufferedReader** object. Here's what the code looks like (note that I terminate the HTTP request with two newline characters):

```
import java.io.*;
import java.net.*;
```

```
public class sockets
{
    public static void main(String[] args)
    {
        try {
            Socket s = new Socket("www.sun.com", 80);

            BufferedReader in = new BufferedReader(new
                InputStreamReader(s.getInputStream()));
            PrintWriter out = new PrintWriter(s.getOutputStream());

            out.print("GET /index.html\n\n");
            out.flush();

            String line;

            while ((line = in.readLine()) != null){
                System.out.println(line);
            }

        } catch (Exception e){}
    }
}
```

Here's the output of this code (sockets.java on the CD):

```
C:\>java sockets
<!DOCTYPE HTML PUBLIC "-//W3C//DTD HTML 4.0 Transitional//EN"
"http://www.w3.org
/TR/REC-html40/loose.dtd">
<HTML>
<HEAD>
<TITLE>Sun Microsystems</TITLE>
    .
    .
    .
```

This example used the Sun Web server's HTTP port to connect to. However, you can create both sides of the connection—the client and the server—in Java. See the next topic.

Creating TCP Clients And Servers

The Big Boss appears and says, "We need a secret way of communicating over the Internet for our spies in the field." "We have spies?" you ask. The BB says, "Set up a client/server program that can communicate over the Internet and make sure you scramble everything." You say, "Hmm."

Using **BufferedReader** and **PrintWriter** objects, you can communicate over the Internet with sockets—all you need is a Domain Name System (DNS) address for the server and a free port on that server (DNS addresses are those groups of four numbers, separated by dots, that specify Internet addresses).

Here's an example. In this case, I'll set up a client program that connects to a server program, sends a message, and gets a message back. In this case, I'll use the DNS 127.0.0.1 (the local host), which means that both the server and the client will be on the same machine. However, you can use any DNS you like as long as you place the server script on the corresponding machine. I'll use an arbitrary port—number 8765. When you're picking a port number, remember that the port cannot be in use and that both the client and server will connect to the same port. Here's the client application, which sends the message "Hello!" to the server and reads what the server sends back:

```java
import java.net.*;
import java.io.*;

class client
{
    public static void main(String args[]) throws Exception
    {
        int character;
        Socket socket = new Socket("127.0.0.1", 8765);

        InputStream in = socket.getInputStream();
        OutputStream out = socket.getOutputStream();

        String string = "Hello!\n";
        byte buffer[] = string.getBytes();
        out.write(buffer);

        while ((character = in.read()) != -1) {
            System.out.print((char) character);
        }
        socket.close();
    }
}
```

Here's the server application, which reads the message from the client and returns it, after prefacing it with the text "The server got this: ":

```java
import java.io.*;
import java.net.*;

public class server
{
    public static void main(String[] args )
    {
        try {
            ServerSocket socket = new ServerSocket(8765);

            Socket insocket = socket.accept( );

            BufferedReader in = new BufferedReader (new
                InputStreamReader(insocket.getInputStream()));
            PrintWriter out = new PrintWriter (insocket.getOutputStream(),
                true);

            String instring = in.readLine();
            out.println("The server got this: " + instring);
            insocket.close();
        }
        catch (Exception e) {}
    }
}
```

To run these applications, you'll need two console windows (for example, in Windows, open two DOS windows). Run the server first in one window, and then the client in the other. When you do, here's what the client reports:

```
C:\>java client
The server got this: Hello!
```

As you can see, the client sent its message to the server, which sent a confirming message back. These applications are client.java and server.java on the CD. Now you're writing Internet client/server applications in Java.

Submitting An HTML Form From Java

"Java's gone all wacky again" the Novice Programmer says. "I've got lots of bells and whistles in my program, but I can't seem to submit an HTML form to the server." "That's because this is Java, not JavaScript," you say, "but there is a way—using sockets."

Many programmers expect that Java has some method of submitting HTML forms, but there's no such method built in. On the other hand, you can create your own technique using sockets and connecting to a Web server's port 80 (the HTTP port). Here's an example in which I submit data to a Perl script, reg.cgi, which lets me register users online by recording their names and email addresses in a file named reg.log:

```perl
#!/usr/local/bin/perl

use CGI;

$co = new CGI;

print $co->header,

$co->start_html(
    -title=>'CGI Example',
    -author=>'Steve',
    -meta=>{'keywords'=>'CGI Perl'},
    -BGCOLOR=>'white',
    -LINK=>'red'
);

if ($co->param()) {
    $! = 0;

    open FILEHANDLE, ">>reg.log";

    print FILEHANDLE "Date: " . `date`;
    print FILEHANDLE "Name: " . $co->param('name') . "\n";
    print FILEHANDLE "email: " . $co->param('email') . "\n";

    close FILEHANDLE;

    unless ($!) {
        print "Thanks for registering.";
    } else {
```

```
        print "Sorry, there was an error: $!";
    }
}
```

```
print $co->end_html;
```

I pass two parameters to this CGI script: name and email. I do that by appending a string beginning with a question mark to the end of this script's URL, making the parameters look like this:

```
?name=Steve&email=me@here
```

Note that you can handle spaces in the parameter's values by using a plus sign (+) instead of a space. To pass this string to reg.cgi, I use an HTTP **GET** request, like this:

```java
import java.io.*;
import java.net.*;

public class reg
{
    public static void main(String[] args)
    {
        try {
            Socket s = new Socket("www.yourserver.com", 80);

            BufferedReader in = new BufferedReader(new
                InputStreamReader(s.getInputStream()));
            PrintWriter out = new PrintWriter(s.getOutputStream());

            out.print("GET " +
                "/yourname/cgi/reg.cgi?name=Steve&email=me@here\n\n");
            out.flush();

            String line;

            while ((line = in.readLine()) != null){
                System.out.println(line);
            }

        } catch (Exception e){}
    }
}
```

That's all it takes. This effectively calls the URL **http://www.yourserver.com/ /yourname/cgi/reg.cgi?name=Steve&email=me@here**. This is how you send data to an HTML form. When you install reg.cgi on the server (using your server name and the correct URL for the script) and run this program (reg.java on the CD), you'll get a confirming Web page back from reg.cgi, which reg.java prints out:

```
C:\>java reg
<!DOCTYPE HTML PUBLIC "-//IETF//DTD HTML//EN">
<HTML><HEAD><TITLE>CGI Example</TITLE>
<LINK REV=MADE HREF="mailto:Steve">
<META NAME="keywords" CONTENT="CGI Perl">
</HEAD><BODY BGCOLOR="white" LINK="red">
Thanks for registering.
</BODY></HTML>
```

That's it. Now you can submit an HTML form from Java.

Using Java Database Connectivity (JDBC)

The Big Boss appears and says, "We need to connect to an ODBC data source." "Good luck," you say. "Not a good answer," the BB says. "Your code is due tomorrow."

You can use Java Database Connectivity (JDBC), as supported by the java.sql package, to connect to a database data source, such as an ODBC data source. Here's the way it works: You get a connection to a data source using an object that implements the **Connection** interface, execute a SQL statement on the data source using an object that implements the **Statement** interface, and get a result sent back from the data source as an object that implements the **ResultSet** interface.

You'll find the fields of the **Connection** interface in Table 24.12 and its methods in Table 24.13, the methods of the **Statement** interface in Table 24.14, and the fields of the **ResultSet** interface in Table 24.15 and its methods in Table 24.16.

*Table 24.12 Fields of the **Connection** interface.*

Field	Does This
static int TRANSACTION_NONE	Indicates that transactions are not supported.
static int TRANSACTION_READ _COMMITTED	Partial reads are prevented; nonrepeatable reads and phantom reads can occur.

(continued)

Table 24.12   Fields of the *Connection* interface (continued).

Field	Does This
static int TRANSACTION_READ _UNCOMMITTED	Partial reads, nonrepeatable reads, and phantom reads can occur.
static int TRANSACTION _REPEATABLE_READ	Partial reads and nonrepeatable reads are prevented; phantom reads can occur.
static int TRANSACTION _SERIALIZABLE	Partial reads, nonrepeatable reads and phantom reads are prevented.

Table 24.13   Methods of the *Connection* interface.

Method	Does This
void clearWarnings( )	Clears all warnings.
void close( )	Releases a connection's database and JDBC resources.
void commit( )	Makes all changes made since the previous commit/rollback.
Statement createStatement( )	Constructs a **Statement** object for sending SQL statements to the database.
Statement createStatement(int result SetType, int resultSetConcurrency)	Constructs a **Statement** object that will generate **ResultSet** objects.
boolean getAutoCommit( )	Gets the current autocommit state.
String getCatalog( )	Gets the connection's current catalog name.
DatabaseMetaData getMetaData( )	Gets the metadata regarding this connection's database.
int getTransactionIsolation( )	Gets this connection's current transaction isolation level.
Map getTypeMap( )	Gets the type map object associated with this connection.
SQLWarning getWarnings( )	Gets the first warning reported by calls on this connection.
boolean isClosed( )	Tests to see whether a connection is closed.
boolean isReadOnly( )	Tests to see whether the connection is in read-only mode.
String nativeSQL(String sql)	Converts the given SQL statement into the system's native SQL grammar.
CallableStatement prepareCall (String sql)	Constructs a **CallableStatement** object for stored procedures.
CallableStatement prepareCall (String sql, int resultSetType, int result SetConcurrency)	Constructs a **CallableStatement** object that will generate **ResultSet** objects.
PreparedStatement prepareStatement (String sql)	Constructs a **PreparedStatement** object for sending parameterized SQL statements to the database.

(continued)

Table 24.13   ***Methods of the Connection interface*** (continued).

Method	Does This
PreparedStatement prepareStatement (String sql, int resultSetType, int result SetConcurrency)	Constructs a **PreparedStatement** object that will generate **ResultSet** objects.
void rollback( )	Discards all changes made since the previous commit/rollback.
void setAutoCommit (boolean autoCommit)	Sets this connection's autocommit mode.
void setCatalog(String catalog)	Sets a catalog name in the database.
void setReadOnly(boolean readOnly)	Makes this connection read-only.
void setTransactionIsolation(int level)	Attempts to change the transaction isolation level.
void setTypeMap(Map map)	Installs the given type map.

Table 24.14   ***Methods of the Statement interface.***

Method	Does This
void addBatch(String sql)	Adds a SQL command to the current batch of commands.
void cancel( )	Cancels this **Statement** object.
void clearBatch( )	Empties the set of commands in the current batch.
void clearWarnings( )	Clears all warnings.
void close( )	Closes this **Statement** object's database and JDBC resources.
boolean execute(String sql)	Executes a SQL statement that may return multiple results.
int[] executeBatch( )	Submits a batch of commands to the database for execution.
ResultSet executeQuery(String sql)	Executes a SQL statement that returns a single **ResultSet**.
int executeUpdate(String sql)	Executes a SQL **INSERT**, **UPDATE**, or **DELETE** statement.
Connection getConnection( )	Gets the **Connection** object that produced this **Statement** object.
int getFetchDirection( )	Gets the direction for fetching rows from database tables.
int getFetchSize( )	Gets the number of result set rows that's the default fetch size.
int getMaxFieldSize( )	Gets the maximum number of bytes allowed for column values.
int getMaxRows( )	Gets the maximum number of rows for a **ResultSet**.
boolean getMoreResults( )	Moves to a statement's next result.
int getQueryTimeout( )	Gets the number of seconds the driver will wait for a statement to execute.
ResultSet getResultSet( )	Gets the current result as a **ResultSet** object.

(continued)

24. Exception Handling, Debugging, And Networking

Table 24.14 Methods of the *Statement* interface (continued).

Method	Does This
int getResultSetConcurrency( )	Gets the result set concurrency.
int getResultSetType( )	Gets the result set type.
int getUpdateCount( )	Gets the current result as an update count. If the result is a **ResultSet** or there are no more results, -1 is returned.
SQLWarning getWarnings( )	Gets the first warning reported by calls on this statement.
void setCursorName(String name)	Defines the SQL cursor name.
void setEscapeProcessing (boolean enable)	Turns escape processing on or off.
void setFetchDirection(int direction)	Sets the fetch direction.
void setFetchSize(int rows)	Sets the number of rows that should be fetched when more rows are needed.
void setMaxFieldSize(int max)	Sets the limit for the maximum number of bytes in a column.
void setMaxRows(int max)	Sets the limit for the maximum number of rows that any **ResultSet** can contain.
void setQueryTimeout(int seconds)	Sets the number of seconds the driver will wait for a statement to execute.

Table 24.15 Fields of the *ResultSet* interface.

Field	Does This
static int CONCUR_READ_ONLY	Concurrency mode for objects that may not be updated.
static int CONCUR_UPDATABLE	Concurrency mode for a **ResultSet** object that may be updated.
static int FETCH_FORWARD	Indicates that rows will be processed first to last.
static int FETCH_REVERSE	Indicates that rows in a result set will be processed last to first.
static int FETCH_UNKNOWN	Indicates that the order in which rows in a result set will be processed is unknown.
static int TYPE_FORWARD_ONLY	Indicates that a cursor may move only forward.
static int TYPE_SCROLL_INSENSITIVE	Indicates that a **ResultSet** object is scrollable but not sensitive to changes made by others.
static int TYPE_SCROLL_SENSITIVE	Indicates that a **ResultSet** object is scrollable and sensitive to changes made by others.

Table 24.16   Methods of the *ResultSet* interface.

Method	Does This
boolean absolute(int row)	Moves to an absolute row.
void afterLast( )	Moves after the last record.
void beforeFirst( )	Moves before the first record.
void cancelRowUpdates( )	Cancels the updates made to a row.
void clearWarnings( )	Clears all warnings.
void close( )	Closes this **ResultSet** object's database and JDBC resources.
void deleteRow( )	Deletes the current row from the result set and the underlying database.
int findColumn(String columnName)	Maps the given **ResultSet** column name to its **ResultSet** column index.
boolean first( )	Moves to the first record.
Array getArray(int i)	Gets a SQL **ARRAY** value from the current row of this **ResultSet** object.
Array getArray(String colName)	Gets a SQL **ARRAY** value in the current row of this **ResultSet** object.
InputStream getAsciiStream (int columnIndex)	Gets the value of a column in the current row as a stream of ASCII characters.
InputStream getAsciiStream (String columnName)	Gets the value of a column in the current row as a stream of ASCII characters.
BigDecimal getBigDecimal (int columnIndex)	Gets the value of a column in the current row as a **java.math.BigDecimal** object with full precision.
BigDecimal getBigDecimal (int columnIndex, int scale)	Deprecated.
BigDecimal getBigDecimal (String columnName)	Gets the value of a column in the current row as a **java.math.BigDecimal** object with full precision.
BigDecimal getBigDecimal (String columnName, int scale)	Deprecated.
InputStream getBinaryStream (int columnIndex)	Gets the value of a column in the current row as a stream of uninterpreted bytes.
InputStream getBinaryStream (String columnName)	Gets the value of a column in the current row as a stream of uninterpreted bytes.
Blob getBlob(int i)	Gets a BLOB (Binary Large Object) value in the current row of this **ResultSet** object.

(continued)

Table 24.16   Methods of the *ResultSet* interface (continued).

Method	Does This
Blob getBlob(String colName)	Gets a BLOB value in the current row of this **ResultSet** object.
boolean getBoolean(int columnIndex)	Gets the value of a column in the current row as a Java boolean.
boolean getBoolean (String columnName)	Gets the value of a column in the current row as a Java boolean.
byte getByte(int columnIndex)	Gets the value of a column in the current row as a Java byte.
byte getByte(String columnName)	Gets the value of a column in the current row as a Java byte.
byte[ ] getBytes(int columnIndex)	Gets the value of a column in the current row as a Java byte array.
byte[ ] getBytes(String columnName)	Gets the value of a column in the current row as a Java byte array.
Reader getCharacterStream (int columnIndex)	Gets a character stream by column index.
Reader getCharacterStream (String columnName)	Gets a character stream by column name.
Clob getClob(int i)	Gets a CLOB (Character Large Object) value in the current row of this **ResultSet** object.
Clob getClob(String colName)	Gets a CLOB value in the current row of this **ResultSet** object.
int getConcurrency( )	Gets the concurrency mode of this result set.
String getCursorName( )	Gets the name of the SQL cursor used by this **ResultSet**.
Date getDate(int columnIndex)	Gets the value of a column in the current row as a **java.sql.Date** object.
Date getDate(int columnIndex, Calendar cal)	Gets the value of a column in the current row as a **java.sql.Date** object.
Date getDate(String columnName)	Gets the value of a column in the current row as a **java.sql.Date** object.
Date getDate(String columnName, Calendar cal)	Gets the value of a column in the current row as a **java.sql.Date** object.
double getDouble(int columnIndex)	Gets the value of a column in the current row as a Java double.
double getDouble(String columnName)	Gets the value of a column in the current row as a Java double.
int getFetchDirection( )	Gets the fetch direction for this result set.
int getFetchSize( )	Gets the fetch size for this result set.
float getFloat(int columnIndex)	Gets the value of a column in the current row as a Java float.
float getFloat(String columnName)	Gets the value of a column in the current row as a Java float.
int getInt(int columnIndex)	Gets the value of a column in the current row as a Java int.

(continued)

Table 24.16   Methods of the *ResultSet* interface (continued).

Method	Does This
int getInt(String columnName)	Gets the value of a column in the current row as a Java int.
long getLong(int columnIndex)	Gets the value of a column in the current row as a Java long.
long getLong(String columnName)	Gets the value of a column in the current row as a Java long.
ResultSetMetaData getMetaData( )	Gets the number, types, and properties of a **ResultSet**'s columns.
Object getObject(int columnIndex)	Gets the value of a column in the current row as a Java object.
Object getObject(int i, Map map)	Gets the value of a column in the current row as a Java object.
Object getObject(String columnName)	Gets the value of a column in the current row as a Java object.
Object getObject (String colName, Map map)	Gets the value in the indicated column as a Java object.
Ref getRef(int i)	Gets a reference column value from the current row.
Ref getRef(String colName)	Gets a reference column value from the current row based on a column name.
int getRow( )	Gets a row.
short getShort(int columnIndex)	Gets the value of a column in the current row as a Java short.
short getShort(String columnName)	Gets the value of a column in the current row as a Java short.
Statement getStatement( )	Gets the statement that produced this **ResultSet** object.
String getString(int columnIndex)	Gets the value of a column in the current row as a Java string.
String getString(String columnName)	Gets the value of a column in the current row as a Java string.
Time getTime(int columnIndex)	Gets the value of a column in the current row as a **java.sql.Time** object.
Time getTime(int columnIndex,	Gets the value of a column in the current row as a **java.sql.Time** object.
Time getTime(String columnName)	Gets the value of a column in the current row as a **java.sql.Time** object.
Time getTime(String columnName, Calendar cal)	Gets the value of a column in the current row as a **java.sql.Time** object.
Timestamp getTimestamp(int columnIndex)	Gets the value of a column in the current row as a **java.sql.Timestamp** object.
Timestamp getTimestamp(int Calendar cal)	Gets the value of a column in the current row as a columnIndex, **java.sql.Timestamp** object.
Timestamp getTimestamp (String columnName)	Gets the value of a column in the current row as a **java.sql.Timestamp** object.

(continued)

Table 24.16 Methods of the *ResultSet* interface (continued).

Method	Does This
Timestamp getTimestamp(String Calendar cal)	Gets the value of a column in the current row as a columnName, **java.sql.Timestamp** object.
int getType( )	Gets the type of this result set.
InputStream getUnicodeStream (int columnIndex)	Deprecated.
InputStream getUnicodeStream (String columnName)	Deprecated.
SQLWarning getWarnings( )	Gets the first warning reported by calls on this **ResultSet**.
void insertRow( )	Inserts the contents of the insert row into the result set and the database.
boolean isAfterLast( )	Returns True if currently after the last record.
boolean isBeforeFirst( )	Returns True if currently before the first record.
boolean isFirst( )	Returns True if the current record is the first record.
boolean isLast( )	Returns True if the current record is the last record.
boolean last( )	Moves to the last record.
void moveToCurrentRow( )	Moves the cursor to the remembered cursor position, usually the current row.
void moveToInsertRow( )	Moves the cursor to the insert row.
boolean next( )	Moves the cursor down one row from its current position.
boolean previous( )	Moves to the previous record.
void refreshRow( )	Refreshes the current row with its most recent value in the database.
boolean relative(int rows)	Moves relative to the current position.
boolean rowDeleted( )	Indicates whether a row has been deleted.
boolean rowInserted( )	Indicates whether the current row has had an insertion.
boolean rowUpdated( )	Indicates whether the current row has been updated.
void setFetchDirection(int direction)	Gives a hint as to the direction in which the rows in this result set will be processed.
void setFetchSize(int rows)	Sets the number of rows that should be fetched from the database when more rows are needed.
void updateAsciiStream(int column Index, InputStream x, int length)	Updates a column with an ASCII stream value.

(continued)

Table 24.16   Methods of the ResultSet interface (continued).

Method	Does This
void updateAsciiStream(String column Name, InputStream x, int length)	Updates a column with an ASCII stream value based on a column name.
void updateBigDecimal(int column Index, BigDecimal x)	Updates a column with a **BigDecimal** value.
void updateBigDecimal(String column Name, BigDecimal x)	Updates a column with a **BigDecimal** value based on a column name.
void updateBinaryStream(int column Index, InputStream x, int length)	Updates a column with a binary stream value.
void updateBinaryStream(String columnName, InputStream x, int length)	Updates a column with a binary stream value based on a column name.
void updateBoolean(int columnIndex, boolean x)	Updates a column with a boolean value.
void updateBoolean(String column Name, boolean x)	Updates a column with a boolean value based on a column name.
void updateByte(int columnIndex, byte x)	Updates a column with a byte value.
void updateByte(String column Name, byte x)	Updates a column with a byte value based on a column name.
void updateBytes(int columnIndex, byte[ ] x)	Updates a column with a byte array value.
void updateBytes(String column Name, byte[ ] x)	Updates a column with a byte array value based on a column name.
void updateCharacterStream(int columnIndex, Reader x, int length)	Updates a column with a character stream value.
void updateCharacterStream(String columnName, Reader reader, int length)	Updates a column with a character stream value based on a column name.
void updateDate(int columnIndex, Date x)	Updates a column with a date value.
void updateDate(String column Name, Date x)	Updates a column with a date value based on a column name.
void updateDouble(int columnIndex, double x)	Updates a column with a double value.

(continued)

Table 24.16   Methods of the ResultSet interface (continued).

Method	Does This
void updateDouble(String column Name, double x)	Updates a column with a double value based on a column name.
void updateFloat(int columnIndex, float x)	Updates a column with a float value.
void updateFloat(String columnName, float x)	Updates a column with a float value based on a column name.
void updateInt(int columnIndex, int x)	Updates a column with an integer value.
void updateInt(String column Name, int x)	Updates a column with an integer value based on a column name.
void updateLong(int columnIndex, long x)	Updates a column with a long value.
void updateLong(String column Name, long x)	Updates a column with a long value based on a column name.
void updateNull(int columnIndex)	Gives a "nullable" column a null value.
void updateNull(String columnName)	Updates a column with a null value.
void updateObject(int columnIndex, Object x)	Updates a column with an object value.
void updateObject(int columnIndex, Object x, int scale)	Updates a column with an object value using a scale.
void updateObject(String column Name, Object x)	Updates a column with an object value based on a column name.
void updateObject(String column Name, Object x, int scale)	Updates a column with an object value based on a column name, using a scale.
void updateRow( )	Updates the underlying database with the new contents of the current row.
void updateShort(int columnIndex, short x)	Updates a column with a short value.
void updateShort(String column Name, short x)	Updates a column with a short value based on a column name.
void updateString(int columnIndex, String x)	Updates a column with a string value.
void updateString(String column Name, String x)	Updates a column with a string value based on a column name.

(continued)

Table 24.16   Methods of the *ResultSet* interface (continued).

Method	Does This
void updateTime(int columnIndex, Time x)	Updates a column with a time value.
void updateTime(String column Name, Time x)	Updates a column with a time value based on a column name.
void updateTimestamp(int column Index, Timestamp x)	Updates a column with a timestamp value.
void updateTimestamp(String column Name, Timestamp x)	Updates a column with a timestamp value based on a column name.
boolean wasNull( )	Indicates whether the last column read had a value of Null.

Here's an example in which I use an ODBC data source named students that has a table named Students, which has Name and Grade fields for a number of students:

```
Name     Grade
- - - - - - - - - - - - - -
| Ann   |   C   |
|------ |------ |
| Mark  |   B   |
|------ |------ |
| Ed    |   A   |
|------ |------ |
| Frank |   A   |
|------ |------ |
| Ted   |   A   |
|------ |------ |
| Mabel |   B   |
|------ |------ |
| Ralph |   B   |
|------ |------ |
| Tom   |   B   |
- - - - - - - - - - - - - -
```

Here, I'll read in this table and display its columns in two choice controls. To do that, I create a new **Connection** object specifying the data source and connection protocol as "jdbc:odbc:students", which indicates I want the JDBC driver to use ODBC to connect to the students data source, as well as a user name and password. Then I execute the SQL statements "SELECT Name FROM Students" and "SELECT Grade FROM Students" to get result sets corresponding to the two fields in the table. Using the **ResultSet** class's **next** method, I can move to the next row in each result set and populate the choice controls with data from the data source. Here's the code (note the line **Class.forName("sun.jdbc.odbc.JdbcOdbcDriver")**, which is necessary to load the JDBC driver):

```java
import java.net.*;
import java.sql.*;
import java.awt.*;
import java.awt.event.*;

public class jdbc extends Frame
{
    Choice students;
    Choice grades;
    Connection connection;
    Statement statement;

    public jdbc()
    {
        students = new Choice();
        grades = new Choice();

        setLayout(new FlowLayout());

        try
        {
            Class.forName("sun.jdbc.odbc.JdbcOdbcDriver");

            connection = DriverManager.getConnection(
                "jdbc:odbc:students", "Steve", "password");

            statement = connection.createStatement();

            String SQL = "SELECT Name FROM Students";
            ResultSet resultset = statement.executeQuery(SQL);
            while (resultset.next())
                students.addItem(resultset.getString(1));

            SQL = "SELECT Grade FROM Students";
            resultset = statement.executeQuery(SQL);
            while (resultset.next())
                grades.addItem(resultset.getString(1));
        }
        catch(Exception e) {}
```

```
        add(students);
        add(grades);
    }

    public static void main (String args[])
    {
        Frame f = new jdbc();

        f.setSize(300, 300);

        f.addWindowListener(new WindowAdapter() {public void
            windowClosing(WindowEvent e) {System.exit(0);}});

        f.show();
    }

}
```

The result appears in Figure 24.5, where you can see the student names as fetched from the Name fields in the Students table. That's it—we've connected to an ODBC data source, executed a SQL statement on that data source, and got the result back. This example is in jdbc.java on the CD.

Figure 24.5   Using JDBC.

Creating Java Servlets

The Novice Programmer is back and says, "Wouldn't it be great if I didn't have to use CGI scripts but could use Java on a Web server instead?" You say, "But you can. Just use Java servlets." The NP says, "Wow!"

You can download the Java Servlet Development Kit (JSDK) from java.sun.com and use it to create servlets. Java servlets are executed on Web servers, and they create Web pages, which makes them extremely powerful. Using servlets, you can create any Web page you want in response to parameters passed to the servlet. The **servlet** class we'll look at here is the abstract **GenericServlet** class, which has this inheritance diagram:

```
java.lang.Object
|____javax.servlet.GenericServlet
```

Requests are passed to a servlet using objects that implement the **ServletRequest** interface, and responses such as Web pages are created using objects that implement the **ServletResponse** interface. You'll find the constructor for the **GenericServlet** class in Table 24.17 and its methods in Table 24.18, the methods of the **ServletRequest** interface in Table 24.19, and the methods of the **ServletResponse** interface in Table 24.20.

Table 24.17   The constructor of the GenericServlet class.

Constructor	Does This
GenericServlet( )	This constructor does nothing because this is an abstract class.

Table 24.18   Methods of the GenericServlet class.

Method	Does This
void destroy( )	Destroys the servlet.
java.lang.String getInitParameter (java.lang.String name)	Gets a string containing the value of the named initialization parameter.
java.util.Enumeration getInit ParameterNames( )	Gets the names of the initialization parameters for this servlet.
ServletConfig getServletConfig( )	Gets a **ServletConfig** object, which sets the servlet initialization parameters.
ServletContext getServletContext( )	Gets a **ServletContext** object, which contains information about the servlet engine.
java.lang.String getServletInfo( )	Gets a string that contains information about the servlet.
void init( )	This is an initialization method, so you do not have to store a **ServletConfig** object to use as a parameter.
void init(ServletConfig config)	Initializes this servlet.
void log(java.lang.String msg)	Writes the servlet class name and a servlet exception message to the servlet log file.

(continued)

Table 24.18   Methods of the *GenericServlet* class (continued).

Method	Does This
void log(java.lang.String message, java.lang.Throwable t)	Writes a system exception message to the servlet log file.
abstract void service(Servlet Request req, ServletResponse res)	Carries out a single request from the client.

Table 24.19   Methods of the *ServletRequest* interface.

Method	Does This
java.lang.Object getAttribute(java.lang.String name)	Gets the value of the named attribute as an object.
java.util.Enumeration getAttribute Names( )	Gets the names of the attributes available to this request.
java.lang.String getCharacter Encoding( )	Gets the name of the character-encoding style.
int getContentLength( )	Gets the length of the content contained in the request.
java.lang.String getContentType( )	Gets the MIME type of the content of the request.
ServletInputStream getInputStream( )	Gets data from the body of the request as a **ServletInputStream**.
java.lang.String getParameter(java.lang.String name)	Gets the value of a request parameter as a string.
java.util.Enumeration getParameter Names( )	Gets the names of the parameters contained in this request.
java.lang.String[ ] getParameterValues (java.lang.String name)	Gets all the values the given request parameter has.
java.lang.String getProtocol( )	Gets the name and version of the protocol the request uses.
java.io.BufferedReader getReader( )	Gets the body of the request as a **BufferedReader**.
java.lang.String getRealPath (java.lang.String path)	Deprecated. Use **ServletContext.getRealPath(java.lang. String)** instead.
java.lang.String getRemoteAddr( )	Gets the Internet Protocol (IP) address of the client that sent the request.
java.lang.String getRemoteHost( )	Gets the fully qualified name of the client that sent the request.
java.lang.String getScheme( )	Gets the name of the protocol used to make this request (such as http, https, or ftp).
java.lang.String getServerName( )	Gets the host name of the server that received the request.
int getServerPort( )	Gets the port number on which this request was received.
void setAttribute(java.lang.String key, java.lang.Object o)	Stores an attribute in the context of this request.

Table 24.20   Methods of the *ServletResponse* class.

Method	Does This
java.lang.String getCharacter Encoding( )	Gets the name of the character-set encoding used.
ServletOutputStream getOutput Stream( )	Gets a **ServletOutputStream** suitable for writing binary data to.
java.io.PrintWriter getWriter( )	Gets a **PrintWriter** object that you can use to send character text to the client.
void setContentLength(int len)	Sets the length of the content the server returns to the client.
void setContentType(java.lang. String type)	Sets the content type of the response.

Here's an example. In this case, I'll just have a servlet return a Web page to a browser with the text "Hello from Java!" in bold. To do that, I extend the **GenericServlet** class and override the **service** method, which is passed a **ServletRequest** object and a **ServletResponse** object. You use the **ServletResponse** object to write the new Web page, like this:

```
import java.io.*;
import javax.servlet.*;

public class servlet extends GenericServlet
{
    public void service(ServletRequest request, ServletResponse
        response) throws ServletException, IOException
    {
        response.setContentType("text/html");
        PrintWriter printwriter = response.getWriter();
        printwriter.println("<B>Hello from Java!</B>");
        printwriter.close();
    }
}
```

You can install this servlet on a server that runs servlets, or you can test it on your own machine. To compile it, you'll need to make sure two JAR files from the JSDK can be found by the Java compiler: servlet.jar and server.jar (that is, adding those JAR files to the CLASSPATH might look something like this in Windows: **SET CLASSPATH=server.jar;servlet.jar;classes;%CLASSPATH%**).

In Windows, you place the compiled class file—servlet.class in this case—into the examples\WEB-INF\servlets directory, which is the directory you installed the JSDK into (for example, C:\jsdk2.1\examples\WEB-INF\servlets). You can start the test server on your machine with the startserver.bat batch file, which comes with the JSDK. After the test server is running on your machine, open a Web browser and navigate to this URL: **http://localhost:8080/examples/servlet/servlet**. The result appears in Figure 24.6, where you can see the Web page created by this applet. That's it. Now you've created and run your own Java servlet. This example is in servlet.java on the CD.

This example completes the Java Black Book. We've come far in this book—from the basics of Java programming to object-oriented programming, from inheritance to inner classes, from AWT to Swing, from I/O streams to multithreading, from JDBC to Java servlets. From the Big Boss, the Novice Programmer, the Programming Correctness Czar, and all the rest—happy Java programming!

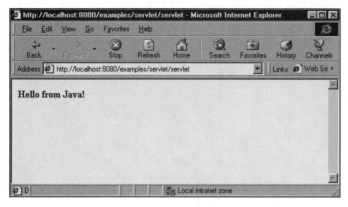

Figure 24.6   Creating and running a servlet.

Index

E

Less than or equal to operator (<=), 132
Libraries. *See* Packages.
lightGray field, 429
Lightweight components, 254, 503
lightWeightPopupEnabled field, 633
LineBorder class, 528
lineno method, 922
LinkedList class, 932, 943–945
List class, 364–366
list command, Java debugger, 1070
List interface, 932, 935–936
list method, 263, 268, 890, 973
List selection modes, 620
ListCellRenderer interface, 624, 645
Listener interfaces. *See* Event listener interfaces.
listenerList field, 507
listFiles method, 890
ListIterator interface, 953–954
listIterator method, 935, 939, 940, 944
listRoots method, 890
Lists, 354, 364–372, 585, 614, 617. *See also specific list classes and interfaces.*
    adding to applets, 364, 367–369
    creating, 618–619
    displaying images, 622–623
    double-click events, 625–627
    models, 622–624
    multiple list selections, 354, 369–372, 617, 620–622
    renderers, 622–623, 624–625
    retrieving user selections, 619, 621
Literals, 62–68
LOAD field, 496
load method, 973
loadImage method, 548, 1044
LOADING field, 436
Loading images into applets, 414, 434–435, 436–438
loadKeymap method, 850
locate method, 263, 268
location method, 263, 343
locationToIndex method, 616, 626
lock field, 908, 909
Logical operators, 120, 128–130
long data type, 61, 68–69. *See also* Integer data types.
long keyword, 19
long literals, 62–63
LookAndFeel class, 538–539. *See also* Pluggable look and feel.
lookupConstraints method, 343
Loop indices, 146, 148
Loop statements, 113
    break statement, 151–152
    continue statement, 152–153
    do-while loops, 145–146
    for loops, 113–115, 146–149
    nested loops, 150
    while loops, 142–144

lostFocus method, 263
lowerCaseMode method, 923
Lowercasing String objects, 99–100
lowerLeft field, 592
lowerRight field, 592
lowestLayer method, 518

M

magenta field, 429
main method, 22–24, 44–45, 180–181, 302–303
Maintainability of Java programs, 47–48
majorTickSpacing field, 600
makeIcon method, 538
makeKeyBindings method, 539
makeVisible method, 366, 834
Managers. *See* Layout managers.
Manifest files, 1023, 1024, 1038, 1051
MANIFEST_NAME field, 1026
Map interface, 933
Map.Entry interface, 933
Maps, 933. *See also specific map classes.*
MARGIN_CHANGED_PROPERTY field, 554
mark field, 899
mark method, 892, 899, 902, 903, 904, 909, 916, 919, 921
markedPos field, 916
marklimit field, 903
markpos field, 903
markSupported method, 892, 899, 903, 909, 916, 919, 921
Math class, 133–134
MatteBorder class, 528
maximizable field, 774
maximumLayoutSize method, 335, 339, 343, 352, 707, 714
maximumRowCount field, 633
MAX_PRIORITY field, 982, 992
MDI. *See* Desktop panes; Internal frames.
MediaTracker class, 436–438. *See also* **ImageObserver** interface.
Memory management, 194–197
MemoryImageSource class, 440, 441–442
Menu bars. *See also* Menus.
    adding menus to menu bars, 470–472, 729
    adding to applets, 729
    adding to frame windows, 469–470
Menu class, 451, 466, 469, 470–471
Menu items
    accelerators and mnemonics, 741–744
    adding and removing, 472–475, 727, 746–748
    changing captions, 744–746
    check box menu items, 482–485, 733–736
    creating at runtime, 748
    enabling and disabling, 481–482, 744–746

R

U